WITHDRAWN

THE UNITED STATES NAVY

THE UNITED STATES NAVY

A CHRONOLOGY, 1775 TO THE PRESENT

JOHN C. FREDRIKSEN

ABC-CLIO

Santa Barbara, California • Denver, Colorado • Oxford, England

Copyright © 2010 by ABC-CLIO, LLC

All rights reserved. No part of this publication may be reproduced, stored in a retrieval system, or transmitted, in any form or by any means, electronic, mechanical, photocopying, recording, or otherwise, except for the inclusion of brief quotations in a review, without prior permission in writing from the publisher.

Library of Congress Cataloging-in-Publication Data
Fredriksen, John C.
  The United States Navy : a chronology, 1775 to the present / John C. Fredriksen.
    p. cm.
  Includes bibliographical references and index.
  ISBN 978-1-59884-431-3 (hard copy : alk. paper) -- ISBN 978-1-59884-432-0 (e-book)
 1. United States. Navy--History. 2. United States. Navy--History--Chronology. I. Title.
  E182.F795 2010
  359.00973--dc22   2010010567

ISBN 978-1-59884-431-3
EISBN 978-1-59884-432-0

14 13 12 11 10 1 2 3 4 5

This book is also available on the World Wide Web as an eBook.
Visit www.abc-clio.com for details.

ABC-CLIO, LLC
130 Cremona Drive, P.O. Box 1911
Santa Barbara, California 93116–1911

This book is printed on acid-free paper ∞
Manufactured in the United States of America

Contents

Introduction, vii

THE CHRONOLOGY, 1775 TO THE PRESENT, 1

Bibliography, 345
Index, 353

Introduction

The United States Navy is viewed presently as the strongest force of its kind in the world, but its origins and survival were decidedly problematic. Its lineal predecessor, the Continental Navy, consisting of a dozen or so frigates authorized by Congress in 1775, found itself pitted against the dominant naval power of its day, Great Britain. Some gifted commanders, such as John Barry and John Paul Jones, scored a series of upset victories in single-ship actions, but the navy was ultimately swept from the sea by the sheer number of British hulls brought to bear against them. Fast-moving, lightly armed privateers, by comparison, enjoyed far more success in raiding British maritime commerce. Little wonder, then, that the Continental Navy was disbanded and its surviving vessels sold off in the postwar period. However, no sooner had independence been gained than President John Adams established the U.S. Navy in 1794 to counter depredations by the Tripolitan pirates. This nascent force cut its teeth in the Quasi-War with France, 1798–1800, fought gallantly during the war with the Barbary pirates, 1801–1805, and garnered a measure of glory during the War of 1812–1815 against its old nemesis, the Royal Navy. However, in all these early contests, the navy remained numerically small and incapable of a strategic impact at sea. Fortunately, its status improved greatly over the next half-century with the founding of the Board of Navy Commissions in 1815, the five Navy Bureaus in 1842, the U.S. Naval Academy in 1845, and the adoption of iron technology, steam propulsion, and enhanced ordnance. The Navy performed splendidly in its limited role throughout the Mexican War, 1846–1848, which concurrently laid the foundations for its first major deployment, the Civil War of 1861–1865. For the first time in its history, the Navy was accorded with sufficient resources, manpower, and vessels to act strategically, and its blockade of the Southern coastline proved a major factor in the Confederacy's ultimate collapse. The creation of revolutionary vessels such as the USS *Monitor* also ushered in new classes of iron vessels that sounded the death knell of the wooden warship.

Three decades of fiscal retrenchment and decline ensued as the Navy was allowed to dwindle from the world's second-largest naval force after Great Britain, to the level of Chile, but this course was quickly reversed following the revolutionary theories of Alfred Thayer Mahan. The navy force was revived in time to win a splendid "little war" against Spain in 1898, through which the United States acquired its first overseas possessions. During this imperial age, naval construction was in vogue around the world, and the battleship was king. But the U.S. Navy remained behind in numbers when compared to the splendid squadrons of England, Germany, Russia, and Japan.

It took two wars of the twentieth century, backed by the nation's massive industrial might, for the navy to finally acquire world-class status. World War I witnessed American implementation of the convoy system and the introduction of naval aviation, both of which were greatly expanded upon during World War II. Moreover, the creation of an entirely new class of warship, the aircraft carrier, gave the Navy power to project military strength far across the globe, while its capable submarine fleet accounted for 56 percent of all Japanese warships sunk. The Navy performed equally well throughout the Cold War, especially in Korea, 1950–1953, and Vietnam, 1964–1974, especially from the standpoint of aerial bombardment. Nor did it lose any technological ground to the large and invigorated Soviet Navy, and pioneered the first use of strategic ballistic submarines as part of a nuclear deterrence, which had helped maintain the peace. Since the collapse of the Soviet Union in 1991, the U.S. Navy remains the world's paramount naval force, and has borne conspicuous roles in the Gulf War of 1991, OPERATION ENDURING FREEDOM in 2001, and OPERATION IRAQI FREEDOM, 2003. It has never failed to give a good account of itself in all its struggles and remains a technically savvy, highly trained, and sophisticated instrument of American policy—and a far cry from the handful of frigates manned by its illustrious but ill-fated forebears.

This chronology is an attempt to capture the great canvass of U.S. Navy history in a relatively modest space. To that end, all the important battles and personages are mentioned to contextualize to military affairs at the time they unfolded. However, great care is also taken to include mention of noted laws, military texts, schools, weapons systems, and occasional political developments that affected military affairs. Overall, this book should impart on lay readers the scope and sweep of navy history, while a detailed bibliography of all the latest scholarship can refer them to greater details. It will also afford prospective researchers a workable time frame or stepping-off point from which they can pursue events and individuals of interest. The author would like to thank editors Pat Carlin and Andrew McCormick for their support and advice in compiling what I hope will be a useful and relevant addition to any library shelf, public or personal.

—*John C. Fredriksen*

1775

MAY 17–18 On Lake Champlain, New York, Colonel Benedict Arnold captures a British sloop and re-christens it the *Enterprise*; this is the first American vessel bequeathed that distinguished name.

Off the coast of Boston, Massachusetts, Captain James Mugford and the sloop *Franklin* capture the transport HMS *Hope*. A cargo of 1,000 barrels of gunpowder and a like number of muskets are acquired and forwarded to the "Army of Observation" outside the town.

JUNE 11 At Machias, Maine, a mob seizes the British transports *Unity* and *Polly*, which are then armed and impressed into American service.

JUNE 12 In Machias Bay, Maine, 40 armed lumbermen under Jeremiah O'Brien sail the captured transports *Unity* and *Polly* against HMS *Margaretta*, which is stormed and boarded after a stiff fight. The British suffer eight killed and five wounded to an American tally of three killed and two wounded. The *Margaretta* becomes the first Royal Navy vessel captured by the Americans, and its guns are transferred to the *Unity*, subsequently renamed *Machias Liberty*.

The Rhode Island Assembly authorizes the construction of two armed sloops; these are the first such vessels approved by a colonial authority.

JUNE 15 On the Providence River, Rhode Island, two armed Rhode Island vessels under Captain Abraham Whipple capture a British tender belonging to the frigate HMS *Rose*. Whipple's vessel *Katy* is subsequently acquired by the Continental Navy and renamed the *Providence*.

AUGUST 3 On the lower Hudson River, a flotilla of American armed galleys under Lieutenant Colonel Benjamin Tupper engages British frigates HMS *Rose* and *Phoenix*. The latter vessel sustains serious damage and retreats; American losses are 4 dead and 14 wounded.

AUGUST 26 In Providence, Rhode Island, the Assembly directs its delegates at the Continental Congress to propose the founding and construction of a new Continental Navy.

AUGUST 28 On the St. Lawrence River, Lower Canada, a colonial flotilla transports 1,000 American militiamen downstream on an amphibious descent against strategic St. Johns.

SEPTEMBER 2 Outside Boston, Massachusetts, General George Washington charters the schooner *Hannah* of Beverly as an armed vessel. Commanded by army officer Nicholas Broughton, the *Hannah* is considered the first American warship, and also the first member of "Washington's Navy," which totals 11 vessels and captures 55 prizes.

SEPTEMBER 5 Near Boston, Massachusetts, the schooner *Hannah*, now outfitted with four small cannon, sails in Continental service under army officer Captain John Broughton. By blockading British forces in the city, it functions as one of the earliest de facto warships of the embryonic Continental Navy.

OCTOBER 3 In Philadelphia, Pennsylvania, Rhode Island delegates at the Continental Congress formally advance legislation for funding and constructing a new Continental Navy.

OCTOBER 10 Near Beverly, Massachusetts, the American vessel *Hannah* is run aground by the sloop HMS *Nautilus*. It is saved from capture by nearby townspeople, who man cannon and drive the British off.

OCTOBER 13   In Philadelphia, Pennsylvania, the Continental Congress authorizes Colonel John Glover, a former sailor, to convert several transports into armed warships. They also approve construction of two formal warships. Furthermore, delegates Silas Deane, Christopher Gadsden, and John Langdon area are appointed to the new marine committee to monitor such matters. For all these reasons, this date is considered the birthday of the U.S. Navy.

OCTOBER 27   In Philadelphia, Pennsylvania, a congressional committee advocates constructing or purchasing five frigates of 32 guns, five of 28 guns, and three of 24 guns. These vessels are intended to serve as the nucleus of the new Continental Navy.

OCTOBER 30   In Philadelphia, Pennsylvania, the Continental Congress authorizes construction of two frigates of 36 and two of 29 guns, for a total of four vessels. Delegates John Adams, Joseph Hewes, Stephen Hopkins, and Richard Henry Lee are also added to the marine committee, a sign of its mounting importance.

NOVEMBER 2   In Philadelphia, Pennsylvania, the naval committee votes $100,000 to purchase, arm, and rename eight merchant vessels as the core of the new Continental Navy: the *Alfred*, 24 guns; *Columbus*, 18 guns; *Andrew Doria*, 14 guns; *Cabot*, 14 guns; *Providence*, 12 guns; *Hornet*, 10 guns; and *Fly*, 8 guns. These will serve as front-line vessels until newer warships are constructed and commissioned.

NOVEMBER 5   In Philadelphia, Pennsylvania, Esek Hopkins of Rhode Island is appointed the first commander in chief of the Continental Navy by the Continental Congress. He apparently received the appointment through the machinations of his brother Stephen Hopkins, who sits on the naval committee.

NOVEMBER 11   Off the coast of Charleston, South Carolina, Captain Simon Tuft and the ship *Defiance* are attacked by the British vessels HMS *Tamer* and *Cherokee*. He manages to scuttle four hulks in the channel and retires without loss.

NOVEMBER 25   In Philadelphia, Pennsylvania, the Continental Congress issues letters of marque to legally commence privateering against English commercial vessels. They also urge creation of admiralty courts in individual colonies to allocate prize money. Significantly, the 1,697 privateers so licensed seize 600 British vessels—three times the amount taken by the entire Continental Navy.

NOVEMBER 28   Off Cape Ann, Massachusetts, Captain John Manley and the armed schooner *Lee* capture the British ordnance brig HMS *Nancy*. Their haul includes 2,000 stands of muskets, 30 tons of shot, and a 2,700-pound mortar, all of which are immediately dispatched to General George Washington's army outside of Boston.

NOVEMBER 28   In Philadelphia, Pennsylvania, John Adams directs the Naval Committee to draw up regulations for the nascent Continental Navy. The ensuing document, entitled *Rules for the Regulation of the Navy of the United Colonies of North America*, dictates rates of pay, rations, discipline, and the all-important division of prize money.

DECEMBER 3   In Philadelphia Harbor, Pennsylvania, Lieutenant John Paul Jones hoists the 13-stripe Grand Union flag over the converted merchant vessel *Alfred* for

December 11–14 In Philadelphia, Pennsylvania, Congress creates a permanent Marine Committee with 13 members, with one from each colony. This body will augment the Naval Committee and is tasked with acquiring and outfitting all warships authorized by the latter. Debate also continues on the proposed construction of 13 modern frigates.

December 22 In Philadelphia, Pennsylvania, the Continental Congress authorizes funding for five 32-gun frigates, five 28-gun frigates, and three 24-gun frigates: the *Hancock*, *Randolph*, *Raleigh*, *Warren*, *Washington*, *Congress*, *Effingham*, *Providence*, *Trumbull*, *Virginia*, *Boston*, *Delaware*, and *Montgomery*. Thus augmented, the Continental Navy will possess 14 vessels and 332 guns. However, it still remains badly outnumbered by the formidable Royal Navy.

Congress also appoints the first 18 officers of the Continental Navy, and Dudley Saltonstall, Abraham Whipple, John B. Hopkins, and Nicholas Biddle become the first commissioned captains. Captain Esek Hopkins of Rhode Island is also confirmed as its first commander in chief.

December 24 Near Cape Ann, Massachusetts, the schooner *Warren* captures the British brig *Sally*. Among the cargo taken is 153 casks of wine, which are promptly forwarded to General George Washington as a Christmas gift.

1776

January 5 Commodore Esek Hopkins is instructed by the Continental Congress to depart Philadelphia and sweep the Virginia and Carolina coasts of marauding British vessels. However, he receives discretionary authority to attack the Bahamas, should the opportunity presents itself.

Barry, John (1745–1803)

John Barry was born in County Wexford, Ireland, on January 1, 1745, migrated to Philadelphia in 1761, and gained prominence as a mariner. In April 1775, Barry donated his vessel *Black Prince* to the Continental Navy while he himself was commissioned captain of the brig *Lexington*. In this capacity he secured the tender HMS *Edward* on April 6, 1776, being the first American naval victory at sea. He commanded a succession of warships, and in February 1780 took charge of the newly built frigate *Alliance*. Barry's first voyage involved conveying Thomas Paine and John Laurens to France and, during the return leg, he captured the British privateers *Minerva* and *Mars* on April 2, 1780. On May 23, 1780, the British warships *Atalanta* and *Trepassy* raked the *Alliance*'s stern in a dead wind, yet Barry, badly wounded, subdued both antagonists once a breeze sprang up. On March 10, 1783, *Alliance* was attacked by no less than three British vessels, but Barry badly crippled HMS *Sybil* in a stiff fight and escaped. In March 1794, he became senior officer of the new U.S. Navy, and oversaw construction of the new 44-gun frigate *United States*. He led several cruises of the Caribbean during the Quasi-War with France, and on February 3, 1799, captured a large privateer off Martinique. Barry finally resigned from active duty in 1801 and died in Philadelphia on September 13, 1803, a harsh yet capable naval leader. Like John Paul Jones, he shares a reputation as "Father of the U.S. Navy."

January 6 In Philadelphia, Pennsylvania, the Continental Congress authorizes the appointment of surgeons and surgeon's mates to vessels, which commences the beginning of American naval medicine.

January 15 Off Newbury, Massachusetts, local volunteers man three whale boats and capture a British provisions ship nearby.

January 17 At Philadelphia, Pennsylvania, Commodore Esek Hopkins sails his eight-ship flotilla down the ice-choked Delaware River, although conditions prevent him from getting to sea. Samuel Tucker is also commissioned a captain and appointed to the frigate *Franklin*.

January 25 Outside Plymouth Harbor, Massachusetts, the schooner *Hancock* seizes two British transports, and thwarts a British schooner attempting to recapture them.

February 17 Commodore Esek Hopkins directs the frigates *Alfred* and *Columbus*, the brigs *Cabot* and *Andrew Doria*, the sloops *Providence* and *Hornet*, and the schooners *Fly* and *Wasp* into open water. This is the Continental Navy's first sortie in strength, and Hopkins has been instructed by Congress to scour the southern coastline of British warships. However, he elects to attack Nassau in the Bahamas instead.

March 1 Commodore Esek Hopkins's squadron rendezvouses off the Bahamian island of Abaco prior to attacking the capital of New Providence (Nassau). Unfortunately, the schooners *Fly* and *Wasp* sustain damage in a collision at sea and limp home.

March 3 Commodore Esek Hopkins captures New Providence on Nassau, the Bahamas, with sailors and 200 marines under Captain Samuel Nicholas. Governor Montfort Browne surrenders after a token defense and no losses are incurred by either side. Hopkins begins confiscating 88 cannon, 15 mortars, and quantities of gunpowder after this, the Continental Navy's first planned offensive, but his dilatory approach enabled Browne to remove 150 casks of gunpowder to safety beforehand.

March 9 On Chariton Creek, Virginia, the Maryland warship *Defense*, assisted by two militia companies, attacks and drives off the HMS *Otter*.

March 13 In Philadelphia, Pennsylvania, the Marine Committee of the Continental Congress purchases the brigantine *Wild Duck* to be rearmed as a warship. It is subsequently renamed *Lexington*, the first of five American naval vessels so christened.

March 17 Commodore Esek Hopkins, laden with booty from his conquest of New Providence, leisurely departs and sails for home waters.

March 19 In Philadelphia, Pennsylvania, a motion by Samuel Chase that would have permitted attacks on British merchant vessels by the Continental Navy in tabled by the Continental Congress. They seek to encourage the practice of privateering instead.

March 23 In Philadelphia, Pennsylvania, the Continental Congress authorizes privateering against British shipping by issuing General Letters of Marque and Reprisal.

April 4 Near Block Island, Rhode Island, Captain Abraham Whipple of the 20-gun frigate *Columbus* seizes the schooner HMS *Hawke*. This is the first prize taken at sea by an American warship.

April 5 In the Atlantic, Commodore Esek Hopkins and the frigate *Alfred* capture the British bomb brig HMS *Bolton*.

April 6 Near Block Island, Rhode Island, Commodore Esek Hopkins's naval squadron engages the Royal Navy's 20-gun frigate HMS *Glasgow* under Captain Tryingham Howe, but fails to capture it after a three-hour running fight. Howe maneuvers brilliantly and severely damages *Alfred's* steering with a lucky shot, and successfully puts into Newport. Hopkins is censured for his slovenly performance; the Americans lose 10 killed and 14 wounded to a British loss of 1 dead and 3 injured.

April 7 Off the Virginia Capes, Captain John Barry and the 16-gun brig *Lexington* captures the British sloop HMS *Edward* after a four-hour battle. This is the first enemy warship taken in a formal ship-to-ship encounter.

April 8 At New London, Connecticut, Commodore Esek Hopkins's squadron concludes its only sortie in strength by dropping anchor. Because most sailors prefer sailing on better-paying privateers, the squadron is broken up and never reconstituted due to a lack of trained manpower.

April 9 In Christina Creek, Delaware Bay, the American schooner *Wasp* captures the British brig *Betsey*.

April 15 At Providence, Rhode Island, the warships *Warren* and *Providence* are launched and commissioned into the rapidly expanding Continental Navy.

May 8–9 On Christina Creek near Wilmington, Delaware, armed row galleys of the Pennsylvania state navy engage the HMS *Roebuck* and *Liverpool*; the British are forced back downstream with minor losses to both sides.

May 10 Lieutenant John Paul Jones assumes command of the 12-gun sloop *Providence*.

May 16 At Philadelphia, Pennsylvania, Captain Thomas Biddle and the 14-gun brig *Andrew Doria* begins cruising between the Delaware Capes and Maine; over the next four months Biddle seizes 10 prizes, including two transports carrying 400 British soldiers.

May 17 Near Nantasket Roads, Massachusetts, Captain John Mugford and the schooner *Franklin* captures the supply ship HMS *Hope*, along with tons of gunpowder and scores of entrenchment tools. That night the British launch 200 men in 12 boats try to capture the *Franklin* and privateer *Lady Washington*, but are bloodily repulsed. The Americans sustain two killed, including Captain Mugford, while the British lose seven dead.

May 21 At Portsmouth, New Hampshire, the *Raleigh* becomes the first Continental frigate launched; it will be captained by John Manley of Boston.

June 7 Near Newburyport, Massachusetts, the 12-gun American privateer *Yankee Hero* surrenders to the frigate HMS *Medford* following a gallant two-hour struggle.

June 16 In Boston Harbor, a squadron under Captain Seth Harding intercepts British transports HMS *George* and *Arabella*. The *George*, partly manned by soldiers of the 71st Highlanders, resists stiffly and surrenders only after losing 12 killed and 13 wounded. Lieutenant Colonel Archibald Campbell, the future conqueror of Georgia, is also taken prisoner.

JUNE 29 Off Cape May, New Jersey, British naval vessels chase the American ship *Nancy*, until it grounds, whereupon Captain Lambert Wickes arrives and orders gunpowder supplies opened and the ship set afire. As the British board the burning vessel, it suddenly explodes, killing several sailors.

JULY 4 In Philadelphia, Pennsylvania, the Continental Congress promulgates the Declaration of Independence. Hereafter, the Americans are fighting to create a nation of their own.

JULY 10 In Philadelphia, Pennsylvania, the Continental frigate *Randolph* is launched and assigned to Captain Nicholas Biddle.

JULY 11 Captain Lambert Wickes and the brig *Reprisal* commence a cruise that seizes four British merchantmen by month's end.

JULY 27 At St. Pierre Harbor, Martinique, the brig *Reprisal* under Captain Lambert Wickes is challenged by the sloop HMS *Shark*, whose captain fails to recognize the new Grand Union flag. Wickes, though towing three prizes, responds with a broadside, and fighting commences between the two vessels. The *Shark* withdraws after a nearby French fort opens fire on them.

AUGUST 8 Lieutenant John Paul Jones advances to captain in the Continental Navy.

AUGUST 12 Near Delaware Capes, the Continental sloop *Sachem* captures the British brigantine *Three Friends* in a two-hour contest.

AUGUST 21–OCTOBER 8 Lieutenant John Paul Jones and the 12-gun sloop *Providence* depart on a cruise between the Delaware Capes and Nova Scotia, and net 16 prizes over the next three months.

AUGUST 24 At Crown Point, New York, energetic General Benedict Arnold assembles a motley collection of schooners, sloops, and gondolas. He intends on sailing down Lake Champlain to engage superior British naval forces.

AUGUST 26 The British frigate HMS *Liverpool* captures the Continental sloop *Warren*, one of General George Washington's original vessels.

SEPTEMBER 3 Lieutenant John Paul Jones of the 12-gun brig *Providence* again departs Delaware Bay to cruise near Bermuda; he ultimately seizes 16 prizes.

SEPTEMBER 5 In Philadelphia, Pennsylvania, the Continental Congress issues the first regulations governing naval uniforms for officers. Their attire consists of a blue coat with red lapels, yellow metal buttons, and a red waistcoat. Wearers remain at liberty to enhance their wardrobe by adding gold embellishments.

SEPTEMBER 7 Near New York City, inventor David Bushnell deploys his experimental submarine *Turtle* to attack Admiral Richard Howe's flagship HMS *Eagle*. Sergeant Erza Lee is tasked with operating the revolutionary vessel, although he is unsuccessful at boring into *Eagle's* copper-sheathed hull to attach an explosive device. History's first submarine attack fails, but hereafter British commanders condemn the Americans for toying with "infernal devices."

OCTOBER 3 In Philadelphia, Congress authorizes purchasing a frigate and two cutters from an unspecified European power.

OCTOBER 4 On Lake Champlain, New York, Governor General Guy Carleton orders his fleet of 5 warships, 20 gunships, and 28 lesser craft to engage General Benedict Arnold's armada in the vicinity of Valcour Island.

OCTOBER 10 In Philadelphia, Pennsylvania, the Continental Congress formally institutes the grade of captain; it ultimately commissions 24 officers with that grade in the Continental Navy.

OCTOBER 11 On Lake Champlain, New York, General Benedict Arnold's ramshackle flotilla of 15 vessels is attacked by a large British armada near Valcour Island. Arnold sequesters his force in shallow water between the island and the shore, and the British initially sail past the Americans, then have to beat back against the wind in order to engage them. During this interval they are savagely pummeled by Arnold's cannon fire. The British, however, gradually overpower their opponents and Arnold draws off under darkness. The American lose 200 men wounded, killed, or captured and two vessels sunk.

OCTOBER 13 On Lake Champlain, New York, the British armada catches up to the fleeing remnants of General Benedict Arnold's flotilla, who mount a desperate rearguard action, but are gradually overwhelmed. Arnold loses all 13 of his remaining vessels, and the crews make their way overland to Crown Point. Governor General Guy Carleton, however, suspends further operations until after winter has passed. This fortuitous decision transforms the tactical defeat at Valcour Island into a significant American strategic victory.

OCTOBER 16 In Philadelphia, Pennsylvania, the Continental Congress censures Commodore Esek Hopkins for disregarding orders and attacking New Providence, Bahamas, instead of clearing the southern coastline.

OCTOBER 30 In Philadelphia, Pennsylvania, the Continental Congress improves the recruitment prospects for the Continental Navy by allowing crewmen up to one-half of all prize money taken. However, most seamen prefer the more lucrative practice of privateering, which also affords looser discipline and better living conditions.

NOVEMBER 1–DECEMBER 18 Captain John Paul Jones commences another cruise with the 24-gun sloop *Alfred*, accompanied by the sloop *Providence* under Captain Hoysted Hacker. The later develops a leak and returns home, but Jones goes on to seize nine prizes off Nova Scotia.

NOVEMBER 6 In Philadelphia, Pennsylvania, the Marine Committee creates the Continental Naval Board. This consists of three members, well-versed in the nuances of maritime affairs, who are tasked with supervising the navy's business matters.

NOVEMBER 12 In the Atlantic, Captain John Paul Jones of the sloop *Alfred* lures the British transport *Mellish* away from an escorting frigate and captures it, along with a valuable cargo of 10,000 winter uniforms. These are hurriedly forwarded to American forces in Pennsylvania.

NOVEMBER 15 In Philadelphia, Pennsylvania, Congress establishes new pay scales for naval officers, and relative ranks between the Army and Navy.

NOVEMBER 16 At St. Eustatius, Dutch West Indies, guns in the nearby fort fire as the Continental brig *Andrew Doria* under Captain Isaiah Robinson enters the harbor. This is the first recorded salute to the Grand Union flag.

NOVEMBER 18 In Philadelphia, Pennsylvania, the Continental Congress authorizes construction of three 74-gun ships of the line and five additional frigates mounting 36 guns apiece. Only one of the former (*America*) and one of the latter (*Alliance*) are constructed by war's end.

NOVEMBER 29 At Quiberon Bay, France, the Continental brig *Reprisal* under Captain Lambert Wickes delivers diplomatic envoys Benjamin Franklin, Silas Deane, and Arthur Lee to the French court. This is also the first Continental warship in European waters.

DECEMBER Off the coast of Puerto Rico, the brig *Andrew* under Captain Isaiah Robinson captures the British sloop *Racehorse* after an action lasting two hours.

DECEMBER 8–9 Off the coast of Nova Scotia, Captain John Paul Jones of the 24-gun brig *Alfred* takes the British prize *John* of 10 guns. Unfortunately, he relinquishes it to the large frigate HMS *Milford* and escapes.

DECEMBER 20 At sea, the Continental brig *Lexington* of 16 guns is captured by the British frigate *Pearle* and outfitted with a prize crew. However, the Americans overpower their captors and sail safely back to Baltimore. Among those captured was Master's Mate Richard Dale, who is convinced to rejoin the Patriot side.

1777

JANUARY 2 In Narragansett Bay, Rhode Island, the British frigate HMS *Diamond* grounds, so Commodore Esek Hopkins resolves to capture it with the sloop *Providence* and a battalion of militia. However, once the tide rises, the *Diamond* floats free, and Hopkins is again criticized for mishandling events.

JANUARY 15 In the Bay of Biscay, Captain Lambert Wickes and the 18-gun brig *Reprisal* cruise along the coasts of France and Spain, netting five prizes. However, his presence in French waters angers the British government, and a diplomatic row ensues to make him depart.

JANUARY 23 In Philadelphia, Pennsylvania, Congress approves construction of two more frigates, one of 38 guns and one of 28, to offset recent losses.

MARCH 3 Near Nova Scotia, Canada, the brig *Cabot* under Captain Joseph Olney runs aground while pursued by the frigate HMS *Milford*. Olney's crew manages to escape, seize a civilian schooner, and sail for home.

MARCH 26 In Philadelphia, Pennsylvania, the Continental Congress is angered by Commodore Esek Hopkins's disparaging remarks about them, and prepares to dismiss him as head of the Continental Navy.

APRIL 19 Off the coast of New York, the 28-gun frigate *Trumbull* under Captain Dudley Saltonstall seizes two British transports.

In Philadelphia, Pennsylvania, the Continental Congress creates the Navy Board of the Eastern Department at Boston, Massachusetts, and appoints James Warren, William Vernon, and James Deshon to serve on it. They answer directly to the Marine Committee and make significant contributions to the war effort.

MAY 1 In the English Channel, Captain Gustavus Conyngham and the 10-gun lugger *Surprise* capture the mail packet *Prince of Orange* and the brig *Joseph* off the Dutch coast, then tow the prizes back to Dunkirk, France. However, a strong diplomatic protest from Great Britain results in Conyngham's arrest.

MAY 10 At Portsmouth, New Hampshire, the Continental sloop *Ranger* is launched and handed over to Captain John Paul Jones.

MAY 21 At Boston, Massachusetts, the 24-gun frigate *Boston* under Captain Hector McNeill and the 32-gun frigate *Hancock* under Captain John Manley begin a North Atlantic cruise.

MAY 28 At Nantes, France, Captain Lambert Wickes, the 18-gun *Reprisal*, the 16-gun brig *Lexington*, and the 10-gun cutter *Dolphin* constitute the first American naval squadron in European waters. They eventually seize 18 English prizes by summer.

JUNE 7 In the North Atlantic, the frigates *Boston* and *Hancock* under Captains Hector McNeill and John Manley, respectively, capture the 28-gun frigate HMS *Fox* after a long running fight. The prize is manned and added to the squadron.

JUNE 14 In Philadelphia, Pennsylvania, Congress approves a new national flag with 13 red and white stripes and a blue field containing 13 stars, one representing each state.

At Portsmouth, New Hampshire, Captain John Paul Jones hoists his standard over the new sloop *Ranger* of 18 guns.

JUNE 27 Captain Lambert Wickes concludes a successful foray into the English Channel and is returning to Nantes, France, with 18 prizes when he is accosted by the ship of the line HMS *Burford*. Wickes is forced to throw all his cannons overboard to lighten *Reprisal* and escape.

JUNE 28 In Delaware, the Continental brig *Nancy* runs aground to escape several pursuing warships. The crews of Continental navy ships *Reprisal* and *Lexington* remove 286 barrels of gunpowder, then set a charge which explodes just as the British clamber aboard to claim it.

JULY 4 At Portsmouth, New Hampshire, the new "Stars and Stripes" flag is unfurled by Captain John Paul Jones on the Continental sloop *Ranger* for the first time.

JULY 7 Off the coast of Halifax, Nova Scotia, a British squadron under Commodore George Collier chases the American 32-gun frigate *Hancock* and the prize ship *Fox*. Captain John Manley should have easily outrun his pursuers, but his mishandling of matters leads to the *Hancock*'s surrender. The 24-gun frigate *Boston* under Captain Hector McNeill sails away, unwilling to assist; McNeill is consequently dismissed from the service.

JULY 17 At Dunkirk, France, Captain Gustavus Conyngham sails the *Revenge* on a profitable cruise of the North and Irish Seas. After taking twenty prizes, he is reviled as the "Dunkirk Pirate."

SEPTEMBER 2–4 In the West Indies, the frigate *Raleigh* under Captain Thomas Thompson and the frigate *Alfred* under Captain Elisha Hinman seize the British transport *Nancy*. The two ships then shadow a British convoy for several days, but are unable penetrate its escort.

SEPTEMBER 14 At St. Malo France, Captain Lambert Wickes is released from prison and allowed to depart aboard the *Reprisal*.

SEPTEMBER 20 Near Ushant, France, the 16-gun American brig *Lexington* under Captain Henry Johnson succumbs to the smaller 10-gun cutter HMS *Alert* after running out of ammunition.

SEPTEMBER 26 Following the fall of Philadelphia, Pennsylvania, to the British, defense of the nearby Delaware River falls upon Commodore John Hazelwood and his armed row galleys of the Pennsylvania State Navy.

SEPTEMBER 27 Near Philadelphia, Pennsylvania, the new 24-gun Continental frigate *Delaware* under Captain Charles Alexander bombards British positions, then runs aground. The vessel strikes its colors after the enemy brings up artillery.

OCTOBER 1 Near Newfoundland, Canada, the dashing Captain Lambert Wickes drowns when the *Reprisal* sinks in a storm.

OCTOBER 6 On the Hudson River, New York, the uncompleted American frigates *Congress* and *Montgomery* are burned to prevent capture by British forces.

OCTOBER 23 On the Delaware River, six British warships sail upstream to bombard Fort Mifflin into submission, but they are attacked by 12 armed galleys under Commodore John Hazelwood; the 64-gun HMS *Merlin* and the 19-gun *Augusta* ground and are burned to prevent capture.

OCTOBER 26 At Marblehead, Massachusetts, the Continental schooner *Lee* completes its final cruise, having previously netted nineteen prizes. This was the last operating vessel of "George Washington's Navy."

NOVEMBER 1 At Portsmouth, New Hampshire, Captain John Paul Jones and the 18-gun sloop *Ranger* sail for France. He carries dispatches bearing news of the victory at Saratoga for the American minister in Paris, Benjamin Franklin.

NOVEMBER 2 In Pennsylvania, General George Washington orders the unfinished Continental frigate *Effingham* burned in the Delaware River to prevent its capture by British forces at Philadelphia, Pennsylvania.

NOVEMBER 21 With the fall of Fort Mifflin, Pennsylvania, Royal Navy warships begin pushing further up the Delaware River, resulting in the scuttling of the brig *Andrew Doria*, the sloops *Hornet*, *Racehorse*, *Wasp*, and *Fly*, and the entire Pennsylvania State Navy.

DECEMBER 2 Captain John Paul Jones and the 18-gun sloop *Ranger,* having taken two British prizes while crossing the Atlantic, drop anchor at Nantes, France.

1778

JANUARY 2 Commodore Esek Hopkins is formally removed as commodore of the Continental Navy, and no officer is appointed to succeed him.

JANUARY 5 On the Delaware River, inventor David Bushnell releases floating mines which kill several British sailors. Hereafter, the Royal Navy expends considerable ordnance detonating mines, which inspires American poet Francis Hopkinson to compose his satirical work, "Battle of the Kegs."

JANUARY 27 New Providence Island (Nassau) in the Bahamas falls to Captain John P. Rathbun of the Continental sloop *Providence*, who also seizes 5 vessels, 1,200 pounds of gunpowder, and 20 American captives.

FEBRUARY 6 In Paris, France, American and French diplomats work out treaties of commerce and alliance between their two nations, slowly converting what was a local revolution into a global conflict.

FEBRUARY 14 At Quiberon Bay, France, the Continental warship *Ranger* under Captain John Paul Jones is saluted by guns of a nearby fort and the warship *Robuste*. This is the first "official" salute to the American flag by a sovereign nation.

FEBRUARY 15 At Boston, Massachusetts, John Adams and his son John Quincy Adams sail on the Continental frigate *Boston* for France. This is the first time two future presidents of the United States sail on the same vessel.

FEBRUARY 26 On the Delaware River, Captain John Barry leads a cutting-out expedition and takes the schooner HMS *Alert* along with four transports.

MARCH 7 Off the coast of Barbados, Captain Nicholas Biddle and the 32-gun frigate *Randolph* engages the 64-gun HMS *Yarmouth*. The two vessels fight in the darkness for 20 minutes until the *Randolph*'s magazine explodes. Biddle and 311 men die; this constitutes the single largest loss of naval personnel until the battleship USS *Arizona* goes down in December 1941. Biddle is also the only Continental Navy officer with professional training, having previously served in the Royal Navy as a midshipman.

MARCH 9 In the West Indies, Captains Elisha Hinman and Thomas Thompson, leading the large frigates *Alfred* and *Raleigh*, engage the British sloops HMS *Ariadne* and *Ceres*. The British should have been overpowered, but the Americans are outmaneuvered and *Alfred* strikes with 181 captives.

MARCH 27 Near Point Judith, Rhode Island, Captain Abraham Whipple deliberately grounds the Continental frigate *Columbus* while pursued by British warships; it is burned to prevent capture.

MARCH 31 In Chesapeake Bay, the new 28-gun frigate *Virginia* under Captain James Nicholson runs aground and is attacked by HMS *Emerald* and *Conqueror*. Worse, Nicholson abandons his vessel and orders Lieutenant Joshua Barney to surrender it for him.

APRIL 10 At Brest, France, Captain John Paul Jones and the 18-gun sloop *Ranger* depart to raid English home waters.

APRIL 22–23 The British town of Whitehaven is taken by Captain John Paul Jones and the 18-gun sloop Ranger. Crew members spike cannon in a local fort, burn several vessels, and return to their ship; this is the first hostile invasion of England since 1667.

APRIL 23 In the Irish Sea, Captain John Paul Jones of the *Ranger* captures the small British island of St. Mary's, intending to kidnap the Earl of Selkirk as a hostage, but finds him absent from his estate. After his men insist on plundering the Selkirk family's silver, Jones purchases it from the men at his own expense and restores it to the family.

APRIL 24 Near Carrickfergus, Ireland, Captain John Paul Jones and the 18-gun sloop *Ranger* captures the 20-gun sloop HMS *Drake*, along with 150 prisoners. American losses are 3 dead and 5 injured to a British tally of 4 killed (including the captain) and 19 wounded.

Near Ocracoke Inlet, North Carolina, the Continental sloop *Independence* under Captain John Young runs aground and is wrecked.

APRIL 27 In Philadelphia, Pennsylvania, the Continental Congress votes to purchase 12 additional warships to offset recent ship losses.

MAY 7 On the Delaware River, Pennsylvania, British raiding parties manage to burn the 32-gun frigate *Washington*, before it ever gets to sea.

MAY 8 At Brest, France, Captain John Paul Jones and the sloop *Ranger* dock with the captured sloop HMS *Drake* and many prisoners.

AUGUST 3 Off the shore of Newfoundland, Canada, the Continental brig *General Gates* engages the British brigantine HMS *Montague*; Captain John Skimmer is killed, but the British vessel strikes its colors.

SEPTEMBER 24–27 Off the Maine coast, Captain John Barry and the 32-gun frigate *Raleigh* is confronted by British warships *Experiment,* 50 guns, and *Unicorn,* 28 guns. Barry loses his mainmast and deliberately grounds his vessel and burns it to prevent capture, then escapes back to Boston on foot with 85 crewmen.

OCTOBER 28 On the Sakonnet River, Rhode Island, Major Silas Talbot of the Continental Army leads the sloop *Hawke* against the schooner HMS *Pigot*. Previously, he had mounted a kedging anchor to his bowsprit, and he rips away *Pigot's* antiboarding nets as he sails by. Talbot boards his adversary so quickly that the *Pigot* and 45 captives are quickly taken.

1779

JANUARY 14 At Boston, Massachusetts, the American-built frigate *Alliance* departs under Captain Pierre Landais and conveys the marquis de Lafayette back to France. This becomes the only warship jointly commanded by the allies.

FEBRUARY 7 In France, Captain John Paul Jones purchases a beat-up French merchant ship, the *Duc de Duras*, which he promptly renames *Bonhomme Richard* in honor of Benjamin Franklin. It takes Jones six months to find guns and other naval implements to outfit his charge for combat.

MARCH 13 At Boston, Massachusetts, a squadron consisting of the *Warren*, 32 guns, under Captain John B. Hopkins, the *Queen of France*, 28 guns, under Captain Joseph Onley, and the *Ranger*, 18 guns, under Captain Thomas Simpson, begins cruising the eastern seaboard.

APRIL 1 The Continental squadron under Captain John B. Hopkins, consisting of frigates *Queen of France* and *Warren* plus the sloop *Ranger*, captures seven British vessels.

MAY 7   Near Cape Cod, Massachusetts, the Continental sloop *Providence* under Captain Hoysted Hacker captures the British brig *Diligent* after a stiff engagement.

JUNE 6   In the Atlantic, the frigate *Confederacy* under Captain Seth Harding, accompanied by the frigate *Boston* under Captain Samuel Tucker, captures the British privateer *Pole* and two merchant vessels.

JULY 7   Off the coast of Rhode Island, Lieutenant Colonel Silas Talbot, commanding the 12-gun sloop *Argo*, captures the British privateer *Lively* after a five-hour battle.

JULY 18   Near Newfoundland, Commodore Abraham Whipple's squadron, consisting of the frigates *Providence* and *Queen of France* and the sloop *Ranger*, stumbles into a 150-ship British convoy. Whipple takes several unsuspecting vessels captive, as does Captain John P. Rathbun of the *Ranger*. The Americans seize a total of 11 ships with cargos totaling $1 million, and convey 9 of them safely back to Boston.

JULY 19   In Boston, Massachusetts, the state government is alarmed by the construction of a British fort on the Bagaduce Peninsula, Maine Territory, and authorizes an amphibious expedition to capture it. This consists of 1,600 men, 19 armed vessels, and 24 transports under Commodore Dudley Saltonstall, assisted by Generals Solomon Lovell and Peleg Wadsworth of the state militia. This is the largest expedition of its kind ever mounted by the Americans, and is undertaken without notifying Congress.

JULY 24   The American naval expedition under Commodore Dudley Saltonstall arrives at the Penobscot River, Maine, and engages the three-ship squadron of Captain Henry Mowat. Saltonstall concludes that the confined waters of Penobscot Bay will not allow him to maneuver, and he declines further naval support until the militia disposes of Mowat's vessels.

AUGUST 2–24   In Chesapeake Bay, the frigate *Deane* under Captain Samuel Nicholson, the frigate *Boston* under Captain Samuel Tucker, and the sloop-of-war *Thorn* under Lieutenant William Wardlow begin a cruise that nets eight prizes.

AUGUST 7   Off the coast of Rhode Island, Lieutenant Colonel Silas Talbot and the *Argo* engage the 14-gun privateer *Dragon*. A four-hour battle ensues until the latter loses its mainmast and surrenders. The British privateer *Hannah* subsequently hoves into view, and is likewise captured.

AUGUST 13   At Penobscot Bay, Maine, Commodore George Collier enters with 10 vessels and 1,600 soldiers, lifting the American blockade. Commodore Dudley Saltonstall retreats upriver and unceremoniously burns his entire squadron of 43 ships, a loss estimated at $8 million. This is the largest American naval defeat of the war.

AUGUST 14   At Isle de Groix, France, Commodore John Paul Jones and the *Bonhomme Richard*, accompanied by French vessels *Alliance*, *Pallas*, *Vengeance*, and *Le Cerf*, departs on a major raid into British home waters.

SEPTEMBER 3   Commodore John Paul Jones's squadron cruises along the eastern coast of England, where he is intent upon raiding Leith, Edinburgh, and Newcastle-upon-Tyne.

SEPTEMBER 6   At Boston, Massachusetts, the frigates *Deane* and *Boston* drop anchor after completing a successful cruise that took 8 prizes and 250 prisoners.

SEPTEMBER 17   Lieutenant Colonel Silas Talbot resigns his commission in the Continental Army, and joins the Continental Navy as a captain. He is the only army officer of this war to do so.

SEPTEMBER 22   Near Flamborough Head, England, Commodore John Paul Jones's squadron captures two British ships, then espies a large convoy anchored at the mouth of the Humber River.

SEPTEMBER 23   Near Flamborough Head, England, Commodore John Paul Jones and the frigate *Bonhomme Richard* encounter a 40-ship convoy escorted by the new, copper-bottomed 44-gun frigate HMS *Serapis* under Captain Richard Pearson. Pearson orders the convoy into port, then bravely interposes his vessel between them and Jones's enemy squadron. The creaking *Bonhomme Richard* and the smartly handled *Serapis* trade broadsides for several hours in the moonlight, until a grenade ignites an ammunition chest on the latter, which convinces Pearson to strike. American casualties are 150 out of 237 present, while the British suffer 170; *Bonhomme Richard* is so riddled that it sinks two days later.

OCTOBER 3   Commodore John Paul Jones's squadron reaches Texel, the Netherlands, after evading pursuit by eight British warships.

OCTOBER 28   In Philadelphia, Pennsylvania, the Continental Congress replaces the Marine Committee with a five-man Board of the Admiralty. This is comprised of two members of Congress and three

Etching depicting the naval battle between John Paul Jones of the Bonhomme Richard and Captain Richard Pearson of the British naval vessel Serapis on September 22, 1779, during the American Revolution. Jones, recognized as the father of the U.S. Navy, scored a decisive victory in this famous battle. (Library of Congress)

commissioners tasked with overseeing naval matters.

NOVEMBER 7   At Martinque, the frigate *Confederacy*, conveying John Jay to serve as Spain's first American minister, is nearly dismasted by a storm, and puts in for repairs.

NOVEMBER 20   Commodore Abraham Whipple's squadron, consisting of the frigates *Boston*, *Providence*, and *Queen of France*, and the sloop *Ranger*, is ordered to Charleston, South Carolina, to help defend the city against combined British forces.

1780

JANUARY 8   In the Atlantic, Captain John Barry sails the 32-gun frigate *Alliance* on a cruise, netting three merchantmen.

MARCH 14   Near Mobile, British West Florida (Alabama), Spanish military efforts are assisted by Captain William Pickles and the American sloop *West Florida* offshore.

MARCH 20   At Charleston, South Carolina, Commodore Abraham Whipple withdraws his small squadron up the Cooper River and sinks several hulks to obstruct the passage of British warships. The Royal Navy under Admiral Marriot Arbuthnot begins maneuvering into bombardment positions and slips five frigates over the sandbar.

MAY 4   In Philadelphia, Congress promulgates the first official Navy seal.

MAY 12   Charleston, South Carolina, falls to a combined British expedition under General Henry Clinton. The squadron of Captain Abraham Whipple, consisting of frigates *Boston* and *Providence* and the sloop *Ranger*, is scuttled to prevent capture.

JUNE 1   North of Bermuda, the 28-gun frigate *Trumbull* under Captain James Nicholson and the 32-gun British privateer *Watt* under Captain John Coulthard engage in one of the most protracted sea fights of the war. Nicholson batters the British hull with broadsides, while Coulthard concentrates on American masts and rigging. After several hours both vessels limp home; the Americans lose 48 men to a British tally of 92.

JUNE 3   Near the Spanish island of Bilbao, the privateer *Pickering* under Captain Jonathan Haraden encounters the larger 22-gun privateer *Golden Eagle*, which he quickly captures. However, he subsequently runs headlong into the larger 42-gun British privateer *Achilles*, drops anchor near the shoals, and forces his adversary to approach head-on. The *Achillies* is seriously damaged by accurate cannon fire and gradually retreats.

JUNE 9   Off the coast of Newfoundland, Canada, the 26-gun Massachusetts frigate *Protector* under Captain John F. Williams defeats the 32-gun privateer *Admiral Duff;* only 55 British are saved after their vessel suddenly explodes.

OCTOBER 9   Off the Delaware Capes, the Continental sloop *Saratoga* under Captain John Young captures three British brigs.

DECEMBER 18   Near the West Indies, Captain John Paul Jones and the 14-gun sloop-of-war *Ariel* meet and subdue the British privateer *Triumph*. This is the last action Jones performs as part of the Continental Navy.

1781

FEBRUARY 7   In Philadelphia, Pennsylvania, the Continental Congress establishes the office Secretary of Marine to replace the Board of Admiralty, but fails to find a compromise candidate to occupy it.

MARCH 14   In Philadelphia, Pennsylvania, the Confederation Congress votes to thank Captain John Paul Jones and his men; he appears in person to accept their accolades.

MARCH 18   Near Cape Francois, Haiti, the Continental 18-gun sloop *Saratoga* under Captain John Young founders and sinks with all hands during a storm.

APRIL 2   Off the French coast, Captain John Barry and the 36-gun frigate *Alliance* is accosted by British privateers *Mars* and *Minerva*; in a striking display of superior seamanship, he subdues both vessels.

APRIL 14   Off the Delaware Capes, the 32-gun frigate *Confederacy* under Captain Seth Harding is cornered by British frigates HMS *Orpheus* and *Roebuck*, and he surrenders without a fight. His vessel is taken into British service as HMS *Confederate*.

MAY 29   In the Atlantic, Captain John Barry and the 36-gun frigate *Alliance* is attacked in calm waters by the 16-gun HMS *Atalanta* and the 14-gun *Trepassy*. The British ships row themselves into raking position near Barry's stern, and he is wounded by grapeshot. He is carried below deck but, after crewmen mention surrendering, Barry orders them to carry him topside. Once the wind springs up, *Alliance* easily outmaneuvers its antagonists, capturing both. American losses are 8 killed and 19 wounded to 12 British dead, 29 injured, and 169 captured.

JUNE 13   In the Atlantic, American privateers *Pilgrim* and *Rambler* encounter, corner, and capture the British sloop *Snake*, 12 guns.

AUGUST 9   Off the Delaware Capes, Captain James Nicholson and the 28-gun frigate *Trumbull* encounter the 32-gun HMS *Iris* and 18-gun brig *General Monck*. Three-fourths of Nicholson's crew, British deserters, refuses to fight, so he, assisted by Lieutenants Richard Dale, Alexander Murray, and a handful of men, resist for half an hour before surrendering. The Americans lose 5 killed, 11 wounded, and 175 prisoners.

AUGUST 29   In Philadelphia, Pennsylvania, the Confederation Congress fails to find a compromise candidate to become Secretary of Marine, so they establish the office of Agent of Marine.

SEPTEMBER 6   Near Charleston, South Carolina, the privateer *Congress* under Captain George Geddes engages the sloop HMS *Savage* and boards it after a four-hour battle.

SEPTEMBER 7   In Philadelphia, Pennsylvania, the Confederation Congress appoints financier Robert Morris to serve as Agent of Marine.

OCTOBER 21 In the Atlantic, the American privateer *Indian* captures the British vessel *Venus*, the first of seven taken on an extended cruise.

DECEMBER 31 After a disastrous year, the Continental Navy has only two vessels, the frigates *Alliance* and *Deane*, still in commission. Two other frigates, *Ariel* and *Pallas*, have been borrowed from France.

1782

APRIL 8 In Delaware Bay, Captain Joshua Barney and the sloop *Hyder Ally* is chased by the brig HMS *General Monk* and the privateer *Fair American* into the restricted waters. Barney quietly instructs his helmsman to do the opposite of whatever commands he yells and the British, listening intently, incorrectly shadow his moves until *Hyder Ally* crosses their bows. The *General Monk* surrenders with a loss of 53 men killed and wounded, while the victorious Barney suffers 15 casualties.

SEPTEMBER 2 In Boston, the Americans turn over the new 74-gun ship of the line *America* to France as compensation for a similar vessel, the *Magnifique*, which previously sank in the harbor. This is the first vessel of its class built in America.

SEPTEMBER 24–28 In the Atlantic, Captain John Barry and the 32-gun frigate *Alliance* capture four British merchant ships headed for Jamaica.

SEPTEMBER 30 Near Tangier Sound, Chesapeake Bay, six British barges attack the Maryland barge *Protector*, capturing 80 prisoners, along with Commodore Hezekiah Whaley. This is one of the final naval encounters of the war.

DECEMBER 20 Off the Delaware Capes, the frigate *South Carolina* under Captain John Joyner surrenders to HMS *Diomede* and HMS *Quebec*; American losses are 6 killed and wounded along with 450 prisoners.

1783

MARCH 10 Off the Florida coast, Captain John Barry of the frigate *Alliance*, accompanied by the French frigate *Duc de Lauzun*, are attacked by the frigates HMS *Alarm* and *Sybil* and the sloop *Tobago*. Barry coolly closes with the *Sybil* to within pistol shot, then unlooses a devastating broadside that cripples the British ship. *Sybil* is dismasted, but Barry moves off to cover the *Duc de Lauzun*, carrying half a million dollars in specie. The Americans lose one killed and nine wounded in this, the final naval engagement of the Revolutionary War.

MARCH 12 At Philadelphia, Pennsylvania, the Continental Navy vessel *George Washington* arrives, bearing a copy of the Treaty of Paris with Great Britain.

MARCH 24 In Philadelphia, Pennsylvania, the Confederation Congress instructs

Agent of Marine Robert Morris to recall all armed Americans vessels, be they Continental Navy or privateer.

April 11 In Philadelphia, Pennsylvania, Congress declares hostilities with Great Britain at an end.

April 15 The Confederation Congress orders all British naval captives to be released.

September 3 In Paris, France, representatives from Great Britain, the United States, and France sign the definitive peace treaty, ending the Revolutionary War.

1784

April 8 In Philadelphia, Pennsylvania, Agent of Marine Robert Morris advises the Continental Congress to sell off existing Continental Navy warships, thereby reducing peacetime expenditures and paying down the national debt.

1785

June 3 In Philadelphia, Pennsylvania, the Confederation Congress orders its final warship, the 36-gun frigate *Alliance*, sold. Consequently, the United States lacks any semblance of naval power for nearly a decade.

July 25 In the Mediterranean, Algerian pirates seize the American vessel *Maria* and hold the crew for ransom. The four Barbary states, Morocco, Algiers, Tunis, and Tripoli, realize that American shipping is no longer protected by the Royal Navy, and they are considered fair game by the pirates. Thus begins a decade-long diplomatic struggle to halt these depredations, made all the more impossible by the nation's utter lack of naval forces.

July 30 In the Mediterranean, Barbary pirates seize a second American vessel, the *Dauphin*, whose crew is held for ransom.

August 1 The distinguished frigate *Alliance*, the last vessel operated by the Continental Navy, is sold on the open market. The United States has rid itself of all former warships.

1787

October 16 In Philadelphia, Pennsylvania, the Confederation Congress unanimously votes Captain John Paul Jones a gold medal for services rendered during the Revolutionary War; he is the only Continental Navy officer so honored.

1788

April 15 In Russia, Captain John Paul Jones accepts an admiral's commission at the behest of Czarina Catherine the Great. He performs useful service against the Turks and the two battles of Liman, but is ultimately frustrated by court intrigues and resigns.

1789

August 7 In Philadelphia, Pennsylvania, Congress orders all present naval matters to be handled by the new Secretary of War's office.

1790

April 4 In Philadelphia, Pennsylvania, the Confederation Congress votes to create a Revenue Marine Service (Coast Guard) for the purpose of suppressing smuggling and increasing revenues. It functions as part of the Treasury Department.

August 4 The Revenue Marine Service arises following the purchase of 10 small boats; this is the origin of the U.S. Coast Guard.

1791

January 6 In New York, Senate Committee on Mediterranean Trade reports that commerce abroad requires the protection of a naval establishment. Since 1783, American shipping has been subject to harassment by the Barbary powers of North Africa (Morocco, Algiers, Tunis, and Tripoli), who seize merchant vessels and exchange them and their crews for ransom and tribute.

March 21 In New York, President George Washington issues his first-ever military commission to Captain Hopley Yeaton of the revenue cutter *Scannel*.

1792

July 18 In Paris, France, Revolutionary War hero John Paul Jones dies in obscurity and is interred in an unmarked grave. His resting place is not rediscovered until 1905.

1793

April 22 In New York, President George Washington recommends a force of six frigates to counter the Algerian piracy in the Mediterranean.

July 8–25 In the Mediterranean, Algerian pirates seize eight American merchantmen.

October 8 In the Mediterranean, American merchant vessels *Dispatch*, *Hope*, and *Thomas* are captured by Algerian pirates and the ships, crews, and cargo are held for ransom. The United States is powerless to respond.

1794

January 2 In New York, Congress adopts a resolution creating a naval establishment for the purpose of protecting American commerce abroad. However, many politicians, especially Thomas Jefferson's Republicans, view navies as overly expensive and dangerously aristocratic in tenor.

March 27 The Naval Act of 1794 authorizes the construction of three 44-gun frigates and three 36-gun frigates. These are built to curtail depredations upon American commerce by Algerian pirates, although Congress can cancel the warships if a peace treaty is signed.

June 28 In Philadelphia, Pennsylvania, shipwright Joshua Humphreys contracts with the government to design two classes of frigates. Among the vessels he constructs, in conjunction with draftsman William Dougherty and English emigrant Josiah Fox, are the *Constitution*, *United States* and *Constellation*.

In concert with the Naval Act of 1794, President George Washington appoints the first six naval officers of the nascent U.S. Navy: Joshua Barney, John Barry, Richard Dale, Samuel Nicholson, Silas Talbot, and Thomas Truxtun.

1795

February 23 In New York, Congress approves The Office of Purveyor of Supplies, a precursor to the Supply Corps.

September 5 To placate the Dey of Algiers, the United States signs a treaty agreeing to pay him a $525,000 ransom for captured crews and ships, a 36-gun frigate as a gift, and $21,000 worth of naval stores as an annual tribute.

1796

March 2 In New York, Congress ratifies the new treaty with Algiers, at which point construction of the six frigates authorized on March 27, 1794, is halted.

MARCH 15 In New York, President George Washington urges Congress to continue funding the six frigates under construction despite the prospects of a treaty with Algiers.

APRIL 20 Congress passes the Naval Act of 1796, a compromise measure allowing completion of three of the frigates authorized by the Naval Act of 1794. The remaining three are suspended in the wake of a peace treaty with Algiers.

NOVEMBER 4 A one-sided treaty is signed with the Pasha of Tripoli in order to end his depredations against American shipping in the Mediterranean.

DECEMBER 6 In his last annual message to Congress, President George Washington endorses creation of a standing navy to protect American commerce on the high seas and garner respect for the flag abroad.

1797

FEBRUARY 27 In New York, Secretary of State Timothy Pickering reports increasing depredations against American shipping in the Caribbean region by vessels of Revolutionary France.

MAY 10 In Philadelphia, Pennsylvania, the 44-gun frigate *United States*, designed by Joshua Humphreys, is launched. This is the first official warship of the U.S. Navy and also the largest of its class in the world. Command is entrusted to Revolutionary War hero Captain John Barry.

MAY 16 In a speech to Congress, President John Adams declares that a standing navy is essential for defending national sovereignty. He further calls for completion of all previously approved warships, and also wants American merchant vessels to arm themselves.

JULY 1 In New York, Congress heeds President John Adams's call to defend American commerce against French privateers, and authorizes crew recruitment for the frigates *Constitution*, *Constellation*, and *United States*. The first set of "Navy Regulations" to govern the service is also approved.

JULY 11 In Philadelphia, Pennsylvania, the 44-gun frigate *United States* is formally commissioned as the nation's first warship; Captain John Barry takes the helm.

AUGUST 14 In Paris, France, the United States signs a peace treaty with Tunis, whereby the former agrees to pay $107,000 to have the latter cease attacks on its shipping.

SEPTEMBER 7 At Baltimore, Maryland, the 36-gun frigate *Constellation* is launched; it is to be captained by Thomas Truxtun. The nascent U.S. Navy begins acquiring real combat capabilities—which will be tested shortly.

OCTOBER 21 At Boston, Massachusetts, the 44-gun frigate *Constitution* is launched under Captain Samuel Nicholson. This is the second such vessel acquired by the Navy and is destined to become its most celebrated warship; it remains in commission today.

1798

MARCH 27 In New York, Congress, responding to rising maritime tensions with France, authorizes the three additional frigates completed in 1797 to be outfitted for active duty.

APRIL 27 In New York, President John Adams is authorized by Congress to purchase 12 armed vessels for the protection of American shipping against French privateers.

APRIL 30 In New York, President John Adams prevails upon Congress to create the Department of the Navy to further strengthen the defensive capability of the nation. This new entity will oversee naval administration previously handled by the Department of War, and is directed by a new Secretary of the Navy.

MAY 3 In Philadelphia, Pennsylvania, the merchant ship *Ganges* is purchased and becomes the first armed vessel ready for deployment in the so-called "Quasi-War" with France. It is commanded by Revolutionary War veteran Captain Richard Dale.

MAY 4 In New York, the purchase or construction of an additional 10 armed vessels is authorized by Congress for use against French privateers in the Caribbean.

MAY 18 In New York, President John Adams appoints Benjamin Stoddert as the first Secretary of the Navy. Despite a grandiose title, he oversees a tiny naval establishment hovering on the cusp of hostilities with France.

MAY 24 At Philadelphia, Pennsylvania, Captain Richard Dale guides the 26-gun ship *Ganges* out to sea, initiating the first cruise of the so-called Quasi-War.

MAY 28 In New York, President John Adams is authorized to order naval commanders to engage any French vessel harassing American commerce at sea. The undeclared naval war is at hand, which is proving ground for the U.S. Navy.

JUNE 18 In New York, Benjamin Stoddert, a former Continental Army officer, takes his oath as the first Secretary of the Navy.

JUNE 23 At Boston, Massachusetts, Captain Samuel Nicholson takes the frigate *Constitution* on its first cruise and begins scouring the coastline for French privateers.

JUNE 25 In New York, Congress authorizes all merchantmen to arm themselves against French privateers.

JUNE 28 In New York, Congress approves the sale of all lawful captures, which will be used to pay prize money to American ship crews.

JUNE 30 In New York, President John Adams receives authorization to expand the U.S. Navy by obtaining 12 additional armed vessels by gift or loan.

JULY 7 In New York, the American government cancels any existing treaties with France.

Near Great Egg Harbor, New Jersey, the U.S. Navy draws its first blood once Captain Stephen Decatur, Sr., and the 20-gun sloop *Delaware* capture the 14-gun French privateer *La Croyable*. This is the first prize of the Quasi-War and it is taken into service as the *Retaliation*.

JULY 9 In New York, President John Adams begins issuing the first of 365

> ### Truxtun, Thomas (1755–1822)
>
> Thomas Truxtun was born on Long Island, New York, on February 17, 1755, the son of an English barrister. He went to sea as a cabin boy and served three years before being impressed onboard HMS *Prudent*, a British warship. He then joined the merchant marine and was commanding his own vessel by the age of 20. When the Revolutionary War broke out in 1775, Truxtun joined the patriot cause and commanded a succession of privateers over the course of the conflict. So skillful was he at running sorely needed supplies to the Continental Army that General George Washington once toasted his service as equal to a regiment's. After the war, Truxtun commanded the merchant vessel *Canton*, and in 1785 he became one of the first Americans to drop anchor in Chinese waters.
>
> In 1798, when hostilities with France culminated in the undeclared Quasi-War, Truxtun became one of the six original captains commissioned in the U.S. Navy. In this capacity he oversaw construction of the 38-gun frigate *Constellation* at Baltimore, Maryland, and on February 9, 1799, he engaged and defeated the frigate *L'Insurgente*. On February 1, 1800, Truxtun fought the larger frigate *La Vengeance* near Guadalupe, roughly handling his adversary until a lucky shot toppled his mainmast. The badly damaged French ship escaped, but Truxtun returned a national hero, and received a gold medal from Congress. The hot-tempered captain resigned his commission in 1802 in a dispute regarding seniority, and died in Philadelphia on May 5, 1822. He was one of the early U.S. Navy's most significant leaders.

Letters of Marque and Reprisal to allow private vessels to be armed and attack French maritime commerce as privateers.

JULY 16 In New York, Congress reverses itself and authorizes construction of the three remaining frigates first authorized in 1794 (*Congress*, *Chesapeake*, and *President*) to continue.

JULY 22 Having completed its shakedown cruise, the frigate *Constitution* departs Boston, Massachusetts, under Captain Samuel Nicholson for a lengthy Caribbean cruise.

JULY 29 Near Dewee's Inlet, South Carolina, the British schooner HMS *Mosquito* mistakenly fires upon the American schooner *Unanimity*, believing it to be French. The *Unanimity* is driven onto a sand bar, but swift diplomatic work minimizes damage between the two nations.

JULY 30 In New York, Secretary of the Navy Benjamin Stoddert outlines his naval strategy to President John Adams. Stoddert intends to offensively deploy American naval assets in the Caribbean, thereby taking the war to the enemy.

AUGUST 8 In New York, Secretary of the Navy Benjamin Stoddert forbids recruiting African Americans for the U.S. Navy; this approach is counter to a trend in effect since the Revolutionary War.

AUGUST 22 In the Caribbean, the frigate *United States* under Captain John Barry captures the French schooner *Sans Pareil* after a 10-hour chase between Dominica and Martinique. This is the first prize taken by an American frigate.

SEPTEMBER 8 Near Cape Hatteras, North Carolina, Captain Samuel Nicholson and the *Constitution* halt the British vessel *Niger*, only to find it has a French captain; it is taken back as a prize.

SEPTEMBER 30 Off the coast of Havana, Cuba, the sloop *Baltimore* and frigate

Constitution are escorting a convoy of 47 merchant vessels when they are infiltrated by the British schooner *Nancy*. The intruder, seeking protection from the French, is expelled. However, several Americans serving on the British ship transfer their services to the *Baltimore*.

NOVEMBER 16   In the Caribbean, British warships accost the 20-gun American sloop *Baltimore* and remove five suspected British deserters for impressment purposes. Once home, Captain Isaac Phillips is cashiered for failing to defend the American flag; henceforth U.S. Navy warships are expressly ordered to use force to resist such practices.

NOVEMBER 20   Off the Carribean Island of Guadalupe, the schooner *Retaliation* under Lieutenant William Bainbridge is seized by the French frigates *L'Insurgente* and *Volontaire*. This becomes the only American warship captured during the "Quasi-War."

In New York, Secretary of the Navy Benjamin Stoddert suggests enhancing U.S. Navy strength by acquiring 12 ships of the line, 12 frigates, and 20 smaller vessels. However, such expenses are way beyond what Congress is willing to appropriate.

DECEMBER 29   In New York, Secretary of the Navy Benjamin Stoddert submits his annual report to Congress for the first time, a practice that continues until 1948.

1799

JANUARY 16   Near Bermuda, Captain Samuel Nicholson and the frigate *Constitution* capture a French vessel, only to learn that it was formerly a British ship captured by the French. Nicholson, lacking authority to liberate English shipping, releases the ship under a prize crew.

JANUARY 17   At St. Kitts, Lesser Antilles, Captain Thomas Truxtun arrives with his American squadron. This port serves as the navy's main base of operations in the Caribbean for the remainder of the conflict.

FEBRUARY 3   In the Caribbean, the frigate *United States* chases and sinks the French privateer *L'Amour de la Paris*. The crew is subsequently exchanged for American prisoners held at Guadalupe.

FEBRUARY 8   Off the coast of Cuba, a convoy escorted by Captain Stephen Decatur, Sr., of the *Delaware* is accosted by the British warship HMS *Solebay*. The British insolently fire shots and demand the right to search for deserters, but Decatur defies them and keeps sailing.

FEBRUARY 9   Off the island of Nevis, Captain Thomas Truxtun of the 38-gun frigate *Constellation* captures the 40-gun French frigate *L'Insurgente*; losses are 2 American dead and 3 wounded to 29 French killed, 41 injured, and 176 captured. This is the first significant ship-to-ship victory of the Quasi-War, and the prize is taken into service as the *Insurgent*.

FEBRUARY 21   Near Cape Nichola Mole, Hispaniola, Captain Thomas Tingey and the *Ganges* are accosted by the British vessel HMS *Surprise*, whose captain demands all English subjects serving on board. The English-born Tingey bristles and threatens to fight the larger vessel, at which point the *Surprise* sails away.

FEBRUARY 25 In New York, Congress authorizes construction of six ships of the line and six sloops-of-war. These represent a considerable naval expansion; however, none of these vessels is built.

MARCH 2 In New York, Congress authorizes the creation of naval pensions and also increases the size of the Marine Corps.

MARCH 5 Near Havana, Cuba, Captain Stephen Decatur, Sr., leads the frigates *Baltimore* and *General Greene* in capturing the French privateer *Le Marsouin*. The French vessel had tried masquerading itself as an unarmed merchantman.

MARCH 12 In New York, Secretary of the Navy Benjamin Stoddert orders U.S. Navy warships to search any suspicious vessels within their grasp and retake any armed prizes.

MAY 12 In the Caribbean, Captain Alexander Murray completes the most impressive cruise of any American naval leader by seizing two French ships, convoying 100 merchantmen ships to safety, and in the course of this he managed to drop anchor at all four American stations in the theater.

MAY 20 At Boston, Massachusetts, the new frigate *Boston* is launched under the auspices of Captain George Little.

MAY 28 At Boston, Massachusetts, Captain Samuel Nicholson is replaced as captain of the frigate *Constitution* by Captain Silas Talbot, a distinguished Revolutionary War veteran.

JUNE 5 At Charleston, South Carolina, the frigate *John Adams* is launched with George Cross as captain.

JUNE 8 At New York, the frigate *Adams* is launched with Captain Richard V. Morris destined to take eventual command of the vessel.

JUNE 26 In New York, President John Adams lifts the embargo of St. Domingo, Hispaniola, but this creates a need for additional naval protection to secure American shipping.

JUNE 28 In the Caribbean, the American brig *Merrimack* dispatches the French schooner *Magicienne* (formerly the *Retaliation*) with a single broadside. The vessel is immediately restored back to American service under its original name.

JULY 27 At Newport, Rhode Island, the frigate *General Greene* drops anchor and concludes its extended cruise of Cuban waters; previously, an outbreak of yellow fever killed 20 crew members and incapacitated 37 others.

AUGUST 1 Captain Thomas Truxtun, angered by a presidential decision to rank him below Captain Silas Talbot, tenders his resignation.

AUGUST 14 The frigate *Insurgent*, recently captured from France, departs for Gibraltar under Captain Alexander Murray.

AUGUST 15 After five years of episodic construction, the 36-gun frigate *Congress* launches at Portsmouth, New Hampshire, under Captain James Sever. It had been first authorized in 1794.

SEPTEMBER 30 At Salem, Massachusetts, the frigate *Essex*, paid for with contributions from the inhabitants of Essex County, is launched under fiery Captain Edward Preble.

October 2 The Washington Navy Yard is established on the future site of Washington, D.C.; it remains the U.S. Navy's oldest shore facility.

November 3 At Newport, Rhode Island, peace envoys Oliver Ellsworth and William Richardson embark on the frigate *United States* and sail for France.

November 18 Off the coast of Guadalupe, the American brig *Pickering* under Lieutenant Benjamin Hillar is attacked by the larger corsair *L'Egypte Conquise*. Hillar, though outgunned, gives battle and forces the French vessel to strike.

December 2 At Norfolk, Virginia, the 38-gun frigate *Chesapeake* launches and will eventually be placed under the command of Captain Samuel Barron. In time it acquires a reputation as an "unlucky vessel."

1800

January 1 Near St. Marc, the armed schooner *Experiment* is attacked by several hundred pirates who mistake it for an unarmed merchantman; the *Experiment* repels its antagonists, sinking two pirate craft.

February 1 Off the coast of Guadalupe, the American frigate *Constellation* under Captain Thomas Truxtun defeats the 50-gun frigate *La Vengeance* in a day-long chase. Superior American gunnery force the French vessel to strike its colors twice, but smoke obscures its capitulation and *Constellation* goes on fighting. *La Vengeance* finally escapes after Truxtun's ship loses its mainmast, and it limps away into Curacao. Truxton's losses total 14 dead and 25 injured; the French sustain an estimated 50 killed and 110 wounded.

February 7 The 32-gun frigate *Essex* under Captain Edward Preble, intent upon reaching the East Indies, becomes the first American warship to dip below the equator.

February 27 Off the coast of Haiti, the frigate *General Greene* under Captain Christopher R. Perry supports Haitian rebels under the famous General Toussaint L'Ouverture, and several French forts are successfully stormed. The general highly praises Perry and his crew.

March 28 The frigate *Essex* under Captain Edward Preble is the first American warship to round the Cape of Good Hope, South Africa, and make sail into the Indian Ocean.

April 5 At Philadelphia, Pennsylvania, the new frigate *Philadelphia* is christened and placed under the command of Captain Stephen Decatur, Sr.

April 10 At New York, the 44-gun frigate *President* launches with the newly restored Commodore Thomas Truxtun at its helm; this is also the last of the original six frigates authorized in 1794.

May 11 Near Puerta Plata, Santo Domingo, Lieutenant Isaac Hull leads a boarding party to the merchant vessel *Sally*, which subsequently pulls alongside the French privateer *Sandwich*. Hull quickly sorties and captures their quarry without loss, then sails away with his prize.

JUNE 12 In Portsmouth, New Hampshire, the Navy buys a 60-acre plot to construct the first shipyard in that state; it is still active to present times.

JUNE 13 In the West Indies, the frigate *John Adams* seizes the French schooner *Decade*, its ninth capture.

JULY 1 In the Sunda Strait, Dutch East Indies, Captain Edward Preble and the frigate *Essex* perform the U.S. Navy's first convoy by escorting 14 merchantmen back home.

AUGUST 3 Near Haiti, the sloop-of-war *Trumbull* seizes the French schooner *Vengeance*. Among the captives are several French army officers and their families fleeing the revolution there.

AUGUST 8 In Philadelphia, Pennsylvania, Captain William Bainbridge leads the sloop *George Washington* to Algeria to deliver a store of lumber and goods to the local dey as tribute. This is the first American warship in Mediterranean waters, and is intended to make an impression upon local pirates.

At Norfolk, Virginia, the late French frigate *Insurgent* sails for the West Indies under Captain Patrick Fletcher, and is lost with all hands en route.

AUGUST 20 At New Castle, Delaware, Lieutenant B. Hillar departs on the revenue cutter *Pickering* for the West Indies, then disappears at sea with all hands.

SEPTEMBER 23 At St. Ana Bay, Curacao, the American sloop *Patapsco* bombards French forces besieging a Dutch fort. The French subsequently evacuate the following day, and it is secured by a party of marines and sailors.

OCTOBER 1 Near St. Barts, the schooner *Experiment* is attacked by two French vessels, when it suddenly turns and captures the schooner *Diana* after a single broadside. General Andre Rigaud is among the captives.

OCTOBER 12 In the Caribbean off Guadalupe, the 28-gun frigate *Boston* under Captain George Little engages and captures the 24-gun corvette *Le Berceau* after an intense night battle. This is one of eight vessels captured by the *Boston*; French losses are 34 men killed and 18 wounded.

OCTOBER 20 In Algiers, Captain William Bainbridge weathers an egregious national insult when the Dey of Algiers orders him to convey an emissary to the Ottoman Empire aboard the warship *George Washington*. Bainbridge angrily refuses, but American consul Richard O'Brien warns him that the dey might resume attacking American shipping if not appeased. Bainbridge is further required to present gifts to the Ottoman government and fly their flag from his masthead; cognizant of his predicament, the Sublime Porte in Istanbul treats him with extreme politeness.

NOVEMBER 28 At New York, the frigate *Essex* under Captain Edward Preble drops anchor following its record 11-month sojourn to the Indian Ocean. *Essex* is also the first American warship to twice round the Cape of Good Hope in one cruise.

DECEMBER 31 In a very active year, the nascent U.S. Navy has captured 49 French privateers and the frigate *Le Berceau* without losing a single vessel of its own.

1801

FEBRUARY 3 In New York, the Senate ratifies the Convention of 1800 which finally ends the Quasi-War with France. The U.S. Navy's 16 warships have performed capably, capturing 85 French privateers and two frigates for a loss of one sloop.

FEBRUARY 18 In New York, Benjamin Stoddert tends his resignation as Secretary of the Navy; five months lapse before his replacement is appointed.

MARCH 3 In New York, the Peace Establishment Act is signed by President John Adams. This authorizes retention of 13 warships for the U.S. Navy, but only 6 of these are maintained on active duty. The budding officer corps is also reduced.

MARCH 4 In Washington, D.C., Thomas Jefferson takes the oath of office. Despite a reputation for pacifism, he proves unhesitating when confronting the Barbary pirates, and orders a naval expedition assembled.

MAY 14 In Tripoli, Pasha Yusuf Karamanli, feeling that the amount of tribute he is receiving from the United States is insufficient, declares war.

MAY 20 In Washington, D.C., the War Department instructs Commodore Richard Dale to form a squadron around the frigates *Essex*, *Philadelphia*, and *President*, accompanied by the schooner *Enterprise*. Officially, he is to show the flag in the Mediterranean but, should war break out with the Barbary States of North Africa, he is to blockade the port of Tripoli.

MAY 22 At Hampton Roads, Virginia, Captain Richard Dale succeeds Thomas Truxtun as commander of the frigate *President*, now serving as the flagship of the new Mediterranean squadron.

MAY 29 At Hampton Roads, Virginia, the squadron assembled by Captain Richard Dale sets sail for the Mediterranean. The United States, after a long hiatus, is about to flex its small but potent naval capacity. Curiously, two batteries of U.S. Army artillerymen are onboard to assist the squadron.

JUNE 10 The illustrious warship *Ganges*, a former merchant craft which captured 11 French vessels during the Quasi War, is sold in accordance with the Peace Establishment Act.

JULY 17 Near Tripoli, North Africa, Commodore Richard Dale's squadron imposes a blockade on the city. The American consul, James Cathcart, futilely tries to convince Pasha Yusuf Karamanli to reduce tribute payments from $250,000 to annual payments of $20,000.

AUGUST 1 Off the coast of Malta, the brig *Enterprise* under Lieutenant Andrew Sterrett captures the 14-gun North African poleacre *Tripoli*, killing 30 Algerians and taking 30 captive. However, because Sterrett is not authorized to take prizes, his catch is disarmed and allowed to sail home. Congress votes him a sword.

SEPTEMBER 29 Outside the Tripoli harbor, the frigates *Essex* and *Philadelphia* fire upon Tripolitan gunboats as they attempt to break the blockade.

1802

February 6 In Washington, D.C., Congress lifts all restrictions inherent in the Peace Establishment Act by voting to allow the president to man, equip, and deploy armed vessels for protecting American commerce. They also belatedly recognize that a de facto state of war exists with the Tripolitan pirates.

March 3 Commodore Thomas Truxtun again resigns his commission over a minor tiff with the Secretary of the Navy. Previously, he had been offered command of a second American squadron for Mediterranean service.

March 10 At Gibraltar, Commodore Richard Dale sails off from the Mediterranean, concluding nine months of fruitless blockade duty. His force proved too weak to either effectively blockade the city or bombard it into submission.

April 27 At Hampton Roads, Virginia, Commodore Richard V. Morris and the frigate *Chesapeake* sail to Tripoli. Once on station there, he will gradually assemble a new squadron in driblets.

May 10 Near Tripoli, the frigate *Boston* engages a flotilla of gunboats, causing one to ground itself.

June 22–August 16 At Tangiers, Morocco, the sultan informs Consul James Simpson of his decision to declare war on the United States. However, news of Commodore Richard V. Morris's impending arrival prompts him to change his mind.

July 22 Off the coast of Tripoli, Captain Alexander Murray and the frigate *Constellation* engage several Tripolitan vessels, sinking two gunboats.

December 15 In Washington, D.C., President Thomas Jefferson, wishing to help preserve inactive warships, entreats Congress to construct a dry dock at the Washington Navy Yard. No action is taken.

1803

February 28 In Washington, D.C., President Thomas Jefferson, determined to enforce trading rights on the Mississippi River, signs Congressional legislation to acquire gunboats for that purpose.

May 12 Near Tripoli, the frigate *John Adams* under Captain John Rodgers captures the brig *Meshuda* as it attempts to enter Tripoli harbor under the Moroccan flag.

May 20 At Boston, Massachusetts, Commodore Edward Preble assumes command of the frigate *Constitution*. A stern disciplinarian, he wields a profound impact on the U.S. Navy's embryonic officer corps.

May 22–26 Near Tripoli, the frigates *John Adams*, *New York*, and *Adams*, accompanied by the schooner *Enterprise*, assume blockading positions. The plucky *Enterprise* also chases an enemy vessel into the city harbor before being hotly engaged by land batteries.

May 23 At Boston, Massachusetts, Captain Edward Preble gains appointment as

> ## Preble, Edward (1761–1807)
>
> Edward Preble was born in Portland, Maine, the son of a merchant marine captain. In 1779 he joined a privateer of the Massachusetts state navy, cruised for prizes during the Revolutionary War, and by 1782 he commanded his own sloop. In 1794 President John Adams established the U.S. Navy, and Preble joined as a lieutenant. During the Quasi-War against France, 1798–1800, he captured the French privateer *L'Egypte Conquise*, then assumed command of the frigate *Essex* and took 14 more prizes in the East Indies. Preble returned home in 1800 and was offered the frigate *Adams*, but he declined due to poor health. However, in 1801 the Dey of Tripoli declared war on the United States to collect larger tribute payments, and President Thomas Jefferson countered by dispatching several naval squadrons to deal with the pirates.
>
> In May 1803 Preble accepted command of a squadron destined for Tripoli, and he arrived off the coast the following November. Unlike previous commanders, he was extremely aggressive and imposed a tight blockade of the city, punctuated by periodic bombardments. In February 1804 he authorized Lieutenant Stephen Decatur to daringly burn the captured frigate *Philadelphia*, which was successfully accomplished. Preble rotated out of the Mediterranean in September 1804 and returned home. He felt his mission had been a failure, and was utterly surprised to learn that Congress had voted him a gold medal for his sterling leadership. He died in Portland on August 25, 1807, having schooled an entire generation of young naval officers in the art of command.

commodore of the Mediterranean Squadron. His aggressive brand of leadership proves infectious to all ranks.

Outside Tripoli, a landing party of 50 sailors and marines under Lieutenant David Porter from the frigate *New York* lands west of the city, sets a dozen beached feluccas (gunboats) on fire, then retires with 15 casualties.

May 27 In Tripoli Harbor, the frigates *John Adams*, *New York*, and *Adams* trade fire with nine gunboats escorting a 14-gun xebec (gunboat) during a protracted night action. The enemy vessels elude capture and return to port.

May 31–June 7 Near Tripoli, the American blockading squadron harasses 10 Tripolitan merchantmen and prevents them from unloading their cargoes. Two of the enemy ships are captured and burned.

June 21 West of Tripoli, a 22-gun Tripolitan polacre is sunk by the frigate *John Adams*, under Captain John Rodgers, and the schooner *Enterprise*. After this diversion, the blockading squadron refocuses its attention toward the city.

In Washington, D.C., Secretary of the Navy Samuel Smith is angered by Commodore Richard V. Morris's unwillingness to communicate his strategy and intention, and takes steps to remove him as head of the Mediterranean squadron.

June 26 Outside Tripoli, Commodore Richard V. Morris unilaterally lifts the naval blockade rather than stir up additional trouble with Morocco.

August 26 Near Cape de Gata, Spain, Captain William Bainbridge and the frigate *Philadelphia* capture the Moroccan warship *Mirboka* and free its American prize, the brig *Celia*, whose crew was being held in irons below deck.

September 14 Near Gibraltar, Commodore Edward Preble assembles the third Mediterranean squadron, consisting of the frigates *Constitution*, *John Adams*, *New York*, and *Philadelphia*, assisted by schooners *Nautilus* and *Vixen*. The youthful officers under his command, none of which are over 30 years old, come to be known collectively as "Preble's Boys." The commodore has also informed Consul James Simpson of his intention to seize any vessels belonging to the sultan of Morocco, should his depredations persist.

SEPTEMBER 17 Commodore Edward Preble learns of the Moroccan seizure of an American vessel at the port of Mogador, and their declared intention to take other ships at sea. Preble determines to impress the sultan with the might of the United States before pressing on to Tripoli.

SEPTEMBER 20 At Gibraltar, Spain, Lieutenant Isaac Hull arrives with the schooner *Enterprise*.

OCTOBER 1 Lieutenant Charles Stewart and the brig *Syren* drop anchor at Gibraltar, Spain.

OCTOBER 12 At Tangiers, Morocco, Commodore Edward Preble and U.S. Consul James Simpson rather indelicately prevail upon Sultan Mulai Suleiman to ratify the peace treaty first concluded in 1787.

OCTOBER 31 In Tripoli harbor, disaster strikes when the frigate *Philadelphia* grounds while chasing an enemy vessel. Captain William Bainbridge struggles to refloat his vessel, but is soon surrounded by gunboats and forced to surrender. His entire crew of 307 is interred as prisoners of war.

NOVEMBER 12 Outside Tripoli, Commodore Edward Preble's squadron establishes an official blockade and warns neutral vessels to steer clear.

NOVEMBER 25 Near Tripoli, a passing British warship informs Commodore Edward Preble of the *Philadelphia's* capture; he immediately begins planning to destroy the vessel at its moorings.

DECEMBER 23 In the Mediterranean, Lieutenant Stephen Decatur, Jr., and the schooner *Enterprise* capture the Tripolitan ketch *Mastico*, which is taken into squadron service as the *Intrepid*.

1804

FEBRUARY 2 At Syracuse harbor, Sicily, Lieutenant Charles Stewart and the brig *Syren* escort Lieutenant Stephen Decatur, Jr., and the captured ketch *Intrepid* on an unknown mission.

FEBRUARY 16 In Tripoli harbor, Lieutenant Stephen Decatur, Jr., leads a cutting-out expedition that recaptures the frigate *Philadelphia*, then burns it under the city's walls. Decatur commands only 60 sailors and marines on the captured Tripolitan ketch *Intrepid*, yet pulls alongside his quarry and storms his objective without loss. This act establishes Decatur as the doyen of the naval officer corps, and he gains promotion to captain at the age of 25, the youngest individual to hold that grade in U.S. Navy history.

APRIL 29 Near Tripoli, the squadron of Commodore Edward Preble manages to capture two small Tripolitan warships attempting to run the blockade.

MAY 13 Commodore Edward Preble convinces the King of Naples to lend him six gun boats and two mortar vessels, and he prepares for immediate offensive action against the Barbary pirates in Tripoli.

JULY 7 Outside Tripoli, a Tripolitan vessel attempt to dodge the brigs *Argus*, *Scourge*, and *Syren* and is run aground; American attempts to capture it are driven off by gunfire.

AUGUST 3 In Tripoli harbor, the frigate *Constitution*, assisted by six Neapolitan gunboats and two mortar vessels, engages Tripolitan gunboats. Captain Stephen Decatur, Jr., then leads a boarding crew that captures two small ships, killing 33 and wounding 19 pirates in the process. However, Decatur's younger brother James dies in action, and three others are wounded.

AUGUST 7 In Tripoli harbor, Commodore Edward Preble boldly arranges his Mediterranean Squadron in bombardment positions and begins shelling the city a second time. His nine ships and nine gunboats manage to sink three gunboats and capture four at a cost of 54 casualties, principally after one of the gunboats explodes. Preble is also joined by the 28-gun frigate *John Adams* under Master Commandant Isaac Chauncey, who informs him that four frigates are being dispatched under Captain Samuel Barron.

AUGUST 11–24 Outside Tripoli, Commodore Edward Preble determines to secure a victory of some kind before his relief arrives, and bombards the city six additional times to force it into surrendering.

AUGUST 27 In Tripoli harbor, Commodore Edward Preble again deploys his squadron in bombardment positions off the city and resumes firing for two hours. Pasha Yusuf Karamanli, however, dispatches a message through the French consul that the American effort fails to impress him.

SEPTEMBER 2 In Tripoli harbor, Commodore Edward Preble again orders gunboats and the frigate *Constitution* into bombardment range for a fifth time, where they engage land batteries and fortifications. This is his final attack on the city, but no serious damage is inflicted.

SEPTEMBER 3 In Tripoli harbor, the captured brig *Intrepid* under Lieutenant Richard Somers silently enters at night. His vessel is packed with five tons of gunpowder, and approaches some enemy gunboats with a view to destroy them. However, the *Intrepid* explodes prematurely, killing Somers and 12 crew members.

SEPTEMBER 9 Outside Tripoli, the aggressive Commodore Edward Preble is relieved by Commodore Samuel Barron of the 44-gun frigate *President*. However, the tight blockade of Tripoli is maintained by the Mediterranean Squadron.

1805

MARCH 2 In Washington, D.C., President Thomas Jefferson signs legislation to construct 25 additional gunboats for the protection of American harbors and commerce. Jefferson prefers the smaller gunboats to ocean-going warships for reasons of economy, which marks a major shift in American naval strategy which, to that point, had been evolving in the direction of a blue-water navy.

MARCH 3   Commodore Edward Preble is surprised to learn that Congress voted him a gold medal for his aggressive actions against Tripoli. He is the first U.S. Navy officer so honored.

APRIL 27   The city of Derna, Tripoli, is captured through the assistance of supporting fire from the brig *Argus* under Master Commandant Isaac Hull, the schooner *Nautilus*, and the sloop *Hornet*.

MAY 22   Off Tripoli, Commodore Samuel Barron is relieved from commanding the Mediterranean squadron by Commodore John Rodgers.

MAY 26   At Tripoli, the frigate *Essex* arrives carrying Colonel Tobias Lear, the U.S. Consul, who begins negotiating an end to the present conflict with Pasha Yusuf Karamanli.

JUNE 3   In Tripoli, a preliminary peace treaty is signed by the United States whereby it pays $60,000 for the release of all prisoners. Tripoli, for its part, waives any claims to future tribute.

JUNE 4   At Tripoli, Captain William Bainbridge and the crew of the *Philadelphia* are freed.

JUNE 12   Near Cadiz, Spain, Royal Navy warships board *Gunboat No. 6* under Lieutenant James Lawrence and impress three sailors from its crew.

JULY 31   Off the Bay of Tunis, Commodore John Rodgers assembles his Mediterranean squadron to induce the local dey into concluding a peace treaty with the United States.

1806

MARCH 25   In Washington, D.C., Congress authorizes funding for new coastal fortifications and additional gunboats. However, a request for six 74-gun ships of the line is defeated, leaving the U.S. Navy frigates as their first line of defense.

APRIL 17   In Washington, D.C., the Senate ratifies the peace treaty with Tripoli, which includes paying a $60,000 ransom for all American citizens and sailors held captive there.

APRIL 21   In Washington, D.C., Congress authorizes a new peacetime naval establishment consisting of 13 captains, 9 master commandants, 72 lieutenants, and 925 sailors.

APRIL 23   In Washington, D.C., President Thomas Jefferson invokes the Nonimportation Act, a ban on specified British products, which will remain in place until Great Britain ceases certain maritime practices, especially the impressment of American sailors.

APRIL 26   Outside New York City, the frigate HMS *Leander* fires across the bow of the American merchantman *Richard*, accidentally killing one sailor. President Thomas Jefferson angrily orders all British warships out of New York harbor.

1807

JUNE 22 Three miles off the coast of Norfolk, Virginia, the 52-gun British warship HMS *Leopard* accosts the smaller 39-gun American frigate *Chesapeake*. The British captain demands the right to search for deserters and, when Commodore James Barron refuses, the *Leopard* pours in several broadsides. Three American sailors are killed and 18 wounded, while 4 alleged British deserters are removed. The attack triggers intense anti-British sentiment nationwide, and Barron is subsequently court-martialed for failing to be at battle stations.

JULY 2 In Washington, D.C., President Thomas Jefferson reacts to the *Chesapeake-Leopard* Affair by ordering all Royal Navy warships out of American waters. Despite intense national resentment toward Great Britain, he nonetheless hopes that peaceful coercion will avert war and result in improved British behavior.

AUGUST 27 At Hampton Roads, Virginia, Captain Stephen Decatur attempts to cobble together a squadron, consisting of the frigate *Chesapeake* and several gunboats, but is unable to muster sufficient manpower to sail. He is thus unable to confront a British squadron anchored offshore.

DECEMBER 18 In Washington, D.C., Congress authorizes the acquisition of an additional 188 gunboats for coastal defense. President Thomas Jefferson still advocates these smaller vessels as a less-expensive alternative to formal warships.

DECEMBER 22 In Washington, D.C., President Jefferson aspires to change European behavior toward the United States by commencing the Embargo Act, which forbids trading with any foreign country. It proves impossible to enforce and almost ruins the American economy.

1809

FEBRUARY The armed ketch *Vesuvius* under Lieutenant Benjamin Reed spends an entire month chasing pirate vessels off the mouth of the Mississippi River, catching three.

FEBRUARY 22 In Washington, D.C., Secretary of the Navy Paul Hamilton persuades Congress to pass a bill for the construction of naval hospitals.

1811

JANUARY 9 Outside Newport, Rhode Island, Lieutenant Oliver Hazard Perry runs the schooner *Revenge* aground and it sinks. He is subsequently exonerated when a court-martial finds the ship's pilot negligent.

JANUARY 22 In Washington, D.C., Secretary of the Navy Paul Hamilton orders naval vessels to patrol the waters off Georgia and South Carolina to search any vessel suspected of engaging in smuggling slaves. The African slave trade has been outlawed since 1808.

May 1 Near Sandy Hook, New York, the 38-gun British frigate HMS *Guerriere* accosts the American merchant brig *Spitfire* and impresses an American seaman. Public outcry forces the government to take action.

May 6 Captain John Rodgers is dispatched in the 44-gun frigate *President* to patrol the waters off Sandy Hook, New Jersey, and stop British vessels from harassing and impressing American seamen.

May 16 Near Sandy Hook, New Jersey, the frigate *President* under Captain John Rodgers encounters an unidentified vessel in the dark. Broadsides are exchanged before the 22-gun corvette HMS *Little Belt* is identified. The British suffer 13 killed and 19 wounded in this one-sided exchange and limp off. The action is hailed as revenge for the British attack on the frigate *Chesapeake* in 1807.

August 7 In the Gulf of Mexico, *Gunboat No. 162* under Midshipman Francis H. Gregory begins patrolling to deter pirate activities. He begins by capturing the pirate schooner *La Franchise*.

August 10 In waters off Mobile, West Florida (Alabama), the pirate schooner *Santa Maria* is captured by Midshipman Francis H. Gregory and *Gunboat No. 162*.

September 11 Midshipman Francis H. Gregory and *Gunboat No. 162*, cruising between Brassa and Barataria, Louisiana, seize three additional pirate schooners.

1812

June 18 In Washington, D.C., Congress declares war against Great Britain, citing impressment at sea and arming of the Indians as underlying causes. The U.S. Navy of 17 warships, 447 guns, and 5,000 men is now arrayed against the mighty Royal Navy, touting 1,048 vessels, 27,800 guns, and 151,500 men.

June 21 At Boston, Massachusetts, Commodore John Rodgers heads a squadron consisting of the frigates *President*, *United States*, and *Congress*, accompanied by the sloop *Hornet* and brig *Argus*. His goal is to raid British commerce in the North Atlantic and force the Royal Navy to concentrate its forces against him, thereby allowing scores of American merchantmen to escape capture.

June 23 In the North Atlantic, the five-ship American squadron under Commodore John Rodgers of the *President* attacks the frigate HMS *Belvidera*. The British vessel escapes after a lengthy chase, and Rodgers suffers a broken leg after a cannon bursts.

July 1 On the Detroit River, the British capture the transport *Cuyahoga*, which carries General William Hull's personal papers. Consequently, British General Isaac Brock knows the exact strength and composition of the American army.

July 3–September 7 At New York, Master Commandant David Porter sails with the 32-gun frigate *Essex* on a North Atlantic cruise.

JULY 17 Near New York, the American brig *Nautilus* under Lieutenant William Crane encounters the ship of the line HMS *Africa* and frigates *Shannon* and *Aeolus,* and is forced to surrender. This is the first American warship lost in the War of 1812.

JULY 17–20 Off the coast of New Jersey, the frigate *Constitution* under Captain Isaac Hull is closely pursued by five British warships, but, by dint of splendid seamanship, escapes undamaged to New York. The exciting chase lasted 66 hours and involved "kedging" (towing) the frigate with rowboats.

JULY 19 On Lake Ontario, Canadian Provincial Marine vessels attack the port of Sackets Harbor, New York, and are driven off by artillery from the sloop *Oneida* under Lieutenant Melancthon T. Woolsey. One of his weapons is a 32-pounder howitzer nicknamed "Old Sow," which fires spent British cannon balls back at the enemy.

AUGUST 9 At Stonington, Connecticut, a British squadron briefly bombards the inhabitants; little damage results.

AUGUST 13 In the North Atlantic, the frigate *Essex* under Captain David Porter captures the 20-gun British sloop HMS *Alert* in only 18 minutes. This is the first British naval vessel taken in the War of 1812.

AUGUST 19 Off the coast of Nova Scotia, Canada, the 44-gun American frigate *Constitution* under Captain Isaac Hull defeats the 38-gun frigate HMS *Guerriere* of Captain James R. Dacres in a two-hour battle. Seven Americans are killed and seven wounded. The British tally is 15 dead and 64 wounded; the enemy vessel is

The USS Constitution *captures the HMS* Guerrière *on August 19, 1812. (Library of Congress)*

so shattered that it is scuttled. Moreover, British cannonballs are seen rebounding off the *Constitution*'s oaken sides, giving rise to the nickname "Old Ironsides."

AUGUST 29 Commodore John Rodgers concludes his four-ship cruise, having seized a paltry seven merchant vessels. Secretary of the Navy Paul Hamilton thereby abandons the strategy of squadron-level cruises, and dispatches individual warships out as commerce raiders.

SEPTEMBER 3 In New York, Captain Isaac Chauncey is ordered to Sackets Harbor on strategic Lake Ontario to assume command of an extensive ship-building program for the Great Lakes.

SEPTEMBER 28 Lieutenant Thomas Macdonough is ordered to the small naval station on Lake Champlain, where he is to construct a fleet of warships.

OCTOBER 8   On Lake Ontario, Commodore Isaac Chauncey's 16-gun brig *Oneida* chases the 22-gun British sloop *Royal George* into Kingston Harbor, where it grounds itself under artillery batteries to prevent capture.

Navy Lieutenant Jesse D. Elliot, assisted by Army Captain Nathan Towson, 2nd Artillery, captures the British brigs *Detroit* and *Caledonia* under the guns of Fort Erie, Upper Canada. One ship grounds and is burned, but the raiders all escape with their prisoners.

OCTOBER 18   In the Atlantic, Captain Jacob Jones of the 18-gun sloop *Wasp* captures the 18-gun British brig *Frolic*, with a loss of 10 Americans to 90 Britons killed and wounded. Both vessels are dismasted in battle, and are subsequently recaptured a few hours later by the ship of the line HMS *Poictiers*.

OCTOBER 25   Off the Madeira Islands (Azores), Captain Stephen Decatur and the 44-gun frigate *United States* score the war's second naval upset by capturing the 38-gun frigate HMS *Macedonian* under Captain John S. Carden in only 30 minutes. Decatur's losses are 5 killed and 7 wounded to a British tally of 36 dead and 68 injured. The prize is towed to New London, Connecticut, and enters American service as the USS *Macedonian*.

OCTOBER 28   Off the Delaware Capes, Captain David Porter and the frigate *Essex* depart on a voyage around Cape Horn and into the Pacific. Porter determines to destroy the British whaling fleet and hopes to possibly raid as far as the Indian Ocean.

NOVEMBER   The Delaware River and Chesapeake Bay are now subject to a blockade by Royal Navy warships.

NOVEMBER 9   On Lake Ontario, a squadron of seven vessels under Commodore Isaac Chauncey bombards British fortifications at Kingston, Upper Canada, until it is forced to withdraw with the onset of bad weather.

NOVEMBER 22   In the West Indies, Lieutenant George W. Read and the 12-gun schooner *Vixen* are captured by the frigate HMS *Southampton* under Captain James L. Yeo.

NOVEMBER 27   Congress, buoyed by the surprising string of victories at sea, authorizes construction of six new 44-gun frigates. However, none of these are completed in time for the war.

DECEMBER 26   In London, England, the British admiralty declares Chesapeake Bay and the Delaware River under a state of blockade. New England and New York waters are unmolested for the time being, possibly as a sop to antiwar Federalists; but as the war continues, the blockade gradually extends from Maine to Georgia.

DECEMBER 29   Off the coast of Brazil, the 44-gun frigate *Constitution* under Captain William Bainbridge defeats the 38-gun British frigate HMS *Java* in a third stunning naval upset. The Americans sustain 9 dead and 25 wounded to a British tally of 48 killed and 102 wounded. The *Java* is so gutted that it has to be sunk at sea. Hereafter, British captains are warned to avoid single-ship duels with their American counterparts.

DECEMBER 31   In Washington, D.C., Secretary of the Navy Paul Hamilton resigns from office rather than face charges of alcoholism and incompetence.

1813

January 2 In Washington, D.C., Congress continues its naval construction frenzy by authorizing four 74-gun ships of the line; none are completed in time for service in this war.

January 13 In Chesapeake Bay, a British squadron under Rear Admiral Sir George Cockburn arrives and enforces the blockade previously announced in December.

January 17 Off the coast of Belize, British Honduras, Lieutenant John D. Henley and the 10-gun brig *Viper* fall prey to the frigate HMS *Narcissus*.

January 19 In Washington, D.C., William Jones takes his oath as the fourth Secretary of the Navy.

February 4 Lieutenant James Lawrence and the brig *Hornet* capture the English brig *Resolution*, which is carrying $23,000 in specie. The cargo is removed, but the prize is burned at sea for want of sufficient crew to man it.

February 14 At Cape Horn, the frigate *Essex* under Captain David Porter rounds the tip of South America, becoming the first American warship to reach the Pacific Ocean.

February 17 At Newport, Rhode Island, Master Commandant Oliver Hazard Perry, languishing as he commands a local gunboat station, is ordered to join the Lake Ontario squadron under Commodore Isaac Chauncey. This proves one of the most fateful naval assignments of the entire war.

February 24 Near British Guiana, the 18-gun American sloop *Hornet* under Master Commandant James Lawrence captures the 20-gun sloop HMS *Peacock*; the British vessel sinks immediately thereafter. The Americans lose 4 killed and 4 wounded to a British tally of 5 dead and 33 wounded.

March 3 In Washington, D.C., Congress, with the urging of Secretary of the Navy William Jones, funds construction of six sloops-of-war similar to the victorious but ill-fated *Wasp*.

March 4 In Chesapeake Bay, Admiral Sir George Cockburn's squadron begins launching small-scale, amphibious attacks ashore to terrorize coastal communities. The local militia fails to mount an effective defense.

March 5 The frigate *Essex*, under Captain David Porter, makes its way up the Chilean coast, becoming the first American vessel to drop anchor there.

March 25 In the Pacific Ocean, Captain David Porter orders the frigate *Essex* to capture the Peruvian privateer *Nereyada* after two American prisoners are discovered in its hold. This is the first American naval victory in that theater.

March 27 At Presque Isle (Erie), Pennsylvania, Captain Oliver Hazard Perry arrives to oversee construction of two brigs, a schooner, and three gunboats constructed from nearby woods and materials hauled overland from Pittsburgh. However, in superseding Captain Jesse Duncan Elliott as station commander, he engenders lasting enmity.

April At Vergennes, Vermont, Lieutenant Thomas Macdonough appeals to local army and militia units for individuals with sailing experience to help man his embryonic fleet. Secretary of the Navy William Jones orders him to desist, however, as this is contrary to naval regulations.

APRIL 9 Off the southern Atlantic coast, Sailing Master James Mork and the 14-gun schooner *Nonsuch* capture the privateer *Caledonia*.

APRIL 27 On Lake Ontario, Commodore Isaac Chauncey's squadron assists General Henry Dearborn's army in the capture of York, the provincial capital of Upper Canada. The schooner *Duke of Gloucester* is captured, and the 24-gun sloop *Sir Isaac Brock* is burned on the stocks. This is the first combined amphibious assault in U.S. military history, and it goes off remarkably well.

APRIL 29 In the Pacific, Captain David Porter employs small boats from the frigate *Essex* to capture the British warship *Montezuma* and the privateers *Policy* and *Georgiana*. David G. Farragut, a future Civil War admiral, is among those present.

MAY 26 In London, England, the British Admiralty extends its blockade of Chesapeake Bay as far south as the Mississippi River, including the ports of Charleston, South Carolina, and Savannah, Georgia.

MAY 27 On Lake Ontario, Commodore Isaac Chauncey's squadron of nine vessels effectively covers the amphibious attack on Fort George, Upper Canada. Master Commandant Oliver Hazard Perry fights with distinction and leads a naval party ashore.

MAY 28 In the Pacific Ocean, the frigate *Essex* and prize vessel *Georgiana* quickly capture four British whaling vessels. Captain David Porter's cruise proves highly destructive to British commercial efforts, and provokes a sharp response from the Royal Navy.

JUNE 1 Outside Boston harbor, Massachusetts, the 38-gun frigate *Chesapeake*, under Captain James Lawrence, engages the crack frigate HMS *Shannon* under Captain Philip B.V. Broke. The Americans are defeated in a bloody, 15-minute engagement in which Lawrence is mortally wounded and Broke critically wounded. American losses are 62 killed and 58 injured to a British tally of 33 killed and 42 wounded. Moreover, Lawrence's dying command of "Don't give up the ship!" passes into U.S. Navy tradition as a battle cry.

At New London, Connecticut, Captain Stephen Decatur's squadron, consisting of the frigates *United States* and *Macedonian* and the brig *Hornet*, is chased into the harbor by a British squadron. The two frigates remain blockaded there for the remainder of the war, and only the *Hornet* manages to slip past British vessels in 1814.

JUNE 3 At the northern end of Lake Champlain, American sloops *Growler* and *Eagle* are trapped in the Sorel River and forced to surrender. This minor disaster tips the balance of power in favor of the British for several months.

JUNE 5 The town of Hampton, Virginia, is sacked and burned by a British amphibious force.

JUNE 18–AUGUST 24 Lieutenant William Henry Allen and the 16-gun brig *Argus* convey U.S. Minister William H. Crawford to France, prior to commencing a spectacular raid into the English Channel.

JUNE 22 Craney Island, Virginia, is attacked by a large British amphibious force, and a detachment of sailors and marines from the nearby frigate *Constellation* mans artillery batteries and drives the British off.

JULY 20 At L'Orient, France, Lieutenant William Henry Allen and the brig *Argus* begin a destructive foray into the English Channel, seizing 19 prizes in 22 days.

JULY 30 On Lake Ontario, Commodore Isaac Chauncey's squadron carries 300 soldiers under Colonel Winfield Scott on a second foray against York (Toronto), Upper Canada. After destroying some public property, the expedition withdraws a day later.

AUGUST 4 On Lake Erie, the British squadron under Captain Robert H. Barclay momentarily abandons its blockade of Presque Isle (Erie), Pennsylvania. Commodore Oliver Hazard Perry then disarms his vessels, passes them over the sandbar blocking the harbor, and painstakingly rearms them in deep water.

AUGUST 7–11 On Lake Ontario, Commodore Isaac Chauncey's squadron of 13 vessels (128 guns) spars with a British force of 6 vessels (99 guns) under Commodore Sir James L. Yeo. The running battle is conducted at long range and little damage results.

AUGUST 8 On Lake Ontario, Commodore Isaac Chauncey loses the schooners *Scourge* and *Hamilton* to stormy weather, and both sink with all hands.

AUGUST 10 On Lake Ontario, two of Commodore Isaac Chauncey's gunboats, the *Growler* and the *Julia*, are cut off and captured by the British.

AUGUST 14 Off the coast of England, the 16-gun sloop *Argus* under Captain William H. Allen is captured by the 21-gun brig HMS *Pelican* under Captain John F. Maples; Allen is mortally wounded in combat. Previously, *Argus* accounted for a total of 27 British vessels since July.

SEPTEMBER 5 Near Portland, Maine, the 16-gun brig *Enterprise* under Lieutenant William Burrows engages the 14-gun brig HMS *Boxer* under Lieutenant Samuel Blythe in a smart action. The British vessel is captured, but Burrows and Blythe are both killed.

SEPTEMBER 10 The Battle of Lake Erie transpires when Commodore Oliver Hazard Perry, commanding nine ships (54 guns), seeks out and engages the six-ship British force (64 guns) under Commodore Robert Heriot Barclay. As Perry closes, his flagship *Lawrence* becomes separated and is forced to strike its colors. Perry, however, coolly transfers his flag to the brig *Niagara* and resumes fighting. Barclay, seriously wounded, finally lowers his flag. "We have met the enemy," Perry laconically wrote, "and they are ours." Casualties in this three-hour slugfest are 27 Americans killed and 96 wounded to 41 British killed and 94 injured. This is also the first time in history that an entire Royal Navy squadron had been captured.

SEPTEMBER 11 On Lake Ontario, Commodore Isaac Chauncey conducts an inconclusive, long-range bombardment of his British counterpart.

SEPTEMBER 22 In the mid-Atlantic, Commodore John Rodgers and the 44-gun frigate *President* seize the British tender *High Flyer*.

SEPTEMBER 26 Commodore John Rodgers and the frigate *President* anchor at Newport, Rhode Island, concluding a five-month cruise that netted 12 English prizes.

SEPTEMBER 27–29 On Lake Erie, Commodore Oliver Hazard Perry's squadron transports 4,500 men of General William Henry Harrison's army to the Canada shore, landing them below Fort Malden. They promptly recapture Detroit and pursue the fleeing British to the Thames River.

SEPTEMBER 28 On Lake Ontario, Commodore Isaac Chauncey's squadron has the better of Commodore James L. Yeo's British force in a running skirmish, and drives them headlong into Burlington Bay. Chauncey, however, does not close, and fails to destroy them.

OCTOBER 4 Offshore at Newport, Rhode Island, Captain John Cahoone and the revenue cutter *Vigilant* seize the British privateer *Dart*.

OCTOBER 5 On Lake Ontario, Lieutenant Arthur Sinclair of the 24-gun brig *General Pike*, assisted by the schooners *Sylph*, *Governor Tompkins*, and *Lady of the Lake*, captures British schooners *Drummond*, *Lady Gore*, *Hamilton*, and *Confiance*.

OCTOBER 25 In the Pacific, the frigate *Essex* under Captain David Porter drops anchor off the Marquesas Islands to conduct badly needed repairs. Local Typee tribesmen resent this intrusion and harass the Americans.

NOVEMBER 16 British admiral John Borlase Warren declares the American seaboard, from New York to the Mississippi River, to be under blockade. Curiously, Federalist New England, hostile to the War of 1812, is unaffected.

NOVEMBER 19 In the Pacific, Captain David Porter of the *Essex* claims the Marquesas chain for the United States, renaming the biggest island, Nukahiva, after President James Madison. However, Congress never recognizes the claim.

DECEMBER 25 In the mid-Atlantic, Captain Thomas Hall and the 14-gun brig *Vixen* (II) are captured by the British frigate HMS *Belvidere*.

DECEMBER 29–30 At Buffalo, New York, British forces burn schooners *Chippewa*, *Little Belt*, and *Trippe*, all formerly part of Commodore Oliver Hazard Perry's Lake Erie squadron.

1814

FEBRUARY 2 At Stono Inlet, North Carolina, Lieutenant Lawrence Kearny wrecks his 8-gun schooner *Ferret* on a sand bar, although without loss of life.

FEBRUARY 25 In the Caribbean, brigs *Enterprise* and *Rattlesnake* catch three prizes, then separate when chased by a British frigate. The *Enterprise* is forced to throw most of its armament overboard to escape.

MARCH 28 Near Valparaiso, Chile, the American frigate *Essex* under Captain David Porter, having lost its topsail in a storm, is attacked and defeated by British warships HMS *Phoebe* and *Cherub*. American losses are 58 dead, 31 drowned, and 66 wounded to 5 British killed and 10 injured. Previously, Porter has captured or destroyed nearly 40 whaling vessels. One of the survivors, 13-year-old midshipman David G. Farragut, subsequently rises to vice admiral during the Civil War.

APRIL 14 The frigate *John Adams*, sailing under a flag of truce, safely conveys peace commissioners Henry Clay and Jonathan Russell to Wargo Island, Norway. Their ultimate destination is Ghent, Belgium.

APRIL 20 In the Florida Straits, the sloop-of-war *Frolic* under Master Commandant Joseph Bainbridge evades frigate HMS *Orpheus* and schooner *Shelburne* for six hours before being forced to surrender.

APRIL 23 In London, England, the British Admiralty extends its blockade to include all of New England. The Royal Navy is becoming a major factor in the near-collapse of the American economy, now suffering from high inflation, severe shortages, and virtual bankruptcy.

APRIL 29 Offshore at Cape Canaveral, Florida, the American sloop *Peacock* under Master Commandant Lewis Warrington defeats the brig HMS *Epervier*. The British vessel, conveying $120,000 in specie, loses 8 dead and 15 injured to 2 American wounded; Warrington receives a Congressional gold medal.

MAY 1 At Newburyport, Massachusetts, the newly launched sloop-of-war *Wasp II* departs on an extended cruise to the English Channel.

MAY 5–6 At Oswego, New York, British land and naval forces under Commodore Sir James Lucas Yeo and Lieutenant General Gordon Drummond capture the American depot. They incur heavy losses and their objective, several heavy cannon intended for the American fleet at Sackets Harbor, had been moved upstream beforehand by Lieutenant Colonel George E. Mitchell, 3rd Artillery.

JUNE 8–10 At St. Leonard's Creek, Maryland, a force of 13 gunboats under Captain Joshua Barney repulses an attack by British barges, then runs an enemy schooner aground.

JUNE 19 On Lake Ontario, Lieutenant Francis H. Gregory and three boatloads of sailors surprise and capture the British gunboat *Blacksnake*.

JUNE 22 Near Cape Sable, Nova Scotia, the 14-gun brig *Rattlesnake* under Lieutenant James Renshaw is captured by the frigate HMS *Leander*.

JUNE 26 On the Patuxent River, Maryland, Captain Joshua Barney's Chesapeake Bay flotilla, consisting of the cutter *Scorpion*, 13 barges, 2 gunboats, and 1 galley, engages the frigates HMS *Loire* and *Narcissus*, forcing them to withdraw downstream.

JUNE 28 In the North Atlantic, the 18-gun sloop *Wasp II* under Master Commandant Johnston Blakeley defeats the 18-gun British brig HMS *Reindeer* in a 19-minute action. The Americans sustain 5 dead and 21 wounded to a British tally of 25 killed and 42 wounded. *Reindeer*, damaged beyond repair, is deliberately sunk.

JULY 1 On Lake Ontario, Lieutenant Francis H. Gregory and some sailors land at Presqu'ile Isle, Upper Canada, burn a 10-gun schooner on the stocks, then escape.

JULY 3 Captain Arthur Sinclair and vessels of the Lake Erie Squadron are tasked with transporting troops from Detroit, Michigan, to Mackinac Island on Lake Michigan.

JULY 14 Off the New England coast, *Gunboat No. 88* under Sailing Master G.

Clement captures the British schooner *Chebacque*.

July 20 At Detroit, Michigan, Commodore Arthur Sinclair leads a small amphibious expedition to Lake Huron for the purpose of recapturing the strategic fur-trading post of Mackinac. He commands the brigs *Niagara, Lawrence,* and *Caledonia,* and schooners *Scorpion* and *Tigress*. En route, the British trading post at St. Joseph's is burned.

July 31 On Lake Ontario, Master Commandant Jesse D. Elliott, directing the 16-gun schooner *Sylph*, runs the British schooner *Magnet* ashore, where it is burned.

August 12 On Lake Erie, outside of Fort Erie, Upper Canada, a British cutting-out expedition storms the American schooners *Somers* and *Ohio*, and sails them off. A third vessel, the *Porcupine*, cuts its cables and drifts to safety. Success here removes potent American firepower from the right flank of British land forces, and induces Lieutenant General Gordon Drummond to assail the fort.

August 14 In Chesapeake Bay, a British naval squadron under Admiral Sir George Cockburn, carrying 5,400 Napoleonic veterans under Major General Robert Ross, prepares to attack the American capital.

August 22 On the Patuxent River, Maryland, Commodore Joshua Barney blows up his Chesapeake Bay Flotilla to prevent its capture. His 400 sailors and Marines subsequently march to join forces defending Washington, D.C.

August 24 In Washington, D.C., British-born Captain Thomas Tingey sets fire to the Washington Navy Yard rather than have it captured by British forces. The flames consume the frigates *Boston, Columbia, General Greene,* and *New York*, along with two ships under construction.

During the Battle of Bladensburg, the American militia is routed, and the only determined resistance is mounted by a combined naval/marine battery commanded by Commodore Joshua Barney. Barney is wounded and captured, then immediately paroled by Admiral George Cockburn.

August 26 A British squadron sails up the Potomac River and bombards Fort Warburton, Maryland, where a lucky shot touches off the gunpowder magazine, destroying it. The garrison has evacuated beforehand.

September 1 In the eastern Atlantic, the sloop *Wasp* under Captain Johnston Blakeley sinks the 18-gun British brig HMS *Avon* in a nighttime engagement; American losses are two dead and one wounded. British casualties total 10 killed and 12 wounded.

September 1–4 On Lake Huron, a British cutting-out expedition under Lieutenant Worsley captures the American schooners *Tigress* and *Scorpion*.

September 3 At Hampden, Maine, Captain John Morris burns the 28-gun frigate *Adams* to prevent its capture. His crew escapes overland back to Boston.

September 11 The Battle of Lake Champlain unfolds as a British squadron under Captain George Downey rounds Plattsburgh Bay, and sails directly into a trap set by Master Commandant Thomas Macdonough. Downey is killed, and Macdonough orders his force rotated by spring lines, which bring the undamaged sides of his warships to bear. For the second time in this war an entire British squadron surrenders; American losses are

52 dead and 59 wounded to a British tally of 84 killed and 100 wounded. Macdonough's victory also forces Governor General Sir George Prevost's invading army to withdraw back to Canada.

SEPTEMBER 16   In Barataria Bay, Louisiana, Commodore Daniel T. Patterson leads the schooner *Carolina* and six gunboats against the holdout of pirate Jean Lafitte at Grand Terre; 11 of their vessels are captured.

SEPTEMBER 21   In the North Atlantic, the American sloop *Wasp* under Captain Johnston Blakeley captures the British brig *Atalanta*; this proves the first of fifteen prizes taken before the *Wasp* mysteriously vanishes.

SEPTEMBER 24   Near Southwest Pass, Louisiana, Lieutenant Isaac McKeever, commanding *Gunboat No. 5*, captures a pirate vessel.

SEPTEMBER 25–26   At Fayal in the neutral Azores, a British squadron consisting of HMS *Plantagenet*, 74 guns, *Rota*, 38 guns, and *Carnation*, 18 guns, attacks the American 8-gun privateer *General Armstrong* under Captain Samuel C. Reid. Reid, however, is well prepared and repulses several boat attacks before scuttling his ship to avoid capture. The damage he inflicts detains the British force for several weeks, hindering their New Orleans offensive.

OCTOBER 9   In the North Atlantic, Master Commandant Johnston Blakeley and the sloop-of-war *Wasp* are last seen by a Swedish vessel, then disappear at sea.

OCTOBER 29   At New York City, Robert Fulton launches the *Demologos* ("Voice of the People"), history's first armored, steam-powered warship. It is 153 long, 56 feet across the beam, and weighs 2,475 tons, being propelled by a steam paddle mounted between two hulls. The vessel is subsequently christened *Fulton the First* to honor the inventor, after he dies the following spring.

NOVEMBER 15   In Washington, D.C., Secretary of the Navy William Jones proffers a sweeping naval reorganization scheme by calling for several ships of the line, standardization of ordnance and equipment, a draft for seamen, a board of inspectors, and a new, national naval academy.

DECEMBER 1   In Washington, D.C., William Jones resigns as secretary of the Navy after suffering bouts of exhaustion.

DECEMBER 13   On Lake Borgne, Louisiana, Sailing Master William Johnson burns the tender *Sea Horse* to prevent its capture by British barges.

DECEMBER 14   On Lake Borgne, Louisiana, 42 British boats crammed with troops attack the six gunboats of Lieutenant Thomas ap Catesby Jones, capturing them. The Americans resist tenaciously, but are gradually overwhelmed with losses of 6 dead, 35 wounded, and 86 captured. British casualties totaled 17 killed and 77 wounded, which delays their approach to New Orleans by several days.

DECEMBER 23–24   On the Mississippi River, Master Commandant John T. Henley and his 14-gun schooner *Carolina* drop down at night and bombard the British encampment at Villere's Plantation, Louisiana. Shooting at camp fires, his heavy fire sows confusion into the enemy's ranks, as troops under General Andrew Jackson attack.

DECEMBER 24   In Ghent, Belgium, British and American diplomats sign a peace treaty ending the War of 1812. Everything reverts back to the prewar status quo, and no mention of impressment, a leading cause of the conflict, is ever made.

DECEMBER 27   On the Mississippi River, British gunners firing red-hot shot sink the 14-gun schooner *Carolina* of Master Commandant John D. Henley, thereby clearing the way for their advance upon New Orleans.

DECEMBER 29–31   At New Orleans, Louisiana, Commodore Daniel T. Paterson directs that cannon from the 16-gun sloop *Louisiana* be landed on the west bank of the Mississippi River, and opposite General Andrew Jackson's defensive lines.

1815

JANUARY 6   On Lake Borgne, Louisiana, a 38-man boat party under Sailing Master William Johnson captures the British 4-gun brig HMS *Cyprus*, along with clothing intended for the army of General Edward Pakenham.

JANUARY 8   At New Orleans, Louisiana, the British army under General Edward Pakenham attacks General Andrew Jackson's main line. They are disastrously repulsed, but a small force landed on the west bank of the Mississippi River routs Kentucky militia stationed there, and storms the naval battery.

JANUARY 13–15   Offshore at Sandy Hook, New Jersey, the 44-gun American frigate *President* under Captain Stephen Decatur is accosted by a four-ship British squadron. Decatur's ship, badly damaged in a storm, nonetheless disables the frigate HMS *Endymion* before finally succumbing to the remaining three vessels. Decatur's losses are 24 dead and 56 wounded; the British sustain 25 casualties.

JANUARY 19–21   On Lake Borgne, Louisiana, Purser Thomas Shields, commanding six boats and 50 men, captures two British schooners and several small craft.

JANUARY 29   Near North Edisto, North Carolina, Lieutenant Lawrence Kearny, commanding 25 men and three barges, captures the tender and launch of the frigate HMS *Hebrus*.

FEBRUARY 7   In Washington, D.C., Congress founds a three-man board of naval commissioners to assist the Secretary of the Navy. The three senior officers chosen, Isaac Hull, David Porter, and John Rodgers, are all confirmed by the Senate.

FEBRUARY 15   In Washington, D.C., Secretary of the Navy Benjamin Crowninshield cancels a second steam-powered warship.

FEBRUARY 17   In Washington, D.C., the U.S. Senate ratifies the Treaty of Ghent, officially ending the War of 1812.

FEBRUARY 20   Off the coast of Madeira, the 44-gun American frigate *Constitution* under Captain Charles Stewart artfully defeats and captures the frigate HMS *Cyane* and sloop *Levant*. American losses are 3 dead and 12 wounded, while the British lose 19 killed and 42 wounded. All three vessels are unaware of the peace treaty.

Decatur, Stephen (1779–1820)

Stephen Decatur was born in Sinepuxent, Maryland, on January 5, 1779, and in 1798 he received a midshipman's commission in the fledgling U.S. Navy. Decatur rose to lieutenant by 1803, then accompanied a squadron against the Barbary pirates of North Africa. On the night of February 16, 1804, he daringly boarded and burned the captured frigate *Philadelphia* in Tripoli harbor with the loss of one man. This act secured Decatur's reputation as a peerless naval officer, and he was promoted to captain at the age of 24. When the War of 1812 commenced, Decatur commanded the 44-gun frigate *United States,* and on October 12, 1812, he handily defeated the slightly smaller 38-gun warship HMS *Macedonian*. The British fleet nonetheless enveloped the American coastline, and Decatur proved unable to get to sea until January 15, 1815. He slipped the frigate *President* out of New York harbor, then grounded on a sand bar before being set upon by a squadron of British ships. He beat off the nearest opponents, but, after a hard pounding, surrendered to the remaining three vessels.

In the summer of 1815 Decatur led a nine-ship squadron back to the Mediterranean and forced the pashas of Algiers, Tunis, and Tripoli to sign peace treaties and pay indemnities for piracy. In November 1815, Decatur was appointed to the new Navy board of Commissioners, and he performed capably over the next five years. However, in 1820 he voted to deny Captain James Barron a long-delayed promotion. Barron blamed Decatur for conspiring behind his back and challenged him to a duel. Decatur was fatally wounded at Bladensburg, Maryland, on March 22, 1820, the naval doyen of his age.

FEBRUARY 27 In Washington, D.C., Congress orders the Navy's gunboat flotilla sold off, while all warships serving on the Great Lakes are placed in storage.

MARCH 3 In Washington, D.C., Congress is angered by new depredations committed against American shipping by Algiers, and declares war against that kingdom. The Dey felt he had not been receiving adequate levels of tribute from the United States, so he resumed seizing ships and hostages.

MARCH 23 Near Tristan de Cunha, South Atlantic, the sloop *Hornet* under Captain Thomas Biddle captures the 19-gun British sloop HMS *Penguin*. American losses are 1 dead and 1 injured to 10 British killed and 28 wounded.

APRIL 15 In Washington, D.C., Secretary Benjamin W. Crowninshield orders Commodore Stephen Decatur, Jr., to assemble a squadron for Mediterranean service, and capture all Algerian ships he may encounter.

MAY 10 In New York, Commodore Stephen Decatur assembles a nine-ship armada (three frigates and six smaller vessels) tasked with ending piratical raids from Algiers. His mission is to establish peace in the Mediterranean with force, if necessary.

MAY 20 Commodore Stephen Decatur, Jr., sails from New York at the head of a nine-ship squadron and prepares to deal directly with the Algerian pirates.

JUNE 17 At sea, Commodore Stephen Decatur, Jr.'s squadron captures the 44-gun Algerian frigate *Mashuda*, killing Admiral Rais Hamida and 30 Muslim sailors, and taking 406 captive. They are assisted by Captain Samuel B. Archer's company, Corps of Artillery, serving the frigate *Guerriere* as gunners.

JUNE 19   Offshore at Cape de Gata, Spain, the 22-gun Algerian brig *Estido* is taken by Commodore Stephen Decatur, Jr.'s, squadron, losing 23 dead and 8 captured.

JUNE 28–30   At Algiers, Commodore Stephen Decatur, Jr., arrives at the head of his squadron and comes ashore to assist American Consul-General William Shaler with peace negotiations. The Dey, awed by American strength, agrees to release all prisoners and vessels, renounce all claims of future tribute, and pay a $10,000 indemnity.

JUNE 30   In the Straits of Sunda, the final naval action of the War of 1812 unfolds when the sloop *Peacock* under Master Commandant Lewis Warrington defeats the 14-gun East India Company brig *Nautilus*. Warrington is then informed that hostilities had ceased, so he releases his quarry; British losses are six killed and eight injured.

JULY 3   At Boston, Massachusetts, Commodore William Bainbridge departs with a nine-ship squadron and sails for the Mediterranean to relieve Commodore Stephen Decatur, Jr.

JULY 14   The brig *Epervier* under Lieutenant John T. Shubrick passes Gibraltar, Spain, on its voyage back home, and disappears at sea.

JULY 26–30   At Tunis, Commodore Stephen Decatur, Jr.'s Mediterranean squadron drops anchor and forces the Dey to stop his harassment of American commerce. Tunis also agrees to pay $46,000 in restitutions for allowing British warships to seize American vessels in its waters during the late war.

AUGUST 5–9   At Tripoli, Commodore Stephen Decatur, Jr.'s, Mediterranean Squadron arrives and persuades the Pasha to sign a treaty halting all attacks on American shipping, free all hostages without ransom, and end tribute payments.

The USS Peacock *encounters the HMS* Nautilus *on the Indian Ocean on June 30, 1815. The* Peacock *attacked the* Nautilus, *which immediately surrendered, citing that the war had ended. Upon confirmation of the peace, Capt. Lewis Warrington gave up the prize and sailed for home. (The Mariners' Museum, Newport News, VA)*

Tripoli agrees to pay $25,000 for vessels it allowed Great Britain to seize in its waters during the War of 1812.

NOVEMBER 12 In New York, Commodore Stephen Decatur, Jr.'s, squadron returns in triumph, having ended all disruptive behavior from the Barbary states of North Africa. His treaties had been, in his own words, "dictated at the mouth of the cannon."

NOVEMBER 20 The newly established Board of Navy Commissioners issues its first report, calling for reorganization of the U.S. Navy. This report suggests a reduction in navy yards, construction of dry docks, naval hospitals, a naval ordnance department, and annual expenditures for shipbuilding. Adopting the rank of admiral is also strongly recommended. Only a few of the board's suggestions come to fruition.

1816

APRIL 29 In Washington, D.C., Congress passes a $1 million naval appropriations bill to acquire nine 74-gun ships of the line, the first such vessels in U.S. Navy history, along with 12 44-gun frigates. From a design standpoint, the Americans are striving for parity in firepower with the Royal Navy.

JUNE 8 The new 74-gun ship-of-the-line *Washington* sails for the Mediterranean as part of Commodore Isaac Chauncey's squadron.

AUGUST At a banquet held in his honor, Commodore Stephen Decatur addresses his guests by thundering, "Our country! In her intercourse with foreign nations may she always be in the right; but right or wrong, our country!" It becomes a signature toast.

DECEMBER 23 In Algiers, a final peace treaty is signed between the United States and the Dey, finally ending the Barbary Wars.

1817

NOVEMBER 16 Captain John D. Henley of the frigate *John Adams* is authorized by President James Monroe to suppress piracy off Amelia Island, East Florida. His orders are subsequently appended to include the Gulf of Mexico as far west as Galveston.

DECEMBER 22 Captain John Henley and the frigate *John Adams* capture Amelia Island, East Florida, thereby depriving pirates of their principal base.

1818

AUGUST 19 In Oregon, Captain James Biddle and the sloop *Ontario* arrive off Cape Disappointment on the Columbia River for the first time. He claims the region for the United States; however, it will be jointly occupied with Great Britain for many years.

SEPTEMBER 2 Captain John Downes of the frigate *Macedonian* is instructed to patrol the Pacific Ocean and protect American commerce from piracy.

1819

FEBRUARY 26 In Washington, D.C., Congress passes legislation instructing the Navy to act against rising piracy in the Caribbean, brought on by Spain's rebellious colonies. Henceforth, Navy vessels commence convoying operations and recapture any vessel unlawfully taken.

MARCH 3 In Washington, D.C., Congress authorizes Navy warships to take an active role in suppressing the slave trade off West Africa. This is the genesis of the African Squadron, which is to also assist the forthcoming nation of Liberia, newly colonized by former slaves.

Congress also adopts the first official naming policy for Navy warships. Henceforth, ships of the line are named after states, frigates are named after rivers, and sloops-of-war are christened after cities.

MARCH 15 The frigate *Macedonian* under Captain John Downes becomes the first Navy warship to deploy on what becomes the Pacific Station.

AUGUST 13 At Trinidad, Captain Oliver Hazard Perry dies of yellow fever while commanding the schooner *Nonsuch* on a diplomatic mission; he was a few days short of his 34th birthday.

1820

MARCH 22 At Bladensburg, Maryland, Commodore Stephen Decatur dies from wounds received in a duel with Captain James Barron. Decatur is only 41 years old, and Barron, the senior American naval officer, is effectively blacklisted and never commands at sea again.

APRIL 5–12 Near present-day Liberia, the frigate *Cyane* under Captain Edward Trenchard seizes five slavers between Cape Mount and the mouth of the Gallinas River.

MAY 16 At Hampton Roads, Virginia, Captain John D. Henley departs with the 36-gun frigate *Congress* and sails for China. This vessel becomes the first American warship to visit the Middle Kingdom the following December.

NOVEMBER 20 At Lima, Peru, Captain John Downes and the frigate *Macedonian* evacuate American and British citizens, then escort a convoy of American and British merchantmen sailing from Callao, Peru.

1821

January 21 At St. Mary's, Georgia, Lieutenant J. R. Madison and the schooner *Lynx* depart for the West Indies and vanish at sea, possibly after striking the Carysfort Reef off the Florida coast.

March 16 Following the capture of Spanish East Florida by General Andrew Jackson, the brig *Hornet* transports captured Spanish soldiers back to Cuba.

March 19 In the Pacific, the frigate *Macedonian* is relieved by the *Constellation* and returns to the United States. In two years and nine months it covered 58,878 miles; 26 sailors died en route.

May 17–25 Off the Gallinas River, West Africa, Lieutenant Robert F. Stockton and the schooner *Alligator* seize four French slave vessels. He also conducts negotiations with tribal leaders to acquire land for the new nation of Liberia to be founded.

October 11 In New York, the new ship of the line *Franklin* sails for the Pacific Ocean where, with the schooner *Dolphin*, it forms the nucleus of the Pacific Squadron. Naval vessels are increasingly necessary to protect American interests from revolutionary movements in South America.

October 16 In waters off Cape Antonio, Cuba, Lieutenant Lawrence Kearny and the brig *Enterprise* capture two pirate vessel and burn two more in a single action He caught them in the act of plundering several American merchantmen.

October 29 Near Santo Domingo, Captain Robert Henley and the brig *Hornet* capture a pirate vessel.

November 5 In the central Atlantic, Lieutenant Robert F. Stockton and the schooner *Alligator* engage the Portuguese vessel *Marianno Flora* for 90 minutes before the latter strikes. Although the Portuguese had fired first, Stockton is admonished for his aggressiveness, and is hereafter restricted to anti-slavery patrols.

November 8 Near Cape San Antonio, Cuba, Lieutenant James Ramage of the schooner *Porpoise* seizes a pirate vessel.

December 21 Offshore near Cape Antonio, Cuba, the brig *Enterprise* under Lieutenant Lawrence Kearney seizes a vessel, then goes ashore and burns a pirate base and five additional ships.

1822

January 7 Outside Bahia Honda, Cuba, Lieutenant James Ramage of the brig *Porpoise* lands sailors and marines ashore, and destroys a pirate base and six vessels.

In the West Indies, a Dutch sloop captured by pirates is recaptured by Lieutenant John H. Elton of the brig *Spark*, who then transports the transgressors back to Charleston, South Carolina, to stand trial.

March 7 In the West Indies, Lieutenant G. W. Hamersley and the schooner *Revenge* seize a pirate barge.

MARCH 8 Off Cape San Antonio, Cuba, Lieutenant Lawrence Kearny of the brig *Enterprise* seizes seven pirate vessels. He then dispatches a landing party of marines and burns their base camp.

MARCH 25 At Key West, Florida Lieutenant Matthew C. Perry of the schooner *Shark* drops anchor and claims the archipelago for the United States.

MARCH 26 The embryonic West India Squadron begins forming under Commodore James Biddle, who is tasked with suppressing piracy, smuggling, and other unlawful activities off Cuba, Puerto Rico, and the coast of Central America. Present are the frigates *Congress*, *John Adams*, *Macedonian*, and *Cyane*, sloops *Hornet* and *Peacock*, brigs *Enterprise* and *Spark*, schooners *Alligator*, *Grampus*, *Porpoise*, *Shark*, and *Revenge*, and *Gunboat No. 168*.

APRIL 30 Near the Windward Islands, the schooner *Alligator* under Lieutenant W. W. McLean captures the Colombian privateer *Cienega*.

MAY 1 Near Sugar Key, Cuba, four pirate vessels and a prize ship are captured by boats that the crews launch from the schooners *Alligator* and *Grampus*.

JUNE Off Cuba's northern coast, the schooners *Shark* under Lieutenant Matthew C. Perry and *Grampus* under Lieutenant Francis H. Gregory seize the pirate vessel *Bandera de Sangre*.

AUGUST 16 Off Puerto Rico, Lieutenant Francis H. Gregory of the schooner *Grampus* captures the pirate vessel *Palmyra*.

SEPTEMBER 28–30 At Bahia Honda, Cuba, the sloop-of-war *Peacock* under Captain Stephen Cassin, assisted by the revenue cutter *Louisiana*, storms a pirate stronghold, seizes five vessels, and releases a prize ship.

NOVEMBER 9 Off Matanzas, Cuba, Lieutenant William Allen of the schooner *Alligator* is killed fighting pirates. His men capture their vessel, killing 14 of its crew; five American merchantmen are also freed.

NOVEMBER 19 Off the Florida coast, Lieutenant W. W. McKean and the schooner *Alligator* are wrecked on Carysfort Reef, without loss of life.

DECEMBER 21 In the Caribbean, the hot-tempered, impetuous Commodore David Porter replaces Commodore James Biddle as commander of the West India Squadron.

1823

FEBRUARY 14 At Norfolk, Virginia, the paddle-wheel *Sea Gull*, the Navy's second steam-powered vessel, makes for the West Indies under Lieutenant William H. Watson. A former Hudson River steamer, it is the first warship of its kind.

MARCH 6 At San Juan, Puerto Rico, Spanish forces fire upon the schooner *Fox*, mistaking it for a pirate vessel, and Lieutenant William H. Cocke is fatally wounded. The Spanish governor issues a formal apology.

APRIL 8 Near Havana, Cuba, the barges *Gallinipper* and *Mosquito*, covered by the sloop *Peacock* under Captain Stephen Cassin, capture a pirate vessel.

APRIL 16 Off the coast of Colorados, Cuba, the sloop *Peacock* captures two pirate vessels.

MAY 22 Near Campeche, Mexico, Lieutenant Francis H. Gregory and the schooner *Grampus* capture two pirate vessels.

JULY At Sigaumpa Bay, Cuba, the barges *Gallinipper* and *Mosquito* under Lieutenants William H. Watson and W. T. Inman, respectively, attack a pirate stronghold. They kill or capture 75 pirates, along with Diabloleto, their leader.

JULY 9 On Little Curacao Island in the West Indies, the veteran brig *Enterprise* under Lieutenant Lawrence Kearny is lost after it breaks up on a reef.

JULY 22 At Cape Cruz, Cuba, the schooner *Greyhound* under Lieutenant Lawrence Kearny, assisted by the schooner *Beagle* under Lieutenant J. T. Newton, shells a pirate stronghold, while landing parties under Lieutenant David G. Farragut come ashore and attack the position from behind.

AUGUST 1 The first unofficial naval medical school, directed by Dr. Thomas Harris, arises at the Philadelphia Navy Yard, Pennsylvania; Thomas runs the venture until it closes in 1843.

NOVEMBER 18 At Corysfort Reef, West Indies, the schooner *Alligator* wrecks after running aground. The crew then burns the vessel to prevent its capture by pirates.

1824

AUGUST 17–26 Offshore at Havana and Bahia Honda, Cuba, the schooner *Terrier* under Lieutenant Thomas Paine, Jr., captures a pirate launch and a schooner.

OCTOBER 20 Near Matanzas, Cuba, Lieutenant Charles W. Skinner and the schooner *Porpoise* capture a pirate schooner, assisted by five small boats directed by Lieutenant William M. Hunter.

OCTOBER 27 At Fajardo, Puerto Rico, Lieutenant Charles Platt anchors the schooner *Beagle* to investigate property allegedly stolen from the U.S. Consul being stored there. He goes ashore with Midshipman Robert Ritchie and is arrested by local authorities, who disbelieve him.

OCTOBER 28 The schooner *Wildcat* under Midshipman L. M. Booth is lost with all hands between Cuba and Thompson's Island in the Caribbean.

NOVEMBER 14 At Fajardo, Puerto Rico, Commodore David Porter lands a force of Marines and sailors and storms a Spanish battery without loss. He does so in response to an alleged Spanish insult to the American flag a few weeks previously. The defenders offer an apology, at which point Porter leaves, but he is subsequently court-martialed for overly aggressive actions.

DECEMBER 27 Command of the West India Squadron passes from Commodore David Porter to Captain Lewis Warrington.

1825

February 4 Off the Cuban coast, the schooner *Ferret* sinks in a storm with a loss of five men. The survivors are rescued subsequently by the schooner *Jackal*.

March 3 In Washington, D.C., Congress authorizes construction of 10 new sloops-of-war to help combat piracy. They also approve legislation to construct a naval yard and depot at Pensacola, Florida.

March 4 At Ponce, Puerto Rico, Lieutenant John D. Sloat of the schooner *Grampus* captures a pirate sloop; he is personally thanked by the governor of the island.

Near Boca del Inferno, West Indies, Lieutenant G. Pendergast, commanding 26 men on a prize sloop, captures a pirate sloop after a 40-minute action.

March 25 At Rio Sagua la Grande near Matanzas, Cuba, Lieutenant Isaac McKeever of the barge *Gallinipper* joins British vessels HMS *Dartmouth*, *Lion*, and *Union* in a combined assault on a pirate base.

September 7 In Washington, D.C., the aged marquis de Lafayette concludes his triumphal tour of the United States and departs for France on the frigate *Brandywine*.

1826

January 9 At the Sandwich Islands (Hawaii), Lieutenant John Percival of the schooner *Dolphin* drops anchor, becoming the first American to do so. Percival is chasing mutineers who have seized the whaling vessel *Globe*.

July 1 Commodore David Porter angrily ends his 28-year career in the U.S. Navy by resigning. He is incensed by his treatment following the so-called "Foxardo Affair," and soon gains appointment as commander in chief of the Mexican Navy.

August 6 At Matavia Bay, Tahiti, Master Commandant Thomas ap Catesby Jones and the sloop *Peacock* arrive, and he negotiates a treaty with local chieftains to protect American commerce in their waters.

September 3 At New York, the frigate *Vincennes* under Master Commandant William B. Finch sails off on a four-year mission to circumnavigate the globe; his is the first U.S. Navy vessel to do so.

December 22 In Hawaii, Master Commandant Thomas ap Catesby Jones of the sloop *Peacock* negotiates a treaty with the tribes to protect American commerce. The United States also receives favored-nation status for trading purposes.

1827

March 3 In Washington, D.C., Congress votes to fund new dry docks at Boston, Massachusetts, and Norfolk, Virginia.

April 2 At Portsmouth, Virginia, work commences on the first U.S. Naval Hospital and continues up through 1833.

OCTOBER 4 In waters off Carabusa, Greece, Master Commandant Lawrence Kearny of the sloop-of-war *Warren* captures a pirate vessel which had been preying upon American and Greek shipping near the Cycades Islands.

OCTOBER 16 In the Adriatic Sea, Lieutenant Benjamin Cooper of the schooner *Porpoise* dispatches sailors and marines to recapture a merchant ship from pirates; they also inflict 40 casualties on them.

OCTOBER 25 On the Mediterranean island of Argenteira, recent attacks on merchant vessels *Cherub* and *Rob Roy* induce the sloop *Warren* under Master Commandant Lawrence Kearny to pursue a pirate brig onto shore, where landing parties scuttle it.

OCTOBER 28 Near Syra, Greece, the sloop *Warren* under Lieutenant Lawrence Kearney recaptures the American brig *Cherub* from pirates.

OCTOBER 30 Off the coast of Mykonos, Greece, the sloop *Warren* under Master Commandant Lawrence Kearny captures a 40-oared pirate galley in the Cycades Islands.

NOVEMBER 1 At Mykonos, Greece, Lieutenant Lawrence Kearney dispatches a landing party from the sloop *Warren* to rescue stolen goods, and arrests five pirates. A pirate vessel is also burned.

NOVEMBER 7 While cruising around Andros Island in the Aegean Sea, a boat crew commanded by Lieutenant William L. Hudson of the sloop *Warren* captures a pirate craft and burns another.

1828

The Navy establishes a new recruiting office at Carlisle, Pennsylvania; this is the first time men are enlisted from regions other than the eastern seaboard.

1829

JUNE 4 In New York, the *Fulton the First*, the world's first steam warship, catches fire and burns; 24 people are killed and another 19 are injured. The vessel performed only minor service as a receiving ship, despite its revolutionary nature.

AUGUST 16 At Pensacola, Florida, the sloop *Hornet* under Lieutenant O. Norris departs on a cruise off the Gulf of Mexico, and is lost at sea with all hands.

1830

JUNE 8 At New York, the sloop *Vincennes* under Master Commandant William B. Finch returns after a four-year hiatus, being the first U.S. Navy warship to circumnavigate the globe.

September 16 In Boston, Massachusetts, Oliver Wendell Holmes writes and publishes the poem "Old Ironsides" in the Boston *Daily Advertiser*, to prevent the aged frigate *Constitution*, "Old Ironsides" of lore, from being sold and broken up. His efforts are so successful that the Navy Department rescinds its order to decommission the vessel.

December 6 In Washington, D.C., the Secretary of the Navy authorizes creation of the Depot of Charts and Instruments in Washington, D.C., to store charts, sailing directions, and navigation instruments. It eventually evolves into the U.S. Naval Observatory.

1831

February Near Quallah Battoo, Sumatra, pirates board the American merchant vessel *Friendship*, kill three crewmen, then plunder its hold. This act results in the first armed intervention in Asia by the United States.

February 3 In Washington, D.C., Congress authorizes construction of three new sloops to be christened *Experiment*, *Enterprise*, and *Boxer*.

June 15 To reduce sailors' affection for grog (rum), Secretary of the Navy Levi Woodbury offers sailors six cents for every ration declined; the effort is largely ignored.

August 28 In Washington, D.C., President Andrew Jackson orders Captain John Downes of the frigate *Potomac* to undertake punitive actions against Sumatran pirates who attacked American shipping in the East Indies.

September 24 In Washington, D.C., Secretary of the Navy Levi Woodbury orders that flogging can only take place in the presence of a ship's captain, and only under his explicit orders.

1832

January 1 In the Falkland (Malvenas) Islands, the sloop *Lexington* under Master Commandant Silas Duncan orders a landing party ashore to obtain redress for the illegal seizure of two American whalers by the Argentinian regime there.

February 6 At Quallah Battoo, Sumatra, Captain John Downes of the *Potomac* lands marines and sailors against pirate strongholds. They destroy four forts, kill 150 pirates, including Rajah Po Mahomet, while losing 2 dead and 11 wounded. The surviving Malays agree to halt further attacks upon American vessels.

March 8 At Boston, Massachusetts, Captain David Geisinger and the sloop *Peacock* convey Edmund Roberts, a State Department official, to the Far East. There Roberts concludes the first commercial treaties between the United States and several Eastern nations.

1833

March 20 In Siam (Thailand), Captain David Geisinger of the *Peacock* and Edmund Roberts of the State Department conclude the first commercial treaty between the United States and that kingdom. This is proof of the growing importance of the Pacific region to American trade.

June 17 In Norfolk, Virginia, the ship of the line *Delaware* enters dry dock for the first time in Navy history. Commodore Lewis Warren is determined to become operational ahead of a similar facility in Boston, and orders the vessel on shore despite the facility's unfinished condition.

June 24 In Boston, Massachusetts, the venerable frigate *Constitution* becomes the first vessel hauled onto the new dry dock there. Vice President Martin Van Buren and Secretary of the Navy Levi Woodbury are on hand to witness the event.

1834

June 30 In Washington, D.C., Congress approves $5,000 for conducting extensive experiments with steam engines for naval vessels. Within a decade, new innovations will revolutionize vessel propulsion.

1835

October 29 The West India Squadron of Commodore Alexander J. Dallas is ordered to deploy along the west coast of Florida and facilitate the removal of Seminole Indians.

November 19 At Guam, the sloop *Vincennes* under Commander John A. Aulick becomes the first American warship to pay a visit to Apra.

1836

January 1 Lieutenant Edward T. Dougherty marches from Pensacola, Florida Territory, with 29 sailors and marines to patrol Tampa Bay and search for recalcitrant Seminole Indians.

January 21 Commodore Alexander J. Dallas is ordered to blockade southern Florida with his West India Squadron and keep Spanish arms and ammunition out of Seminole hands. The blockade remains in place throughout the war.

January 28 At Pensacola, Florida, Master Commandant Thomas T. Webb departs with the sloop-of-war *Vandalia* for Tampa Bay to assist in the defense of Fort Brooke.

March 16–30 Captain Ezekiel Jones and the U.S. Revenue Cutter *Washington* scouts the shores of Charlotte Harbor (Tampa), Florida, looking for Seminoles. When none are sighted, he lands parties ashore that penetrate 10 miles inland, without success.

March 17–28 In Tampa Bay, Florida, Lieutenant Levin M. Powell leads a boat expedition from the sloop *Vandalia* to reconnoiter the mouth of the Manatee River.

April 1 Near Tampa Bay, Florida, Lieutenant Levin M. Powell's second expedition dispatches a boat crew under Lieutenant Stephen C. Rowan, who attacks Seminoles in their camp; two Indians are killed and several wounded in the ensuing fire fight.

May 18 In Washington, D.C., Congress authorizes the government's first scientific and oceanic surveying expedition. It ultimately consists of six vessels under Lieutenant Charles Wilkes.

June 19–July 27 On the Chattahoochee River, Alabama, the armed steamers *American*, *Major Dade*, and *Lieutenant Izard* commence patrols against potentially hostile Creeks, to assist General Winfield Scott's land operations.

July 12 Charles H. Haswell becomes the Navy's first commissioned engineer, a sign that technology is becoming of paramount importance to that service. Over the next 16 years, he compiles the first engineering books and other technical treatises.

October 6–November 20 At Pensacola, Florida, the sloop *Vandalia* and revenue cutter *Washington* sail for Key West to scout out hostile Seminoles along the coast. Lieutenant Levin M. Powell is also tasked with conducting sweeps inland along various waterways, including the Everglades. This is the Navy's first experience with riverine warfare.

1837

February 8 On Lake Monroe, Florida, Navy gunboats aid a beleaguered army detachment by providing close support fire. Their intervention breaks a determined Seminole assault.

September 24 In Florida, Lieutenant Levin M. Powell is pleased with his expedition into the Everglades and writes the Secretary of the Navy to conduct similar operations on a much large scale. Powell's suggestions serve as the basis for combined Army-Navy operations in the same area later that year.

December 13 At New York, the new, oceangoing sidewheel steamer *Fulton* (II) is the first seaworthy vessel of its class in the U.S. Navy.

1838

January 15 In the Everglades, southern Florida, Lieutenant Levin M. Powell leads 200 soldiers, sailors, and marines on a fourth boat foray down the Jupiter River, Florida. At length they encounter a large Seminole encampment and attack. The Americans suffer 4 dead and 22 wounded in a stiff action and withdraw back downstream, battered but intact.

MARCH 22–23   In the Florida Everglades, Lieutenant Colonel James Bankhead leads a combined naval/military force in pursuit of Seminoles until they reach an island, and skirmishing ensues. Bankhead's operation is the first deep penetration of previously inaccessible Seminole territory.

MAY 18   In Washington, D.C., Lieutenant Charles Wilkes receives command of the U.S. Exploring Expedition, the first government-funded attempt to acquire scientific knowledge from around the globe.

MAY 31   In Florida, Lieutenant John McLaughlin receives command of the former yacht *Wave,* and uses it to patrol Florida waters and keep Spanish traders from supplying Seminole Indians with firearms and gunpowder.

AUGUST 18–JULY 6, 1842   At Hampton Roads, Virginia, Lieutenant Charles Wilkes of the sloop *Vincennes* leads his six-ship exploring expedition into the Pacific and Antarctic oceans. This four-year endeavor is the first scientific expedition funded by the Federal government, and the numerous scientists and specialists on board will report on hydrography, geology, botany, and geography.

The USS Vincennes, *with Lt. Charles Wilkes at the helm, plows through ice during the U.S. Exploring Expedition's survey of the Antarctic shelf in 1840. (National Oceanic and Atmospheric Administration)*

AUGUST 19   Near Cape Florida, Lieutenant John Faunce of the revenue-cutter *Campbell* leads 24 men ashore and surprises a party of Seminoles, killing three. This was retaliation for the massacre of three boat crews who had recently grounded in a gale.

SEPTEMBER 18   Along the east coast of Florida, Lieutenant John McLaughlin and the converted yacht *Wave* engage a body of Seminoles while approaching the wrecked brig *Alna,* killing three Indians and wounding several more.

1839

JANUARY 1–2   At Quallah Battoo, Sumatra, Commander John C. Read of the East India Squadron directs the frigate *Columbia* and sloop *John Adams* to attack pirate forts. This action comes in retaliation for continuing attacks on American commerce; five forts are destroyed, two villages are completely burned. Moreover, the survivors pay reparations and promise to halt further attacks.

APRIL 5 Off southern Florida, Commodore Isaac Mayo takes charge of the steamer *Poinsett* and joins the yacht *Wave* as a blockading squadron designed to assist Army efforts further inland. This force becomes known as the Florida Expedition.

APRIL 26 Off the Chilean coast, the pilot boat *Sea Gull* becomes detached from the Wilkes Expedition and is lost somewhere in the South Atlantic.

JULY 30 In Florida, landing parties from the steamer *Poinsett* accost Seminoles under Catsha Tustenuggee, arresting them for the murder of 12 whites a week earlier. The killings violated a truce arranged by General Alexander Macomb.

AUGUST 26 Near Montauk Point, New York, the Spanish slaver ship *Amistad*, which was taken over by Africans in a bloody uprising, is stopped by the revenue cutter *Washington*. The slaves are removed to Hartford, Connecticut, win a celebrated trial to regain their freedom, and return to their homeland.

DECEMBER 2 In south Florida, Lieutenant John McLaughlin takes charge of the embryonic "Mosquito Squadron," a flotilla of small craft utilized for operations in the Everglades. He also succeeds Commander Isaac Mayo of the Florida Expedition.

1840

JANUARY 19 Approaching the South Pole, Lieutenant Charles Wilkes of the sloop *Vincennes* glimpses Antarctica for the first time. The region he spots subsequently becomes known as Wilkes Land.

APRIL 10 At Cape Sable, Florida, the Mosquito Fleet schooner *Otsego* lands a party of 24 sailors and marines to scout the shoreline, when they are attacked by a large party of Seminoles. The Indians withdraw as reinforcements from the schooners *Wave* and *Flirt* approach.

JULY 26 At Maolo, Fiji Islands, Lieutenant Charles Wilkes leads a landing party ashore that destroys the towns of Sualib and Arro in retaliation for the murder of two of the expedition's officers.

AUGUST 6–7 At Indian Keys, Florida, a Seminole raiding party under Chakaika attacks a settlement, killing 13 people and torching the buildings. This is the only known amphibious assault made by Native Americans, who paddled to their objective by canoe.

SEPTEMBER Near Bahia, Brazil, the schooner *Enterprise* under Lieutenant Louis M. Goldsborough apprehends a pirate brig.

SEPTEMBER 27 At West Point, New York, future naval theorist Alfred Thayer Mahan is born. His father, Dennis Hart Mahan, is an instructor at the U.S. Military Academy.

DECEMBER 31 In the Florida Everglades, Lieutenant Colonel William S. Harney and Navy Lieutenant John T. McLaughlin lead a force of 100 sailors and marines and 90 soldiers on a deep penetration mission into the Seminole heartland. They keep paddling, and emerge on Florida's west coast 19 days later, being the first whites to traverse that swampy region.

1841

JANUARY 7 In New York, the new steam frigate *Missouri* is launched, becoming the first side-paddle warship in Navy history. Given the transitional nature of technology at this time, the vessel also carries conventional sails and rigging.

FEBRUARY 1 In Washington, D.C., the Navy Department issues its first dress regulations for enlisted personnel, who, up til now, had been at liberty to wear almost whatever they liked.

FEBRUARY 21 At Upolu, Samoa, the sloop *Peacock* lands sailors and marines ashore, who burn three native villages in consequence of their murder of an American merchant seaman.

APRIL 9 On Drummond Island in the Gilberts, the sloop *Peacock* lands 80 sailors and marines, who rout 800 warriors and burn two villages after failing to rescue a sailor previously kidnapped by the inhabitants.

JULY 7 In Washington, D.C., the House Naval Affairs Committee reacts to a war scare with Great Britain by creating a Home Squadron to patrol the American coast and the Newfoundland Fishing Banks.

JULY 18 Near the Columbia River, Oregon Territory, the sloop-of-war *Hornet* under Lieutenant William L. Hudson wrecks on a sand bar; no lives are lost.

OCTOBER 10–27 In south Florida, sailors and marines of the "Mosquito Squadron" traverse the Everglades along the Shark River to snare Seminole leader Sam Jones. The attempt is abandoned after 17 days, and they return.

NOVEMBER 3–DECEMBER 23 In south Florida, the "Mosquito Squadron" of Lieutenant John T. McLaughlin completes two more unsuccessful forays through the Florida Everglades. No Seminoles are encountered, and nearly a quarter of McLaughlin's men are incapacitated by disease by the time they withdraw.

DECEMBER 19 In the Pacific, Lieutenant Charles Wilkes and the sloop *Vincennes* come upon an atoll consisting of three small islets. This is the future site of Wake Island, a famous World War II battleground.

1842

In Connecticut, pistol manufacturer Samuel Colt begins experimenting with a submarine battery, or underwater mines.

FEBRUARY 11 In south Florida, the "Mosquito Squadron" under Lieutenant John T. McLaughlin begins its latest sweep through the Everglades, Florida, which continues over the next two months. Another party under Lieutenant John B. Marchand ventures inland from the west, but no Seminoles are encountered, and all hands suffer heavily from illnesses.

JUNE 10 In New York, the United States Exploring Expedition under Lieutenant Charles Wilkes returns after covering

90,000 miles and visiting 200 islands. Work on his published report continues until 1844, and runs five volumes.

JUNE 20 In Florida, the "Mosquito Squadron" is disbanded, having provided the U.S. Navy with its first extensive exposure to riverine warfare.

JUNE 29 In Washington, D.C., Lieutenant Matthew Fontaine Maury is assigned to the Superintendent of the Depots of Charts and Instruments after a leg injury disqualifies him from sea duty. Here Maury lays the foundation for oceanography, and earns the title "Pathfinder of the Seas."

JULY 4 In Connecticut, the old gunboat *Boser* is sunk by an electrically detonated "torpedo" (mine) developed by Samuel Colt, the pistol manufacturer.

AUGUST 9 The new Webster-Ashburton Treaty settles an American/Canadian boundary dispute, and formalizes anti-slave patrols off West Africa by the Royal and the U.S. Navies.

AUGUST 31 In Washington, D.C., Congress abolishes the old Board of Navy Commissioners and substitutes the five bureaus of Yards and Docks, Construction and Repair, Provisions and Clothing, Ordnance and Hydrography, and Medicine and Surgery. Congress further institutes an engineer in chief for the U.S. Navy, and authorizes deployment of a chief engineer on every steam vessel.

OCTOBER 2 In the Mozambique Channel, Africa, the sloop *Concord* under Commander William Boerum is wrecked, and three sailors are drowned.

OCTOBER 13 In China, Commodore Lawrence Kearney and his East India Squadron arrive and begin comprehensive diplomatic and commercial negotiations with Manzu officials.

OCTOBER 20–21 Off the California coast, Commodore Thomas ap Catesby Jones of the East Pacific Squadron seizes the Mexican settlement of Monterrey, California, being under the false impression that the United States and Mexico are at war. He is abruptly corrected by American consul Thomas O. Larkin, apologizes, and departs; Jones is subsequently relieved of command.

DECEMBER 1 Commander Alexander S. Mackenzie hangs three individuals for allegedly plotting mutiny on the brig *Somers*. One individual, 19-year-old Midshipman Philip Spencer, is the son of Secretary of War John C. Spencer. Mackenzie is subsequently court-martialed for the executions, but is exonerated; this is the only instance of mutiny aboard a U.S. Naval warship.

1843

MARCH 11 En route from Charleston, South Carolina, to Norfolk, Virginia, Lieutenant A. E. Downes and the schooner *Grampus* are lost at sea with all hands.

AUGUST 25 At Gibraltar, Spain, the sidewheel steamer *Missouri* becomes the first side-paddle steam vessel to cross the Atlantic Ocean. However, the vessel is destroyed by an accidental fire the following evening.

SEPTEMBER 9 At Philadelphia, Pennsylvania, the revolutionary screw sloop *Princeton* is launched, becoming the first U.S. Navy vessel driven by a propeller.

The ship was designed by Swedish engineer John Ericsson, and Captain Robert F. Stockton is appointed its commander.

December 5 At Erie, Pennsylvania, the *Michigan*, the Navy's first all-iron vessel and the world's first prefabricated warship, is assembled by sections and successfully launched. This vessel was constructed in parts at Pittsburgh before being transported overland to Lake Erie.

December 15 On Africa's Ivory Coast, Commodore Matthew C. Perry visits Little Berebee village, accompanied by 200 sailors and marines. Negotiations with King Ben Krako commence, until fighting suddenly breaks out and the king and several natives are killed. The surviving tribal leaders consequently agree not to harass missionaries in the area.

1844

February 25 In Washington, D.C., the new Naval Appropriations Act limits manpower ceilings to 7,500 men, which induces the Secretary of the Navy to phase out the few remaining ships of the line from active duty.

February 28 On the Potomac River outside Washington, D.C., Secretary of State Abel P. Upshur, Secretary of the Navy Thomas Gilmer, and six others are killed by an accidental cannon burst on the steam frigate *Princeton*. The weapon, nicknamed "Peacemaker," was specifically designed by Commodore Thomas F. Stockton, who was also injured.

March 29 Contentious Uriah Philips Levy becomes the first Jewish naval officer to gain the rank of captain.

1845

January 29 In Washington, D.C., the Secretary of the Navy orders the bureau chiefs to evaluate Captain George W. Taylor's ambitious plans for developing diving bells, submarines, and torpedoes (mines).

February 26 In Washington, D.C., the Secretary of the Navy issues a General Order clearly delineating the duties of engineering officers on board Navy vessels. He seeks to clarify the command relationship between engineering officers and those of the line.

March 11 In Philadelphia, Pennsylvania, William Chauvenet of the navy school contacts Secretary of the Navy George Bancroft with an idea for transforming the present short course for prospective officers into two years of formal instruction. Bancroft is intrigued by the idea, but feels that Annapolis, Maryland, would be a better venue for the new school. Specifically, he has his eye on the old Army post at Fort Severn as a possible site.

March 20 Commodore David Conner is ordered to sail the Home Squadron into Mexican waters, thereby underscoring Congressional support for a resolution favoring the annexation of Texas.

MARCH 25–29 In the Rio Pongas, West Africa, Lieutenant S. F. Blunt accompanies a joint American/British boat expedition to capture the slave vessel *Spitfire*.

JUNE 2 In Philadelphia, Pennsylvania, the Naval Asylum board contemplates the suitability of Annapolis, Maryland, as a potential site for the new naval academy. Three officers are selected to begin planning for such an institution.

JUNE 4 In New York, the ship of the line *Columbus* and sloop-of-war *Vincennes* depart under Commodore James Biddle. He is conveying Alexander H. Everett, who will deliver a ratified copy of the breakthrough Treaty of Wangxia promoting American trade with China.

JULY 25 At Nueces Bay, Texas, a convoy escorted by the sloop-of-war *St. Mary's* arrives, and General Zachary Taylor's army disembarks on St. Joseph's Island.

AUGUST 15 After Fort Severn, Annapolis, Maryland, is transferred from the Army to the Navy, Commander Franklin Buchanan is appointed to serve as the first superintendent of the new U.S. Naval Academy.

AUGUST 29–SEPTEMBER 2 In Washington, D.C., President James K. Polk's cabinet agrees that U.S. Navy warships should blockade Mexican ports along the gulf coast in the event of war. They further decide to treat foreigners operating under Mexican Letters of Marque as pirates.

AUGUST 31 In Washington, D.C., the Secretary of the Navy issues a General Order that grants naval rank to surgeons, but excuses them of any corresponding command authority.

OCTOBER 10 At Annapolis, Maryland, Secretary of the Navy George Bancroft attends opening ceremonies of the Naval School (U.S. Naval Academy after 1850), with 56 midshipmen in attendance at the time. Initially, all midshipmen are to serve one year at school, complete a three-year tour of duty at sea, then return to finish a second and final year before being commissioned. Fortunately, Commander Franklin Buchanan effectively lays the curriculum groundwork for the first graduating class of 1854.

OCTOBER 31 Near Veracruz, Mexico, the government orders Commodore David Conner's Home Squadron out of national waters before they will receive Louisiana Congressman John Slidell as the new American ambassador.

NOVEMBER 30 Near Kabenda, Africa, the sloop *Yorktown* seizes the American slaver *Pons*; this is the first of three such vessels seized during a short cruise there.

DECEMBER 24 At Macao, China, Commodore James Biddle drops anchor and proceeds to Guangzhou with a ratified copy of the Treaty of Wanghia. This document allows trade relations and the establishment of the first U.S. diplomatic delegation to that nation.

1846

JANUARY 17 Off the coast of Veracruz, Mexico, Commodore David Conner takes his Home Squadron in support of General Zachary Taylor's army operating along the Rio Grande.

APRIL 1   At Monterey, California, Commodore John D. Sloat of the Pacific Squadron instructs the sloop *Portsmouth* to anchor there, and protect American lives and property in the event of war.

APRIL 17   On the Rio Grande, the brig *Lawrence* and the revenue cutter *Woodbury* aggressively intercept several vessels bound for Matamoros, Mexico, to prevent supplies from reaching Mexican forces opposing General Zachary Taylor.

APRIL 23   In Mexico City, Mexico, President Mariano Paredes y Arrillaga declares war on the United States.

MAY   In Washington, D.C., President James K. Polk declares the Mexican coastline along the Gulf of Mexico and the Pacific Ocean to be under a state of blockade.

MAY 4   With war declared, Commodore David Conner and the Home Squadron depart Veracruz, Mexico, and sail directly for the mouth of the Rio Grande.

MAY 13–14   In Washington, D.C., Secretary of the Navy George Bancroft orders Commodore David Conner's Home Squadron to blockade Mexican ports and intercept all enemy vessels in the Gulf of Mexico. In the Pacific, Commodore John D. Sloat is directed to blockade the California coast while awaiting reinforcements from warships stationed off Brazil and China.

MAY 15   In Washington, D.C., Secretary of the Navy George Bancroft instructs Commodore John D. Sloat's Pacific Squadron to capture San Francisco, Monterey, and other ports along the California coast.

MAY 16   In Washington, D.C., all 11 revenue cutters are ordered to support military and naval operations in the war against Mexico.

MAY 19–25   In Washington, D.C., Secretary of the Navy George Bancroft orders shallow-draft steamers and schooners, originally intended for the Mexican Navy, purchased from the New York firm Brown and Bell. These are subsequently employed in amphibious operations.

MAY 24   In the Gulf of Mexico, the sloop *Falmouth* under Commander Joseph R. Jarvis and the brig *Somers* under Commander Duncan J. Ingraham capture the Mexican schooners *Criolla* and *Amada*. Both are subsequently released after learning that the Mexican government generously allowed four American vessels to depart Veracruz despite a state of war.

JUNE 8   Tampico, Mexico, is briefly shelled by the 20-gun sloop *St. Mary's* under Commander John L. Saunders.

JUNE 14   Offshore at Tampico, Mexico, the sloop *St. Mary's* launches a nighttime boat expedition against Mexican forts along the Panuco River. The effort fails after the boat runs aground on a sandbar, alerting the defenders.

JULY 7–9   At Monterey, California, the frigate *Savannah* and the sloop *Cyane* send landing parties ashore, whereby Commodore John D. Sloat claims California for the United States.

JULY 9   At Yerba Buena (San Francisco), California, Commander John B. Montgomery of the sloop-of-war *Portsmouth* takes possession of the area without resistance.

JULY 20   At Edo (Tokyo) Bay, Japan, Commodore James Biddle and his East India Squadron unsuccessfully parlay with the Tokugawa shogunate to establish diplomatic relations. This is the first visit of American warships to the Land of the Rising Sun, but local authorities rebuff his efforts and he departs empty-handed.

JULY 29   Off the California coast, Commodore Robert F. Stockton arrives to replace Commodore John D. Sloat as commander of the Pacific Squadron. He intends to expand upon Sloat's initial success by capturing the settlement of Los Angeles, in concert Major John C. Fremont's land forces.

Near San Diego, California, the sloop *Cyane* under Captain William Mervine anchors and sends Lieutenant Stephen C. Rowan ashore to seize the settlement. His vessel is also carrying the California Battalion of Captain John C. Fremont, U.S. Army.

AUGUST 4   Offshore at Santa Barbara, California, the frigate *Congress* under Commodore Samuel F. Du Pont anchors and sends a landing party ashore to seize the settlement.

AUGUST 7   In the Gulf of Mexico, the nine ships of Commodore David Conner's Home Squadron assume bombardment positions off Alvarado, Mexico, and begin shelling forts and gunboats guarding the entrance of the Alvarado River. The action ceases following the onset of poor weather.

AUGUST 10   In Washington, D.C., President James K. Polk signs a bill elevating naval manpower strength from 7,500 to 10,000.

AUGUST 13   Near Los Angeles, California, Commodore Robert F. Stockton leads 360 sailors and marines ashore, joins forces with Captain John C. Fremont's California Battalion, and subdues that settlement without violence.

AUGUST 14   Near Tampico, Mexico, the brig *Truxtun* under Commander Edward W. Carpenter runs aground at Tuxpan Reef and he is forced to surrender. A week later, a party from the sloop *Princeton* burns the *Truxtun* where it rests.

AUGUST 29   In the Gulf of Mexico, Commodore David Conner receives orders to be wary of Mexican privateers near Key West, Florida. He is also instructed to secure geographical information about the Veracruz area for a possible amphibious landing there.

SEPTEMBER 2   Off the coast at San Blas, Baja California, Lieutenant Stephen C. Rowan and the sloop *Cyane* drop anchor, capture a Mexican sloop, then send landing parties ashore to seize an enemy fort and spike 24 cannon.

SEPTEMBER 6–8   At Mazatlan, Mexico, the sloop *Warren* takes up blockading positions and seizes the Mexican brigs *Malek Adhel* and *Carmelita* as they try to slip by.

SEPTEMBER 10   At the mouth of the Columbia River, Oregon Territory, the schooner *Shark* under Lieutenant Neil M. Howison is wrecked without the loss of life.

SEPTEMBER 14   Near La Paz, Baja, California, the sloop *Cyane* seizes an additional nine Mexican vessels while enforcing a strict blockade.

OCTOBER 1   In the Gulf of California, Mexico, the sloop *Cyane* anchors off Loreto on the western shore, capturing two schooners.

OCTOBER 7 Offshore at Sonora, Mexico, Commander Samuel F. Du Pont of the sloop *Cyane* shells Guaymas and sinks two gunboats, while a landing party seizes a merchant brig.

OCTOBER 7–8 Near Los Angeles, California, a landing detachment from the frigate *Savannah* attacks rebellious inhabitants, only to be repulsed by local cavalry equipped with cannon.

OCTOBER 15 At Alvarado, Mexico, warships of Commodore David Conner's Home Squadron again try to capture Mexican forts, until the steamer *McLane* grounds on a sandbar and the attempt is cancelled.

OCTOBER 23–25 On the Tabasco River, Mexico, seven vessels under Commodore Matthew C. Perry capture the village of Frontera, then sail 25 miles upstream to seize the settlement of Tabasco. Seven vessels are captured and, despite some shelling from the defenders, no damage is inflicted, and the Americans return to gulf waters.

NOVEMBER 14 On the Panuco River, Mexico, American sailors and marines from Commodore David Connor's Home Squadron seize the Mexican port of Tampico, along with five enemy schooners; four of these are taken into U.S. service as gunboats.

NOVEMBER 15 Off the coast of the Bahamas, the sloop *Boston*, sailing to join the Home Squadron in the Gulf of Mexico under Commander George F. Pearson, encounters a squall and wrecks on Eleuthra Island.

Bombardment of San Juan de Ulúa, Mexico, by the U.S. Navy under Commodore Matthew C. Perry in 1846. (Ridpath, John Clark, Ridpath's History of the World, *1901)*

NOVEMBER 19 On the Panuco River, Mexico, Commodore Josiah Tattnall leads the side-wheel steamer *Spitfire* and the schooner *Petrel* to capture the town of Tampico, where a number of cannon are destroyed. This settlement remains in American hands for the rest of the conflict.

NOVEMBER 26 Off Veracruz, Mexico, a cutting-out expedition under Lieutenant James L. Parker from the brig *Somers* burns the Mexican brig *Criolla* under the guns of Fortress San Juan de Ulúa. It turns out that this was actually a spy ship that Commodore David Conner had allowed to pass.

DECEMBER 8 In the Gulf of Mexico, the brig *Somers* under Lieutenant Raphael Semmes is caught in a squall and sinks, with 32 sailors drowned and 7 more captured.

DECEMBER 21 In the Bay of Campeche, Mexico, Commodore Matthew C. Perry's four-ship squadron captures the town of Carmen without resistance.

DECEMBER 29 Outside Los Angeles, California, Commodore Robert F. Stockton leads 600 sailors and marines overland in a bid to recapture that settlement.

1847

JANUARY 12 In Washington, D.C., Lieutenant John A. Dahlgren is assigned to the Bureau of Ordnance and Hydrography. However, his real talent turns out to be designing naval ordnance.

JANUARY 14 In the Gulf of Mexico, the sloop *St. Mary's* anchors off South Padre Island, Texas, while protecting transport vessels intended for General Winfield Scott's army.

JANUARY 22 Offshore at California, Commodore William B. Shubrick replaces Commodore Robert F. Stockton as head of the Pacific Squadron.

FEBRUARY 5 Off the island of Lobos, Mexico, boating parties from the sloop *St. Mary's* burn the grounded troop transport *Ondiaka* to prevent it from capture.

MARCH 3 In Washington, D.C., the new Naval Appropriations Act provides funding for dry dock facilities at the Pensacola Navy Yard, Florida, and thereby facilitates the repair of vessels operating in the Gulf of Mexico.

MARCH 6 In the Gulf of Mexico, transports conveying the invasion force of General Winfield Scott depart Lobos Island and rendezvous with Commodore David E. Conner's Home Squadron.

MARCH 9 At Veracruz, Mexico, Commodore David Conner's Home Squadron effectively posits the 8,000-man army of General Winfield Scott on Collado Beach without a single casualty. This is the first major amphibious operation conducted by the U.S. Navy since the capture of York, Upper Canada, in 1813.

MARCH 10 Near Veracruz, Mexico, Commander Josiah Tattnall orders the steamer *Spitfire* to bombard the Mexican fort at San Juan de Ulúa, diverting their attention from General Winfield Scott's approaching army.

United States general Winfield Scott lands 10,000 men and artillery at the port city of Veracruz on March 9, 1847. The Mexicans surrendered at the Battle of Veracruz after suffering 21 days of shelling, a tactic criticized by Mexico, Europe, and even the United States itself as cruel and inhumane. (Library of Congress)

MARCH 21 In the Gulf of Mexico, Commodore Matthew C. Perry replaces Commodore David Conner as commander of the Home Squadron.

MARCH 22 In waters off Veracruz, Mexico, six vessels of the Home Squadron begin bombarding Mexican positions in support of Army operations ashore; little damage is inflicted by enemy counterfire.

At Monterey, California, Commodore James Biddle succeeds William B. Shubrick as commander of the Pacific Squadron.

MARCH 23 Near Veracruz, Mexico, Commander Josiah Tattnall pushes the steamers *Spitfire* and *Vixen* to within 600 yards of Mexican fortifications, suffering little damage in return. His bold dash is accompanied by several gunboats.

MARCH 24–25 At Veracruz, Mexico, a naval land battery of two 32-pounders and three eight-inch guns goes into action under Captain John H. Aulick of the frigate *Potomac*. They trade fire with Mexican artillery at nearby Fort Santa Barbara. The sailors sustain six dead and nine wounded, until their ammunition runs out the following day.

MARCH 30 In Baja California, a landing party under Lieutenant Benjamin F. B. Hunter of the sloop *Portsmouth* takes temporary possession of the Mexican port at San Jose del Cabo.

MARCH 31 The town of Alvarado, Mexico, falls to landing parties under Lieutenant Charles G. Hunter of the steamer *Scourge*, who also burns one schooner and seizes three others. However, insomuch as this operation interferes with efforts to capture Mexican horses and supplies in the area, an irate Commodore Matthew C. Perry orders him court-martialed.

APRIL 13 At Baja California, a landing party under Lieutenant John S. Missroon of the sloop *Portsmouth* seizes the capital of La Paz.

APRIL 18–22 In the Gulf of Mexico, Commodore Matthew C. Perry's Home Squadron, escorting 30 troop barges, captures the town of Tuxpan. After destroying the forts and batteries, they withdraw four days later.

MAY 12 On the Gulf of Campeche, Mexico, two vessels from Commodore Matthew C. Perry's Home Squadron pass up the Coatzacoalcos River and approach the village of Minatitlan, 24 miles downstream, to gather intelligence.

MAY 16 In the Gulf of Mexico, landing parties from Commodore Matthew C. Perry's Home Squadron capture the Mexican town of Carmen.

JUNE 14–16 On the Tabasco River, Mexico, Commodore Matthew C. Perry directs 1,713 men in 47 boats upstream against the village of Villahermosa; four forts are captured. However, the onset of yellow fever forces him to evacuate the premises on July 22.

JULY 19 At California, Commodore James Biddle departs the Pacific Squadron, and command reverts back to Commodore William B. Shubrick.

AUGUST 4 In Washington, D.C., Secretary of the Navy John Y. Mason instructs Commodore Matthew C. Perry not to capture any more Mexican ports.

OCTOBER 5 At Loreto, Baja California, Lieutenant T. A. M. Craven leads a landing party of sailors and marines ashore, seizing three cannon.

OCTOBER 20 Offshore at Guaymas, Sonora, Mexico, the frigate *Congress* under Captain Ellie A. F. La Vallette and the sloop *Portsmouth* under Commander John B. Montgomery begin shelling various defensive positions. Once the Mexicans withdraw, the settlement is occupied by a landing party.

NOVEMBER 11 In the Pacific, a landing force assembled from the frigates *Congress* and *Independence* and the sloop *Cyane* capture Mazatlan, Mexico's most important port in the region.

NOVEMBER 17 Off the coast of Guaymas, Sonora, Mexico, Commander Thomas O. Selfridge of the sloop *Dale* lands with 67 sailors and Marines in a show of force, only to be attacked by a force of 250 Mexicans. Selfridge is wounded and his men are hard pressed, until the *Dale* intervenes with a well-directed fire that scatters the attackers.

NOVEMBER 20 At Urias, south of Matzatlan, Mexico, landing parties under Lieutenants George C. Selden and Stephen C. Rowan scatter a Mexican infantry company by attacking at dawn.

DECEMBER 12 Ten miles from Matzatlan, Mexico, a detachment of 43 sailors and marines under Lieutenant Montgomery Lewis attacks a Mexican camp after sunset, scattering them.

1848

JANUARY 12 In the Pacific, landing parties from the bark *Whiton* and storeship *Lexington,* under Lieutenant Frederick Chatard, capture a battery defending the Pacific Mexican port of San Blas.

JANUARY 17   At Manzanillo, Mexico, Lieutenant Frederick Chatard of the *Whiton* again goes ashore with a landing party, and occupies the port.

JANUARY 30   Eight miles east of Guaymas, Sonora, Mexico, a landing party under Lieutenant T. A. M. Craven from the sloop *Dale* attacks at dawn and disperses a Mexican detachment.

FEBRUARY 2   The Treaty of Guadalupe Hidalgo ends the Mexican-American War, although skirmishing will continue for several weeks.

FEBRUARY 13   Four miles north of Guaymas, Sonora, Mexico, Lieutenant Fabius Stanly of the sloop *Dale* leads a detachment of 60 sailors and marines ashore, which routs a Mexican force at Bocachicacampo.

APRIL 8–MAY 10   In the Middle East, Lieutenant William Lynch and a survey party map the Sea of Galilee, and venture down the Jordan River until they encounter the Dead Sea.

APRIL 9   Near Guaymas, Mexico, Lieutenant Fabius Stanly leads a detachment of sailors and marines from the sloop *Dale*, marches 12 miles inland, and spikes a three-gun Mexican battery. These are the final shots fired by U.S. Navy personnel during the war.

MAY 6   Off the California coast, Commodore William B. Shubrick relinquishes command of the Pacific Squadron to the reinstated Commodore Thomas ap Catesby Jones.

1849

MARCH 3   In Cambridge, Massachusetts, Lieutenant Charles H. Davis founds the Nautical Almanac Office at Harvard University. This act establishes him as a leading scientific figure in naval circles.

APRIL 17   At Okinawa, the sloop *Preble* becomes the first American vessel to drop anchor. Japan proper, however, remains off-limits.

AUGUST 16   At New York, a scientific expedition under Lieutenant James M. Gilliss departs to demonstrate the practicality of using astronomical observations as a navigational tool. However, the bulk of his work unfolds at an observatory he constructs near Santiago, Chile.

1850

MAY 26   In New York, an expedition under Lieutenant Edward J. De Haven sails in the brigs *Advance* and *Rescue* in an attempt to find the missing Arctic explorer Sir John Franklin, who disappeared in 1847. Because this endeavor is underwritten by philanthropist Henry Grinnell, it is known as the Grinnell

Expedition. Both vessels are destroyed that fall owing to the onset of icy conditions, and expedition members do not return home until the summer of 1851.

JULY 1   At Annapolis, Maryland, the U.S. Navy School is formally renamed the U.S. Naval Academy. The curriculum is also extended to four years, but students still endure a three-year stint at sea after two years of classroom instruction.

SEPTEMBER 2   In Washington, D.C., Congress finally abolishes the practice of flogging to enforce discipline on warships.

SEPTEMBER 6   In the Cape Verde Islands, the sloop *Yorktown* under Commander John Marston is lost when it wrecks on Isla de Mayo; no lives are lost.

1851

MAY 21   At Lima, Peru, an expedition under the command of Lieutenant William L. Herndon is dispatched, to explore the feasibility of navigating up the Amazon basin.

AUGUST 6–7   On Johanna Island (Grande Comore), Indian Ocean, Commander William C. Pearson of the sloop *Dale* demands that King Selim pay an indemnity for illegally jailing a New England merchant captain. When the king refuses to comply, Pearson bombards the town, and he changes his mind.

NOVEMBER 15   At Annapolis, Maryland, the U.S. Naval Academy adopts a new curriculum requiring midshipmen to remain in class for four continuous years, with midshipman cruises during the summer months. Previously, cadets interrupted their studies after two years to complete a three-year tour at sea.

1852

FEBRUARY 3   At Buenos Aires, Argentina, Commodore Isaac McKeever of the Brazilian Squadron dispatches landing parties ashore, to protect American lives and property in a period of unrest.

APRIL 11   Para, Brazil, is reached by an exploring expedition, under Lieutenant William L. Herndon, which sailed 4,366 miles up the Amazon River. This endeavor was accomplished to demonstrate the feasibility of navigating upstream.

SEPTEMBER 30   In New York, the brig *Dolphin* departs under Lieutenant S. P. Lee; his mission is to test the theories of Lieutenant Matthew Fontaine Maury regarding winds and currents in the Atlantic.

NOVEMBER 24   From Norfolk, Virginia, a four-ship squadron commanded by Commodore Matthew C. Perry departs for Japan to establish diplomatic relations with the Tokugawa shogunate. This dynasty has deliberately sealed itself off from the outside world for the past two and a half centuries, so Perry's task is daunting.

Perry, Matthew C. (1794–1858)

Matthew Calbraith Perry was born in South Kingston, Rhode Island, on April 10, 1794. He was a younger brother of Oliver Hazard Perry, victor of the Battle of Lake Erie. He joined the U.S. Navy as a midshipman in 1809, and over the next three decades emerged as one of the foremost naval officers of his generation. Perry rose to captain in 1837 and assumed command of the USS *Fulton* (II), the navy's first side-paddle steamship. In 1839 he assumed command of the navy's first gunnery school off Sandy Hook, New Jersey, handled his responsibilities adroitly, and rose to commodore in June 1841. During the Mexican War, Perry replaced Commodore David F. Conner as commander of the Gulf Coast Squadron, and assisted the landing of General Winfield Scott's army at Veracruz. He returned to New York in 1848 before accepting one of the most significant diplomatic missions ever assigned to a naval officer.

In 1853 President Millard Fillmore ordered Perry to take a squadron of steam vessels across the Pacific and establish diplomatic relations with Japan. Perry's four vessels appeared suddenly in Edo Bay on July 8, 1853, and the commodore, a tall, dignified man, met with panic-stricken shogunate couriers, handed them a letter from President Fillmore, and then departed. The Americans returned in February 1854 and found Japanese officials willing to negotiate. Perry returned home to a hero's greeting, and served on the Navy's efficiency board. He died in New York City on March 4, 1858, the man who opened Japan up to the world.

1853

JANUARY 19 At Baltimore, Maryland, Lieutenant Thomas J. Paige and the sidewheel steamer *Water Witch* begin a three-year exploratory survey of River Plate in South America.

FEBRUARY 15 In Washington, D.C., President Millard Fillmore authorizes a 46-chapter "System of Orders and Instructions" intended to closely govern corporal punishments administered in the U.S. Navy.

MAY 30 In New York, naval surgeon Dr. Elisha Kent Kane takes the steamer *Advance* on an exploring expedition toward the Arctic region. This is better known as the Second Grinnell Expedition, being underwritten by philanthropist Henry Grinnell, which also comes to grief on the Arctic ice pack.

JUNE 11–OCTOBER 19, 1855 Commander Cadwallader Ringgold begins the North Pacific Surveying and Exploring Expedition by charting the Hawaiian Islands, prior to sailing off for the Aleutians and Japan. En route he is replaced by his subordinate, Commodore John Rodgers, son of the War of 1812 hero.

JUNE 21 At Smyrna, Turkey, Commander Duncan N. Ingraham of the sloop *St. Louis* prepares to engage Austrian warships if they fail to release naturalized American citizen and former Hungarian revolutionary Martin Kostza. Kostza is freed, the crisis subsides, and Congress subsequently awards Ingraham a gold medal.

JULY 8 In Edo (Tokyo) Bay, Japan, mouths are agape as the side-wheel steamers *Mississippi* and *Susquehanna*, and sloops *Plymouth* and *Saratoga*, all under Commodore Matthew C. Perry, enter unannounced. He is ordered to establish diplomatic relations between the two nations, primarily to end the cruel practice of killing or abusing shipwrecked American sailors. The xenophobic Japanese distrust the Americans, but Perry, an urbane, commanding figure, impresses local officials by his dignity and courtesy.

JULY 14 In Edo (Tokyo), Japan, Commodore Matthew C. Perry presents shogunate officials with a letter from President Millard Fillmore and invites them to open diplomatic relations. He grants them several months to consider the offer, then departs.

AUGUST 31 In Washington, D.C., the Franklin Board recommends adoption of the new nine-inch Dahlgren gun, designed by Lieutenant John A. Dahlgren. This is the first of many weapons created by Dahlgren, who becomes the Navy's most talented ordnance designer.

1854

JANUARY 19 At Caledonia, Panama, Lieutenant Isaac G. Strain of the sloop *Cyane* leads 25 officers and men across the Isthmus of Panama, looking for terrain to build a canal stretching from the Atlantic to the Pacific. It proves a difficult endeavor in which nine members perish.

FEBRUARY 13 At Yokohama, Japan, Commodore Matthew C. Perry's squadron again drops anchor, and he awaits the Emperor's reply toward establishing trade and diplomatic relations with the United States. The Japanese cannot help but notice that his squadron has increased from six vessels to eight.

MARCH 8–31 At Yokohama, Japan, Commodore Matthew C. Perry negotiates the Treaty of Kanagawa with the Tokugawa shogunate. Japan has finally opened up to the world on the basis of peace and amity, although commercial relations will be established later.

APRIL 4–5 At Shanghai, China, Commander John Kelly of the sloop *Portsmouth* lands 90 men which attack a body of Taipei rebels that were threatening Western interests there; one American dies and three are wounded.

JULY 11 On the Loo Choo (Ryukyu) Islands south of Japan, Commodore Matthew C. Perry signs the Treaty of Naha with the local regency to promote peace and amity.

JULY 13 Near Greytown, Nicaragua, the sloop *Cyane* under Commander George N. Hollins arrives, demanding an apology and an indemnity for the detainment of an American ambassador. When he receives neither, *Cyane* levels the settlement, an action that meets with State Department approval.

SEPTEMBER 16 Outside San Francisco, California, Commander David G. Farragut occupies Mare Island, which evolves into a significant shipyard.

SEPTEMBER 21 The brig *Porpoise* under Lieutenant K. Bridge is last seen passing through the Formosa Straits, then disappears with all hands.

SEPTEMBER 29 The sloop-of-war *Albany* under Commander James T. Gerry departs Aspinwall, Panama, for New York, and disappears at sea with all hands.

NOVEMBER 17 At Okinawa, the sloop *Vincennes* lands a detachment ashore to enforce provisions of the recent Treaty of Naha.

1855

FEBRUARY 1 The paddle-wheel steamer *Water Witch*, surveying down the Paraguay River in South America, is inexplicably fired upon by Paraguayan forces.

JULY 24 In the Arctic Circle, the exploring party of naval surgeon Dr. Elisha Kent Kane finally breaks free from the ice after two years, and completes an 83-day sledge journey back to Upernavik, Greenland.

AUGUST 4 Near Hong Kong, China, the frigate *Powhatan*, assisted by the British sloop *Rattler*, attacks and destroys 17 pirate junks lurking in Ty-Ho Bay.

SEPTEMBER 12 At Nukulau, Fiji Islands, the sloop *John Adams* under Commander E. B. Boutwell dispatches a landing party ashore to obtain compensation for recent attacks on American citizens.

SEPTEMBER 22 At Viti Levu, Fiji Islands, a landing party from the sloop *John Adams* under Commander E. B. Boutwell arrests the local king, hauls him onboard, and makes him sign a treaty requiring him to compensate American citizens for the destruction of their property.

OCTOBER 28–31 On Viti Levu, Fiji Islands, Commander E. B. Boutwell and the sloop *John Adams* return to find provisions of a recent treaty have not been honored. Lieutenant Louis C. Sartori consequently brings a landing party ashore and burns several villages; he loses one man killed and three wounded.

NOVEMBER 27 At Montevideo, Uruguay, the sloop *Germantown* under Lieutenant Augustus S. Nicholson sends landing parties ashore to guard the American consulate during a local insurrection. He is joined by forces from three other navies.

1856

JANUARY 26 Offshore near Seattle, Washington Territory, the sloop *Decatur* under Commander Guert Gansevoort provides close supporting fire, which repels an Indian attack upon a local settlement.

FEBRUARY 3 The paddle-wheel steamer *Water Witch* returns to New York under Lieutenant Thomas J. Paige, following a three-year surveying expedition on the River Plate, South America.

OCTOBER 23 At Guangzhou, China, the sloops *Portsmouth* and *Levant* land sailors and marines ashore to protect American lives and property.

NOVEMBER 15–16 At Guangzhou, China, the Chinese Barrier Forts on the

Pearl River fire upon American warships attempting to retrieve the detachment landed there in October. This act draws a particularly sharp response from the U.S. Navy.

NOVEMBER 20–22 At Guangzhou, China, Commander Andrew H. Foote of the East India Squadron land sailors and marines ashore, which storm the Chinese Barrier Forts, supported by fire from the sloops *Portsmouth* and *Levant*. The forts and 170 cannon are all destroyed; the Americans lose 42 casualties, while Chinese losses are approximately 400.

1857

OCTOBER 2 At Mare Island Navy Yard, California, the venerable 74-gun ship of the line *Independence* becomes a receiving vessel, and functions in that capacity for the next 55 years.

1858

JULY 29 In the North Atlantic, the steam frigate *Niagara* under Captain William L. Hudson, assisted by the HMS *Agamemnon*, successfully lays down the first transatlantic cable.

OCTOBER 6 At Waya, Fiji Islands, the sloop *Vandalia* lands 44 sailors and marines, under Lieutenant C. H. B. Caldwell, who destroy a local village in revenge for the recent murder of two American merchants.

OCTOBER 17 Off the South American coast, Flag Officer William B. Shubrick leads the 19-vessel Brazilian Squadron against Paraguay for its firing on the survey vessel *Water Witch* in 1855. This is the largest armada of American naval warships assembled to date, and Shubrick is ordered to extract an indemnity as compensation.

1859

JANUARY 25 At La Plata, Paraguay, Flag Officer William B. Shubrick's Brazilian Squadron anchors, and he successfully secures an indemnity for that nation's attack on the paddle-wheel steamer *Water Witch* in 1855. A new commercial treaty is also concluded.

APRIL 21 Off the mouth of the Congo River, West Africa, the sloop *Marion* under Commander W. F. Blunt captures the first of five slavers netted by the U.S. Navy that year.

JUNE 25 At the mouth of the Bai He River, China, Commodore Josiah Tattnall's East India Squadron assists British gunboats attacking the Chinese Dagu Forts by towing reinforcements in the chartered steamer *Toey-Wan*. Tattnall remarks, "Blood is thicker than water," during the action, and the State Department subsequently approves of his actions.

1860

February 6 Off the coast of West Africa, the U.S. Navy's African squadron captures the first of 13 slave trade vessels captured over the ensuing year.

September 25 The sloop-of-war *Levant* under Commander William E. Hunt, sailing from Hilo, Hawaii, to Aspinwall, Columbia, disappears at sea with all hands.

October 10 In the South Atlantic, the slaver *Bonito* is apprehended by the screw steamer *San Jacinto*. U.S. Navy vessels have apprehended 18 such vessels over the past 19 months.

November 1 In Washington, D.C., the Navy Department reaffirms its commitment to modernization by releasing plans to convert seven sailing ships to steam power at a cost of $3 million.

November 6 The election of Abraham Lincoln as president-elect puts in motion a chain of events leading to the bloodiest conflict in American history, the Civil War.

November 15 At Key West, Florida, Lieutenant Thomas A. Craven, commanding the naval installation there, orders landing parties to secure nearby Forts Taylor and Jefferson against possible seizure by secessionists.

1861

January 5 At New York, the supply vessel *Star of the West* departs for Fort Sumter, South Carolina, carrying food supplies and reinforcements. However, General Winfield Scott detains the warship *Brooklyn*, originally intended for the mission, as he feels that civilian vessel appears less provocative.

January 9 Near Charleston, South Carolina, Confederate shore batteries fire on the unarmed transport *Star of the West*, as it attempts to deliver supplies to the garrison of Fort Sumter. These are the first hostile shots of the war.

January 10 In Florida, the Pensacola Navy Yard is occupied by state forces once the U.S. garrison is withdrawn to Fort Pickens, offshore.

January 23 In Washington, D.C., Commander John A. B. Dahlgren removes several cannon and tons of ammunition from the Washington Navy Yard, to preclude their possible capture by secessionists.

January 29 At Pensacola, Florida, Captain William S. Walker and the screw sloop *Brooklyn* arrive, but he is ordered not to reinforce the garrison there unless it is attacked by Confederate forces.

February 15 Southern-born Commodore Raphael Semmes resigns his commission from the U.S. Navy. He subsequently gains infamy commanding the Confederate raider *Alabama*.

February 20 In Montgomery, Alabama, the Provisional Confederate Congress authorizes a Confederate Department of the Navy.

February 21 Floridian Stephen R. Mallory, the former congressman and chairman of the House Naval Affairs

Committee, is appointed the Confederate secretary of the navy.

FEBRUARY 27 In Washington, D.C., Congress authorizes the Navy Department's request for seven heavily armed steam sloops to augment existing naval strength to 47 vessels.

MARCH 7 In Washington, D.C., Gideon Welles, a former Connecticut newspaper editor, is sworn in as the 24th secretary of the navy. He proves surprisingly effective and far-sighted in this wartime role.

MARCH 20 At Fort Pickens, Pensacola, Florida, Confederate forces seize the sloop *Isabella* after it attempts to deliver supplies to the Union garrison there.

MARCH 21 Near Charleston, South Carolina, former naval officer Gusavtus V. Fox reconnoiters Fort Sumter and Charleston harbor with a view toward relieving the garrison there. He suggests to President Abraham Lincoln that two shiploads of troops escorted by the screw sloop *Pawnee* and the revenue cutter *Harriet Lane* should be sent.

APRIL 3 On Morris Island, Charleston harbor, Confederate artillery fires upon the Union vessel *Rhoda H. Shannon*.

APRIL 5 In Washington, D.C., Secretary of the Navy Gideon Welles instructs Captain Samuel Mercer to take the sidewheel steamer *Powhatan*, the screw sloop *Pawnee*, and revenue cutter *Harriet Lane* to relieve the Army garrison at Fort Sumter, South Carolina.

APRIL 10 In New York, the steamer *Baltic* departs in a second attempt to relieve the garrison at Fort Sumter, Charleston. It is joined off Hampton Roads, Virginia, by the screw sloop *Pawnee*.

At the Norfolk Navy Yard, Virginia, Captain Charles S. McCauley is ordered to prepare the steam frigate *Merrimack* for transfer to a northern port before Confederate forces attack his position.

At Pensacola, Florida, Lieutenant John L. Worden arrives on official business and receives permission from General Braxton Bragg to visit Fort Pickens offshore.

APRIL 12–13 At Charleston, South Carolina, the screw sloop *Pawnee*, the revenue cutter *Harriet Lane*, and the steamer *Baltic*, all commanded by Gustavus V. Fox, arrive with food supplies for Fort Sumter. Being too late to assist the garrison, they remain passive spectators while the bombardment continues.

At Fort Pickens, Florida, the frigate *Sabine*, sloops *Brooklyn* and *St. Louis*, and screw steamer *Wyandotte* deposit troops and marines, to secure that post from the Confederates.

APRIL 13 At Charleston, South Carolina, the garrison of Fort Sumter is evacuated back north by the ships of Gustavus V. Fox's squadron.

At Fort Pickens, Florida, Lieutenant John L. Worden returns to Washington, D.C. However, he is arrested by Confederate authorities near Montgomery, Alabama, and imprisoned for several months.

APRIL 17 At Fort Pickens, Florida, the steam frigate *Powhatan* under Lieutenant David D. Porter debarks an additional 600 troops to bolster the garrison, securing that important post for the remainder of the war.

At Montgomery, Alabama, President Jefferson Davis invites prospective Confederate privateers to apply for letters of marque and reprisal.

APRIL 19 In Washington, D.C., President Abraham Lincoln declares a naval blockade of the Confederate coastline, a task covering 3,549 miles of coastline and 180 ports. The sheer extent of this mission so overwhelms the relatively small U.S. Navy that any blockade can only be implemented gradually, by stages. By 1865 it reaches stranglehold proportions and becomes a major factor in the economic collapse of the Confederacy.

April 18 At Norfolk, Virginia, an expedition headed by Captain Hiram Paulding occupies the Gosport Navy Yard, burns nine vessels, sets fires to various facilities, and tows away the sloop *Cumberland*. However, the damage inflicted proves insufficient.

April 20 At Norfolk, Virginia, Captain Charles S. McCauley prematurely orders the Gosport Navy Yard burned and evacuated. However, the dry docks become operative again in a few weeks, and the Confederates retrieve 1,200 heavy naval cannon, many of which are implanted at fortifications as far west as Vicksburg, Mississippi. McCauley's botched withdrawal proves an embarrassing windfall for the Confederacy.

At Annapolis, Maryland, the U.S. Naval Academy is abandoned and transferred north to Newport, Rhode Island, for the duration of the war. The existing campus buildings ultimately serve as barracks for Union troops.

April 21 In Washington, D.C., Secretary of the Navy Gideon Welles instructs commandants of the Philadelphia, New York, and Boston navy yards to collect shallow-draft vessels for coastal operations. Similar vessels are also acquired nearby, and are armed and manned for the protection of the capital.

At Norfolk, Virginia, Confederate forces reoccupy Gosport Navy Yard and begin salvaging the old steam frigate *Merrimack*. In a few months this vessel reemerges as the ironclad ram *Virginia*.

April 22 At Annapolis, Maryland, the steamer *Boston* disgorges the 7th New York Regiment, which marches overland for the defense of Washington, D.C.

At the Washington Navy Yard, D.C., Captain Franklin Buchanan tends his resignation in anticipation of Maryland's secession from the Union. After it remains loyal, he reapplies for reinstatement and is denied, so Buchanan joins the Confederacy anyway. Captain John A. B. Dahlgren subsequently takes charge of the navy yard.

April 24 At Annapolis, Maryland, the venerable frigate *Constitution* under Captain George S. Blake is towed to safety by the steam ship *R. R. Cuyler*. The entire Naval Academy faculty and all midshipmen are on board; they are to be relocated to Newport, Rhode Island.

April 27 In Washington, D.C., President Abraham Lincoln extends the Union blockade to encompass the coasts of Virginia and North Carolina after they secede. Secretary of the Navy Gideon Welles also authorizes the capture of all Confederate privateers.

May 3 In Washington, D.C., President Abraham Lincoln appeals for the enlistment of 18,000 sailors to help suppress the rebellion.

May 6 In Richmond, Virginia, the Confederate Congress acknowledges a state of war with the United States and begins issuing Letters of Marque and Reprisals to prospective privateers. However, most private vessels engage in blockade running, owing to lesser risks and higher profits.

May 7 At Newport, Rhode Island, the U.S. Naval Academy staff, students, and supplies arrive onboard the steamer *Baltic* and the venerable frigate USS *Constitution*. They remain in place for the rest of the war.

May 9 In Richmond, Virginia, Confederate Secretary of the Navy Stephen R. Mallory orders Commander James D. Bulloch to England as the Confederacy's naval agent. His machinations result in acquisition of the noted commerce cruisers *Alabama*, *Florida*, and *Shenandoah*, the purchase of which must be disguised owing to strict neutrality laws.

May 10 At Charleston, South Carolina, the new screw frigate *Niagara* under Captain William W. McKean arrives to strengthen the blockade.

In Richmond, Virginia, Confederate Secretary of the Navy Stephen R. Mallory alerts the Committee of Naval Affairs in Congress that the acquisition of a heavily armored steamship is of the highest priority. Only such ships are capable of challenging the Union blockade.

May 13 Near Pensacola, Florida, the frigate *Sabine* under Captain N. S. Adams establishes a blockade.

May 15 The brig *Bainbridge* under Lieutenant Thomas M. Brasher is ordered to Aspinwall, New Granada (Panama), to escort gold-laden transports arriving from California back to New York. They would prove a natural target for Confederate privateers.

May 16 The Navy Department orders Commodore John Rodgers, Jr., to Ohio to commence construction of shallow-water gunboats intended for use on western waters. Such vessels prove a key to Union victory out west.

May 18 At Sewell's Point (Norfolk), Virginia, several small U.S. Navy craft commit their first offensive action by bombarding nearby Confederate batteries.

May 24 Offshore at Alexandria, Virginia, Commander Stephen C. Rowan of the Potomac Flotilla directs the screw sloop *Pawnee*, screw steamer *Anacostia*, tug *Resolute*, and gunboat *Thomas Freeborn* to bombard the town; fortunately, it surrenders without a fight.

May 26 Union vessels have since blockaded New Orleans, Louisiana; Mobile, Alabama; Savannah, Georgia; and the mouth of the Mississippi River. The latter is covered by Commander Charles H. Poor of the side-wheel steamer *Powahtan*, while Mobile is watched by Lieutenant David Dixon Porter and the steamer *Union*.

May 29 Near Savannah, Georgia, a Union blockade is established by the steamer *Union* under Commander John R. Goldsborough.

May 29–June 1 At Aquia Creek, Virginia, the Potomac flotilla under Commander S. C. Rowan trades fire with nearby Confederate artillery batteries.

May 30 At Norfolk Navy Yard, Virginia, the scuttled steam frigate *Merrimack* is finally raised by Confederate forces.

June 10 In Norfolk, Virginia, Confederate Lieutenant John M. Brooke, a gifted naval engineer, begins converting the former steam frigate *Merrimack* into a new vessel, the ironclad ram *Virginia*.

June 25 In Washington, D.C., the Secretary of the Navy is apprised of Confederate efforts to construct an "infernal machine" (submersible) at New Orleans,

Louisiana. This eventually emerges as the *Hunley*.

JUNE 27   In Washington, D.C., the newly created Blockade Strategy Board convenes between representatives of the army, navy, and Coast Survey. It emerges as a key planning body whose policies remain in effect throughout the war.

At Mathias Point, Virginia, Confederates repel the gunboats *Pawnee* and *Thomas Freeborn* as they attempt to land parties ashore. Commander James H. Ward is killed, becoming the Navy's first officer fatality.

JUNE 28   In Washington, D.C., the Blockade Strategy Board resolves to seize ports along the coasts of South Carolina and Georgia, which will serve as coaling stations to sustain the blockade effort offshore.

Confederate agents under Captain George N. Hollins, disguised as passengers, capture the steamer *St. Nicholas* as it sails between Washington, D.C., and Baltimore, Maryland. They subsequently capture three merchant vessels by ruse, then escape.

JUNE 30–JANUARY 18, 1862   Off the coast at New Orleans, Louisiana, Captain Raphael Semmes of the CSS *Sumter* evades the *Brooklyn* and begins his celebrated career as a commerce raider. This initial cruise nets 18 prizes over the ensuing six months.

JULY 2   Near Galveston, Texas, Commander James Alden and the screw steamer *South Carolina* establish a blockade.

JULY 3   Near Cuba, Captain Raphael Semmes and the Confederate raider *Sumter* capture the vessel *Golden Rocket*. Over the next three days he quickly seizes an additional seven prizes.

JULY 6   At Havana, Cuba, the Confederate raider *Sumter* under Captain Raphael Semmes docks with six Union prizes in tow.

JULY 8   On the Potomac River, the screw tug *Resolute* retrieves two mysterious-looking objects which turn out to be the first Confederate "torpedoes" (mines). In time these devices become the bane of Union vessels.

JULY 14   Offshore at Wilmington, North Carolina, Commander Samuel Lockwood and the screw steamer *Daylight* establish a blockade.

JULY 16   In the Atlantic, the Confederate prize crew aboard the *S. J. Waring* is overpowered by its crew, led by William Tilghman, an African American sailor. The ship docks in New York six days later.

JULY 19   In Havana, Cuba, the Spanish Captain-General of the island orders all the Northern prizes possessed by Captain Raphael Semmes of the *Sumter* immediately released.

JULY 24   In Washington, D.C., Congress authorizes President Abraham Lincoln to temporarily expand the U.S. Navy by whatever extent he deems necessary.

AUGUST 1   In Washington, D.C., Gustavus V. Fox gains appointment as the first Assistant Secretary of the Navy, an office that was created on July 22.

AUGUST 3   In Washington, D.C., Congress authorizes the design and construction of three ironclad prototypes. An "Ironclad Board" is also constituted to facilitate the acquisition and deployment of ironclad warships. They also appropriate $1.5 million to undertake this significant project.

Naval aeronautics is born off Sewell's Point, Virginia, when John La Mountain takes a balloon aloft while it is tethered to the steamer *Fanny*. From there he makes aerial observations of nearby Confederate batteries.

AUGUST 7 In Washington, D.C., the Navy Department authorizes engineer James B. Eads of St. Louis, Missouri, to construct several gunboats for riverine service. These vessels, known as "Pook's turtles," on account of their distinct humpbacked shape, prove instrumental in asserting Union power along strategic western waterways.

AUGUST 12 Near Cairo, Illinois, newly constructed gunboats *Conestoga*, *Lexington*, and *Tyler* guard the confluence of the Ohio and Mississippi rivers from Confederate control.

AUGUST 24 At Hampton Roads, Virginia, Commodore Silas H. Stringham assembles a combined expedition mounting 143 rifled cannon. Stringham, a veteran of the Mediterranean Squadron, is well-versed in the latest fort-reducing tactics perfected during the Crimean war. His objective is to capture Confederate forts at Cape Hatteras, North Carolina.

In Ohio, Captain Andrew H. Foote replaces the temperamental Captain John Rodgers as commander of the gunboat flotilla.

AUGUST 27 At Hatteras Inlet, North Carolina, the expedition of Commodore Silas H. Stringham prepares to attack nearby forts Clark and Hatteras. These are garrisoned by 350 men of the 7th North Carolina, and are poorly situated to resist such a powerful force.

AUGUST 28–29 At Pamlico Sound, North Carolina, Commodore Silas H. Stringham's squadron of eight warships and two transports take up bombardment positions off Hatteras Inlet, North Carolina. He forms his vessels into a fast-moving circle offshore, and continuously bombards Confederate positions with a plunging fire. At length the Forts Hatteras and Clark are occupied by 900 men of Major General Benjamin F. Butler, conveyed there by the transports. This is also the Civil War's first amphibious operation.

AUGUST 30 Offshore near Newport News, Virginia, the Confederate tug *Harmony* sorties and damages the Union frigate *Savannah*.

SEPTEMBER 6 In Kentucky, the gunboats *Tyler* and *Lexington* under Commander John Rodgers support General Ulysses S. Grant's occupation of Paducah and Smithland. This action places the mouths of the Tennessee and Cumberland Rivers under Union control.

SEPTEMBER 10 At Lucas Bend, Missouri, a Confederate battery is silenced by the gunboats *Conestoga* and *Lexington*. These small vessels continue to demonstrate their utility to the North.

SEPTEMBER 14 At Pensacola, Florida, Lieutenant John H. Russell sails the frigate *Colorado* past Confederate batteries at night, then leads 100 sailors and marines on a cutting-out expedition that seizes several vessels and destroys the schooner *Judah*.

SEPTEMBER 16 In Washington, D.C., the Ironclad Board recommends the construction of three new ironclad warships—*Monitor*, *Galena*, and *New Ironsides*—to Secretary of the Navy Gideon Welles. The *Monitor* is a revolutionary turreted design by Swedish emigre engineer John Ericsson, and all vessels of this class profoundly impact naval warfare.

SEPTEMBER 16–17 At Beacon Island, North Carolina, landing parties from the screw sloop *Pawnee* land, destroy enemy batteries, and close the Ocracoke Inlet to blockade runners.

SEPTEMBER 18 Flag Officer Samuel F. Du Pont becomes commander of the South Atlantic Blockading Squadron, destined to blockade the Confederate city of Charleston, South Carolina.

SEPTEMBER 19 Commodore Louis M. Goldsborough's North Atlantic Blockading Squadron commences operations off the North Carolina and Virginia coasts.

SEPTEMBER 22 In the Gulf of Mexico, Flag Officer William W. McKean assumes command of the Gulf Blockading Squadron.

SEPTEMBER 25 In Washington, D.C., Secretary of the Navy Gideon Welles instructs Flag Officer Samuel F. Du Pont to enlist African Americans into the naval service for the first time in several decades.

OCTOBER 1 In Washington, D.C., Secretary of the Navy Gideon Welles opposes issuing Letters of Marque and Reprisal against the South on the grounds that these imply de facto national sovereignty.

At Pamlico Sound, North Carolina, a Confederate squadron consisting of the side-wheel steamer *Curlew*, the tug *Junaluska*, and the gunboat *Raleigh* under Flag Officer William F. Lynch seize the Union steamer *Fanny*. Many troops are captured along with valuable supplies; this is also the first Union vessel captured by the South.

OCTOBER 4 In Washington, D.C., President Abraham Lincoln approves contracts to acquire the U.S. Navy's first ironclad warships; among them is John Ericsson's revolutionary *Monitor*.

OCTOBER 7 At Norfolk, Virginia, the steam-powered ironclad *Virginia* (formerly *Merrimack*), now armored and redesigned by Confederate naval engineer John M. Brooke, makes a brief debut off Hampton Roads.

OCTOBER 12 At New Orleans, Louisiana, the new Confederate ram *Manassas* under Commodore George N. Hollins ventures down the Mississippi River, accompanied by the armed steamers *Ivy* and *James L. Day*. Hollis then confronts the Union vessels *Richmond* and *Vincennes* at the Head of Passes, ramming both and running them aground. The victorious Southerners then depart, but both Union ships are raised and repaired.

At Charleston, South Carolina, Confederate agents James Mason and John Slidell take the side-wheel steamer *Theodora* past blockading Union vessels. They then head for Cuba to board the British mail steamer *Trent*.

OCTOBER 17 In Washington, D.C., Commodore Samuel F. Du Pont informs Secretary of the Navy Gideon Welles that Port Royal, South Carolina, would constitute an important asset to the blockading effort if captured. An expedition to do so begins assembling.

OCTOBER 23 In New York, crew members of the Confederate privateer *Savannah* are tried for piracy and threatened with execution. They are convicted, but their sentences are never carried out, to avoid reprisals against Union naval prisoners.

OCTOBER 25 At Greenpoint, New York, the capable Swedish engineer John Ericsson oversees construction of his revolutionary ironclad warship *Monitor*.

OCTOBER 29 Near Hampton Roads, Virginia, Flag Officer Samuel F. Du Pont conducts a combined expedition of 17 warships, 25 supply vessels, and 25 transports conveying General Thomas W. Sherman and 13,000 Federal troops. This force is the largest American armada assembled to date, and is sailing to capture Port Royal, South Carolina, to place a Union lodgement between Charleston, South Carolina, and Savannah, Georgia.

NOVEMBER 4 At Port Royal, South Carolina, the naval expedition of Commodore Samuel F. Du Pont anchors. Confederate vessels under Commodore Josiah Tattnall then fire upon the Coast Survey ships *Vixen* and *Ottawa* as they begin reconnoitering the two-mile-wide channel entrance.

NOVEMBER 5 At Port Royal Sound, South Carolina, the screw sloop *Pawnee*, assisted by gunboats *Ottawa*, *Pembina*, and *Seneca*, destroy Confederate shipping, in anticipation of a major amphibious assault there.

NOVEMBER 7 At Port Royal Sound, South Carolina, 77 vessels of the South Atlantic Blockading Squadron under Commodore Samuel F. Du Pont debark General Thomas W. Sherman's 16,000 troops halfway between Charleston and Savannah, Georgia. Naval fire quickly neutralizes nearby Forts Walker and Beauregard, and the Union acquires a second lodging on the Confederate coastline. Port Royal quickly emerges as a major entrepot for the blockading squadron.

At Belmont, Missouri, the gunboats *Lexington* and *Tyler* handily demonstrate their utility to army operations by covering the withdrawal of General Ulysses S. Grant's army back to the Mississippi River.

NOVEMBER 8 In Old Bahama Channel, the screw sloop *San Jacinto* under Captain Charles Wilkes boards the British mail packet *Trent* and removes Confederate envoys James M. Mason and John Slidell. This egregious violation of international law threatens to embroil the United States in a war with Great Britain.

NOVEMBER 9 Beaufort, South Carolina, is seized by Union gunboats, cutting overland communications between Charleston and Savannah, Georgia.

NOVEMBER 11 In the Potomac River, another shipboard aerial reconnaissance unfolds as Professor Thaddeus Lowe rides a balloon up from the deck of the *G. W. Parke Custis*.

NOVEMBER 12 At Savannah, Georgia, the British-built steamer *Fingal* arrives and is taken into Confederate service as the commerce raider *Atlanta*.

NOVEMBER 15 At Fortress Monroe, Virginia, the *San Jacinto* under Captain Charles Wilkes arrives with Confederate emissaries James M. Mason and John Slidell. Wilkes is hailed in the press as a hero, but the government now has to deal with an enraged Great Britain.

NOVEMBER 18 Commodore David D. Porter is assigned with gathering gunboats and supplies for the long-anticipated campaign against New Orleans, Louisiana.

NOVEMBER 22 At Pensacola, Florida, the steam frigate *Niagara* and steam sloop *Richmond* commence a two-day bombardment of Confederate-held Fort McRee in the Pensacola Navy Yard. They are assisted by several Army batteries.

NOVEMBER 24 In Boston, Massachusetts, the *San Jacinto* under Captain John Wilkes drops anchors, whereupon Confederate envoys James M. Mason and John Slidell are incarcerated at Fort Warren. Great Britain demands their immediate release.

Near Savannah, Georgia, Commander John Rodgers leads a five-ship squadron into the harbor and effortlessly seizes Tybee Island, offshore.

DECEMBER 2 In Washington, D.C., Secretary of the Navy Gideon Welles issues his first annual report and touts the apprehension of 153 Confederate vessels. He also states the upcoming strength of the U.S. Navy at 264 ships, mounting 2,557 guns.

DECEMBER 10 On the Ashepoo River, South Carolina, Otter Island is captured by landing parties launched from the screw steamer *Isaac Smith*.

DECEMBER 17 Off the coast at Savannah, Georgia, Union blockaders sink seven old ships filled with stones off the harbor entrance. This act initiates what becomes known as the "Stone Fleet," which does not prove particularly effective at barring Confederate vessels.

DECEMBER 21 In Washington, D.C., Congress institutes the Navy Medal of Honor as the nation's highest award granted to that service. It is originally intended for enlisted ranks, and officers remain ineligible until 1915. The Army Medal of Honor emerges on July 12, 1862.

DECEMBER 26 Near Savannah, Georgia, Commodore Josiah Tattnall leads a small squadron of Confederate vessels out from the Savannah River and attacks, temporarily incapacitating the Union blockade there.

DECEMBER 31 At Port Royal Ferry, South Carolina, gunboats *Ottawa*, *Pembina*, and *Seneca* land parties along the Coosaw River, thwarting Confederate attempts to isolate Union forces on Port Royal Island.

Biloxi, Mississippi, is captured by landing parties from the paddle-wheel steamer *Water Witch*, the screw steamer *New London*, and the *Henry Lewis*, which also destroy a Confederate battery and schooner.

1862

JANUARY 6 Commodore Andrew H. Foote, seeking to resolve critical shortages of trained manpower, suggests drafting soldiers for service on his gunboat fleet. The Army is reluctant to comply, until General Ulysses S. Grant suggests that guardhouses be emptied to provide the requested "sailors."

JANUARY 7 On the Cumberland River, Tennessee, Lieutenant Samuel L. Phelps and the gunboat *Conestoga* closely reconnoiter Confederate-held Fort Henry and Fort Donelson. A Union offensive appears pending

JANUARY 9 In the Gulf of Mexico, Flag Officer David G. Farragut assumes control of the Western Gulf Blockading Squadron. Though Southern-born, he is tasked with capturing New Orleans, Louisiana, an essential part of overall Union strategy.

JANUARY 11 Near Lucas Bend, Missouri, gunboats *Essex* and *St. Louis* bombard Confederate craft on the Mississippi River, forcing the Southerners to withdraw.

JANUARY 12 At Hampton Roads, Virginia, Flag Officer Louis M. Goldsborough's 100-vessel naval expedition sails for an attack upon strategic Roanoke Island, North Carolina. His transports are conveying 15,000 Union troops under General Ambrose E. Burnside.

January 13   Lieutenant John L. Worden gains appointment as commander of the revolutionary ironclad *Monitor*, which is nearing completion at Montauk Point, New York.

At Hatteras Inlet, North Carolina, Commodore Louis M. Goldsborough's 100-ship expedition drop anchors and prepares to engage Confederate defenses. His gunners are equipped with the latest Bormann fuses fitted to 9-inch shrapnel shells.

January 16   At Cedar Keys, Florida, the screw sloop *Hartford* dispatches sailors and marines ashore; they destroy a battery, seven vessels, a railroad depot, and a telegraph office. This action underscores the vulnerability of the Confederate coastline to attack from the sea.

At Cairo, Illinois, Flag Officer Andrew H. Foote announces that seven of the new Eads gunboats are commissioned and ready for service. These vessels are instrumental in turning the tide of the war in the west.

January 17   On the Tennessee River, gunboats *Conestoga* and *Lexington* closely reconnoiter Confederate-held Fort Henry, and the intelligence they convey helps formulate plans for its reduction.

January 20   In the Gulf of Mexico, the Union Gulf Blockading Squadron is reorganized into the East Gulf Blockading Squadron and the West Gulf Blockading Squadron. The latter formation is led by Commodore David G. Farragut, who commands 17 steam warships and 19 mortar boats under Commander David D. Porter, his foster brother.

January 26   At Wassaw Sound, Georgia, gunboats *Ottawa* and *Seneca* escort transports carrying 2,400 soldiers under General Horatio G. Wright on a reconnaissance mission near Fort Pulaski. Their mission completed, the force returns safely.

January 28   In Illinois, Flag Officer Andrew H. Foote advises General Henry W. Halleck to commence riverine operations against Forts Henry and Donelson before subsiding water levels on the Tennessee and Cumberland Rivers make it impractical.

January 30   At Greenpoint, Long Island, John Ericsson's revolutionary ironclad *Monitor* is launched amidst thunderous applause. Though derided by many onlookers as "a cheese box on a raft," acceptance trials begin immediately.

February 3   In Washington, D.C., the federal government resolves to treat Confederate privateersmen as prisoners of war, rather than prosecute them as pirates. This eliminates the chance that Union naval personnel could be hanged in retaliation.

February 4   On the Tennessee River, Commodore Henry H. Foote's gunboat squadron sounds out Confederate defenses at Fort Henry, and several moored "torpedoes" (mines) that have been worked free by the fast current are examined closely.

February 6   On the Tennessee River, Flag Officer Andrew H. Foote leads four ironclads and three wooden gunboats against Fort Henry, opening fire at 1,700 yards. Confederate general Lloyd Tilghman remains behind with 100 artillerists and mounts an "honorable defense" while his garrison escapes intact. Once the position falls, it is renamed "Fort Foote."

FEBRUARY 7–8   At Albemarle Sound, North Carolina, the squadron of Flag Officer Louis M. Goldsborough attacks Roanoke Island. Fortunately, this strategic point is poorly situated to repel an attack of this magnitude, and it is occupied by troops under Brigadier General Ambrose M. Burnside.

On the Tennessee River, the gunboat *Conestoga* engages Confederates, forcing them to burn three steamers to spare them from capture.

FEBRUARY 10   At Norfolk, Virginia, Captain Franklin Buchanan complains that he lacks the necessary crewmen to render the steam ram *Virginia* operational. Nonetheless, he is being pressured to break the Union blockade as soon as possible.

On the Pasquotank River, North Carolina, Union vessels under Commander Stephen C. Rowman pursue Flag Officer William F. Lynch's gunboats upstream. Five Confederate "Cottonclads" are destroyed, along with several land batteries near Elizabeth City. Quarter Gunner John Davis wins the Navy's first Medal of Honor for passing gunpowder to gun crews during a fire on the steamer *Valley City*.

FEBRUARY 14   On the Cumberland River, Tennessee, Commodore Andrew H. Foote's gunboat flotilla bombards Fort Donelson, closing at one point to within 400 yards. Confederate guns, situated on a 150-foot-high bluff overlooking the river, nonetheless subject the Union fleet to a plunging fire. The *Louisville* and *St. Louis* are damaged, and Foote receives a foot injury that requires him to retire.

FEBRUARY 17   In Norfolk, Virginia, the formidable ironclad ram *Virginia* is commissioned under Captain Franklin Buchanan. His immediate objective is to raise the nearby Union blockade.

FEBRUARY 19   On the Cumberland River, Tennessee, Commodore Andrew H. Foote's gunboats assist in the capture Fort Defiant and Clarksville, Tennessee, which are hastily evacuated upon his approach. Foote subsequently urges General William F. Smith to advance on Nashville while the river is running high.

FEBRUARY 20   In Washington, D.C., Secretary of the Navy Gideon Welles, cognizant that the Confederate ironclad *Virginia* is nearly ready to sail, orders the new vessel *Monitor* to sail from New York for Hampton Roads, Virginia, without delay.

FEBRUARY 21   At Ship Island, Mississippi, newly promoted Flag Officer David G. Farragut arrives to take command of the West Gulf Blockading Squadron prior to leading it against New Orleans, Louisiana. This proves to be one of the most decisive events in all naval history.

FEBRUARY 24   At Norfolk, Virginia, Captain Franklin Buchanan is ordered by Confederate Secretary of the Navy Stephen R. Mallory to sortie his James River Squadron against the Union blockade off Hampton Roads. Much is expected of his flagship, the ironclad ram CSS *Virginia*.

FEBRUARY 25   At Long Island, New York, the new ironclad *Monitor* passes its sea trials and is commissioned under Lieutenant John L. Worden. This revolutionary design features a rotating turret housing two 11-inch Dahlgren smoothbore cannon. It also sits extremely low in the water, and does not offer enemy gunners much of a target.

MARCH 2   Union gunboats *Cincinnati* and *Louisville* make a reconnaissance in force of Confederate positions at Columbus, Kentucky. The Southerners, correctly anticipating a Federal move upon their works, begin evacuating that position.

March 3 Flag Officer Samuel F. Du Pont's squadron captures Cumberland Island, Georgia, along with Fernandina and Amelia Islands, Florida. Fort Clinch, Georgia, is also seized by a crew from the *Ottawa*, becoming the first Federal installation retaken during the war.

March 8 Near Hampton Roads, Virginia, the ironclad ram *Virginia* under Captain Franklin Buchanan engages wooden vessels of the Union blockading squadron. Buchanan rams the sloop *Cumberland* and riddles the frigate *Congress* with heavy gunfire, while a third ship, the *Minnesota*, grounds itself rather than be sunk. It is been a fateful day, whereby the death knell of wooden warships has sounded. Meanwhile, the ironclad *Monitor* under Lieutenant John L. Worden survives a perilous transit from New York and arrives off Hampton Roads, Virginia, that evening. However, Buchanan is wounded in action and misses the dramatic sequel to the day's events.

March 9 At Norfolk, Virginia, Lieutenant Catesby ap Roger Jones sorties the ironclad ram *Virginia* back to Hampton Roads, where he is startled to see the strange-looking *Monitor* sailing up to meet him. The iron giants duel at close range over the next four hours, but both vessels, heavily armored, fail to inflict any serious damage. Jones returns to Norfolk as water levels recede before the contest subsides, and *Monitor* has preserved the Union blockade at Norfolk. This dramatic engagement heralds the dawn of iron warships. However, the largely intact *Virginia* still denies union forces unfettered use of the James River.

March 10 President Abraham Lincoln pays a bedside visit to Lieutenant John L. Worden, who sustained an eye wound during his clash with the CSS *Virginia*.

The USS Monitor *(right foreground) and the CSS* Virginia *(formerly the USS* Merrimack, *left foreground) on March 9, 1862. Although the two ironclads sparred for almost four hours, neither vessel was badly damaged. Neither the Union nor the Confederacy could claim outright victory, but both acknowledged that history had been made, as the two ships revolutionized naval warfare. (National Archives)*

MARCH 13 At New Madrid, Missouri, Confederate forces are evacuated, covered by three gunboats of Flag Officer George N. Hollis's river squadron.

MARCH 14 On the Neuse River, North Carolina, Commander Stephen C. Rowan's 13 warships assist Brigadier General Ambrose's 12,000-man army in capturing the city of New Bern.

MARCH 16 On the Mississippi River, Commodore Andrew H. Foote's 6 gunboats and 12 mortar boats begin a sustained bombardment of Confederate defenses on Island No. 10.

MARCH 17 Near Beaufort, North Carolina, the Confederate commerce raider *Nashville* slips past blockading vessels *Cambridge* and *Gemsbock*. A distraught Assistant Secretary Gustavus V. Fox pronounces it "a Bull Run for the Navy."

On the Mississippi River, Flag Officer Andrew H. Foote orders the gunboats *Benton*, *Cincinnati*, and *St. Louis* bound together into one large floating battery. These proceed to bombard Confederate batteries on Island No. 10.

MARCH 22 From Liverpool, England, Confederate Acting Master John Low guides the steam cruiser *Oreto* to the Bahamas, where it will be armed and impressed into service as the commerce raider CSS *Florida*.

MARCH 25 In Richmond, Virginia, Confederate Secretary of the Navy Stephen R. Mallory orders Commodore Josiah Tattnall to Norfolk, Virginia, where he is to replace the wounded Captain Franklin Buchanan.

At Pass Christian, Mississippi, Confederate side-paddle steamer *Pamlico* and gunboat *Oregon* attack the Union screw steamer *New London*; little damage is inflicted in a two-hour battle, and the vessels draw off.

MARCH 27 In Washington, D.C., Secretary of War Edwin M. Stanton orders naval engineer Charles Ellet to construct several steam rams at Pittsburgh, Pennsylvania, and Cincinnati, Ohio. Moreover, these have to be large enough to cope with the new Confederate ironclad being assembled at Memphis, Tennessee.

MARCH 28 At Jacksonville, Florida, a boat party under Lieutenant Thomas F. Stevens returns from a foray up the St. John's River with the captured CSS *Memphis*, formerly the famous British racing yacht *America*. It enters U.S. Navy service as the USS *America*.

APRIL 1 On the Mississippi River, a landing party from the gunboat *St. Louis* spikes a Confederate battery on Island No. 1, as the noose slowly tightens around strategic Island No. 10.

APRIL 4 On the Mississippi River, the ironclad *Carondelet* under Commander Henry W. Walke dashes past Confederate batteries on Island No. 10 at night, covered by a rain storm. This cuts the Southerners off from possible reinforcements, whereas General John Pope's forces can safely cross over to the Tennessee shore.

APRIL 6 At Shiloh, Tennessee, Federal gunboats *Tyler* and *Lexington* assist the last-ditch Union defenses at Pittsburgh Landing with heavy and accurate cannon fire. They prove instrumental in dissuading a final Confederate advance.

APRIL 7 At Gibraltar, Spain, Commander Raphael Semmes lays up the Confederate raider CSS *Sumter* after its boiler breakdowns. So far Semmes has accounted for 18 Union prizes.

On the Mississippi River, the ironclad *Pittsburgh* under Commander Egbert Thompson slips past Island No. 10 and joins the *Carondelet* in covering General

John Pope's army, as ferries cross to the Tennessee shore.

APRIL 8 On the Mississippi River, Commodore David G. Farragut runs his West Gulf Blockading Squadron vessels over the Southwest Pass sandbar, and makes for Head of Passes with 24 warships and 19 mortar ships under Commander David D. Porter.

On the Mississippi River, the captured Confederate vessel *Red Rover* is converted into the Navy's first hospital ship. It is partly manned by the Nurses of the Holy Cross, an antecedent of the Navy Nurse Corps.

APRIL 9 In Richmond, Virginia, Confederate Secretary of the Navy Stephen R. Mallory is convinced that the Mississippi River Squadron of Commodore Andrew H. Foote is the biggest threat to New Orleans, Louisiana. Therefore he refuses Confederate vessels at Fort Pillow, Tennessee, to reinforce that vital port.

APRIL 14 On the Mississippi River, Commodore Andrew H. Foote's mortar boats bombard Fort Pillow, Tennessee. This post is 60 miles south of newly captured Island No. 10, and guards the northern approaches to Memphis.

APRIL 16 On the Mississippi River, Commodore David G. Farragut masses 17 warships of the West Gulf Blockading Squadron below Forts Jackson and St. Philip, Louisiana. These aged structures, situated 12 miles above Head of Passes, mount 90 cannon and are assisted by a "mosquito squadron" under Captain George N. Hollis.

APRIL 18 On the Mississippi River, Commodore David G. Farragut dispatches Commander David D. Porter with 20 mortar boats to bombard Forts Jackson and St. Philip. He begins pelting them with 200-pound mortar shells over the next five days, convinced they can be subdued through firepower alone.

In Richmond, Virginia, the Confederate Congress orders the construction of six large ironclads, with payment to be made in cotton. These vessels will be used

---

Farragut, David G. (1801–1870)

David Glasgow Farragut was born in Campbell's Station, Tennessee, on July 5, 1801, the son of a U.S. Navy officer. Orphaned at an early age, he was adopted by Captain David Porter, and in 1813 he accompanied his stepfather on the frigate *Essex* during its heroic sortie into the Pacific Ocean. He survived Porter's defeat at the hands of HMS *Phoebe* and *Cherub* in February 1814, then returned to the United States onboard a cartel (exchange) vessel. Over the next 45 years Farragut functioned ably, rose to captain in 1855, and was residing in Norfolk, Virginia, when the Civil War erupted in 1861. Because of his Southern origins, Farragut was not entirely trusted by the Navy Department, and only the direct intervention of his stepbrother, Captain David Dixon Porter, gained him appointment as commander of the West Gulf Blockading Squadron in January 1862. Farragut then successfully captured the vital Confederate port of New Orleans on April 25, 1862, which placed Union forces at the mouth of the Mississippi River and was a leading cause of the Confederacy's downfall.

On August 5, 1864, Farragut confronted his greatest challenge by attacking Mobile, Alabama, the last remaining gulf port of the Confederacy. His fleet was required to run a gauntlet of minefields; they took some losses and he exclaimed, "Damn the torpedoes! Full speed ahead!" After Mobile surrendered on August 23, 1864, Farragut became the first rear admiral in U.S. history. In 1866 he was promoted to full admiral, then commanded the European Squadron on a goodwill mission from 1867 to 1868. Farragut died at Portsmouth, New Hampshire, on August 14, 1870, an effective combat officer.

to break the Union blockade of Southern ports.

APRIL 20 On the Mississippi River, the gunboats *Itasca* and *Pinola* penetrate an obstacle constructed from heavy chains and sunken hulks strewn below New Orleans, Louisiana. The path is now cleared for Flag Officer David G. Farragut's West Gulf Blockading Squadron to advance.

APRIL 21 In Richmond, Virginia, the Confederate Congress authorizes the store ship *Patrick Henry*, anchored below Drewry's Bluff, to serve as a Southern naval academy. Its first class consists of 52 midshipmen.

APRIL 24 On the Mississippi River, an impatient Commodore David G. Farragut runs his entire squadron past Forts Jackson and St. Philip rather than bombard them further. General Johnson K. Duncan's Confederates unleash a heavy cannonade, inflicting little damage. Eight Southern ships are sunk, while Union casualties amount to 39 dead and 171 injured. With this decisive stroke, the fate of New Orleans is decided.

APRIL 25 Commodore David G. Farragut's West Gulf Blockading Squadron captures the city of New Orleans, Louisiana, after exchanging with Confederate gunners at the English Turn. The Confederacy loses its largest and wealthiest seaport, which the North utilizes as a base for operations further up the Mississippi River. The huge ironclad CSS *Mississippi*, then under construction, is also destroyed to prevent capture.

APRIL 26 A combined operation under Commander Samuel Lockwood and Brigadier General John G. Parke results in the fall of Fort Macon, North Carolina.

APRIL 27 On Bastian Bay, Louisiana, U.S. Naval forces capture Fort Livingston, and crewmen from the *Kittatinny* hoist the Stars and Stripes over its ramparts. Forts Quitman, Pike, and Wood capitulate later that day.

APRIL 28 Below New Orleans, Louisiana, the isolated defenders of Forts Jackson and St. Philip capitulate to Flag Officer David G. Farragut's squadron. Beforehand, they destroy the unfinished ironclad *Louisiana*, along with two other vessels.

At Nassau, the Bahamas, the British steamer *Oreto* under Acting Master John Low waits to be manned by Confederate sailors, and it is taken into Southern service as the commerce raider CSS *Florida*.

MAY 6–7 At West Point, Virginia, Commander William Smith of the screw sloop *Wachusett*, assisted by gunboats *Chocura* and *Sebago*, conveys army transports along the York River.

MAY 8 At Sewell's Point, Virginia, the ironclad *Monitor*, accompanied by the steam sloop *Dacotah* and screw steamer *Naugatuck*, bombards Confederate positions, forcing two Southern vessels to flee up the James River.

MAY 9 Above Fort Pillow, Tennessee, Captain Charles H. Davis relieves the ailing Commodore Andrew H. Foote, who was wounded at the capture of Fort Donelson.

MAY 10 At Norfolk, Virginia, Union forces reoccupy the Norfolk Navy Yard.

On the Mississippi River, the ramshackle Confederate River Defense Fleet under Captain James E. Montgomery sortie at Plum Run Bend, north of Fort Pillow, Tennessee. The eight vessels engage seven Navy ironclads under Commodore Charles H. Davis in one of the few squadron actions of the Civil

War. Once the formidable ironclad *Carondelet* moves into firing range, Montgomery withdraws back to the safety of Fort Pillow.

In light of the fall of New Orleans, Confederate forces hastily abandon Pensacola, Florida, and the navy yard is reoccupied by Union troops.

MAY 11 Near Craney Island, Virginia, Commodore Josiah Tattnall scuttles the large ironclad ram CSS *Virginia,* because it draws too much water to operate further up the James River. The Northern Blockading Squadron can now advance upstream as far as Drewry's Bluff.

MAY 12 At Drewry's Bluff, Virginia, crewmen of the CSS *Virginia* assemble under Lieutenant Catesby ap Roger Jones to man an artillery battery. Theirs is a formidable position rising 100 feet above the river, and only seven miles from Richmond, Virginia.

MAY 13 Outside Charleston Harbor, South Carolina, harbor pilot Robert Smalls and eight fellow African Americans abscond with the Confederate steamer tug *Planter,* surrendering it to the steamer *Onward* offshore.

MAY 15 Seven miles below Richmond, Virginia, Commodore John Rodgers leads the ironclads *Monitor, Galena,* and *Nauguatuck* up the James River until they encounter Confederate defenses along Drewry's Bluff. The Union ships, outgunned and unable to circumvent obstacles in their path, take a pounding, so Rodgers leads them back to Norfolk.

MAY 17 On the Pamunkey River, Virginia, the steamers *Sebago* and *Currituck* escort troop transport *Seth Low* for several miles, forcing the Confederates to scuttle 17 vessels to prevent capture. The river at this point narrows dramatically, and the vessels are obliged to run backwards for some distance before turning their bows around.

MAY 18 Near Vicksburg, Mississippi, Commander Stephen D. Lee demands the city's surrender, but Confederate General Martin L. Smith refuses. A year will pass before the "Gibraltar of the West" succumbs to Union land forces, assisted by naval vessels on the Mississippi River.

MAY 20 On the Stono River, South Carolina, Union gunboats bombard Confederate positions on Cole's Island to prepare for operations against Charleston.

JUNE 4–5 On the Mississippi River, Union gunboats bombard the Confederate defenders of Fort Pillow, Tennessee, which they abandon. The city of Memphis is also poorly garrisoned, save for a weak naval squadron.

JUNE 6 Two miles north of Memphis, Tennessee, Commander Charles H. Davis's gunboat squadron heads directly for the city, until a small Confederate squadron of steam rams under Captain James E. Montgomery sorties to confront them. Davis feigns retreating, and Montgomery pursues until he is surprised in midstream by Union rams sailing four abreast. Confederate losses in the ensuing rout total around 100 killed with another 100 captured. Davis brooks no delay in making Memphis his prize. The Mississippi River can now be navigated as far south as Vicksburg, Mississippi.

JUNE 17 On the White River, Arkansas, Commander Augustus H. Kilty leads ironclads, gunboats, and transports down as far as St. Charles, where troops land and capture a Confederate battery. However, the vessel *Mound City* takes a hit that ruptures steam lines, killing or wounding 150 crewmen.

JUNE 28 Outside Vicksburg, Mississippi, Admiral David G. Farragut and Commander David D. Porter slip their respective squadrons past Confederate gun emplacements, suffering 15 killed and 30 wounded. This is a trifling loss, considering the ordnance poured upon them by Southern batteries.

JULY 1 On the Mississippi River above Vicksburg, Flag Officer David G. Farragut's West Gulf Blockade Squadron unites with Flag Officer Charles H. Davis's Western Gunboat Flotilla.

JULY 1 At Malvern Hill, Virginia, accurate gunfire from the ironclad *Galena* and gunboats *Aroostoock* and *Jacob Bell* enfilade the right flank of General Robert E. Lee's attacking Confederates, contributing to their bloody repulse.

JULY 4 On the James River, Virginia, the side-wheel steamer *Maratanza* under Lieutenant T. H. Stevens captures the Confederate minelayer *Teaser*; this is the first vessel of its kind, and it is inspected closely by Union officials.

JULY 5 In Washington, D.C., Congress passes a naval reorganization act which increases the amount of bureaus to eight. They are Docks and Yards, Equipment and Recruiting, Navigation, Ordnance, Construction and Repair, Steam Engineering, Provisions and Clothing, and Medicine and Surgery.

JULY 7 At Harrison's Landing, Virginia, the schooner *Ariel* transports President Abraham Lincoln and his entourage for talks with General George B. McClellan.

JULY 12 On the Yazoo River, the Confederate ironclad *Arkansas* under Lieutenant Isaac N. Brown sorties into the Mississippi River and heads south toward Vicksburg, Mississippi. He is forced into action by receding water levels.

JULY 14 In Washington, D.C., Congress finally outlaws alcoholic rations on board Navy vessels, and all sailors will receive an additional five cents per day in lieu of their traditional grog.

JULY 15 On the Yazoo River, Mississippi, Commodore Charles H. Davis's gunboat squadron attacks the newly built Confederate ironclad CSS *Arkansas* of Lieutenant Isaac N. Brown. Damage is inflicted on both sides, but the *Arkansas* escapes to the Mississippi River and berths at Vicksburg. It remains a menace to Union shipping for several weeks.

JULY 16 In Washington, D.C., Congress promotes David G. Farragut to rear admiral, becoming the first officer in the U.S. Navy to hold such rank. President Abraham Lincoln also signs legislation conferring similar promotions on all sitting flag officers. The ranks of commodore and lieutenant commander are also introduced, while the number of ranking officers increases to 9 rear admirals, 18 commodores, 36 captains, and 72 commanders.

JULY 21 On the Ohio River, landing parties from the gunboats *Clara Dolsen* and *Rob Roy* recapture Henderson, Kentucky, from Confederate partisans.

JULY 22 Near Vicksburg, Mississippi, the ironclad *Essex* under Captain William B. Porter, accompanied by the ram *Queen of the West,* attacks the Confederate ironclad CSS *Arkansas*. The Union vessels are driven off without seriously damaging their opponent, which defiantly challenges the Federals to fight.

JULY 24 At Vicksburg, Mississippi, falling water levels on the Mississippi River induce Rear Admiral David G. Farragut to return to New Orleans, Louisiana, after two months upstream. His experience outside Vicksburg convinces him that the city cannot be taken by naval forces alone.

JULY 29 At Liverpool, England, Ship "209," christened *Enrica*, departs for "sea trials." It is actually headed for Nassau, the Bahamas, to join the Confederate navy as the commerce raider CSS *Alabama*.

AUGUST 5 On the Mississippi River, the large Confederate ironclad *Arkansas* under Lieutenant Henry K. Stevens steams down to assist an expedition against Baton Rouge, Louisiana. His mission is to neutralize Union gunboats in the area, but *Arkansas* sustains a broken propeller shaft en route and is unable to support the military effort ashore.

AUGUST 6 Near Baton Rouge, Louisiana, Commander David D. Porter's gunboat squadron attacks and further damages the Confederate ironclad *Arkansas*. That vessel is crippled by a broken propeller shaft and, once it grounds, Lieutenant Henry K. Stevens orders it scuttled.

AUGUST 10 At Green Cay, Bahamas, the English-built commerce cruiser CSS *Florida* secretly arrives and it is taken into Confederate naval service by Lieutenant John N. Maffitt. This is the first of several foreign-made warships acquired by the South.

AUGUST 16 On the Yazoo River, Mississippi, the side-wheel steamer *General Bragg*, gunboats *Benton* and *Mound City*, and steam rams *Monarch*, *Lioness*, *Samson*, and *Switzerland* commence an armed expedition upstream, landing troops occasionally and capturing some batteries and vessels.

AUGUST 18 Near Corpus Christi, Texas, four vessels under Acting Lieutenant John W. Kittredge land parties ashore, but these withdraw following the appearance of Confederate cavalry.

AUGUST 22 In Virginia, Rear Admiral Louis M. Goldsborough is ordered to detach ships from his North Atlantic Blockading Squadron and assist the Army of the Potomac on shore.

AUGUST 24 At Terciera, Azores, the English-built commerce raider CSS *Alabama* is armed and commissioned into Confederate service by Captain Raphael Semmes. Its notorious 22-month cruise will result in the destruction of 68 Union vessels.

AUGUST 26 Captain Franklin Buchanan advances to rear admiral for his conduct in the CSS *Virginia* on March 8, 1862. He is the first Confederate naval officer so honored.

SEPTEMBER 1 In Virginia, Rear Admiral Stephen Lee replaces Rear Admiral Louis M. Goldsborough as commander of the North Atlantic Blockading Squadron.

SEPTEMBER 4 Outside Mobile Bay, Alabama, Confederate raider CSS *Florida* under Lieutenant John N. Maffitt plunges past Union vessels and safely anchors. This action results in an official rebuke for local commanders and renewed emphasis on tighter blockade efforts.

SEPTEMBER 5 Near the Azores, the CSS *Alabama* under Captain Raphael Semmes commences its celebrated raiding career by burning the Union vessel *Ocmulgee*.

SEPTEMBER 8 In the Caribbean, Commodore John Wilkes assembles his West India Squadron, tasked with halting depredations by Confederate raiders *Alabama* and *Florida*.

SEPTEMBER 20 At Charleston, South Carolina, Admiral Samuel F. Du Pont warns Assistant Secretary of the Navy Gustavus V. Fox of the perils involved in attacking the heavily armed harbor. Unfortunately, his warnings go unheeded by the Navy Department.

SEPTEMBER 25 At Sabine, Texas, the screw steamer *Kensington*, assisted by *Henry James* and *Rachel Seaman*, destroy Confederate batteries. Landing parties also go ashore and destroy a railroad bridge.

SEPTEMBER 26 Near South Carolina, Rear Admiral Samuel F. Du Pont suggests using a vessel converted into a floating coal hulk, capable of carrying a thousand tons of coal at sea, to support the blockading fleet. This is the origin of modern-day refueling at sea.

OCTOBER 1 In the western theater, all Army vessels belonging to the Western Gunboat Fleet are transferred from the War Department to the Navy Department. Command of the newly designated Mississippi Squadron also switches to Rear Admiral David D. Porter, who replaces the less aggressive Rear Admiral Charles H. Davis.

OCTOBER 3–9 Near Galveston, Texas, a flotilla of five Union gunboats under Commander William B. Renshaw begins bombarding Confederate positions; the city capitulates six days later.

OCTOBER 11 In the Atlantic, Confederate raider CSS *Alabama* under Captain Raphael Semmes burns the Union vessel *Manchester*. He reads from captured New York newspapers the dispositions of the U.S. Navy warships out searching for him.

OCTOBER 12 Near Charleston, South Carolina, Confederate oceanographer Matthew F. Maury pilots the *Herald* past the Union blockade. He subsequently sails for England to purchase warships for the South.

OCTOBER 15 At Taylor's Bayou, Texas, landing parties from the screw steamer *Kensington* and the schooner *Rachel Seaman* destroy a railroad bridge, along with the Confederate schooners *Lone Star* and *Stonewall*.

OCTOBER 24 At Hopefield, Arkansas, a landing party from the gunboat *Baron De Kalb* tangles with Southern guerrillas, and pursues them on horseback for nine miles before capturing them.

OCTOBER 28 In Chesapeake Bay, a Confederate boat party under Lieutenant John Taylor Wood captures and burns the Union vessel *Alleghanian*.

OCTOBER 30 In Washington, D.C., the Navy Department announces a $500,000 reward for the capture of Confederate raider "290" (*Alabama*). Several warships are sent off in a futile pursuit.

OCTOBER 31 In Richmond, Virginia, the Confederate Congress authorizes a Torpedo Bureau and an embryonic Naval Submarine Battery Service. The numerous devices tested and deployed are a menace to Union vessels at sea, in harbors, and especially on rivers, ultimately accounting for 40 ships.

Near Plymouth, North Carolina, a force of U.S. Navy steamers, accompanied by the Army gunboat *Vidette*, bombards nearby Confederate positions on shore.

NOVEMBER 3 In Berwick Bay, Louisiana, the Confederate steamer *Cotton* engages four Union vessels and damages several before retreating back to safety.

NOVEMBER 15 In Washington, D.C., President Abraham Lincoln and several Cabinet members have a narrow escape when an experimental Hyde rocket explodes at the Washington Navy Yard.

NOVEMBER 18 At Martinique, the Confederate raider CSS *Alabama* slips past the screw frigate *San Jacinto* in bad weather and escapes.

NOVEMBER 19 At Ossabaw Sound, Georgia, the gunboat *Wissahickon* and the screw steamer *Dawn* are relieved from blockading duty and sent up the Ogeechee River to shell Confederate-held Fort McAlister.

NOVEMBER 23 At Jacksonville, North Carolina, the side-wheel steamer *Ellis* grounds after being bombarded by Confederate batteries. Lieutenant William B. Cushing orders it burned to prevent capture, and escapes on its two prizes.

NOVEMBER 29 In Texas, General John B. Magruder has the Confederate steamers *Bayou City* and *Neptune* "armored" with bales of cotton, transforming them into "cotton-clads." They figure prominently in the attack upon Galveston.

DECEMBER 1 In Washington, D.C., Secretary of the Navy Gideon Welles releases his second annual report, which places the U.S. Navy at 427 vessels mounting 1,577 guns. They are manned by 28,000 officers and enlisted men.

DECEMBER 2 Near Padre Island, Texas, Confederate steamer *Queen of the Bay* runs aground and is attacked by Union boats from the gunboat *Sachem*, but the Southerners drive off their antagonists with rifle fire.

DECEMBER 8 In Washington, D.C., President Abraham Lincoln recommends Captain John L. Worden for a vote of thanks from Congress due to his role in commanding at Hampton Roads that spring.

DECEMBER 9 In the Gulf of Mexico, command of the East Gulf Blockading Squadron passes to Rear Admiral Theodorus Bailey.

DECEMBER 12 On the Yazoo River, Mississippi, the ironclad *Cairo* under Commander Thomas O. Selfridge strikes a Confederate "torpedo" (mine) and sinks, becoming the first of 40 Union vessels lost to submerged Confederate ordnance.

DECEMBER 20–27 At Helena, Arkansas, Rear Admiral D. Dixon Porter confers with General William T. Sherman in anticipation of a combined effort against Vicksburg, Mississippi. Porter's command has grown exponentially and now equals the U.S. Navy at the commencement of the Civil War.

DECEMBER 26 On the Yazoo River, gunboats under Commodore David D. Porter begin shelling the Confederate defenses on Hayne's Bluff to cover the landing of General William T. Sherman's forces.

DECEMBER 27 At points along Drumgould's Bluff, Mississippi, Confederate batteries bombard Union naval forces, clearing the Yazoo River of mines and other obstacles.

DECEMBER 31 Off Cape Hatteras, North Carolina, the ironclad *Monitor* sinks in a gale while under tow. 16 crewmen perish, and 47 are rescued by the nearby *Rhode Island*.

1863

JANUARY 1 Near Galveston, Texas, Confederate "cotton-clads" *Bayou City* and *Neptune* under Major Leon Smith sortie against the Union blockading squadron of Commander William B. Renshaw. Renshaw, perceiving the battle lost, orders his squadron into deeper water, but he and 12 other Union sailors perish once the demolition charges on his vessel explode prematurely. Galveston remains in Southern hands for the rest of the war.

JANUARY 4–11 On the Arkansas River, Rear Admiral David D. Porter's gunboats pound the strong Confederate works of Fort Hindman (Arkansas Post) into submission with point-blank artillery fire; 4,700 prisoners are taken. The fort is immediately occupied by 30,000 accompanying Union troops under Major General David McClernand.

JANUARY 9 At St. Joseph's, Florida, landing parties from the bark *Ethan Allen* destroy a salt factory. This commodity is of increasing importance to the Confederate economy.

JANUARY 11 Near Galveston, Texas, the paddle steamer *Hatteras* is approached at night by the Confederate raider CSS *Alabama* under Captain Raphael Semmes. *Alabama* sinks the *Hatteras* in a fierce engagement of only 13 minutes, and Semmes rescues the entire crew.

JANUARY 13–14 In Arkansas, Army and Navy forces operating along the White River inflict retaliatory damage on Mound City in retaliation for recent guerrilla attacks.

JANUARY 16–AUGUST 23 At Mobile, Alabama, the Confederate raider CSS

Confederate attack on the Union gunboat flotilla at Galveston, Texas, on January 1, 1863. As a major port for the western Confederacy and potential anchor for the Union blockading fleet, the island city of Galveston was considered vital by Confederate and Union authorities alike. (Library of Congress)

Florida again evades Union blockaders and successfully escapes to sea under Lieutenant John N. Maffitt. Over the ensuing months Maffit takes 22 prizes in the South Atlantic.

JANUARY 21   Near Sabine Pass, Texas, Confederate steamer *Josiah Bell* and gunboat *Uncle Ben* capture Union blockaders *Morning Light* and *Velocity* in a surprise attack.

JANUARY 27   On the Ogeechee River, Georgia, the ironclad monitor *Montauk* under Captain John L. Worden spearheads a Federal assault upon Fort McAllister. Admiral Samuel F. Du Pont is disappointed by the results, especially the slow rate of fire and inaccuracy of his vessels. Again, the Navy Department ignores his warning not to attack Charleston, South Carolina.

JANUARY 30   On the Stono River, South Carolina, the gunboat *Isaac Smith* under Acting Lieutenant Francis S. Conover is captured by Confederates while reconnoitering downstream.

In Mississippi, Admiral David D. Porter's squadron sweeps the Yazoo River of cotton supplies, to deprive the Confederacy of this valuable commodity. The captured bales are employed as additional "armor" on his ships.

JANUARY 31   At Charleston, South Carolina, the Confederate steam rams *Palmetto State* and *Chicora* under Commanders Duncan R. Ingraham and John R. Tucker sortie against the South Atlantic Blockading Squadron. A stiff fight ensues, and several Union vessels are damaged before the Confederate vessels withdraw. The blockade, while dented, has not been broken.

FEBRUARY 1   On the Ogeechee River, Georgia, the *Montauk* of Captain John L. Worden, assisted by ironclads *Seneca*, *Wissahickon*, *Dawn*, and mortar boat *C. P. Williams*, again attack Fort McAllister. The *Montauk* sustains 48 hits in the four-hour exchange, but little damage is inflicted on the enemy.

FEBRUARY 2–3   On the Mississippi River, the steam ram *Queen of the West* conducts a successful foray downstream, heavily damages the Confederate steamer *City of Vicksburg*, and captures three transports loaded with provisions.

FEBRUARY 3   In Tennessee, a surprise Confederate attack against Fort Donelson is foiled by the presence of Commander Le Roy Fitch's gunboat squadron.

In Washington, D.C., Congress votes Captain John L. Worden its thanks for services rendered as captain of the *Monitor* at Hampton Roads in 1862.

FEBRUARY 6–MARCH 17   In Mississippi, Admiral David D. Porter orders his vessels through the levee at Yazoo Pass, and begins ascending the Yazoo River to attack the city of Vicksburg from behind. It is an audacious plan but proves impractical.

FEBRUARY 14   On the Red River, Louisiana, the steam ram *Queen of the West* and screw steamer *Indianola* venture upstream to attack Confederate vessels at Gordon's Landing. Instead, they are attacked by artillery batteries along the shore line; *Queen of the West* grounds and is abandoned. It then enters Confederate service.

FEBRUARY 24   Near Wharton, Mississippi, Confederate vessels *William H. Webb* and *Beatty*, assisted by newly captured *Queen of the West*, attack the ironclad *Indianola* below Warrenton. Outnumbered and outmaneuvered, the *Indianola* sustains serious damage, and Commander George Brown surrenders.

FEBRUARY 25 Off the coast at St. Thomas in the Caribbean, the *Vanderbilt* boards the British merchant vessel *Peterhoff*, sparking a diplomatic row over the disposition of mail found onboard. President Abraham Lincoln orders the craft and all confiscated mail returned to their rightful owners.

In Mississippi, Confederates destroy the newly captured screw steamer *Indianola* once alerted that a large Union vessel is heading toward them down the Red River. This proves to be a ruse conjured up by Admiral David D. Porter; the "gunboat" is nothing but an unmanned barge with trees mounted as guns.

FEBRUARY 28 On the Ogeechee River, Georgia, the ironclad *Montauk* under Captain John L. Worden sinks the blockade-runner *Rattlesnake* under the guns of nearby Fort McAllister. The victorious vessel then strikes a mine, and is deliberately grounded on a mud bank to make repairs.

MARCH 3 On the Ogeechee River, Georgia, the ironclads *Nahant*, *Passaic*, and *Patapsco* bombard Confederate-held Fort McAllister for six hours. Through these repeated actions, Union vessels are perfecting their bombardment techniques for the assault upon Charleston, South Carolina.

MARCH 11 The Mississippi Squadron under Admiral David D. Porter, having cleared the Yazoo Pass, next attacks Fort Pemberton on the Tallahatchie River. Four union vessels are heavily damaged while dueling with land emplacements at a distance of only 800 yards.

MARCH 13 On the Neuse River, North Carolina, gunboats *Ceres*, *Netzel*, *Hunchback*, and *Shawsheen* under Commander Henry K. Davenport assist troops to repel a Confederate night attack against Fort Anderson.

On the Tallahatchie River, Mississippi, the steamer *Chillicothe* and gunboat *Baron de Kalb* make a second attack on Fort Pemberton. However, the former vessel receives 38 hits in 90 minutes and withdraws.

MARCH 14 At Port Hudson, Louisiana, Admiral David G. Farragut's squadron of seven ships runs past Confederate batteries. His flagship, the screw sloop *Hartford*, is lashed alongside the gunboat *Albatross* and makes the passage intact. However, accompanying vessels *Monongahela* and *Richmond* are turned back, and Farragut is cut off from part of his force for several weeks.

In Mississippi, Admiral David D. Porter pushes his gunboats, mortar boats, and four tugs up the Yazoo River to secure Steele's Bayou above Vicksburg. First they have to surmount dense forest and overhangs, compounded by river obstacles placed by the Confederates.

MARCH 16 In Mississippi, gunboats of the Yazoo River Expedition engage Fort Pemberton at Greenwood, and the ironclad *Chillicothe* sustains another eight direct hits and drifts helplessly. Rear Admiral David D. Porter's failure here concludes General Ulysses S. Grant's second attempt to circumvent the northern defenses of Vicksburg.

MARCH 25 On the Mississippi River, steam rams *Switzerland* and *Lancaster* fail to run past Vicksburg's batteries. The former suffers a boiler hit and drifts downstream, while the latter is sunk outright.

APRIL 2 In Mississippi, Admiral David D. Porter hosts Generals Ulysses S. Grant and William T. Sherman on a grand reconnaissance of the Yazoo River as far as Hayne's Bluff. The stark terrain and other imposing obstacles convince Grant to shift his attention to operations below the city.

APRIL 7   At Charleston, South Carolina, Admiral Samuel F. Du Pont's ironclads launch their long-anticipated attack against the harbor. In the course of several hours his slow-firing monitors fire only 139 rounds, while well-handled Confederate artillery pours 2,000 shells upon them. All nine of Du Pont's vessels are struck repeatedly, with the *Keokuk* taking 90 hits near or below the waterline, which render it uncontrollable. Du Pont, who had anticipated much worse, suspends the action at dusk, entirely thankful that the battle was "a failure instead of a disaster."

APRIL 8   Outside Charleston, South Carolina, the battered ironclad *Keokuk* sinks, and its signal book is eventually recovered by the Confederates. They can now discern the blockading squadron's communications.

APRIL 9–OCTOBER 28   Off the coast of France, Commander William L. Maury secretly converts the merchantman *Japan* into the Confederate commerce raider CSS *Georgia*, which proceeds on a cruise to the Cape of Good Hope, South Africa.

APRIL 15   Near Fernando de Noronha, Brazil, Confederate commerce raider CSS *Alabama* under Captain Raphael Semmes burns the Union whalers *Kate Cory* and *Lafayette*.

APRIL 16–17   At Vicksburg, Mississippi, the transports of Admiral David D. Porter make a nighttime run past Confederate batteries posted on nearby bluffs. The action lasts two-and-a-half hours, but most of his vessels only sustain light damage. The squadron then berths off New Carthage, Mississippi, and prepares to transport General Ulysses S. Grant's army over to the Confederate shore.

APRIL 20   On the Nansemond River, Virginia, Army and Navy forces cooperate in the capture of a Confederate redoubt at Hill's Point.

Near Butte a la Rose, Louisiana, the side-wheel gunboat *Estrella* under Lieutenant Commander A. P. Cooke bombards Confederate-held Fort Burton, into submission.

APRIL 21   At Vicksburg, Mississippi, a convoy of additional army transports passes the city's batteries at night and under fire, before joining the main fleet at New Carthage. All hands are hastily preparing to transport General Ulysses S. Grant across the river, a singular feat that proves one of the most decisive improvisations of the war.

APRIL 29   On the Mississippi River, Admiral David D. Porter's gunboats bombard Confederate batteries at Grand Gulf, Mississippi. Porter's army transports skirt the remaining batteries without incident, and Federal forces subsequently bypass Grand Gulf altogether.

APRIL 30   On the Mississippi River, Rear Admiral David D. Porter's gunboats and transports ferry the army of General Ulysses S. Grant from Hard Times, Mississippi, to Bruinsburg, 10 miles below Grand Gulf. Consequently, Confederate defenses at Vicksburg are compromised and can now be attacked from the rear. Union Army and Navy cooperation has never been more manifest, and culminates in a decisive victory.

MAY 3   On the Mississippi River, Rear Admiral David D. Porter's ironclads move back to engage Confederate batteries at Grand Gulf, Mississippi, only to find that the defenders have hastily fled inland.

MAY 4   On the Red River, Louisiana, Rear Admiral David D. Porter sails upstream with his ironclads *Arizona*, *Benton*, *Estrella*, *Lafayette*, *Pittsburgh*, and

Switzerland. Once he arrives, Admiral David G. Farragut departs for New Orleans.

May 5 On the Red River, Louisiana, Rear Admiral David D. Porter's gunboat squadron approaches Fort De Russy, which has also been abandoned by Confederate forces.

May 6 Off the Brazilian coast, the brig *Clarence* is captured by the Confederate raider CSS *Florida* and pressed into Confederate service under Lieutenant Charles W. Read. He then steams north to raid the mid-Atlantic seaboard.

May 7 Admiral David D. Porter sails his Mississippi Squadron further up the Red River, Louisiana, and occupies the town of Alexandria, until army forces can arrive.

May 12 On the Tennessee River, Union gunboats support Army actions against the Confederate cavalry gathered at Linden, Tennessee. They ferry Union troopers across while providing supporting fire during the ensuing action; the Southerners withdraw.

May 18 On the Mississippi River, Admiral David D. Porter orders six gunboats under Lieutenant Commander John G. Walker to bombard Confederate positions along Snyder's Bluff, Mississippi, to provide a diversion for General Ulysses S. Grant, who is marching inland.

May 19 On the Mississippi River, Rear Admiral David D. Porter's gunboat squadron commences bombarding Confederate fortifications at Vicksburg, Mississippi, in support of General Ulysses S. Grant.

As five Union gunboats proceed up the Yazoo River, Mississippi, Confederate Commander Isaac N. Brown is forced to scuttle three steam rams being constructed at Yazoo City.

May 21 On the Yazoo River, Mississippi, five Union gunboats under Commander John G. Walker reach Yazoo City, inducing the Confederates to destroy their navy yard.

May 24–30 On the Yazoo River, Mississippi, five Union gunboats burn several Confederate steamers that have grounded on a sand bar. They subsequently sail 10 miles down the Sunflower River, destroying additional caches of food stocks and vessels.

May 27 At Vicksburg, Mississippi, the gunboat *Cincinnati* under Lieutenant George M. Bache attacks Confederate rifle pits outside the city, but is riddled by cannon fire and sinks. A total of 25 sailors are killed and wounded, while another 15 drown.

May 31 Near Perkins Landing, Louisiana, the gunboat *Carondelet* assists Union troops during a serious Confederate attack there. A transport then successfully evacuates the troops, covered by heavy supporting fire.

June 7 At Milliken's Bend, Louisiana, the gunboats *Choctaw* and *Lexington* help Union troops defeat a determined Confederate assault with heavy concentrations of shell, canister, and grapeshot delivered at close range.

June 8–11 Near Pass a l'Outre, Louisiana, a Confederate boat party led by Master James Duke captures the steam tug *Boston*. Duke uses his prize to burn two additional vessels before finally running the blockade outside Mobile, Alabama.

June 9 Near Vicksburg, Mississippi, Union mortar boats resume their protracted bombardment to cut off resupply efforts and undermine civilian morale. They hurl 175 heavy explosive shells into the city every day, forcing its inhabitants to cower in nearby caves.

JUNE 17 In Wassaw Sound, Georgia, the ironclad *Weehawken* under Captain John Rodgers, assisted by the *Nahant*, engage Commander William A. Webb of the steam ram *Atlanta*. *Atlanta* grounds in the channel during its approach and is subsequently worked free, but its rudder is damaged. Rodgers then slips into point-blank range, and pounds his adversary into submission.

JUNE 18 On the Mississippi River, Union rams *General Sterling Price* and *Mound City* conclude a three-day raid that captures or destroys 60 enemy skiffs, barges, and boats.

JUNE 24 In Washington, D.C., Admiral John A. B. Dahlgren is relieved of duties at the Washington Navy Yard, and ordered to succeed Admiral Samuel F. Du Pont as commander of the South Atlantic Blockading Squadron.

JUNE 25 In Japan, the steamer *Pembroke* is fired upon by cannon belonging to Prince Nagata, as it journeys through the Shimonoseki Straits. This event provokes a direct American response.

JUNE 26 In New York City, the distinguished Rear Admiral Andrew H. Foote dies of wounds received in the siege of Fort Donelson in February 1862.

Near Portland, Maine, the Confederate schooner CSS *Archer* under Lieutenant Charles W. Read sinks the revenue cutter *Caleb Cushing*, but subsequently surrenders to the *Forest City* after expending its ammunition. Read, in the span of only 19 days, captures 22 vessels, despite numerous Union craft looking for him.

JULY 3 At Vicksburg, Mississippi, the onset of surrender negotiations ceases the bombardment of the city by Admiral David D. Porter's Mississippi River Squadron. During the siege, Porter's men had fired 16,000 rounds from a variety of ships, gunboats, and mortar craft, and 13 naval guns hauled ashore.

JULY 4 At Helena, Arkansas, the gunboat *Tyler* under Lieutenant Commander James M. Prichett successfully supports Union forces attacked by superior numbers of Confederates.

JULY 6 Near Port Royal, South Carolina, Admiral John A. B. Dahlgren relieves Admiral Samuel F. Du Pont as commander of the South Atlantic Blockading Squadron. Du Pont's removal is due as much to poor relations with Secretary of the Navy Gideon Welles as it is his failure before Charleston.

JULY 9 On the Ohio River, Union gunboats under Lieutenant Commander Le Roy Fitch go into action against the daring mounted raider of General John H. Morgan.

JULY 10 At Charleston, South Carolina, Admiral John A. B. Dahlgren initiates a second siege by bombarding Morris Island. The ironclads *Nahant, Weehawken, Catskill,* and *Montauk* are all damaged by Confederate shore batteries, though none seriously.

At Boston, Massachusetts, the screw sloop *Shenandoah* and bark *Ethan Allen* begin pursuing the Confederate raider CSS *Florida*, which has been sighted nearby.

JULY 13 Outside Yazoo City, Mississippi, the gunboat *Baron de Kalb* strikes a mine and sinks while escorting several transports. The troops these carry capture the town, forcing the Southerners to scuttle 19 vessels to prevent capture.

JULY 14   On the James River, Virginia, eight gunboats under Rear Admiral Samuel D. Lee assist Union forces in the capture of Fort Powhatan.

JULY 16   On the Stono River, South Carolina, the screw sloop *Pawnee* and the gunboat *Marblehead* assist Union troops to repel a determined Confederate attack against Grimball's Landing.

At Shimonoseki, Japan, the screw sloop *Wyoming* under Captain David McDougal sinks three of Prince Nagata's warships. This action comes in retaliation for their firing on an American merchant vessel.

JULY 18   In Charleston harbor, South Carolina, Rear Admiral John A. B. Dahlgren's ironclad squadron lends supporting fire during the assault on Battery Wagner. His vessels close to within 300 yards of Confederate works, but the moment they cease fire, the defenders suddenly emerge to repel the Union troops.

JULY 21   On the Mississippi River, Confederate artillery fire disables the transport *Sallie Ward,* and it grounds on Island No. 82.

JULY 22   In Charleston harbor, South Carolina, Rear Admiral John A. B. Dahlgren orders a naval battery constructed on Morris Island to help bombard Fort Sumter.

JULY 29   On the Ohio River, Union gunboats under Lieutenant Commander Le Roy Fitch attack General John H. Morgan's Confederate raiders on Buffington Island, while army troops attack his rear; 3,000 Confederates surrender, but Morgan escapes.

AUGUST 1   In the West, Admiral David D. Porter succeeds Admiral David G. Farragut to command all naval forces along the Mississippi River. The ailing Farragut is going on extended leave to recover his health.

AUGUST 5   On the James River, Virginia, the side-wheel steamer *Commodore Barney* is damaged when a 1,000-pound, electrically detonated mine is exploded a short distance away. Confederate underwater ordnance is acquiring technical sophistication and considerable lethality.

AUGUST 7   At Charleston, South Carolina, General Pierre G. T. Beauregard asks authorities in Mobile, Alabama, if a "submarine boat" being constructed there can be transferred overland by rail. He intends to use it to break the Union blockade of the city.

AUGUST 12   At Charleston, South Carolina, the experimental submarine *Hunley* arrives. This vessel is a waterproofed iron steam boiler fitted with tapered bow and stern sections. Moreover, it is 40 feet long, 3.5 feet in diameter, and propelled by five men operating a crankshaft-driven propeller. General Pierre G. T. Beauregard seeks to impress it into active service as soon as testing is completed.

AUGUST 16   On the Stono River, South Carolina, the screw sloop *Pawnee* sails down until four electrically detonated mines explode nearby. No damage results, but the attack underscores the sophistication of submerged Confederate ordnance.

AUGUST 17   At Charleston harbor, South Carolina, Union ironclads under Rear Admiral John A. B. Dahlgren commence a five-day bombardment of Fort Sumter.

AUGUST 21   In Charleston harbor, South Carolina, the Confederate torpedo boat *Torch* tries to attack the ironclad *New Ironsides* at Morris Islands at night; the mission aborts due to steering problems.

AUGUST 22   At New Topsail Inlet, North Carolina, Acting Ensign Joseph C. Cony leads two boats of sailors against blockade runner *Alexander Cooper*, which he burns; then he also destroys a salt works.

AUGUST 23   Near Windmill Point on the Rappahannock River, Virginia, a Confederate cutting-out expedition under Lieutenant John Taylor Wood captures the Union steamers *Reliance* and *Satellite*.

At Brest, France, Confederate commerce raider CSS *Florida* under Lieutenant John N. Maffitt anchors after an eight-month cruise that netted 22 prizes. Still, the *Florida* needs a refit, and six months lapse before it puts to sea again.

AUGUST 25   Near the mouth of the Rappahannock River, Virginia, Lieutenant John T. Wood uses captured gunboats *Reliant* and *Satellite* to seize three additional schooners. All five vessels are subsequently burned and scuttled, owing to a lack of sufficient coal to operate them.

AUGUST 29   In Charleston harbor, South Carolina, the experimental submarine *Hunley*, under Lieutenant John A. Payne, sinks on a trial run, killing all six crew members. General Pierre G. T. Beauregard orders it raised and recommissioned.

SEPTEMBER 1–2   In Charleston harbor, South Carolina, Admiral John A. B. Dahlgren's ironclads commence a five-hour night action against Fort Sumter. They steam to within 500 yards of the embattled fortress before firing, while sustaining 70 hits from batteries at Fort Moultrie. The action ceases at daybreak.

SEPTEMBER 6   In Charleston Harbor, Union picket boats capture three Confederate barges, as the Southerners abandon Battery Wagner at night by water.

SEPTEMBER 7   At Charleston harbor, South Carolina, Admiral John A. B. Dahlgren demands Fort Sumter's surrender; after it refuses, he conducts a reconnaissance in force with the ironclads *Weehawken* and *New Ironsides*. *Weehawken*, however, grounds in the channel, so *New Ironsides* interposes itself between it and Fort Moultrie, taking 50 hits.

SEPTEMBER 8   At Sabine Pass, Texas, a combined expedition under Major General William B. Franklin, commanding 4,000 men, and Acting Volunteer Lieutenant Frederick Crocker, with four gunboats, attempts to capture this strategic position, but is thwarted by a 42-man garrison at Fort Griffin. Lieutenant Richard Dowling allows the vessels to approach to within point-blank range before opening fire, which disables two vessels and drives the rest off. The *Clifton* and *Sachem* are both captured, along with 315 officers and men.

SEPTEMBER 8–9   In Charleston harbor, South Carolina, Admiral John A. B. Dahlgren launches a nighttime assault against Fort Sumter, with 413 sailors and U.S. Marines under Commander Thomas H. Stevens. The Southerners, having secured a code book from the sunken *Keokuk*, can decipher Union signals, and the attackers are rebuffed with a loss of 100 prisoners.

SEPTEMBER 19–23   In Chesapeake Bay, a Confederate boat expedition under Acting Masters John Y. Beall and Edward McGuire burns four schooners.

SEPTEMBER 24   In New York, eight Russian warships pay an official visit. Although the move is widely interpreted as a sign of diplomatic support for the North, they are actually seeking refuge once Great Britain and France threaten war over the Polish insurrection. In this manner, another squadron of six vessels also anchors at San Francisco, California.

OCTOBER 5   In Charleston harbor, South Carolina, the torpedo boat *David*, equipped with an exploding spar, steams out intending to fatally jab *New Ironsides* below the waterline. The latter sustains heavy damage, but the *David*, its boilers extinguished by the blast, drifts alongside its victim for several minutes before escaping in the dark.

OCTOBER 9   At Birkenhead, England, the government seizes two very large steam Laird rams being constructed for the Confederacy. These vessels represent the most advanced naval technology available to any nation, and the United States has threatened to declare war if they end up in Confederate hands.

OCTOBER 15   In Charleston harbor, South Carolina, the experimental Confederate submarine *Hunley* founders a second time, killing all seven crew members including Horace L. Hunley, its inventor. Once again, General Pierre G. T. Beauregard orders the craft raised and refitted.

OCTOBER 26–DECEMBER 4   In Charleston harbor, South Carolina, Union ironclads commence a two-week bombardment of Fort Sumter, firing 9,306 shells on that position. Fort Sumter, still defiant throughout this latest ordeal, is reduced to rubble.

OCTOBER 28   From the Cape of Good Hope, South Africa, Commander William L. Maury leads the commerce raider CSS *Georgia* back to European waters after an unspectacular cruise. He has only taken nine prizes owing to the poor sailing characteristics of the ship, which is subsequently sold.

NOVEMBER 16   In Charleston harbor, South Carolina, the tug *Leigh* runs aground, and five members of its crew row a line out to the ironclad *Nahant* under enemy fire, which tows them all to safety. All five members receive the Congressional Medal of Honor.

DECEMBER 6   In Charleston harbor, South Carolina, the ironclad *Weehawken*, under Commander James M. Duncan, accidentally sinks, and 24 sailors drown.

DECEMBER 7   In Washington, D.C., Secretary of the Navy Gideon Welles releases his third annual report and declares that the Union blockade covers 3,549 miles of Southern coastline. The strength of the U.S. Navy is also up to 588 vessels, 4,443 guns, and 34,000 personnel.

DECEMBER 10   At St. Andrew's Bay, Florida, Union vessels land parties which destroy a Confederate salt works, along with most of the adjacent town.

DECEMBER 17   Near Halifax, Nova Scotia, the gunboats *Annie* and *Ella* under Acting Lieutenant Frederick Nichols recover the Union steamer *Chesapeake* from John C. Braine and fifteen Confederate sympathizers, who escape overland.

1864

JANUARY 18   At Mobile, Alabama, Rear Admiral David G. Farragut conducts a close reconnaissance of the harbor defenses. Fully recovered, he is now tasked with planning a major offensive against this vital port.

FEBRUARY 2 On the Neuse River, North Carolina, Lieutenant John T. Wood's Confederate cutting-out expedition captures the steamer *Underwriter*, then burns it under fire from land batteries. The Confederate Congress gives him a vote of thanks.

FEBRUARY 12 At Brest, France, Lieutenant Charles M. Morris leads the commerce raider *Florida* out to sea and eludes the blockading screw sloop *Kearsarge* under Captain John A. Winslow; he takes 15 additional prizes over the next eight months.

FEBRUARY 16 Near Mobile, Alabama, Rear Admiral David G. Farragut begins his campaign, with a preliminary bombardment of Fort Powell to test Confederate defenses.

FEBRUARY 17 In Charleston harbor, South Carolina, the Confederate submarine *H. L. Hunley* under Lieutenant George E. Dixon sinks the Union screw sloop *Housatonic*. The *Hunley* survived the explosion and signaled that it was returning, then sank a third time with all hands. Nonetheless, *Housatonic* enjoys the melancholy distinction of being the first warship sunk by a submarine.

FEBRUARY 20 At Charleston, South Carolina, Admiral John A. B. Dahlgren is alarmed by the successful Confederate submarine attack, and suggests that the Navy Department offer a $20–30,000 reward for the capture or destruction of any such craft.

FEBRUARY 29 At Smithville, North Carolina, Lieutenant William B. Cushing leads men ashore to capture General Louis Hebert in his tent; unfortunately, the general is absent, and the raiders snare a Confederate army captain.

MARCH 5 Near Cherrystone Point, Virginia, Confederate raiders under Commander John T. Wood seize a Union telegraph office and the steamers *Aeolus* and *Titan*. Wood destroys the vessels and makes his escape.

MARCH 6 Near Charleston, South Carolina, the screw steamer *Memphis* is attacked by a Confederate torpedo boat on the North Edisto River. It survives after the explosive spar fails to detonate under its waterline, and the attacker escapes in the night.

MARCH 8 On the Mississippi River below Grand Gulf, the gunboat *Conestoga* is struck by the ram *General Sterling Price* and sinks; two sailors drown.

MARCH 12 On the Red River, Louisiana, Admiral David D. Porter leads 13 ironclads, 4 tinclads, and 4 wooden gunboats upstream as part of the Shreveport Expedition of General Nathaniel P. Banks. This campaign is viewed as preparation for invading Texas to cut off Confederate supplies.

MARCH 16 On the Red River, landing parties from the ironclad *Osage* under Commodore Thomas O. Selfridge occupies the town of Alexandria, Louisiana, until army troops provide a garrison. The balance of Rear Admiral David D. Porter's squadron also arrives offshore later that day.

MARCH 25 At Paducah, Kentucky, gunboats *Paw Paw* and *Peosta* provide effective supporting fire that repels a Confederate attack against that town.

APRIL 1 In the St. John's River, Florida, the transport *Maple Leaf* strikes a Confederate mine, and sinks.

APRIL 3 On the Red River, Louisiana, three transport steamers and nine gunboats from Rear Admiral David D. Porter's squadron convey General Andrew J. Smith's army corps from Alexandria to Grand Ecore. Once there the latter will march overland to join the main force under General Nathaniel P. Banks.

APRIL 9   Near Newport News, Virginia, the steam frigate *Minnesota* under Lieutenant Commander John H. Upshur is damaged by the Confederate torpedo boat *Squib*, which escapes under heavy fire.

APRIL 10   On the Red River, Louisiana, Rear Admiral David D. Porter's squadron steams to within 30 miles of its objective at Shreveport, only to find that Confederates have sunk a large steamer in his path. He also learns of the Union defeat at Sabine Crossroads, after which General Nathaniel P. Banks retreated. Faced with declining water levels on the river, Porter likewise decides to return downstream.

APRIL 12   On the Red River, Louisiana, Admiral David D. Porter's squadron is shelled by Confederate batteries at Blair's Landing. Fire from the gunboat *Lexington* silences enemy cannon, and kills Brigadier General Thomas Green.

APRIL 15   On the Red River, Louisiana, the gunboat *Eastport* under Commander S. Ledyard Phelps strikes a Confederate mine, and grounds itself eight times to make repairs before finally being scuttled.

APRIL 16   The transport *General Hunter* strikes a Confederate mine on the St. John's River, Florida, and sinks.

APRIL 17   Near Plymouth, North Carolina, supporting fire from the gunboats *Miami* and *Southfield* helps repulse a Confederate attack on Union positions.

APRIL 19   Outside Plymouth, North Carolina, the huge Confederate steam ram *Albemarle* under Commander James W. Cooke attacks the Federal blockading squadron, sinking the *Southfield* and killing Commander C. W. Flusser. Once the surviving Union vessels draw off, the nearby army garrison surrenders the following day.

APRIL 21   On the Yazoo River, Mississippi, Union forces attack Confederate positions at Yazoo City, and the gunboat *Petrel* is severely damaged by artillery fire. The damaged craft drifts and is ultimately captured.

APRIL 26–27   On the Red River, Louisiana, Admiral David D. Porter's squadron struggles against Confederate opposition along the banks, until it finally reaches Alexandria. Navy losses are two gunboats disabled and one captured; Porter's flagship, the *Cricket*, is struck repeatedly.

APRIL 28   On the Red River, Louisiana, Admiral David D. Porter's flotilla is trapped by receding water levels. The admiral is resigned to the necessity of scuttling his entire squadron, and he advises Secretary of the Navy Gideon Welles that "you may judge my feelings at having to perform so painful a duty." Only a miracle can save the vessels.

APRIL 29   On the Red River, Mississippi, the engineer Colonel Joseph Bailey constructs a series of dams of logs to raise the water levels and keep Admiral David D. Porter's gunboat squadron afloat. This proves one of the most daring and imaginative military innovations of the entire war.

APRIL 30   In Richmond, Virginia, Confederate Secretary of the Navy Stephen Mallory confirms the weakness of Southern naval forces. Presently he commands only 13 ships and 1 floating battery for service in the east.

May 4–7 Near Tampa, Florida, steamers *Sunflower* and *Honduras* capably assist an amphibious attack ashore.

May 5 Near Plymouth, North Carolina, the Confederate ironclad ram *Albemarle* under Commander James W. Cooke, escorted by gunboats *Bombshell* and *Cotton Planter*, steams into Albemarle Sound to engage the Federal blockading squadron. Captain Melanchton Smith, however, keeps the Southerners under a hot fire, and once *Albemarle* is badly damaged, Cooke orders the vessels back up the Roanoke River for repairs.

May 5 On the Red River, Louisiana, Confederate land forces engage the wooden steamers *Covington*, *Signal*, and *Warner* near Dunn's Bayou, Louisiana, destroying all three vessels.

May 6 On the James River, Virginia, the side-wheel steamer *Commodore Jones* is struck by a 2,000-pound, electrically detonated mine and is completely destroyed, along with 40 of her crew.

On the Cape Fear River, North Carolina, Confederate Flag Officer William F. Lynch and the ironclad ram *Raleigh* engage the Union blockaders *Britannia* and *Nansemond*. This action allows a Southern blockade runner to slip out, but *Raleigh* grounds while returning upstream and is destroyed to prevent capture.

On the Red River, Louisiana, Confederate forces battling Rear Admiral David D. Porter's squadron capture the side-wheel steamers *Granite City* and *Wave* at the Calcasieu Pass.

May 7 On the James River, Virginia, Confederate forces capture the Union side-wheel steamer *Shawsheen* under Acting Ensign Charles Ringot off Chaffin's Bluff.

May 10 On the Red River, Louisiana, the dam constructed by Colonel Joseph Bailey is breached, and ironclads *Mound City*, *Pittsburgh*, and *Carondelet* successfully shoot-run the rapids. Admiral David D. Porter informs Secretary of the Navy Gideon Welles that "The passage of these vessels was a beautiful sight, only to be realized when seen."

On the St. John's River, Florida, the army transport *Harriet A. Ward* strikes a Confederate mine and sinks.

May 12 Near Virginia, Rear Admiral Samuel Lee organizes an "anti-torpedo" squadron of three steamers outfitted to drag the James River for mines.

May 13 On the Red River, Louisiana, the *Louisville*, *Chillicothe*, and *Ozark*, last of Admiral David D. Porter's gunboats, dash over a wing dam and float off to safety. The ingenuity of Colonel Joseph Bailey's engineers saved an entire squadron from capture.

May 23 At Horse Landing on the St. John's River, Florida, the tug *Columbine* grounds and fights Confederate forces for several hours before surrendering. The Southerners burn their prize to prevent its recapture.

May 25 On the Roanoke River, North Carolina, five volunteers from the gunboat *Mattabesett* unsuccessfully attack the anchored Confederate steam ram *Albemarle*. One sailor is captured, but all five receive the Congressional Medal of Honor.

June 3 In Ossabow Sound, Georgia, the side-wheel steamer *Water Witch* is captured by a 130-man Confederate cutting-out expedition under Lieutenant Thomas P. Pelot; Pelot is killed in action.

June 11 At Cherbourg, France, Captain Raphael Semmes and the Confederate raider *Alabama* anchor to complete badly needed repairs. His arrival is noted by the American vice-consul in the city, who informs naval authorities.

JUNE 14   Outside Cherbourg, France, the screw sloop *Kearsarge* under Captain John A. Winslow arrives and begins blockading the notorious Confederate raider *Alabama* in port.

JUNE 19   Outside Cherbourg, France, the Union screw sloop *Kearsarge* under Captain John A. Winslow engages the CSS *Alabama* of Captain Raphael Semmes. Both vessels handle their guns well; *Kearsarge* receives 28 hits, but Union gunners inflict tremendous hull damage, puncturing the *Alabama* repeatedly. Within an hour the ship is listing; Semmes abandons ship and is picked up by the English yacht *Deerhound*; only 41 crew members survive from 149 present. The South's most celebrated commerce runner has met an ignominious end.

JUNE 24   On the White River, Arkansas, the side-wheel steamer *Queen City* is captured by Confederate cavalry and artillery near Clarendon.

JULY 5   On the Stono River, South Carolina, Union ironclads attack Confederate rifle pits and other fortifications, driving the defenders from their positions.

JULY 10   Off the Maryland coast, the Confederate commerce raider CSS *Florida* sinks the bark *General Berry*. Consequently, the screw steamer *Mount Vernon* and gunboat *Monticello* put to sea to apprehend the elusive vessel.

JULY 25   On the Roanoke River, North Carolina, a four-man reconnaissance team led by Acting Master's Mate John Woodman pinpoints the exact location of the huge Confederate ram *Albemarle*.

Outside Mobile Bay, Alabama, Union boat crews at night locate and neutralize

The USS Kearsarge *sinks the CSS* Alabama *off Cherbourg, France, during the American Civil War on June 19, 1864. (Chaiba Media)*

Confederate mines deployed near the entrance of the bay, a process that continues over several nights.

AUGUST 1–4 McIntosh Court House, Georgia, is stormed by a raiding party from the sloop *Saratoga*, which seizes civilians trying to form a coastal guard.

AUGUST 5 At Mobile Bay, Alabama, Admiral David G. Farragut launches an all-out attack against Confederate defenses. After the ironclad *Tecumseh* detonates a torpedo and sinks, Farragut declares, "Damn the torpedoes, full speed ahead!" He next confronts the large steam ram *Tennessee* under Rear Admiral James Buchanan, but Farragut easily dodges his slower adversary while his squadron pummels it with cannon fire. Buchanan finally lowers his flag at 10:00 A.M., and Farragut's bold gambit closes the Confederacy's final port on the Gulf Coast.

AUGUST 6–23 At Wilmington, North Carolina, the Confederate steamer *Tallahassee* departs under Commander John T. Wood, and, over the next two weeks, he nets 31 Union prizes.

AUGUST 9 At City Point, Virginia, a Union army transport explodes and sinks on the James River after two Confederate agents place a time bomb on board; damage to General Ulysses S. Grant's base of supply is severe.

At Mobile, Alabama, the former Confederate ram *Tennessee*, now manned by Union sailors, helps bombard Fort Morgan into submission.

AUGUST 10 Off the New York coast, the Confederate raider *Tallahassee* under Commander John T. Wood takes the first of 31 prizes, forcing the Navy to dispatch several warships in pursuit.

SEPTEMBER 2 In Washington, D.C., Secretary of the Navy Gideon Welles is authorized to mount an amphibious assault against Fort Fisher, Wilmington, North Carolina, the South's remaining seaport.

SEPTEMBER 19 On Lake Erie, a Confederate raiding party under Acting Master John Yates Beall seizes and burns two steamers. His objective is to free Confederate prisoners held at Johnson's Island, Sandusky, Ohio, but Beall is apprehended and eventually hung as a spy.

SEPTEMBER 28 In a major command shake-up, Rear Admiral David D. Porter yields command of the Mississippi Squadron to Rear Admiral Stephen D. Lee, while Porter takes charge of his North Atlantic Blockading Squadron.

SEPTEMBER 29 Near Fort Harrison, Virginia, the Confederate James River Squadron under Flag Officer John K. Mitchell provides supporting fire for Confederate operations at Fort Harrison.

Off the Cuban coast, Confederate sympathizers under John C. Braine hijack the steamer *Roanoke* at sea, then burn it at Bermuda.

OCTOBER 7 At Bahia, Brazil, the screw sloop *Wachusett* under Commander Napoleon Collins attacks the Confederate commerce raider CSS *Florida*, after learning that Lieutenant Charles M. Morris and most of his crew were ashore. Because this is a blatant violation of Brazilian neutrality, diplomatic protests are issued.

OCTOBER 12 In the Gulf of Mexico, Rear Admiral Cornelius K. Stribling assumes command of the East Gulf Blockading Squadron.

OCTOBER 19 In the Madeiras Islands, the British-built vessel *Sea King* arrives at Las Desertas; it is taken into Confederate service as the commerce raider CSS

Shenandoah under Lieutenant James I. Waddell.

OCTOBER 22 In Richmond, Virginia, Confederate Secretary of the Navy Stephen R. Mallory writes President Jefferson Davis and defends his decision to deploy the *Tallahassee* and *Chickamauga* as commerce raiders rather than assigning them to the defense of Wilmington, North Carolina. He feels their activity would draw Union vessels off from the blockading service, thereby decreasing the pressure on Wilmington.

OCTOBER 27 On the Roanoke River, North Carolina, a spar torpedo operated by 21-year-old Lieutenant William B. Cushing sinks the imposing Confederate ram *Albemarle*. Cushing's own vessel sinks, and he is forced to swim to shore. Only he and one other member of the expedition return to Union lines, the remaining 13 are captured or killed.

OCTOBER 28 At Wilmington, North Carolina, Lieutenant John Wilkinson leads the Confederate raider CSS *Chickamauga* past the Union blockade. He takes seven prizes over the next three weeks, then slips back safely during a fog.

OCTOBER 29–NOVEMBER 1 Offshore at Plymouth, North Carolina, Union naval forces under Commander W. H. Macomb bombard Confederate positions, then put landing parties ashore to plant powder charges. This successful action closes the Carolina Sounds to the Confederacy.

OCTOBER 29–NOVEMBER 7 Near Wilmington, North Carolina, the Confederate commerce raider CSS *Olustee* (originally *Tallahassee*) under Lieutenant William H. Ward dodges Union blockaders, then performs a week-long cruise that takes seven prizes.

OCTOBER 30 South of the Azores, the Confederate commerce raider CSS *Olustee* captures the bark *Alina*, its first prize.

On the Tennessee River, the gunboat *Undine* and two transports are captured by Confederate under General Nathan B. Forrest near Johnson City, Tennessee.

NOVEMBER 2 On the Tennessee River, the paddle-wheel steamers *Key West* and *Tawah* recapture the former Union gunboats *Undine* and *Venus* from audacious Confederate cavalry.

NOVEMBER 4 On the Tennessee River, General Nathan B. Forrest sinks three more Union paddle-wheelers near Johnsonville, Tennessee, with artillery fire. By the time he concludes his raid, 4 gunboats, 14 steamers, 17 barges, 33 cannon, 150 captives, and 75,000 tons of supplies worth $6.7 million are ruined.

NOVEMBER 27 On the James River, Virginia, the Union steamer *Greyhound*, functioning as the floating headquarters of General Benjamin F. Butler, explodes and sinks with a high-level conference in progress. This event is most likely a result of Confederate sabotage, whereby a "coal torpedo" was inadvertently shoveled into the *Greyhound*'s boiler. Fortunately, Butler, General Robert Schenck, and Admiral David D. Porter escape unharmed.

NOVEMBER 29 On the James River, Virginia, Union monitors *Onondaga* and *Mahopac* trade shots with Confederate batteries for three hours without serious damage.

NOVEMBER 30 At Grahamville, South Carolina, Commander George H. Preble leads a Union naval brigade into action at Honey Hill in support of Union land forces. The 500 sailors and marines have been drawn from the South Atlantic Blockading Squadron.

DECEMBER 3–4   On the Cumberland River, Union gunboats recapture three transports, then duel with Confederate batteries at Bell's Mills, Tennessee.

DECEMBER 5   In his third annual report, Secretary of the Navy Gideon Welles states that the Navy consists of 671 vessels mounting more than 4,600 guns, and has taken 1,400 prizes. He also lauds the Union blockade as the lengthiest in history.

At Tulifinny Crossroads, Georgia, the Naval Brigade under Commander George H. Preble supports Army operations aimed at cutting the Savannah-Charleston railroad. The attempt fails, but the sailors fight competently.

DECEMBER 6   On the Cumberland River, Lieutenant Commander LeRoy Fitch and the ironclad *Neosho* attempt running past Confederate batteries at Bell's Mills, Tennessee. However, his vessel sustains over 100 hits in a three-hour struggle, and Fitch concludes that the position is unapproachable.

DECEMBER 7   In Mobile Bay, Alabama, the tug *Narcissus* under Acting Ensign William G. Jones hits a Confederate mine and sinks in only fifteen minutes.

DECEMBER 9   On the Roanoke River, North Carolina, the tug *Bazely* and the side-wheel steamer *Otsego* engage Confederate batteries along Rainbow Bluff, then both strike mines and sink.

DECEMBER 13   In New York City, an ailing and fatigued Admiral David G. Farragut again arrives onboard the screw sloop *Hartford,* receiving another hero's welcome by its inhabitants.

DECEMBER 14–21   On Ossabaw Sound, Georgia, Union gunboats begin reducing Savannah's outer ring of defenses by attacking and capturing Forts Beaulieu and Rosedew.

DECEMBER 15–16   On the Cumberland River, Tennessee, seven gunboats under Commander LeRoy Fitch provide heavy supporting fire for Union forces engaged in the Battle of Nashville. The Confederate Army of Tennessee under Major General John B. Hood is nearly annihilated.

DECEMBER 20   In New York harbor, Rear Admiral David G. Farragut lowers his flag from the screw sloop *Hartford* for the last time.

DECEMBER 21   At Savannah, Georgia, retreating Confederate forces destroy the *Savannah, Isondiga, Firefly*, and *Georgia* to prevent them from being captured by General William T. Sherman's approaching army.

DECEMBER 23   In Washington, D.C., President Abraham Lincoln signs congressional legislation creating the rank of vice admiral. David G. Farragut becomes the first naval officer so honored, which gives him the rank equivalent to that of lieutenant general.

DECEMBER 23–24   Outside Wilmington, North Carolina, the explosive-laden vessel *Louisiana*, intended to be detonated under the guns of Fort Fisher, ignites 250 yards from its objective. Because this fails to damage the Confederate defenses as planned, Rear Admiral David D. Porter's 60 vessels begin a bombardment that strikes the fort with 155 shells per minute. However, the expedition retires after General Benjamin F. Butler withdraws his 2,000 troops from the beach.

1865

JANUARY 1 At No Name Cay in the Bahamas, the screw frigate *San Jacinto* under Captain R.W. Meade strikes a reef, and is scuttled with loss of life.

JANUARY 2 In Washington, D.C., Secretary of the Navy Gideon Welles impresses upon Secretary of War Edwin M. Stanton the dire necessity for capturing Wilmington, North Carolina, the only port through which supplies can reach the Confederacy.

JANUARY 4 In North Carolina, Rear Admiral David D. Porter establishes his strategy for the reduction of Fort Fisher at Wilmington. He intends to hit the fort frontally with his naval brigade, consisting of 1,200 sailors and marines under Lieutenant Commander K. R. Breese, while army troops maneuver toward the rear.

JANUARY 12 At Wilmington, North Carolina, Admiral David D. Porter arrives with 59 warships and 8,000 men under General Alfred H. Terry. This is the largest Union armada assembled during the war, and also the largest amphibious expedition.

JANUARY 13 In Georgia, Lieutenant Stephen B. Luce of the gunboat *Pontiac* confers with General William T. Sherman, and becomes convinced that a naval war college is needed to better impart the principles of war on naval officers.

JANUARY 14 At Fort Fisher, North Carolina, Admiral David D. Porter's armada begins its reduction of Confederate defenses. Porter moves his ships to within 1,000 yards of the fort to deliver a storm of shot and shell. The bulk of Fort Fisher's armament has been dismounted or made useless within a few hours.

JANUARY 15 At Wilmington, North Carolina, Admiral David D. Porter orders his ironclad monitors to within point-blank range of Fort Fisher, then orders his naval brigade to land. The naval brigade is repelled in three desperate charges and suffers 309 casualties, but they distract the defenders from Army troops circling from behind. For their role in this victory, no less than 35 sailors and marines receive the Congressional Medal of Honor.

In Charleston harbor, South Carolina, the ironclad *Patapsco* under Lieutenant Commander S. P. Quackenbush strikes a Confederate mine and sinks with half of its crew.

JANUARY 23–24 In Virginia, the James River Squadron under Commodore John K. Mitchell attacks City Point, the main supply base for General Ulysses S. Grant's army. However, it encounters heavy resistance from Union shore batteries and ironclads *Massasoit* and *Onondaga* at Trent's Reach, then withdraws with a loss of three vessels.

JANUARY 27 On the James River, Virginia, a boat party under Acting Ensign Thomas Morgan refloats the Confederate torpedo boat *Scorpion* which had been previously sunk by cannon fire, and delivers it to Union lines.

JANUARY 28 At Colerain, North Carolina, the steam gunboat *Valley City* provides close fire support to Union troops during a surprise Confederate attack.

Near Mobile, Alabama, Lieutenant Commander William W. Low and the Confederate torpedo boat *St. Patrick* ram the side-wheel steamer *Octorara*. Its explosive torpedo spar fails to explode, and neither vessel suffers damage.

FEBRUARY 9 On the North Edisto River, South Carolina, the screw sloop *Pawnee*, the side-wheel steamer *Daffodil*, and the gunboat *Sonoma* engage Confederate batteries. The vessels all sustain several hits before the enemy guns are silenced.

FEBRUARY 10 In Virginia, Captain Raphael Semmes, celebrated commander of the *Alabama*, advances to rear admiral in charge of the James River Squadron.

FEBRUARY 15 Off the Florida coast, the steam frigate *Merrimack* takes on water after its pumps fail, and it is abandoned.

FEBRUARY 17 In North Carolina, Rear Admiral David D. Porter's squadron ferries two divisions of General William T. Sherman's army along the Cape Fear River, pausing only to bombard Fort Anderson in the ensuing assault. The ultimate goal for both men is the capture of Wilmington.

FEBRUARY 17–18 Charleston, South Carolina, is evacuated by Confederate forces, who destroy the ironclads *Charleston*, *Chicora*, and *Palmetto State* to prevent their capture. The city had been under siege for 567 days.

FEBRUARY 19–22 On the Cape Fear River, North Carolina, Admiral David D. Porter's gunboats train their guns on Fort Strong to assist in the capture of Wilmington.

FEBRUARY 25 On the Pee Dee River, South Carolina, Ensign Allen K. Noyes directs a landing party from armed tug *Catalpa* that defeats the Confederate cavalry at nearby Georgetown.

FEBRUARY 29 In Winyah Bay, South Carolina, Rear Admiral John A. Dahlgren's flagship, the side-wheel steamer *Harvest Moon*, strikes a mine and sinks. The admiral is unhurt.

MARCH 4 At Mussel Shoals, Alabama, a Confederate force under Brigadier General Philip D. Roddey abandons its encampment to the side-wheel gunboats *General Burnside* and *General Thomas*.

MARCH 12 On the Blakely River, Alabama, the tug *Althea* strikes a mine while performing dredging operations and sinks.

MARCH 24 Outside El Ferrol, Spain, Commander Thomas J. Page guides the French-built ironclad ram CSS *Stonewall Jackson* past the out-gunned blockading vessels *Niagara* and *Sacramento* under Commander Thomas T. Craven. Craven is subsequently court-martialed for not engaging the enemy, but Secretary of the Navy Gideon Welles ignores the verdict.

MARCH 27 In Washington, D.C., Secretary of the Navy Gideon Welles orders the screw sloop *Wyoming*, the screw sloop *Wachusett*, and the steam sloop *Iroquois* to search for the elusive Confederate raider CSS *Shenandoah*.

MARCH 28 On the Blakely River, Alabama, the ironclad monitor *Milwaukee* under Commander J. H. Gillis strikes a Confederate mine and sinks.

MARCH 29 On the Blakely River, Alabama, the ironclad monitor *Osage* is sunk by a Confederate mine.

APRIL 1 On the Blakely River, Alabama, the tinclad *Rodolph* under Master N. M. Dyer sinks after striking a Confederate mine.

April 2 In Virginia, ships of the Confederate James River Squadron, including the ironclads *Virginia* (II), *Fredericksburg*, and *Richmond*, along with seven gunboats and smaller craft, are all scuttled to prevent their capture by Union forces advancing after the fall of Richmond.

April 3 In Virginia, Admiral Raphael Semmes collects sailors of the James River Squadron into a naval brigade that will serve under the command of General Robert E. Lee.

April 8 At Mobile, Alabama, a naval bombardment forces the Spanish Fort and Fort Alexis to capitulate, clearing the way for a general assault on Mobile itself.

April 13 In Mobile Bay, Alabama, the armed tug *Ida* under Ensign F. Ellms strikes a Confederate mine near Choctaw Pass and sinks.

April 14 In Mobile Bay, Alabama, the gunboat *Sciota* strikes a Confederate mine and sinks.

April 17–25 In Washington, D.C., suspects implicated in the assassination of President Abraham Lincoln are retained on the ironclads *Montauk* and *Saugus* anchored offshore.

April 22 At Mound City, Illinois, the side-paddle steamer *Black Hawk* catches fire and burns at its moorings.

April 24–25 On the Mississippi River, Lieutenant Charles W. Read leads the Confederate side-wheel ram *Webb* downstream in an attempt to reach the open sea. After passing New Orleans at night, he encounters the steam sloop *Richmond* and runs aground; Read and his crew are captured in a nearby swamp.

April 28 On the Mississippi River, boilers on the steamer *Sultana* explode, hurling crew and passengers alike into the frigid waters. Help arrives from Memphis, Tennessee, two hours later, but only 600 survivors are fished from the waters alive. Over 1,700 people have perished from burns and hypothermia, making *Sultana* the biggest maritime disaster in United States maritime history. In terms of carnage it even eclipses the more famous *Titanic* disaster, 47 years hence.

May 19 At Havana, Cuba, Confederate Commander Thomas J. Page turns the ironclad vessel CSS *Stonewall Jackson* over to Spanish authorities after learning that the Civil War has ended.

May 20 In Washington, D.C., Secretary of the Navy Gideon Welles orders every aspect of the U.S. Naval Academy to be examined by a board commissioned for that purpose.

June 3 In Washington, D.C., the Navy Department reconstitutes the Mediterranean Squadron for the first time in four years.

June 9 In Washington, D.C., Secretary of the Navy Gideon Welles orders a major peacetime consolidation, whereby the East and West Gulf squadrons are united into the Gulf Squadron, while the North and South Atlantic Blockading squadrons are joined into the Atlantic Squadron.

June 23 In Washington, D.C., President Andrew Johnson declares that the Union naval blockade of all Southern states has officially ended.

June 28 In the Bering Sea, the Confederate raider CSS *Shenandoah* under Lieutenant James I. Waddell fires the last shots of the Civil War and captures 10 Union whalers. Waddell has heard rumors that the war has ended from his captives, but remains unconvinced.

July 31 The East India Squadron is reconstituted under Commodore Henry H. Bell.

August 2 In the Pacific, Lieutenant James I. Waddell of the CSS *Shenandoah* is informed by the British vessel *Barracouta* that the Civil War has ended in a complete Union victory. Fearing that he and his crew will be charged with piracy, Waddell orders the vessel to England over the objection of many crew members.

August 12 Near Bahia, Brazil, Rear Admiral Sylvanus Gordon assumes command of the resurrected Brazilian Squadron.

August 28 At Newport, Rhode Island, Admiral David D. Porter becomes the sixth superintendent of the U.S. Naval Academy, and he orchestrates its transfer back to Annapolis, Maryland.

November 3 In Washington, D.C., Secretary of the Navy Gideon Welles instructs U.S. Navy vessels to render proper honors as they enter English ports. Such behavior is resumed only after the British government has retracted its recognition of belligerent status from the defunct Confederacy.

November 5 At Liverpool, England, Lieutenant James I. Waddell docks the CSS *Shenandoah*, after covering 58,000 miles and seizing 38 Union prizes. His is the final Confederate flag struck.

December 4 In Washington, D.C., Secretary of the Navy Gideon Welles reconstitutes the West India Squadron under the aegis of Commodore James S. Palmer.

December 27 In Washington, D.C., Secretary of the Navy Gideon Welles issues his final wartime report, cataloging U.S. Navy strength at no less than 700 warships of every description. This represents a far cry from the paltry 42 vessels in commission in 1861, and manpower has mushroomed from 7,600 to 51,000 men during this same period. Welles lauds the successful Union blockade, which played a major role in the economic collapse of the Confederacy.

1866

January 4 Off the Florida coast, the armed tug *Narcissus* under Acting Ensign Isaac S. Bradbury strikes the Egmont Reef and sinks, with the loss of 32 sailors.

May 6 At New York, the ironclad *Miantonomoh*, accompanied by the sidewheel vessels *Ashuelot* and *Augusta,* is the first vessel of its class to cross the Atlantic Ocean under its own power. Assistant Secretary of the Navy Gustavus Fox is on board to oversee a technical mission in Europe.

June 20 Near Yingkou, China, the screw sloop *Wachusett* under Lieutenant John W. Philip lands parties of sailors and marines ashore to seize a local bandit who had been attacking American interests. Apparently the local authorities had declined to do so.

June 21 In Washington, D.C., Congress establishes the Hydrographic Office to continue the oceanic mapping activities previously handled by the Hydrographical Office. This is the brainchild of the distinguished sailor-scientist Admiral Charles H. Davis.

JULY 25   In Washington, D.C., Congress creates the rank of full admiral and awards it to Vice Admiral David G. Farragut in honor of his exemplary service during the Civil War service. His stepbrother, Rear Admiral David D. Porter, also becomes the Navy's second vice admiral.

1867

JUNE 11   On Kanghoa Island, Korea, the latest attempt to establish diplomatic relations with the "Hermit Kingdom" ends in tragedy, when Navy Lieutenant Hugh W. McKee is fatally speared.

JUNE 13   On Formosa (Taiwan), screw sloops *Wyoming* and *Hertford* under Commander George C. Belknap conduct a punitive raid against natives who massacred the crew of the shipwrecked merchant bark *Rover*. A landing party scatters the defenders, although Lieutenant Alexander S. Mackenzie dies in combat.

JUNE 19   Near Madras, India, the screw sloop *Sacramento* under Captain Napoleon Collins wrecks on a bar, without the loss of life.

JULY 22   The ironclad *Miantonomoh*, the gunboat *Ashuelot*, and the side-wheel steamer *Augusta* return safely after covering 17,700 miles, while traveling to 10 nations in Europe without mishap.

AUGUST 28   On Midway Island, 1,300 miles northwest of Hawaii, the screw sloop *Lackawana* under Captain William Reynolds drops anchor and claims that atoll for the United States. The name derives from the fact that it lies midway between the ports of San Francisco, California, and Yokohoma, Japan.

The United States officially has little interest in it, but the China Mail Steamship Company seeks to utilize it as a coaling station.

DECEMBER 28   In Washington, D.C., Congress formally annexes the Central Pacific atoll of Midway Island as part of American territory.

1868

FEBRUARY 4   Near Hiogo, Japan, parties of sailors and marines are sent ashore by the screw sloop *Oneida* for the protection of American lives and property.

FEBRUARY 7–26   At Montevideo, Uruguay, Rear Admiral Charles H. Davis and the screw sloops *Guerriere* and *Quinnebaug*, along with three smaller vessels, drop anchor to protect American interests during an insurrection.

FEBRUARY 8   At Nagasaki, Japan, the screw sloop *Shenandoah* lands sailors and marines ashore to safeguard American lives and property.

FEBRUARY 11   The screw-powered cruiser *Wampanoag* is the Navy's fastest vessel and can hit sustained speeds of 17 knots; this record is not eclipsed until 1889.

JULY 9   Off Vancouver Island, British Columbia, the side-wheel gunboat *Suwanee* strikes a hidden rock in the Queen Victoria Sound and sinks; no lives are lost.

JULY 27   In Washington, D.C., Congress passes legislation allowing Japanese midshipmen to attend the U.S. Naval Academy at Annapolis, Maryland. A total of 16 Japanese nationals graduate between 1869 and 1906, and several of these become admirals in their own service.

AUGUST 13   Near Arica, Peru, the bark *Fredonia* and the gunboat *Wateree* are hit by a tidal wave during a hurricane. This carries both vessels 1,500 feet inland before sinking them; 27 sailors drown.

DECEMBER 8   At Annapolis, Maryland, Jiunzo Matsumura becomes the first Japanese national admitted to the U.S. Naval Academy. He graduates in 1873, and eventually rises to vice admiral in the Imperial Japanese Navy.

1869

APRIL 26   In Washington, D.C., Congress authorizes the Good Conduct Medal, a Maltese Cross made from nickel, for distribution to enlisted naval personnel.

JUNE 9   In Washington, D.C., Secretary of the Navy Adolf E. Borie authorizes the Navy's first torpedo station on Goat Island off Newport, Rhode Island.

JUNE 18   The Navy Department, still commanding a force transitioning from sail power to steam, orders ships to rely upon wind power unless circumstances are "most urgent."

JUNE 28   In Washington, D.C., William M. Wood is appointed the first Surgeon General of the Navy.

SEPTEMBER 21   Offshore at Yokohama, Japan, a typhoon cripples the sailing vessel *Idaho*; it is reduced to a floating hulk that is decommissioned and sold in 1874.

DECEMBER 1   At Annapolis, Maryland, distinguished Civil War veteran Commodore John L. Worden replaces Vice Admiral David D. Porter as seventh superintendent of the U.S. Naval Academy.

1870

JANUARY 22   Off the Panama coast, the gunboat *Nipsic* under Commander Thomas O. Selfridge, Jr., begins surveying the Isthmus of Darien for constructing a canal. He recommends four possible routes, and releases his official report in 1874.

JANUARY 24   Near Yokohama, Japan, the screw sloop *Oneida* sinks after colliding with the British vessel *City of Bombay*, losing 117 crewmen and 3 senior officers. However, the British vessel refuses to render assistance.

JUNE 17   On the Teacapan River, Mexico, several boat-loads of sailors from the screw sloop *Mohican* row upstream in search of pirates, then burn their vessel, a former British gunboat.

August 11–13 In Egypt, the gunboat *Palos* becomes the first American warship to pass through the Suez Canal.

August 14 Admiral David G. Farragut dies in Portsmouth, New Hampshire, aged sixty-nine years. He was one of history's outstanding naval commanders and battle captains.

October 29 Near Ocean Island, mid-Pacific, the side-wheel steamer *Saginaw* under Commander Montgomery Siccard strikes a reef. Consequently, a boatload of five volunteers under Lieutenant John G. Talbot sets off for Hawaii to obtain help—a distance of 1,500 miles.

December 20 At Hawaii, a boatload of five volunteers under Lieutenant John G. Talbot reaches landfall after sailing 31 days and covering 1,500 miles. Tragically, their vessel capsizes in heavy surf coming ashore and only Coxswain William Halford survives. His shipmates on Ocean Island are consequently rescued, and Halford receives a Congressional Medal of Honor.

1871

March 3 In Washington, D.C., Congress establishes the Pay Corps (later Supply Corps).

May 30 Near Chelmpo (Inchon), Korea, Rear Admiral John Rodgers, the screw frigate *Colorado*, and several smaller vessels ascend the Han River. He is carrying Frederick Low, U.S. Minister to China, to establish relations with the "Hermit Kingdom." However, several land forts fire upon the intruders, to which Rodgers promptly responds in kind; two sailors are wounded.

June 10–11 On the Han River, Korea, American warships *Monocacy* and *Palos* land 700 sailors and marines under Commander L. A. Kimberly ashore; they storm and destroy several Korean forts which had fired on the American squadron a few days previous. The defenders resist to the last man, and 243 are ultimately killed. American losses are 3 dead and 7 wounded—fifteen Congressional Medals of Honor are awarded to sailors and marines in this action.

June 29 At New York, Captain Charles F. Hall sails with the screw tug *Polaris* on an expedition to the Arctic.

1872

September 21 At Annapolis, Maryland, James Henry Conyers is the first African American admitted to the U.S. Naval Academy as a cadet. However, he resigns because of deficiencies in mathematics and French; Annapolis does not graduate a black candidate until 1949.

1873

May 7–12 In Panama, the screw sloop *Tuscarora* lands 200 sailors and marines ashore to protect American lives and property during an insurrection.

September 23 In Panama, continuing violence prompts the screw steamer *Pensacola* and the screw sloop *Benicia* to land 190 men ashore protect the railroad there.

October 9 At Annapolis, Maryland, 15 naval officers, seeking an outlet for dissident opinions, form a professional society that eventually emerges as the United State Naval Institute. They also begin publishing their *Proceedings* to sound opinions from members.

October 31 In the Caribbean, the steamer *Virginius* is captured by the Spanish warship *Tornado* as it conveys weapons for insurrectionists in Cuba. Spanish authorities execute 30 members, including Captain Joseph Fry, a U.S. Naval Academy graduate. Their deaths provoke indignation and cries for war.

1874

February 12 At Honolulu, Hawaii, the sloop *Portsmouth,* under Commander Joseph S. Skerret, and the screw sloop *Tuscarora,* under Commander George E. Belknap, put 150 sailors and marines ashore to protect Americans during unrest accompanying the coronation of King Kalakaua.

July 31 At Boston, Massachusetts, the screw steamer *Intrepid* is commissioned as the Navy's first experimental torpedo ram; however, its service life is short and unsuccessful.

1875

January 5 At Norfolk, Virginia, Commander E. R. Lull conducts the latest expedition to Panama to find a suitable route to construct a canal.

June 18 Near Vancouver, British Columbia, the side-wheel steam sloop *Saranac* under Captain Walter W. Queen strikes a rock in the Seymour Narrows and sinks, without loss of life.

1877

November 24 Offshore at Nags Head, North Carolina, the steam sloop *Huron* under Commander George P. Ryan shipwrecks in a storm, with a loss of 98 sailors out of 132.

1878

January 17 Samoa concludes a treaty with the United States, whereby the harbor of Pago Pago serves as a Pacific coaling station for the U.S. Navy.

June 18 In Washington, D.C., Congress establishes the United States Life-Saving Service, the first such organization in the world, as part of the Treasury Department. In 1915 it is amalgamated with the Revenue Cutter Service to become the U.S. Coast Guard.

December 7 From Hampton Roads, Virginia, Commodore Robert W. Shufeldt sails the screw sloop *Ticonderoga* on a global voyage lasting two years. This is also the first steam-powered American vessel to perform such a mission.

1879

August 7–March 23, 1882 At San Francisco, California, Lieutenant George W. DeLong sails the converted steam bark *Jeanette* with 28 men on an ill-fated attempt to explore waters of the North Pole via the Bering Strait. This endeavor is underwritten by *New York Herald* publisher James G. Bennett, who had purchased and outfitted the *Jeanette* for that purpose.

1880

November 9 At Hampton Roads, Virginia, the screw sloop *Ticonderoga* under Commander Robert W. Shufeldt returns, concluding a two-year sojourn covering 36,000 miles and calling on over 40 ports worldwide.

1881

In New Jersey, Irish naval engineer John Holland invents the first practical submarine for naval warfare, drawing inspiration from Jules Verne's novel *Twenty Thousand Leagues under the Sea*. He hopes his invention will be used against the Royal Navy, but the U.S. Navy reacts tepidly to it.

June 28 In Washington, D.C., Secretary of the Navy William H. Hunt establishes a Naval Advisory Board under Admiral John Rodgers to combat the service's dilapidated condition. The board recommends an immediate construction program to acquire modern steel-hulled vessels.

September 12 In the Arctic, the yacht *Jeanette* under Lieutenant George W. DeLong is abandoned after being crushed by the ice. The crew marches in freezing weather to the edge of the Arctic ice pack, and DeLong orders three boats they hauled overland to try to reach the mainland.

NOVEMBER 3 At Louisville, Kentucky, Captain William Devan commands the first inland station of the U.S. Life Saving Service. He will assist shipwrecked passengers and sailors along the Ohio River, and makes his first rescue four days later.

NOVEMBER 30 In St. Lawrence Bay, Canada, the steamer *Rodgers*, scouting for the ill-fated *Jeanette* expedition, catches fire and sinks, with the loss of one life.

1882

MARCH 23 In Washington, D.C., the Office of Naval Intelligence (ONI) is founded by the Secretary of the Navy.

On the Lena Delta, Siberia, a rescue party under Chief Engineer George W. Melville of the *Jeanette* finds the frozen remains of Lieutenant George W. DeLong and 14 companions. Fortunately, the expedition's records are recovered intact.

MAY 16 In Washington, D.C., Samuel Powhatan Carter is elevated to rear admiral in the U.S. Navy. During the Civil War, Carter also served as a major general in the Union Army, thus he becomes the only senior military officer to have attained the ranks of both general and admiral.

MAY 19–22 In Korea, Commodore Robert W. Shufeldt of the screw sloop *Swatara* arrives and commences diplomatic negotiations for a commercial treaty with that reclusive kingdom.

JULY 14 At Alexandria, Egypt, the gunboat *Nipsic* and the screw sloop *Lancaster* put sailors and marines ashore to guard the American consul during a brief, nationalist rebellion against Great Britain.

NOVEMBER 15 In London, England, Lieutenant French Ensor Chadwick becomes the navy's first naval attaché. His mission is to observe and report European navies and the most recent technological developments.

1883

FEBRUARY 18 Near the mouth of the Swatow River, China, the gunboat *Ashuelot* under Commander Horace E. Mullan strikes a rock and sinks, with a loss of 11 lives.

MARCH 3 In Washington, D.C., Secretary of the Navy William E. Chandler convinces Congress to fund construction of three protected (steel) cruisers, *Atlanta*, *Boston*, and *Chicago*, and a dispatch vessel, the *Dolphin*. These are the first modern vessels acquired since the Civil War, and herald the age of the new "Steel Navy."

JUNE 7–AUGUST 21 In New York, the screw steamer *Trenton* is the first naval vessel fitted with electrical lighting while berthed. The Edison Lighting Company installs 238 lamps inside and outside the ship at a cost of $5,500.

DECEMBER 4 In Washington, D.C., President Chester A. Arthur vows to Congress that the United States will not become embroiled in a naval arms race such as the one presently unfolding in Europe between the empires of Germany and Great Britain.

1884

APRIL 25–MAY 10 At New York, Commander Winfield Scott Schley leads the steamers *Alert*, *Bear*, and *Thetis* to Lady Franklin Bay for possible survivors from Lieutenant Adolphus W. Greely's expedition. These have been missing since 1881.

JUNE 22 On Cape Sabine, Arctic Circle, Commander Winfield S. Schley's relief expedition reaches Lieutenant Adolphus W. Greely's scientific observatory on Grinnell Land (Ellesmere Island). Only 6 of its 24 members have survived, on a diet of moss, lichen, and seal skin.

JULY 7 In Washington, D.C., Congress appoints Professor James R. Soley to reorganize the Office of Naval Records. Soley had previously administered the Navy Library since 1882.

OCTOBER 6 At Newport, Rhode Island, the U.S. Naval War College is founded under the aegis of Commodore Stephen B. Luce, who also serves as its first president. This is the world's first graduate-level military establishment, and Commander Alfred Thayer Mahan, a noted naval theorist, is appointed one of the earliest instructors.

Mahan, Alfred Thayer (1840–1914)

Alfred Thayer Mahan was born in West Point, New York, on September 27, 1840, and graduated from the U.S. Naval Academy in 1859. When the Civil War broke out in 1861, he performed blockading duty with Admiral John A. D. Dahlgren, and was retained in the peacetime establishment after 1865. Mahan rose to captain in 1885, enjoying a reputation for sterling scholarship. The following year he delivered a series of lectures at the U.S. Naval War College at Newport, Rhode Island. These activities spurred him to research the nuances of naval power, and in 1890 he published his famous treatise, *The Influence of Sea Power upon History, 1660–1783*. Mahan held that great nations and empires require adequate naval forces to ensure their safety and continuing viability. It cemented his reputation as America's leading naval theorist, and, being widely endorsed by politicians such as Theodore Roosevelt, provided political impetus for continuing naval rearmament.

In 1892 Mahan followed up his initial success by writing *The Influence of Sea Power upon the French Revolution and Empire*, another classic examination of naval strategy. That year he served as president of the War College, and in 1893 he captained the cruiser USS *Chicago* on a goodwill tour of Europe. He was feted by the British government and received honorary degrees from both Cambridge and Oxford, and afterwards he served on the U.S. delegation to the peace conference at The Hague in 1899. Mahan died in Washington, D.C., on December 1, 1914, among the most influential naval theorists in history.

1885

MARCH 31   At Colon, Panama (Colombia), a landing detachment of sailors and marines goes ashore from the screw sloop *Galena* to secure the western end of the rail line from civil unrest.

SEPTEMBER 3   In Newport, Rhode Island, the Naval War College conducts its first formal classes. The first graduating class consists of eight officers.

1886

AUGUST 3   In Washington, D.C., Secretary of the Navy William C. Whitney argues for Congress to fund two ironclads, an armored cruiser, and a motor torpedo boat as part of his ongoing naval modernization program. Whitney also reorients the service toward modernity by embracing the latest technology. The United States will boast the world's third-largest navy by the turn of the century.

AUGUST 6   In Washington, D.C., Congress authorizes funding for the 6,000 ton armored cruiser *Maine* and the battleship *Texas*, with the former mounting 10-inch guns, and the latter 12-inch guns, in two main turrets. Acquisition of these vessels also marks the introduction of modern battleships into American service.

1887

MARCH 3   In Washington, D.C., the trend toward naval expansion and modernization continues as Congress authorizes construction of the protected cruisers *Philadelphia* and *San Francisco*, along with two gunboats.

1888

MAY 17   Massachusetts is the first state to establish a naval militia, which ultimately spurs creation of a new Naval Reserve.

JUNE 19   At Chemulpo, Korea, a 25-man landing party from the screw steamer *Essex* marches into the capital of Seoul for the protection of American citizens living there. In 1950 this same port gains lasting fame, after it is renamed Inchon.

SEPTEMBER 7   In Washington, D.C., naval modernization continues as Congress funds construction of the steel cruiser *New York* and six smaller vessels.

DECEMBER   In Samoa, German naval forces suppressing an uprising briefly seize a small American ship flying the national flag. The U.S. vice consul in Apia wires the matter to Washington, D.C., and requests the presence of a naval squadron to protect American interests.

December 20 At Port-au-Prince, Haiti, the warships *Galena* and *Yantic* drop anchor, inducing authorities there to free a wrongfully detained American steamer.

1889

January 12 Admiral Lewis A. Kimberly is dispatched to Samoa with the warships *Trenton*, *Nipsic*, and *Vandalia*. This action comes in response to recent German activity there.

March 15–16 At Apia, Samoa, a hurricane scatters the one British, three American, and three German warships anchored there in a test of wills. The gunboat *Nipsic* is beached while the screw steamer *Trenton* and screw sloop *Vandalia* are sunk, with a loss of 49 lives. Three German vessels are likewise destroyed.

1890

January 7 The cruiser *Baltimore* becomes the first American naval vessel rigged specifically as a mine layer.

January 23 At Bristol, Rhode Island, the *Cushing* is launched, the first torpedo boat in American naval history. It is subsequently assigned to the so-called Squadron of Evolution for testing and evaluation purposes.

April 23 In Narragansett Bay, Rhode Island, the *Cushing* is commissioned as the navy's first torpedo boat. Only 104 feet in length, it is manned by 22 crew members and boasts a top speed of 23 knots.

May At Newport, Rhode Island, Captain Alfred Thayer Mahan publishes his seminal work, *The Influence of Sea Power Upon History, 1660–1783*. Once translated into several languages, it becomes the de facto official policy for naval establishments around the world. Moreover, it influences political and military thinkers in the United States to reevaluate their traditional isolationism in this increasingly imperial age.

June 30 In Washington, D.C., Secretary of the Navy Benjamin F. Tracy's first annual report calls for the construction of no less than 20 armored battleships to defend the nation's home waters. Congress, however, votes to pay for only three: *Indiana*, *Massachusetts*, and *Oregon*. These 19,000-ton vessels are a third larger than existing designs, and mount their main armament in centerline turrets.

August 8 The cruiser *Baltimore* carries the body of Swedish naval engineer John Ericsson back to his homeland for burial. During the Civil War he designed the famous ironclad *Monitor*.

November 29 Initiating a long and fierce sports rivalry, the U.S. Naval Academy football team ventures to the U.S. Military Academy, West Point, for the first time. Navy wins the first-ever interservice academy game, 24–0.

1891

March 3 In Washington, D.C., James Russell Soley, a former Naval Academy professor, is tapped to fill the newly resurrected office of assistant secretary of the Navy.

July 4 Near Irquique, Chile, the *Charleston* seizes the Chilean rebel vessel *Itata* after allegations that it violated American neutrality by purchasing arms for rebels at San Diego, California.

October 16 In Valparaiso, Chile, two American sailors from the *Baltimore* under Captain William S. Schley are killed by a mob at the True Blue Saloon, and 16 others are injured. The locals are apparently angered by the recent seizure of a boat carrying arms for local rebels.

1892

January 21–27 In Washington, D.C., President Benjamin Harrison issues an ultimatum to the government of Chile, demanding an apology for insulting remarks made by its foreign minister. Upon further reflection, Chile apologizes and pays an indemnity of $75,000 to the families of two sailors killed.

July 19 In Washington, D.C., Congress authorizes construction of a sixth steel battleship, the *Iowa*.

1893

January 16 Near Honolulu, the cruiser *Boston* lands 150 sailors and marines ashore during the revolt of American settlers against Queen Liliukalani, who issued a new constitution limiting their influence.

August 1 The U.S. Navy acquires its first modern warship, the 8,150-ton cruiser *New York*. This vessel is both heavily armed and armored, with a top speed of 21 knots.

1894

January 29 In Rio de Janeiro, Rear Admiral A. E. K. Benham breaks a blockade established by Brazilian monarchist rebels attempting to subvert the republic. In time he is joined by several British vessels.

February 2 Off the coast of Central America, the venerable screw sloop *Kearsarge* strikes the Roncador reef off and sinks. Its name is subsequently transferred to a new battleship under construction; this is the only vessel of its class not christened after a state.

July 6 Near Bluefields, Nicaragua, the cruiser *Columbia* sends sailors and marines ashore to protect American lives and property.

SEPTEMBER 17 In Korea, Philo McGiffen, who graduated from Annapolis in 1882 and served with the Chinese, becomes the first American to command a battleship when he takes charge of the *Chen Yuen* during the Battle of Yalu against Japan.

1895

MARCH 2 In Washington, D.C., Congress continues its modernizing trend by funding construction of the new battleships *Kearsarge* and *Kentucky*.

MARCH 13 In New York, the John P. Holland Company contracts with the Navy Department to construct its first submarine.

AUGUST 15 The *Texas* becomes the first armored battleship to serve in the Navy. However, because its armament is designed off-center, the ship is classified as a second-class warship once more modern designs, enjoying centerline battery turrets, arrive.

SEPTEMBER 17 The *Maine*, an armored cruiser reclassified as a second-class battleship, is commissioned into service. It serves for only three years before being destroyed by an accidental explosion—which helps brings on a war.

NOVEMBER 20 The *Indiana*, the first modern American battleship fitted with a centerline turret armament, is commissioned. The *Massachusetts* and *Oregon* also constitute this class of vessel.

1896

MAY 2–4 At Cortino, Nicaragua, the gunboat *Alert* sends sailors and marines ashore to safeguard American interests and property.

JUNE 10 In Washington, D.C., an experimental ship-model testing tank is authorized by Congress to facilitate the construction of modern warships. It is eventually built at the Washington Navy Yard.

JUNE 16 The newly commissioned battleship *Iowa* resides as the only vessel of its class.

1898

JANUARY 1 Off the Dry Tortugas, Florida, Admiral Montgomery Sicard positions his North Atlantic Squadron in anticipation of war with Spain.

JANUARY 24–25 At Havana Harbor, Cuba, the battleship *Maine* under Captain Charles D. Sigsbee drops anchor. It is ostensibly on a goodwill call, but actually deploys here to protect American lives and property at a time of unrest.

FEBRUARY 7   Near San Juan del Sur, Nicaragua, the gunboat Alert under Commander Eugene H. C. Leutze dispatches sailors and marines ashore to protect the U.S. Consulate during a period of unrest.

FEBRUARY 15   In Havana harbor, Cuba, the 6,700-ton battleship *Maine* under Captain Charles D. Sigsbee explodes and sinks while anchored, with the loss of 260 sailors out of a total complement of 358, apparently from an internal explosion. However, the American press treats this matter as an act of sabotage, and "Remember the Maine!" becomes a stirring battle cry for intervention in Cuba.

FEBRUARY 23   In Washington, D.C., the Navy Department orders additional warships concentrated at Key West, Florida, in anticipation of hostilities with Spain.

FEBRUARY 25   In Washington, D.C., Assistant Secretary of the Navy Theodore Roosevelt secretly cables Commodore George Dewey at Hong Kong that, if war with Spain breaks out, he is to attack the Pacific Squadron of Admiral Patricio Montojo in the Philippines.

MARCH 6   At Puget Sound, Washington, the 10,200-ton battleship *Oregon* sails for Key West, Florida, under Captain Charles E. Clark. The fact that it takes 67 days and 14,760 miles to round Cape Horn and deploy underscores the need for a Central American canal.

MARCH 8   In Washington, D.C., Congress appropriates $50 million to be spent by presidential discretion for national defense.

MARCH 17   At the Crescent Shipyard, New Jersey, the *Holland* becomes the Navy's first commissioned submarine, and is launched under Lieutenant H. H. Caldwell.

MARCH 18   In the Atlantic, Acting Commodore Winfield S. Schley accepts command of the "Flying Squadron," consisting of battleships *Texas* and *Massachusetts*, and cruisers *Brooklyn*, *Columbia*, and *Minneapolis*. Schley's mission is to guard the Eastern Seaboard against possible attack by Spain.

MARCH 19   At San Francisco, California, the battleship *Oregon* under Captain Charles B. Clark departs for Florida. The ensuing 67-day voyage covers 14,700 miles at an average speed of 12 knots, the first time a warship of this size has accomplished such a feat.

MARCH 24   In the Atlantic, Captain William T. Sampson replaces Rear

The decorated wreck of the USS Maine in Havana Harbor, Cuba, photographed on May 30, 1902. The Maine was sunk on February 15, 1898, increasing hostilities between the United States and Spain that eventually led to war later that year. (Library of Congress)

Admiral Montgomery B. Sicard as commander of the North Atlantic Squadron; his own promotion to admiral is forthcoming.

MARCH 28 In Washington, D.C., the Navy Department forwards its official report on the loss of the battleship *Maine* to Congress. It chooses to ignore the evidence, and intimates that the vessel was sunk by an underwater explosion, possibly from a mine. It has since been deduced that a fire in a coal bunker ignited a nearby ammunition magazine, destroying the vessel.

APRIL 19 In Washington, D.C., Congress authorizes President William McKinley to expel Spanish forces from Cuba. Moreover, the Teller Amendment attached to the War Resolution prevents the Americans from annexing the island.

APRIL 22 In Florida, Rear Admiral William T. Sampson departs from Key West to impose a naval blockade around the island of Cuba, previously declared by President William McKinley.

In the Gulf of Mexico, the gunboat *Nashville* under Commander Washburn Maynard draws the first blood by capturing the Spanish steamer *Buenaventura*.

APRIL 23 The ships of Rear Admiral William T. Sampson's North Atlantic Squadron begin closing the ports of Havana, Mariel, Matanzas, Cardenas, and Cienfuegos, Cuba.

APRIL 25 In Washington, D.C., Congress votes to declare war on Spain, dating it retroactively to April 21. Secretary of the Navy John D. Long immediately orders Commodore George Dewey's squadron to attack the Spanish fleet in the Philippines.

APRIL 27 At Hong Kong, China, Commodore George Dewey sorties the modern steel cruisers *Olympia*, *Boston*, *Baltimore*, and *Raleigh*, as well as the gunboats *Petrel* and *Concord*, and steers directly toward Manila Bay in the Philippines. He intends to seek out and destroy Admiral Patricio Montojo's Pacific Squadron.

Near Matanzas, northwestern Cuba, Rear Admiral William T. Sampson's squadron silences Spanish batteries with fire from the cruisers *New York* and *Cincinnati*, assisted by the monitor *Puritan*.

APRIL 28 At San Vincente, Cape Verde Islands, Admiral Pascual Cervera's Atlantic Fleet sails for Cuba with the antiquated cruisers *Infanta Maria Theresa*, *Vizcaya*, *Almirante Oquendo*, and *Cristobal Colon*, plus destroyers *Furor*, *Pluton*, and *Terror*. However, its exact whereabouts is a mystery to the American fleet, prompting fears of an attack on the United States coastline.

APRIL 29 At Cienfuegos, Cuba, the cruiser *Marblehead* and armed yacht *Eagle* briefly exchange fire with the Spanish gunboats *Galacia* and *Vasco Nunez de Balboa*; little damage is inflicted.

APRIL 30 At Rio de Janeiro, Brazil, the battleship *Oregon* and the gunboat *Marietta*, having rounded Cape Horn, arrive to take on coal. They are also on the lookout for the Spanish destroyer *Temerario*, which is reportedly nearby.

Near Luzon, the Philippines, the Asiatic Squadron of Commodore George Dewey arrives and looks for the Spanish navy, which has relocated inside Manila Bay.

MAY 1 In the Atlantic, Rear Admiral William T. Sampson finally receives intelligence that Rear Admiral Pascual Cervera's Spanish fleet, consisting of four cruisers and three destroyers, has departed Cape Verde. Sampson is convinced they are headed for the Caribbean and not the U.S. coast.

In the Philippines, the Battle of Manila Bay ensues as Commodore Admiral George Dewey's squadron attacks Admiral Patricio Montojo's vessels, which are anchored in line abreast formation. After barking, "You may fire when ready, Gridley," *Olympia* joins cruisers *Boston*, *Baltimore*, *Raleigh*, *Concord*, and gunboat *Petrel* in a shooting spree against the obsolete Spanish vessels. Montojo loses all seven vessels and 371 killed and wounded; Dewey sustains 9 wounded. The lopsided nature of this decisive victory renders the admiral an immediate national hero.

MAY 2–3 At Cavite, Philippines, the gunboat *Petrel* dispatches a landing party that captures the Spanish naval arsenal. Other troops disembark from the cruisers *Baltimore* and *Raleigh* and capture Corregidor Island in Manila Bay.

MAY 4 In Washington, D.C., Congress funds 3 additional battleships, 16 torpedo boat destroyers, 12 torpedo boats, and 1 gunboat. This constitutes the largest wartime naval construction program since the Civil War.

MAY 8 On Cardenas Bay, northwestern Cuba, heavy fire from Spanish gunboats *Ligera*, *Alerta*, and *Antonio Lopez* drive off the torpedo boat *Winslow*.

MAY 11 The Torpedo boat *Winslow* reenters Cardenas Bay, Cuba, this time supported by the cruiser *Machias* and gunboats *Hudson* and *Wilmington*. The vessels are ambushed by a masked Spanish battery, which kills five and wounds five on the *Winslow* in an hour-long duel. Ensign Worth Bagley become the navy's first and only officer fatality in this war. However, Gunner's Mate George F. Brady and Chief Machinist's Mate Thomas C. Cooney receive Congressional Medals of Honor for bravery under fire. The Spanish suffer 2 dead and 12 wounded while the gunboats *Ligera* and *Antonio Lopez* receive heavy damage.

Offshore at Cienfuegos, Cuba, the cruiser *Marblehead* and the gunboat

---

Dewey, George (1837–1917)

George Dewey was born at Montpelier, Vermont, on December 26, 1837, and he graduated from the U.S. Naval Academy in 1858. During the Civil War he accompanied the squadron of Captain David G. Farragut. He rendered useful service at the capture of New Orleans and during operations along the Mississippi River. Afterwards Dewey successively rose to commander in 1872, captain in 1884, and commodore by 1896. The Navy at this time was undergoing a period of transition from sail to steam, and Dewey immersed himself in the nuances of modern propulsion and ordnance. In 1897 he requested sea duty, and Assistant Secretary of the Navy Theodore Roosevelt appointed him commander of the Asiatic Squadron, based at Hong Kong. No sooner had the Spanish-American War erupted in 1898 than Roosevelt ordered him to destroy all Spanish naval forces in the Philippines.

On May 1, 1898, Dewey led four modern cruisers and two gunboats into Manila Bay against an older but similarly sized Spanish force. The Americans completely outgunned their adversaries, sinking all the Spanish ships, and victory here rendered him a national hero. Dewey was consequently promoted to rear admiral, and the Democratic Party openly courted him to run as their presidential candidate. In 1899 he received the special rank admiral of the navy, the highest grade ever held by an American naval officer, which required him to remain on active duty for life. Dewey published his memoirs in 1913; he died in Washington, D. C., on January 26, 1917, an architect of American global naval power.

Nashville launch several boatloads of sailors to sever communication cables between Havana and Madrid, but they are driven off by heavy artillery fire. Still, the Revenue Cutter *Windom* races close to shore and brings down the local lighthouse with its four-inch gun. Four Americans die and five are wounded; 54 Congressional Medals of Honor are awarded.

In Washington, D.C., Assistant Secretary of the Navy Theodore Roosevelt resigns from office to join a New York volunteer cavalry unit.

MAY 12   Near San Juan, Puerto Rico, Admiral William T. Sampson's squadron bombards Spanish positions with the battleships *Indiana* and *Iowa,* cruisers *Detroit* and *New York*, and several monitors and gunboats. Once Sampson is apprized that the main Spanish squadron is not anchored there, he sails for Key West, Florida, to refit.

MAY 13   East of San Juan de Puerto Rico in the Caribbean, Captain C. F. Goodrich orders the armed auxiliary *Saint Louis* to dredge the seabed and cut the underwater cable to St. Thomas.

In Manila Bay, Philippines, Admiral George Dewey cables the Navy Department and requests 5,000 Army troops to capture and occupy the city.

MAY 14   Near Havana, Cuba, the gunboats *Vicksburg* and *Annapolis* perceive the small Spanish vessels *Conde de Venadito* and *Nueva España* attempting to run their blockade. They are reinforced by the auxiliaries *Mayflower, Wasp, Tecumseh,* and *Osceola,* and the Spanish make for the safety of the harbor.

Admiral Pascual Cervera's Spanish squadron puts briefly into Willemsted, Curacao, to recoal. He is last seen steering for Puerto Rico before altering his course to the northwest and Santiago, Cuba.

MAY 16   Near Santiago, Cuba, cruisers *Saint Louis* and *Wompatuck* find and cut the telegraphic cable leading to Jamaica, although fire from shore batteries gradually drives them back to deep water.

MAY 17   From Key West, Florida, Admiral William T. Sampson's flagship *New York* departs and begins searching for the Spanish fleet. At one point he accosts the vessel *Carlos F. Rosas* off Havana, Cuba, where his fleet gradually joins him over the next two days.

In Santiago Bay, Cuba, the cruisers *Saint Louis* and *Wompatuck* reenter and cut another underwater telegraph cables before being driven off by land batteries.

MAY 18   Back at Key West, Florida, Commodore William T. Sampson learns that the Spanish fleet under Rear Admiral Pascual Cervera had coaled at Curacao, Netherlands West Indies, and is headed in the direction of Cuba.

MAY 19   At Santiago Harbor, Cuba, Spanish Admiral Pascual Cervera's fleet of four cruisers and three destroyers arrives and joins the 19,000 man garrison of General Arsenio Linares. The Americans, meanwhile, remain ignorant of Cervera's whereabouts, and suspect he is going to bombard the United States coastline. As a precaution Commodore Winfield S. Schley takes his "Flying Squadron" and blockades the port at Cienfuegos, Cuba.

MAY 20   In the Caribbean, the *Wompatuck* cuts the underwater cable connecting Guantanamo, Cuba, to Cape Mole, Haiti.

MAY 21   At Key West, Florida, Rear Admiral William T. Sampson again departs to patrol the Nicholas Channel along the northern coast of Cuba to intercept the Spanish fleet if it makes for Havana.

Near Cavite, Manila Bay, the boiler room on the *Concord* catches fire and Seamen William A. Krause and John Walter receive Congressional Medals of Honor for extinguishing the flames.

MAY 24 At Jupiter Inlet, Florida, the battleship *Oregon*, having sailed 14,000 miles from Puget Sound, Washington, concludes its 67-day transit in time to rendezvous with Admiral Winfield S. Schley's squadron. Their lengthy sojourn highlights the dire need for a Panama Canal to obtain a shorter passage between the Atlantic and Pacific oceans.

From Cienfuegos, Cuba, Admiral William T. Sampson sails his squadron toward Santiago, then, running short of coal, he orders it back to Key West, Florida.

MAY 26 Outside Santiago Harbor, Cuba, Commodore Winfield S. Schley shepherds the battleships *Massachusetts* and *Texas,* cruisers *Brooklyn* and *Marblehead,* and three armed auxiliaries to within 20 miles of harbor. Schley is subsequently reinforced by the cruiser *Minneapolis* and two more armed auxiliaries, but is unaware that the Spanish fleet is already anchored nearby.

MAY 27 Near Florida, Rear Admiral William T. Sampson is informed by the auxiliary vessel *Harvard* that he is to immediately proceed to Santiago, Cuba, and possibly intercept the main Spanish squadron. He accordingly turns his bows away from Key West and sails east.

MAY 28 In Santiago harbor, Cuba, the cruiser *Marblehead* under Commander Bowman H. McCalla scouts ahead of Commodore Winfield S. Schley's squadron, and perceives the Spanish squadron of Admiral Pascual Cervera anchored there.

At Cardenas, Cuba, cannon fire from the armed tugs *Uncas* and *Leyden* flatten a Spanish blockhouse.

MAY 29 Outside Santiago, Cuba, Commodore Winfield S. Schley, having inadvertently discovered the fleet of Admiral Pascual Cervera anchored in the harbor, assumes blockading positions. Meanwhile, Rear Admiral William T. Sampson's squadron also hastens to the spot from Key West, Florida.

MAY 31 Outside Santiago, Cuba, Admiral Winfield S. Schley tests the defenses of the harbor by having battleships *Massachusetts* and *Iowa* exchange fire with shore batteries. Little damage results, and the Americans withdraw leisurely, while the Spanish stretch a boom across the harbor entrance.

JUNE 1 Admiral William T. Sampson finally arrives at Santiago, Cuba, and immediately confronts a strategic impasse. While the U.S. fleet is stronger, it cannot enter the narrow channels of Santiago, which are covered by powerful artillery batteries and are presumably mined. However, Admiral Pascual Cervera does not dare leave the safe confines of the harbor.

JUNE 3 In Santiago Harbor, Cuba, Lieutenant Richmond P. Hobson attempts to scuttle the collier *Merrimac* to trap the Spanish fleet there. However, his vessel is sunk by Spanish artillery at the edge of the channel. Hobson and seven volunteers are captured, but all receive the Congressional Medal of Honor; Hobson, as an officer, is ineligible for the award at this time, but will be awarded one in 1933 through a special act of Congress.

In Washington, D.C., Congress authorizes the Dewey Medal to all officers and men present at Battle of Manila Bay. This is also the first campaign medal issued.

June 6 At Santiago, Cuba, Admiral William T. Sampson's squadron enters Santiago Harbor and begins shelling the defenders. They withdraw after inflicting 3 Spanish dead and 14 injured ashore, and a further 5 killed and 14 wounded on the antiquated cruiser *Reina Mercedes*.

June 7 Outside Caimanera, Cuba, Commander Bowman H. McCalla directs the cruiser *Marblehead* to bombard and destroy a Spanish battery at Playa del Este. The cruiser *St. Louis* subsequently runs the harbor boom, and anchors off Fisherman's Point to receive two Cuban guerrillas carrying intelligence about Spanish defenses.

June 10 In the Caribbean, the gunboat *St. Louis* intercepts the British collier *Twickenham* carrying 3,000 tons of coal for the Spanish fleet.

June 13 Near Cienfuegos, Cuba, the Spanish torpedo boat *Galicia* mistakenly approaches the converted cruiser *Yankee* and is driven off by cannon fire.

June 14 Off the coast of Cuba, the American squadron is strengthened by the arrival of the 930-ton cruiser *Vesuvius*. This experimental vessel is armed with high explosive gun-cotton ordnance and is nicknamed the "dynamite cruiser."

At Tampa, Florida, the 17,000-man V Corps of Major General William T. Shafter departs on transports under a naval escort and heads for Santiago, Cuba.

June 15 In Guantanamo Bay, Cuba, the cruiser *Marblehead* under Commander Bowman H. McCalla, the auxiliary cruiser *Suwanee,* and the battleship *Texas* destroy a Spanish fort at Cayo Toro. This vital port subsequently functions as the principle coaling station for the main fleet outside Santiago, and also a major entrepot for the invasion of Puerto Rico.

June 17 In the Philippines, German warships under Admiral Otto Von Diedrichs disregard blockade rules established by Commodore George Dewey and sails into Manila Harbor. The Germans are seeking to lease bases in the region.

June 20 Outside Santiago, Cuba, Major General William R. Shafter confers with Admiral William T. Sampson as to strategy for taking Santiago, Cuba.

June 21 Offshore at Guam, a task force under Captain Henry Glass of the cruiser *Charleston* hails the Spanish garrison with a gunshot, then sends a messenger ashore to find out why they fail to retaliate. The Spanish commander, who has not been informed as to the state of war, explains his complete lack of ammunition.

June 22 Offshore at San Juan, Puerto Rico, a sortie by Spanish cruiser *Isabel II* and destroyer *Terror* is rebuffed by the auxiliary *Saint Paul* under Captain Charles D. Sigsbee. *Isabel II* safely withdraws, but *Terror* ends up being beached.

Transport and naval vessels land the 17,000 men of Major General William R. Shafter's V Corps at Daiquiri, Cuba, east of Santiago.

June 28 In Washington, D.C., President William McKinley declares the entire southern coast of Cuba under a naval blockade.

At San Juan, Puerto Rico, the auxiliary cruiser *Yosemite* under Commander William H. Emory drives the Spanish transport *Antonio Lopez* ashore, destroying it. This is despite covering fire from two Spanish cruisers and a torpedo boat nearby.

June 30 In Niquero Bay, Cuba, the armed yachts *Hornet* and *Hist* sink a small

Spanish gunboat. After being joined by the armed tug *Wompatuck*, the three vessels venture into Manzanillo harbor and sink the Spanish vessel *Centenila*.

JULY 1   At Manzanillo, Cuba, the gunboats *Scorpion* and *Osceola* return to the harbor to engage Spanish land batteries, but encounter heavy fire and withdraw after several hours. Seaman Frederick Muller wins a Congressional Medal of Honor for conspicuous bravery under fire.

In Manila Bay, Philippines, the American Expedition Force of 115 officers and 2,386 men disembarks while escorted by the cruiser *Charleston*.

JULY 2   In Santiago, Cuba, Spanish authorities order the squadron of Admiral Pascual Cervera to sortie immediately, if only to salvage national honor. Cervera complies, withdraws 1,200 sailors manning the city's defenses, and prepares to make way.

Outside the city, Major General Willam R. Shafter is alarmed by his heavy losses at the battles of El Caney and San Juan Hill, so he requests Admiral William T. Sampson to seize the entrance of Santiago Bay. A resentful Sampson interprets this as a plea for him to capture the entire city, and the two make arrangements to confer ashore at Siboney on the following day.

JULY 3   From Santiago, Cuba, Rear Admiral William T. Sampson leaves the fleet for consultations with Major General William T. Shafter, just as Admiral Pascual Cervera attempts to run for the open sea. However, the American Commodore Winfield S. Schley intercepts him with battleships *Indiana*, *Iowa*, *Oregon*, and *Texas*, plus the cruiser *Brooklyn*, and Cervera, possessing only four cruisers and two destroyers, loses all his vessels along with 474 killed and wounded, along with 1,800 captured. The Americans lose only 1 dead and 10 injured. Admiral William T. Sampson, who returns toward the close of the battle, insists that the victory be considered his.

Sailors prepare to fire a round during the Battle of Santiago in the Spanish-American War. (Wildside Press)

July 4 Outside Santiago Harbor, Cuba, the battleships *Massachusetts* and *Texas* sink the Spanish cruiser *Reina Mercedes* to stop it from being scuttled and blocking the channel. This vessel is subsequently raised and becomes a receiving ship at the U.S. Naval Academy.

Seven miles west of Havana, Cuba, the Spanish mail steamer *Alfonzo* runs aground and is burned by the armed yacht *Hawk* and the gunboat *Castine*.

July 8 Near Manila, Philippines, Admiral George Dewey seizes Isla Grande before moving on the city. The German gunboat *Irene* is also ordered out of the vicinity.

July 10 At Santiago, Cuba, the battleships *Indiana* and *Texas*, joined by the cruisers *Brooklyn* and *New York*, bombard Spanish positions in the city.

July 12 At Piedras Point, southwestern Cuba, the *Eagle* chases the Spanish blockade runner *Santo Domingo* aground, burning it.

July 13 In the Philippines, Commodore George Dewey orders the *Raleigh* and *Concord* to seize Grande Island in Subic Bay. Several Germans vessel retire upon their approach.

July 16 The northeastern port of Gibara, Cuba, surrenders to rebels assisted by the cruiser *Nashville*.

July 17 Santiago, Cuba, surrenders to American forces, concluding seven days of non-stop naval bombardment. Eight vessels are also captured, including the gunboat *Alvarado*.

July 18 Near Manzanillo, Cuba, the gunboats *Wilmington* and *Helena*, and several smaller vessels, attack and destroy six Spanish gunboats and a blockade runner.

July 21 From Guantanamo, Cuba, transports carrying 3,400 volunteers under Major General Nelson A. Miles make for Puerto Rico, escorted by the battleship *Massachusetts* and cruisers *Columbia*, *Dixie*, *Gloucester*, and *Yale*.

On the northeastern coast of Cuba, gunboats *Annapolis* and *Hunter* enter Nipe Bay and sink the dispatch vessel *Jorge Juan*; this is the final hostile naval encounter of the war.

July 23 At Bahia Honda, Cuba, the *Wanderer* comes under Spanish artillery fire at the mouth of the Manimai River and is disabled. The vessel eventually reaches safety, thanks to Lieutenant John Heard, 3rd Cavalry, who remains on deck shouting instructions to the engine crew.

July 25–26 The port town of Guanica, Puerto Rico, is captured by landing parties from the *Gloucester* under Lieutenant Henry P. Huse. This is in preparation for landing the invasion force under Major General Nelson A. Miles, which disembarks the following day.

July 28 Ponce, Puerto Rico, surrenders to the auxiliary cruiser *Dixie* under Commander C. H. Davis without a shot being fired.

August 1 Guayama, Cuba, is captured with assistance from the cruisers *Cincinnati* and *St. Louis*.

August 6 Offshore at San Juan, Puerto Rico, a naval landing party from the *Amphitrite*, assisted by gunfire from the cruiser *Cincinnati*, captures a lighthouse.

August 12–13 Near Manzanillo, Cuba, an American task force consisting of the cruiser *Newark* under Captain Caspar F. Goodrich and five lesser vessels silences several Spanish batteries, while Cuban guerrillas harass the garrison. The city is then captured before word that the war has ended arrives.

AUGUST 13 In Manila Bay, Philippines, the cruiser *Olympia* and gunboat *Petrel* bombard Spanish-held Fort San Antonio into submission; the transport *Zafiro* subsequently disembarks 600 troops which seize the post. The American flag is subsequently raised over Manila by Lieutenant Thomas N. Brumby.

AUGUST 14 Outside Caibarien, Cuba, the armed lighthouse ship *Mangrove* under Lieutenant Command D. D. Stuart engages two Spanish gunboats. Stuart then learns of the armistice after a white flag is raised; his are the concluding shots of the war.

NOVEMBER 14 In the Caribbean, the cruiser *Potomac*, en route to Nassau from Cat Island, experiences dangerous problems in its boiler room, but prompt action by Lieutenant Thomas Cavanaugh resolves the crisis. He receives a Congressional Medal of Honor.

NOVEMBER 23 In the Philippines, Paymaster W. B. Wilcox and Cadet Leonard R. Sargent issue a study which accurately predicts that the inhabitants will resist any attempt by the United States to impose a new colonial regime.

DECEMBER 10 In Paris, France, a treaty is signed between Spain and the United States which formally ends the Spanish-American War.

DECEMBER 23 In Washington, D.C., the Navy Department accepts responsibility for administering the newly acquired island of Guam.

1899

JANUARY 17 In the Central Pacific, Wake Island is claimed for the United States by Commander E. D. Taussig of the gunboat *Bennington*.

FEBRUARY 5 Near Manila, Philippines, the cruiser *Charleston*, the monitor *Monadnock*, and the gunboats *Callao* and *Concord* provide supporting fire for army operations against Filipino guerrillas under Emilio Aguinaldo.

FEBRUARY 11 At Ilo-ilo City, Philippines, the gunboat *Petrel* bombards a rebel fort, and a landing party goes ashore to secure the position.

FEBRUARY 22 Near Cebu, Philippines, the gunboat *Petrel* dispatches a landing party which seizes the island.

FEBRUARY 24 At Bluefields, Nicaragua, the gunboat *Marietta* lands sailors and marines ashore for the protection of American lives and property.

MARCH 2 In Washington, D.C., Congress creates the rank Admiral of the Navy for Admiral George Dewey; he is the only officer in American naval history so honored. This becomes the first military rank to waive mandatory retirement age.

MARCH 3 In Washington, D.C., Congress authorizes construction of three new battleships, three armed cruisers, and six protected cruisers. Having acquired an overseas empire, it is imperative to show the flag abroad. They also approve the Naval Personnel Act of 1899, which merges line and engineering officers to end intractable hostilities among the officer corps. Curricula at the U.S. Naval Academy is also expanded to include more engineering courses.

APRIL 1   At Apia, Samoa, the protected cruiser *Philadelphia* lands sailors and marines ashore to protect the American consulate during an uprising on the island.

JUNE 10–13   At Cavite, Philippines, Filipino insurgents are bombarded by monitors *Monadnock* and *Monterey* and four gunboats, then Army units sweep them from the banks of the Zapote River.

JULY 29   At Katbalogan, Samar, Philippines, guerrillas tangle with sailors acting as infantry, and Gunner's Mate Andrew V. Stoltenberg wins a Congressional Medal of Honor.

SEPTEMBER 18–23   At Olongapo, Luzon, cruisers *Charleston* and *Baltimore*, assisted by several gunboats, bombard Filipino insurgents at the head of Subic Bay. The transport *Zafiro* subsequently lands troops, which take their position.

SEPTEMBER 25   On the Pampanga River, Luzon, Filipino guerrillas ambush the armed boat *Urdaneta* under Naval Cadet Welborn C. Wood. Four crewmen die, four are captured, and *Urdaneta* becomes the only naval vessel lost in the Philippine Insurrection.

NOVEMBER 2   Near Camiguin Island, Philippines, the cruiser *Charleston* under Captain C. W. Pigman hits a reef and shipwrecks, without the loss of life.

NOVEMBER 7   At Lingayen Gulf, Luzon, Commander Henry Knox directs six vessels, as they land 2,500 Army troops ashore at San Fabian.

NOVEMBER 26   North of the Lingayen Gulf, the battleship *Oregon* and the cruiser *Baltimore* dispatch landing parties who seize and occupy Vigan. They are relieved by Army troops two days later.

DECEMBER 10   On Subic Bay, Philippines, the battleship *Oregon* and the cruiser *Baltimore* dispatch landing parties which seize the former Spanish Navy yard at Olongapo.

1900

JANUARY 11   The gunboat *Princeton* under Commander Harry Knox disgorges landing parties that seize the Bataan Islands, northern Philippines, from insurgents.

FEBRUARY   In the Philippines, Navy gunboats spend the month supporting army operations in the captures of Biniktigan village, Perez, and Pasacao from Filipino insurgents.

FEBRUARY 10   On Samoa, Commodore Seaton Schroeder gains appointment as the first naval governor of the island, which is to be administered by the Navy Department.

FEBRUARY 20   The new battleship *Kearsarge* is commissioned, being the vessel of its class not named after a state.

MARCH 13   In Washington, D.C., the Secretary of the Navy founds a General Board of senior admirals which functions in an advisory capacity only. He is reluctant to copy the Army general staff that would centrally control naval planning, and Admiral George Dewey is appointed to head the board initially.

April In the Philippines, the gunboat *Paragua* seizes the insurgent vessel *San Jose*, then supports capturing the towns of Bailer and Calaguaquin.

April 11 In New York, the *Holland* finally becomes the first operational submarine in the U.S. Navy. This vessel is 53 feet long, slightly over 10 feet at the beam, and can operate submerged for two hours—a far cry from the *Turtle* of 1776!

May Near Leyte, the Philippines, the gunboats *Pampanga* and *Paragua* assist in the reduction of Masing and Santa Margarita, and four insurgent vessels are also captured or sunk.

June 10 At Tianjin, China, allied forces gather for a relief expedition to Peking (Beijing). The American contingent consists of 112 sailors and marines from the cruiser *Newark* under Captain Bowman H. McCalla.

June 16 After only two months of operating in Philippine waters, the gunboat *Villalobos* captures its 22nd Filipino insurgent craft.

June 17 Near Dagu, China, the gunboat *Moncacy* is shelled by Chinese forts, but is ordered not to return fire along for fear of precipitating a war with the Manchu regime.

July Around Samar and Mindanao, Philippines, Navy gunboats continue supporting Army operations inland, while also capturing or sinking 12 more insurgent craft.

August 2 In the Philippines, the gunboat *Pampanga* destroys nine insurgent *bancas* (coastal craft) during a very active month of operations.

September 8 Off the Philippine coast, the gunboat *Panay* sweeps the region of insurgent craft, sinking four small vessels.

October Off the Philippine coast, gunboats *Panay* and *Callao* support Army operations aimed at capturing Carles, Balsen, Estabcia, and Malabung; two insurgent vessels are also taken.

November 12 On Samar, Philippines, the gunboat *Bennington* supports Army troops attacking insurgent positions at Borongon. Heavy fire from the warship drives the insurgents off before they burn the town down.

December 13 At Apia Harbor, Guam, the station ship *Yosemite* is struck by a typhoon and sinks, with five sailors lost.

1901

January 2–3 Near Cavite, the Philippines, Navy gunboats under Lieutenant F. R. Payne attack and capture 18 insurgent vessels operating along the Imus River.

January 17 Near Luzon, the Philippines, the unarmored cruiser *Don Juan of Austria* under Commander T. C. McLean bombards three insurgent villages, which are then captured.

January 28 Maringondon, Luzon, Philippines, is seized by Army troops covered by gunfire from the gunboat *Don Juan of Austria* under Commander T. C. McLean.

February 24–March 3 On Lubang Island, Philippines, Army troops operating at Loorg Bay receive fire support from the gunboat *Villalobos* under Lieutenant Henry P. Huse.

March 18–23 On Palawan Island, Philippines, the gunboat *Vicksburg* under Commander E. B. Barry supports Army operations ashore.

March 23 In the Philippines, the gunboat *Vicksburg* supports the attempt to capture insurgent leader Emilio Aguinaldo. This successful action signals the end of the Philippine insurrection.

July 1 By this date, 60 new warships are under construction for the Navy, which is a useful gauge of America's new global responsibilities.

July 3–17 On Samar Island, the Philippines, the armed vessel *Basco* under Naval Cadet J. H. Comfort trades fire with Moro (Muslim) insurgents on the Gandara River.

July 19 During an action near Samar, Philippines, Gunner's Mate Frederick T. Fisher receives a Congressional Medal of Honor for bravery onboard the cruiser *Philadelphia*.

September 16 The new battleship *Illinois* is commissioned; it serves in various capacities until 1956.

November 2–16 On Samar Island, the Philippines, the gunboat *Vicksburg* bombards Moro insurgents near Nipanipa, then lands parties of sailors ashore to support Marine Corps operations.

November 16 Outspoken Lieutenant William S. Sims writes directly to President Theodore Roosevelt, complaining about the poor quality of American naval gunnery. He thereupon suggests they adopt the British gunnery system developed by Captain Percy Scott of the Royal Navy. Roosevelt agrees, and eventually appoints Sims to be inspector of target practice.

On Samar Island, the Philippines, the gunboat *Vicksburg* under Lieutenant Commander J. H. Glennan lands shore parties to support an expedition against Moro insurgents on the Basey River.

December 13 The bitter dispute between Rear Admirals William T. Sampson and Winfield S. Schley intensifies following the report of a court of inquiry requested by the latter. Schley is criticized for his slovenly search for the Spanish fleet, but finally receives credit for the victory at Santiago. President Theodore Roosevelt then declares the matter closed.

1902

April 16–19 At Boca del Toro, Panama, the gunboat *Machias*, the cruiser *Cincinnati*, and several lesser vessels place landing parties ashore to restore order. Admiral Silas Casey is enabled to enforce a truce between local rebels and the Colombian troops.

September 17 At Colon, Panama, the cruiser *Cincinnati* lands sailors and marines ashore to protect American lives and property.

SEPTEMBER 18   At Panama City, Panama, a landing party of sailors and marines goes ashore from the survey ship *Ranger*.

SEPTEMBER 23   In Panama, Rear Admiral Silas Casey refuses Colombian forces the right of passage across Panama to attack rebel forces, and again arranges a temporary truce between them.

NOVEMBER 24   The *Bainbridge* (DD-1) is commissioned as the Navy's first torpedo-boat destroyer. Such high-speed vessels are specifically designed to outrun and destroy torpedo boats, from which they acquire their name.

DECEMBER 22   A new battleship *Maine* is christened and replaces the one lost in Havana Harbor in 1898; the two others vessel of this class are *Missouri* and *Ohio*.

Representing the birth of the U.S. Navy's destroyer fleet, the USS Bainbridge *measured 250 feet in length, displaced 420 tons, and was in service during the Spanish-American War and World War I. (U.S. Naval Historical Center)*

1903

JANUARY 17   After German warships shell Fort San Carlos, Venezuela, in an attempt to wrest back payments out of the government, President Theodore Roosevelt orders Admiral George Dewey to conduct maneuvers in the Caribbean with a fleet of 50 warships. Roosevelt is determined to enforce the Monroe Doctrine by force, if necessary.

FEBRUARY 23   In Washington, D.C., President Theodore Roosevelt signs a lease for utilizing Guantanamo Bay, Cuba, as a naval base. Being spacious and strategically located, it affords Navy vessels immediate access to the Windward Passage.

SEPTEMBER 7–13   Near Beruit, Syria (Lebanon), the cruiser *San Francisco* sends landing detachments ashore during a period of civil strife.

OCTOBER 17   In Washington, D. C., the General Board issues a secret plan to obtain 48 battleships and auxiliaries by 1920. This decision, kept from public scrutiny, influences naval funding for two decades.

NOVEMBER 4   At Colon, Panama, the gunboat *Nashville* under Commander John Hubbard lands parties of sailors and marines ashore, to prevent Colombian soldiers from taking a train to Panama City and crushing the rebellion there.

1904

JANUARY 5–APRIL 23 Off the coast at Seoul, Korea, the transport *Zafiro* lands sailors and marines ashore for the purpose of protecting the U.S. Legation there.

JANUARY 17 At Puerto Plata, Dominican Republic, the screw sloop *Detroit* dispatches sailors and marines ashore to protect American citizens.

FEBRUARY 11 Near Santo Domingo, Dominican Republic, rebels fire on the steamer *New York*, and a force of 300 sailors and marines from the cruisers *Columbia* and *Newark* land and chase them out from the city.

APRIL 13 A powder accident onboard the battleship *Missouri* results in the deaths of 36 sailors; however, Robert Edward Cox, Mons Monssen, and Charles S. Schepke receive Congressional Medals of Honor for extinguishing the resulting fire.

OCTOBER 7 In Seattle, Washington, the battleship *Nebraska* is the first modern capital ship constructed from the keel up for the Navy.

1905

JANUARY 18 At the Dominican Republic, landing parties go ashore from the cruiser *Detroit* to preclude intervention by foreign military forces attempting to collects debts.

JANUARY 20 In the Dominican Republic, naval personnel take over the national customs service to stabilize the collection of revenues and pay off national debts.

MARCH 3 In Washington, D.C., Congress approves construction of the battleship *South Carolina*. To date, President Theodore Roosevelt has authorized 10 battleships, 4 armored cruisers, and 17 lesser vessels as part of his overall program of naval expansion.

APRIL 7 In Paris, France, the unmarked grave of Revolutionary War hero John Paul Jones is uncovered. The United States government intends to escort the remains back home under a Guard of Honor.

JULY 21 At San Diego, California, the gunboat *Bennington* suffers a boiler explosion, whereby 60 sailors die and 40 more are injured. No less than 10 Congressional Medals of Honor are awarded for heroism in saving lives on board.

JULY 23 In the North Atlantic, the remains of Revolutionary War naval hero John Paul Jones are escorted from France to Annapolis, Maryland, by Rear Admiral Charles D. Sigsbee and the cruisers *Brooklyn, Chattanooga, Galveston*, and *Tacoma*, accompanied by the French cruiser *Jurien de la Graviere* as an escort. Rear Admiral Robley D. Evans provides an additional escort of eight battleships once they reach Nantucket Shoals.

JULY 24 In Annapolis, Maryland, the remains of John Paul Jones are laid to rest in the crypt below the U.S. Naval Academy Chapel. Along with John Barry, he is considered one of the founding fathers of the U.S. Navy.

1906

MARCH 8 On Jolo Island, the Philippines, a landing detachment from the gunboat *Pampanga* under Ensign H. D. Cooke, Jr., assists Army troops in storming Moro positions at Bad-Dajo.

APRIL 13 Near Cape Cruz, Cuba, a turret fire onboard the battleship *Kearsarge* kills eight sailors and injures four. Sailor George Breeman and Chief Boatswain Isidor Nordstrom receive Congressional Medals of Honor for saving shipmates.

APRIL 18 In San Francisco, California, Navy and Marine personnel from the Mare Island Navy Yard restore order in the wake of a destructive earthquake there.

APRIL 21 In the Arctic Circle, Commander Robert E. Peary reaches latitude 87 degrees 6 minutes north; this is the closest any man has come to the North Pole.

SEPTEMBER 14 Offshore at Cienfuegos, Cuba, the gunboat *Marietta* under Commander William Fullam sends half its crew ashore to protect American sugar mills from rebels.

SEPTEMBER 26 In Washington, D.C., the General Board of the Navy faces the prospects of fighting a Pacific War with Japan by conceiving the Orange War Plan. This strategy mandates a surface fleet consisting of 48 capital warships, three times larger than the one at present. Thus armed, the United States could engage the Japanese across a vast and distant arena with good prospects for success.

NOVEMBER 9 President Theodore Roosevelt becomes the first chief executive to travel abroad on a naval vessel, when he boards the battleship *Louisiana* on an inspection tour of the Panama Canal.

1907

JANUARY 8 In Washington, D.C., President Theodore Roosevelt directs that American naval vessels be prefixed with "United States Ship" (USS).

DECEMBER 16 At Hampton Roads, Virginia, President Theodore Roosevelt dispatches Rear Admiral Robley D. "Fighting Bob" Evans with his "Great White Fleet" of 16 modern battleships. The name arises from the gleaming white hulls of the vessels. Evans conducts his charge on a 15-month, round-the-world excursion to South America, Australia, and Japan without mishap, dispelling notions that such global missions are technologically unfeasible.

1908

FEBRUARY 1 The battleship *Mississippi* is commissioned; it is destined to become the first ship of its class to launch and handle airplanes on board.

APRIL 1   In Washington, D.C., President Theodore Roosevelt asks Congress to provide funding for an additional four battleships. The new battleship *Idaho* is also commissioned, being the last of the older, pre-dreadnought-class battleships employed by the Navy.

MAY 13   At the Naval Hospital in Washington, D. C., the new U.S. Navy Nurse Corps recruits its "Sacred Twenty." They are employed and enjoy military status, but are not considered enlisted personnel.

JULY 6   In New York, an Arctic expedition under Commodore Robert E. Peary departs on the icebreaker *Roosevelt*, intent on reaching the North Pole.

JULY 7   Near Batangas, the Philippines, the destroyer *Decatur* under Ensign Chester W. Nimitz runs aground. Nimitz, a future Navy leader, is court-martialed and found guilty of "neglect of duty," but remains on active duty.

AUGUST 15   The battleships *Illinois* and *Rhode Island* and the transport *Prairie* become the first naval vessels with onboard post offices.

SEPTEMBER 3–17   At Fort Myer, Virginia, Navy Lieutenant George C. Sweet and Naval Constructor William McEntee are on hand to observe the first military trial of the Wright brothers' aircraft.

DECEMBER 2   In Washington, D.C., Chief of the Bureau of Equipment Rear Admiral William S. Cowles hands over Lieutenant George C. Sweet's report to the Secretary of the Navy. Sweet has

The "Sacred Twenty" women of the Navy Nurse Corps, ca. 1908, were the first women to serve in the U.S. Navy. Three of the women pictured here in the bottom row (fifth, sixth, and seventh from the left) would serve as superintendents of the corps during its early years: Josephine Beatrice Bowman (1922–1935), Lenah H. Sutcliffe Higbee (1911–1922), and Esther Voorhees Hasson (1908–1911). (Naval Historical Center)

examined the specifications for an aircraft capable of working in conjunction with the surface fleet, and recommends the acquisition of several aircraft for research along these lines.

DECEMBER 4 In London, England, the United States and nine other naval powers attend a Naval Conference to better articulate the rules of naval warfare. Their final declaration clarifies blockades, contraband, convoy, destruction of neutral prizes, and compensation for ships seized illegally.

1909

JANUARY 27 In Washington, D.C., the Commission on Naval Reorganization forms under President Theodore Roosevelt. They immediately advocate separating the Navy Department into five divisions, the heads of which would act as a council advising the Secretary of the Navy. The scheme plan is not adopted, but highlights the trend toward administrative reform.

FEBRUARY 22 At Hampton Roads, Virginia, the "Great White Fleet" under Rear Admiral Charles Sperry returns, after circumnavigating the globe across 46,000 miles without a single vessel breaking down. This carefully choreographed exercise impressed host nations with American sea power, while underscoring the need for additional coaling stations world-wide and new auxiliary vessels like destroyers and cruisers.

APRIL 6 At the North Pole, the small expedition headed by Commander Robert Edwin Peary reaches 90 degrees north for the first time. Accompanied only by four Inuit Indians and Matthew Henson, his African American assistant, Peary raises the American flag and claims the region for the United States. In the course of seven Polar expeditions, Peary has lost all but two toes to frostbite.

AUGUST 16 In Washington, D.C., the Navy Bureau of Equipment requests that the Secretary of the Navy purchase two "heavier than air flying machines." However, the secretary demurs, noting that the Navy has no use for them in their present state of development.

SEPTEMBER 1 In Paris, France, Commander Frederick L. Chapin, the naval attache, reports his observations of the recent aviation meet at Rheims. Here he prophetically states that aircraft will probably employ catapults to launch them from battleship and cruiser turrets, as well as flat-decked vessels acting as seaborne airfields.

NOVEMBER 11 In Washington, D.C., the Navy Department draws up plans to turn Pearl Harbor on the island of Oahu, Hawaii, into a major naval facility.

DECEMBER 1 In Washington, D.C., the Navy Department adopts a new administrative scheme with four new bureaus to administer fleet operations, matériel, inspections, and personnel. The head of each division also reports directly to the secretary of the Navy in an advisory capacity.

1910

January 4 The new battleship *Michigan* is commissioned; it is patterned after the revolutionary British vessel *Dreadnaught*, then the most modern warship of its class. *Michigan* displaces 16,000 tons and carries its main armament of twelve 8-inch guns in mainline turrets. The "big gun battleship" will dominate naval thinking for the next three decades.

April 4 The new battleship *Delaware* is commissioned, which displaces 20,380 tons and is armed with 12-inch guns.

May 19 Near Bluefields, Nicaragua, the gunboats *Dubuque* and *Paducah* land parties of sailors and marines ashore to protect American lives during a local insurgency. Commander William W. Gilmer of the latter forbids a Nicaraguan gunboat from shelling the city.

July 11 Near Provincetown, Massachusetts, the submarine *Bonita* collides with the gunboat *Castine* in the first recorded underwater accident. *Bonita* escapes with minor damage, but *Castine* is beached to prevent it from sinking.

September 26 In Washington, D.C., the Secretary of the Navy appoints Captain Washington I. Chambers, Assistant to the Aid for Material, to serve as the correspondent for all civilian inquires regarding naval aviation. In this capacity he responds to inquires from the civilian U.S. Aeronautical Reserve, which advocates the military application of aeronautics. These exchanges constitute the first awareness of aviation within the Navy Department.

October 7 In Washington, D.C., Captain Hutch I. Cone informs the Chief of the Bureau of Steam Engineering that aircraft are improving technically, which underscores their usefulness to the Navy. He therefore requests that an aircraft be acquired for the cruiser *Chester*, along with instructors to teach the first naval aviators.

October 11 In Washington, D.C., the Navy General Board alerts the Secretary of the Navy that continuing interest should be maintained in aeronautics for the advantages it might convey to the Navy. They seek to berth airplanes on all news classes of scouting vessels.

October 13 In Washington, D.C., the Secretary of the Navy orders that two officers report on all progress in the field of aviation, especially as it relates to naval applications.

October 18 Near Cape Hatteras, North Carolina, Commander Walter Wellman crashes the 228-foot-long dirigible *America* during a transatlantic flight. The crew is rescued by a British steamer, yet still it has established a new 71-hour, 1,000-mile duration record.

October 22–30 At Belmont Park, New York, Captain Washington I. Chambers, a former battleship commander, attends the International Air Meet and is impressed by the military potential of aircraft. Chambers becomes a staunch advocate of naval aviation at a time when such views are unpopular.

October 31 In Washington, D.C., the Chief of the Bureau of Construction and Repair advises the Secretary of the Navy that one or more airplanes should be acquired, along with funding to modify a turret on the battleship *Texas* to launch aircraft.

NOVEMBER 14   Near Hampton Roads, Virginia, a Curtiss pusher biplane flown by civilian pilot Eugene B. Ely flies from a wooden platform on the bow of the cruiser *Birmingham*; this is the first time an aircraft launches from a warship.

NOVEMBER 29   Aeronautical pioneer Glenn H. Curtiss offers his services as a pilot instructor to the Secretary of the Navy, providing they use his aircraft.

DECEMBER 23   At San Diego, California, Lieutenant Theodore G. Ellyson is ordered to earn his wings by training on a Curtiss A-1 Triad at North Island.

DECEMBER 31   By this date the U.S. Navy boasts 717,202 tons of vessels, making it the second-largest surface force in the world after the Royal Navy. An additional 824,162 tons of shipping is presently under construction.

1911

JANUARY 18   In San Francisco Bay, California, a Curtiss pusher biplane flown by Eugene B. Ely lands a wooden platform on the armored cruiser *Pennsylvania*. This is the first aerial landing on a ship. He then turns his craft around and takes off, demonstrating the viability of naval aviation.

JANUARY 26   At North Island, San Diego, California, aeronautical pioneer Glenn H. Curtiss impresses Navy authorities with his amphibious hydroaeroplane, or "flying boat."

JANUARY 28   At San Diego, California, Lieutenant Theodore G. Ellyson becomes the first naval officer to fly, when he taxies his Curtiss pusher too hard and accidently lifts off.

FEBRUARY 1   At San Diego, California, aeronaut Glenn H. Curtiss successfully demonstrates his hydroaeroplane, which employs a single centerline float. This leads to adoption of the "sled profile float" which is in widespread use prior to World War I.

FEBRUARY 10   The Wireless Station at Point Loma Linda, California, is instructed by the Assistant Secretary of the Navy to cooperate with Captain Harry S. Harkness, U.S. Aeronautical Reserve. Harkess is conducting experiments involving wireless transmission (radio) from airborne aircraft.

FEBRUARY 17   In San Diego Harbor, California, aviator Glenn H. Curtiss lands his flying boat alongside the armored cruiser *Pennsylvania*; it is then hoisted on board by a crane. Once lowered back into the water, Curtiss takes off and returns to base.

MARCH 4   In Washington, D.C., Congress approves the first Naval Appropriations Act containing funds for the nascent naval aviation program. The $25,000 appropriated will be administered by the Bureau of Navigation for flight testing purposes.

MARCH 9   The Wright Company of Dayton, Ohio, offers to train a Navy pilot if they will purchase a $5,000 Wright flier.

MARCH 17   Navy Lieutenant John Rodgers is dispatched to the Wright Company, Dayton, Ohio, for flight instructions. He will become Naval Aviator No. 2.

April 1 In Washington, D.C., aviation-minded Captain Washington I. Chambers reports for duty with the Navy General Board. The move was suggested by Admiral George Dewey, since the Aid for Operations office lacked the space.

April 12 At San Diego, California, Lieutenant Theodore G. Ellyson passes through the Curtiss Aviation Center as Naval Aviator No. 1.

April 14 In Washington, D.C., the nascent Office of Naval Aviation transfers from the General Board to the Bureau of Navigation, another sign of increasing significance.

May 8 In Washington, D.C., Captain Washington I. Chambers prevails upon the Navy's Chief of the Bureau of Navigation to issue its first contract for obtaining two Curtiss A-1 Triad biplanes. This marks the birth of naval aviation, which sets the taxpayers back $25,000.

June 27 At Hammondsport, New York, Lieutenant John H. Towers reports to the Curtiss facility for flight instructions; he is Naval Aviator No. 3.

July 1 At Lake Keuka, Hammondsport, New York, aeronautical pioneer Glenn H. Curtiss demonstrates his A-1 Triad aircraft, built for the Navy, by flying off the lake for five minutes at an altitude of 25 feet.

July 3 At Lake Keuka, Hammondsport, New York, Navy lieutenant Theodore G. Ellyson makes the first night flight by a naval aviator in his Curtiss A-1 Triad, without the aid of lights.

July 6 At Annapolis, Maryland, Captain Washington I. Chambers arrives at the U.S. Naval Academy to select a site for the Navy's first aviation base. The site chosen, Greenbury Point, is not formally occupied until the fall.

An airplane takes off from a modified warship. During World War I, airplanes served as scouts, discovering and reporting the location and strength of the enemy forces. (Reynolds and Taylor, Collier's Photographic History of the European War, *1916)*

JULY 10   At Hammondsport, New York, aeronaut Glenn H. Curtiss makes the first amphibious flight of a naval aircraft of by lifting off from on land, raising his wheels, then landing on water with pontoons.

JULY 19   At Annapolis, Maryland, a Wright Type B airplane arrives and is fitted with pontoons to become the Navy's first seaplane.

AUGUST 23   At Dayton, Ohio, and Hammondsport, New York, naval aviators are ordered to Annapolis, Maryland, to work with the Engineering Experiment Station, U.S. Naval Academy, and set up the naval aviation base at Greenbury Point.

AUGUST 31   Captain William S. Benson, a future Chief of Naval Operations, takes charge of the new battleship *Utah*.

SEPTEMBER   At Annapolis, Maryland, the Navy establishes an aviation camp at Greenbury Point, directly across the Severn River from the U.S. Naval Academy. As a good indication of the low reputation of naval aeronautics, it shares property with the midshipman's rifle range.

SEPTEMBER 7   At Hammondsport, New York, Lieutenant Theodore G. Ellyson successfully tests a shipboard launching device by gliding his Curtiss Triad down an inclined wire from the beach to the water.

SEPTEMBER 16   To cut down on exposure while flying open aircraft, Lieutenant Theodore G. Ellyson recommends that the Navy Department purchase leather helmets, goggles, fur-lined jackets, leather pants, rubber galoshes, and life preservers for aviation personnel.

SEPTEMBER 20   In Washington, D.C., the Bureau of Navigation requests the U.S. Naval Observatory that they lend a boat compass for work with aerial navigation from airplanes.

SEPTEMBER 24   On Basilan Island, the Philippines, the gunboat *Pampanga* disgorges a landing party which captures the village of Mundang after fierce fighting with Moro rebels; five Congressional Medals of Honor are awarded.

OCTOBER 10   At the Washington Navy Yard, Washington, D.C., Lieutenant Holden C. Richardson gains appointment as naval aviation's first engineering and maintenance officer.

OCTOBER 17   In a very prescient letter, Captain Washington I. Chambers approaches aeronaut Glenn H. Curtiss about the future use of turbine (jet) propulsion in aircraft. He also mentions the possibility of diesel propulsion.

OCTOBER 25   Over Virginia, a Curtiss A-1 Triad flown by Lieutenants Theodore G. Ellyson and John H. Towers experiences a leaking radiator flying from Annapolis, Maryland, to Fortress Monroe, and set down; they still covered 112 miles in 122 minutes.

NOVEMBER 4   The Navy contacts the Burgess Company of Marblehead, Massachusetts, to convert its Wright B-1 landplane into a hydroaeroplane by installing a suitable float.

NOVEMBER 24   The armored cruiser *Saratoga* departs Shanghai and makes for Dagu, China, where its landing party will guard foreign missionaries residing there.

DECEMBER 14   At Pearl Harbor, Hawaii, the armored cruiser *California* is the first American capital warship to enter the channel. Beforehand, civilian contractors widened the channel by 1,100 feet and to a uniform depth of 35 feet.

DECEMBER 20 At Annapolis, Maryland, a Curtiss A-1 Triad flown by Lieutenant John H. Towers and Ensign Charles H. Maddox experiments with airborne wireless transmissions. This is accomplished by reeling out a radio wire behind the aircraft as an antenna, but the signals are too weak to be received.

DECEMBER 26 In Washington, D.C., Captain Washington I. Chambers, looking for a practical launching device for shipborne aircraft, reports that the Bureau of Ordnance has considered devices used for launching torpedoes.

DECEMBER 29 In Washington, D.C., the Navy Departments orders all aviators transferred from Annapolis, Maryland, to North Island, San Diego, California, to establish a new aviation camp.

1912

FEBRUARY 11 In Havana, Cuba, the sunken battleship *Maine* is raised from the harbor by the U.S. Army Corps of Engineers.

FEBRUARY 14 The *Skipjack* becomes the U.S. Navy's first diesel-powered submarine. Commanded by Captain Chester W. Nimitz, it serves as a test bed for underwater radio transmissions and gyrocompass navigation.

MARCH 9 In Washington, D.C., Assistant Naval Constructor Holden C. Richardson evinces one of the earliest expressions of interest in steel and aluminum as building materials for aircraft.

MARCH 11 In Washington, D.C., the Secretary of the Navy displays interest in early helicopter-type aircraft, however, he authorizes expenditures of not higher than $50 in developing working models.

MARCH 23 At Mare Island Navy Yard, San Francisco, California, wireless equipment mounted in a dummy airplane fuselage and elevated to 85 feet emits signals that are received at Point Richard, 20 miles distant.

APRIL 6 In Washington, D.C., Captain Washington I. Chambers suggests using the word "airplane" to replace "aeroplane," then in usage. He also suggests such commonplace terms as "landing gear" and "fuselage."

MAY 11 At Salem, Massachusetts, Rear Admiral Bradley A. Fiske is the first flag officer to take off and land on water in a Wright B-1 hydroaeroplane. The experience reaffirms his belief that airplanes are potentially useful as scouting craft at sea.

MAY 19 The cruiser *Birmingham* begins patrolling the North Atlantic on the first-ever ice patrol. This comes in consequence of the *Titanic* tragedy, and within two years this activity is conducted by the U.S. Coast Guard.

MAY 28 Near Guantanamo and Nipe Bays, Cuba, American gunboats *Paducah*, *Nashville*, and *Petrel* send sailors and marines ashore to protect American-owned sugar mills from rebel activity.

JUNE 21 Over Annapolis, Maryland, Lieutenant Theodore G. Ellyson flies his Curtiss A-1 to 900 feet in only 3 minutes and 30 seconds.

JULY 16 In Washington, D.C., the Patent Office issues a patent to Rear Admiral Bradley Fiske for his air-launched torpedo, one of many innovative designs he pioneers with military applications.

JULY 25   In Washington, D.C., the Secretary of the Navy releases "Requirements for Hydroaeroplanes," the first aircraft specifications requiring standardized construction and safety features from manufacturers.

JULY 27   Over Chesapeake Bay, a Wright B-1 hydroaeroplane flown by Lieutenant John Rodgers and Midshipman Charles Maddox transmits the Morse code letter "D" while airborne. Their signal is received by the torpedo boat *Bailey*, one mile away.

JULY 31   At Annapolis, Maryland, Lieutenant Theodore G. Ellyson attempts the first launch of an aircraft using compressed air. His A-1 roars off the Santee Wharf and cartwheels into the Severn River; Ellyson remains unhurt.

AUGUST 4   In Nicaragua, revolutionary violence against President Adolfo Diaz prompts the gunboat *Annapolis* to land 100 sailors and marines ashore, which march overland to guard the American legation in Managua.

AUGUST 17   At Bluefields, Nicaragua, the cruiser *Tacoma* lands parties of sailors and marines ashore to maintain order and protect lives.

AUGUST 28   Near Cortino, Nicaragua, the armored cruiser *California* lands 364 sailors and marines ashore to maintain order.

AUGUST 30   At San Juan del Sur, Nicaragua, sailors and marines come ashore from the cruiser *Denver* to maintain order.

SEPTEMBER 5   At Cortino, Nicaragua, an additional 343 sailors and marines from the armored cruiser *Colorado* are sent ashore to bolster landing parties already there.

OCTOBER 3–4   At the Naval Proving Ground, Indian Head, Maryland, a recoilless gun designed by Commander Cleland Davis undergoes initial testing. This is intended to fire shells large enough to sink a submarine from an aircraft.

OCTOBER 6   Over Annapolis, Maryland, Lieutenant John H. Towers sets an American endurance record of 6 hours, 10 minutes, and 35 seconds in his Curtiss A-2.

OCTOBER 8   At the Engineering Experimental Station, Annapolis, Maryland, the Navy conducts tests with the Gyro 50-horsepower rotary engine. Significantly, this is the first engine scientifically evaluated with laboratory equipment, including a dynamometer.

OCTOBER 26–DECEMBER 18   Over Chesapeake Bay, Lieutenant John H. Towers attempts to spot submerged submarines from the air for the first time. He reports that 800 feet appears to be the optimum altitude for scouting, although subs can only be seen a few feet below the surface if the water is murky.

NOVEMBER 12   On the Anacostia River, D.C., Navy Lieutenant Theodore G. Ellyson's Curtiss A-1 Triad hydroaeroplane is successfully catapulted from a specially designed barge. This technology is viewed as essential if aircraft are to be launched from warships at sea in a future war.

NOVEMBER 30   At Lake Keuka, Hammondsport, New York, a Curtiss C-1 is piloted by Lieutenant Theodore G. Ellyson. This becomes the Navy's first flying boat, an operational type lasting up through the Vietnam War.

DECEMBER 19 In Washington, D.C., President William H. Taft calls for a "Commission on Aerodynamic Laboratory" to explore the best methods of establishing such an institution for naval aviation.

1913

JANUARY 6 At Guantanamo Bay, Cuba, naval maneuvers unfold which employ the entire naval aircraft inventory. These are launched for the first time from the collier *Sterling* and tested for their ability to scout, spot submarines and mines, and serve as visual adjuncts to the battle fleet.

FEBRUARY 1 At Annapolis, Maryland, the Naval Postgraduate School opens its doors in the former Marine Barracks at the U.S. Naval Academy; it is ultimately transferred to Monterey, California.

FEBRUARY 26 In Washington, D.C., the Chief Constructor of the Navy approves plans to acquire a first wind tunnel and scientifically study aerodynamic properties. It is finally constructed at the Washington Navy Yard, remaining in service up through the end of World War II.

MARCH 4 In Washington, D.C., Congress passes the Naval Appropriations Act of 1914, which includes a 35-percent increase for flight pay for naval aviators.

MARCH 5 Outside Guantanamo Bay, Cuba, Lieutenant John H. Towers reports that submarines can be aerially spotted at depths of 30–40 feet, provided the water is not murky.

Dr. Harry E. Harvey goes aboard the hospital ship *Solace* as the first certified dentist to serve on a naval vessel.

MARCH 6 Near Guantanamo Bay, Cuba, Lieutenant John H. Towers and Ensign Godfrey DeC. Chevalier successfully perform spotting flights in concert with surface vessels. Here they espy a column of battleships and alert a squadron of destroyers, who attack.

MARCH 13 Captain Washington I. Chambers is awarded by the Aeronautical Society for advancing the state of aviation, as it applies to seaplanes and catapult technology.

MARCH 31 In Washington, D.C., the Navy Department issues regulations mandating that the Burgess Company and Curtiss D-1 be outfitted with a compass, altimeter, inclinometer, speed indicator, chart board, radio, and generator. Hereafter, these become standard equipment on all naval aircraft.

APRIL 7 The collier *Jupiter* becomes the Navy's first electrically powered vessel, although in 1922 it is converted into the *Langley* (CV-1), the first aircraft carrier.

APRIL 10 In Washington, D.C., the Secretary of the Navy's office issues new performance standards to qualify for the position of Navy Air Pilot. The Navy touts them as "more exacting" than those affecting Army pilots or required by the Federation Aeronautique Internationale.

APRIL 28 In Washington, D.C., Rear Admiral Victor Blue, Chief of the Bureau of Navigation, authorizes the Navy Department, the Glenn Curtiss Company, and the Sperry Corporation to jointly develop gyroscopic stabilizers for aircraft.

MAY 3   In Washington, D.C., Captain Washington I. Chambers and Lieutenant Holden C. Richardson become naval representatives on an advisory committee at the Langley Aerodynamical Laboratory, Virginia.

JUNE 12   In Washington, D.C., the Secretary of the Navy dispatches Lieutenant Jerome C. Hunsaker to the Massachusetts Institute of Technology for developing a course in aeronautical engineering.

JUNE 13   Over Annapolis, Maryland, Lieutenant Patrick N. L. Bellinger sets an American altitude record for seaplanes by reaching 6,200 feet in his Curtiss A-3.

JUNE 20   Over Annapolis, Maryland, Ensign William D. Billingsley becomes the Navy's first aviation-related fatality when he is thrown from his Wright B-2 hydroaeroplane and falls 1,500 feet to his death. Lieutenant J. H. Towers, his passenger, is also tossed overboard, but clings to the aircraft until it crashes in the water; he sustains serious injuries. In consequence, safety belts become standard equipment on all naval aircraft.

JUNE 23   In Washington, D.C., a Navy General Order finally recognizes the Aviation Bureau and grants it equal status to those associated with naval vessels.

AUGUST 30   In Washington, D.C., Admiral George Dewey and the General Board of the Navy strongly recommend to the Secretary of the Navy that an "efficient Naval Air Service" should be established as quickly as possible.

Over Hammondsport, New York, Lieutenant Patrick N. L. Bellinger tests a Curtiss C-2 flying boat fitted with a Sperry gyroscopic stabilizer (automatic pilot) for the first time.

OCTOBER 5   At Hammondsport, New York, the Navy conducts its first trials of Curtiss E-1 amphibian flying boats; these are Curtiss A-2 aircraft outfitted with a flying-boat hull and three-wheeled landing gear.

OCTOBER 7   In Washington, D.C., Secretary of the Navy Josephus Daniels appoints an Aeronautical Board under Captain Washington I. Chambers. Their first act is recommending an aeronautical center at Pensacola, Florida, plus the assignment of at least one scout aircraft to every battleship and cruiser in the fleet. An aviation office is also established within the secretary's office.

DECEMBER 17   In Washington, D.C., Captain Mark L. Bristol becomes the Navy Department's new special duty officer in charge of aviation matters.

1914

JANUARY 1   In Washington, D.C., Secretary of the Navy Josephus Daniels institutes off-duty education for all enlisted men to try to raise academic standards. He also begins the practice of allowing 100 enlisted men to compete yearly for entrance into the U.S. Naval Academy.

JANUARY 7   In Washington, D.C., the Office of Aeronautics transfers from the Bureau of Navigation to the Division of Operations within the Office of the Secretary of the Navy. This is another sign of aviation's growing significance to the service.

JANUARY 10   In Washington, D.C., Secretary of the Navy Josephus Daniels declares that aeronautics has technically evolved to where it is a vital element of naval forces for both offensive and defensive purposes.

JANUARY 20   At Pensacola, Florida, the naval aviation force arrives from Annapolis, Maryland, to establish a flying school. Presently it musters 9 officers, 23 enlisted men, and seven aircraft under Lieutenant John H. Towers.

JANUARY 31   At Pensacola, Florida, the first naval air station is formally inaugurated.

FEBRUARY 16   Near Pensacola, Florida, a Burgess D-1 crashes 200 feet from shore and kills Lieutenant James M. Murray.

In Washington, D.C., Congress creates a national naval militia force to supplement the standing establishment in wartime.

MARCH 9   In Washington, D.C., the pioneering wind tunnel constructed at the Washington Navy Yard begins calibration tests over the next three months.

MARCH 12   The new battleship *Texas* is commissioned; it still resides at San Jacinto, Texas, as a war memorial.

MARCH 27   In Washington, D.C., the Navy Department issues official aircraft designations with A for heavier than air, D for dirigible or airships, B for balloons, and K for kites. The second letter, L, H, B, X, N, and C indicate land machines, hydroaeroplanes, flying boats, amphibians, and convertibles.

APRIL 9   At Tampico, Mexico, a boatload of American sailors from the *Dolphin* under Assistant Paymaster Charles W. Copp goes ashore at Tampico to purchase supplies; they are arrested by Mexican authorities and briefly detained. The local commander, General Ignacio Morelos Zaragoza, orders the captives released and apologizes to the U.S. Consul. Nevertheless, Admiral Henry T. Mayo, commanding the Atlantic Fleet's Fourth Division, demands a 21-gun salute to the American flag; the Mexicans refuse.

APRIL 11   In Mexico City, Mexico, General Victoriano Huerta apologizes for the arrest of American sailors at Tampico, but he declines to hoist the American flag there and salute it.

APRIL 14   In Washington, D.C., President Woodrow Wilson supports Admiral Henry T. Mayo and orders the Atlantic Fleet into Tampico Bay. He also gives the Mexican government until April 18 to fire an official salute to the American flag as demanded.

APRIL 18   At Veracruz, Mexico, U.S. Consul William W. Canada notifies the State Department that the German transport *Ypiranga* is carrying a huge cache of weapons and ammunition for General Victoriano Huerta's regime. President Woodrow Wilson determines that the arms should not reach the Mexican dictator.

APRIL 20   At Pensacola, Florida, the cruiser *Birmingham* conveys an aviation detachment for service off Tampico, Mexico. This consists of 3 pilots, 12 enlisted men, and three aircraft under Lieutenant John H. Towers.

In Washington, D.C., the Navy Department alerts Admiral Frank F. Fletcher, commanding the First Division of the Atlantic Fleet off Veracruz, Mexico, that the German transport *Ypiranga* must discharge its cargo of guns and ammunition in port.

APRIL 21–22   At Pensacola, Florida, the battleship *Mississippi* conveys a second aviation detachment under Lieutenant Patrick N. L. Bellinger for use at Veracruz, Mexico.

At Veracruz, Mexico, Admiral Frank F. Fletcher lands a Naval Brigade of 800 marines and sailors ashore to seize all customs facilities and prevent General Victoriano Huerta's regime from receiving German arms. Street fighting costs the Americans 17 dead and 63 wounded to a Mexican tally of 126 killed and 195 injured; 55 Congressional Medals of Honor are awarded, the highest ever granted for a single action.

APRIL 22 In Washington, D.C., the Bureau of Navigation authorizes formal flight instruction and mechanical repair courses at the Flying School in Pensacola, Florida.

APRIL 24 At Veracruz, Mexico, the battleship *Mississippi* arrives with the 2nd Aero Section under Lieutenant Patrick N. L. Bellinger.

APRIL 25 Over the Gulf of Mexico, Lieutenant Patrick N. L. Bellinger flies a Curtiss AB-3 flying boat off the battleship *Mississippi*. He scouts for mines in Veracruz's harbor, becoming the first American pilot to operate in a combat zone.

APRIL 28 Over Veracruz, Mexico, Lieutenant Patrick N. L. Bellinger and Ensign Walter D. LaMont perform one of the earliest-known reconnaissance flights by photographing harbor installations.

MAY 2 Near Tejar, Mexico, an AH-3 hydroaeroplane flown by Lieutenant Patrick N. L. Bellinger and Ensign W. D. LaMont perform the first recorded ground support mission by buzzing guerrillas who have fired on a party of marines.

MAY 6 Over Veracruz, Mexico, Lieutenant Patrick N. L. Bellinger's Curtiss AH-3 hydroaeroplane takes anti-aircraft fire; Lieutenant Richard C. Saufley, his observer, is wounded, becoming America's first aerial casualty.

MAY 24 The cruiser *Birmingham* arrives outside Veracruz, Mexico, carrying with it the 1st Aero Section under Lieutenant John H. Towers. In light of a lack of military urgency, they resume training activities.

MAY 26 Lieutenant Holden C. Richardson recommends that the Navy purchase two Burgess-Dune hydroaeroplanes for expanded evaluation; these eventually enter the service as the AH-7 and AH-10.

JULY 1 In Washington, D.C., the Office of Naval Aeronautics under Captain Mark I. Bristol becomes a branch within the Division of Operations under the Secretary of the Navy. They are tasked with facilitating future development in aerial operations. The secretary also orders wine rations eliminated from flag and wardroom messes of all U.S. Navy vessels; these have remained dry ever since.

JULY 11 At Quincy, Massachusetts, the new battleship *Nevada*, the first naval vessel to utilize fuel oil for propulsion, slides off the stays. This enhanced design is also capable of bringing 10 14-inch guns to bear on targets.

AUGUST 15 In Panama, the Panama Canal officially opens. It is a highly significant strategic asset that shortens the transit of warships shuttling between the Atlantic and Pacific Oceans.

AUGUST 21 Three naval officers are dispatched to Paris, France, for a two-day inspection of aircraft factories and nearby aerodromes. This is the first time that Naval Aviators have been sent abroad as foreign observers.

OCTOBER 10–12 In Panama, the collier *Jupiter* is the first Navy vessel to pass through the Panama Canal, en route to Philadelphia from the West Coast.

NOVEMBER 16 At Pensacola, Florida, aviation administration shifts from command vessels offshore to land facilities. Henceforth the base receives the official designation of Naval Aeronautical Station (NAS), Pensacola.

NOVEMBER 23 In Washington, D.C., Captain Mark L. Bristol is officially appointed "Director of Naval Aeronautics," and reports directly to the Secretary of the Navy in that capacity.

DECEMBER 1 In Washington, D.C., the noted naval theorist Alfred Thayer Mahan dies at the age of 74. His publications invigorated naval construction programs around the world, particularly in the United States.

DECEMBER 17 In Washington, D.C., Secretary of State William Jennings Bryant dispatches the gunboat *Machias* to Port au Prince, Haiti, to seize the $500,000 gold reserve of the national bank and prevent revolutionaries from looting the treasury.

DECEMBER 25 In Washington, D.C., Director of Naval Aeronautics Captain Mark L. Bristol authorizes installment of meteorological equipment to measure wind gusts and squalls.

1915

JANUARY 21 In Washington, D.C., the Bureau of Navigation issues its first seven Navy pilot "Certificates."

The cruiser *San Diego* suffers a boiler explosion, and Fireman Second Class Telesforo Trinidad wins a Congressional Medal of Honor for rescuing several shipmates.

JANUARY 23 Near Cap-Haiten, Haiti, the cruiser *Washington* under Captain Edward L. Beach arrives for scheduled meetings with rebel leader General Sam.

JANUARY 28 In the South Atlantic, the American cargo ship *William P. Frye* is torpedoed without warning by the German auxiliary cruiser *Prinz Eitel Friedrich*. This becomes the first American merchant vessel sunk in World War I.

JANUARY 30 In Washington, D.C., Congress creates the new U.S. Coast Guard by combining the Revenue Cutter Service and the Life Saving Service. This serves under the Treasury Department in peacetime, and is tasked with suppressing contraband trade and patrolling nearby sea lanes. In the event of war, the Coast Guard functions within the Navy Department.

FEBRUARY 1 In Washington, D.C., the Bureau of Navigation's Division of Naval Militia Affairs creates an aeronautic corps within state naval militias.

MARCH 3 In Washington, D.C., Congress approves the Naval Act of 1915, which increases personnel assigned to naval aviation units to 48 officers and 96 men. Moreover, enlisted men and student pilots are eligible for increased pay and benefits once they qualify as aviators. The act also stipulates creation of the U.S. Naval Reserve and a new senior post, the Chief of Naval Operations (CNO).

MARCH 8 The *Baltimore*, a former cruiser, becomes the world's first dedicated mine-laying ship.

MARCH 22 The Navy Department authorizes use of the term "Naval Aviator" to signify those naval officers qualified by flying credentials.

MARCH 25 Offshore at Honolulu, Hawaii, the submarine *F-4* sinks with the loss of all 21 crew members. These are also the first American submarine casualties.

APRIL 16 Near Pensacola, Florida, an AB-2 flying boat flown by Lieutenant Patrick N. L. Bellinger is successfully catapulted from a barge.

APRIL 17 Near Honolulu, Hawaii, diver William F. Loughman's air hose becomes ensnared during salvage operations to raise the submarine *F-4*; Chief Gunner's Mate Frank W. Crilley dons a diving suit and rescues him, receiving a Congressional Medal of Honor.

APRIL 23 Over Pensacola, Florida, Lieutenant Patrick N. L. Bellinger sets a new American record for seaplanes by working his Burgess-Dunne AH-10 to an altitude of 10,000 feet.

MAY 1 Off the Scilly Isles, southwest England, the tanker *Gulflight* is sunk by a U-Boat, and three sailors are killed. The German government promises to make speedy reparations, but German Ambassador Count von Bernstoff reiterates a warning for neutral civilians not to travel on vessels carrying war materials for the allies.

MAY 7 Off the Irish coast, the huge Cunard liner *Lusitania* sinks in 18 minutes after being torpedoed by the German U-20. Casualties are enormous with 1,198 of its 1,924 passengers dead, including 128 Americans (63 children among them). This single act dramatically shifts American public opinion against Germany, but President Woodrow Wilson clings steadfastly to isolationism.

MAY 8 Near Pensacola, Florida, Lieutenant Melvin L. Stolz dies in the crash of an AH-9 hydroaeroplane.

MAY 11 In Washington, D.C., Admiral William S. Benson gains appointment as the first Chief of Naval Operations (CNO), despite the fact he was never closely identified with naval reform.

MAY 28 The Flying School at Pensacola, Florida, announces that refresher flights are available to limited numbers of aviators in the Naval Militia.

JUNE 1 Connecticut Aircraft Company, New Haven, contracts with the Navy to build the dirigible DN-1, its first lighter-than-air vehicle.

JULY 1 Offshore at Cap Haitien, Haiti, continuing unrest prompts the cruiser *Washington* to send parties of sailors and marines ashore to secure American lives and property. Admiral William B. Caperton also comes ashore to oversee radio communication between his vessel and the American consulate.

JULY 7 In Washington, D.C., Secretary of the Navy Josephus Daniels solicits cooperation with the civilian sector to mobilize the latest scientific and technological developments for the Navy. Ultimately, the Naval Consulting Board is founded to assist the service during World War I.

JULY 10 In Washington, D.C., the emphasis on scientific testing manifests in the new Aeronautical Engine Laboratory at the Washington Navy Yard. This organization is tasked with testing all machinery associated with naval aviation.

The Navy Department issues a General Order to create organizational unity on the Naval Militia's aeronautical units. Accordingly, each will consist of 6 officers and 28 enlisted men, with two sections forming a division, while the highest rank allowed is lieutenant commander.

JULY 16 In Panama, the battleships *Missouri*, *Ohio*, and *Wisconsin* are the first capital ships to pass through the Panama Canal, confirming its utility as a strategic asset.

JULY 21 In Washington, D.C., President Woodrow Wilson requests Secretary of War Lindley M. Garrison and Secretary of the Navy Josephus Daniels to promulgate plans for increased defense expenditures.

JULY 22 In Washington, D.C., the Director of Naval Aeronautics issues exacting standardized equipment requirements for all naval aircraft, including: air speed meter, incidence indicator, tachometer, skidding and sideslip indicator, altitude barometer, oil gauge, fuel gauge, compass, course and distance indicator, magazine camera, binoculars, clock, and sextant.

AUGUST 5 At Fortress Monroe, Virginia, Lieutenant Patrick N. L. Bellinger spots mortar fire for Army batteries for the first time while flying a Burgess-Dunne AH-10.

AUGUST 11 In Rochester, New York, the Eastman Kodak Company is approached by the Navy to develop aerial cameras capable of clear reconnaissance photography at altitude of 1,000–2,000 feet.

AUGUST 12 In Haiti, elections arranged by Admiral William B. Caperton make Sudre Dartiguenave Haiti's seventh president in as many years. Caperton also imposes a military government at Cap Haitien to preclude a rival administration under Dr. Rosalvo Gonaives from arising.

The Panama Canal was completed in 1914, just as World War I began. United States military presence at the canal was strong because of the canal's strategic and economic importance. (U.S. Naval Historical Center)

August 17 In Washington, D.C., Secretary of the Navy Josephus Daniels requests that the Secretary of War provide Navy and Marine aviators with training to operate aircraft from land.

September 9 Chief Watertender Eugene P. Smith wins the Congressional Medal of Honor for rescuing injured sailors after an explosion aboard the destroyer *Decatur*.

October 12 In Washington, D.C., the Navy Department abolishes the Office of the Director of Naval Aeronautics and transfers its responsibilities to the Chief of Naval Operations (CNO).

October 15 In Washington, D.C., the Secretary of the Navy approaches the General Board with Captain Mark L. Bristol's proposal that a merchant ship be equipped to operate aircraft. He also urges the board to figure out how to employ the battleship *North Carolina*, which is outfitted with a catapult for launching aircraft.

October 19 At New London, Connecticut, the Navy founds a major submarine station.

November 5 Near Pensacola, Florida, Lieutenant Commander Henry C. Mustin is successfully catapulted off the battleship *North Carolina* in a AB-2 flying boat. This is also the first shipboard launching of an aircraft from a vessel underway; announcement of the feat is made by Assistant Secretary of the Navy Franklin D. Roosevelt.

November 11 In Haiti, Rear Admiral William B. Caperton persuades the government to allow American officials to administer local customs houses and collect revenues to reduce public debt.

December 1 At Pensacola, Florida, the Naval Flying School formally opens with an officer, 3 instructors, and 12 mechanics. This day Congress also earmarks $1 million for military aviation, its largest expenditure ever.

December 3 Over Pensacola, Florida, Lieutenant Richard C. Saufley establishes a new American altitude record of 11,975 feet in a Curtis AH-14 hydroaeroplane.

December 4 In Washington, D.C., Rear Admiral Frank F. Fletcher is the first officer of his grade awarded a Congressional Medal of Honor for his actions at Veracruz, Mexico, in April 1914.

December 7 In Washington, D.C., President Woodrow Wilson advances a naval expansion program totaling $500 million. This is intended to purchase no less than 10 battleships, 6 battle cruisers, 10 cruisers, 50 destroyers, and 100 submarines.

1916

January 6 At Pensacola, Florida, flight instruction for enlisted men commences. The Navy Flying School has since mushroomed to 58 officers, 431 enlisted men, and 33 seaplanes.

January 11 In Washington, D.C., the Naval Observatory forwards two British Creigh-Osborne magnetic compasses to the Flying School, Pensacola, Florida, for operational testing. These devices will be widely used on naval aircraft throughout World War I.

January 21 The Superintendent, Radio Service, instructs the Pensacola Radio

Station to begin large-scale experiments with aircraft radio; by summer 50 radio sets are on order.

JANUARY 24 After a room aboard the battleship *New York* fills with dangerous gases, Gunner's Mate Wilhelm Smith wins a Congressional Medal of Honor for rescuing several shipmates.

FEBRUARY 10 In Washington, D.C., the Bureau of Construction and Repair authorizes assigned numbers to aircraft for identification purposes. This is the genesis of serial numbers assigned to all naval aircraft.

MARCH 4 In Washington, D.C., Captain Mark L. Bristol, Director of Naval Aeronautics, is reassigned to the battleship *North Carolina* as the new Commander of the Air Service. He is responsible for supervising aircraft, air stations, and developments connected with naval aviation.

MARCH 11 The new battleship *Nevada* is commissioned; the other ship in this class is the *Oklahoma*.

MARCH 25 In Washington, D.C., the Navy Department issues a General Order refining qualifications for officers and enlisted men in the Naval Militia; these are brought much closer to standard Navy requirements.

MARCH 29 Over Pensacola, Florida, Lieutenant Richard C. Saufley establishes a new American altitude record of 16,010 feet, flying a Curtiss hydroaeroplane.

MARCH 30 At Pensacola, Florida, Lieutenants Charles E. Sugden and Elmer F. Stone become the first Coast Guard officers to receive flight training.

APRIL 15 In Washington, D.C., the Bureau of Construction and Repair issues regulations for aircraft identification markings. All Navy airplanes now carry an anchor and a two-digit numeral painted in blue against a white background on the upper and lower wing surfaces, and both sides of the fuselage.

MAY 13 In Washington, D.C., the Chief of Naval Operations orders development of gyroscopic modifications for airplane instruments; these ultimately include compasses, bombsights, and turn and bank indicators.

MAY 14 In Santo Domingo, Dominican Republic, Rear Admiral William B. Caperton confers with General Desiderio Arias, who has taken up arms against President Juan Isidro Jimenez, convincing him to peacefully remove his followers from the city.

MAY 20 In Washington, D.C., the Bureau of Ordnance allocates $750 to the Sperry Gyroscope Corporation for a gyroscopically operated bombsight.

MAY 22 At the Naval Aeronautical School, Pensacola, a Hess-Ives Corporation color camera is tested to evaluate whether or not color photography can be applied to aerial reconnaissance.

JUNE In Seattle, Washington, William E. Boeing flies the first airplane made at his new Boeing Airplane Company, convincing Navy representatives to purchase 50 Model C floatplanes.

JUNE 1 At Puerta Plata, Santo Domingo, sailors and marines from the gunboat *Sacramento* go ashore and skirmish with rebels forces.

JUNE 3 At Pensacola, Florida, the Naval Flying School still offers free and captive ballooning courses to prospective naval aviators.

JUNE 9 Near Pensacola, Florida, Lieutenant Richard C. Saufley fatally crashes his AH-9 hydroaeroplane on Santa Rosa Island. He had managed to stay aloft 8 hours and 51 minutes while attempting a new endurance record.

JUNE 12 The new battleship *Pennsylvania* is placed in commission.

JUNE 17 The troop ship *Henderson* is the first Navy transport vessel specifically designed to carry Marines and their equipment.

JUNE 20 In Washington, D.C., the Navy Department issues a General Order providing bureau recognition to lighter-than-air machines in its inventory.

JULY 12 In Pensacola Bay, Florida, Lieutenant Godfrey deC. Chevalier makes his final calibration launch off the battleship *North Carolina* in an AB-3 flying boat. The *North Carolina* is the first capital ship outfitted for aircraft operations.

JULY 17 At Norwich, Connecticut, Navy Inspector Lieutenant George D. Murray observes flight tests of the Gallaudet seaplane. This is a revolutionary design with a propeller mounted mid-way down the fuselage.

JULY 18 In Washington, D.C., the Secretary of the Navy issues clothing allowances to all naval flight personnel; pilots receive helmets, goggles, and safety jackets, while enlisted men receive wool head covers, suits, and boots.

JULY 22 In Washington, D.C., Chief Constructor Rear Admiral David W. Taylor approaches the Aluminum Company of America to develop lighter alloys for possible use in dirigible construction.

AUGUST 8 In Washington, D.C., the Secretary of the Navy directs that the General Board is responsible for providing desired numbers and characteristics of new aircraft, whereas the Bureau of Construction is tasked with aircraft procurement and development.

AUGUST 10 In Washington, D.C., the Bureau of Construction negotiates with Glenn H. Curtiss for the acquisition of 30 J-9 trainers. These are delivered between November 1916 and February 1917, and function as the Navy's most popular training aircraft.

AUGUST 12 In Washington, D.C. the secretaries of War and the Navy agree that the Deperdussin system of flight controls will become standardized equipment on aircraft of both services.

AUGUST 17 At Pensacola, Florida, the mission of the Naval Aeronautical Station becomes restricted to flight instruction for commissioned and enlisted personnel. All manufacturing, experimental test, inspection, and related functions are henceforth being transferred to a forthcoming Aeronautics School.

AUGUST 19 In Washington, D.C., the Navy Department formally organizes the U.S. Navy Reserve Force.

AUGUST 29 In Washington, D.C., Congress passes the Naval Appropriations Act of 1917 which founds a Naval Flying Corps with 150 officers and 350 enlisted men, which includes a Naval Flying Reserve Corps of six classes.

The first Coast Guard Aviation Division is also established, but, because funding does not materialize until 1926, Coast Guard pilots train and operate within Navy aviation units.

Furthermore, the Naval Preparedness Act ("Big Navy") passed this day enlarges the Navy for possible conflict in European waters. The $500 million appropriated will acquire 10 battleships, 6 battle cruisers, 10 scout cruisers, 60 destroyers, and 67 submarines over a three-year period. This crash expansion renders the U.S. Navy as second to none.

Near Santo Domingo, Dominican Republic, the cruiser *Memphis* under Captain Edward L. Beach is struck by a tidal wave and sinks, with the loss of 40 sailors. Three Congressional Medals of Honor are awarded, including one posthumously, for bravery while saving shipmates.

SEPTEMBER 2   Over North Island, San Diego, California, two naval aviators transmit and receive radio telegraph messages for the first time at a distance of two miles. In-flight communication is becoming technically feasible and is a tremendous boon to aerial operations.

SEPTEMBER 7   In Washington, D.C., the United States Shipping Board arises to acquire merchant ships for naval purposes, especially for shipping military forces abroad.

SEPTEMBER 9   In Washington, D.C., the Secretary of the Navy initiates a program of formal flight testing for accepting all new aircraft into the service. This is accompanied by establishment of proper procedures to ensure safe aircraft operations.

SEPTEMBER 12   At Amityville, Long Island, New York, Lieutenant T. W. Wilkinson, Bureau of Ordnance, observes the first successful flight of an airplane guided by a gyroscope invented by Elmer Sperry. This device ensures the accuracy and safety of long-distance flights.

SEPTEMBER 20   In Washington, D.C., the Navy Department issues color regulations for all Curtiss N-9 training machines to be finished in bright yellow varnish—a warning that neophytes are at the controls!

OCTOBER 11   In Washington, D.C., the Secretaries of War and the Navy agree to a joint Aeronautics Board to evaluate the requirements for lighter-than-air machines currently in service.

OCTOBER 17   The new battleship *Arizona* is commissioned; it remains entombed at the bottom of Pearl Harbor, the victim of a 1941 Japanese aerial attack.

OCTOBER 24   In Washington, D.C., the Bureau of Steam Engineering instructs the Philadelphia Navy Yard to develop a radio directional finder employing wavelengths from 600 to 4,000 meters.

OCTOBER 27   In Washington, D.C., the Chief of Naval Operations orders that all aircraft loaned or donated to Naval Militia units receive the designation NMAH.

NOVEMBER 8   At the Naval Proving Ground, Indian Head, Maryland, a pair of naval aviators die when the bomb they are carrying detonates prematurely.

NOVEMBER 17   In Washington, D.C., Chief Constructor David W. Taylor solicits design proposals from various companies to acquire new seaplanes capable of flying between 50 to 95 miles per hour, remain aloft for two-and-a-half hours, and carry a radio.

NOVEMBER 29   In the Dominican Republic, Captain Harry S. Knapp is appointed military governor, and the entire island is placed under the military jurisdiction of the United States.

DECEMBER 7   At the Naval Air Station, Pensacola, Florida, Lieutenant Commander Henry C. Mustin extolls the Eastman Aero Camera, which has produced satisfactory photographs from altitudes of between 600 to 5,100 feet.

DECEMBER 12   The tasks of Commander of the Air Service are transferred to Rear Admiral Albert Gleaves, Commander Destroyer Force, Atlantic Fleet.

December 22 In New York, inventor Elmer B. Sperry files a patent application for his "aerial torpedo," an unmanned airplane piloted by a gyrostabilizer.

December 30 In Washington, D.C., the Commission of Navy Yards and Naval Stations recommends that a joint Army-Navy Board should jointly decide the location of new air bases, with a view towards enhancing national defense.

1917

January 6 In Washington, D.C., the Secretaries of War and the Navy are encouraged by a joint Army-Navy Board to acquire lighter-than-air ships based on the German Zeppelin design. Future funding will be evenly split between the two services, and a joint board with three officers from each service arises to ensure close cooperation.

January 8 Above Pensacola, Florida, a Benet-Mercie machine gun, mounted on a Burgess-Dunne AH-10, is fired successfully from altitudes of 100 and 200 feet.

January 10 In Washington, D.C., the Naval Observatory places its first order for 20 Aero Cameras from the Eastman Kodak Company. This is the first such equipment acquired for American military aircraft.

January 13 Near Eureka, California, the cruiser *Milwaukee* grounds while attempting to refloat the sunken submarine *H-3*, and wrecks without loss of life.

February 4 In Washington, D.C., the Secretary of the Navy issues a contract for 16 nonrigid, Class B airships from the Connecticut Aircraft Corporation, the Goodyear Tire & Rubber Company, and the B. F. Goodrich Company.

February 5 In Washington, D.C., the Chief of Naval Operations urges that eight aeronautical coastal patrol stations be constricted at strategic points along the Eastern Seaboard. European affairs are beginning to weigh heavily on national security.

February 12 At Cuba, the gunboat *Paducah* sends the bulk of its crew members ashore to protect American lives and property during a period of unrest.

February 15 Outside Santiago Harbor, Cuba, Commander Dudley Knox of the gunboat *Petrel* drops anchor and strikes a bargain with local rebels. In exchange for not allowing governmental vessels to enter the harbor, the rebels pledge not to scuttle a ship in the channel.

February 26 In Washington, D.C., President Woodrow Wilson asks Congress to pass the Armed Ship Bill for arming merchant vessels. However, a group of pacifist senators under Robert La Follette filibusters its passage.

February 28 At North Island, San Diego, California, the successful experiments with radio/voice communications between aircraft and ground stations transpire for the first time.

March 1 In Washington, D.C., Congress overcomes opposition to a law permitting the arming of merchant vessels to defend themselves against U-boat attacks.

March 4   In Washington, D.C., President Woodrow Wilson signs the Naval Appropriations Bill of $157 million. This is the largest naval expenditure in history to that date.

March 8   In Santiago, Cuba, large numbers of Cuban rebels surrender to landing parties from the *San Francisco*, *Olympia*, and *Machias* rather than turn themselves over to government forces.

March 9   In Washington, D.C., President Woodrow Wilson orders merchant vessels armed without the consent of Congress. The deck weapons in question are to be manned by Navy gun crews, and Navy vessels are also ordered to return fire if attacked.

March 12   In Washington, D.C., the Secretaries of War and the Navy sign the first-ever interservice cooperative agreement regarding the development of aeronautical technology.

March 13   In Washington, D.C., the Bureau of Construction and Repair updates regulations regarding airplane coloring, and orders all seaplanes finished in an overall yellow color.

March 14–21   German U-boats, waging unrestricted warfare against neutral shipping, sink five American merchant vessels.

March 17   In Washington, D.C., the Navy Department authorizes recruitment of women "yeomanettes" to perform clerical tasks and other functions. Ultimately, 11,275 are recruited during World War I.

March 24   At West Palm Beach, Florida, 29 men from the First Yale Unit enlist in the Naval Reserve Force and begin military training.

March 26   In Washington, D.C., the Joint Army-Navy Airship Board arises to facilitate their application to military uses.

March 31   In the Virgin Islands, Rear Admiral James H. Oliver is appointed the first governor of this territory, recently acquired from Denmark.

April 6   In Washington, D.C., the Secretary of the Navy establishes standard flight-clothing issues for the Naval Flight Service, including long coats, helmets, goggles, gloves, boots, and life belts.

The declaration of war against Imperial Germany finds the Navy at a strength of 4,376 officers and 69,680 enlisted men. Though small by European standards, it is well-trained and -led.

April 7   In Washington, D.C., President Woodrow Wilson signs an executive order transferring the Coast Guard to the Navy for operational purposes.

April 9   Rear Admiral William S. Sims is dispatched to London to establish high-level contacts with Royal Navy authorities, and is shocked to learn that Great Britain is within weeks of losing the war to a U-Boat blockade. Sims consequently implores the Navy Department to forward every available destroyer or patrol vessel to counter the threat. He also urges that the Navy adopt a convoy system advocated by several British officers.

April 13   In New York City, the battleship *New Mexico* is launched. This is the first capital ship utilizing a turbine electric drive, and it is commissioned a year later.

April 14   In Washington, D.C., the Naval Consulting Board suggests appropriating $50,000 for developing "aerial torpedoes" in the form of automatically controlled airplanes that carry high explosives. This project is the Navy's first guided-missile program.

> ### Sims, William S. (1858–1936)
>
> William Sowden Sims was born in Port Chester, Ontario, on October 15, 1858, and raised in Orbisonia, Pennsylvania. He graduated from the U.S. Naval Academy in 1880 and fulfilled routine duties at sea for several years. In 1900 Sims encountered Captain Percy Scott of the Royal Navy, who had invented a new, continuous aiming and firing method, and urged its adoption. When the Navy Department ignored his recommendation, Sims violated the chain of command by appealing directly to President Theodore Roosevelt, an avowed naval reformer, who appointed him inspector of target practice as a lieutenant commander. Over the next five years, Sims helped transform Navy gunnery into the world's finest. In 1907 he became the youngest naval officer to command a capital ship by taking charge of the battleship *Minnesota*. Sims also visited England, and made an unauthorized pledge of U.S. support in the event of a war with Germany, which drew a reprimand from President William Howard Taft.
>
> Sims advanced to rear admiral in 1917 and also served as president of the U.S. Naval War College in Newport, Rhode Island. Following President Woodrow Wilson's declaration of war against Germany, Sims suddenly found himself in charge of all U.S. naval forces in European waters. He was on particularly good terms with the Royal Navy's hierarchy, whom he admired, and he integrated all American naval assets under British control. For his role in helping win the war, Sims received a temporary promotion to admiral in December 1918. He died in Boston, Massachusetts, on September 28, 1936, an outspoken advocate of naval modernization.

APRIL 18 In the North Atlantic, the American transport *Mongolia*, carrying a Navy armed guard, fires upon a surfaced U-boat in the Atlantic and wrecks its conning tower.

APRIL 20 At Pensacola, Florida, the DN-1, the Navy's first rigid airship, performs unsatisfactorily and is grounded after three flights.

APRIL 24 At Boston, Massachusetts, Destroyer Squadron Eight under Commander Joseph K. Taussig, consisting of the *Porter*, *Conyngham*, *Wadsworth*, *McDougal*, *Davis*, and *Wainwright*, sails directly for Queenstown, Ireland.

APRIL 26 At the Mare Island Navy Yard, California, the armored cruiser *Huntington* performs pioneering dead-load tests on its aircraft catapult.

MAY 1 In Washington, D.C., the Navy Department adopts a training program for prospective aircraft and dirigible pilots. These are to be offered every three months, and include provisions for instructing enlisted men as mechanics and quartermasters.

MAY 4 At Squantum, Massachusetts, and Bay Shore, New York, the naval militia stations are taken over by regular Navy officers. These are used to expand flight training programs, until more permanent stations are constructed.

At Queenstown (Cobh), Ireland, Commander Joseph K. Taussig of Destroyer Squadron Eight, anchors with the *Conyngham*, *Davis*, *McDougal*, *Porter*, *Wainwright*, and *Wadsworth*, and reports for duty. When his British superior inquires how much time is necessary before his ships are ready for action, Taussig declares, "We are ready now, sir."

MAY 5 In Washington, D.C., the Secretaries of War and the Navy continue the trend towards standardization and interservice cooperation by convening a "joint technical board" to standardize the design and performance of forthcoming aircraft.

At Pensacola, Florida, a synchronized Berthier machine gun is successfully test-fired through the propeller arc of a Curtiss R–3 as it taxies on water.

MAY 15 In Washington, D.C., the Secretary of the Navy lists aircraft acquisitions as the ninth of 20 major priorities for wartime preparations.

MAY 17 In Washington, D.C., the Chief of Naval Operations authorizes the purchase of 50 machine guns and synchronizing equipment in the naval air arm's first armament program. Captain Noble E. Irwin also replaces Lieutenant John H. Towers as Officer-in-Charge of the aviation desk, Matériel Branch, Chief of Naval Operations.

At Newport News, Virginia, the Curtiss Exhibition Company contracts to train 20 men of the Naval Reserve Flying Force.

MAY 18 Representatives of the Army and Navy Bureau of Standards observe the first demonstration of self-sealing fuel tanks for aircraft. These are essential to keep aircraft from catching on fire once damaged.

MAY 19 In Washington, D.C., the Chief of Naval Operations requisitions two small seaplanes and one pilot for continuing radio experiments at Pensacola, Florida.

MAY 23 In Washington, D.C., the Joint Technical Board on Airplanes recommends that the Navy acquire 30 school trainers, 200 service seaplanes, 100 speed scouts, and 100 large seaplanes.

MAY 24 At Hampton Roads, Virginia, the first American convoy bound for England departs under armed escort. This combination is the key to defeating Germany's U-Boat menace.

MAY 28 Near Mare Island, San Francisco, California, the armored cruiser *Huntington* conducts quixotic aeronautical experiments involving manned kite balloons.

MAY 29 In the North Atlantic, the Navy commences routine convoy duty by escorting the first of 911,047 Army troops and millions of tons of supplies and equipment safely to the European theater. The deed is accomplished by the newly formed Cruiser and Transport Force of Rear Admiral Albert Gleaves, and, considering the lethality of U-boats, the results are impressive.

JUNE 5–6 At Bordeaux and St. Nazaire, France, the 1st Aeronautical Detachment under Lieutenant Kenneth Whiting lands. It is the first naval aviation unit deployed to Continental Europe. It is conveyed there by the colliers *Jupiter* and *Neptune*, the first of 500 aircraft and 16,000 men to follow. The Navy also constructs 16 naval air stations in France, 5 in Ireland, 3 in England, and 2 in Italy.

JUNE 9 In New York, 6 armed yachts of the U.S. Patrol Squadron sail for Brest, France, to assist antisubmarine and mine-sweeping operations. The patrol force expands to include 38 destroyers and 16 armed yachts under Rear Admiral Henry B. Wilson.

JUNE 14 At Montauk, Rockaway, and Bay Shore, New York, the Navy contracts to acquire its first permanent aerial-patrol stations on the eastern seaboard.

JUNE 17 Major Raynal C. Bolling and a joint Army-Navy aviation board are dispatched to Europe by the Aircraft Production Board. There they will study, evaluate, and help to incorporate advanced manufacturing techniques in aircraft production at home.

JULY In Washington, D.C., the Navy Department determines to neutralize Germany's U-boats by suspending capital

British convoy steering a zig-zag path to avoid possible U-boat attack. The convoy system successfully carried almost half of the American land forces to Europe. (Hammerton, Sir J. A., A Popular History of the Great War, 1917)

ship construction, in favor of acquiring larger numbers of smaller ships capable of antisubmarine warfare.

JULY 9   At Ontario, Canada, Ensign Frederick S. Allen conducts a group of 24 future Naval Aviators to the University of Toronto to train under the auspices of the Canadian Royal Flying Corps. Ultimately, 100 naval aviators will be trained by the Canadians.

JULY 10   A plan for training officers in the Naval Reserve Flying Corps emerges and consists of three parts: a Ground School for indoctrination, a Preliminary Flight School featuring up to 10 hours of solo flying, and a Completing Flight School to hone abilities as Naval Aviators. The plan is ultimately implemented, although official sanction is lacking

JULY 23   At Cambridge, Massachusetts, prospective Naval Aviators receive ground instruction at the Massachusetts Institute of Technology (MIT). Similar programs are also established at the University of Seattle, Washington, and Dunwoody Institute, Minneapolis, Minnesota.

In the South Atlantic, the cruiser *Pittsburgh* suffers a deadly casemate explosion; Lieutenant Willis Winter Bradley and Seamen Ora Graves receive Congressional Medals of Honor for saving their shipmates.

JULY 27   North Island, San Diego, California, is appropriated by the Army and Navy for establishing permanent training facilities. It emerges as one of the Navy's most important air stations along the west coast.

In Pennsylvania, the Naval Aircraft Factory begins building at the Navy Yard, Philadelphia. This government company is tasked with developing and constructing aircraft intended for use in naval aviation.

AUGUST 8   In Washington, D.C., the Secretary of the Navy approves a plan of overseas base construction, which includes one aviation-training and three coastal-patrol stations in France. By war's end, 27 such bases are operational in France, England, Ireland, and Italy.

AUGUST 14   Over Huntington Bay, New York, Lieutenant Edward O. McDonnell conducts the first experimental torpedo drop from an aircraft. In practice, the dummy ordnance ricochets off the water and strikes the craft, nearly downing it.

AUGUST 25   In Washington, D.C., Chief Constructor David W. Taylor requests that a large seaplane capable of flying across the Atlantic in wartime be developed. The result is the Curtiss NC flying boat, which arrives too late for combat.

SEPTEMBER 7   At Pensacola, Florida, messages from Simon radio transmitters are received at Naval Radio Station New Orleans, Louisiana, 140 miles away. Consequently, an additional 300 transmitters are purchased.

SEPTEMBER 8   At Hampton Roads, Virginia, an air training and patrol base arises at the Naval Operating Base, which also conducts experimental work in seaplane aviation.

SEPTEMBER 16   Near Mine Head, Ireland, the *U-61* unsuccessfully attacks the destroyer *Cassin*. Gunner's Mate Osmond K. Ingram responds by attempting to roll a depth charge over the side, but he is thrown overboard instead, the first American sailor killed in action. Ingram receives a posthumous Congressional Medal of Honor.

SEPTEMBER 17   An observation kite balloon released by the cruiser *Huntington* crashes after the pilot is ensnared in the rigging and is dragged underwater; Ships Fitter Patrick McGunigal dives overboard, rescues him, and wins a Congressional Medal of Honor.

SEPTEMBER 18   In Washington, D.C., the Joint Technical Board on Aircraft outlines a production program to acquire 1,700 naval aircraft.

SEPTEMBER 25   Off the Florida coast, a Navy plane crashes, and Chief Machinist's Mate Francis E. Ormsbee wins a Congressional Medal of Honor for his failed attempt to save the pilot.

OCTOBER 6   In Washington, D.C., the Secretary of War authorizes the Navy to utilize part of the Army landing field at Anacostia, D.C., where a seaplane hangar is erected.

OCTOBER 11   In the Brooklyn Navy Yard, New York, the battleship *North Carolina* is stripped of all its catapult-launching equipment. It had previously played an important role in the rise of naval aviation.

OCTOBER 13   The armored cruiser *Huntington* is stripped of all its aeronautical equipment prior to being deployed on convoy duty.

OCTOBER 16   The Naval Aircraft Factory at Philadelphia, Pennsylvania, rolls out its first completed aircraft only 67 days after construction began.

OCTOBER 24   At Naval Air Station, Moutchic, France, flight and ground instruction commences. All naval air units deployed in Europe will pass through this base before becoming operational.

NOVEMBER 2   At Buffalo, New York, the 12 men of the Second Yale Detachment who had obtained pilot training at their own expense become ensigns in the U.S. Navy Reserve Force, as well as Naval Aviators.

NOVEMBER 5   Off the French coast, U-boat *UC-71* torpedoes and sinks the motor patrol yacht *Alcedo*, with a loss of 22 men. This is the first U.S. Navy vessel lost in World War I.

When Seaman Tedford H. Cann discovers a leak in a flooded compartment on board the steam yacht *May*, he risks his life closing it; Cann receives a Congressional Medal of Honor.

NOVEMBER 14   In Washington, D.C., Secretary of War Newton D. Baker grants priority to the Navy's efforts to develop seaplanes and seaplane bases for the war effort. Most Army aircraft will be purchased in Europe.

NOVEMBER 17   Off the coast of Ireland, destroyers *Fanning* under Lieutenant Arthur S. Carpender and *Nicholson* under Commander Frank D. Berrien spot a German submarine, roll depth charges, and sink *U-58*. This is the first and only enemy vessel destroyed by American warships during World War I.

NOVEMBER 18   At Naval Air Station, Le Croisic, France, Lieutenant William M. Corry's unit conducts the first flying-boat patrols of the war by operating near the mouth of the Loire River. Curiously, they are flying French-built Tellier seaplanes.

NOVEMBER 19   Near Gibraltar, Spain, the British merchantman *Rose* accidently rams and sinks the American destroyer *Chauncey*, killing 21 crew members including Commander Walter E. Reno.

NOVEMBER 21   At Amityville, New York, the Navy successfully demonstrates a pilotless Curtiss-built N-9 "aerial torpedo" (flying bomb).

NOVEMBER 22–24   Off the French coast, an armed patrol by a Navy-piloted seaplane ends embarrassingly, when the aircraft is forced down by mechanical malfunctions and drifts for two days. The crew is rescued by a French destroyer.

NOVEMBER 24   In Washington, D.C., the Chief of Naval Operations notes that current aircraft cannot carry more than 600 pounds of ordnance, so aerial torpedoes developed under this restriction would be insufficient to sink or even seriously damage a modern warship.

DECEMBER 1   In France, Naval Air Station Pauillac becomes an active assembly and repair station for all remaining naval air stations in the theater.

DECEMBER 4   At Newport, Rhode Island, the submarine *E-1* (formerly *Skipjack*) departs and becomes the first vessel of its kind to cross the Atlantic under its own power. It eventually patrols waters between Ponta and Delgada in the Azores to deny their ports to German U-boats.

DECEMBER 6   Off the Isles of Scilly, *U-53* torpedoes and sinks the destroyer *Jacob Jones*, which sinks in only eight minutes. Only 38 of the 108-man crew survive. The German commander chivalrously radios the Americans at Queenstown (Cobh), Ireland, the coordinates of the sinking.

DECEMBER 7   In Washington, D.C., the Secretary of the Navy authorizes the Curtiss Company to begin development of its HA or "Dunkirk Fighter." This is a single-pontoon seaplane armed with two forward-firing machines guns and a dual set, flexibly mounted in the rear cockpit. This is the first fighter-type aircraft under consideration by the Navy.

At Pensacola, Florida, the Naval Aeronautical Station there is officially redesignated a Naval Air Station (NAS).

In the Atlantic, Rear Admiral Hugh Rodman conducts Battleship Division Nine, consisting of the *Delaware*, *Florida*, *New York*, *Texas*, and *Wyoming*, to Scapa Flow, northern Scotland. They will join the British Grand Fleet as the Sixth Battle Squadron.

DECEMBER 17   Near San Pedro, California, submarine *F-1* collides with its stablemate *F-3* and sinks, killing 19 sailors.

In the Bay of Biscay, Boatswain's Mate John Mackenzie of the motor patrol boat *Remlik* secures a loose depth charge by hand during a heavy storm. He holds on until it can be discharged overboard, winning a Congressional Medal of Honor.

December 27 Near Queensland, Ireland, a German torpedo slices into the converted yacht *Santee*; it limps back into port with no casualties.

1918

January 1 Naval Air Station, Hampton, Virginia, becomes the new home for the Experimental and Test Department formerly located at Pensacola, Florida. The facility is now closer to manufacturing and industrial areas.

January 3 Commander Charles Belknap takes charge of the newly established Naval Overseas Transport Service (NOTS), tasked with shipping vast quantities of military supplies to Europe. It ultimately consists of 450 transport vessels, of which 8 are lost in combat.

February 3 At Camp Taliaferro, Fort Worth, Texas, Canadian Royal Flying Corps instructors provide aerial gunnery sessions for Naval Aviators.

February 6 In the North Atlantic, the passenger ship *Tuscania*, carrying the 32nd Division (Michigan and Wisconsin National Guard), is torpedoed by *U-77* and sunk. This is the first American troopship lost to hostile fire, and 267 men are killed.

February 7 In Washington, D.C., the Joint Army/Navy Technical Board arises to standardize instrumentation used by Army and Navy aircraft.

February 8 In Washington, D.C., the Navy Department updates national insignia regulations by adopting concentric red and blue circles on wing surfaces and fuselages.

February 21 Naval Air Station, Bolsena, Italy, is founded; it is the first of two such facilities established in Italy, and serves primarily for training purposes.

February 22 In Washington, D.C., the Director of Naval Communications requests that five naval air stations along the Atlantic Seaboard, plus those at San Diego, California, and Coco Solo, Panama, be fitted with modern wireless transmitters. This equipment will permit pilots to communicate with their home base while on patrol.

Naval Air Station, Queenstown, Ireland, is founded under Lieutenant Paul J. Peyton as an assembly and repair depot.

February 26 In Washington, D.C., the Chief of Naval Operations draws up a list for aerographic equipment deployed at naval air stations abroad to better gauge the impact of meteorology on aerial operations.

March 1 Paimboeuf, France, is established by Lieutenant Commander Louis H. Maxfield to serve as a dirigible station.

March 3 At Naval Air Station, Paimboeuf, France, naval aviators first go aloft in a borrowed AT-1 dirigible; this is the first of 12 such vehicles acquired by the Navy.

March 4 In the West Indies, the collier *Cyclops* under Lieutenant Commander

George W. Worley hoists anchor at Barbados and sails off, only to disappear without a trace.

March 7 In Washington, D.C., the Office of the Chief of Naval Operations establishes the new Office of the Director of Naval Aviation.

March 9 In Washington, D.C., the Navy Department upgrades its training program for Naval Aviators by allowing elementary and advanced specialization courses.

March 15 In Washington, D.C., the Bureau of Construction and Repair decrees that naval aircraft will be painted in low-visibility gray enamel.

March 19 Near Heligoland in the North Sea, Ensign Stephen Potter, flying long-range patrol missions with the Royal Flying Corps, become the first naval aviator to shoot down an enemy seaplane. On April 25, Potter dies while fighting seven enemy seaplanes near Felixstowe, England.

Off the Irish coast, the destroyer *Manley* under Commander Robert L. Berry accidentally collides with the British auxiliary cruiser HMS *Motagua*, and several depth charges stored above deck detonate. The *Manley* loses 56 crewmen, and limps into port with the rear third of its hull under water.

March 25 Ensign John F. McNamara, flying out of NAS Portland, England, conducts the Navy's first aerial attack by bombing a U-boat sighted off the English coast.

March 27 At the Navy Yard, Philadelphia, Pennsylvania, the first H-16 flying boat rolls out, being the first airplane constructed at the Naval Aircraft Factory. This large craft carries five crewmen, five machine guns, and two 230-pound bombs.

March 30 The Navy Department orders the Curtiss 18-T, a two-seater, single-engine triplane, from the Curtiss Engineering Corporation. This is armed with two fixed, forward-firing machine guns and two flexible guns operated by the rear gunner.

April 11 Near Corsewell Light, Scotland, the *UB-73* torpedoes and sinks the NOTS cargo ship *Lake Moor;* 46 lives are also lost.

April 17 In Quiberon Bay, France, the munitions vessel *Florence H.* endures an internal explosion. Ship's Cook Jesse Whitfield and Quartermaster Frank Monroe Upton from the nearby destroyer *Stewart* dive overboard and rescue a drowning man; both receive Congressional Medals of Honor.

April 23 At Naval Air Station, Pauillac, France, the first shipment of Liberty engines arrives.

In France, Lieutenant Commander Alexander Gordon Lyle, a Navy dentist serving with the 5th Marine Regiment, rescues a wounded corporal under heavy fire, winning a Congressional Medal of Honor.

April 27 At Naval Air Station, Paimboeuf, France, airship AT-1 under Lieutenant Frederick P. Culbert completes a 25-hour aerial patrol while escorting three convoys through a mine zone. This is the longest mission ever performed by this type of airship, and Culbert is commended by the French Minister of Marine.

April 30 In Washington, D.C., the Secretary of the Navy approves a proposal by the General Board and U.S. Naval Forces in Europe to create a specialized unit for operations against German U-boat pens in the Dunkirk-Zeebrugge region. This force is incarnated as the Northern Bombing Group.

May 6 Naval Air Station Coco Solo, Panama, arises under Lieutenant Ralph G. Pennoyer to patrol seaward approaches to the Panama Canal.

May 8 In the Mediterranean, Lieutenant Commander Richard P. McCullough and the armed yacht *Lydonia* cooperate with the destroyer HMS *Basilisk* to sink the *UB-70*.

May 12 In Great Britain, six 100-foot long, high-speed, wooden U.S. Navy subchasers, the genesis of what becomes known as the "Splinter Fleet," arrive. Of 121 such vessels committed to combat, only 2 are lost to mines.

May 15–16 In Washington, D.C., the Bureau of Steam Engineering announces in-flight results with the Marconi SE 1100 radio transmitter. Direct voice communication is now possible at distances of 50 miles, and code communications reach out to 120 miles. The SE 1100 becomes the first tube-set radio installed in naval aircraft.

May 18 In Washington, D.C., the Chief of Naval Operations orders eight training squadrons established, with two at Key West, Florida, four at Miami, Florida, and two at Bay Shore, New York. Six advanced-training squadrons are also to be assembled at Pensacola, Florida, for instruction in patrolling and night bombing.

May 20 At the New York Navy Yard, the battleship *New Mexico*, the first capital warship driven by electric power, is officially commissioned. This vessel displaces 32,000 tons and is 624 feet long.

May 21 Off the coast of Scotland, the *UC-58* torpedoes and sinks the Naval Overseas Transport Service (NOTS) tanker *William Rockefeller*, killing three crewmen.

On the converted yacht *Christabel*, Ensign Daniel Augustus Joseph Sullivan single-handedly secures depth charges scattered on the deck by a depth charge detonation; he receives a Congressional Medal of Honor.

May 24 At Pauillac, France, the first contingent of American-built HS-1 flying boats arrives onboard the vessels *Houston* and *Lake Placid*.

Near Murmansk, Russia, the cruiser *Olympia* under Captain Bion B. Bierer sends a landing party ashore as part of the Anglo-American occupation force. These have arrived to keep a large stockpile of war matériel from being captured by the Bolsheviks.

May 25 Near Cape Charles, Virginia, German U-boats begin infesting American coastal waters. The *U-151* attacks and damages three small schooners, but little is accomplished by such raids.

May 31 In the North Atlantic, *U-90* torpedoes the NOTS transport *President Lincoln*, sinking it with the loss of 26 crewmen. Lieutenant Edouard V. Izak is captured and closely observes German submarine techniques and tactics. He then stages a daring escape from prison and imparts this valuable military intelligence, winning a Congressional Medal of Honor.

June 8–September 20 On the North Sea, American vessels under Rear Admiral Joseph Strauss assist the Royal Navy in laying an extensive mine field (barrage) 240 miles across from Scotland to Norway. They ultimately deploy four-fifths of the 70,263 mines deposited there to curtail U-boat operations, and as many as six

June 13 At Naval Air Station, Pauillac, France, an HS-1 flying boat becomes the first American-made warplane assembled in Europe.

June 19 At Pensacola, Florida, upper atmospheric weather soundings are taken for the first time with a balloon device. Better information on wind velocity and direction is necessary for navigational flight training.

June 22 In the Bay of Biscay, the cargo vessel *California* of the Naval Overseas Transport Service strikes a mine and sinks.

June 30 In Great Britain, a group of Naval Aviators takes special training with British units, then joins RAF Squadron 214 on a night bomb run as observers. This is the genesis of the Navy's Night Wing, Northern Bombing Group.

July 1 In Washington, D.C., Congress modifies laws relating to the National Naval Volunteers (NNV), allowing the president to transfer all members at their present rank or rating to the Naval Reserve, the Naval Flying Reserve, or the Marine Corps Reserve.

Offshore at Brest, France, the *U-86* torpedoes and sinks the transport *Covington*, killing six crewmen.

July 7 At the Philadelphia Navy Yard, the Naval Aircraft Factory completes its first 50 H-16 flying boats.

July 11 Off the French coast, German submarine *U-92* sinks the transport *Westover*, killing 11 sailors.

July 19 Near Fire Island, New York, the armored cruiser *San Diego* strikes a German mine and sinks, with the loss of six crewmen. This is the only major warship lost in World War I; the device had been laid by *U-156*, which is itself sunk crossing the North Sea mine field while returning home.

July 20 In England, RAF Station Killingholme becomes a naval air station under Lieutenant Commander Kenneth Whiting; the Navy has flown patrols out of there since February.

July 21 At Naval Air Station, Chatham, Massachusetts, two seaplanes sortie and attack the surfaced *U-156*, driving it back underwater. Previously, the submarine *U-156* had fired 80 rounds at the tugboat *Perth Amboy* and four barges off nearby Nauset Bluffs. Some of the shells strike the mainland; this is the only enemy action on American soil in World War I.

July 24 Naval Air Station, Porto Corsini, Italy, becomes operational under Lieutenant Wallis B. Haviland. This remains the only active U.S. Navy seaplane base on the peninsula.

July 25 In Washington, D.C., the Navy Department assumes responsibility for developing all rigid airships for military purposes.

July 27 At the Philadelphia Navy Yard, the N-1 experimental fighter successfully test-fires its Davis gun, striking several targets moored in the nearby Delaware River. This is one the earliest naval fighter designs.

August 5 At Naval Air Station, Killingholme, England, Ensign Ashton W. Hawkins completes the first night-patrol mission of an American aircrew. However, they land in poor weather and nearly out of fuel.

AUGUST 11 At Mineola, New York, Ensign James B. Taylor takes the Loening M-2 Kitten prototype aloft; this is the first monoplane constructed for the U.S. Navy.

AUGUST 15 In northern France, the Northern Bombing Group begins independent bombing operations with a raid against German submarine pens at Ostend, Germany. Its first foray consists of a single Caproni bomber flown by Ensign Leslie R. Taber.

AUGUST 19 Naval Air Station, Halifax, Nova Scotia, reaches operational status under Lieutenant Richard E. Byrd; it is one of two patrolling stations established in Canada.

Trial runs of the Kirkham 18-T triplane fighter reach airspeeds of 162 miles per hour.

AUGUST 21 Over the Adriatic Sea, a Macchi M.5 flying boat flown by Ensign George Ludlow is downed by Austrians near their naval base at Pola, so a second craft piloted by Quartermaster Charles H. Hammann lands and rescues him, winning a Congressional Medal of Honor.

AUGUST 23 At Bantry Bay, Ireland, Rear Admiral Thomas S. Rodgers and the battleships *Nevada*, *Oklahoma*, and *Utah* arrive to preclude German battle-cruiser attacks on North Atlantic convoys.

AUGUST 27 Near Long Island, New York, the armed transport vessel *S. Feliz Taussig* mistakenly opens fire on the subchaser *SC 209*, killing or injuring 18 crewmen.

SEPTEMBER 1 The Commander, U.S. Naval Aviation Forces, Foreign Service, becomes the new Aide to Aviation on the staff of the Commander, U.S. Naval Forces Operating in European Waters.

SEPTEMBER 3 At Naval Air Station, Lough Foyle, Ireland, the Navy commences patrolling the North Channel entrance up to the Irish Sea.

SEPTEMBER 6 Near Soissons, France, a battery of five 14-inch (346mm) naval railway cannon under Rear Admiral Charles R. Plunkett commences fire upon German forces. Such large naval ordnance has rarely been brought to bear in a land engagement.

SEPTEMBER 15 Off the French coast, the transport *Mount Vernon* is torpedoed 200 miles west of Ushant, losing 36 crewmen. Fortunately, it manages to stay afloat and limps back to Brest.

At Thiaucourt, France, Hospital Apprentice David E. Hayden dashes forward to save a wounded Marine under fire; he receives a Congressional Medal of Honor.

SEPTEMBER 16 Off the Spanish coast, the cargo vessel *Buena Ventura* is torpedoed by *U-46* and sinks, with a loss of 19 crew members.

SEPTEMBER 23 At Copiague, Long Island, New York, the so-called "flywheel catapult" successfully launches a flying bomb. This device, jointly developed by the Sperry Company and the Bureau of Ordnance, is the precursor of catapults installed on the carriers *Lexington* and *Saratoga* in the 1930s.

SEPTEMBER 24 Over Nieuport, France, Lieutenant David S. Ingalls, flying a British Sopwith Camel with No. 213 Squadron, Royal Air Force, shoots down a German Rumpler two-seater. This is his fifth aircraft in six weeks of flying, and the Navy's first and only ace of World War I.

SEPTEMBER 25 Outside Pensacola Bay, Florida, Chief Machinist's Mate Francis Edward Ormsbee observes a training aircraft crash in the waters, dives in, saves the gunner, and makes several unsuccessful attempts to rescue the pilot; he wins a Congressional Medal of Honor.

SEPTEMBER 26 In the Bristol Channel, England, German *UB-91* sinks the Coast Guard Cutter *Tampa*, and the entire crew of 115 men is lost.

SEPTEMBER 29 Off the Delaware Capes, the battleship *Minnesota* strikes a German mine and is slightly damaged, without casualties.

SEPTEMBER 30 In the North Atlantic, the Naval Overseas Transport Service (NOTS) ship *Ticonderoga* wages a two-hour surface battle with *U-152* before being sunk. Only 24 out of 237 crewmen survive, but Lieutenant Commander James J. Madison wins a Congressional Medal of Honor.

OCTOBER 2 In the Adriatic, 11 American subchaser units clear mines and screen against submarines during a large allied naval raid against the Austrian base at Durazzo.

OCTOBER 4 At Naval Air Station Rockaway, New York, the first Curtiss NC flying boat makes its maiden flight under Commander Holden C. Richardson.

OCTOBER 14 Over Thielt, Belgium, eight DH-4 bombers of the Navy's Northern Bombing Group attack German-held railway yards for the first time. This unit consists of a Navy Night Wing and a Marine Corps Day Wing.

OCTOBER 17 At Copiague, Long Island, New York, a Curtiss N-9 rigged as a "flying torpedo" is successfully launched, and flies a prescribed course. Suddenly, the distance gear malfunctions, and it continues flying out of sight at an altitude of 4,000 feet.

OCTOBER 21 In Berlin, Germany, the German government agrees to President Woodrow Wilson's demand for an immediate cessation of submarine warfare as a precondition for armistice negotiations.

NOVEMBER 1 On the burning schooner Hjeltenaes, Boatswain's Mate John Otto Siegel rescues several sailors before nearly dying from smoke inhalation; he receives a Congressional Medal of Honor.

NOVEMBER 9 Near Fenwick Island, Delaware, the Naval Overseas Transport Service (NOTS) cargo ship *Saetia* strikes a German mine and sinks.

NOVEMBER 17 At Naval Air Station, Hampton Roads, Virginia, a Curtiss H-16 flying boat, operating a British radio direction finder, picks up a radio station in Arlington, 150 miles away.

NOVEMBER 21 Near the Firth of Forth, Scotland, American battleships assigned to the British Grand Fleet watch in awe as 14 German capital ships sail into Scapa Flow and surrender. Vice Admiral William S. Sims and Rear Admiral Hugh Rodman are present on the battleship *Texas*.

NOVEMBER 22 At the Naval Aircraft Factory, Philadelphia, Pennsylvania, a 400-pound dummy torpedo is dropped by a Curtiss F-5L flying boat for the first time.

NOVEMBER 27 At Rockaway Beach, New York, the new Curtiss NC-1 flying boat is flown with 51 people on board, a new world record for passengers aloft.

DECEMBER 1 At Naval Air Station, Hampton Roads, Virginia, the Navy dirigible *C-7* is the first American airship to go aloft with helium gas, instead of the more explosive hydrogen.

DECEMBER 30 Over Pensacola, Florida, an H-16 flying boat flown by Lieutenant Thomas C. Holden wins a Curtiss Marine Trophy race by carrying 11 passengers over 670 statute miles.

1919

January 23 At Naval Air Station, Miami, Florida, an HS-2L flying boat flown by Ensign Fitzwilliam W. Dalrymple remains aloft for 9 hours and 21 minutes, through use of special fuel tanks.

February 4 In Washington, D.C., the Navy Distinguished Service Medal and the Navy Cross, rating second and third behind the Congressional Medal of Honor, are instituted by Congress.

February 28 The new destroyer *Osmond Ingram* is launched to honor Gunner's Class Osmond K. Ingram, the first enlisted man killed when the destroyer *Cassin* was torpedoed in 1917.

March 7 At Naval Air Station, Hampton Roads, Virginia, a Curtiss N-9 piloted by Lieutenant Frank M. Johnson launches from a powered sea sled capable of reaching 50 knots.

March 9 At Guantanamo Bay, Cuba, Lieutenant Commander E. O. McDonnell launches his Sopwith Camel from a platform fixed to a turret on the battleship *Texas* for the first time.

March 12 Lieutenant Harry Sadenwater demonstrates the utility of aerial radio broadcasts by conversing with the Secretary of the Navy in a flying boat, 65 miles from Washington, D.C.

April 26 At Naval Air Station, Hampton Roads, Virginia, a Curtis F-5L flying boat piloted by Lieutenant H. D. Grow turns in a record flight of 1,250 miles in 20 hours and 19 minutes.

May 8 At Air Station Rockaway, New York, Seaplane Division One, under Commander John H. Towers, lifts off and wings its way east to Portugal via Newfoundland and the Azores. This early flyover involves three Curtiss NC flying boats (NC-1, NC-3, and NC-4).

May 27 At Lisbon, Portugal, a Curtiss NC flying boat under Lieutenant Commander Albert C. Read sets down after traversing the Atlantic via Newfoundland and the Azores. This 18-day voyage is the first transatlantic crossing by large aircraft, a considerable accomplishment given the primitive level of aviation technology.

May 28 In Washington, D.C., the General Board of the Navy recommends that the great construction programs contained in the Naval Act of 1916 be completed, despite the onset of peace.

May 31 In England, Lieutenant Commander A. C. Read finally touches down on the coast with his Curtiss NC flying boat. He, his four crewmen, and squadron leader Commander John H. Towers receive Congressional gold medals for their efforts.

June 28 In France, the Treaty of Versailles is signed by all major powers, which ends World War I. However, because of provisions requiring creation of the new League of Nations, the document is not ratified by the U.S. Senate.

July 11 In Washington, D.C., Congress passes the Naval Appropriations Act of 1919, which funds converting the collier *Jupiter* into the Navy's first aircraft carrier, the *Langley*. Two rigid airships and two merchant vessels, modified into seaplane tenders, are paid for. The Navy Department also renames the Pay Corps the Supply Corps.

July 30 Near New London, Connecticut, the submarine *G-2* sinks drowning three sailors.

August 9 At Philadelphia, Pennsylvania, the Navy begins constructing its first rigid airship, the dirigible ZR-1 *(Shenandoah)* at the Naval Aircraft Factory. This device is 682 feet in length and inflated by helium, a much safer gas than the hydrogen employed by European machines.

October 6 On the Hudson River, New York, the submerged submarine *Nautilus* successfully transmits a radio message to its home base at New London, Connecticut.

November 20 At the Mare Island Navy Shipyard, San Francisco, the battleship *California* is the first capital ship constructed on the west coast.

December 23 In Philadelphia, Pennsylvania, the Navy launches the *Relief*, the first vessel constructed entirely as a hospital ship. The vessel boasts a 500-bed capacity and houses the most modern medical facilities available.

In China, the Navy organizes several gunboats into the Yangtze Patrol (YangPat) under Captain T. A. Kearney. This is undertaken to protect American interests along that vital Chinese waterway.

1920

January 17 The Coast Guard assumes maritime duty to enforce provisions of the Volstead Act at sea, now that Prohibition is in effect.

January 20 In Washington, D.C., the Bureau of Steam Engineering is authorized to spend $100,000 on developing a 200-horsepower, radial air-cooled engine with by the Lawrence Aero Engine Corporation.

January 22 The Naval Aviation Program, which imparts flight training to enlisted men, commences. It will be maintained up through 1947.

March 18 Near Santa Margarita Island, California, the submarine *H-1* grounds on a shoal, killing three sailors. The vessel is lost six days later during salvage operations.

March 27 At Hampton Roads, Virginia, a Curtiss F-5L flying boat successfully tests a Sperry gyrostabilized autopilot system while in flight.

June 28 At Philadelphia, Pennsylvania, a flight of six F-5Ls under Lieutenant Commander Bruce G. Leighton completes a seven-month tour of the West Indies. His aircraft flew 12,731 nautical miles without mishap, including 4,000 performed as part of fleet maneuvers.

July 6 At Hampton Roads, Virginia, a Navy Curtiss F-5L seaplane makes the first flight assisted by a radio compass for navigation purposes. To this end it ventures out 94 miles at sea to the battleship *Ohio*, then flies home guided entirely by signals relayed at Norfolk.

July 12 In Washington, D.C., the Navy Department reorganizes its surface assets into the Atlantic, Pacific, and Asiatic fleets. The unit types are also finalized as Battleship, Cruiser, Destroyer, Submarine, Mine, Air, and Train.

JULY 17   In Washington, D.C., the Navy Department adopts letter symbols to identify ship types, such as "BB" for battleship and "DD" for destroyer. The same system extends to aircraft, with lighter-than-air machines designated "Z" and heavier-than-air as "V." The letters F, O, S, P, T, and V likewise designate fighter, observation, scouting, patrol, torpedo, and level bombing activities.

JULY 18   Near Hampton Roads, Virginia, Navy bombers sink the former German light cruiser *Frankfurt* in a major bombing experiment. These results do not go unnoticed by the Army.

JULY 29   In the Mediterranean, the cruiser *St. Louis* and six destroyers are sent to help evacuate American citizens displaced by the Greco-Turkish War.

SEPTEMBER 1   Off the Delaware Capes, the submarine *S-5* sinks in 194 feet of water. Fortunately, the crew fills the aft ballast tanks and it rises stern-first to the surface, whereupon they escape through a hole cut in the hull.

SEPTEMBER 10   At Philadelphia, Pennsylvania, the cruiser *St. Louis* departs to help evacuate the thousands of refugees from the Russian Civil War.

OCTOBER 2   Near Hartford, Connecticut, a Curtiss JN-4 Jenny crashes, and pilot Lieutenant Commander William M. Corry is thrown clear. However, he perishes while attempting to rescue Lieutenant Arthur C. Wagner, and receives a posthumous Congressional Medal of Honor.

OCTOBER 14–NOVEMBER 1   In Tangier Sound, Chesapeake Bay, the Navy conducts aerial bombing tests against the old battleship *Indianapolis* to see how well ship hulls withstand the destructive effect of near misses by heavy bombs.

1921

JANUARY 20   In Washington, D.C., the Bureau of Ordnance and Bureau of Engineering receive permission to develop radio-controlled aircraft as potential weapons.

FEBRUARY 26   Off the Panamanian coast, the destroyer *Woolsey* collides with the freighter *Steel Inventor* and sinks, with a loss of 16 sailors.

MARCH 7   In Washington, D.C., Captain William A. Moffett becomes the new Director of Naval Aviation; this is a very significant appointment, for Moffett proves himself far-sighted.

MARCH 15   In Philadelphia, Pennsylvania, the Naval Aircraft Factory reports that chromium-vanadium steel alloys possess superior strength and are ready for manufacture as aircraft fittings. This is the beginning of high-strength components for aircraft construction in the United States.

MARCH 25   From Mare Island, California, the ocean-going tug *Conestoga* departs for Samoa, and her 56-man crew vanishes without a trace.

JULY 12   In Washington, D.C., Congress founds the Bureau of Aeronautics to administer naval aviation, and Rear Admiral William A. Moffett gains appointment as its first chief. It is tasked with overseeing every phase of development, deployment, and repair of aircraft assigned to Navy units. However, its existence is not immediately revealed to the public.

JULY 21   Near Hampton Roads, Virginia, General William "Billy" Mitchell of the Army Air Service sinks the captured German battleship *Ostfriesland* and three other vessels with his Martin MB-2 bombers. Despite this impressive display of air power, the Navy considers the results inconclusive. Mitchell, however, somewhat prematurely declares the end of all surface warships.

JULY 21   The battleship *Maryland* is commissioned as the Navy's newest capital ship; two other vessels constitute the class.

AUGUST 10   In Washington, D.C., the Navy Department publicly announces the existence of the Navy Bureau of Aeronautics, the first new department since the Civil War. Rear Admiral William A. Moffett is also revealed as its first chief.

At Hampton Roads, Virginia, an Aeromarine 39B flown by Lieutenant Alfred M. Pride taxies onto a dummy carrier deck, and is snared by wires stretched across its path. This is the genesis of carrier arresting gear.

AUGUST 24   Near Hull, England, the dangers of lighter-than-air aircraft are underscored when the British-built U.S. Navy dirigible *R-38* crashes into the Humber River, killing 22 British and 16 American passengers, including Commander Louis H. Maxfield, U.S.N.

OCTOBER 3   From Philadelphia, Pennsylvania, the cruiser *Olympia* sails for Le Havre, France, to retrieve the remains of the Unknown Soldier.

OCTOBER 26   At the Philadelphia Navy Yard, Pennsylvania, an N-9 seaplane under Commander Holden C. Richardson successfully launches from a compressed air catapult.

NOVEMBER 3   At Omaha, Nebraska, a Curtiss-Navy racer flown by Bert Acosta wins the Pulitzer Race with an average air speed of 176.7 miles per hour.

NOVEMBER 9   At Washington, D.C., the cruiser *Olympia* docks, carrying the remains of the Unknown Soldier. The vessel fires a salute and the coffin goes ashore for internment at Arlington National Ceremony.

NOVEMBER 11   In Washington, D.C., the First International Conference on Limitation of Naval Armaments is convened, with delegates from Belgium, China, France, Great Britain, Italy, the Netherlands, Portugal, and the United States in attendance. The idea originated with Senator William E. Borah, who feared triggering an arms race between the United States, Great Britain, and Japan.

NOVEMBER 19   At Newport News, Virginia, the battleship *West Virginia*, possessing the heaviest defensive armor of any capital ship, is launched. This is also the last vessel of its class launched before provisions of the Washington Naval Treaty become law.

DECEMBER 1   At Norfolk, Virginia, the Navy's non-rigid *C-7* is the first American airship to utilize non-flammable helium instead of the highly explosive hydrogen gas. Lieutenant Commander Ralph F. Wood takes it on a round-trip test hop from Norfolk to Washington, D.C.

1922

February 6 In Washington, D.C., the Five Power Treaty (the United States, Great Britain, Japan, France, and Italy) establishes the warship ratio between nations, respectively, at 5:5:3:1.75:1.75. A 10-year moratorium is then imposed which outlaws the construction of warships with greater than 10,000 tons displacement and 8-inch guns, while capital vessels cannot exceed 35,000 tons and 16-inch guns. The U.S. and England are also required to halt building fortifications in the Pacific, while Japan is allowed to enhance its homeland defenses.

February 7 At the Washington Navy Yard, D.C., the 200-horsepower Lawrence J-1 radial air-cooled engine completes 50 hours of testing. Radial engines will be exclusively employed by Navy aircraft to replace more complex and vulnerable water-cooled inline engines.

March 20 At Norfolk, Virginia, the Navy commissions the *Langley* as its first operational aircraft carrier; Commander Kenneth Whiting takes charge. Its ungainly appearance results in the moniker "Covered Wagon."

March 29 In Washington, D.C., the Navy General Board issues its "United States Naval Policy," mandating creation of a naval force "second to none" although within treaty provisions.

April 22 In Washington, D.C., the Secretary of the Navy assigns one spotter aircraft to all of its battleships and cruisers, and orders the feasibility that additional aircraft might be carried to be tested.

April 25 The Stout Engineering Laboratory ST-1 torpedo plane debuts as the Navy's first all-metal airplane. It does not achieve operational status, but nonetheless constitutes a significant milestone to all-metal aircraft.

May 24 The battleship *Maryland* launches a Vought VE-7 with its turret-mounted compressed air catapult at sea. Hereafter, such launches become routine.

July 1 The recent Five Power Treaty allows the United States to construct two aircraft carriers of 33,000 tons apiece, so Congress authorizes the conversion of heavy cruisers *Lexington* and *Saratoga* into flattops.

July 17 In Washington, D.C., the Chief of Naval Operations instructs the various Bureaus to convene a board for the purpose of drawing up tactical doctrines for aerial spotting aircraft and fleet fire control.

September 16 At Smyrna, Turkey, a three-destroyer force under Commander Halsey Powell assists in the evacuation of thousands of Greek refugees fleeing the Greco-Turkish War. A total of 262,578 people are eventually rescued.

September 27 Off the Virginia Capes, a force of 18 PT torpedo planes score "hits" on the battleship *Arkansas* as it maneuvers at full speed. This is the first mass torpedo launch made against warships under steam, and demonstrates that such ordnance can be made to run straight.

At the Naval Aircraft Radio Laboratory, Anacostia, D.C., Albert H. Taylor and Leo C. Young make the first "radar observations."

October 17 At the York River, Virginia, Commander Virgil C. Griffith flies a Vought VE-7 off the deck of the

Langley. This is the first carrier launch in history.

OCTOBER 26 Offshore at Cape Henry, Virginia, Lieutenant Commander Godfrey DeC. Chevalier lands his Aeromarine 39B on the deck of the carrier *Langley* for the first time in history.

OCTOBER 27 The Navy League of the United States sponsors the first national celebration of what becomes Navy Day. Ironically, it coincides with the birthday of President Franklin D. Roosevelt, a former assistant secretary of the Navy.

NOVEMBER 18 At the York River, Virginia, a PT aircraft flown by Commander Kenneth Whiting becomes the first aircraft successfully catapulted from the deck of the carrier *Langley*.

NOVEMBER 20–DECEMBER 18 The cruisers *Denver* and *Cleveland* are dispatched with emergency supplies to assist victims of the severe earthquake in Chile.

DECEMBER 6 In Washington, D.C., the Navy Department unites the Atlantic and Pacific fleets into the United States Fleet under Admiral Hilary P. Jones. This entity is subdivided again into the Scouting Fleet and the Battle Fleet.

DECEMBER 16 Near Istanbul, Turkey, the destroyer *Bainbridge* rescues 482 people from the French transport *Vinh-Long*, despite violent explosions that eventually sink it. Lieutenant Commander Walter A. Edwards receives a win Congressional Medal of Honor for his efforts.

1923

FEBRUARY 6 In Washington, D.C., the Aeronautical Engine Laboratory transfers from the Washington Navy Yard to the Naval Aircraft Factory, Philadelphia, Pennsylvania. This location consequently becomes the center of naval aviation development.

FEBRUARY 12 In Washington, D.C., the Bureau of Navigation decrees that, following graduation from flight school, Naval Aviators are no longer subject to two years of mandatory service in an operating unit to gain their wings.

FEBRUARY 18–22 In the Caribbean, Fleet Problem I, the defense of the Panama Canal is undertaken by ship of the U.S. Fleet to evaluate the threat of potential air attacks against the Canal region, gets underway. Fleet exercises become an annual event, and aircraft figure prominently throughout.

FEBRUARY 21 Deck handling tests with Aeromarine 39Bs on the carrier *Langley* demonstrate that a minimum of two minutes is necessary to prepare the deck after each landing. With better experience, three aircraft can be landed and secured in only seven minutes.

APRIL 15 In Philadelphia, Pennsylvania, experiments conducted by the Naval Aircraft Factory result in a F-5L seaplane being remotely guided at a distance of 10 miles from the transmitter.

APRIL 26 In Washington, D.C., the General Board recommends enlarging naval facilities at Pearl Harbor, Hawaii, Guam, and the Philippines. They also urge development of a surface fleet capable of sustained operations over the vast Pacific reaches in the event war with Japan breaks out.

MAY 26 In Washington, D.C., the Navy Bureau of Aeronautics and the Chief of the Air Service agree that it is best for both services to work under identical aeronautical specifications wherever possible, to avoid duplication of effort and better harmonize research efforts .

JUNE 6–7 At San Diego, California, Navy aviators set 15 speed, distance, duration, and altitude records for various Class C seaplanes such as Douglas DTs and Curtiss F-5Ls.

JUNE 11 At Norfolk Navy Yard, Virginia, a boiler explosion on the destroyer *Bruce* induces Machinist's Mate William R. Huber to pull a shipmate to safety; he receives a Congressional Medal of Honor.

JUNE 12 At San Diego, California, a Douglas DT torpedo plane flown by Lieutenant Mainrad A. Schur establishes three world records for Class C Seaplanes, including a speed of 70.49 miles per hour, a distance of 792.25 miles, and a flying time of 11 hours, 16 minutes.

JUNE 13 At San Diego, California, a TS seaplane flown by Lieutenant Ralph A. Ofstie hits 121 miles per hour, establishing a world speed record for Class C seaplanes.

JULY 31 In Washington, D.C., the Bureau of Aeronautics adopts the policy of assigning experimental aircraft to fleet squadrons for operational testing.

SEPTEMBER 1 In Yokohama, Japan, Ensign Thomas J. Ryan wins the Congressional Medal of Honor for rescuing a woman trapped in a burning building following a devastating earthquake.

SEPTEMBER 4 At Naval Air Station, Lakehurst, New Jersey, the *Shenandoah*, the Navy's first rigid airship, performs its maiden flight under Captain Frank R. McCrary.

SEPTEMBER 5 Near Yokohama, Japan, ships of the U.S. Asiatic Fleet anchor to lend assistance and humanitarian aid in the wake of a devastating earthquake.

SEPTEMBER 8 Offshore at Point Pedernales, Santa Barbara, California, Destroyer Squadron 11 runs completely aground attempting to navigate the Santa Barbara Channel in a thick fog. All six vessels are wrecked, and the *Young* capsizes, killing 22 sailors.

OCTOBER 10 The large rigid airship *Shenandoah* is commissioned into service. The Navy entertains high hopes for its lighter-than-air machines.

OCTOBER 28 In Limon Bay, Panama, submarine *O-5* is struck by the steamer *Abangarez*; Torpedoman Second Class Henry Breault refuses to abandon a man in the forward section and remains with him 31 hours until rescued; he wins a Congressional Medal of Honor.

NOVEMBER 5 At Hampton Roads, Virginia, diminutive Martin MS-1 scout aircraft is stored, transported, then reassembled and launched from the submarine *S-1*. Other experiments ensue, but sub-stowed aircraft are never adopted by the Navy.

NOVEMBER 16 In Washington, D.C., the Bureau of Aeronautics mandates that aircraft attached to vessels of the fleet will receive complete overhauls every six months. This is done in the interest of enhancing operational safety.

December 3 In Washington, D.C., the Chief of Naval Operations approves a special service squadron for the purpose of developing long-range patrolling aircraft. The task is assigned to VS-3 operating out of Anacostia, D.C.

December 6 In Guangzhou, China, escalating civil war results in several destroyers of the U.S. Asiatic fleet being dispatched to protect foreign lives and property.

1924

January 16 The light cruiser *Tacoma* strikes the Blanquilla Reef off Veracruz, Mexico, and sinks, losing four sailors including the captain.

February 4 In Washington, D.C., the Bureau of Aeronautics revises paint scheme regulations and decrees that all aircraft sport naval gray schemes. However, aircraft deployed abroad could carry bright yellow upper wings to increase visibility in the event of a crash landing.

March 21 In Washington, D.C., the Bureau of Aeronautics orders all Navy aviation personnel to wear parachutes while airborne.

April 21 In Washington, D.C., the Bureau of Steam Engineering is authorized to develop a small radio capable of transmitting and receiving signals over 20 miles, yet small enough to be carried by fighter aircraft.

June 12 The battleship *Mississippi* experiences a turret explosion, killing 3 officers and 44 enlisted men.

August 8–September 18 In Narragansett Bay, Rhode Island, the airship *Shenandoah* is moored to a special mast on the oiler *Patoka* prior to conducting aerial exercises with the fleet. This is the first time a mooring mast has been mounted on a vessel for extended airship operations.

August 11 Over Greenland, Navy scout planes from the cruiser *Raleigh* reconnoiter the coast from Angmagsalik to Cape Farewell for emergency landing sites that Army pilots, completing the last leg of their circumnavigation flight, might need as they cross the Atlantic via Iceland.

September 1 At Naval Air Station Lakehurst, New Jersey, the Navy, unwilling to rely further on the Army, opens its own parachute school.

September 15 Over the Naval Proving Grounds, Dahlgren, Virginia, a Curtiss N-9 seaplane flies 40 minutes under radio control. It subsequently sinks after experiencing a hard landing, but radio-directed flight is increasingly practical.

October 7–25 At Lakehurst, New Jersey, the airship *Shenandoah* completes a round-trip flight to and from the west coast, covering 9,317 miles in 258 hours.

October 15 At Lakehurst, New Jersey, the German-built dirigible ZR-3 touches down after flying 5,000 miles, and is taken into Navy service as the *Los Angeles*.

October 16 Over Coronado, California, Gunner William M. Coles is the first naval enlisted man saved by a parachute after his JN trainer collides with another aircraft.

OCTOBER 20 Near Norfolk, Virginia, the light cruiser *Trenton* experiences an explosion in its forward gun turret. Two sailors, who refuse to flee and attempt preventing the fire from reaching the magazines, receive posthumous Congressional Medals of Honor.

NOVEMBER 11 In San Diego harbor, California, Lieutenant Dixie Kiefer is launched at night for the first time from a turret of the anchored battleship *California*. His flight is assisted by searchlights trained 1,000 yards ahead of the aircraft to guide it.

NOVEMBER 14 In Washington, D.C., the Chiefs of the Bureau of Aeronautics and the Bureau of Medicine and Surgery establish the qualifications for Flight Surgeon. Prospective candidates will complete a three-month course at the U.S. Army School of Aviation, followed by three months of active duty at Naval Aviation in order to qualify.

NOVEMBER 17 The converted collier *Langley* joins the fleet as the first operational flagship of Aircraft Squadrons, Battle Fleet, following two years in experimental status. This is also the Navy's first aircraft carrier.

NOVEMBER 25 At Naval Air Station Anacostia, Washington, D.C., ceremonies christening the rigid airship *Los Angeles* are presided over by Mrs. Calvin Coolidge.

DECEMBER 13 At Philadelphia, Pennsylvania, the Naval Aircraft Factory rolls out its NM-1, an early all-metal airplane intended for Marine Corps aviators during expeditionary forays.

DECEMBER 14 At Bremerton, Washington, the battleship *Mississippi* successfully launches a Martin MO-1 aircraft with a new gunpowder catapult. The system is then adopted for use by battleships and cruisers.

1925

JANUARY 17 In Washington, D.C., Admiral Edward W. Eberle submits a report from a special board he had chaired, and stresses the growing importance of naval aviation to the fleet. He endorses the new carriers *Lexington* and *Saratoga*, argues that a new 23,000-ton carrier be built, and seeks a comprehensive aircraft production program to acquire the most modern designs.

JANUARY 22 Near San Diego, California, VF-2 becomes the first naval aviation squadron to train as a carrier squadron on the carrier *Langley*.

FEBRUARY 4 In Washington, D.C., the Navy Department drops a regulation, mandating six-month overhauls for all naval aircraft, for being impractical. Such responsibilities are now entrusted to commanding officers.

MARCH 2–11 Off the California coast, the carrier *Langley* participates in a Fleet Problem V for the first time, with airplanes performing scouting missions. It is becoming apparent that more durable aircraft are needed to withstand the stress of operations from a carrier deck.

MARCH 4 In Washington, D.C., Congress institutes the Naval Reserve Officer Corps Training (NROTC) program at six universities, beginning the following year. They also lend official recognition to the Navy Band, making it a permanent organization headed by a senior lieutenant; it begins its first national tour by visiting 300 cities and towns.

MARCH 13   In Washington, D.C., Rear Admiral William A. Moffett is appointed to serve a second term as Chief of the Bureau of Aeronautics.

APRIL 1   Offshore at San Diego, California, Lieutenant Commander John D. Price of VF-1 performs the first nighttime landing by a Navy aircraft, touching down on the carrier *Langley* at night. Nocturnal operations are considered extremely hazardous and do not become routine until after World War II.

MAY 1–2   Over Philadelphia, Pennsylvania, a PN-9 flying boat constructed by the Naval Aircraft Factory sets a world endurance record for Class C seaplanes. This aircraft, which remains aloft for 28 hours, 35 minutes, 27 seconds, is also one of the first naval aircraft with an all-metal hull.

MAY 5   In Washington, D.C., the Secretary of the Navy orders the U.S. Naval Academy, Annapolis, Maryland, to promote aviation classes as a central part of its curriculum.

JUNE 17   In Boston, Massachusetts, Lieutenant Commander Richard E. Byrd conducts the Naval Air Detail assigned to the Macmillan Arctic Expedition. He commands three Loening OL amphibians stored on the destroyer *Peary*.

AUGUST 1   At Etah, Greenland, Lieutenant Commander Richard E. Byrd's Naval Air Detail arrives, prior to aerial exploration covering 30,000 square miles.

SEPTEMBER 1   From San Francisco, California, a PN-9 flying boat under Commander John Rodgers departs, intending to reach Hawaii flying non-stop. Unfortunately, he runs out of fuel 1,841 miles out and settles down on the Pacific Ocean. He next orders canvass stripped from the upper wing to form a makeshift sail, and the winds push him to within a few miles of the Hawaiian coast 10 days later.

SEPTEMBER 3   Over Ava, Ohio, the Navy airship *Shenandoah* crashes in a severe storm, killing 14 of 43 crewmen present, including Lieutenant Commander Zachary Lansdowne.

SEPTEMBER 25   Near Block Island, Rhode Island, submarine *S-51* collides with the vessel *City of Rome*, drowning 33 of 36 crew members.

OCTOBER 27   Oleo shock-absorbing landing gear is fitted to NB-1, FB-1, UO-1, and SC-2 aircraft under construction, to ensure smoother carrier landings.

DECEMBER 18   At Anacostia, D.C., flight trials between Consolidated, Curtiss, and Huff-Deland prototypes result in selection of the Consolidated NY trainer. This aircraft becomes a mainstay of Naval Aviation up through the 1930s.

1926

JANUARY 14   In Sumatra, scientists from the Naval Observatory observe a solar eclipse; Lieutenant H. C. Keller also collects 9,000 rock specimens for the Smithsonian Institution.

APRIL 21   In Washington, D.C., the Secretary of the Navy orders that all Annapolis graduates receive 25 hours of flight instruction during their first tour of sea duty. Accordingly, new training facilities are established at Hampton Roads, Virginia, and San Diego, California.

MAY 9   At Spitzbergen, Norway, Lieutenant Commander Richard E. Byrd and civilian pilot Floyd Bennett fly their Fokker F.VII-3m aircraft *Josephine* over the North Pole for the first time. The round trip covers 1,600 miles and takes 15.5 hours, and both men receive Congressional Medals of Honor.

JUNE 16   The Bureau of Aeronautics announces that crash barriers installed on the carrier *Langley* prevent aircraft landing on the flight deck from crashing into parked aircraft.

JUNE 24   In Washington, D.C., Congress votes to provide the Navy with funding to expand its aerial force to 1,000 aircraft within five years. They also decree that command of air units and air stations must belong to Naval Aviators.

JULY 1   In Washington, D.C., the Secretary of the Navy announces new regulations mandating that a minimum of 30 percent of Naval Aviators on active duty be drawn from the enlisted ranks.

JULY 10   In Washington, D.C., Congress, reacting to the Morrow Board findings, creates the post of Assistant Secretary of the Navy for Aeronautics. Edward P. Warner is the appointee.

JULY 28   On the Thames River, New London, Connecticut, a Cox-Klemin XS-2 scout seaplane is assembled on the deck of submarine *S-1*, flown off by Lieutenant D. C. Allen, recovered, disassembled, then stored. However, the concept is never adopted by the U.S. Navy.

OCTOBER 22   Near San Pedro, California, six Curtiss F6C-2 Hawks under Lieutenant Commander Frank D. Wagner stage mock dive-bombing attacks against battleships at sea. Rear Admiral Joseph M. Reeves, air commander of Battle Fleet, considers the maneuver a resounding success.

OCTOBER 24   On the Isle of Pines, the Caribbean, light cruiser *Milwaukee* and destroyer *Goff* arrive with medical supplies and food to assist survivors of a severe hurricane.

NOVEMBER 1   At Ten Pound Island, Gloucester, Maine, the Coast Guard Air Service commences with the arrival of two Loening amphibian aircraft; these are outfitted with radios and machine guns to circumvent smugglers.

NOVEMBER 19   The battleship *Maryland* tests the Mark XIX antiaircraft fire control system, to counter the growing threat posed by aircraft to capital ships. This device incorporates a stabilized line of sight to track approaching aircraft.

DECEMBER 13   In Washington, D.C., Rear Admiral Joseph M. Reeves, head of Aircraft Squadrons, Battle Fleet, reports results of a recent dive bombing exercise. He notes that the Curtis F6Cs and Boeing FB-5s of VF-2 under Lieutenant Commander Frank D. Wagner scored 19 "hits" with 45 bombs released from 2,500 feet. Impressed, the Navy increases its development of dive bombers.

1927

JANUARY 5   In recognition for his historical flight over the North Pole, Lieutenant Commander Richard E. Byrd receives a Congressional Medal of Honor; his civilian

> ### Byrd, Richard E., (1888–1957)
>
> Richard Evelyn Bird was born in Winchester, Virginia, on October 25, 1888, and he graduated from the U.S. Naval Academy in 1912. Byrd could not perform sea duty due to a sports injury, so he joined the fledgling naval aviation service. During World War I he commanded patrol bombers based in Canada. Thereafter, he became intrigued by the prospects of transoceanic flight, and on May 9, 1926, he accompanied Floyd Bennet in a Fokker transport across the North Pole for the first time. In 1928–1930 Byrd shifted his attention southward to Antarctica, and on November 29, 1929, he and pilot Bernt Balchen flew over the South Pole for the first time. In 1934 Byrd, now an admiral, also manned a weather-observation shack south of the main base, where carbon dioxide from a faulty heater nearly killed him.
>
> During World War II Byrd served with the U.S. Antarctic Service, and functioned capably with the Chief of Naval Operations staff. In 1946–1947 he orchestrated a huge Antarctic expedition called Operation Highjump, which utilized 41,000 men, 13 ships, 19 aircraft, and 4 helicopters. Byrd thus became the only man to fly a plane over the South Pole twice. In 1957 he performed similar work, commanding Operation Deepfreeze for the International Geophysical Year (IGY), and flew over the pole a third and final time. Illness necessitated his returning to Boston, Massachusetts, to recuperate, and he died there on March 11, 1957, a noted naval explorer.

accomplice, Floyd Bennett, also receives a medal.

JANUARY 18   In Washington, D.C., Lieutenant Commander John R. Poppen is appointed head of the new Aviation Section of the Naval Medical School. This also constitutes the start of flight surgeon training.

FEBRUARY 9   Off the coast at Nicaragua, Rear Admiral Julian L. Latimer's Special Service Squadron, consisting of the cruisers *Galveston*, *Milwaukee*, and *Raleigh*, are ordered to land detachments ashore and seize control of the Cortino-Managua railway to keep service from being disrupted.

MARCH 9   At Naval Air Station Anacostia, D.C., the Navy receives its first large transport, a Ford JR-1 trimotor, for testing purposes.

MAY 23   In Philadelphia, Pennsylvania, the Naval Aircraft Factory reveals a major advance in the maintenance of aviation metal, by applying anodic coatings to prevent corrosion of aluminum by salt water.

MAY 27   In Washington, D.C., the Commander in Chief, Battle Fleet, is directed to perform extensive testing and evaluation of dive bombing. VF-5S is subsequently appointed to help develop the specialized equipment and tactics employed by this offensive tactic.

JUNE 11   At the Washington, D.C., Navy Yard the light cruiser *Memphis* docks after transporting Charles Lindbergh and his *Spirit of St. Louis* from France.

JUNE 30–AUGUST 4   In Geneva, Switzerland, delegates from the United States, Great Britain, and Japan convene a Naval Conference to place limitations on warships not covered by the existing Washington Naval Treaty; an agreement proves fleeting.

NOVEMBER 16   The new 36,000-ton *Saratoga* is commissioned as the Navy's first combat-capable aircraft carrier. Having been converted from a heavy cruiser, the vessel possesses a 900-foot flight deck and is faster and more capable than its predecessor, the converted collier *Langley*.

DECEMBER 14   The new carrier *Lexington* is commissioned; this is another converted cruiser and the fourth vessel carrying that proud name.

DECEMBER 17   Near Provincetown, Massachusetts, submarine *S-4* collides with the Coast Guard cutter *Paulding*, with a loss of all 39 crew members. Chief Gunner's Mate Thomas Eadie receives a Congressional Medal of Honor for rescuing a salvage diver whose air line became entangled in the wreckage.

1928

JANUARY 27   The dirigible *Los Angeles* successfully lights upon the flight deck of the carrier *Saratoga*, transferring passengers and taking on supplies.

FEBRUARY 27   In Chesapeake Bay, Commander Theodore C. Ellyson, Naval Aviator No. 1, dies with two companions when his Loening OL amphibian crashes during a night flight.

FEBRUARY 28   In San Diego, California, Consolidated Aircraft Corporation sign a naval contract to construct the XPY-1 prototype, a large, monoplane flying boat.

JUNE 12   In the Pacific, the carrier *Lexington* makes a high-speed run from San Pedro, California, to Honolulu, Hawaii, covering the distance in a record 72 hours and 34 minutes. This exercise confirms the Navy's ability to project power far from America's shores—and quickly.

JUNE 30   In Baltimore, Maryland, the Martin Company contracts with the Navy to build its XT5M-1 dive bomber prototype. This enters into production as the BM-1, the first Navy dive bomber capable of dropping a 1,000-pound bomb.

AUGUST 25   Over Antarctica, Admiral Robert E. Byrd begins his ambitious expedition to fly to the South Pole. This is also the first time that aircraft have been used to explore the region.

DECEMBER 14   The carrier *Saratoga* receives 14 radio telephone sets for fighter aircraft belonging to VB-2B Squadron. This is the first communication equipment installed in single-seat aircraft.

1929

JANUARY 16   In Washington, D.C., the Navy Department revises regulations for Navy and Marine Corps aviators to have experience night flying; prospective candidates now must accumulate 10 hours of night flying and execute 20 landings.

JANUARY 21   The Naval Proving Ground recommends that Mark XI Norden bombsight be placed into production and installed on Navy bombers. This accurate device is capable of guiding bombs to within 25 feet of a target.

January 23–27 In the Atlantic, Fleet Problem IX becomes the first annual exercize staged with aircraft carriers. Rear Admiral Joseph M. Reeves orders the *Saratoga* detached from the battle fleet to stage a surprise "attack" upon the Panama Canal. Success here demonstrates the offensive potential of carrier aviation to operate independently of the main fleet.

February 13 In Washington, D.C., Congress passes the Cruiser Act to fund construction of 15 such vessels, along with the aircraft carrier *Ranger*. The latter is the first vessel built from the keel up as a carrier. The ill-fated heavy cruiser *Indianapolis* of World War II fame is also among those constructed.

March 13 In Washington, D.C., Rear Admiral William A. Moffett is again appointed Chief of the Bureau of Aeronautics.

May 8 The successful testing of a Martin T4M torpedo bomber equipped with brakes allows the Navy to dispense with fore-and-aft arresting gear on carrier decks.

In a major development, Lieutenant Charles B. Momsen invents the so-called "Momsen Lung," in conjunction with Chief Gunner Clarence L. Tibbals and civilian engineer Frank Hobson. This ingenious device uses carbon dioxide from exhaled air and replaces it with oxygen; it is the first device allowing submariners to escape sunken vessels in relatively deep water.

May 10 In Washington, D.C., Naval Aviator Lieutenant Alford J. Williams receives a Distinguished Service Cross for pioneering violent maneuvers and inverted flight profiles for more accurate methods of aircraft testing.

June 4 A Wright Apache Seaplane flown by Lieutenant Apollo Soucek establishes a new altitude record of 38,560 feet for Class C seaplanes.

August 20 At Lakehurst Naval Air Station, New Jersey, Lieutenant Adolphus W. Gorton hooks his UO-1 aircraft to a trapeze attached to the airship *Los Angeles*. This experiment confirms the feasibility of aircraft operating directly from dirigibles.

November 28–29 In Antarctica, a Ford Trimotor, with Commander Richard E. Byrd acting as navigator, successfully flies over the South Pole for the first time. It returns safely to the base camp at "Little America" (McMurdo Sound) after a flight of 19 hours.

December 18–January 16 In Tacoma, Washington, the carrier *Lexington* provides electricity to the city following the failure of its power plant. This is one of the earliest vessels fitted with a turbo-electric generator.

1930

January 29 At Naval Air Station, Hampton Roads, Virginia, a new type of hydraulic arrester gear is tested to absorb the energy of aircraft landing on carrier decks.

January 31 Over Lakehurst, New Jersey, the rigid dirigible *Los Angeles* drops a glider flown by Lieutenant Ralph S. Barnaby from 3,000 feet; he pilots his craft to a safe landing.

FEBRUARY 14   At Naval Air Station Anacostia, D.C., the Boeing Model 205 prototype fighter is delivered for testing; this is the first monoplane design evaluated by the Navy. It is not accepted into production, but stimulates additional development of the type.

FEBRUARY 15   In Philadelphia, Pennsylvania, the Naval Aircraft Factory begins designing retractable landing gear aircraft to reduce drag and boost airspeeds on aircraft.

MARCH 21   In Baltimore, Maryland, the Martin XT5M-1 prototype dive bomber passes its strength and performance tests, including the successful delivery of a 1,000-pound bomb.

APRIL 22   In England, the London Naval Conference finds Great Britain, the United States, and Japan agreeing to limitations on cruiser tonnage at a ratio of 10:10:7 ships per nation. Furthermore, terms of the existing Washington Naval Treaty are extended by another five years, which has the net effect of weakening American naval capabilities in the Pacific.

MAY 15   At Portsmouth, New Hampshire, the submarine *Narwal* is the first of a new class of successful, streamlined submersibles; it displaces 2,730 tons and measures 371 feet in length.

JUNE 4   Over Anacostia Naval Air Station, Washington, D.C., Lieutenant Apollo Soucek works his Wright Apache seaplane to a new altitude of 43,166 feet.

JULY 21   At Anacostia Naval Air Station, Washington, D.C., Captain Arthur H. Page establishes a world record instruments-only flight of 1,000 miles while flying in from Omaha, Nebraska.

NOVEMBER 5   In Washington, D.C., the Director of the Naval Research Laboratory reports that experiments with radio waves have detected airplanes overhead. Success here spurs developments in the new field of radar.

NOVEMBER 28   In Washington, D.C., Chief of Naval Operations Admiral William V. Pratt orders naval aviation to become an integral part of the battlefleet, and directly commanded by the Commander in Chief, U.S. Fleet. Consequently, the offensive role of aviation at sea is emphasized, while its participation in coastal defense becomes a secondary concern.

1931

JANUARY 8   At the Naval Proving Grounds, Dahlgren, Virginia, a trapeze-type invention is tested that swings a bomb past the propeller arc before releasing it. This greatly reduces the danger for dive bombers and keeps their propellers from being damaged.

JANUARY 9   In Washington, D.C., an agreement is reached between Chief of Naval Operations William V. Pratt and Army Chief of Staff Douglas A. MacArthur, whereby the Army Air Corps assumes primary responsibility for coastal defense. Hereafter naval aviation will concentrate on mobile operations with the fleet.

JANUARY 22   At Naval Air Station, Hampton Roads, Virginia, the Pitcairn XOP-1 autogyro, an early aircraft/helicopter hybrid, arrives for testing and evaluation purposes.

MARCH 2 The Hamilton Standard Propeller Company contracts with the Navy to develop variable-pitch propellers to maximize aircraft performance.

MARCH 3 In Pasadena, California, the Navy assigns two officers from the postgraduate engineering group to take advanced courses at the California Institute of Technology (CalTech).

MARCH 31 The carrier *Lexington* and hospital ship *Relief* are dispatched to Nicaragua to lend assistance in the wake of a large earthquake, and five airplanes are to carry food and medical supplies to the survivors.

APRIL 1 In Washington, D.C., the Navy Department reorganizes the U.S. Fleet into Battle, Scouting, Submarine, and Base Forces.

APRIL 2 The Navy accepts its first design proposal from the Grumman Aircraft to construct the two-seat XFF-1 fighter. This visionary machine has retractable landing gear, an enclosed cockpit, and all-metal construction, and is expected to yield great improvements in performance.

APRIL 9 In Baltimore, Maryland, the Martin Company contracts with the Navy to construct 12 BM-1 dive bombers capable of delivering a 1,000-pound bomb. These are the first specifically designed aircraft acquired by the Navy.

SEPTEMBER 10 In Washington, D.C., Rear Admiral William A. Moffett expands and expedites testing of variable-pitch propellers, based on highly successful trial runs with a Curtiss F9C fighter.

SEPTEMBER 23 The large airship *Akron* enters operational service with the U.S. Navy; it is also the first dirigible specifically designed to house and deploy onboard fighter aircraft. The Navy also begins testing the Pitcarin XOP-1 autogyro off and on the deck of the carrier *Langley*.

SEPTEMBER 26 At Newport News, Virginia, the keel of the new 14,500-ton *Ranger* is laid; this is the first American aircraft carrier specifically designed for that purpose.

OCTOBER 7 The Navy successfully tests the new and highly accurate Mark XV bombsight developed by Carl J. Norden, and bombs dropped from 5,000 feet scored a hit rate of 50 percent on the aged armored cruiser *Pittsburgh*. These devices remain the most advanced bombsights of their kind through World War II.

At Naval Air Station Lakehurst, New Jersey, testing begins on the K-1 airship. This is the largest non-rigid airship employed by the Navy to date, and features an all-metal car and a 320,000-cubic foot envelope.

OCTOBER 27 At Naval Air Station, Lakehurst, New Jersey, the large rigid dirigible *Akron* (ZRS 4) is commissioned under Lieutenant Commander Charles E. Rosendahl and begins active deployment.

NOVEMBER 3 Over Lakehurst, New Jersey, the dirigible *Akron* flies for 10 hours with 207 people, establishing a record for the number of individuals carried aloft.

DECEMBER 9 Off the New England coast, the carrier *Langley* cruises frigid winter waters to test protective flight clothing and carrier deck gear under adverse weather conditions.

1932

JANUARY 9 In Washington, D.C., the Secretary of the Navy informs the Secretary of War of progress with radio detection (Radar) equipment at the Naval Research Laboratory; he also inquires if the Army is interested in conducting similar work on its own.

MAY 2 In Washington, D.C., the Bureau of Aeronautics orders hydraulic-type carrier arresting gear installed and tested on the carrier *Langley*.

JUNE 30 At Naval Air Station, Lakehurst, New Jersey, the dirigible *Los Angeles* is decommissioned for reasons of economy. Over the past eight years it has traveled over 5,000 miles by air without serious mishap.

1933

FEBRUARY 25 At Newport News, Virginia, the new carrier *Ranger* of 15,575 tons is christened by Mrs. Herbert Hoover. This vessel carries 140 aircraft and heralds a new chapter in naval aviation.

APRIL 4 Near Barnegat Light, New Jersey, the giant airship *Akron* under Commander Frank McCord crashes into the Atlantic during a storm, killing Admiral William A. Moffett, Chief of the Bureau of Aeronautics, and 72 crewmen.

JUNE 13 The Navy contracts with the Washington Institute of Technology to develop radio equipment capable of allowing blind landings on carriers.

JUNE 16 In Washington, D.C., Congress passes the National Industrial Recovery Act, which earmarks $238 million for the construction of 32 new warships over the next three years. These vessels include the new fleet carriers *Yorktown* and *Enterprise*, along with 290 additional aircraft.

JUNE 23 At Akron, Ohio, the rigid airship *Macon* is commissioned. This also the last such craft procured by the Navy, despite the fact it possesses an onboard hangar capable of carrying five fighter airplanes.

AUGUST 8 The Navy initiates widespread use of variable-pitch propellers when Boeing F4B fighter on the carriers *Langley* and *Saratoga* are fitted with such devices for upcoming exercises.

AUGUST 29 In Washington, D.C., Acting Secretary of the Navy Admiral W. H. Standley informs Robert H. Goddard that adapting his novel rocket propulsion system to depth charges and anti-aircraft projectiles appears impractical.

SEPTEMBER 7–8 Six Consolidated P2Y-1 flying boats under Lieutenant Commander Herman F. Halland of Patrol Squadron 5F perform a non-stop flight from Norfolk, Virginia, to Coco Solo, Panama, covering covered 2,059 miles in 25 hours and 19 minutes.

OCTOBER 12 From Naval Air Station, Lakehurst, New Jersey, the rigid airship *Macon* flies to Sunnyvale, California, whereby it covers 2,500 miles in only 70 hours.

OCTOBER 24   In Philadelphia, Pennsylvania, the Naval Aircraft Factory begins work designing a special abdominal belt to prevent pilots from blacking out while dive bombing.

OCTOBER 28   In San Diego, California, the Consolidated Aircraft Company contracts with the Navy to produce the XP3Y-1 prototype, the famous PBY Catalina flying boat.

NOVEMBER 17   The National Industrial Recovery Act, passed on June 16, 1933, includes $7.5 million for the Navy to procure sufficient new aircraft and equipment to both maintain a 1,000-plane fleet and equip them with the latest radio and navigation devices.

1934

JANUARY 10–11   Lieutenant Commander Knefler McGinnis conducts a flight of six Consolidated P2Y-1 flying boats from San Francisco, California, to Pearl Harbor, Hawaii. The flight covers 2,399 miles in 24 hours and 35 minutes, which constitutes a new record for C Class seaplanes.

MARCH 14   At the Naval Research Laboratory, Dr. A. Hoyt Taylor begins researching pulse radar devices capable of emitting bursts of radio energy that echo back the distance to an oncoming target. His progress is abetted by new cathode ray tubes, high power transmitting tubes, and special receiving tubes designed for that purpose.

MARCH 27   In Washington, D.C., Congress passes the Vinson-Trammel Act which increases the Navy to its authorized strength as prescribed in the Five Powers Treaty. Presently, it possesses only 65 percent of assigned tonnage, and funding is provided to continue construction over the next eight years; among the new ships authorized is the carrier *Wasp*.

JUNE 4   The 14,500-ton aircraft carrier *Ranger* is commissioned and placed in service. This is the first American vessel expressly designed for that role.

JUNE 30   In Los Angeles, California, Douglas Aircraft contracts with the Navy to construct its XTBD-1 prototype torpedo bomber. When entering the service as the TBD Devastator, it becomes the first all-metal monoplane in naval service.

JULY 19   At sea, the rigid airship *Macon* releases two Curtiss F9C-1 fighters from its onboard hanger. The two aircraft subsequently return by re-latching onto a trapeze device that raises them back inside.

NOVEMBER 1   In Philadelphia, Pennsylvania, the Naval Aircraft Factory begins designing and manufacturing a flush-deck hydraulic catapult Type H, Mark I. This device gains widespread adoption on all U.S. carriers.

NOVEMBER 18   The Northrop Corporation contracts with the Navy to produce its XBT-1 prototype dive bomber. This machine is eventually acquired by Douglas Aircraft and further refined into the famous SBD Dauntless of World War II.

DECEMBER 15   The Navy contracts with the Curtiss Aircraft to acquire X03C-1 biplane observation seaplanes; these enter the service as the SOC-1 Seagull.

Curtiss SOC-1 ("Seagull") scout-observation aircraft in flight, July 2, 1939. (U.S. Naval Historical Center)

1935

JANUARY 14 Aircraft from the carrier *Ranger* make mid-winter flights to Hartford, Connecticut, and Buffalo, New York, to test cold-weather equipment.

FEBRUARY 9 In Philadelphia, Pennsylvania, the prototype XN3N-1 is ordered from the Naval Aircraft Factory. This primary trainer becomes known as the "Yellow Peril" on account of its bright yellow paint scheme.

FEBRUARY 12 Near Point Sur, California, the giant Navy dirigible *Macon* under Commander Herbert V. Wiley crashes, killing two crew members. This accident also ends further military interest in lighter-than-air ships until World War II.

MARCH 22 On Long Island, New York, the Grumman XF3F-1 prototype flies for the first time. This aircraft, nicknamed the "Flying Barrel" on account of its rotund fuselage, enters production as the F3F and is the Navy's last biplane fighter. It also features retractable landing gear and the first fully enclosed cockpit on a Navy plane.

APRIL 15 In Washington, D.C., Congress passes the Aviation Cadet Act to increase the number of qualified pilots available to the Navy and Marine Corps Reserve. Qualified candidates perform three years of active duty, then receive $1,000 bonuses and inactive reserve commissions.

In Los Angeles, California, the Douglas TBD Devastator enters production, becoming the first American naval aircraft with hydraulically folding wings for storage on carriers.

MAY 1 The Navy department revises its pilot training program to include 300 hours of flight school and 465 hours of ground school, all covered in one year.

JUNE 12–JULY 10 In the Pacific, Fleet Problem XVI unfolds across five million square miles of ocean. This operation includes deployment of 520 carrier aircraft, and is tasked with gauging how efficiently the fleet could fend off probable attacks against Hawaii and the west coast.

JULY 30 At San Diego, California, Lieutenant Frank Akers lands his Berliner-Joyce OJ-2 observation craft on the carrier *Langley* while flying blind. The technology making this feat possible had been jointly developed with the Washington Institute of Technology; this is also the first time it has been attempted on a carrier, and Akers receives a Distinguished Flying Cross.

OCTOBER 5 At Naval Air Station, Lakehurst, New Jersey, the first G-Class airship, a Goodyear G-1, arrives for training purposes.

OCTOBER 14–15 Lieutenant Commander Knefler McGinnis sets a 3,443-mile record by flying a Consolidated XP3Y-1 flying boat non-stop from Cristobal Harbor, Panama, to Alameda, California.

NOVEMBER 15 In Washington, D.C., the Chief of the Bureau of Aeronautics announces a competition between the Brewster XF2A-1 and the Grumman XF4F-3 fighter designs. Curiously, they enter service as the Buffalo and Wildcat, respectively.

DECEMBER 9 In London, England, a second Naval Conference transpires between delegates from the United States, Great Britain, Italy, France, and Japan. The effort fails when several countries balk at new limitations, and warship construction resumes in earnest.

1936

MARCH 18 At Naval Air Station, Pensacola, Florida, the Naval Aircraft Factory XN3N-1 trainer aircraft successfully concludes its testing phase.

APRIL 28 The Naval Research Laboratory successfully tests a pulsed radio-wave detection device (radar) which detects a moving aircraft 25 miles away.

JULY 23 In San Diego, California, Consolidated Aircraft contracts with the Navy to construct the XPB2Y-1 four-engine flying boat. This large aircraft subsequently enters the service as the *Coronado*.

AUGUST 19 Off the Virginia Capes, Martin T4M bombers sink the old submarine *R-8* by causing extensive damage from deliberate near-misses.

SEPTEMBER 18 Rear Admiral Arthur P. Fairfield conducts a squadron to Spain to evacuate American citizens trapped by the internecine civil war raging there.

1937

May 30 The Navy contracts with the Martin Company to build its prototype XPMB-1 twin-engined flying boat. It enters into service as the PBM Mariner and sees distinguished service during World War II.

June 21–22 Lieutenant Robert W. Morse conducts 12 PBY Catalinas, Patrol Squadron Three, from San Diego, California, to Coco Solo, Panama, and covers the 3,292 miles distance in 27 hours and 58 minutes.

July 2 In Washington, D.C., President Franklin D. Roosevelt orders a battleship, four destroyers, and a minesweeper to look for missing aviatrix Amelia Earhart in the southeast Pacific.

September 30 The new carrier *Yorktown* is commissioned; it plays a major role in the early days of World War II.

December 12 On the Yangtze River, China, Japanese aircraft sink the American gunboat *Panay* under Lieutenant Commander James J. Hughes, killing 2 crew members and wounding 43 others. This is despite the fact the vessel has its American markings prominently displayed.

December 14 The Japanese government apologizes for the sinking of the *Panay*, and agrees to pay reparations to the families of the dead. This incident does little to soothe relations between the two nations.

December 17 The Hall Aluminum Aircraft Company contracts with the Navy to construct its prototype XPTBH-2. This is the last twin-float torpedo aircraft acquired for Naval Aviation, and it is cancelled before entering production.

1938

February 2 Two Consolidated PBY Catalinas collide in the dark, and Lieutenant Carlton B. Hutchins maintains control of his stricken craft long enough for his crew to bail out; he receives a posthumous Congressional Medal of Honor.

April In the Pacific, the carrier *Saratoga* stages a mock surprise attack on naval facilities at Pearl Harbor, Hawaii, as part of Fleet Exercise XIX. This is an eerie anticipation of what actually transpires on December 7, 1941.

May 1–3 Along the east coast of the United States, a force of 220 aircraft and 3,000 officers and men participate in mock air raids against the fleet to establish if air power alone could repel a seaborne invasion. Results are encouraging but still inconclusive, overall.

May 12 The new carrier *Enterprise* is commissioned; it will emerge as the Navy's most decorated vessel of World War II.

May 17 In Washington, D.C., Congress passes the Naval Expansion Act of 1938 and appropriates $1 billion for new capital ships, cruisers, aircraft carriers (including the *Essex*), and 3,000 modern naval aircraft.

JUNE 25   In Washington, D.C., Congress further authorizes construction of two battleships, one carrier, two light cruisers, and several smaller vessels.

JULY 1   The new post of Commander, Carrier Air Group, arises while carrier squadrons are organized into groups and designated by their carrier's name.

AUGUST 23   In Baltimore, Maryland, the Martin Company contracts with the Navy to build a huge XPBM-1 four-engine flying boat; this enters service as the JRM Mars, of which only six are built during World War II.

AUGUST 24   The JH-1, the Navy's first radio-controlled target drone, is successfully tested on board the carrier *Ranger*. Radio-controlled aircraft are rapidly becoming a practical reality.

SEPTEMBER 14   In the first demonstration of an air-to-ground missile, the battleship *Utah* is subjected to simulated dive bomb attacks by a radio-controlled N2C-2 target drone.

OCTOBER 15   The Navy Department revises color regulations for all training aircraft, which are now to be finished in bright orange-yellow paint scheme. Service aircraft will continue with bare aluminum fuselages and orange yellow upper wing surfaces, as they have since 1925.

DECEMBER 1   In Washington, D.C., the Hepburn report highlights the need for enlargement of 11 airbases in the United States. It also recommends the construction of 16 additional airbases overseas, including 6 in the Pacific (including Wake, Midway, and Guam).

DECEMBER 9   Shipboard radar developed by the Naval Research Laboratory is successfully tested on the battleship *New York*; during World War II, American vessels outfitted with such devices enjoy huge advantages over their Japanese counterparts.

DECEMBER 16   At Naval Air Station Lakehurst, New Jersey, the Navy tests the non-rigid K-2 blimp for use as an anti-submarine weapon; no less than 135 of these craft are acquired during World War II, and prove highly successful at combating U-boats.

1939

APRIL 7   In San Diego, California, the Consolidated Company is contracted to build an amphibian version of the PBY Catalina flying boat with retractable landing gear. This variant, the PBY-5A, sees widespread service during World War II.

MAY 15   Curtiss Aircraft contracts with the Navy to construct the XSB2C-1 dive bomber prototype, which sees service in World War II as the Helldiver.

MAY 17   Off the coast of China, the destroyer *Whipple* and gunboats *Asheville* and *Tulsa* send sailors and marines ashore to protect the U.S. Consulate after Japanese forces move into the area.

MAY 23   Near Portsmouth, New Hampshire, the submarine *Squalus* sinks in 240 feet of water, and 33 (out of 59) surviving crew members are rescued by the new McCann Rescue Chamber (diving bell).

The submarine itself is raised in a salvage effort directed by Rear Admiral Ernest J. King, and reenters service as the *Sailfish*.

JUNE 11–13   Off the west coast, the carrier *Saratoga* and fleet oiler *Kanawaha* undertake refueling exercises at sea; this practice proves invaluable in the Pacific during World War II, where bases are inaccessible.

JULY 7   The Navy's Lighthouse Bureau is absorbed into the U.S. Coast Guard.

JULY 13   In Washington, D.C., the Chief of Naval Operations authorizes a Fleet Air Tactical Unit to research the operational use of new aircraft entering the service.

AUGUST 4   Carriers *Yorktown* and *Enterprise* successfully launch SBC-3 and O3U-3 aircraft from hangar decks directly below the flight deck, using hydraulic flush-deck catapults mounted there.

AUGUST 30   Lieutenant Commander Thurston B. Clark repeatedly lands a twin-engined XJO-3 aircraft on the deck of the carrier *Lexington*, demonstrating the practicality of operating multi-engine aircraft at sea.

SEPTEMBER 1   World War II begins as German tanks blitzkrieg their way across Poland; the British and French governments promptly declare war two days later, as Europe is engulfed in another costly struggle.

SEPTEMBER 5   In Washington, D.C., President Franklin D. Roosevelt orders Chief of Naval Operations Admiral Harold R. Stark to commence a "Neutrality Patrol" to monitor potentially hostile foreign vessels entering American waters. This activity stretches out 300 miles off the Eastern Seaboard.

SEPTEMBER 8   In Washington, D.C., President Franklin D. Roosevelt authorizes the Navy to increase its manpower from 110,813 to 145,000. In light of the world situation, retired officers, enlisted men, and even nurses are called back to the colors. He also declares a "Limited National Emergency" as a pretext for continued military preparations.

SEPTEMBER 11–13   In the Caribbean, PBY Catalinas of VP-33 and VP51 operate from new bases in Panama and Puerto Rico while patrolling the region for potentially hostile vessels.

SEPTEMBER 21   In the Philippines, 14 PBY Catalinas of VP-21 arrive from Pearl Harbor, Hawaii; they serve as the first patrol unit assigned to the Asiatic Fleet since 1932.

OCTOBER 1   The Navy orders its pilot-training syllabus concentrated so that cadets gain their wings in 6 months instead of 12. Ground school for mechanics is also shortened from 33 weeks to 18.

OCTOBER 5   The Hawaiian Detachment, consisting of the carrier *Enterprise*, two heavy cruiser divisions, two destroyer squadrons, and auxiliary vessels, departs the west coast for Pearl Harbor, Hawaii. It is hoped their presence will deter Japanese aggression in the Pacific.

OCTOBER 14   In Philadelphia, Pennsylvania, the Naval Aircraft Factory begins testing radio-control equipment for possible flight testing of aircraft. In this manner, such violent maneuvers as dive and pullouts could be accomplished without risking a pilot's life.

DECEMBER 1   Submarine Division 14's six vessels are ordered to the Asiatic Station as a precaution in the event of war. The ships in question are the *Perch, Permit, Pickerel, Pike, Porpoise,* and *Tarpon.*

DECEMBER 14–19   The German passenger liner *Columbus,* pursued by British destroyers, is scuttled 450 miles off the American coast to prevent capture; the heavy cruiser *Tuscaloosa* rescues 573 passengers and takes them to New York City.

DECEMBER 20   The Navy contracts with Consolidated Aircraft to purchase 200 PBY Catalina patrol planes to meet demands of the Neutrality Patrol. This also constitutes the largest single order for naval aircraft since 1917.

1940

JANUARY 11   Near Culebra, Puerto Rico, Fleet Landing Exercise No. 6 unfolds with the former destroyer-turned-transport *Manley* being the only vessel capable of putting marines ashore.

JANUARY 15–22   Offshore at Monterey, California, joint Army and Navy forces rehearse amphibious landings to familiarize themselves with embarking and landing procedures. Such experience proves vital to both services during World War II.

FEBRUARY 15   In Washington, D.C., the Commander in Chief, U.S. Fleet, orders the Bureaus of Aeronautics and Ordnance to accelerate procurement of naval aircraft with better armor and self-sealing fuel tanks. This comes in response to tactical combat intelligence reports arriving from Europe.

FEBRUARY 27   The Vought Aircraft Company contracts with the Navy to develop its radical V-173 prototype, featuring a near-circular wing; because of its peculiar shape it becomes known as the "Flying Flapjack."

MARCH 22   The Naval Aircraft Factory experiments with a radio system for its torpedo-carrying TG-2 flying drone, one of the first guided-missile systems.

APRIL 7–13   Off the Panama Canal Zone, the destroyer *J. Fred Talbott* rendezvouses with the Japanese freighter *Arimasa Maru* to assist an injured crew member.

APRIL 20   At Camden, New Jersey, the *Curtiss* becomes the first seaplane tender designed specifically for the Navy.

APRIL 25   The new aircraft carrier *Wasp* is commissioned.

MAY 7   In Washington, D.C., President Franklin D. Roosevelt orders ships of the U.S. Fleet to remain at Pearl Harbor as a show of force to Japan. However, when Admiral James Richardson forcefully protests that its defensive facilities are woefully inadequate, the president responds by removing him from command the following February.

MAY 16   In Washington, D.C., President Franklin D. Roosevelt requests and additional $1.18 billion in defense appropriations from Congress.

MAY 17   In Washington, D.C., President Franklin D. Roosevelt orders that 35 World War I destroyers, presently laid up (mothballed), be recommissioned.

MAY 27   In Washington, D.C., the Secretary of the Navy orders the new destroyers

Pringle, Stanly, Hutchins, Stevens, Halford, and *Leutze* to be outfitted with catapults and plane-handling equipment.

JUNE 11 In Washington, D.C., Congress passes the Naval Supply Act, which provides a further $1.5 billion in defense appropriations.

JUNE 14–15 In Washington, D.C., President Franklin D. Roosevelt signs the Naval Expansion Act of 1940, authorizing an 11 percent increase in naval strength. The measure, which includes provisions for 4,500 new aircraft, is increased to 10,000 the following day.

JUNE 17 In Washington, D.C., Congress, upon the urging of Chief of Naval Operations Admiral Harold R. Stark, passes a $4 billion appropriations bill. This further increases naval strength by 70 percent to achieve a true "Two Ocean Navy" and doubles the existing 1.2 million tons of vessels, while raising naval aircraft acquisitions to 15,000. This new Naval Expansion Act is signed into law on July 19.

JUNE 20 In Washington, D.C., the Navy Department orders the Bureau of Construction and Repair merged with the Bureau of Engineering to form the new Bureau of Ships. The position Undersecretary of the Navy is also created.

At Montevideo, Uruguay, the cruiser *Quincy* arrives in South America to counter German propaganda there. The cruiser *Wichita* subsequently joins it on a goodwill tour of the region.

JUNE 25 In Washington, D.C., the Chief of Naval Operations expands existing flight training programs to include 300 new entrants per month.

The Naval Construction Corps is abolished, and its officers are merged into the navy line; henceforth all members receive "engineering duty only" classifications.

AUGUST 22 At Baltimore, Maryland, the Martin Aircraft Company begins construction of its huge PB2M (JRM) Mars flying boat; only six are constructed.

AUGUST 25 In Pittsburgh, Pennsylvania, the Navy contracts with Carnegie University's Department of Terrestrial Magnetism to develop fuzing technology for antiaircraft weapons. This research culminates in the radio VT proximity fuze that proves lethal to Japanese aircraft across the Pacific.

SEPTEMBER 3 The United States and Great Britain agree to the exchange of 50 aged destroyers for rights to construct air and sea facilities in Newfoundland, Bermuda, and the British West Indies. This agreement also marks the genesis of the Lend-Lease Program, whereby the United States functions as a de facto weapons supplier to the western allies. Prime Minister Winston Churchill characterized this deal as a matter "of life and death."

SEPTEMBER 6 The first eight "flush-deck" destroyers configured for the Lend-Lease Program are dispatched to Great Britain.

SEPTEMBER 9 In Washington, D.C., President Franklin D. Roosevelt signs a supplemental defense appropriation bill, of which the Navy receives $3 billion. This is part of the largest naval procurement bill in history and calls for construction of 210 vessels, including 12 carriers and seven battleships.

OCTOBER 3 In London, England, the U.S. Naval Attache is instructed to procure examples of British radio echo (radar) equipment. This technology is to be evaluated for aircraft interception (AI), surface vessel detection (ASV), and aircraft identification (IFF) purposes.

OCTOBER 9 In Washington, D.C., the Secretary of the Navy authorizes plans to equip select submarines for carrying aviation gasoline and refueling patrol planes at sea.

OCTOBER 12 The carrier *Wasp* launches Army Air Corps P-40s and O-47s to evaluate their takeoff runs; this is the first time Army aircraft have operated from a carrier.

OCTOBER 25 In Shanghai, China, Japanese aircraft drop bombs 300 yards from the gunboat *Tutuila* and the U.S. Embassy; their government apologizes and blames equipment malfunctions.

NOVEMBER 18 In Washington, D.C., the Chief of Naval Operations orders that the acronym "radar" be officially adopted; it stands for "radio detection and ranging." This is one of the most important new technologies developed and deployed during World War II.

DECEMBER 30 In Washington, D.C., the Navy Department again revises its aircraft camouflage scheme, whereby Navy planes are to be painted light gray. However, patrol aircraft receive blue-gray top surfaces.

1941

JANUARY 1 At this date, on the cusp of entering World War II, U.S. Navy personnel stands at 383,150 officers and men. It will expand tenfold by 1945.

JANUARY 2 In Washington, D.C., President Franklin D. Roosevelt unveils a naval construction program aimed at producing 200 7,500-ton cargo vessels. These ungainly but essential craft acquire a degree of immortality as "Liberty Ships."

JANUARY 6 At Simonstown, South Africa, the heavy cruiser *Louisville* loads $148 million in British gold for transportation to the United States.

JANUARY 9 In the Central Pacific, the first contractors arrive to construct an air station on Wake Island.

FEBRUARY 1 In Washington, D.C., the Navy Department revives the old designation of Atlantic and Pacific Fleets. These are commanded by Admirals Ernest J. King and Husband E. Kimmel, respectively. The Asiatic Fleet is headed up by Admiral Thomas C. Hart.

FEBRUARY 7 At Annapolis, Maryland, the Naval Academy's Class of 1941 graduates four months early in light of the world situation.

MARCH 17 In Washington, D.C., the Chief of Naval Operations founds a special committee tasked with reviewing jet propulsion, and possible applications for both flight and assisted takeoffs.

MARCH 27 In Washington, D.C., the United States, Great Britain, and Canada conclude the ABC-1 Staff Agreement to help frame strategic cooperation. A Combined Chiefs of Staff with officers from member countries arises, and the U.S. Atlantic Fleet will also convoy ships to Britain in concert with the Royal Navy.

APRIL 9   The modern battleship *North Carolina* is commissioned, being the first vessel of its class since 1923.

APRIL 10   In the North Atlantic, the destroyer *Niblack* under Lieutenant Commander E. R. Durgin rescues survivors from a torpedoed Dutch freighter, then drops depth charges on a sonar contact believed to be a German U-boat. This is the first aggression by a United States warship toward the Axis.

APRIL 11   In Washington, D.C., President Franklin D. Roosevelt orders U.S. Navy vessels to extend patrolling activities to west longitude, 26 degrees. The Germans simply ignore this posturing and continue attacking allied shipping.

APRIL 26   The Naval Aircraft Factory reports that a radio-controlled O3U-6 aircraft was successfully tested in flight regimens far exceeding the safety margins of piloted flight. The information gathered proves useful in high-speed flutter analysis.

MAY 2   The Naval Aircraft Factory, Philadelphia, Pennsylvania, embarks on Project Roger to test airborne radar equipment with the Massachusetts Institute of Technology and the Naval Research Laboratory.

MAY 15   Following the fall of France, President Franklin D. Roosevelt orders French-registered vessels in American ports secured to prevent them from falling into German hands. This haul includes the great luxury liner *Normandie*.

MAY 21   Off the coast of Brazil, the American merchantman *Robin Moore* is sunk by German submarines despite American flags being prominently displayed on its hull. This is the first American ship lost in World War II.

In Louisiana, the new bow-ramp version of the Higgins landing craft is deemed superior to more conventional craft employed by the Navy; this is the forerunner of the famous Landing Craft Vehicle Personnel, or LCVP.

MAY 26   Over 300 miles off the French coast, a British PBY Catalina flown by U.S. Navy Ensign Leonard B. Smith spots the German battleship *Bismark* circling. The vessel is located and sunk the following day by the main British fleet. Lieutenant Commander Joseph H. Wellings is also on board the battleship *King George V* as an observer, and witnesses the battle first-hand.

MAY 27   In Washington, D.C., a state of "Unlimited National Emergency" is declared by President Franklin D. Roosevelt.

JUNE 2   At Newport News, Virginia, the former merchant vessel *Mormacmail* is converted into the first escort carrier, the *Long Island*. These nondescript craft are essential for ending the U-boat menace in the Atlantic.

JUNE 4   The Naval Aircraft Factory reports that television technology has progressed to the point where it is possible to transmit signals to an aircraft and control its course in flight.

JUNE 6   In Philadelphia, Pennsylvania, the mine-laying vessel *Terror* becomes the first Navy vessel solely designed for this purpose.

JUNE 12   In Washington, D.C., President Franklin D. Roosevelt orders the U.S. Naval Reserve mobilized.

JUNE 15   Near Shanghai, China, lightning strikes twice as Japanese warplanes again drop bombs alarmingly close to the gunboat *Tutuila*. Their government apologizes, declaring the incident "wholly unintentional."

JUNE 20   Near Portsmouth, New Hampshire, the submarine *O-9* sinks during a test dive, and all 33 crewmen perish.

JULY 1   Atlantic Fleet commander Admiral Ernest J. King begins organizing 10 "task forces" to convoy neutral merchant vessels between the United States and Iceland. This action comes as a result of a recent treaty between the two, whereby the United States agrees to occupy and defend the island.

In Washington, D.C., the Navy Department organizes the American coastline into six "sea frontiers." Each of these has assigned forces with responsibilities covering convoy escorts, patrols, and antisubmarine warfare. Two additional sea frontiers are designated for Hawaii and the Philippines.

JULY 30   At Chongqing, China, Japanese aircraft drop bombs close to the American gunboat *Tutuila* a third time. However, their government dismisses the affair as another accident and apologizes again.

AUGUST 5   At Vineland Sound, Massachusetts, President Franklin D. Roosevelt secretly boards the heavy cruiser *Augusta* and steams north to Argentia, Newfoundland, for talks with Prime Minister Winston Churchill.

AUGUST 9–12   At Placentia Bay, Newfoundland, President Franklin D. Roosevelt and British Prime Minister meet aboard the cruiser *Augusta* and battleship *Prince of Wales*. They then sign the Atlantic Charter, which reaffirms American intentions to assist Great Britain should they enter the war.

SEPTEMBER 1   On this date the U.S. Navy is assigned responsibility for convoying transatlantic merchant ships from Argentia, Newfoundland, to a mid-ocean meeting point south of Iceland.

SEPTEMBER 4   Southwest of Iceland, the destroyer *Greer* trades depth charges and torpedoes with *U-652*. Both vessels miss their intended target, but the incident highlights growing tensions in the Atlantic.

SEPTEMBER 11   In Washington, D.C., President Franklin D. Roosevelt responds to U-boat attacks upon American shipping by instructing Navy vessels and aircraft to "shoot on sight" any Axis vessels caught within the defensive zone established on April 11.

SEPTEMBER 16   The Navy Department announces it will protect allied and neutral shipping in the Atlantic Ocean as far east as Iceland. This is consistent with provisions of the ABC-1 Staff Agreement so American and Canadian warships will accompany North Atlantic convoys to a "mid-ocean meeting point," after which Royal Navy vessels will escort them for the remainder of the trip to England.

SEPTEMBER 17   At Halifax, Nova Scotia, the U.S. Navy conducts its first escort when Rear Admiral A. B. Cook convoys 20,000 Commonwealth troops to England.

SEPTEMBER 27   At Baltimore, Maryland, the *Patrick Henry* becomes the first of 2,742 "Liberty Ships" constructed in World War II. Slow and ungainly, these prove seaworthy and carry tremendous amounts of supplies around the world.

OCTOBER 14   At Boston, Massachusetts, the Coast Guard Cutter *Bear* arrives with the 20 German prisoners seized near

Greenland on the freighter *Busko*. This vessel was flying a Norwegian flag at the time, and among those taken is a Gestapo agent.

OCTOBER 16   For the first time, Navy destroyers escorting Convoy SC 48 in the North Atlantic encounter and engage German U-boats. The *Livermore* drops depth charges on *U-553* to thwart an attack.

OCTOBER 17   Southwest of Iceland, the *U-553* torpedoes the destroyer *Kearny* under Lieutenant Commander A. L. David, killing 11 sailors and wounding 22. The *Kearny* had previously dropped depth charges to discourage a possible attack upon Convoy CS 48, which it was escorting.

OCTOBER 20   The new carrier *Hornet* is commissioned under Captain Marc A. Mitscher.

OCTOBER 30   In the North Atlantic, the *U-106* torpedoes the American tanker *Salinas* 700 miles off the Newfoundland Coast, and it limps into port safely. The destroyer *Bernadou* drops depth charges in retaliation.

OCTOBER 31   Off the coast of Iceland, the *U-562* sinks the American destroyer *Reuben James* as it escorts convoy HX 156; 115 lives are lost. This is the first American warship lost in the so-called "undeclared war," and President Franklin D. Roosevelt now grants navy ships permission to shoot German submarines on sight.

NOVEMBER 1   In Washington, D.C., President Franklin D. Roosevelt moves the United States closer to a wartime footing by placing the Coast Guard under operational command of the Navy Department.

NOVEMBER 6   In the central Atlantic, the cruiser *Omaha* and destroyer *Somers* apprehend the German blockade runner *Odenwald*, disguised as the American merchantman *Willmoto*.

NOVEMBER 17   In Washington, D.C., Congress votes to allow merchant vessels to arm themselves with the assistance of a Coast Guard gun crew.

NOVEMBER 20   In Washington, D.C., President Franklin D. Roosevelt signs an amendment to the Neutrality Act of 1939; this allows merchant vessels to arm themselves and call at ports belonging to friendly belligerents.

NOVEMBER 26   In the Kuriles Islands, Japan, Vice Admiral Chuichi Nagumo leads an armada of six aircraft carriers, two battleships, three cruisers, nine destroyers, and various tankers and submarines under strict radio silence. They are to attack American naval installations at Pearl Harbor, Hawaii, unless a diplomatic agreement is concluded by December 5.

NOVEMBER 27   In Washington, D.C., Chief of Naval Operations Admiral Harold R. Stark issues a "war warning" to the U.S. Fleet in the Atlantic and Pacific regions. This is one day after Japanese task forces have set sail for Hawaii.

NOVEMBER 28   From Pearl Harbor, Hawaii, Admiral William F. Halsey leads the carrier *Enterprise* to deliver Marine Corps F4F Wildcats to the garrison at Wake Island. He also issues "War Order No. 1," declaring that the vessel is to operate under war conditions.

NOVEMBER 29   In Washington, D.C., President Franklin D. Roosevelt instructs the Commander in Chief, Asiatic Fleet, to purchase three small vessels, raise the American flag on their masts, and station them in the West China Sea and the Gulf of Siam. If attacked by Japanese forces, it would be considered an act of war.

DECEMBER 2   A Coast Guard Armed Guard gun detachment arrives on the merchant vessel *Dunboyne*, being the first of 145,000 men to serve in the Coast Guard during the war. They ultimately man 6,236 merchant ships.

DECEMBER 5   From Pearl Harbor, Hawaii, the carrier *Lexington* sails for Midway Island to deliver a squadron of Marine Corps Vought SB2U Vindicators to the garrison.

DECEMBER 7   At Pearl Harbor, Hawaii, a "Day of Infamy" unfolds as Japanese carriers launch 353 aircraft that sink 8 American battleships along with 11 other vessels; American losses are 2,403 soldiers, sailors, and civilians dead and a further 1,178 wounded. Admiral Isaac C. Kidd of the ill-fated battleship *Arizona* becomes the first American flag officer killed in World War II when he goes down with his ship. A total of 15 Congressional Medals of Honor are awarded for various acts of heroism and self-sacrifice. Japanese losses are 29 aircraft and 3 midget submarines, totaling 100 men. This is one of the most devastating aerial attacks in military history, superbly planned, staged, and executed.

Six troop transports and nine cargo vessels bound for the Philippines are forced by the outbreak of war to return to ports on the west coast; two elect to drop anchor at Brisbane, Australia.

DECEMBER 8   In Washington, D.C., President Franklin D. Roosevelt characterizes December 7 as a "date that will live in infamy," and asks Congress for a declaration of war against Japan.

Near Shanghai, China, the crew of the gunboat *Wake* capitulates to Japanese forces after the crew proves unable to scuttle it; this is the only Navy vessel of this conflict to strike its colors.

The USS West Virginia *burns in Pearl Harbor. The attack on Pearl Harbor was the worst naval disaster in U.S. history, with 16 ships damaged or destroyed. (National Archives)*

A captured Japanese photograph shows the smoke rising from Hickam Field during the attack on Pearl Harbor on December 7, 1941. (National Archives)

DECEMBER 9 The submarine *Swordfish*, 150 miles west of Manila, Philippines, launches the first American torpedo attack of the war against a Japanese merchant vessel. The sub claims a sinking, but it is not borne out in postwar records.

DECEMBER 10 In Hawaiian waters, a SBD Dauntless launched from the carrier *Enterprise* draws first blood by sinking the Japanese submarine *I-70*; this is the first confirmed victory by a Navy carrier aircraft. This submarine had scouted out military facilities in Hawaii just prior to the Pearl Harbor attack.

At Cavite, Philippines, a Japanese air raid sinks one vessel and damages others; the Navy's first air-to-air kill occurs after Chief Boatswain Earl D. Payne of Patrol Squadron 101 flames an attacking A6M2 Zero from his PBY Catalina gun blister.

On Guam, Captain George J. McMillin, the island governor, surrenders his small Marine garrison to overwhelming Japanese forces.

DECEMBER 12 In Washington, D.C., the Naval Air Transportation Service is created.

DECEMBER 14 At Cavite, Philippines, PBY Catalinas of VP-10 begin wending their way toward Australia via the Netherlands East Indies. The lumbering amphibians are easy targets for nimble Japanese fighter aircraft.

DECEMBER 15 At Pearl Harbor, Hawaii, Rear Admiral Frank J. Fletcher conducts Task Force 14—the carrier *Saratoga*, three heavy cruisers, four destroyers, the oiler *Neches*, and seaplane tender *Tangier*—to Wake Island to rescue the heroic garrison.

DECEMBER 16 The submarine *Swordfish* sinks the Japanese cargo ship *Atsutasan Maru*, being the first recorded victory of a U.S. submarine in World War II.

DECEMBER 17 At Pearl Harbor, Hawaii, command of the Pacific Fleet passes from the disgraced Admiral Husband E. Kimmel to Admiral William S. Pye.

DECEMBER 19 In Annapolis, Maryland, the class of 1942 graduates six months early due to the national emergency.

DECEMBER 22 In Washington, D.C., President Franklin D. Roosevelt and Prime Minister Winston Churchill meet in the "Arcadia Conference," whereby the allies adopt a "Germany first" strategy. However, they agree that a supreme commander should be appointed to both the Atlantic and Pacific theaters of operation.

On Luzon, the Philippines, Japanese troops begin landing unopposed at Aparri.

The first convoy of American troops arrives in Brisbane, Australia, escorted by the cruiser *Pensacola*.

DECEMBER 23 Wake Island, having heroically resisted repeated attacks since December 11, is overwhelmed by Japanese forces, and Commander Winfield Scott Cunningham surrenders.

The Wake Island relief force under Rear Admiral Frank J. Fletcher, whose progress from Pearl Harbor has been dictated by the 12-knot oiler *Neches*, is 425 miles from its destination when that island finally succumbs to superior Japanese forces; they are recalled.

DECEMBER 24 In the Philippines, General Douglas MacArthur orders Major General Lewis H. Brereton evacuated to Australia by a Navy PBY.

DECEMBER 30 Admiral Ernest J. King, brilliant, hard-edged, and a confirmed Anglophobe, is appointed Commander in Chief, U.S. Fleet.

DECEMBER 31 At Pearl Harbor, Hawaii, Admiral Chester W. Nimitz, a quiet and reflective officer, gains appointment as Commander in Chief of the Pacific Fleet.

1942

JANUARY 1 The post of Commander in Chief, U.S. Atlantic Fleet, is delegated to Admiral Royal E. Ingersoll.

JANUARY 2 Manila, Philippines, falls to advancing Japanese forces, and with it, the naval base at Cavite falls also.

JANUARY 3 At Singapore, the unified ABDA (American, British, Dutch, Australian) command is devised under General Sir Archibald Wavell to defend the Southwest Pacific against Japan.

JANUARY 5 Just eight miles outside of Tokyo Bay, Japan, the submarine *Pollack* sinks a Japanese freighter; it torpedoes two more over the next four days.

In Washington, D.C., a joint Army-Navy communiqué declares that all American aircraft are to receive a distinct name and number designation for identification purposes.

JANUARY 6 Manila, Philippines, falls to Japanese forces, who also capture 11 Navy nurses; these spend the next 37 months as prisoners.

JANUARY 11 In the Central Pacific, the *I-6* torpedoes the *Saratoga* as the latter returns from Midway Island to Pearl Harbor, Hawaii. The vessel is forced back to the west coast for repairs, weakening American carrier strength to three.

JANUARY 12 In Washington, D.C., Congress increases Navy manpower levels to 500,000 men.

JANUARY 14 In Washington, D.C., the first Washington Conference (or Arcadia) transpires between President Franklin D. Roosevelt, Prime Minister Winston Churchill, and their respective staffs. While agreeing that Germany must be defeated first, a communications line is established in the Pacific from Australia, through American Samoa, New Caledonia, and the Fijis, which is to be defended by the United States at all costs.

JANUARY 15 In the western Pacific, Admiral Thomas C. Hart assumes command of all naval forces operated by the ABDA coalition.

JANUARY 16 A TBD Devastator from the carrier *Enterprise* runs out of fuel while on a search mission, and, observing the strictest radio silence, crashes into the ocean. The three-man crew under Aviation Chief Machinist's Mate Harold F. Dixon survives 31 days in a raft and drifts 1,200 miles before reaching the Danger Islands.

JANUARY 20 Near Darwin, Australia, the destroyer *Edsall* under Lieutenant Joshua J. Dix assists three Australian corvettes in sinking the Japanese submarine *I-124*. This is the first submersible sunk by American surface forces.

In the Makassar Strait, Borneo, the submarine *S-36* under Lieutenant John S. McKnight, Jr., patrols the poorly charted waters until it hits a reef and is scuttled. His crew is rescued by Dutch warships.

JANUARY 23–24 On Bataan, Philippines, a Naval Battalion forms under Commander Francis J. Bridget to assist in defending the peninsula.

JANUARY 24 In the Gulf of Panama, submarine *S-26* is accidentally rammed and sunk by the subchaser *PC-460*; only three men survive.

The Battle of Makassar Straits, Borneo, commences as four ships of Destroyer Division 59, under Commander Paul H. Talbot, raid the Japanese landing site at Balikpapan. The Americans sink three transports and a cargo ship, then escape undamaged; this is the first surface action waged by the U.S. Navy in World War II.

JANUARY 26 At Pearl Harbor, Hawaii, a Board of Inquiry investigating the Pearl Harbor disaster finds Chief of the Pacific Fleet Admiral Husband E. Kimmel and commander of the Hawaiian Department General Walter C. Short guilty of dereliction of duty. Both are dismissed from the position with a court-martial being held.

JANUARY 27 The First Naval Construction Battalion (Seabees) departs the United States for Bora Bora.

In the Central Pacific, the submarine *Gudgeon* under Lieutenant Commander E. H. Grenfell sinks the Japanese submarine *I-173* west of Midway Atoll. This is the first enemy submersible sunk by its American counterpart; 23 enemy submarines meet their fate in this manner.

JANUARY 28 Off the coast of Newfoundland, Canada, a PBO Hudson patrol bomber flown by Aviation Machinist's Mate First Class Donald F. Mason attack a surfaced U-boat and radios back, "Sighted sub, sank same"; however, the kill is not verified in postwar records.

FEBRUARY 1 In the Central Pacific, Vice Admiral William F. Halsey conducts the first American carrier strikes of the war when his Task Group 8, based around the *Enterprise*, attacks Japanese bases on Kwajalein, Marshall Islands, while heavy cruisers

Northampton and *Salt Lake City*, assisted by the destroyer *Dunlap*, sink a gun boat and an auxiliary subchaser. Concurrently, Task Group 17, centered upon the *Yorktown*, hits targets in the Gilbert Islands.

FEBRUARY 3   At Corregidor, Philippines, the submarine *Trout* under Commander Frank W. Fenno delivers food and ammunition to the defenders, then takes on 20 tons of gold and silver for safekeeping and departs.

FEBRUARY 4   In the Java Sea, an Allied task force under Dutch Admiral Karel W. F. M. Doorman is attacked by land-based Japanese medium bombers. The American cruisers *Houston* and *Marblehead* are heavily damaged, and the latter is forced back to the United States for repairs.

FEBRUARY 7   In Washington, D.C., President Franklin D. Roosevelt authorizes creation of the War Shipping Administration under Rear Admiral Emory S. Land. This body is tasked with consolidating and coordinating all merchant-vessel activities throughout the war effort.

FEBRUARY 9   In New York, the confiscated French luxury liner *Normandie*, now outfitted as a troop transport, catches fire and sinks at the dock.

FEBRUARY 11   East of the Celebes, Dutch East Indies, the submarine *Shark* under Lieutenant Commander Louis Shane is sunk by the Japanese destroyer *Yamakaze*; this is the first American submersible lost in combat.

FEBRUARY 14   At Java, Dutch and English leaders force Admiral Thomas C. Hart to step down as commander of Allied Naval Forces, Southwest Pacific; his replacement is Vice Admiral C. E. L. Helfrich, Royal Netherlands Navy.

FEBRUARY 17   At Bora Bora, the 1st Naval Construction Battalion arrives; it becomes the first unit of the fabled Seabees to arrive in theater.

FEBRUARY 19   Port Darwin, Australia, is attacked by Japanese aircraft launched from the carriers *Akagi*, *Hiryu*, *Kaga*, and *Soryu* surprise. The destroyer *Peary* under Lieutenant Commander J. M. Bermingham is sunk with a loss of 80 men, along with two transports. A PBY Catalina flown by Lieutenant Thomas H. Moorer, a future chairman of the Joint Chiefs of Staff, is shot down, and the crew is rescued by a transport—which is itself also sunk.

FEBRUARY 19–20   Near Bali, Dutch East Indies, the Battle of Badoeng Strait unfolds between an Allied force under Rear Admiral Karel W. F. M. Doorman and Japanese warships. Several vessels are damaged on both sides, and the American destroyer *Stewart* is forced into drydock at Surabaya, Java.

FEBRUARY 20   As the carriers *Lexington* and *Yorktown* steam toward Japanese-held Rabaul under Vice Admiral Wilson Brown, they are attacked by a squadron of Mitsubishi G4M bombers. Two Grumman F4F Wildcats led by Lieutenant Edward H. ("Butch") O'Hare move to intercept; their number drops to one when the wingman's guns malfunction. O'Hare nonetheless tackles the bombers, shooting down four bombers and damaging two more. The carriers are saved from imminent destruction, and O'Hare receives a Congressional Medal of Honor.

At Mariveles, Philippines, the submarine *Swordfish* conveys President Manuel Quezon and Vice President Sergio Osmena, along with their families, to nearby Panay Island.

February 22 At Surabaya, Java, the damaged destroyer *Stewart* falls off its keel blocks while in drydock, and is scuttled to prevent capture. Japanese forces subsequently raise and employ it as a patrol boat until its recapture at Kure, Japan, in 1945.

February 23 In Washington, D.C., the Bureau of Aeronautics revises its training regimen for naval aviators, whereby new candidates receive 11 months of instruction for one- and two-engined craft, and 12-and-a-half months for four-engined ones. Classes are also to receive the designations Primary, Intermediate, and Advanced.

Near Santa Barbara, California, Japanese submarine *I-17* surfaces at night and shells the Ellwood oil refinery; damage is slight but adds to local war jitters.

February 24 Wake Island is struck by Task Group 16 under Vice Admiral William F. Halsey. Aircraft from the carrier *Enterprise* bomb and strafe the atoll, while heavy cruisers *Northampton* and *Salt Lake City* and destroyers *Balch* and *Maury* bombard land facilities.

At Manila Bay, Philippines, Francis B. Sayre, U.S. High Commissioner, is evacuated by the submarine *Swordfish* to Java and safety.

February 25 The U.S. Coast Guard assumes responsibility for the protection of all American ports. It presently boasts a strength of 25,000 men, but ultimately expands to 175,000 regulars and reservists.

February 27 South of Tjilatiap, Java, Japanese land-based bombers heavily damage the seaplane tender *Langley*. It has to be scuttled, along with its cargo of 32 Curtiss P-40 fighters intended for the 17th Pursuit Squadron.

February 27–28 The Battle of the Java Sea unfolds as American, British, and Dutch naval forces under Rear Admiral Karel W. F. M. Doorman sustain a crushing defeat at the hands of Rear Admiral Takeo Takagi. Dorman's 5 cruisers and 11 destroyers are battered by superior Japanese gunnery and torpedoes, which sink 2 destroyers and the Dutch light cruisers *De Ruyter* and *Java*. Doorman is killed, and all surviving vessels flee for the supposed safety of Australia.

February 28 Off the Delaware Capes, the destroyer *Jacob Jones* under Commander H. D. Black is sunk by a German submarine, losing most of its crew.

February 28–March 1 The Battle of Sunda Strait, Java, unfolds as the heavy cruiser *Houston* under Captain Albert H. Rooks and the Australian light cruiser *Perth* are attacked by three heavy cruisers and nine destroyers under Admiral Takeo Kurita. Both Allied vessels are sunk in a stiff engagement, and, of *Houston*'s 1,000 crew members, only 368 sailors are captured; Rooks receives a posthumous Congressional Medal of Honor.

March 1 Off Newfoundland, a Lockheed Hudson bomber flown by Ensign William Tepuni of VP-82 sinks *U-656*; this is the first American victory over a German submarine in World War II.

Near Java, the destroyer *Pope* under Lieutenant Commander W. C. Blinn is attacked by Japanese vessels and sunk by aircraft from the carrier *Ryujo*; Lieutenant Richard N. Antrim, the vessel's executive officer, wins a Congressional Medal of Honor while in captivity. Meanwhile, Japanese battleships *Hiei* and *Kirishima* fire 1,141 heavy shells at the elusive destroyer *Edsall* under Lieutenant J. J. Nix, but it succumbs to an air attack; five crew members survive and are subsequently executed.

South of Christmas Island, Japanese aircraft from the carriers *Akagi*, *Hiryu*, *Kaga*, and *Soryu* sink the oiler *Pecos*.

With the fall of Java imminent, the ABDA Command is disbanded.

MARCH 2 Near Surabaja, Netherlands East Indies, the destroyer *Pillsbury* under Commander H. C. Pound is sunk by the Japanese cruisers *Atago* and *Takao* while fleeing to Australia.

MARCH 3 Offshore at Surabaja, Netherlands East Indies, the submarine *Perch* under Lieutenant Commander David A. Hurt endures three days of depth-charge attacks before being scuttled; the entire crew of 59 falls captive.

South of Java, the gunboat *Asheville* is sunk by Japanese destroyers *Arashi* and *Nowaki*; only one crewman is captured.

MARCH 4 Marcus Island, 800 miles northwest of Wake Island, is struck by SBD Dauntless dive-bombers launched from the carrier *Enterprise*, which damage several Japanese facilities.

MARCH 5 In Washington, D.C., the Navy Department grants the newly established Naval Construction Battalion (CB) the official designation of "Seabees."

MARCH 7 Near New London, Connecticut, the K-5 blimp's experimental radio sonobuoy detects the submerged submarine *S-20* at a distance of five miles. Blimps so equipped play a major role in defeating the U-boat menace.

MARCH 10 Over northern New Guinea, aircraft from the carriers *Enterprise* and *Yorktown* under Vice Admiral Wilson Brown attack Japanese shipping at Lae and Salamuna. 4 small enemy vessels are sunk

Seabees

The origins of the Naval Construction Battalion (CB) lay with the foresight of Admiral Ben Moreel, chief of the navy's Bureau of Yard and Docks. Shortly after the Japanese attack on Pearl Harbor in December 1941, and being cognizant of the far-flung nature of the Pacific War, he proposed that the Navy dispense with civilian contractors, who could not be legally employed in a war zone, and create its own specialized construction/engineering force. The first battalions were raised and trained at Davisville, Rhode Island, in the summer of 1942, and placed under the aegis of the Navy's Civilian Engineer Corps. Throughout World War II, the construction battalions, or, as they were popularly known, Seabees, numbered 325,000 men. They built airfields, housing, roads, and other projects on 6 continents and 300 islands. They performed yeoman work, usually under trying or nearly impossible conditions, yet were invariably successful and completed their objectives on time. They declined to 10,000 men during the Korean War, but were actively engaged with the marines at Inchon by constructing docks and causeways under fire, and added additional luster to their reputation. Another huge endeavor was construction of the Naval Air Station (NAS) at Cubi Point in the Philippines, which had to be carved out of mountainous, jungle terrain in five years, at a cost of $100 million. During the Vietnam War they also distinguished themselves by building roads, schools, and hospitals, along with fortifications and installations. Seabee units continue rendering distinguished service to the Navy in Iraq and Afghanistan, and are the most accomplished construction and engineering force in military history.

and 10 others damaged, which prompts Japan to dispatch its own carriers to the region for offensive purposes.

MARCH 11–14 In the Philippines, Lieutenant John D. Bulkeley transports General Douglas A. MacArthur and Rear Admiral Francis W. Rockwell 560 miles to Mindanao in a PT boat; he receives a Congressional Medal of Honor.

MARCH 12 In Washington, D.C., President Franklin D. Roosevelt orders the offices of Chief of Naval Operations and Commander in Chief, U.S. Fleet, combined. This merger grants Admiral Ernest J. King unprecedented control over naval operations—and he proves himself a masterful coordinator.

MARCH 15 Near Argentia, Newfoundland, a Lockheed Hudson bomber of VP-82 sinks *U-503* as it escorts an allied convoy.

MARCH 17 The new post of Commander, Naval Forces Europe, is assigned to Vice Admiral Robert L. Ghormley.

MARCH 19 Near Virginia, the destroyer *Dickerson* is accidentally struck by fire from the freighter *Liberator*; three men are killed including the captain.

At Negros, Philippines, President Manuel Quezo, along with his family and staff, are evacuated at Mindanao by motor torpedo boat *PT-41*.

MARCH 20 The new battleship *South Dakota* is commissioned; it is among the first warships of its class mounting a radar-directed firing system.

MARCH 25 At Portland, Maine, the carrier *Wasp*, battleship *Washington*, heavy cruisers *Tuscaloosa* and *Wichita*, and eight destroyers sail to Scapa Flow, Orkney Islands, to reinforce the British Home Fleet. Tragically, Task Force 39 commander Rear Admiral John W. Wilcox, Jr., is washed overboard and replaced by Rear Admiral Robert C. Giffen.

In the Atlantic, the heavily armed merchantman (Q-Ship) *Atik* engages the *U-123* and is sunk, with all hands lost.

MARCH 26 In Washington, D.C., Admiral Harold R. Stark steps down as Chief of Naval Operations and is replaced by Admiral Ernest J. King. As Chief, U.S. Fleet, King also holds unprecedented responsibilities, which have been combined into the CNO position through an executive order.

MARCH 27 In Washington, D.C., the Department of the Navy is tasked with controlling all anti-submarine activity along both coastlines. This authority also extends to Army Air Force units engaged in such activity.

APRIL 3 In Washington, D.C., greater interservice harmony is promoted when Admiral Chester W. Nimitz is appointed Commander in Chief, Pacific Ocean Area (CINCPOA), while General Douglas A. MacArthur is designated Commander, Southwest Pacific Area. Such a division of responsibility is unprecedented, but is intended to placate the touchy MacArthur.

APRIL 6 In Manila Bay, Philippines, four Japanese landing barges crammed with troops are sunk by the gunboats *Mindanao* and *Oahu*.

APRIL 8 At Corregidor, Philippines, the submarine *Seadragon* evacuates specialists, such as radio communications intelligence officers, before the island surrenders.

APRIL 9 In Narragansett Bay, Rhode Island, a TG-2 radio-controlled drone fitted with a television camera successfully "attacks" the destroyer *Aaron Ward*, when

> ### Nimitz, Chester W. (1885–1965)
>
> Chester William Nimitz was born in Fredericksburg, Texas, on February 24, 1885, and he graduated from the U.S. Navy Academy in 1905. He accidentally ran the destroyer *Decatur* aground in July 1908, but a court-martial simply reprimanded him. Nimitz proved himself to be a far-sighted naval officer. During World War I he pioneered refueling techniques at sea. In 1939 Nimitz became chief of the Bureau of Navigation, where his quiet, affable manner and grasp of strategy caught the attention of Secretary of the Navy Frank Knox. After the Japanese attack on Pearl Harbor, Knox recommended that President Franklin D. Roosevelt appoint him commander in chief of the Pacific Fleet as a full admiral. Nimitz received the position, although his authority was restricted to the Central Pacific, because the Southwest Pacific was reserved for the prickly General Douglas A. MacArthur.
>
> Nimitz now faced the task of uprooting Japanese forces from their Pacific strongholds. He did so by fighting the Japanese navy to a draw at Coral Sea in May 1942, then crushing them at Midway in June. Over the next three years Nimitz orchestrated a steady advance through the Central Pacific with victories at Tarawa, Saipan, and Tinian. In December 1944 he advanced to five-star fleet admiral, and organized the successful captures of Iwo Jima and Okinawa that spring. Nimitz was present at surrender ceremonies in Tokyo Bay in September 1945, signing documents for the United States. Shortly thereafter he succeeded King as Chief of Naval Operations. He died in San Francisco, California, on February 20, 1966, a master of modern sea power.

it releases a torpedo that passes within 300 feet of its target.

In the Philippines, the submarine tender *Canopus*, minesweeper *Bittern*, tug *Napa*, and drydock *Dewey* are scuttled following the surrender of Bataan.

Near Cebu Island, Philippines, the Japanese light cruiser *Kuma* and torpedo boat *Kiji* are attacked by motor patrol boats *PT-34* and *PT-41*. The Americans score several hits, but defective torpedoes fail to explode. The *PT-34* is subsequently attacked by floatplanes and scuttled.

APRIL 10 The Navy Department reorganizes the U.S. Pacific fleet into the various commands and commanders: Carriers (Vice Admiral William F. Halsey, Jr.); cruisers (Rear Admiral Frank J. Fletcher); Destroyers (Rear Admiral Robert A. Theobald); Service Force (Vice Admiral William L. Calhoun); Amphibious Force (Vice Admiral Wilson Brown, Jr.); Submarine Force (Rear Admiral Thomas Withers); Patrol Wings (Rear Admiral John S. McCain).

APRIL 14 On the North Carolina coast, the destroyer *Roper* sinks *U-85* with depth charges; this is the first German vessel sunk off the Eastern Seaboard.

APRIL 18 The carrier *Hornet* under Vice Admiral William F. Halsey, Jr., 800 miles off the Japanese coast, launches 18 North American B-25 *Mitchell* medium bombers under Colonel James "Jimmy" Doolittle. These aircraft strike targets in Tokyo, Yokosuka, Yokohama, Kobe, and Nagoya, Japan, before crash-landing in China. The damage inflicted proves minor, but the Japanese Navy loses considerable face for failing to protect the home islands. Several fighter units are subsequently recalled to guard Japanese airspace.

At Naval Air Station, Quonset Point, Rhode Island, the Night Fighter Development Unit is established to develop equipment for Navy and marine aviators.

At Timor, Dutch East Indies, the submarine *Searaven* evacuates the remaining Royal Australian Air Force personnel to safety.

APRIL 19   In Chesapeake Bay, a television-guided BG-1 drone operated by Utility Squadron VJ-5 scores a direct hit on a raft towed at eight knots. Moreover, it is guided to the target by a control airplane flying 11 miles distant.

APRIL 20   In the Mediterranean, 58 Royal Air Force Spitfires fly off the carrier *Wasp* under Captain J. W. Reeves, Jr., to reinforce the Malta garrison.

APRIL 25   At Norfolk, Virginia, Andrew Higgins's 50-foot tank lighter is accepted into Navy service as the Landing Craft Mechanized (LCM). This it is the first vessel capable of landing armored vehicles during amphibious operations.

APRIL 26   Near Key West, Florida, the destroyer *Sturtevant* under Lieutenant Commander C. L. Weigle runs afoul of a poorly charted American mine field, strikes a mine, then sinks with a loss of 15 men.

APRIL 28   At Scapa Flow, Orkney Islands, the battleship *Washington*, heavy cruisers *Wichita* and *Tuscaloosa*, and four American destroyers assist Royal Navy vessels while escorting convoy PQ 15 to Murmansk, Soviet Union.

APRIL 30   Admiral Harold R. Stark is appointed commander, U.S. Naval Force Europe.

MAY 1   Near Honshu, Japan, the 9,000-ton seaplane tender *Mizuho* is sunk by the submarine *Drum* under Commander Robert H. Rice.

MAY 3   At Corregidor, Philippines, the submarine *Spearfish* evacuates nurses and specialist personnel for the last time before the Japanese storm the island.

MAY 4   In the Solomon Islands, aircraft from the carrier *Yorktown* strike Japanese shipping off Tulagi; four transports are sunk.

MAY 6   After the minesweeper *Quail* under Lieutenant Commander John H. Morrill is scuttled in Manila Bay, Philippines, his 18-man crew sails off in a motor launch and reaches Darwin, Australia, on June 6, 1942.

MAY 7–8   In the Coral Sea, United States and Japanese warships wage the first naval encounter where the opposing fleets never sight each other. The battle turns completely on naval air strikes: Rear Admiral Frank J. Fletcher's Task Force 17 loses the heavy carrier *Lexington,* the destroyer *Sims,* and oiler *Neosho,* while the *Yorktown* is heavily damaged. Vice Admiral Takeo Takagi loses light carrier *Shoho* and six smaller vessels, while the large carriers *Shokaku* and *Zuikaku* are heavily damaged. A Japanese invasion force, intended for Port Moresby, New Guinea, has been turned back for the first time. On the *Neosho,* Chief Watertender Oscar V. Peterson closes bulkhead stop valves and saves his shipmates, winning a posthumous Congressional Medal of Honor.

MAY 9   In the Mediterranean, the carrier *Wasp* under Captain J. W. Reeves delivers a second cargo of 47 Royal Air Force Spitfires to Malta; Prime Minister Winston Churchill subsequently quips, "Who said a *Wasp* couldn't sting twice!"

MAY 10   Off the Gold Coast, West Africa, the carrier *Ranger* launches 68 Army Curtiss P-40s fighters, which land at Accra.

MAY 13   In Washington, D.C., the Bureau of Navigation acquires the new designation Bureau of Personnel. Previously, its scientific functions had been transferred to the chief of naval personnel's office.

May 20 The position of Commander, Air Forces, South Pacific, is given to Rear Admiral John S. McCain, whose efforts prove pivotal in the forthcoming Guadalcanal campaign.

May 21 Command of the new North Pacific Force falls upon Rear Admiral Robert A. Theobald, who is responsible for operations in Alaskan waters.

May 25 Near Martinique, French West Indies, a torpedo from *U-156* blows 60 feet off the bow of the destroyer *Blakeley*, killing six sailors. Fortunately, the destroyer survives and is repaired.

In the Central Pacific, Japanese and American flotillas begin converging upon Midway Island, setting the stage for a decisive showdown. Unknown to Japan, Commander Joseph J. Rochefort's code breakers at Pearl Harbor have cracked their military codes and are aware of their plans.

June 1 Acting upon orders from President Franklin D. Roosevelt, the Navy and Marine Corps reverse a decades-old policy by formally recruiting African Americans into their respective war effort.

June 3–6 In the Central Pacific, Rear Admiral Frank J. Fletcher's Task Force 17, seconded by Task Force 16 under Rear Admiral Raymond Spruance, decisively wins the Battle of Midway, waged entirely with carrier aircraft. Vice Admiral Chuichi Nagumo loses 17 ships, including carriers *Kaga*, *Akagi*, *Hiryu*, and *Soryu*, 275 airplanes, and scores of irreplaceable pilots, plus the heavy cruiser *Mikuma* and 4,800 men. American losses are 300 men, the carrier *Yorktown*, and the destroyer *Hammann*, along with 132 aircraft lost. Midway proves a turning point in the Pacific War, for the United States assumes the strategic offensive.

A handful of new Grumman TBF Avenger torpedo bombers debut at Midway with Torpedo Squadron 8. Most are shot down, but they become the widely utilized torpedo bomber in naval aviation.

June 15 At Naval Air Station, Lakehurst, New Jersey, a K-2 airship outfitted with Long Range Navigation Equipment (LORAN) homes in on the beacon and rides it directly toward the middle of the hangar from a distance of 75 miles.

June 16 In Washington, D.C., Congress authorizes the purchase of 200 lighter-than-air craft in recognition of their utility as antisubmarine craft.

June 18 Bernard Robinson is the first African American to receive an officer's commission in the Navy by becoming an ensign in the U.S. Naval Reserve.

June 19 Near Amchitka Island, Aleutians, the submarine *S-27* under Lieutenant Herbert K. Jukes runs aground and is scuttled; the crew is subsequently rescued by PBY Catalinas.

Command of the new South Pacific Area, and its South Pacific Force, reverts to Vice Admiral Robert L. Ghormley.

June 30 Near Bermuda, a PBM Mariner of VP-74 sinks *U-158* with depth charges.

July 1 Outside Manila Bay, Philippines, the submarine *Sturgeon* sinks the Japanese transport *Montevideo Maru*, unaware it is transporting 1,050 Allied prisoners.

July 3 At Goldlake, California, a PBY-5A successfully fires a retro-rocket antisubmarine weapon for the first time. This device was designed at the California Institute of Technology, and reaches operational status early in 1943.

July 7 In the Pacific, Rear Admiral Richmond K. Turner's transport fleet and

Rear Admiral Frank J. Fletcher's Task Force 17 are collared for an offensive in the Solomon Islands. This marks the beginning of an Americans strategic offensive in the Pacific.

JULY 10   In the Aleutian Islands, a Consolidated PBY observes a nearly intact Mitsubishi A6M3 Zero fighter that has crash-landed in a bog. Once recovered, it proves a major intelligence coup, and reveals its strengths and weaknesses to Allied aircraft designers.

JULY 13   Near Panama, the subchaser *PC 458* and the destroyer *Landowne* sink the *U-153*, assisted by Army aircraft.

JULY 15   Near North Carolina, the freighter *Unicoi* rams the surfaced *U-576*, which is then sunk by an OS2U Kingfisher of VS-9.

JULY 18   Rear Admiral Richmond K. Turner assumes command of the new Amphibious Force, South Pacific, in preparation for an offensive in the Solomon Islands.

JULY 19   Off the Gold Coast of Africa, the carrier *Ranger* delivers a second wave of 72 Army P-40 fighters to Accra.

JULY 20   In Washington, D.C., Admiral William D. Leahy is appointed President Franklin D. Roosevelt's Chief of Staff. He also serves as chairman of the Joint Chiefs of Staff and plays a major role in the formulation of Allied strategy.

JULY 30   In Washington, D.C., President Franklin D. Roosevelt establishes the Women Accepted for Volunteer Emergency Service (WAVES), under Lieutenant Commander Mildred H. McAfee. By war's end, 86,291 women are serving in the ranks.

Off the Aleutian Islands, the submarine *Grunion* under Lieutenant Commander Mannert L. Abele makes a final radio transmission, then vanishes. The wreck is discovered on October 3, 2008,

Waves

For most its history, the U.S. Navy applied stringent gender restrictions to its personnel by employing males only. However, on July 30, 1942, President Franklin D. Roosevelt signed Public Law 689 which created the Women Accepted for Volunteer Emergency Service, famously known as the acronym WAVES. This act legally allowed women to join the Navy Reserve and serve in World War II, although with restrictions as to combat arms and locale. They were headed by Lieutenant Commander Mildred McAfee, president of Wesley College, who began training her initial cadre of officers at Smith and Mount Holyoke colleges, Massachusetts, in the fall of 1942. Wholesale recruitment commenced in February 1943, and by war's end 81,000 WAVES had enlisted and passed through the training facility at Hunter College in New York City. A further 5,000 women served in the Coast Guard and the Marine Corps. In practice, WAVES were forbidden from serving on vessels or in combat capacities, but were otherwise exposed to the full regimen of Navy training and discipline. The occupations they held included hospital service, parachute rigging, gunnery training, mail service, and air-traffic control. Furthermore, many of the 10,500 women officers went on to receive specialized instruction in aeronautics, navigation, ship design, inventory management, and naval intelligence. Thus situated, they released enough men to man 10 battleships, 10 aircraft carriers, 28 cruisers, ands 50 destroyers. Overall, the Navy's experience with its WAVES was extremely successful, and in July 1948 President Harry S. Truman signed the Women's Armed Services Integration Act which abolished the Women's Reserve and allowed them to join the regular naval establishment.

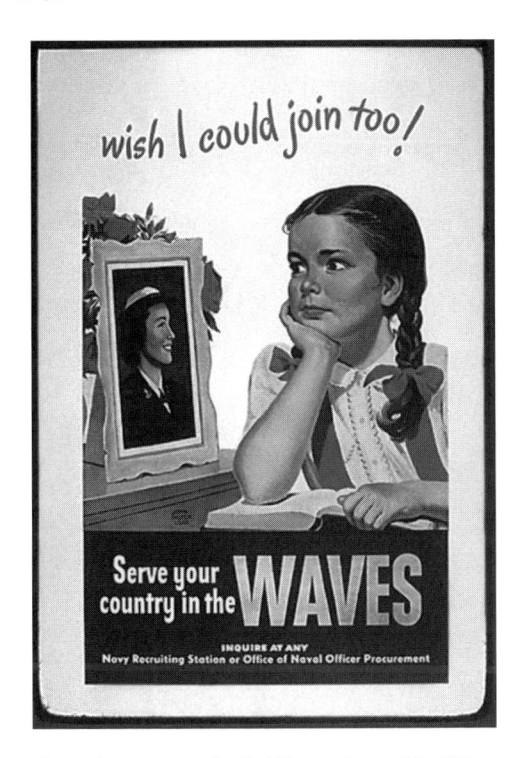

A recruitment poster for the Women Accepted for Volunteer Emergency Service (WAVES) encourages women to join the military during World War II. (National Archives)

by a survey crew who were hired by Abele's three sons.

AUGUST 4 Near Espiritu Santo, New Hebrides, the destroyer *Tucker* under Commander W. R. Terrell strikes a mine in the Segond Channel and sinks, with a loss of six men.

AUGUST 7 In the lower Solomon chain, Admiral Richmond K. Turner directs OPERATION WATCHTOWER, the amphibious invasion of Guadalcanal, Florida, Tulagi, Gavutu, and Tanambogo islands. The 1st Marine Division goes ashore supported by the guns and aircraft of Admiral Frank J. Fletcher's fleet. Unknown at the time, an internecine six-month struggle is about to commence, as costly as it is protracted.

AUGUST 8 Near Guadalcanal, the destroyers *Mugford* and *Jarvis* and transports *Barnett* and *George F. Elliott* are damaged by an intense Japanese air strike, causing the latter to be scuttled.

AUGUST 9 Near Guadalcanal, the Battle of Savo Island erupts as Japanese heavy and light cruisers and destroyers under Vice Admiral Gunichi Mikawa slip unnoticed into Ironbottom Sound at night. The American cruisers *Astoria*, *Quincy*, and *Vincennes* are sunk, along with the Australian cruiser *Canberra*, which is scuttled. Fortunately, Mikawa loses his nerve and does not swoop down upon the helpless transports, but the sheer magnitude of this defeat impels Admiral Frank J. Fletcher to depart immediately with his surviving carriers.

The destroyer *Jarvis* under Lieutenant Commander W. W. Graham is attacked by Japanese aircraft while steaming to Australia for repairs, and sinks with all hands.

AUGUST 10 Near Kavieng, New Ireland, the Japanese light cruiser *Kako* is sunk by the antiquated submarine *S-44* under Lieutenant Commander John R. Moore, becoming the first major warship destroyed by an American submersible.

AUGUST 12 Over Chesapeake Bay, the light cruiser *Cleveland*, armed with new radar-activated VT proximity fuzes, shoots down three target drones in quick succession. This new ammunition grants American warships a tremendous boost in defensive firepower for thwarting aerial attacks.

AUGUST 14 Near Rossel Island in the Pacific, the submarine *S-39* under Lieutenant Commander Francis E. Brown grounds and is scuttled; an Australian vessel rescues the survivors.

AUGUST 16 Off the California coast, a mystery unfolds as airship *L-8* of Blimp Squadron 32 lands at Dale City under its own power, but the two-man crew is missing without a trace.

AUGUST 17–18   In the Gilbert Islands, the large, troop-carrying submarines *Nautilus* and *Argonaut* land marine raiders on the Japanese-held atoll of Makin, then support them with deck gunfire.

AUGUST 22   Near Guadalcanal, the Japanese destroyer *Kawakaze* torpedoes the American destroyer *Blue* at night, killing 9 crewmen and wounding 21; the vessel is scuttled the following day.

AUGUST 23   A convoy carrying two Royal Air Force Squadrons to Murmansk, Russia, is escorted by heavy cruiser *Tuscaloosa* and destroyers *Rodman* and *Emmons*.

AUGUST 24   The Battle of the Eastern Solomons unfolds as a Japanese flotilla makes a determined effort to reinforce the garrison on Guadalcanal. They are intercepted by Rear Admiral Frank J. Fletcher's carriers *Saratoga* and *Enterprise*, which sink the carrier *Ryujo* and destroyer *Mutsuki*. However, the *Enterprise* is badly damaged by planes from *Shokaku* and *Zuikaku*, and returns to Pearl Harbor for repairs.

AUGUST 28   From Henderson Field, Guadalcanal, Navy and Marine SBD Dauntless dive bombers attack a Japanese convoy headed for that island; the destroyer *Asagiri* sinks while *Shirakumo* and *Yugiri* are damaged.

Near Florida Island in the Solomons, the mine-layer *Gamble* sinks the submarine *I-123*.

In the Caribbean, a PBY Catalina of VP-92 assists Canadian corvette HMCS *Oakville* in sinking the *U-94*.

AUGUST 30   Near Kukum Point, Guadalcanal, Japanese aircraft sink the transport *Colhoun* under Lieutenant Commander G. B. Madden, killing 51 crew members.

AUGUST 31   The carrier *Saratoga*, steaming 260 miles southeast of Guadalcanal, is torpedoed by the submarine *I-26* and forced back to Pearl Harbor for repairs.

Near Atka Island, the Aleutians, the destroyer *Reid*, in concert with PBY Catalinas from VP 42 and 43, sinks the submarine *RO-61*.

At Bethesda, Maryland, the National Naval Medical Center is dedicated; it has a 2,000-bed capacity.

SEPTEMBER 1   On Guadalcanal, the 6th Naval Construction Battalion lands at Lunga Point; this is the first Seabee unit committed to combat operations.

The new position of Commander Air Force, Pacific Fleet, is given to Vice Admiral Aubrey W. Fitch.

SEPTEMBER 5   Near Lunga Point, Guadalcanal, the destroyers *Yudachi*, *Hatsuyuki*, and *Murakumo* sink the high-speed transports *Gregory* and *Little*; the Japanese are inadvertently assisted by a flare dropped by a patrolling PBY Catalina.

SEPTEMBER 10–14   In the North Atlantic, U-boats enjoy considerable success hunting allied merchant vessels, sinking 12 ships from Convoy ON-127, en route from North America to Great Britain.

SEPTEMBER 11   In the South China Sea, Pharmacist's Mate First Class Wheeler B. Lipes of the submarine *Seadragon* successfully performs an appendectomy while submerged.

SEPTEMBER 15–16   In the Central Pacific, Japanese submarine *I-19* unleashes a torpedo spread that brackets Task Force 18, escorting a supply convoy to Guadalcanal. The battleship *North Carolina*, the destroyer *O'Brien*, and the *Wasp* are struck, and Captain Forrest P. Sherman orders the carrier scuttled; the vessel loses 193 killed and 366 wounded.

SEPTEMBER 27   In the South Atlantic, the armed merchantman *Stephen Hopkins* trades cannon shots with German auxiliary cruiser *Stier*; both vessels sink, and Lieutenant Kenneth W. Willet, commanding the Armed Guard detachment, wins a posthumous Navy Cross. The *Hopkins's* surviving 15 crew members remain in a lifeboat for 31 days before reaching Brazil.

OCTOBER 5   Off the coast of Iceland, a PBY Catalina belonging to VP-73 sends *U-582* to the bottom.

At Bougainville, the Solomons, dive bombers from the *Hornet* strike at Japanese vessels near Buin-Tonolei and Faisi, damaging two destroyers and seaplane tenders.

In the Solomon Islands, a PBY Catalina sinks Japanese submarine *I-22*; the aircraft in question belongs to the Commander Aircraft South Pacific.

OCTOBER 11   The Battle of Cape Esperance rages off Guadalcanal as a Japanese force of three heavy cruisers and two destroyers under Rear Admiral Aritomo Goto engages Task Force 64 (heavy cruisers *San Francisco* and *Salt Lake City*, light cruisers *Boise* and *Helena*, and five destroyers) under Rear Admiral Norman Scott. Goto dies in combat and loses the heavy cruiser *Furutake* and destroyer *Fubuki*. Several American vessels are also damaged, and the destroyer *Duncan* is scuttled.

OCTOBER 12   Navy and Marine dive bombers launch from Henderson Field, Guadalcanal, and sink the destroyers *Natsugumo* and *Murakumo*.

OCTOBER 15   Near San Cristobal Island, the Solomons, Japanese aircraft from the *Zuikaku* attack an American supply convoy near Guadalcanal, sinking the destroyer *Meredith* under Lieutenant Commander Harry E. Hubbard.

OCTOBER 16   Near San Cristobal Island, Solomons, dive bombers from the *Hornet* strike a Japanese supply convoy, sinking three cargo vessels.

The submarine *Thresher* lays mines at the entrance of Bangkok harbor, Thailand; this is the first time a submarine has deployed such weapons.

OCTOBER 18   Admiral Chester W. Nimitz relieves Vice Admiral Robert L. Ghormley as commander of the South Pacific Area and South Pacific Force, replacing him with Vice Admiral William F. "Bull" Halsey, Jr. Nimitz seeks more aggressive American naval leadership, and Halsey, a known fire-eater, does not disappoint him.

OCTOBER 19   Near Samoa, the destroyer *O'Brien*, previously damaged on September 15, sinks while sailing home for repairs.

OCTOBER 20   Near San Cristobal, Solomon Islands, the heavy cruiser *Chester* is torpedoed by *I-176*, losing 11 dead and 12 wounded; the ships sails off to Espiritu Santo for repairs.

OCTOBER 25   Navy, Marine, and Army aircraft sortie from Henderson Field, Guadalcanal, and damage the light cruiser *Yura*, and it has to be scuttled.

OCTOBER 26–27   The Battle of the Santa Cruz Islands unfolds as Vice Admiral Chuichi Nagumo's task force tangles with American forces under Rear Admiral Thomas C. Kinkaid. Carriers *Zuiho*

> ### Halsey, William F. (1882–1959)
>
> William Frederick Halsey was born in Elizabeth, New Jersey, on October 30, 1882, and he graduated from the U.S. Naval Academy in 1904. During World War I Halsey received the Navy Cross, although it was not until 1935 that he attended the naval flight school in Pensacola, Florida, and won his wings at the age of 52. In 1940 he commanded Carrier Division Two, consisting of the *Enterprise* and *Yorktown*, and, after the devastating Japanese raid on Pearl Harbor, Hawaii, he led the first American air strikes against enemy installations on the Gilbert and Marshall Islands. In April 1942 he garnered national renown by transporting 16 U.S. Army Air Force B-25 land-based bombers under Colonel James H Doolittle on their famous raid against Tokyo.
>
> Halsey missed the decisive carrier clashes at Coral Sea and Midway in the summer of 1942 owing to illness, but that fall he assumed command of American naval forces in the South Pacific and decisively defeated Japanese forces off Guadalcanal on November 12–15. In October 1944, Halsey took charge of the Third Fleet and assisted General Douglas MacArthur's return to the Philippines. He then weathered controversy by sailing his fleet through two destructive typhoons in December 1944 and June 1945. In September 1945 the Japanese delegation signed surrender documents on board his flagship, the battleship USS *Missouri*. Halsey retired in April 1947 and died on Fisher's Island, New York, on October 16, 1959, a hard-hitting naval commander.

and *Shokaku* are damaged, as are the heavy cruiser *Chikuma* and destroyer *Terusuki*. However, the carrier *Hornet* is so badly damaged that it is scuttled, while the *I-122* also sinks the destroyer *Porter*. Nagumo wins a tactical victory, but because the U.S. Navy remains at Guadalcanal, this remains a strategic victory for the Americans.

OCTOBER 29 Near San Cristobal, Solomon Islands, a PBY Catalina from VP-11 sinks the Japanese submarine *I-172*.

NOVEMBER 4 East of Iceland, the merchant vessel *John H. B. Latrobe* is attacked by German He-115 seaplanes and defended by members of the Armed Guard; all seven torpedoes miss, but three of the guards are wounded, and the vessel returns to Iceland.

NOVEMBER 5 Near Iceland, a PBY Catalina of VP-84 sinks German submarine *U-408*.

The British submarine *Seraph*, temporarily commanded by U.S. Navy Captain Jerauld Wright, evacuates French General Henri-Honoré Giraud from Vichy, France.

NOVEMBER 8–10 Near Casablanca, Morocco, OPERATION TORCH, commanded by British Admiral Sir Andrew B. Cunningham and seconded by U.S. Navy Admiral H. Kent Hewitt, commences as the battleship *Massachusetts* bombards the French fleet anchored there. The battleship *Jean Bart* is damaged, while dive bombers from the carrier *Ranger* sink the light cruiser *Primaguet* and four destroyers. The fleet also lands 100,000 British and American troops ashore between French Morocco and Algiers.

NOVEMBER 12 The struggle for Guadalcanal intensifies as a huge Japanese convoy, laden with 11,000 reinforcements, enters the northern chain, or "Slot," escorted by two battleships, a cruiser and 11 destroyers. Admiral Hiroaki Abe's raiding force of 2 battleships, 1 light cruiser, and 14 destroyers is also sent on ahead to soften up Henderson Field.

NOVEMBER 13 North of American Samoa, Captain Eddie Rickenbacker, Colonel Hans C. Anderson, and Private John F. Bartek are rescued by an OS2U Kingfisher; their aircraft had ditched 21 days earlier.

The Battle of Guadalcanal begins as Rear Admiral Daniel J. Callaghan's 2 heavy cruisers, 3 light cruisers, and 8 destroyers engage Vice Admiral Hiroaki Abe's 2 battleships, 1 cruiser, and 14 destroyers off Lunga Point. A bloody nighttime action ensues, whereby the light cruiser *Atlanta* and four destroyers are lost while the light cruiser *Juneau* is torpedoed by *I-26* and sinks in 20 seconds; there are only 10 survivors. Admiral Callaghan and Rear Admiral Norman Scott are both killed, as are all five Sullivan brothers, who perish on the *Juneau*. The Japanese battleship *Hiei* is scuttled and sunk by aircraft from the carrier *Enterprise*, along with the destroyers *Akatsuki* and *Yudachi*. Moreover, the Japanese are forced back without shelling Guadalcanal.

NOVEMBER 14 Near Guadalcanal, Navy and Marine dive bombers from Henderson Field and the carrier *Enterprise* fall upon the "Tokyo Express" of Rear Admiral Raizo Tanaka. The heavy cruiser *Kinugasa* and seven transports and freighters carrying the 38th Division are sunk, and only 2,000 men of the original 10,000 are landed.

NOVEMBER 15 Near Guadalcanal, Rear Admiral Willis A. Lee's Task Force 64, consisting of the radar-equipped battleships *Washington* and *South Dakota* and four destroyers engages Vice Admiral Nobutake Kondo's battleship *Kirishima*, four cruisers, and nine destroyers. The Americans lose three destroyers while *Kirishima* and one destroyer are sunk. The Japanese never again mount a resupply effort on this scale, which decides the fate of remaining troops on Guadalcanal.

NOVEMBER 16 Near Morocco, the destroyers *Woolsey*, *Swanson*, and *Quick* destroy the *U-173*; this is the first American naval victory in the Mediterranean.

NOVEMBER 30 The Battle of Tassafaronga rages near Guadalcanal as Rear Admiral Raizo Tanaka's "Tokyo Express" of eight destroyers engages Task Force 67 under Rear Admiral Carleton H. Wright. Japanese "long lance" torpedoes damage the heavy cruisers *Pensacola*, *Northhampton*, *New Orleans*, and *Minneapolis*; within hours the *Northhampton* and the destroyer *Takanami* sink. This action establishes "Tenacious" Tanaka as one of Japan's finest destroyer leaders.

DECEMBER 8–9 Near Guadalcanal, eight motor torpedo boats repel eight Japanese destroyers carrying troops; the next evening the submarine *I-3* is sunk by *PT-59*.

DECEMBER 11 Near Guadalcanal, five motor torpedo boats engage a Japanese convoy escorted by the "Tokyo Express"; they sink the destroyer *Terusuki* while losing *PT-44*. This is also the last Pacific surface action of 1942.

DECEMBER 15 On Henderson Field, Guadalcanal, the all-black PBY Catalinas of VP-12 begin operations. The lumbering craft become known as the "Black Cat Squadron" and are rigged to drop torpedoes in night-attack missions against enemy shipping.

December 18 Near northern New Guinea, the Japanese light cruiser *Tenryu* is sunk by the submarine *Albacore* under Commander Richard C. Lake.

December 31 The new 27,100-ton carrier *Essex* is commissioned; it first of a class of 10 fast carriers which will see extensive service in the Pacific War.

1943

January 5 Near Munda, New Georgia, Admiral Walden L. Ainsworth's Task Force 67 bombards Japanese land positions; an aerial counterattack is launched, and the light cruiser *Helena* is the first warship to splash an enemy dive-bomber with VT proximity fuze ammunition.

January 6 Off the coast of Brazil, a PBY Catalina belonging to VP-83 sinks *U-164*.

January 10 Offshore at New Britain, the troop-carrying submarine *Argonaut* under Lieutenant Commander John R. Pierce attacks a Japanese convoy, but is sunk, with a loss of 105 sailors.

January 11 Near Cape Esperance, Guadalcanal, a Japanese convoy of 8 destroyers is attacked by 11 motor torpedo boats; one destroyer is damaged, and *PT-112* is sunk.

January 13 Off the coast of Brazil, *U-507* is attacked and sunk by a PBY Catalina from VP-83.

January 14–23 In Casablanca, Morocco, President Franklin D. Roosevelt and Prime Minister Winston Churchill confer as to allied strategy for the upcoming year. For the U.S. Navy, this will entail a large amphibious offensive through the Central Pacific region toward the Marshalls and Carolinas.

January 14–February 7 Off the coast of northern New Guinea, the submarine *Wahoo* under Commander Dudley W. Morton begins a highly successful cruise by sinking a Japanese destroyer with a "down the throat" (bow) torpedo shot, then sending three transports to the bottom. Consequently, "Mush" Morton receives a Navy Cross and the Distinguished Service Cross.

January 20 At the Mare Island Navy Yard, San Francisco, California, the *Brennan* is the first destroyer escort (DE) launched. Small, fast, and heavily armed, they prove the bane of German U-boats and Japanese submarines.

January 24 Near Kolombangara, the Solomon Islands, Admiral Walden L. Ainsworth's Task Force 67 bombards Japanese fuel and supply depots; they are soon joined by air strikes launched from Guadalcanal.

January 29–30 Near Rennell Island, Solomons, Japanese aircraft attack Task Force 18 under Rear Admiral Robert C. Giffen, crippling the heavy cruiser *Chicago*; it sinks the following day. Enemy aircraft have also unveiled a new tactic, using flares to light up the water near intended targets.

February At Brisbane, Australia, three American submarines, the *Amberjack* under John A. Bole, the *Grampus* under Commander John R. Craig, and the *Triton* under Lieutenant Commander George K.

MacKenzie, depart on their final war cruises this month before vanishing at sea.

FEBRUARY 1–2 Near Guadalcanal, Japanese dive bombers sink the destroyer *DeHaven* under Commander C. E. Tolman, while mines laid by mine-layers *Montgomery*, *Preble*, and *Tracy* claim the destroyer *Makigumo* near Savo Island.

FEBRUARY 1–8 On Guadalcanal, the "Tokyo Express" under Rear Admiral Raizo Tanaka brilliantly executes OPERATION KE by evacuating 11,000 Japanese troops under the noses of American forces. The Navy assumed he was bringing reinforcements to the island, as expected.

FEBRUARY 7 Near Rabaul, the surfaced submarine *Growler* is preparing to attack the Japanese ship *Hayasaki*, when it suddenly turns and charges. Commander Howard Gilmore rams the enemy vessel, while enemy gunners rake his conning tower, mortally wounding him. Gilmore orders *Growler* to dive and abandon him; he receives a posthumous Congressional Medal of Honor.

FEBRUARY 11 In the Coral Sea, the submarine *I-18* is sunk by the destroyer *Fletcher*, working in concert with a Curtiss Seagull floatplane launched from the light cruiser *Helena*.

FEBRUARY 12 At Brisbane, Australia, the submarine *Grampus* commences its sixth war cruise; it vanishes at sea.

FEBRUARY 14 Near New Britain, the submarine *Amberjack* radios that it is under attack, then vanishes; it was probably sunk by the torpedo boat *Hiyo* and submarine chaser *Ch-18*.

FEBRUARY 21 Near the Russell Islands, 30 miles north of Guadalcanal, the campaign for the Central Solomons commences as aircraft from the *Saratoga* support amphibious landings; they come ashore unopposed.

FEBRUARY 22 The *Iowa*, the first vessel of the new battleship class, is commissioned; this is also the first of its class of capable of doing 33 knots to keep up with fast carrier groups.

MARCH 1–20 In the North Atlantic, German U-boats come perilously close to shutting down sea lanes of communication by sinking 85 allied vessels at a cost of 6 submersibles.

MARCH 5 The auxiliary escort carrier *Bogue* serves as the nucleus for the new hunter-killer group, consisting of destroyer escorts and airplanes. This tactical grouping proves particularly lethal to U-boats in the North Atlantic, who had been enjoying unparalleled success against allied shipping.

MARCH 6 Near Kolombangara, Rear Admiral A. Stanton Merrill's force of three light cruisers and three destroyers bombards Japanese positions at Vila, sinking the destroyers *Mionegumo* and *Murasame*.

MARCH 8 Near Trindad, the German *U-156* is sunk by a PBY Catalina from VP-53.

MARCH 10 In the South Atlantic, the German blockade runner *Karin* is accosted by light cruiser *Savannah* and the destroyer *Eberle*. After scuttling charges explode, killing 7 Americans and wounding 2; *Eberle* rescues 72 German survivors.

MARCH 11 In the Pacific, the submarine *Triton* radios that it sank a Japanese cargo vessel, then vanishes at sea.

> ### King, Ernest J. (1878–1956)
>
> Ernest Joseph King was born in Lorain, Ohio, on November 23, 1878, and he graduated from the U.S. Naval Academy in 1901. He spent World War I as aide to Admiral Henry T. Mayo, and advanced to captain at the relatively young age of 39. He subsequently passed through the Naval War College in 1933, and succeeded Admiral William A. Moffett as Chief of the Bureau of Aeronautics. In 1941 King received command of the Atlantic Fleet, along with promotion to the rank of full admiral, and orchestrated the undeclared war against German U-boats in the Atlantic.
>
> Shortly after the Japanese attack on Pearl Harbor on December 7, 1941, President Roosevelt appointed King Chief of Naval Operations and Commander in Chief of all naval forces. He was the first naval officer in American history to combine both titles and to be entrusted with divining naval strategies for the European and Pacific theaters. Brash and irascible, King consented to the "Germany First" priority of the Allied High Command, but insisted that tactical offensives be maintained in the Pacific. Such noted naval leaders as William F. Halsey, Raymond A. Spruance, and Marc A. Mitscher were all under his direct command, and King, a brilliant strategist, made very few mistakes. By 1945 the size of the Navy had increased tenfold to 3 million men and 92,000 vessels of every description. Congress elevated King to five-star admiral in 1944. He spent several years as a senior adviser before dying at Portsmouth, New Hampshire, on June 25, 1956.

MARCH 12 West of the Azores, the destroyer *Champlin* sinks *U-130* as it stalked a convoy.

MARCH 15 In Washington, D.C., Admiral Ernest J. King imposes a new system of numbering fleets, with the Atlantic receiving even numbers and the Pacific odd. The practice persists to modern times.

MARCH 23 Near Formosa (Taiwan), the submarine *Kingfisher* survives an intense Japanese depth charging by piping air bubbles and an oil slick to the surface; the enemy, convinced that their target is destroyed, departs, and *Kingfisher* silently escapes.

MARCH 25 In the Yellow Sea, Lieutenant Commander D. W. "Mush" Morton and the submarine *Wahoo* sink four Japanese transports in a single day.

MARCH 26 Off the Kormandorski Islands (Aleutians), Rear Admiral Charles H. McMorris's Task Group 16.6 (one heavy cruiser, one light cruiser, four destroyers) engages Vice Admiral Boshiro Hosogaya's two heavy cruisers, two light cruisers, and four destroyers. A prolonged running battle ensues, and McMorris prevents them from reinforcing the garrison on Kiska; heavy cruisers *Nachi* and *Salt Lake City* are damaged.

APRIL 1 The new Naval Air Station Patuxent, Maryland, is founded for flight-testing purposes and is the future home of the Naval Test Pilot Center.

APRIL 5 Near Russell Islands, Central Solomons, the destroyer *O'Bannon* catches submarine *RO-34* operating while surfaced, and sinks it.

APRIL 7 Near Honshu, Japan, the submarine *Pickerel* under Lieutenant Commander A. H. Alston sinks a Japanese transport, before all contact is lost.

APRIL 7–16 Admiral Isoroku Yamamoto orders carrier aircraft and the Eleventh Air Fleet to attack American shipping at Tulagi in the Solomon Islands; at length the destroyer *Aaron Ward* and oiler *Kanawaha* are sunk.

April 9 In Washington, D.C., the Navy Department reintroduces the rank of commodore.

April 14 Fleet Radio Unit, Pacific Fleet, deciphers a Japanese naval communique intimating that Admiral Isoroku Yamamoto will visit Bougainville on an inspection tour. The exact time, date, and escort force are also known. Admiral Chester Nimitz assigns the highest priority on intercepting his flight.

April 15 Near Brazil, a PBY Catalina flown by VP-83 sinks the Italian submarine *Archimede*.
In China, Commander Milton E. Miles becomes the American liaison to Chinese general Tai Li as the new Sino-American Cooperative Organization takes form. It is created to instruct Chinese operatives in guerrilla warfare, intelligence gathering, and other clandestine endeavors.

April 16 The Navy Department changes the traditional khaki working uniform to slate gray, which proves so unpopular with officers that it is dropped in October 1946, and khaki is readopted.

April 18 Rear Admiral Marc A. Mitscher, alerted by decrypted intelligence that Fleet Admiral Isoroku Yamamoto is arriving at Kahili, arranges for a flight of 16 Army Air Force P-38 Lightnings from Guadalcanal to intercept his bomber, killing him. He is succeeded by Admiral Mineichi Koga.

April 22 Off the Malaysian coast, the submarine *Grenadier* under Lieutenant Commander John Fitzgerald is scuttled after being damaged by Japanese aircraft; the crew is captured and harshly treated.

April 27 Near Halifax, Nova Scotia, the German *U-174* is sunk by a PV-1 Ventura patrol-bomber of VP-125, as it escorts Convoy SC 128.

May A turning point is reached in the Battle of the Atlantic when Convoy ONS 5, consisting of 43 merchantmen and 9 escorts, is attacked by 51 German U-boats; 6 U-boats are sunk for a loss of 13 cargo ships, an attrition rate the Germans cannot sustain.

May 7 In Long Island Sound, New York, the merchant tanker *Bunker Hill* serves as a launching platform for the Sikorsky XR-4 helicopter, which performs 15 consecutive takeoffs and landings with the vessel in motion. This experiment convinces the Navy of the utility of helicopters at sea.

May 8 In the Solomon Islands, American mines and airstrikes sink Japanese destroyers *Kuroshio*, *Kagero*, and *Oyashio*.

May 11–13 The invasion of Attu, the Aleutians, is supported by Rear Admiral Thomas C. Kincaid's Task Forces 16 and 51, as soldiers of Major General A. E. Brown's 7th Infantry Division storm ashore. The destroyers *Edwards* and *Farragut* also sink the submarine *I-31*.

May 14 In the Vitaiz Strait, New Guinea, the submarine *RO-182* is sunk by motor patrol boats *PT-150* and *PT-152*.

May 15 Near Cuba, an OS2U Kingfisher floatplane aircraft belonging to VS-62 sinks the *U-176*.

May 16 Near the Madeira Islands, the destroyer *MacKenzie* sinks the *U-182*.

May 17 In the South Atlantic, a PBM Mariner from VP-74 damages *U-128*, which is then finished off by the destroyers *Moffett* and *Jouett*.

May 17–25 In Washington, D.C., President Franklin D. Roosevelt and Prime Minister Winston Churchill conclude the so-called Trident Conference, which reaffirms the "Germany first" policy, yet allows a major offensive across the Central Pacific.

May 20 In Washington, D.C., Admiral Ernest J. King, the Chief of Naval Operations, establishes Headquarters, Tenth Fleet, to better coordinate the anti-submarine campaign in the Atlantic.

May 22 In the North Atlantic, TBF Avengers from the escort carrier *Bogue* under Captain Giles E. Short sink *U-569* and damage *U-305* as they stalk Convoy ON 184. This is the first kill registered by the ungainly but deceptively deadly escort carriers.

May 23 The *New Jersey*, the second *Iowa*-class battleship, is commissioned.

May 24 In Berlin, Germany, Admiral Karl Doenitz, head of the German Navy, orders U-boats out of the Atlantic to end prohibitive losses. This concludes the wolfpack threat to Atlantic supply convoys.

May 25 Near Iceland, *U-467* is sunk by a PBY Catalina of VP-84.

May 26 On Basilan Island, Philippines, the submarine *Trout* lands a party ashore to organize coastwatchers and assist Filipino guerrillas.

May 27 At Midway Island, the submarine *Runner* puts to sea on its third war patrol, and vanishes at sea.

June 2 Off the Virginia Capes, subchaser *PC-565* engages in a lengthy battle with the *U-521*, sinking it with depth charges and 20-mm cannon fire.

June 5 Near the Canary Islands, *U-217* is sunk by TBF Avengers of VC-9.

June 9 At Annapolis, Maryland, the, U.S. Naval Academy's Class of 1943 is graduated a year early due to the national emergency.

June 10 After the tanker *Esso Gettysburg* is torpedoed by *U-66*, Ensign John S. Arnold mans a machine gun and fires at the submarine. He wins a Navy Cross; only 15 of 72 crewmen survive.

Near Shemya Island, Aleutians, submarine chaser *PC-487* forces *I-24* to surface, then sinks it by ramming.

June 12 Submarine *R-12* sinks during a training exercise near Key West, Florida, killing all 42 crewmen.

Near the Canary Islands, a TBF Avenger from the escort carrier *Bogue* sinks *U-118*.

June 13 Offshore at Kiska, Aleutian Islands, the destroyer *Frazier* rolls depth charges on a periscope it has sighted, sinking the *I-9*.

June 20 Off the Iceland coast, a PBY Catalina belonging to VP-84 sinks *U-420* with a new Mark 24 homing torpedo.

June 22 Near Kiska, the Aleutians, the destroyer *Monaghan* attacks and runs the submarine *I-7* aground; on December 7, 1941, this same vessel sank a Japanese midget submarine at Pearl Harbor.

June 23 In the Pacific, the Japanese submarine *RO-103* sinks cargo ships *Aludra* and *Deimos* as they sail toward Guadalcanal.

June 30 On New Georgia, Solomon Islands, OPERATION TOENAIL unfolds as Rear Admiral Richmond K. Turner's Task Force 31 commences amphibious landings covered by the ships and aircraft of Admiral William F. Halsey's Task Force 36; the attack transport *McCawley* is torpedoed and damaged.

Off the coast of northern New Guinea, Admiral Daniel E. Barbey's Seventh Amphibious Force (Task Force 76) deposits Army troops on Woodlark and Kiriwina islands.

JULY 1   In Washington, D.C., the Navy Department establishes its V-12 program for training Navy and Marine enlistees at selected universities for officer commissions.

JULY 5–6   In Kula Gulf, between New Georgia and Kolombangara, a clash at sea results in the destroyer *Strong* under Commander J. H. Wellings sinking, with a loss of 46 lives.

JULY 6   Over Greenwich Island, a PB4Y-1 Privateer flown by Lieutenant Commander Bruce A. Van Voorhis (VB-102) makes a daring raid upon Japanese installations and is shot down; Voorhis is awarded a posthumous Congressional Medal of Honor.

Near New Georgia, Solomon Islands, the Battle of Kula Gulf unfolds when Rear Admiral Walden L. Ainsworth's Task Group 36.1 fights a night battle with destroyers of the "Tokyo Express" under Rear Admiral Teruo Akiyama. The light cruiser *Helena* sinks, while the Japanese lose two destroyers sunk and three damaged. This is Japan's fourth failed attempt to resupply the garrison on Kolombangara.

JULY 9   Near the mouth of the Amazon River, Brazil, *U-590* is sunk by a PBY Catalina from VP-94.

In the Mediterranean, a smoke pot accidentally ignites on *LST-375*, and Ensign John J. Parle heroically picks it up and hurls it overboard. In the process, Parle is fatally burned. He receives a posthumous Congressional Medal of Honor.

JULY 10   Near Sicily, Italy, OPERATION HUSKY commences as Vice Admiral H. Kent Hewitt's Western Naval Task Force conveys the Seventh Army of Lieutenant General George S. Patton ashore, while the Eastern Naval Task Force under British Vice Admiral Sir Bertram H. Ramsay lands the Eighth Army under Field Marshall Bernard Montgomery. Over 1,400 vessels of various sorts participate and cover a landing zone stretching 100 miles; this is the largest amphibious landing to date. Three new classes of amphibious vessels, the Landing Ship Tank (LST), Landing Craft tank (LCT) and Landing Craft Infantry (LCI), also debut for the first time.

Near Gela, Sicily, German dive bombers sink the destroyer *Maddox* under Lieutenant Commander E. R. Sarsfield, with heavy loss of life.

JULY 11   Near Sicily, Italy, Axis air attacks damage several landing craft and smaller ships, but light cruisers *Boise* and *Savannah* press close to shore, destroying 13 German tanks of the Hermann Goering Panzer Division near Gela.

JULY 12   Near Kolombaranga, Solomon Islands, the Japanese submarine *RO-107* is sunk by the destroyer *Taylor*.

JULY 13   Near the Azores, *U-487* is sunk by a TBF Avenger bomber launched from the auxiliary aircraft carrier *Core*.

In the Solomon Islands, the Battle of Kolombaranga unfolds as Rear Admiral Walden L. Ainsworth's 3 light cruisers and 10 destroyers engage Admiral Shunji Izaki's light cruiser and 5 destroyers. Izaki is killed when his flagship *Jintsu* sinks, along with destroyer *Yukakaze*; Ainsworth's 3 cruisers are also damaged and the destroyer *Gwin* is scuttled. Some of the troop-laden Japanese destroyers land reinforcements at Kolombangara.

JULY 14   South of the Azores Islands, the *U-160* is sunk by TBF Avengers launched from the auxiliary carrier *Santee*.

JULY 15   West of the Canary Islands, *U-135* is sunk by a PBY Catalina belonging to VP-92.

South of the Azores, *U-509* is sunk by a TBF Avenger from the auxiliary carrier *Santee*.

South of Haiti, *U-159* is sunk by a PBM Mariner belonging to VP-32.

JULY 16   In the Atlantic, *U-67* is sunk by a TBF Avenger bomber from the auxiliary carrier *Core*.

JULY 17–18   Large numbers of naval aircraft join their Army, Marine Corps, and New Zealand counterparts in bombing Japanese positions and vessels throughout Bougainville; one destroyer is sunk and three are damaged.

JULY 18   In the Florida Straits, *U-134* surfaces and engages blimp K-74 in a fire fight, shooting the latter down. This is the only blimp lost in combat during the war.

JULY 19   Off the mouth of the Amazon River, *U-513* is sunk by a PBM Mariner of VP-74.

JULY 19–20   Near Choiseul, northern Solomons, Japanese destroyers *Yugure* and *Kiyonami* are sunk by Navy and Marine Corps aircraft attacks.

As of this date, the submarine *Runner* under Lieutenant Commander Joseph H. Bourland fails to report in, and is presumed lost.

JULY 21   Off the mouth of the Amazon River, Brazil, *U-662* is sunk by a PBY Catalina belonging to VP-94.

JULY 22   In the Bougainville Strait, Navy aircraft sink the seaplane carrier *Nisshin*.

JULY 23   In England, VP-63 becomes the first Navy patrol squadron stationed there; it is tasked with patrolling the Bay of Biscay for U-boats in concert with the Royal Air Force Coastal Command.

South of the Azores, *U-527* is sunk by TBF Avengers launched from the carrier *Bogue*.

Off the Brazilian coast, *U-598* is sunk by PB4Y-1 Privateers from VB-107.

South of the Azores, *U-613* is sunk by the destroyer *George E. Badger*.

JULY 26   Near Haiti, the submarine *U-359* is sunk by a PBM Mariner of VP-32.

JULY 28   At Kiska, Aleutian Islands, Vice Admiral Shiro Kawase's task force evacuates the 5,183-man garrison from under the noses of American forces nearby.

JULY 30   Near Brazil, a Lockheed PV-1 Ventura of VB-127 flying top cover for convoy TJ 2 sinks *U-591*.

In the Atlantic, *U-43* is sunk by TBF Avenger bombers launched from the escort carrier *Santee*.

Off the Tunisian coast, the submarine chaser *PC-624* sinks *U-375*.

JULY 31   Off the mouth of Rio de Janeiro, Brazil, *U-199* is sink by a PBM Mariner.

AUGUST 2   Near Kolombangara, the destroyer *Amagiri* rams and sinks *PT-109* under Lieutenant John F. Kennedy. Kennedy herds 11 survivors to the nearest island and is rescued there on August 7; he receives the Navy and Marine Corps Medal.

AUGUST 3 North of Dutch Guiana, *U-572* is sunk by a PBM Mariner belonging to VP-205.

Near Tunisia, the Italian submarine *Argento* is sunk by the destroyer *Buck*.

AUGUST 5 Offshore at Cape Henry, New Jersey, *U-566* sinks the gunboat *Plymouth*.

AUGUST 6 In Vella Lavella Gulf, seven American destroyers under Commander Frederick Moosbrugger engage four Japanese destroyers in a wild nighttime melee; the *Arashi*, *Hagikaze*, and *Kawakaze* are all sunk. This is the Navy's first unequivocal victory in a night action.

AUGUST 7 In the North Atlantic, *U-84* is sunk by a PB4Y-1 Privateer from VB-105.

AUGUST 7–9 West of the Azores Islands, German submarines *U-117* and *U-664* are sunk by TBF Avengers from the escort carrier *Card*.

AUGUST 11 In the South Atlantic, incessant air attacks by U.S. Navy patrol aircraft result in the *U-604* being scuttled.

AUGUST 14–24 At the Quebec Conference, President Franklin D. Roosevelt, Prime Minister Winston Churchill, and their combined Chiefs of Staff continue to refine war strategy for the remaining year. The U.S. Navy remains tasked with an offensive against the Marianas in the Central Pacific.

AUGUST 15 At Kiska, the Aleutians, Vice Admiral Thomas C. Kinkaid's task force conducts a major amphibious operation—only to discover that the Japanese have long since evacuated the island chain.

At Vella Lavella, Solomon Islands, Rear Admiral Theodore S. Wilkinson's Task Force 34 conducts amphibious landings to "leap frog" over Japanese strong points and neutralize heavily garrisoned Kolombangara. Here they land the 58th Seabee Construction Battalion and commence building new airfields.

AUGUST 17–24 In Quebec, Canada, the Quadrant Conference unfolds as President Franklin D. Roosevelt, Prime Minister Winston Churchill, and their combined chiefs of staff draw up the year's strategy, which includes increased naval support for the Pacific theater.

AUGUST 19 Near Australia, the *1-17* is sunk by a Vought OS2U Kingfisher from VS-57 working in conjunction with the New Zealand corvette *Tui*.

AUGUST 25 Near San Cristobal, Solomon Islands, the submarine *RO-35* is sunk by the destroyer *Patterson*.

AUGUST 27 In the Atlantic, *U-847* is sunk by TBF Avenger bombers from the escort carrier *Card*.

AUGUST 31 On Marcus Island, 800 miles northwest of Wake, Rear Admiral Charles A. Pownall's Task Force 15 launches air strikes against Japanese installations This action marks the combat debut of the *Essex* and *Independence* carriers, along with the Grumman F6F Hellcat fighter—nemesis of the Japanese A6M Zero.

SEPTEMBER 1 In Washington, D.C., the Navy Department assumes complete responsibility for airborne-operations warfare against German submarines in the Atlantic theater.

On Baker Island, Central Pacific, the *Ashland* is the first landing ship dock (LSD) committed to combat operations, when it participates in landings there.

September 3 Near Espiritu Santo, the submarine *I-25* is sunk by the destroyer *Ellet*.

September 4 At Lae, New Guinea, Rear Admiral Daniel E. Barbey's Seventh Amphibious Force lands the 9th Australian Division and its equipment. The Japanese respond with an air raid, damaging the destroyer *Conyngham* and two tank carrying vessels. On *LST-473*, Seaman First Class Johnny D. Hutchins is wounded by a bomb blast, yet he mans the pilot house and steers his ship clear of an oncoming torpedo; he receives a posthumous Congressional Medal of Honor.

September 9 In the South China Sea, the submarine *Grayling* under Lieutenant Commander Robert M. Brinker is rammed and sunk by a Japanese transport.

September 9–16 Near Salerno, Italy, Vice Admiral H. Kent Hewitt's Task Force 80 lands General Mark W. Clark's Fifth Army ashore. When German counterattacks threaten the beachhead, the fleet provides supporting fire and destroys several panzers.

September 11 Near Salerno, Italy, the destroyer *Rowan* under Lieutenant Commander Joel C. Ford is sunk by German motor torpedo boats, killing 202 of 273 men. Overhead, Luftwaffe Do-217 bombers badly damage the light cruiser *Savannah* with rocket-propelled bombs, killing a further 197 sailors.

U.S. Coast Guardsmen and Navy beach battalion men hug the shaking beach at Paestum, Italy, during a German bomber attack in October 1943. The Allied advancements on the Italian beaches during Operation Avalanche *were slow but successful. (Library of Congress)*

September 15 East of San Cristobal, Solomon Islands, a PBY Catalina of VP-23, acting in concert with the destroyer *Saufly*, sinks the submarine *RO-101*.

September 18 Japanese defenses on Tarawa, Gilbert Islands, are struck by aircraft from Task Force 15 under Rear Admiral C. A. Pownell.

September 19 At Darwin, Australia, the submarine *Cisco* under Commander James W. Coe departs on a war cruise and vanishes at sea.

September 22 At Finschhafen, New Guinea, Rear Admiral Daniel E. Barbey's Seventh Amphibious Force lands the 20th Australian Brigade at Huon Bay, overcoming strong resistance from Japanese Special Naval Landing Forces.

September 23 On the northeast coast of Bougainville, the submarine *Gato* deposits a Navy-Marine scouting party, while the submarine *Guardfish* debarks another at Empress Augusta Bay.

September 24 In the Gulf of Salerno, Italy, *U-593* sinks the minesweeper *Skill*, which goes down in 20 minutes with 32 survivors out of 103 crewmen.

September 25 In the Pacific, the submarine *Pompano* under Commander Willis M. Thomas radios that it has sunk a transport off the Japanese coast, then vanishes.

September 27 Near Brazil, *U-161* is sunk by a PBM Mariner of VP-74.

September 28 In the Sulu Sea off Panay Island, the submarine *Cisco* is apparently sunk by Japanese warships.

October 3 Off Finschhafen, New Guinea, *RO-108* sinks the destroyer *Henley* under Commander A. R. Theobald, with a loss of 17 lives.

October 4 Near Bodo, Norway, the carrier *Ranger*, heavy cruiser *Tuscaloosa*, and several destroyers under Read Admiral Olaf M. Hustvedt assist the British Home Fleet on a raid that sinks several German freighters.

North of the Azores Islands, *U-460* and *U-422* are sunk by TBF Avengers launched from the escort carrier *Card*. They were part of a group of four submarines performing resupply functions on the surface.

Southwest of Iceland, the submarine *U-279* is sunk by a PV-1 Ventura of VP-128.

October 5–6 In the Central Pacific, Wake Island is attacked by aircraft launched from six carriers belonging to Rear Admiral Alfred E. Montgomery's Task Force 14; his cruisers also shell Japanese installations.

October 6–7 The Battle of Vella Lavella commences as destroyers *O'Bannon*, *Chevalier*, and *Selfridge* engage Rear Admiral Matsuji Ijuin's convoy, which is conveying troopships to the island. The destroyer *Yugumo* is sunk and the *Chevalier* is scuttled. This is the final naval engagement in the central Solomon Islands, after which the Japanese garrison is successfully evacuated.

October 7 Near the Kuriles Island, Japan, the destroyer *Ishigaki* sinks the submarine *S-44* under Lieutenant Commander Francis E. Brown in a surface action.

October 9 In the Gulf of Salerno, Italy, the destroyer *Buck* under Lieutenant Commander Michael J. Klein is torpedoed by the *U-616*, sinking in four minutes, with a loss of 166 sailors.

OCTOBER 13 North of the Azores Islands, the *U-402* is sunk by a TBF Avenger launched from the escort carrier *Card*.

Off the Algerian coast, the *U-371* sinks the destroyer *Bristol* under Commander J. A. Glick, with a loss of 52 lives.

OCTOBER 17 Near Honshu, Japan, the far-ranging German surface raider *Michel* is sunk by the submarine *Tarpon* under Commander Thomas L. Wogan.

OCTOBER 20 North of the Azores Islands, *U-378* is sunk by TBF Avengers launched from the escort carrier *Core*.

OCTOBER 21 In the Atlantic the tanker *Bulkoil* collides with the destroyer *Murphy*, slicing off its bow. The latter is towed back to port and eventually repaired.

OCTOBER 24 In the Atlantic, the submarine *Dorado* under Lieutenant Commander Earl K. Schneider fails to report, and is presumed lost at sea.

OCTOBER 31 North of the Azores, *U-584*, on its tenth war patrol, is sunk by TBF Avengers from the escort carrier *Card*.

Near Vella La Vella, an F4U Corsair flown by Lieutenant H. D. O'Neil, makes the Navy's first radar-equipped night fighter kill by splashing a Japanese G4M bomber.

NOVEMBER 1 North of the Azores, the old destroyer *Borie* under Lieutenant Commander Charles H. Hutchins engages the German submarine *U-405* in a desperate night engagement. *Borie* then rams its adversary, which surrenders, but the old ship gradually sinks from bow damage.

At Empress Augusta Bay, Bougainville, Rear Admiral Theodore S. Wilkinson's Third Amphibious Force lands soldiers and marines in a major amphibious assault.

Near Shortland Island, South Pacific, Rear Admiral Aaron S. Merrill's Task Force 39 dispatches destroyers and cruisers to bombard Japanese positions, assisted by aircraft from the *Saratoga* and *Princeton*.

NOVEMBER 2 The Battle of Empress Augusta Bay unfolds as Rear Admiral Aaron S. Merrill's four light cruisers and eight destroyers of Task Force 39 encounter Rear Admiral Sentaro Omori's two cruisers, two light cruisers, and six destroyers. The light cruiser *Sendai* and destroyer *Hatsukaze* are sunk, while four American vessels also receive damage. This is also the first battle where Captain Arleigh A. Burke distinguishes himself.

South of Honshu, Japan, submarines *Seahorse*, *Halibut*, and *Trigger* ravage a Japanese convoy, sinking five transports.

NOVEMBER 5 Southwest of Ascension Island, *U-848* is sunk by Navy PB4Y Privateers of VB-107 and Army Air Force B-25 Mitchells of the 1st Composite Squadron.

In the Pacific, 97 aircraft from Rear Admiral Frederick C. Sherman's Task Force 38 surprise Japanese installations on Rabaul, New Britain. 9 vessels are heavily damaged, including the heavy cruisers *Atago*, *Chikuma*, *Maya*, *Mogami*, and *Takao*; 10 aircraft are lost.

NOVEMBER 6 Near Cape Bougaroun, Algeria, German aircraft sink the destroyer *Beatty* under Lieutenant Commander W. Outerson and the transport *Santa Elena*, which is part of allied convoy.

NOVEMBER 9 In the Sea of Japan, the submarine *Wahoo* under Captain Dudley W. ("Mush") Morton disappears on its fifth war patrol; previously, it had sunk four additional Japanese transports.

NOVEMBER 10 In the Bay of Biscay, *U-966* is sunk by Navy PB4Y-1 Privateers, assisted by Royal Air Force aircraft.

NOVEMBER 11 Over Rabaul, New Britain, Rear Admiral Alfred E. Montgomery's Task Group 50.3 under joins Task Force 28 under Rear Admiral Frederick C. Sherman in a joint air strike. This attack marks the debut of the new Curtiss SB2C Helldivers, which sink one destroyer and four minor warships.

NOVEMBER 12 President Franklin D. Roosevelt boards the new battleship *Iowa* for a voyage to Cairo, Egypt, and Tehran, Iran, to confer with Prime Minister Winston Churchill and Soviet Premier Joseph Stalin.

In the Bay of Biscay, the submarine *U-508* is sunk by a PB4Y-1 Privateer from VB-103.

NOVEMBER 13 In the Gilbert and Marshall Islands, American carrier aircraft attack Japanese installations in preparation for a major drive across the central Pacific.

NOVEMBER 14 In the Bay of Biscay, *U-508* is sunk by a PB4Y-1 Privateer from VB-103.

In the Atlantic, the destroyer *William D. Porter* accidentally launches a torpedo at the battleship *Iowa*, then carrying President Franklin D. Roosevelt; disaster is averted by quick maneuvering.

NOVEMBER 16 South of Truk, Caroline Islands, the submarine *Corvina* under Commander Robert S. Rooney is sunk by the *I-176*; this is only instance where an American submersible is destroyed by its Japanese opposite.

NOVEMBER 17 Near Bougainville, Solomon Islands, Japanese aircraft sink the high-speed destroyer transport *McKean* under Lieutenant Commander Ralph L. Ramey; 116 men belonging to the 21st Marines are also lost.

NOVEMBER 19 North of Truk, Central Pacific, the submarine *Sculpin* under Commander Fred Connaway is sunk by destroyer *Yamagumo*; Captain John P. Cromwell, head of Submarine Division 43, is also on board, and goes down with the ship rather than face capture and reveal details about the forthcoming Gilbert Islands offensive; he receives a posthumous Congressional Medal of Honor.

NOVEMBER 20–23 In the Gilbert Islands, Central Pacific, Rear Admiral Kelly R. Turner's Task Force 54 launches OPERATION GALVANIC, against the Tarawa Atoll, which falls after heavy fighting. The carrier *Independence* and destroyer *Ringgold* are damaged in the fighting.

NOVEMBER 22 Off the Gilbert Islands, the *I-35* is forced to the surface by destroyers *Frazier* and *Meade*, whereupon the *Frazier* sinks it by ramming.

NOVEMBER 24 Off the Gilbert Islands, the escort carrier *Liscombe Bay* under Captain I. D. Wiltse is sunk by Japanese submarine *I-175*; as this is the flagship of Task Group 52.3, among the dead is Rear Admiral Henry M. Mullinix, along with 644 sailors.

NOVEMBER 25 In the South Atlantic, *U-849* is sunk by a PB4Y-1 Privateer of VB-107.

Near Cape St. George, New Ireland, Captain Arleigh Burke's Destroyer Squadron 23 engages a similar force under Captain Kiyoto Kagawa at night; in a smart reverse, Burke sinks three enemy vessels without taking a single hit.

North of the Gilbert Islands, Central Pacific, the *I-19* is sunk by the destroyer *Radford*.

In the South Atlantic, submarine U-849 is sunk by a PB4Y-1 Privateer from VB-107.

NOVEMBER 28–29 Northwest of the Marian Islands, Central Pacific, a Japanese convoy is attacked by submarines *Pargo* and *Snook*, which sink three vessels.

NOVEMBER 29 At Cape Torokina, Bougainville, the 1st Marine Parachute Battalion is successfully evacuated as destroyers *Fullam*, *Lardner*, and *Lansdowne* rush close to shore and give direct fire support.

Off the coast of eastern New Guinea, the Australian transport *Duntroon* accidentally rams into the destroyer *Perkins* under Lieutenant Commander G. L. Ketchum, sinking it.

DECEMBER 2 In the Makassar Strait, Borneo, the submarine *Capelin* under Commander Elliott E. Marshall is declared missing after failing to report in; it probably struck a mine.

DECEMBER 4 In the Marshall Islands, Central Pacific, aircraft from Rear Admiral Charles A. Pownall's Task Force 58 strike Japanese shipping at Kwajalien and Wotje; four vessels are sunk, and seven others are damaged.

Near Honshu, Japan, the submarine *Sailfish* under Lieutenant Commander Robert E. Ward sinks the Japanese escort carrier *Chuyo*; tragically, this vessel carries survivors of the submarine *Sculpin*, lost a month earlier.

DECEMBER 9 After high-level conferences in Cairo, Egypt, and Tehran, Iran, President Franklin D. Roosevelt embarks on the battleship *Iowa* and returns to the United States.

DECEMBER 13 West of the Canary Islands, *U-172* is sunk by American destroyers and aircraft from the escort carrier *Bogue*; the destroyer *Osmond Ingram* suffers damage from the submarine's deck gun.

Near Algiers, *U-593* is sunk by the destroyer *Wainwright* and British corvette *Calpe* after a 32-hour chase.

DECEMBER 15 At Arawe, New Britain, Rear Admiral Daniel E. Barbey's Seventh Amphibious Force lands Army troops to secure the Vitaz and Dampier straits between New Guinea and New Britain.

DECEMBER 20 Southwest of the Azores Islands, *U-850* is sunk by TBF Avengers from the escort carrier *Bogue*.

DECEMBER 24 In the North Atlantic, the destroyer *Leary* under Commander James E. Kyes is sunk by the *U-645*, which is in then sunk in turn by the destroyer *Schenk*.

DECEMBER 26 Near Cape Gloucester, New Britain, Rear Admiral Daniel E. Barbey's Seventh Amphibious Force lands the 1st Marine Division under Major General William H. Rupertus. Rear Admiral Victor A. C. Crutchley's Task Force 74 provides supporting gunfire; the destroyer *Brownson* under Lieutenant Commander J. B. Maher is sunk by enemy dive-bombers.

DECEMBER 28 In the Bay of Biscay, a German destroyer and two motor patrol boats are sunk by a PB4Y-1 Privateer of VB-105, which acts in concert with two British light cruisers.

DECEMBER 29 Near Palau, Central Pacific, a Japanese convoy is attacked by the submarine *Silversides*, which sinks three transports.

1944

JANUARY 2 In the Atlantic, the German blockade runner *Weserland* is spotted off Ascension Island by a PB2Y-1 Privateer of VB-107; the information is relayed to the destroyer *Somers*, which sinks the *Weserland* with a single salvo.

At Saidor, New Guinea, Rear Admiral Daniel E. Barbey's Task Force 76 lands Army troops ashore.

JANUARY 3 In the Ambrose Channel, New York, an internal explosion onboard the destroyer *Turner* under Commander H. S. Wygant kills 100 sailors; the vessel subsequently sinks.

JANUARY 4–5 Off the Brazilian coast, light cruiser *Omaha* and destroyer *Jonett* accost German blockade runners *Rio Grande* and *Burgenland*; both vessels are scuttled to prevent capture.

JANUARY 5 In the mid-Pacific, the submarine *Scorpion* rendezvouses briefly with the submarine *Herring*, only to vanish at sea.

JANUARY 10–11 North of Okinawa, a Japanese convoy is attacked by the submarine *Seawolf*, which sinks three cargo vessels.

JANUARY 11 In the North Atlantic, two TBF Avengers from the escort carrier *Block Island* launch rockets against a surfaced German U-boat for the first time.

JANUARY 15 At Pearl Harbor, Hawaii, Service Squadron 10 is created under Captain Worrall R. Carter, to facilitate mobile logistical operations for the upcoming Central Pacific Campaign.

JANUARY 16 In the Atlantic, *U-544* is sunk by a TBF Avenger from the escort carrier *Guadalcanal*.

JANUARY 22 Near San Cristobal, Solomon Islands, the oiler *Cache* is sunk by the submarine *RO-27*'s torpedoes, which is sunk in turn by the destroyer *Buchanan*.

JANUARY 22–24 Near Anzio, Italy, Admiral Frank K. Lowry's Anglo-American Task Force 81 puts allied troops ashore, despite heavy German air attacks and mines. Mine and air attacks account for one minesweeper sunk and three ships damaged.

JANUARY 28 Off the Shannon River estuary, Ireland, *U-271* is sunk by a PB4Y-1 Privateer of VB-103.

JANUARY 29–FEBRUARY 6 In the Central Pacific, aircraft from Rear Admiral Marc A. Mitscher's Task Force 58 commences preliminary bombardment of Kwajalein, Wotje, Eniwetok, and Taora in the Marshall Islands, in preparation for an impending amphibious assault.

JANUARY 30–FEBRUARY 9 Japanese-held Wake Island is struck by waves of naval aircraft launched from Midway Island; their goal is to neutralize a new airfield there prior to invading the Marshall Islands.

JANUARY 31–FEBRUARY 22 In the Marshall Islands, the Central Pacific offensive continues as Vice Admiral Raymond A. Spruance's Fifth Fleet lands Army troops and Marines on Kwajalein and neighboring atolls.

FEBRUARY 1 At Pearl Harbor, Hawaii, the tenacious and aggressive Vice Admiral Richmond K. Turner is appointed commander of Amphibious Forces, Pacific Fleet.

February 2 Off the Marshall Islands, the destroyer *Walker* sinks the submarine *RO-39*.

February 3 The Kurile Islands of northern Japan are shelled by U.S. Navy warships; this constitutes the first attack on the enemy home islands since Doolittle's raid of April 1942.

February 5 North of Jaluit, Marshall Islands, *I-21* is sunk by the destroyer *Charrette*.

February 6 West of Ascension Island, Atlantic, *U-177* is sunk by a PB4Y-1 Privateer belonging to VB-107.

February 15 On the Green Islands, 55 miles east of New Ireland, Rear Admiral Theodore S. Wilkinson's Task Force 31 lands the 3rd New Zealand Division to help encircle the Japanese garrison at Rabaul.

February 15–18 Near Kavieng, New Ireland, a PBY Catalina flown by Lieutenant Nathan G. Gordon lands repeatedly under heavy fire to rescue 15 stranded airmen; he receives a Congressional Medal of Honor.

February 16 Northwest of Kwajalein, Marshall Islands, the destroyer *Phelps* and the minesweeper *Sage* sink the submarine *RO-40*.

February 17 On Truk, Carolina Islands, aircraft from Admiral Raymond Spruance's Task Force 58 sink the light cruiser *Naha*, along with three destroyers, while 265 enemy aircraft are destroyed. The battleships *Iowa* and *New Jersey* also sink the light cruiser *Katori* and another destroyer. However, Japanese pilots manage to torpedo and damage the carrier *Intrepid*.

Northwest of the Marshall Islands, the submarine *I-11* is sunk by the destroyer *Nicholas*.

February 18–19 Eniwetok, Marshall Islands, is invaded by Rear Admiral Harry W. Hill's Task Group 51.11, which puts Marines ashore.

February 19 In the South China Sea, a Japanese convoy of six tankers is attacked by the submarine *Jack*, which sinks four.

February 23 In the Marianas, Rear Admiral Marc A. Mitscher's Carrier aircraft from Task Groups 58.2 and 58.3 begin preliminary attacks on Japanese positions on Guam, Rota, Saipan, and Tinian in anticipation of an upcoming invasion.

February 24 In the Straits of Gibraltar, *U-761* is attacked by PBY Catalinas of VP-63 which employ the latest Magnetic Anomaly Detection (MAD) equipment to for the first time; the submarine is damaged and scuttled.

February 27 In the East China Sea, the submarine *Grayback* under Commodore John A. Moore is sunk, apparently by Japanese aircraft.

February 29 Off the Marianas Islands, the submarine *Trout* under Lieutenant Albert H. Clark sinks a Japanese transport before being sunk in turn by its escorts.

February 29–March 9 On Los Negros, Admiralty Islands, Rear Admiral William M. Fechteler's Task Group 76.1 puts Army troops ashore; the objective is secured by April 3, further tightening the encirclement of Rabaul.

March 1–2 In the North Atlantic, *U-603* is sunk by the destroyer escort *Bronstein*; the following day it is joined by destroyer escorts *Thomas* and *Bostwick,* and the three claim the *U-709.*

MARCH 6   In the East China Sea, the submarine *Scorpion* under Commander Maximillan G. Schmidt is declared overdue and assumed lost, probably to a minefield.

MARCH 9   In the North Atlantic, the destroyer escort *Leopold* under Lieutenant Commander K. C. Phillips is sunk by *U-255;* 28 survive out of 199 crewmen.

MARCH 13   In the North Atlantic, *U-575* is sunk by TBF Avengers from the escort carrier *Bogue,* a British patrol bomber, and several U.S. and Canadian vessels.

Near Yokosuka, Japan, the submarine *Sand Lance* under Lieutenant Commander Malcolm E. Garrison sinks the light cruiser *Tatsuta* and cargo ship *Kokuyo Maru.* Escorting destroyers drop 105 depth charges on the submarine for the next 18 hours in retaliation, but it escapes.

MARCH 15   Admiral William F. Halsey orders the seizure of Emirau Island, northwest of Rabaul, to completely isolate the 100,000-strong Japanese garrison there.

MARCH 16   In the Straits of Gibraltar, *U-392* is detected by a PBY Catalina of VP-63 using MAD detection equipment, and finally sunk by the British corvette *Affleck.*

MARCH 17   West of the Cape Verde Islands, *U-801* is sunk by TBF Avengers from the escort carrier *Block Island,* in conjunction with the destroyer *Corry* and destroyer escort *Bronstein.*

MARCH 19–MAY 11   Southwest of Dakar, West Africa, *U-1059* is sunk by a TBF Avenger from the escort carrier *Block Island.*

MARCH 20   Kavieng, New Ireland, is bombarded by warships of Rear Admiral Robert M. Griffin's Task Force 37, while Commodore Lawrence F. Reifsnider's Task Group 31.2 lands the 4th Marine Division on Emirau Island, in the Bismark Archipelago.

MARCH 25   In Pacific waters south of Wotje, the destroyer escort *Manlove* and patrol craft *PC-1135* corner and sink the Japanese submarine *I-32.*

MARCH 26   North of the Palaus Islands, the submarine *Tullibee* under Commander Charles F. Brindupke is accidently sunk by a malfunctioning torpedo that circles back and strikes it.

MARCH 30–APRIL 1   Airplanes launched from Task Force 58 bombard Japanese positions in the Palaus and Carolines. This is also the first time that Navy carrier bombers drop mines in daylight during the Pacific War.

APRIL 7   In Atlantic waters, the destroyer *Champlin* rams and sinks the *U-856;* Captain John J. Shaffer, however, dies of shrapnel wounds.

Off the South Pacific island of New Hanover, the destroyer *Saufley* sinks the submarine *I-2.*

APRIL 9   Near Madeira Island, *U-515* and *U-68* are sunk by TBF Avengers from the escort carrier *Guadalcanal* and destroyer escorts *Pillsbury, Pope, Flaherty,* and *Chatelain.*

APRIL 15   The new battleship *Wisconsin* is commissioned; this is the third member of the high-speed *Iowa* class.

APRIL 17   In the North Atlantic, *U-986* is sunk by minesweeper *Swift* and submarine chaser *PC-619.*

APRIL 18 Southwest of Iwo Jima, the submarine *Gudgeon* is sunk, most likely by a Japanese aircraft.

APRIL 19 At Sabang, Netherlands East Indies, the carrier *Saratoga* assists the newly arrived British carrier HMS *Illustrious* in attacking Japanese shipping; three vessel are reported sunk.

APRIL 20 Near Algeria, the destroyer *Lansdale* Lieutenant Commander D. M. Swift is damaged by German aircraft as it escorts convoy UGS 38; it sinks with a loss of 47 crewmen.

Off the Marianas Islands, Central Pacific, the submarine *Seahorse* sinks the *RO-45*.

APRIL 21 West of the Marianas Islands, the submarine *Stingray* sinks after colliding with an underwater pinnacle.

APRIL 22 At Tanahmerah and Humboldt Bay, Netherlands New Guinea, Rear Admiral Daniel E. Barbey's Seventh Amphibious Force lands two Army divisions of Lieutenant General Robert L. Eichelberger's I Corps, covered by aircraft from Rear Admiral Marc A. Mitscher's Task Force 58.

APRIL 26 Near Slapton Sands, England, several Allied troop transports rehearsing "Exercise Tiger" for the Normandy Invasion are sunk by German E-boats. Over 750 soldiers and sailors are killed, and the disaster is kept hidden from public scrutiny.

Off the Canary Islands, *U-488* is sunk by destroyer escorts *Frost*, *Huse*, *Barber*, and *Snowden*.

Off the Aleutian Islands, *I-180* is sink by the destroyer escort *Gilmore*, which pursues a sonar contact and drops several depth charges.

APRIL 27 Off the Caroline Islands, the submarine *Bluegill* under Commander Eric L. Barr sinks the Japanese light cruiser *Yubari*.

APRIL 28 In Washington, D.C., James V. Forrestal becomes the new Secretary of the Navy following the untimely death of Frank Knox.

APRIL 29–MAY 1 Aircraft from Vice Admiral Marc A. Mitscher's Task Force 58 attacks Japanese installation on Truk in the Caroline Islands. Battleships and cruisers under Admirals Jesse B. Oldendorf and Willis A. Lee, Jr., also shell enemy shore installations on Satawan Island and Ponape.

A TBF Avenger from the light carrier *Monterey* assists destroyers *MacDonough* and *Stephen Potter* in sinking the Japanese submarine *I-174*.

MAY 4 In the Luzon Straits, Philippines, a Japanese convoy is attacked by submarines *Bang*, *Parche*, and *Tinosa*, which sink five cargo ships.

MAY 6 West of the Cape Verde Islands, the destroyer escort *Buckley* and *U-66* engage in a close-quarter battle which ends only after the submarine sinks.

MAY 13 Southwest of the Azores, the destroyer escort *Francis M. Robinson* sinks the *RO-501* as it returns from a voyage to Germany.

MAY 15 Near Tangiers, *U-731* is sunk by PBY Catalinas of VP-63, assisted several British warships.

MAY 16 North of the Solomon Islands, the destroyers *Franks*, *Harrad*, and *Johnston* sink the submarine *I-176*.

MAY 17 Near Algeria, *U-616* is damaged by eight American destroyers, aided by a British bomber, and is subsequently scuttled.

At Surabaja, Java, aircraft from an Allied task force under Admiral Sir James F. Somerville attack Japanese shipping and shore installations.

MAY 17–18 On the northern New Guinea Coast, Rear Admiral William M. Fechteler directs the Seventh Amphibious Force as it lands the 163rd Infantry Regiment on the Island of Wakde, 120 miles west of Japanese-held Hollandia.

MAY 19 Off the Algerian coast, *U-960* is sunk by destroyers *Niblack* and *Ludlow*, assisted by British aircraft.

Near New Ireland, Central Pacific, the destroyer escort *England* under Lieutenant Commander Walton B. Pendleton sinks the Japanese submarine *I-16*, the first of six vessels claimed in 12 days.

MAY 19–22 Northeast of Wake Island, aircraft from Rear Admiral A. E. Montgomery's Task Force 58.6 strike at Japanese positions on Marcus Island; they also pay Wake a visit three days later.

MAY 27 In the Schouten Islands, New Guinea, Rear Admiral William M. Fechteler's Seventh Amphibious Force lands the 41st Infantry Division under Major General H. H. Fuller on Biak.

MAY 29 Off the Azores Islands, *U-549* sinks the escort carrier *Block Island* under Captain Francis M. Hughes after penetrating its screen of escort destroyers; this is the only carrier lost during the Battle of the Atlantic. The submarine is sunk in turn by destroyer escorts *Ahrens* and *Eugene E. Elmore*.

MAY 31 Near Matsuwa in the Kurile Islands, submarines *Barb* and *Herring* attack a Japanese convoy, sinking all five of its ships.

JUNE 1 Off the Kurile Islands, Japan, the submarine *Herring* under Lieutenant Commander David Zabriskie sinks the freighter *Hiburi Maru*, and then is itself sunk by shore batteries.

JUNE 4 Off the African coast, *U-505* surfaces and is seized intact by ships of Task Group 22.3; this is the first enemy vessel captured at sea by the Navy since 1815. Lieutenant Albert L. David leads a boarding party from the destroyer escort *Pillsbury* and disarms scuttling charges, winning a Congressional Medal of Honor. As for *U-505*, it is on permanent display at the Museum of Science and Industry in Chicago, Illinois.

JUNE 6 At Normandy, France, Rear Admiral Alan G. Kirk's Western Task Force plays a direct role in the Army's success during OPERATION OVERLORD by transporting troops ashore, providing close support fire, and maintaining an endless stream of transport vessels to the beach areas. Several Seabee units also come ashore with Army troops to clear away obstacles, taking severe losses. The destroyer *Corry* is sunk by a mine, becoming the first of 165 small craft lost over the next three weeks.

JUNE 7 Near Reauville, France, the troopship *Susan B. Anthony* is sunk by a mine; valuable equipment belonging to the 90th Infantry Division is lost.

JUNE 8 Off Normandy Beachhead, France, mines damage destroyer escorts *Glennon, Meredith*, and *Rich*; the latter sinks after losing 50 feet of its stern with 27 dead, 73 wounded, and 62 missing.

JUNE 8–9 Near Biak, New Guinea, Rear Admiral V. A. Crutchley's Task Force 75 intercepts a Japanese convoy carrying reinforcements, and forces it to withdraw. He commands the Australian cruiser

HMAS *Australia*, light cruisers *Bosie* and *Phoenix*, and 14 destroyers.

JUNE 9 Off Normandy Beachhead, France, the destroyer *Meredith* under Commander George Knuepfer sinks after striking a mine.

Near Tawi Tawi, Philippines, the submarine *Harder* sinks three Japanese destroyers, survives protracted depth charge attacks, and rescues coastwatchers from the island of Borneo; Commander Samuel D. Healy receives a Congressional Medal of Honor.

JUNE 10 Near Normandy, France, a German shore battery sinks the destroyer *Glennon* under Commander C. A. Johnson, which was previously damaged by a mine.

Northeast of Kaving, New Ireland, the destroyer *Taylor* sinks the submarine *RO-111*.

Northeast of Kwajalein, the destroyer escort *Bangust* sinks the submarine *RO-42*.

JUNE 11 The Missouri, last of the four-ship Iowa-class battleships, is commissioned; this is also the last U.S. Navy battleship accepted in service.

JUNE 11–12 Near Normandy, France, battleships support the 101st Airborne Division as it seizes Carentan.

JUNE 11–14 Over the Marianas, Central Pacific, Task Force 58 unleashes F6F Hellcat fighters on a sweep of enemy airfields; Japanese air power is eviscerated, and 19 small vessels are sunk.

JUNE 13 East of Saipan, Marianas Islands, the destroyer *Melvin* sinks the Japanese submarine *RO-36*.

JUNE 13–15 Saipan and Tinian in the Marianas are shelled by Rear Vice Admiral Willis A. Lee's Task Group 58.7.

Task Groups 52.17 and 52.18 under Rear Admirals Jesse B. Oldendorf and Walden L. Ainsworth add their battleships to the effort a day later.

Near Honshu, Japan, the submarine *Golet* under Lieutenant James S. Clark is lost and presumed sunk by Japanese aircraft.

JUNE 15 Iwo Jima, Bonin Islands, is struck for the first time by carrier aircraft from Task Force 58 to prevent aerial attacks against operations at Saipan and Tinian.

At Saipan and Tinian, Marianas, Vice Admiral Richmond K. Turner's Task Force 58 unleashes OPERATION FORAGER with amphibious landing. Admiral Raymond A. Spruance's Fifth Fleet covers them with their guns and aircraft. The Americans have to cross 700 miles of open water to reach their objective, long held as the centerpiece of the Central Pacific offensive.

In the South Atlantic, the submarine *U-860* is sunk by TBM Avengers from the escort carrier *Solomon*.

JUNE 16 Near Tinian, Marshall Islands, destroyers *Melvin* and *Wadleigh* sink the submarine *RO-114*.

Near Eniwetok, destroyer escort *Burden R. Hastings* and sinks the submarine *RO-44*.

Vice Admiral Raymond A. Spruance cancels forthcoming landings on Guam, once intelligence is received that the main Japanese fleet has sortied from the Philippines.

JUNE 17 Near Truk, Caroline Islands, *RO-117* is sunk by a PB4Y-1 Privateer from VB-109.

JUNE 19 Off the coast of Guam, Central Pacific, *I-184* is sunk by TBF Avengers from the escort carrier *Suwanee*.

JUNE 19–20 The Battle of the Philippine Sea erupts as Vice Admiral Jisaburo Ozawa launches aircraft against Vice Admiral Marc A. Mitscher's Task Force 58 off Saipan. This aerial armada is eviscerated by the Navy combat air patrol, which shoots down 326 attackers at a cost of 30 Americans. Commander David Campbell of the *Essex* splashes seven aircraft in one day, making him a leading contender to become the Navy's top-scoring ace. On the following day Mitscher replies with a counterstrike at the Japanese fleet, sinking carrier *Hiyo* and two oilers, and damaging three other carriers, a battleship, and four other ships. The American warplanes return that evening, and Mitscher daringly orders all carrier lights to help them land. The lopsided tally in this engagement leads to the nickname "Great Marianas Turkey Shoot."

In the Philippine Sea, submarines *Albacore* under Commander James W. Blanchard and *Cavalla* under Lieutenant Commander Herbert J. Kossler penetrate Japanese defenses and sink carriers *Taiho* and *Shokaku*, respectively.

JUNE 21 North of Saipan, Marianas Islands, the destroyer *Newcomb* and minesweeper *Chandler* sink the *I-185*.

JUNE 24 Southwest of the Azores Islands, the Japanese submarine *I-52* is sunk by TBM Avengers from the escort carrier *Bogue*.

In the Koshiki Straits, Japan, the submarine *Tang* attacks a Japanese convoy, sinking three freighters and a tanker.

JUNE 25 Near Cherbourg, France, a task force under Rear Admiral Morton L. Deyon shells German land batteries which manage to damage the battleship *Texas* and four destroyers; the port falls the following day.

JULY 2 Southeast of the Azores Islands, *U-543* is sunk by a TBM Avenger from the escort carrier *Wake Island*.

On Noemfoor Island, New Guinea, Rear Admiral William M. Fechteler's Task Force 77 lands the 168th Infantry as part of the ongoing "leapfrogging" campaign over Japanese defenses.

JULY 3 Near Madeira in the Atlantic, *U-154* is sunk by destroyer escorts *Frost* and *Inch*.

JULY 4 At Saipan, Marianas Islands, the destroyer *David W. Taylor* and destroyer escort *Riddle* sink the *I-10*.

Near Oahu, Hawaii, the submarine *S-28* sinks during a training exercise; all hands are lost.

In the Bonin Islands, aircraft and warships of the Fifth Fleet bombard and shell Japanese positions on Chichi Jima, Haha Jima, and Iwo Jima.

JULY 5 Near Nova Scotia, Canada, the mine-laying submarine *U-233* is forced to the surface by destroyers *Thomas* and *Baker*, where it is rammed and sunk by *Thomas*.

JULY 8 At Deptford, England, tank-landing ships *LST-312* and *LST-384* are damaged by German V-1 missiles, being the first vessels damaged by such weapons.

JULY 8–19 At Guam, Rear Admiral R. L. Connolly's task force dumps 15,500 16-inch battleship rounds and 16,214 5-inch cruiser shells on the dug-in defenders; this is the longest and most protracted bombardment of the war.

JULY 9 On Saipan, Admiral Chuichi Nagumo, who orchestrated the successful attack on Pearl Harbor, commits suicide.

JULY 12–17 Near Luzon, Philippines, Captain William O'Reagan's Task Group

17.16 attacks Japanese vessels in coastal waters, sinking nine.

JULY 14 At Tinian, Marianas Islands, the destroyer escort *William C. Miller* and high-speed transport *Gimer* sink the *I-6*.

JULY 17 At Port Chicago, California, the merchant vessel *E. A. Bryant* explodes at dockside, killing 320 workers. The bulk of casualties are African American munition loaders, and the survivors refuse to return to work. A total of 258 are court-martialed but, after the war, all receive honorable discharges.

JULY 17–20 Off the coast of Guam, Marianas Islands, underwater demolition teams (UDT) neutralize 940 obstacles and mines to facilitate landings there.

JULY 19 At Tinian, Marianas Islands, the destroyer escort *Wyman* sinks the *RO-48*.

In the South China Sea, the Japanese light cruiser *Oi* is sunk by the submarine

The U.S. Marines salute the U.S. Coast Guard after the battle of Guam in August 1944. Once the island was conquered, the U.S. Navy built five large airfields on the island and used it as a home base for B-29 bombers attacking the Western Pacific and mainland Japan. (National Archives)

Flasher, under Commander Reuben T. Whitaker.

July 21–24 On Guam, Central Pacific, Rear Admiral Richard L. Conolly's Task Force 53 commences OPERATION STEVEDORE by landing marines under an umbrella of close support gunfire.

July 24 On Tinian, Marianas Islands, Read Admiral Harry W. Hill directs Task Force 51 as it conducts amphibious landings by marines and other troops. This subsequently serves as a major air base for launching B-29 raids against the Japanese homeland.

July 25–28 In the Caroline Islands, aircraft from the carriers of Admiral Marc A. Mitscher's Task Force 58 strike Japanese installations on Yap, Ulithi, Fais, Ngulu, Sorol, and Palau.

July 26 Near Palawan Island, Philippines, the submarine *Robalo* under Lieutenant Commander Manning M. Kimmel vanishes, probably after striking a mine.

July 26–29 At Pearl Harbor, Hawaii, President Franklin D. Roosevelt arrives on the cruiser *Baltimore* for a four-day conference with senior military leaders Admiral Chester W. Nimitz and General Douglas A. MacArthur. One of the biggest strategic dilemmas facing them is whether to continue the Central Pacific offensive onto Taiwan or the Philippines. Both are valid targets, yet MacArthur articulates a moral imperative for liberating the Philippines first.

July 28 East of Tinian, Marianas Islands, the destroyers *Wyman* and *Reynolds* sink the submarine *I-55*.

July 30–31 In New Guinea, Rear Admiral William M. Fechteler's Seventh Amphibious Force lands Major General Franklin C. Sibert's 6th Army Division on Cape Sansapour and Cape Opmari, bringing the campaign to a victorious conclusion.

July 31 South of Formosa (Taiwan), a submarine group commanded by Commander Lewis S. Parks ravages a Japanese convoy, sinking four ships and damaging three more. The *Parche* under Commander Lawson P. Ramage makes a daring surface attack and remains surfaced to draw fire from the other subs; he receives a Congressional Medal of Honor.

August 2 East of Newfoundland, Canada, *U-804* sinks the destroyer escort *Fiske* under Lieutenant John A. Comly, with a loss of 30 lives.

August 3 In Washington, D.C., the Office of the General Counsel is created by the Navy Department.

August 4–5 Off the Bonin Islands, Rear Admiral Joseph J. Clark's Task Group 58.1 attack a Japanese convoy with gunfire and aircraft, sinking eight vessels. The following day Rear Admiral Alfred E. Montgomery's Task Group 58.3 appears, and the two launch concerted air strikes against Japanese installations on Chichi Jima and Haha Jima.

August 7 Near Kyushu, the light cruiser *Nagara* is sunk by the submarine *Croaker* under Commander John E. Lee.

August 13 In the Balabac Strait, north of Borneo, the submarine *Flier* under Commander John D. Crowley strikes a mine and sinks; only eight crewmen survive.

August 15 Off the coast of southern France, Vice Admiral H. Kent Hewitt's Western Naval Task Force facilitates OPERATION DRAGOON by landing three divisions of Army troops ashore.

AUGUST 18 In waters off of Luzon, Philippines, the submarines *Rasher* and *Redfish* attack a Japanese convoy, sinking four vessels and damaging two more.

In the San Bernadino Strait, the Japanese light cruiser *Natori* is sunk by the submarine *Hardhead* under Commander Fitzhugh McMaster.

AUGUST 20 In the North Atlantic, *U-1229* is sunk by TBM Avengers from the escort carrier *Bogue*.

AUGUST 21–24 Off the coast of Philippines, the submarine *Harder* under Commander Samuel D. Dealey sinks several Japanese vessels before succumbing to a coastal defense vessel; Dealey, who had previously sunk 16 Japanese vessels, receives a posthumous Congressional Medal of Honor.

AUGUST 31–SEPTEMBER 2 Aircraft from Read Admiral Ralph E. Davison's Task Force 38.4 strike Iwo Jima and Chichi Jima in the Bonin Island, south of Japan. A TBF Avenger flown by Lieutenant George H. W. Bush, a future President of the United States, is shot down, and he is rescued by the submarine *Finback*.

SEPTEMBER 6–8 Vice Admiral Marc A. Mitscher's Task Force 38 directs air strikes against the Palaus and western Caroline Islands.

SEPTEMBER 9–10 Aircraft from Vice Admiral Marc A. Mitscher's Task Force 38 strike Japanese airfields on Mindanao in the southern Philippines.

SEPTEMBER 10–16 Aircraft from Admiral Marc A. Mitscher's Task Force 38 bomb Japanese land installations in the Palaus, the Visayas, and Mindanao, southern Philippines, in preparation for an impending invasion.

SEPTEMBER 11–16 In Quebec, Canada, President Franklin D. Roosevelt, Prime Minister Winston Churchill, and their Combined chiefs of staff convene the Second Quebec Conference. The role of the Royal Navy in the Pacific theater and the impending invasion of the Philippines are at the center of discussions; Admiral Ernest J. King, an Anglophobe, ardently opposes British participation, but is overruled by Roosevelt. A decision is also reached to move the invasion date of Leyte, Philippines, up from December 20 to October 20, at the behest of Admiral Chester W. Nimitz and General Douglas A. MacArthur.

SEPTEMBER 12–13 At the Philippines, Task Force 58 launches air strikes against Japanese airfields and shipping around Visayas, sinking 38 vessels. The following day Cebu, Negros, and Legaspi are also struck.

SEPTEMBER 13 In the North Atlantic, a storm sinks the destroyer *Warrington* under Commander Frank Quarles.

Off Anguar, Palau Islands, the minesweeper *Perry* sinks after striking a mine.

SEPTEMBER 15 On Peleliu, Palau Islands, Vice Admiral Theodore S. Wilkinson's Third Amphibious Force conducts OPERATION STALEMATE II by landing the 1st Marine Division ashore.

On Morotai, midway between New Guinea and the Philippines, Rear Admiral Daniel E. Barbey's Seventh Amphibious Force lands the 41st Infantry Division; the island serves as a logistical springboard for the upcoming invasion of Leyte.

SEPTEMBER 16 At Wasile Bay, Halmahera Island, East Indonesia, *PT-489* and *PT-363* under Lieutenant Arthur M. Preston endure navigate Japanese minefields and dodge shore batteries to rescue downed allied pilot Ensign Harold A. Thompson; Preston receives a Congressional Medal of Honor.

Southeast of Hong Kong, the submarine *Barb* under Commander Eugene B. Fluckey sinks the 20,000-ton escort carrier *Unyo* and the tanker *Azusa* with one salvo of torpedoes.

Near Yokosuka, Japan, the submarine *Sea Devil* sinks the *I-364*.

SEPTEMBER 17   On Anguar, Palau Islands, Rear Admiral William H. P. Blandy's Task Group 32.2 lands the 81st Infantry Division to construct an airfield capable of supporting operations in the Philippines.

SEPTEMBER 21–22   Near Luzon, Philippines, Vice Admiral Marc A. Mitscher's Task Force 38 launches carrier raids against Japanese shipping Cebu and San Fernando, sinking nine vessels.

SEPTEMBER 23   At Ulithi, Caroline Islands, Rear Admiral William H. Blandy's Task Group 32.2 lands troops ashore; this locale serves as a forward supply base for the Pacific Fleet.

At Pearl Harbor, Hawaii, the battleship *West Virginia* returns to service after being heavily damaged on December 7, 1941. This is the last veteran of the initial Japanese attack to rejoin the fleet.

SEPTEMBER 24   Over the central Philippines, Vice Admiral's Mac A. Mitscher's Task Force 38 launches carrier raids against enemy shipping off the Visayan islands, sinking 15 vessels.

SEPTEMBER 25   Near Le Havre, France, the mine-layer *Miantonomah* sinks after striking a mine; 58 men are lost.

SEPTEMBER 27   Over Bougainville, Solomon Islands, Special Air Task Force 1 debuts as a modified TBM Avenger launches radio-controlled TDR-1 drones at a beached freighter serving as an antiaircraft battery.

SEPTEMBER 29   In the South Atlantic, *U-863* is sunk by PB4Y-1 Privateers of VP-107.

In San Francisco, California, Admirals Chester W. Nimitz and Forrest P. Sherman finally convince Chief of Naval Operations Admiral Ernest J. King that invading Formosa (Taiwan) is impractical because the Army lacks the manpower necessary to garrison the island. Consequently, the American high command focuses its attention toward Luzon, Iwo Jima, and Okinawa as future objectives.

SEPTEMBER 30   West of the Cape Verde Islands, the destroyer escort *Fessenden* sinks the *U-1063*.

OCTOBER 1   In Washington, D.C., Vice Admiral Richard S. Edwards is promoted to Deputy Commander in Chief, U.S. Fleet, and Deputy Chief of Naval Operations.

OCTOBER 3   In Washington, D.C., the Joint Chiefs of Staff finally authorize General Douglas MacArthur to invade Luzon, the Philippines, while Admiral Chester W. Nimitz is to capture the islands of Iwo Jima and Okinawa.

Near Morotai, Netherlands East Indies, the destroyer escort *Shelton* under Lieutenant Commander L. G. Salomon is sunk by the submarine *RO-41*. The destroyer escort *Richard M. Rowell* counterattacks, and mistakenly sinks the American submarine *Seawolf* under Commander Albert M. Bontier, who is operating in the area.

Near Angaur, Palau Islands, the destroyer escort *Samuel S. Miles* sinks the *I-177*.

OCTOBER 10   Okinawa, Japan, is heavily attacked by aircraft from Admiral Marc A. Mitscher's Task Force 38; they sink 30 vessels of varying tonnage. Formosa (Taiwan), the Pescadores, and Luzon, Philippines, will be struck by similar raids.

OCTOBER 12–15   Aircraft from Admiral Marc A. Mitscher's Task Force 38 attack airfields and other Japanese installations on

Formosa (Taiwan), sinking 17 vessels of various sizes. Japanese aerial units then counterattack and damage the carrier *Franklin Hancock*, the heavy cruiser *Canberra*, and the light cruiser *Houston*.

OCTOBER 17 After this date all contact ceases with the submarine *Escolar* under Commander W. J. Millican; it mostly likely struck a mine shortly after communicating with the submarine *Perch*.

Admiral Soemu Toyoda, Commander in Chief of the Japanese Combined Fleet, puts in motion OPERATION SHO-1 ("Victory") to defeat American naval forces in the Leyte Gulf, Philippines.

In Leyte Gulf, Philippines, a task force commanded by Rear Admiral Arthur D. Struble lands the 6th Ranger Battalion ashore on Suluan and Dinagar Islands to prevent the Japanese garrison from detecting the main Philippine invasion. However, they arrive too late, and the message is sent.

OCTOBER 17–18 Over the Philippines, aircraft from Admiral Marc A. Mitscher's Task Force 38 strikes Japanese shipping in Manila Bay, Luzon, sinking 12 vessels. The island of Cebu is also struck, and another dozen ships are claimed.

OCTOBER 19 Near Luzon, Philippines, Vice Admiral Thomas C. Kinkaid's Seventh Fleet unleashes his battleships and cruisers as they bombard landing beaches.

OCTOBER 20 Near Luzon, Philippines, Admiral Thomas C. Kinkaid's Seventh Fleet lands four divisions of General Walter P. Krueger's Sixth Army ashore, covered by battleships and carriers of the Third Fleet. Japanese counterattacks damage the escort carrier *Sangamon* and light cruiser *Honolulu*.

OCTOBER 23 The Battle of Leyte Gulf commences as the submarine *Darter* under Commander Bladen D. Claggett detects Vice Admiral Takeo Kurita's First Striking Force steaming for Leyte, Philippines. *Darter*, joined by the *Dace* under Commander David H. McClintock, sinks the heavy cruiser *Atago*, Kurita's flagship, and the heavy cruiser *Maya*. A third heavy cruiser, *Takao*, is heavy damaged and withdraws.

OCTOBER 24 Outside Leyte Gulf, Philippines, aircraft from Admiral Marc A. Mitscher's Task Force 38 ravage Admiral Takeo Kurita's surface fleet as it slips through the Sibuyan Sea. The giant battleship *Musashi* is sunk after receiving 19 torpedoes and 17 bombs, along with the destroyer *Wakaba*; two battleships, two heavy cruisers, and three destroyers are also severely damaged. Thoroughly chastised, Kurita turns his surviving vessels around.

In the skies above Leyte Gulf, Commander David Campbell takes in F6F Hellcat and attacks a formation of 60 Japanese aircraft. He and his wingman knock down 15 aircraft, and Campbell claims 9. He wins a Congressional Medal of Honor and becomes the Navy's top fighter ace with 34 kills.

In the Pacific, Japanese sink the light carrier *Princeton*, which explodes with such force that nearby escorting vessels are damaged; 229 men are killed and 426 are wounded. *Princeton* is scuttled, being the only *Essex*-class carrier lost in World War II.

Near Leyte, the Philippines, the first use of kamikazes by the Japanese occurs when several attack the freighters *Augustus Thomas* and *David Dudley Field*.

No sooner does Task Force 38 refuel its aircraft, then they are sent against another Japanese force under Vice Admiral Shoji Nishimura that is approaching through the Sulu Sea; they damage two battleships and sink a destroyer.

In the Palawan Passage, Philippines, the submarine *Darter* runs aground on

Bombay Shoal, and is scuttled; the crew is rescued by the submarine *Dace*.

East of Surigao Strait, Philippines, the destroyer escort *Richard M. Rowell* sinks the Japanese submarine *I-54*.

In the Formosa Strait, the *Tang* under Commander Richard H. O'Kane sinks two freighters before a malfunctioning torpedo circles back and strikes the submarine. Nine crewmen survive, including O'Kane, who wins the Congressional Medal of Honor.

Somewhere in the Philippines, the submarine *Shark* under Commander Edward N. Blakely ceases all contact, and is presumed lost in action.

OCTOBER 25 The Battle of Suriago Strait unfolds as Rear Admiral Jesse B. Oldendorf's Task Group 77.2, assisted by Task Group 77.3 and 29 motor torpedo boats, tackles Japanese forces under Vice Admiral Shoji Nishimura. The latter's torpedoes sink the battleship *Fuso* and three other warships while damaging the battleship *Yamashiro*. The American battleships, most Pearl Harbor survivors, sink all remaining Japanese warships; only a single destroyer survives. The destroyer *Albert W. Grant* is heavily damaged.

Admiral William F. Halsey moves the bulk of his fleet north to intercept Vice Admiral Jisaburo Ozawa's surface forces, and his aircraft sink four carriers. However, Halsey's departure leaves the northern approach to Leyte guarded by escort carriers and destroyers, and Admiral Takeo Kurita's Center Force heads directly toward the San Bernardino Straits. A handful of destroyers and escort carriers under Rear Admiral Clifton F. Sprague, near Samar, are all that stand between Kurita and the American landing zones. The escort carrier *Gambier Bay* and three destroyers (*Hoel, Johnston,* and *Samuel B. Roberts*) are sunk before aircraft from Task Force 38 damage several battleships and sink the heavy cruisers *Chikuma, Chokai,* and *Suzuya*. At this point Kurita, unnerved, withdraws. Commander Ernest E. Evans of the doomed destroyer *Johnston* goes down with his ship, winning a posthumous Congressional Medal of Honor.

OCTOBER 26 Near Leyte Gulf, Philippines, aircraft from Admiral William F. Halsey's Third Fleet attack the remaining Japanese fleet, sinking an additional five vessels. The submarine *Jallao* under Commander Joseph B. Icetower also sinks the light cruiser *Tama*. Their total loss over the past two days is four carriers, three battleships, eight cruisers, nine destroyers, and a submarine, after which Japanese naval power ceases to exist.

Off the coast of the Philippines, Japanese kamikaze pilots score one of their earliest successes by sinking the escort carrier *St. Lo* Under Captain F. J. McKenna.

In the Visayan Sea, Rear Admiral Thomas L. Sprague's Taffy 2 force launches aircraft that sink light cruiser *Kinu* and the destroyer *Uranami*.

OCTOBER 27 Near Negros Island, Philippines, carrier aircraft sink the Japanese light cruiser *Abukuma*.

OCTOBER 28 In waters off the Philippines, the submarine *I-46* is sunk by TBF Avengers from the escort carrier *Belleau Wood*, assisted by the destroyers *Helm* and *Gridely*.

At Leyte, Philippines, the Japanese submarine *I-45* sinks the destroyer escort *Eversole* under Lieutenant Commander George E. Marix, before being sunk in turn by the destroyer escort *Whitehurst*.

OCTOBER 29–30 In the Philippines, Japanese kamikazes lash Task Force 38 savagely and damage the carriers *Intrepid, Franklin,* and *Belleau Wood*.

NOVEMBER 1 Near Leyte, Philippines, kamikazes sink the destroyer *Abner Read* while conventional bombs damage five others.

NOVEMBER 5–6 Aircraft from Vice Admiral John S. McCain's Task Group 38.1 attack Japanese airfields on Luzon, Philippines, sinking the heavy cruiser *Nachi* and four lesser vessels.

NOVEMBER 7 Offshore at Hokkaido, Japan, the submarine *Albacore* under Lieutenant Commander Hugh R. Rimer sinks after striking a mine; all hands are lost.

NOVEMBER 8 Near Mindoro, Philippines, the submarine *Growler* under Commander Thomas B. Oakley is sunk by Japanese surface vessels.

NOVEMBER 10 In the Java Sea, the submarine *Flounder*, alerted by decoded naval intelligence, sinks the German *U-537* en route to Japan.

At Manus, Admiralty Islands, the transport *Mount Hood* sinks after 3000 tons of explosives accidently ignite; 36 nearby vessels are also damaged.

NOVEMBER 11 In Ormoc Bay, Philippines, carrier planes launched by Task Force 58 sink destroyers *Hamanami*, *Naganami*, *Shimakaze,* and *Wakatsuki*.

NOVEMBER 12 South of Yap, Caroline Islands, the destroyer *Nicholas* sinks the Japanese submarine *I-37*.

NOVEMBER 13 In Manila Bay, Philippines, aircraft from the Third Fleet attack Japanese shipping and sink the light cruisers *Kiso* and destroyers *Akebono*, *Akishimo*, *Hatsuharu*, and *Okinami*.

In mid-Pacific waters between Hawaii and California, the frigate *Rockford* and the minesweeper *Ardent* sink the Japanese submarine *I-12*.

NOVEMBER 13–14 Aircraft from Task Force 38 again strike Japanese shipping in Manila Bay, Philippines, sinking 25 small vessels.

NOVEMBER 17 In the Philippine sea, the Japanese submarine *I-41* is sunk by the destroyer escort *Lawrence C. Taylor*, assisted by TBM Avengers from the escort carrier *Anzio*.

In the Yellow Sea, the submarine *Spadefish* under Commander Gordon Underwood sinks the 21,000-ton Japanese escort carrier *Shinyo*.

NOVEMBER 17–18 In the East China Sea, Japanese convoy MI 27 is ravaged by U.S. submarines, which sink five vessels.

NOVEMBER 19 West of the Palau Islands, the destroyer escorts *Conklin* and *McCoy* sink the Japanese submarine *I-37*.

NOVEMBER 21 Offshore at Formosa (Taiwan), the submarine *Sealion* under Commander Eli T. Riech sinks the Japanese battleship *Kongo* and destroyer *Urakaze*; *Kongo* is the first battleship claimed by an American submersible.

NOVEMBER 25 Near Luzon, Philippines, aircraft from Task Force 38 strike Japanese shipping, sinking eight vessels, including the heavy cruisers *Kumano* and *Yasojima*. Kamikaze aircraft hit back, damaging carriers *Essex*, *Intrepid*, and *Hancock*.

NOVEMBER 27–29 Near the Philippines, kamikaze aircraft damage another six vessels belonging to Task Force 38.

NOVEMBER 28 In Leyte Gulf, Philippines, destroyers *Saufley*, *Waller*, *Renshaw*, and *Pringle* sink the submarine *I-46*.

NOVEMBER 29 In Tokyo Bay, the huge, 64,000-ton carrier *Shinano*, originally designed as a battleship, is torpedoed and sunk by the submarine *Archerfish* under Commander Joseph F. Enright. This is the biggest single sinking, in terms of tonnage, of the entire war.

DECEMBER 2–3   In Ormoc Bay, Leyte, Philippines, Destroyer Division 120 engages Japanese forces at night; the *Cooper* sinks with a loss of 191 lives in exchange for the destroyer *Kuwa*.

DECEMBER 6–7   Off the coast of the Philippines, Japanese convoy TAMA 34 is struck by Navy submarines, which sink four vessels and force the grounding of another four.

DECEMBER 7   At Leyte, Philippines, Rear Admiral Arthur D. Struble's Task Force 78.3 lands the 77th Infantry Division at Ormoc Bay while lashed by kamikazes; destroyers *Lamson* and *Mahan* are heavily damaged and scuttled.

DECEMBER 11   Near Leyte, Philippines, kamikazes sink the destroyer *Reid* under Commander S. A. McCornock, as it resupplies at Ormoc Bay.

DECEMBER 14   In Washington, D.C., Admirals William D. Leahy, chairman of the Joint Chiefs of Staff, Admiral Ernest J. King, Chief of Naval Operations, and Chester W. Nimitz, Commander in Chief, Pacific Fleet, all receive promotion to the new five-star rank.

DECEMBER 15   Near Mindoro, Philippines, Rear Admiral Arthur D. Struble's Task Force 78.3 lands Army troops ashore, while kamikaze aircraft cripple the escort carrier *Marcus Island*, sink two landing craft, and damage two destroyers.

DECEMBER 16   In Subic Bay, Philippines, aircraft from Task Force 38 sink the Japanese freighter *Oryoku Maru*, unaware that 1,600 Americans prisoners are confined below deck.

DECEMBER 18   East of the Philippines, Admiral William F. Halsey's Third Fleet is badly battered by a typhoon; destroyers *Hull, Monaghan,* and *Spence* capsize with a loss of 765 men, while 21 other vessels are also damaged. This represents heavier losses than have been inflicted by the Japanese. Ironically, Halsey had decided against dodging the storm.

DECEMBER 19   Southeast of Shanghai, China, the submarine *Redfish* under Commander Louis D. McGregor sinks the carrier *Unryu*, but the ensuing depth-charge attack forces it to limp home in damaged condition.

DECEMBER 21   South of Tokyo Bay, the submarine *Scamp* under Commander John C. Hollingsworth is declared overdue and presumed missing in action.

DECEMBER 24   Near Cherbourg, France, *U-486* sinks the Belgium-operated troopship SS *Leopoldville*, and 500 men of the 262nd and 264th Infantry Regiments drown in the freezing water.

DECEMBER 26   At Mindoro, Philippines, American troops landing ashore are set upon by Rear Admiral Masanori's heavy cruiser, light cruiser, and destroyers. The Japanese bombard the beachhead, losing one destroyer to American warplanes.

Somewhere in the Pacific, the submarine *Swordfish* disappears at sea during its 13th war patrol.

DECEMBER 28–30   Near Mindoro, the Philippines, kamikazes lash an American convoy, sinking two freighters and damaging the destroyers *Pringle* and *Gansevoort*.

1945

JANUARY 1 Worldwide, U.S. Navy personnel amounts to 3.4 million, making it the largest naval force in military history.

JANUARY 3–4 Aircraft from Rear Admiral John McCain's Task Force 38 strike Japanese shipping off Formosa (Taiwan), sinking 10 vessels. A protracted carrier raid ensues throughout the Western Pacific and South China Sea.

JANUARY 3–8 In the Lingayen Gulf, Philippines, Vice Admiral Jesse B. Oldendorf's Task Group 77.2 is struck by kamikazes, which heavily damage escort carrier *Ommaney Bay*, scuttling it, and sink the destroyer *Hovey*. Battleships *California* and *New Mexico*, heavy cruiser *Louisville*, and light cruiser *Columbia* are also damaged; Commander George F. Davis of the destroyer *Walke*, who refuses to abandon ship after five kamikaze strikes and serious wounds, receives a posthumous Congressional Medal of Honor.

JANUARY 3–9 Japanese airfields and installation on Formosa (Taiwan) and Luzon, Philippines, are struck by aircraft from Admiral William F. Halsey's Third Fleet, which mounts over 3,000 sorties.

JANUARY 5 In the Bonin Islands, Rear Admiral Allan E. Smith's Cruiser Division 5 bombards shore installations on Iwo Jima, Haha Jima, and Chichi Jima. Off Paramushiro, Kurile Islands, Rear Admiral J. L. McRea's cruiser force also shells Japanese positions.

JANUARY 6–9 At Pearl Harbor, Hawaii, the first detachment of WAVES deploys, the first of 4,009 assigned there; this is the only post outside the continental U.S. where women are permanently stationed.

JANUARY 7–8 On the Lingayen Gulf, Philippines, Vice Admiral Jesse B. Oldendorf's Task Group 77.2 shells Japanese shore installations prior to landing troops. Japanese aircraft bomb and sink the minesweeper *Palmer*, while kamikazes damage the cruiser HMAS *Australia*.

JANUARY 8 In the Lingayen Gulf, the Philippines, Admiral Thomas C. Kinkaid's Task Force 77 is attacked by kamikazes which damage escort carriers *Kadashan Bay* and *Kitkun Bay*. Such resistance forces Task Force 38 carriers to shift air strikes against Japanese airfields on the mainland to curtail further attacks.

Off the coast of Formosa (Taiwan), American submarines from Task Group 17.21 under Commander Charles E. Loughlin ravage a Japanese convoy, sinking three vessels and damaging three.

JANUARY 9 At Lingayen Bay, Philippines, Rear Admiral Thomas C. Kinkaid's Task Force 77 lands 68,000 Army troops ashore while supporting them with air strikes and naval gunfire. The Japanese counter with kamikaze attacks, and the new battleship *Missouri* is hit repeatedly. The Americans are also attacked by naval kamikazes employing high-speed boats crammed with explosives; one transport vessel is sunk by these weapons.

JANUARY 12 Near French Indochina (Vietnam), aircraft from Rear Admiral John S. McCain's Task Force 38 strike Japanese installations, sinking 31 vessels. McCain next shifts his sights to Hong Kong and the Chinese coast.

Near Okinawa, the submarine *Swordfish* under Commander Keats E. Montross is lost after reconnoitering island waters.

JANUARY 13   Northeast of Truk, Caroline Islands, the destroyer escort *Fleming* sinks submarine *I-362*.

JANUARY 16   Near the Azores Islands, destroyer escorts *Otter*, *Hubbard*, *Hayter*, and *Varian* sink the *U-248*.

JANUARY 21–22   Off the Chinese coast, Vice Admiral John S. McCain's Task Force 38 is heavily attacked by kamikazes that damage carriers *Ticonderoga* and *Hancock*, the light carrier *Langley*, and the destroyer *Maddox*.

JANUARY 23   President Franklin D. Roosevelt boards the heavy cruiser *Quincy* for a trip to Yalta (Crimea) in the Soviet Union to confer with Prime Minister Winston Churchill and Soviet Premier Joseph Stalin.
Near Yap, Caroline Islands, destroyer escorts *Conklin*, *Corbesier*, and *Raby* sink the *I-48*.

JANUARY 25   Off the Bonin Islands, Rear Admiral Oscar C. Badger's task force, including the battleship *Indiana*, bombards Japanese positions on Iwo Jima.

JANUARY 26   Admiral Raymond A. Spruance succeeds Admiral William F. Halsey, and his command is renamed from Third Fleet to Fifth Fleet.

JANUARY 29   At Guadalcanal, Solomon Islands, the cargo ship *Serpens* accidentally explodes, killing all 255 men on board.

JANUARY 29–31   On Luzon, the Philippines, Rear Admirals Arthur D. Struble's Task Groups 78.3 and Rear Admiral William M. Fechteler's Task Force 78.2 outflank Japanese defenders on Luzon by landing 30,000 Army troops at Subic and Manila Bay.

JANUARY 31   South of Manila Bay, Philippines, Rear Admiral William M. Fechteler directs Amphibious Group 8 to put the 11th Airborne Division ashore at Nasugbu.

FEBRUARY 1   Southwest of Manila, Philippines, destroyers *Jenkins*, *O'Bannon*, and *Bell*, assisted by destroyer escort *Moore*, sink the *RO-115*.

FEBRUARY 4   In the South China Sea, the submarine *Barbel* is apparently sunk by Japanese aircraft.

FEBRUARY 7   Near Luzon, Philippines, the destroyer escort *Thomason* sinks the Japanese submarine *RO-55*.

FEBRUARY 9–12   Off the Philippine coast, Japanese submarines, *RO-115*, *RO-112*, and *RO-113* are sunk by the *Batfish* under Commander John K. Fyfe in four days, a Navy record.

FEBRUARY 13   In Manila Bay, Philippines, Rear Admiral R. S. Berkey orders minesweepers attached to his Task Group 77.3 to begin clearing the waters.

FEBRUARY 14   Near Corregidor, the Philippines, Japanese batteries sink the minesweeper *YMS-48* and damage the destroyers *Hopewell* and *Fletcher*. On the latter, Watertender First Class Elmer C. Bigelow rushes into a magazine and extinguishes a fire; winning a posthumous Congressional Medal of Honor.

FEBRUARY 15   In the Philippines, Rear Admiral Arthur D. Struble's Task Group 78.3 increases the pressure on Japanese defenders by landing Army troops at Mariveles Harbor, Bataan, and Luzon.

FEBRUARY 16 Over Tokyo, Japan, aircraft from Admiral Marc A. Mitscher's Task Force 58 attack military targets; this is also the first time that the capital has been raided by carriers.

Near Iwo Jima, Bonin Islands, Rear Admiral William H. Blandy deploys his battleships and cruisers and begins bombarding Japanese shore positions in anticipation of an amphibious invasion.

Off the coast of the Philippines, the submarine *Barbel* under Lieutenant Commander Conde L. Raguet is declared overdue and presumed lost in action.

FEBRUARY 17 On Iwo Jima, Bonin Islands, Underwater Demolition Teams (UDT) begin scouring the beaches for possible obstructions. After Japanese artillery badly damages LCI (G)-449, Lieutenant Rufus G. Herring, although badly wounded, refuses to quit his post until all the frogmen are recovered; he receives a Congressional Medal of Honor.

At Pearl Harbor, Hawaii, Boatswain's Mate Second Class Owen F. P. Hammerberg rescues two fellow divers who become trapped during a salvage operation. He is himself injured and dies, but received a posthumous Congressional Medal of Honor.

FEBRUARY 19–23 Near Iwo Jima, Bonin Islands, Admiral Marc A. Mitscher's Task Force 58 launches waves of fighters and dive-bombers against Japanese positions. Fighting on the island remains intense and costly.

FEBRUARY 21 Near Iwo Jima, Bonin Islands, massed kamikazes sink the escort carrier *Bismark Sea* under Captain J. L. Pratt, with a loss of 218 crewmen. The carrier *Saratoga* also sustains five hits which effectively end its combat career, while the light carrier *Langley* also receives a hit but recovers.

FEBRUARY 25 Over Japan, Admiral Marc A. Mitscher's Task Force 58 launches carrier strikes against targets around Tokyo, until bad weather cancels flying operations.

FEBRUARY 26 Near Iwo Jima, Bonin Islands, the Japanese submarines *I-368* and *RO-43* are sunk by TBM Avengers from the escort carrier *Anzio*; further south, the destroyer escort *Finnegan* sinks the *I-370*.

FEBRUARY 27 In the English Channel, a PB4Y-1 Privateer of VPB-112 assists Royal Navy ships in sinking the *U-327*.

FEBRUARY 28 On Palawan Island, southern Philippines, Rear Admiral William M. Fechteler's Task Group 78.2 and Rear Admiral Ralph S. Riggs's Task Force 74.2 land Army troops on Puerto Princesa.

On Iwo Jima, Pharmacist's Mate First Class John H. Willis throws out eight Japanese grenades from a trench holding a wounded Marine; he is killed by the ninth, winning a Congressional Medal of Honor posthumously.

MARCH 1 At Orlando, Florida, the Naval Research Laboratory Underwater Sound Reference Division (USRD) is commissioned and commences research operations.

Over Okinawa, Ryukyu Islands, Vice Admiral Marc A. Mitscher's Task Force 58 launches aircraft against Japanese shipping, sinking 15 small vessels.

MARCH 2 On Corregidor Island, the Philippines, Rear Admiral Arthur D. Struble's Task Group 78.3 provides supporting fire for Army troops going ashore.

In the Ryukyu Islands, Rear Admiral F. E. M. Whiting's Task Group 58, a mixed force of cruisers and destroyers, bombards Japanese shore positions on Okino Daito.

MARCH 3 On Iwo Jima, Bonin Islands, Pharmacist's Mate Third Class Jack Williams ignores serious wounds to treat several injured Marines; he is shot returning to American lines, and wins a posthumous Congressional Medal of Honor.

Nearby, Pharmacist's Mate Second Class George E. Whalen also ignores his own wounds while attending wounded Marines, and in one instance he crawls 50 yards under fire to render assistance; he receives a Congressional Medal of Honor.

MARCH 6 On Iwo Jima, Bonin Islands, Ensign Jane Kendeigh arrives by plane as the battle rages, becoming the first Navy nurse serving in an active combat zone.

MARCH 8 Phyllis Daley is commissioned an ensign in the Navy Nurse Corps, becoming the first African American woman to do so.

MARCH 10 On Mindanao, Philippines, Rear Admiral Forrest B. Royal's Task Force 78.1 lands Army troops ashore at Zamboanga, despite accurate Japanese artillery fire.

Near Okinawa, the submarine *Kete* reports sinking three Japanese cargo ships, then vanishes at sea.

MARCH 11 Off the Isles of Scilly, a PB4Y-1 Privateer of VPB-103 sinks *U-681*.

At Ulithi, Caroline Islands, a Japanese bomber launched from the mainland on a one-way mission hits the carrier *Randolph*, killing 25 sailors and wounding 106.

In Germany, several hundred Navy landing craft are hauled overland in preparation for a major crossing at Bad Neuenahr; they are commanded by Commander William J. Whiteside.

MARCH 15 In the Boston Navy Yard, Massachusetts, a faulty torpedo door leads to the submarine *Lancetfish* accidentally sinking.

MARCH 16 On Iwo Jima, Pharmacist's Mate Second Class Francis J. March is wounded while tending wounded Marines, and draws a pistol to draw fire away from his patients; he receives a Congressional Medal of Honor.

MARCH 18 Near Nova Scotia, Canada, destroyer escorts *Mosley*, *Pride*, and *Lowe* sink the *U-866*.

Over Japan, aircraft from Vice Admiral Marc A. Mitscher's Task Force 58 raid airfields and other targets on the mainland. They claim 102 Japanese airplanes shot down and 275 destroyed on the ground. However, kamikazes lash back, damaging carriers *Intrepid*, *Enterprise*, *Hornet*, and *Wasp*.

In the Philippines, Rear Admiral Arthur D. Struble's Task Force 78.3 lands the 40th Infantry Division of Major General Rapp Brush on Panay Island.

At Long Beach, California, the prototype Douglas AD Skyraider flies for the first time. Developed too late to see service in World War II, it renders distinguished service as a bomber up through the Vietnam conflict.

MARCH 18–21 Over Japan, aircraft from Vice Admiral Marc A. Mitscher's Task Force 58 again strike Japanese ports and installations on the main island of Kyushu.

MARCH 19 Off the Japanese mainland, a solitary bomber strikes the carrier *Franklin*, and a blazing inferno results. A total of 772 are killed and 265 wounded out of 3,450 crewmen present. Lieutenant Donald A. Gary risks his life rescuing sailors trapped below decks, assisted by Commander Joseph T. O'Callaghan, the Catholic chaplain, who hurls burning ammunition overboard; both receive Congressional Medals of Honor.

MARCH 20 Between Japan and Okinawa, the submarine *Kete* under Lieutenant Commander Edward Ackerman is reported overdue and is declared missing in action.

MARCH 23 In Germany, landing craft operated by Task Unit 122.5.1 ferry General George S. Patton's Third Army across the Rhine River despite heavy German fire.

In the Philippine Sea, the destroyer *Haggard* rams Japanese submarine *I-371*, sinking it.

MARCH 23–APRIL 1 Over the Ryukyu Island, aircraft from Vice Admiral Marc A. Mitscher's Task Force 58 begin a preliminary bombardment of Japanese positions on Okinawa.

MARCH 25 At Okinawa, Ryukyu Islands, Rear Admiral Morton L. Deyo's Task Force 54 begins preliminary bombardment of Japanese positions.

MARCH 26 At Okinawa, Ryukyu Islands, as Rear Admiral Morton L. Deyo's Task Force 54 continues bombarding Japanese shore installations, kamikazes damage the battleship *Nevada* and light cruiser *Biloxi*; the destroyer *Halligan* under Lieutenant Commander T. E. Grace also sinks after striking a mine.

On Kerama Retto, Ryukyu Islands, Rear Admiral Ingolf N. Kiland's Task Group 51.1 land the 77th Infantry Division under Major General W. H. Arnold.

In the Philippines, Captain Albert T. Sprague's Task Group 78.2 lands the Americal Division, under Major General William H. Arnold, on Talisay Point, Cebu.

MARCH 27 The submarine *Trigger* under Commander David R. Connole is declared missing in action during its 12th Pacific war patrol.

In Manila Bay, Philippines, Navy destroyers and rocket-firing PT boats help the 151st Regimental Combat Team wipe out a Japanese garrison on Caballo Island.

MARCH 29 Over Japan, aircraft from Vice Admiral Marc A. Mitscher's Task Force 58 strikes targets in Kagoshima Bay, Kyushu, sinking 12 vessels.

In the Philippines, Task Group 78.3 under Rear Admiral Arthur D. Struble lands the 185th Regimental Combat Team ashore on Negros Island.

MARCH 31 At Okinawa, Ryukyu Islands, the destroyers *Morrison* and *Stockton* sink the submarine *I-8*. Kamikazes also strike Admiral Raymond A. Spruance's flagship, the heavy cruiser *Indianapolis*, and he transfers his flag to the battleship *New Mexico*.

APRIL 1 OPERATION ICEBERG, the invasion of Okinawa, commences as Task Force 51 under Vice Admiral Richmond K. Turner's Joint Expeditionary Force puts 183,000 men of the III Amphibious Corps ashore, covered by the guns and aircraft of Admiral Raymond A. Spruance's Fifth Fleet.

At Okinawa, kamikaze aircraft damage the battleship *West Virginia* and two attack transports.

Near Legaspi, Luzon, Philippines, Captain Homer F. McGee's Task Group 78.4 lands Army troops ashore.

In the Formosan Straits, the submarine Queenfish sinks the Japanese ship *Awa Maru* in poor visibility. However, because that vessel was on a humanitarian mission delivering supplies to Allied prisoners in Malaysia, and marked with Red Crosses, Lieutenant Commander Charles E. Loughlin is court-martialed and receives a letter of reprimand.

APRIL 5 Near Okinawa, Ryukyu Islands, the destroyer *Hudson* sinks the Japanese submarine *RO-41*.

APRIL 6 Over Okinawa, Ryukyu Islands, Admiral Soemu Toyoda commences OPERATION TEN-GO by unleashing 355 kamikazes and 669 conventional aircraft against the American invaders; the destroyers *Bush* and *Calhoun*, along with transports *Hobbs Victory* and *Logan Victory*, are sunk outright, while 12 other vessel receive damage. This is the first of nine massed aerial attacks, dubbed *kikusui*, or "floating chrysanthemums," by the Japanese.

APRIL 7 Near Okinawa, Ryukyu Islands, kamikaze aircraft damage six vessels including carrier *Hancock* and battleship *Maryland*.

The huge Japanese battleship *Yamato*, the light cruiser *Yahagi*, and eight destroyers sortie on a one-way mission against the American fleet at Okinawa. They are intercepted by 386 carrier aircraft from Vice Admiral Marc A. Mitscher's Task Force 58, and all but four destroyers are sunk with terrific loss of life; Admiral Seiichi Ito goes down with 2,767 men on his flagship. This is the Imperial Japanese Navy's last sortie, and costs the Americans 10 aircraft and 12 airmen.

In Bima Bay, Netherlands East Indies, submarines *Gabilan* under Commander William B. Parham and *Charr* under Commander Francis D. Boyle jointly sink the Japanese light cruiser *Isuzu*.

APRIL 8 In the Pacific, the submarine *Snook* rendezvouses with the submarine *Tigrone*, then vanishes.

APRIL 9 Near Okinawa, Ryukyu Islands, the destroyers *Mertz* and *Monssen* sink the Japanese submarine *RO-56*.

APRIL 11 Near Okinawa, Ryukyu Islands, kamikaze attacks damage another six vessels, including the battleship *Missouri* and carrier *Enterprise*. The carrier *Essex*, three destroyers, and several landing craft are also struck by bombs.

APRIL 12 In Warm Springs, Georgia, President Franklin D. Roosevelt dies and is succeeded by Vice President Harry S. Truman.

Near Formosa, the submarine *Snook* under Commander John F. Walling is apparently lost in action through enemy action.

APRIL 12–13 Offshore at Okinawa, Ryukyu Islands, 380 Japanese aircraft attack the U.S. fleet, including the first rocket-powered Baka suicide bombs; the destroyer *Mannert L. Abele* is struck by one and sinks. The landing craft *LCS (L)-33* also sinks, while 18 vessels are heavily damaged. However, Task Force 58 fighters claim 298 enemy aircraft.

APRIL 14 In the Yellow Sea, a large Japanese convoy is attacked by the submarine *Tirante* under Lieutenant Commander George L. Street III, who sinks three vessels while still surfaced; Street receives a Congressional Medal of Honor.

APRIL 15 At Okinawa, Ryukyu Islands, the destroyer *Laffey* is singled out by 22 separate kamikaze attacks; 6 attackers are shot down and another 6 crash into it. *Laffey* loses 109 men, but survives and is towed off to safety.

APRIL 15–16 West of the Azores Islands, the destroyer escorts *Frost* and *Stanton* sink the *U-1235*; a day later the duo also sinks the *U-880*.

APRIL 16 Near Okinawa, Ryukyu Islands, kamikazes sink the destroyer *Pringle* under Lieutenant Commander J. L. Kelley, with a loss of 62 men, and badly damage the battleship *Missouri* and carrier *Intrepid*.

APRIL 16–21   On the west coast of Okinawa, Rear Admiral L. F. Reifsnider's Task Force 53 lands Major General A. D. Bruce's 77th Infantry Division on the island of Ie Shima.

APRIL 17–MAY 11   On the west coast of Mindanao, Philippines, Rear Admiral A. G. Noble's Task Group 78.2 successfully lands the X Corps of Major General F. C. Silbert ashore.

APRIL 18   Near Okinawa, Ryukyu Islands, the *I-56* is sink by a TBM Avenger from the light carrier *Bataan*, assisted by four destroyers.

At Wake Island, Central Pacific, the submarine *Sea Owl* sinks the *RO-46* 400 yards from the beaches.

APRIL 19   Off the coast of Nova Scotia, Canada, the destroyer escorts *Buckley* and *Reuben James* sink the *U-548*.

APRIL 22   Near the Azores, destroyer escorts *Neal A. Scott* and *Carter* sink the *U-518*.

APRIL 23   In the Java Sea, the submarine *Besugo* intercepts and sinks the German submarine *U-138*.

Near Balikpapan, Borneo, Navy PB4Y Privateers of VBP-109 launch several radio-controlled "Bat" missiles at Japanese targets, damaging several freighter and oil installations. These are the first automatic homing missiles employed during World War II, although their accuracy is problematic.

APRIL 24   East of Newfoundland, Canada, *U-546* sinks the destroyer escort *Frederick C. Davis*, under Lieutenant J. R. Crosby, then is sunk in turn by seven other destroyer escorts.

APRIL 25   At Brest, France, *U-326* is sunk by a PB4Y-1 Privateer of VPB-103.

APRIL 26   In the Philippines, Commander W. V. Deutermann's Task Unit 78.3.3 conveys Army troops to the island of Negros.

APRIL 27   At Okinawa, Ryukyu Islands, kamikazes sink the transport *Canada Victory* and damage three destroyers and the hospital ship *Comfort*.

APRIL 28–30   Near Okinawa, Ryukyu Islands, an additional fifteen warships are damaged by repeated kamikaze attacks.

APRIL 29   Near Okinawa, the *I-44* is sunk by a TBM Avenger from the escort carrier *Tulagi*.

APRIL 30   Off the Virginia Capes, the destroyer escorts *Thomas*, *Bostwick*, *Coffman*, and *Natchez* sink the *U-879*.

Near Brest, France, a PBY Catalina belonging to VP-63 sinks the *U-1107*.

MAY 1   On Tarakan Island, Borneo, Rear Admiral Forrest B. Royal's Task Group 78.1 puts the 26th Brigade of the Australian 9th Division troops ashore; they are covered by the guns of Rear Admiral Russell S. Berkey's Task Force 74.3.

MAY 2   On Okinawa, Hospital Apprentice Second Class Robert E. Bush is attacked by Japanese soldiers as he treats a wounded Marine. Bush shoots down six attackers with his carbine and loses an eye in the process, but refuses to be evacuated; he receives a Congressional Medal of Honor.

MAY 3   Near Okinawa, Ryukyu Islands, the destroyer *Little* and the medium landing ship *LSM-195* are sunk by kamikazes; four other vessels are heavily damaged

In the Gulf of Siam, the submarine *Legarto* under Commander Frank D. Latta is sunk by the minesweeper *Hatsutaka* as it decimates a Japanese convoy.

May 4 At Okinawa, Ryukyu Islands, the destroyers *Luce* and *Morrison* are sunk by kamikazes with a loss of 300 men; an additional 12 vessels receive heavy damage.

May 4–10 Seaplanes of Patrol Wing 1 sweep through the Tsushima Strait and the coastline of Korea, sinking 21 vessels.

May 6 At Block Island, Rhode Island, the destroyer escort *Atherton* and the frigate *Moberley* sink the *U-853*.

In the North Atlantic, the destroyer escort *Farquhar* sinks the German submarine *U-881*; this is also the final German vessel destroyed by American forces during World War II.

May 9 At Okinawa, Ryukyu Islands, kamikazes strike the destroyer escort *Oberrender* under Lieutenant Commander Samuel Spencer, sinking it.

May 11 At Okinawa, Ryukyu Islands, a kamikaze strikes the carrier *Bunker Hill*, Vice Admiral Marc A. Mitscher's flagship, which suffers severe damage but manages to limp back to the United States. The ship loses 373 sailors killed and 264 injured. Several destroyers are also struck and damaged, while Mitscher is forced to transfer his flag to the carrier *Enterprise*.

On Okinawa, Pharmacist's Mate Second Class William D. Halyburton shields a wounded marine with his own body and is mortally injured; he receives a posthumous Congressional Medal of Honor.

May 13–14 Determined to thwart kamikaze attacks, Admiral Marc A. Mitscher directs Rear Admiral J. J. Clark's Task Group 58.1 under and Rear Admiral Forrest P. Sherman's Task Group 58.3 to strike Japanese airfields on Kyushu and Shikoku, Japan.

May 14 At Okinawa, the carrier *Enterprise*, Vice Admiral Marc A. Mitscher's new flagship, is seriously damaged by another kamikaze strike.

May 18 At Naha, Okinawa, Japanese artillery batteries shell the destroyer *Longshaw* under Commander C. W. Becker after it runs aground; 86 men die after the forward magazines explode.

May 23–25 At Okinawa, Ryukyu Islands, the high-speed transport *Bates* and the medium landing ship *LSM-135* are sunk by kamikazes; seven other vessels sustain heavy damage.

May 27 In the latest command shake-up, Admiral William F. Halsey succeeds Vice Raymond Spruance as commander of the Fifth Fleet, which is subsequently redesignated the Third Fleet. Vice Admiral John S. McCain also replaces Rear Admiral Marc A. Mitscher as head of Task Force 38.

May 28 At Okinawa, Ryukyu Islands, kamikazes sinks the destroyer *Drexler* with a loss of 168 dead and 52 injured; three other destroyers are damaged.

May 30 At Okinawa, Ryukyu Islands, *I-361* is sunk by a TBM Avenger from the escort carrier *Anzio*.

June 2–3 Over Japan, Rear Admiral Arthur W. Radford's Task Group 38.4 unleashes aircraft raids against Japanese airfields on Kyushu.

June 5 Near Okinawa, Ryukyu Islands, Admiral William F. Halsey's Third Fleet is again badly battered by a typhoon, which damages four battleships, eight carriers, seven cruisers, and numerous smaller vessels. The heavy cruiser *Pittsburgh* loses its entire bow and has to sail to Australia for repairs. Halsey and his subordinate, Vice

Admiral John S. McCain, are subsequently found negligent for taking inadequate precautions.

JUNE 6 At Annapolis, Maryland, the U.S. Naval Academy, Class of 1946, is graduated a year early to assist the war effort.

JUNE 7 Over Okinawa, the Japanese make their final massed kamikaze attack against the U.S. Navy, damaging two minesweepers and a landing craft.

JUNE 8 Over Japan, Rear Admiral Arthur W. Radford's Task Group Task 38.4 launches air raids against the Kanoya airfield on Kyushu.

On Okinawa, Ryukyu Islands, Hospital Apprentice First Class Fred F. Lester is critically wounded aiding an injured Marine. He refuses all medical assistance and tends the wounded Marine until he dies, winning a posthumous Congressional Medal of Honor.

JUNE 9–20 In the Sea of Japan, Commander Earl T. Hydeman commit his nine-submarine wolfpack, "Hydeman's Hellcats," against Japanese vessels. In three weeks they sink 54,578 tons of shipping at the cost of one submarine, the *Bonefish* under Lieutenant Commander Lawrence Edge. OPERATION BARNEY is consequently one of the most successful submarine patrols of the entire war.

JUNE 10 At Brunei Bay, Borneo, Admiral Forrest P. Royal's Task Group 78.1 lands part of the 9th Australian Division, under Major General W. T. Wooten. Rear Admiral Russell S. Berkey's Task Group 74.3 covers the invasion force with its guns and aircraft.

At Okinawa, Ryukyu Islands, kamikazes sink the destroyer *William D. Porter* under Commander C. M. Keyes and its crew is rescued by the landing craft *LCS (L)-122*.

JUNE 11 At Okinawa, landing craft *LCS (L)-122* is struck by a kamikaze and the commanding officer, Lieutenant Richard M. McCool, is severely wounded, but he refuses to quit his post and helps free men trapped in a burning compartment. He wins the Congressional Medal of Honor.

JUNE 16 At Patuxent River, Maryland, the new Naval Air Test Center is founded and commences operations.

At Okinawa, Ryukyu Islands, the destroyer *Twiggs* under Commander George Philip becomes the 12th destroyer lost in the campaign; all 22 of its officers are killed or wounded in action.

JUNE 21 At Okinawa, Ryukyu Islands, a final Japanese kamikaze attack succeeds in sinking a landing ship and also damages four vessels. The 89-day campaign cost the U.S. Navy 36 ships sunk and 243 damaged, along with over 4,900 sailors killed and 4,824 wounded. This is the most costly naval campaign in American history.

JUNE 27 East of Saipan, the *I-16* is sunk by a PV-1 Ventura from VPB-142.

JULY 1 At Balikpapan, Borneo, Rear Admiral Albert G. Noble's Task Group 78.2 lands the 7th Australian Division of Major General E. J. Milford ashore. This is also the last major amphibious operation of the Pacific War.

Vice Admiral John S. McCain's Task Force 38 departs Leyte Gulf for protracted operations in Japanese home waters.

JULY 2 At Kaiyho Island, Kuriles, the *Barb* bombards shore installations in the first American use of submarine-launched tactical rockets.

JULY 7 President Harry S. Truman boards the heavy cruiser *Augusta* on his voyage to Potsdam, Germany, to confer with Prime Minister Winston Churchill and Soviet premier Joseph Stalin.

July 10 Over Japan, Aircraft from Vice Admiral John S. McCain's Task Force 38 strike airfields in Tokyo. Resistance is light, as the Japanese are husbanding their strength for a final defense of the homelands.

July 14 On Honshu, Japan, Rear Admiral John F. Shafroth's Task Unit 34.81, including the battleships *Indiana*, *Massachusetts*, and *South Dakota*, and heavy cruisers *Chicago* and *Quincy*, begins the first bombardment of the Japanese homeland by shelling the Japan Iron Company at Kamaishi, Honshu.

July 14–15 Over Japan, Vice Admiral John S. McCain's Task Force 38 launches strikes against Japanese shipping near northern Honshu and Hokkaido. These targets are beyond B-29 range and require 1,391 sorties to complete; 46 vessels are claimed to have been sunk.

July 15 In Japan, Rear Admiral Oscar P. Badger's Task Unit 38.8.2, including the large and modern battleships *Iowa*, *Missouri*, and *Wisconsin*, bombard Muroran and Hokkaido and destroys the Nihon Steel Company by firing 860 shells.

July 16 Off Yokohama, Japan, the *I-13* is sunk by a TBM Avenger launched from the escort carrier *Anzio*.

July 17–18 Over Japan, Rear Admiral John S. McCain's Task Force 38 launches air strikes against around Tokyo and Yokosuka Naval Base.

Near Japan, Rear Admiral Oscar C. Badger's Task Unit 34.8.2, reinforced by the battleships *Alabama* and *North Carolina*, shells industrial targets at Hitachi, north of Tokyo.

July 24 Near Japan, Rear Admiral John S. McCain's Task Force 38 launches strikes against naval bases at Kure and Kobe, sinking the hybrid battleship-carrier *Hyuga*, the battleships *Haruna* and *Ise,* and heavy cruisers *Tone* and *Aoba*. This is one of the most devastating carrier raids of the entire war.

At Luzon, Philippines, the destroyer *Underhill* under Lieutenant Commander R. M. Newcomb is struck by kaitens (suicide submarines) released by the Japanese submarine *I-153*, and sinks, with a loss of 112 lives.

July 26 At Tinian, Marianas Islands, the cruiser *Indianapolis* delivers the components for the first atomic bomb, nicknamed "Fat Boy."

July 28 Near Okinawa, Ryukyu Islands, kamikazes sink the destroyer *Callaghan* under Commander C. M. Bertholf, with a loss of 120 crewmen; this is the 13th and last vessel lost.

July 29 Over Honshu, Japan, Rear Admiral John S. McCain's Task Force 38 launches air strikes against Maizuru Naval Base, sinking 3 small vessels and 12 merchant ships.

July 30 In the western Pacific, the heavy cruiser *Indianapolis* is sunk by the *I-58* under Lieutenant Commander Mochitsura Hashimoto. It goes under before distress signals can be transmitted; consequently, 800 survivors spend the next several days in shark-infested waters. Only 316 men survive the ordeal, and Captain Charles B. McVay III is court-martialed for failing to take adequate anti-submarine measures.

August 6 Over Hiroshima, Japan, Navy Captain William S. Parsons accompanies the *Enola Gay* mission and arms the Little Boy weapon in flight.

Near the Lombok Strait, the submarine *Bullhead* under Lieutenant Commander Edward R. Holt is lost in action, apparently to a Japanese aircraft.

AUGUST 9   Over Nagasaki, Japan, the B-29 named *Bock's Car* delivers a second atomic bomb, forcing the Japanese government to finally capitulate.

AUGUST 9–10   Over Japan, Admiral John S. McCain's Task Force 38 unleashes air strikes against airfields on northern Honshu, destroying 251 aircraft.

AUGUST 12   At Buckner Bay, Okinawa, a Japanese aerial torpedo strikes the battleship and Pearl Harbor survivor *Pennsylvania*; it is the final major American warship damaged in World War II.

AUGUST 13   Over Japan, Rear Admiral John S. McCain's Task Force 38 launches air strikes against airfields on the Kanto Plain, destroying 254 aircraft; a further 18 warplanes are claimed by Navy fighter craft.

AUGUST 14   In the wake of two atomic bombing at Hiroshima and Nagasaki, the government of Japan unconditionally surrenders to the Allies.

AUGUST 15   In Japan, Rear Admiral John S. McCain's Task Force 38 launches the last air strike of the war—although news of the Japanese surrender forces the second wave to abort and return.

Southeast of Shanghai, China, the submarine *Spikefish* sinks the *I-373*.

AUGUST 21   On the Chinese coast between Haimen and Shanghai, a junk carrying Japanese troops attacks another junk manned by Chinese guerrillas and American sailors under Lieutenant Livingston Swentzel, Jr. The allies slaughter their adversaries with machine guns, bazookas, and hand grenades; Swentzel wins a Congressional Medal of Honor. This is also the final surface engagement of the war.

AUGUST 25   Outside Tokyo Bay, Japan, Admiral William F. Halsey conducts the victorious Third Fleet into Sagomi Wan; this is an imposing armada that stretches for miles.

AUGUST 29   At Omari, Japan, landing craft arrive with U.S. troops, and the first prisoner of war camp is liberated.

SEPTEMBER 2   In Tokyo Bay, Japan, representatives of Japan and the victorious allies assemble on the battleship *Missouri* to sign surrender documents. Admiral Chester W. Nimitz pens the document for the United States. By this time, U.S. Navy consists of 1,300 combat vessels and 11,000 smaller vessels, manned by 3.3 million officers and enlisted men.

SEPTEMBER 10   The large carrier *Midway* becomes the first vessel of its class, but is commissioned too late to see wartime service.

SEPTEMBER 11   OPERATION MAGIC CARPET begins, whereby warships are rigged as temporary transports and return thousands of servicemen back to the United States.

SEPTEMBER 23   In Washington, D.C., the Navy Department creates a new Office of Naval Material, along with five new Deputy Chiefs of Naval Operations for Personnel, Administration, Naval Operations, Logistics, and Aviation.

SEPTEMBER 29   In Washington, D.C., the post of Commander in Chief, U.S. Fleet, is eliminated by executive order.

Japanese signatories arrive aboard the USS Missouri *in Tokyo Bay, to participate in World War II surrender ceremonies on September 2, 1945. (National Archives)*

OCTOBER 19 In Washington, D.C., the Senate Military Affairs Committee weighs legislation merging the War and Navy Departments into a single entity. This unification also threatens the Marine Corps, as they duplicate many tasks performed by the Army.

OCTOBER 27 In Washington, D.C., President Harry S. Truman presides over launching ceremonies for the new aircraft carrier *Franklin D. Roosevelt*.

NOVEMBER 5 A Ryan FR-1 Fireball, a propeller/jet hybrid fighter flown by Ensign Jake West, successfully lands on the escort carrier *Wake Island*; technically, is the first landing of a jet aircraft on a naval vessel.

NOVEMBER 15 Off the coast of Manchuria, and in a portent of things to come, a PBM Mariner flying is fired upon by Soviet fighters; no damage results.

DECEMBER 5 At Naval Air Station, Fort Lauderdale, Florida, a flight of five TBM Avengers lifts off on a routine training flight—then vanishes without a trace. A PBM Mariner sent after them also mysteriously disappears. These events add to the growing myth of the "Bermuda Triangle."

DECEMBER 15 In Washington, D.C., Fleet Admiral Chester W. Nimitz is appointed the 10th Chief of Naval Operations.

1946

January 1 The U.S. Coast Guard, which has functioned as part of the Navy since 1941, reverts back to control of the Treasury Department.

March 1–22 In the Arctic Circle, OPERATION FROSTBITE unfolds as the carrier *Midway* steams off the Davis Strait, Greenland, to conduct cold-weather operational testing.

April 5–14 In the eastern Mediterranean, the battleship *Missouri* makes goodwill tours of Istanbul, Turkey, and Athens, Greece, as a show of force on behalf of American interests. It also returns the remains of the Turkish ambassador to the U.S., who died in 1944.

June 13 The Navy Flight Demonstration Team, famously known as the Blue Angels, performs for the first time.

July 1 In the Marshall Islands, OPERATION CROSSROADS unfolds as an atomic device is detonated over an anchored armada, centered upon the old battleship *Nevada*.

July 21 Near Camp Henry, Virginia, a jet-powered McDonnell FD-1 Phantom touches down on the flight deck of the carrier *Franklin D. Roosevelt*; this is the first pure jet aircraft to land on a naval vessel.

July 25 In the Marshall Islands, OPERATION CROSSROADS continues with Test Baker, whereby an underwater nuclear device is detonated that sinks or damages 75 test vessels.

August 8–October 4 In the Mediterranean, the carrier *Franklin D. Roosevelt* arrives to join the battleship *Missouri* in raising the American profile there in a show of support of the Greek government, which is battling a Communist insurgency.

August 13 Because the U.S. Naval Academy is deemed incapable of providing the sheer number of qualified officers for a true, global navy, Rear Admiral James L. Holloway formats a plan to have a regular influx of officers from NROTC programs with pay; Congress approves the plan, and President Harry S. Truman signs it.

August 21 In Washington, D.C., the Navy Department authorizes the Office of Naval Research to conduct high-end scientific research.

September 29 At Columbus, Ohio, the P2V Neptune *Truculent Turtle* under Commander Thomas Davis completes a 1,235.6 mile, non-stop flight from Perth, Australia. Total flying time is 55 hours and 17 minutes.

October 1 In light of the strategic significance of the Mediterranean to Western security in the rapidly unfolding Cold War, the U.S. Naval Forces, Mediterranean Command, is created. It becomes better known as the Sixth Fleet in 1950.

At Point Mugu, California, the Navy establishes the Naval Air Missile Test Center to develop and acquire new military technology along these lines.

December 6 Attack Squadron 19A is the first Navy formation to operate new Douglas AD Skyraiders, some of the finest propeller-driven carrier aircraft ever flown.

1947

January 1 The post of Commander in Chief, Pacific Command, passes to Admiral John H. Towers, who is also the Navy's third aviator. He is the first naval aviator so honored.

January 11 The prototype McDonnell XF2H-1 Banshee flies for the first time; this twin-engine jet fighter serves with distinction throughout the Korean War.

January 29 Off the coast of Antarctica, Rear Admiral Richard E. Byrd lifts off the carrier *Philippine Sea* with six R-4D transports to take command of OPERATION HIGHJUMP, an extensive mapping expedition.

March 15 Long-standing racial barriers begin to fall as Ensign John W. Lee is the first African American ensign commissioned in the regular naval service. He had previously served with the Naval Reserve.

May 1 At Point Mugu, California, the submarine *Cusk* launches a Loon rocket (a navalized version of the infamous German V-1), becoming the first American submersible to do so.

September 6 A German V-2 ballistic missile is successfully launched for the first time at sea from the deck of the carrier *Midway*.

September 18 In Washington, D.C., the army, air force, and navy departments are unified into a single Department of Defense through terms of the National Security Act of 1947.

September 23 In Washington, D.C., James Forrestal, a former secretary of the Navy, is appointed the first Secretary of Defense.

November 21 The Grumman XF9F Panther jet prototype flies for the first time; it performs yeoman work during the Korean War.

1948

March 11 At Key West, Florida, Secretary of Defense James Forrestal conducts a spell of interservice diplomacy by consulting with the Joint Chiefs of Staff, including Navy and Air Force representatives. Hereafter, the Navy grants the Air Force a monopoly on strategic bombing, while the Air Force no longer opposes construction of large, flush-deck aircraft carriers.

April 1 At Naval Air Station, Lakehurst, New Jersey, the Navy activates the Helicopter Utility Squadron 1 (HU-1) as the first in the service.

April 30 The large Martin XP5M Marlin flying-boat prototype flies for the first time; it serves with distinction up through the Vietnam War.

May 6 The light carrier *Saipan* hosts Fighter Squadron 17A, the Navy's first operational all-jet fighter squadron, equipped with McDonnell FH-1 Phantoms.

JUNE 12 In Washington, D.C., the new Women's Armed Services Integrated Act allows women to serve in the regular Navy and Marine Corps for the first time, not simply the reserves.

AUGUST 20 At Newport, Rhode Island, Defense Secretary James Forrestal holds a second gathering of the Joint Chiefs of Staff at the Naval War College, whereby the Air Force accepts temporary control of all atomic weapons.

SEPTEMBER 9 The Navy founds Composite Squadron (VC) 5 in an attempt to outfit carrier aircraft with strategic capabilities. This entails converting P2V Neptunes for carrying nuclear weapons and developing the requisite tactics and procedures.

OCTOBER 1 The Navy commissions the *Norton Sound*, a former seaplane tender converted into its first guided-missile test ship.

NOVEMBER 9 During the Berlin Airlift, Navy transport squadrons VR-6 and VR-8 commence regular flights in and out of that beleaguered city; by the time operations cease on July 31, 1949, they will have logged 45,990 flight hours while carrying 129,989 tons of cargo.

NOVEMBER 16 At the Boston Navy Yard, Massachusetts, the new cruiser *Des Moines* is commissioned and features fully automatic 8-inch cannon.

1949

APRIL 4 In light of rising tensions with the Soviet Union and its Eastern European allies, the United States joins the North Atlantic Treaty Organization (NATO), the first peace-time military alliance it has ever belonged to.

APRIL 23 In Washington, D.C., a minor furor erupts when Secretary of Defense Louis Johnson cancels the supercarrier *United States*—without informing the Navy Department; Chief of Naval Operations Admiral Louis E. Denfield resigns in consequence.

JUNE 3 At Annapolis, Maryland, Ensign Wesley A. Brown becomes the first African American to graduate from the U.S. Naval Academy.

AUGUST 1 The Navy Department establishes the Seventh Task Fleet to serve as its forward deployed force in the Western Pacific.

AUGUST 9 Over Walterboto, South Carolina, Lieutenant J. L. Fruin is forced to eject from his F2H Banshee fighter, marking the first time an American ejection seat is used in an emergency situation.

AUGUST 26 Off the coast of Norway, the submarine *Cochino* sinks, following an internal battery explosion, while conducting top-secret surveillance operations. Its crew is rescued by the submarine *Tusk*.

OCTOBER 1 To facilitate the shipping of troops abroad, the army and navy transportation services unite to form the new Military Sea Transport Services; it will be controlled by the Secretary of the Navy.

OCTOBER 5–17 In Washington, D.C., Congressman Carl Vinson opens hearings of the House Naval Affairs Committee, whereby Chief of Naval Operations

Keel plate laid for USS United States *on April 18, 1949. (U.S. Navy)*

Admiral Louis E. Denfield complains that the Navy is being neglected and cites the recent cancellation of the supercarrier *United States*. The following spring, a committee issues a report favorable to the Navy. Denfield's forceful presentation is considered the beginning of the "Revolt of the Admirals."

NOVEMBER 1 In Washington, D.C., the Secretary of the Navy relieves Admiral Louis E. Denfield as Chief of Naval Operations over his charged testimony before Congress. President Harry S. Truman approves of the decision, and appoints Admiral Forrest P. Sherman to succeed him.

1950

JANUARY 17 Near Hampton Grounds, Virginia, the battleship *Missouri* runs aground, resulting in a court-martial for all its senior officers.

FEBRUARY 12 In the Mediterranean, U.S. Naval forces operating there receive the new designation of Sixth Fleet. The Seventh Task Fleet in the Pacific also receives the designation Seventh Fleet.

MARCH 16 At Pearl Harbor, the submarine *Pickerel* surfaces, after completing a record 5,195-nautical-mile voyage from Hong Kong while submerged and relying solely on its snorkel.

April 8 Over the Baltic Sea, a Navy PB4Y Privateer is shot down by Soviet fighters; the 10-man crew is presumed killed in action.

April 21 The North American AJ-1 Savage, the first Navy bomber expressly designed to carry nuclear weapons, is successfully launched from the flight deck of the carrier *Coral Sea*.

June 25 On this fateful day, North Korean forces roll across the Demilitarized Zone into South Korea, triggering the first military crisis of the Cold War.

June 26 At Inchon, South Korea, the destroyers *De Haven* and *Mansfield* evacuate 700 Americans and foreign nationals from danger.

June 27 In Washington, D.C., President Harry S. Truman authorizes American air and naval forces to support South Korea during the Communist attack.

June 29 Offshore at Okkye, South Korea, the light cruiser *Juneau* under Captain Jesse D. Sowell fires the first fire-support mission of the war by striking enemy troop concentrations.

July 1 In Japan, ships of the Military Sea Transport Service begin transferring Army troops and their equipment to Pusan, South Korea.

July 2 At Chumunjin, North Korea, four torpedo boats attack the cruisers *Juneau* and HMS *Jamaica* and the frigate *Black Swan*; three of the attackers are quickly sunk by naval gunfire. This is also the only purely naval engagement of the war.

July 3–4 Aircraft from Vice Admiral Arthur D. Struble's Task Force 77, including the carriers *Valley Forge* and HMS *Triumph*, bombard Communist positions in Pyongyang, North Korea, in the first naval airstrikes of the war. F9F Panthers from *Valley Forge* also score the first jet victories by downing two Yak-9 fighters.

July 4 In Washington, D.C., President Harry S. Truman places the North Korean coast under a naval blockade.

July 9 Commander Michael J. Luosey is appointed commander of the South Korean Navy.

July 11 At Rashin, North Korea, a party of 10 marines and sailors under Commander W. B. Porter leaves the cruiser *Juneau* and successfully destroys a railroad tunnel.

July 18 The oil refinery at Wonsan, North Korea, is destroyed by aircraft from the carrier *Valley Forge*.

July 18–19 At Pohang, South Korea, Rear Admiral James H. Doyle's Amphibious Group One puts the Army's 1st Cavalry Division ashore, which helps establish defensive lines along the port of Pusan.

July 19 Over Kangmyong-ni, North Korea, a Navy AD Skyraider of VA-55 is shot down during a strafing attack; Ensign Donald E. Stevens becomes the first naval aviator killed in this war.

July 25 Off the coast of North Korea, Task Force 96.5 arises for the purpose of blockading the east coast of the peninsula. The west coast is covered by the British Commonwealth force under Rear Admiral William G. Andrewes.

Responding to an urgent request from Lieutenant General Walton H. Walker, aircraft from the carrier *Valley Forge* begin lending tactical air support for Army troops holding the vital Pusan perimeter.

In San Francisco, California, the hospital ship *Benevolence* sinks after colliding with the freighter *Mary Luckenbach*; 13 crew members die.

AUGUST 15–16 Along Korea's eastern coast, an Underwater Demolition Team (UTD) from the high-speed transport *Bass* makes several nighttime raids ashore, destroying railroad bridges and tunnels.

AUGUST 16 At Yonghae, South Korea, the 3rd Division, Republic of Korea (ROK) is evacuated by the vessels of Task Force 96.51, covered by guns of the cruiser *Helena*.

AUGUST 21 Over Pyongyang, North Korea, warplanes from the carriers *Valley Forge* and *Philippine Sea* complete 202 sorties, setting a new, one-day operational record.

SEPTEMBER 12 At Korea, blockading forces are reorganized into Task Force 95, although responsibility for the west coast remains in the hands of Commonwealth vessels.

SEPTEMBER 14 At Samchok, South Korea, the newly arrived battleship *Missouri* destroys a bridge with its 16-inch projectiles.

SEPTEMBER 15 At Inchon, South Korea, Admiral James H. Doyle's Amphibious Group One successfully lands Major General Edward M. Almond's X Corps ashore, taking North Korean defenders completely by surprise. This is one of the greatest amphibious assaults of military history.

SEPTEMBER 18 At Samchok, South Korea, the battleship *Missouri*, cruiser *Helena,* and four destroyers cover the evacuation of 725 South Korean troops.

SEPTEMBER 25–29 Near Chuksan, North Korea, the minesweeper *Magpie* strikes a

Landing Ship Tanks (LSTs) of the Military Sea Transportation Service (MSTS) deploy the 31st Infantry Regiment at Inchon Harbor, Korea, on September 18, 1950. The MSTS was a U.S. unified logistics organization established to handle ocean transportation of all military services. (National Archives)

mine and sinks, becoming the first U.S. Navy vessel lost in this conflict. The destroyers *Brush* and *Mansfield* are also heavily damaged.

OCTOBER 9 In Korea, the carrier *Leyte* deploys after transferring from the Atlantic Fleet.

OCTOBER 12–25 The North Korean harbor of Wonsan is cleared by the minesweepers in anticipation of a landing there by the Army X Corps; over 3,000 contact and magnetic mines are present, and the operation concludes five days behind schedule. The minesweepers *Pirate* and *Pledge* also sink after striking mines.

NOVEMBER 9 An F9F Panther, flown by Lieutenant Commander W. T. Amen (from the carrier *Philippine Sea*), is the first Naval aviator to shoot down a vaunted Soviet-built MiG-15 jet fighter.

DECEMBER 4 Over Hagaru-Ri, North Korea, an F4U Corsair flown by Ensign Jesse L. Brown, the Navy's first African American pilot, is shot down. His wingman, Lieutenant Thomas J. Hudner, crash-lands nearby but cannot extricate him from his cockpit. Brown dies before he can be rescued, winning a posthumous Flying Cross. Hudner receives a Congressional Medal of Honor.

DECEMBER 5 At Chinampo on the west coast of North Korea, Navy and Commonwealth vessels evacuate 7,700 U.S. and South Korean forces in the face of a massive Chinese offensive.

DECEMBER 7 Inchon, South Korea, is evacuated by U.S. naval forces who remove 32,400 troops and 57,700 tons of supplies by January 5, 1951.

DECEMBER 10–24 At Hungnam, North Korea, Rear Admiral James H. Doyle's Task Force 90 performs an efficient evacuation of 105,000 U.S. and South Korean troops, 91,000 civilians, and 350,000 tons of supplies and equipment in the face of a surging Chinese offensive.

DECEMBER 18 Over Korea, Patrol Squadron VP-892 becomes the first Naval Air Reserve unit called into combat operations.

1951

JANUARY 29 Vice Admiral Arthur D. Struble's Task Force 77 is ordered to commence air strikes against the rail system and bridge network along the east coast of North Korea; Struble protests the mission, feeling his aircraft were better employed for close support.

FEBRUARY 2 At Wonsan, North Korea, the minesweeper *Partridge* under Lieutenant B. M. Clark strikes a mine and sinks, with a loss of eight dead and six wounded; this is the last such vessel lost in the war.

FEBRUARY 5–8 Five AJ Savages of VC-5 fly from Norfolk, Virginia, nonstop to Port Lyautey, French Morocco. These are the Navy's first aircraft specifically designed to deliver nuclear weapons.

FEBRUARY 16 At Wonsan, North Korea, U.S. naval forces commence an 861-day naval siege of that major port through blockades and occasional shelling of troops ashore. The harbor also serves as a haven for pilots to ditch their damaged aircraft and be quickly rescued by waiting helicopters.

March 14–19 Off North Korea, the battleship *Missouri* employs highly accurate cannon fire to destroy eight railroad and seven highway bridges at Kyojo Wan, Songjin, Chaho, and Wonsan.

March 29 On the carrier *Boxer*, the Carrier Air Group 101 becomes the first reserve formation of its kind committed to combat operations in the war.

April 1 F9F Panther jets from VF-191 (*Princeton*) attack and destroy the bridge at Songjin, North Korea. This is the first bombing raid by navy jets in the war, and this particular squadron is composed largely of personnel from the Blue Angels Flight Demonstration Team.

April 5 In South Korea, Hospital Corpsman Richard D. DeWert dashes forward under enemy fire four times to rescue injured marines; he is fatally wounded on his fourth attempt and receives a posthumous Medal of Honor.

April 7 At Chongjin on the east coast of North Korea, Royal Marine Commandoes go ashore and destroy a railroad, covered by the cruiser *St. Paul* and two destroyers.

April 26 The North Korean port of Hungnam is placed under siege by U.S. naval forces.

May 1 Over North Korea, eight AD Skyraiders from Attack Squadron (VA) 195 and Composite Squadron (VC) 35 attack the Hwachon Dam with torpedoes, completely flooding the Han and Pukhan River Valleys.

May 20 At Wonsan, Korea, land batteries bracket the destroyer *Brinkley Bass*, then score a direct hit, killing one sailor and wounding nine.

May 21 The North Korean coastal town of Kangsong is shelled by the battleship *New Jersey*, which had recently reached the theater of operations.

June 5–September 20 Operation Strangle commences as warplanes of Task Force 77, the 1st Marine Air Wing, and the Fifth Air Force begin an aerial interdiction campaign against Communist supply lines. It concludes four months later, having basically failed in its objectives.

June 12 Near Hungnam, North Korea, the destroyer *Walke* strikes a mine, losing 26 sailors dead and 35 wounded.

June 14 At Songjin, North Korea, land batteries strike the destroyer minesweeper *Thompson* 14 times, killing three sailors and wounding four.

June 18 In the Mediterranean, Admiral Robert B. Carney gains appointment as Commander, Allied Command Southern Europe.

July 3 Over North Korea, Lieutenant John K. Koelsch, having volunteered to look for a Marine pilot downed in rough terrain, has his HO3S helicopter shot down, and he is captured. He steadfastly refuses to aid his captors and dies in captivity, winning a posthumous Congressional Medal of Honor.

July 10 At Kaesong, North Korea, Vice Admiral C. Turner Joy, Commander, U.S. Naval Force, Far East, functions as the principal UN negotiator. He is soon joined by Rear Admiral Arleigh A. Burke, Commander, Cruiser Division 5.

July 28 In the Haeju-Man channel, South Korea, the cruiser *Los Angeles* suddenly slips in and demolishes several

North Korean land batteries, demonstrating UN control of the Ongjin Peninsula.

AUGUST 11   In North Korea, the minesweepers *Dextrous* and *Redstart* are shelled by shore batteries in the vicinity of Hodo-pando; *Dextrous* takes two direct hits that kill one sailor and wound three.

AUGUST 21   The Navy signs a $29 million contract with the Electric Boat Company of Groton, Connecticut, to construct the *Nautilus*, the world's first nuclear-powered submarine.

AUGUST 25   Over Rashin, North Korea, Air Force B-29 bombers are escorted by F9F Panther and F2H Banshee jets from the carrier *Essex*. Their target is the rail center at Rashin, a few miles south of the Soviet border.

SEPTEMBER 7   The missile test ship *Norton Sound* successfully test-fires a Terrier surface-to-air missile, downing an F6F drone.

OCTOBER 3   At Naval Air Station, Key West, Florida, the Navy commissions HS-1, the world's first helicopter anti-submarine squadron. This is the debut of rotary-wing aircraft in the field of ASW.

OCTOBER 29   At Kapsan, North Korea, AD Skyraiders from the carrier *Essex* attack local Communist Party headquarters during a meeting, killing an estimated 500 members. They had been tipped off by good military intelligence.

NOVEMBER 6   In the Sea of Japan off the coast of Siberia, Soviet warplanes shoot down a P2V Neptune patrol plane over international waters; the crew of 10 is killed.

NOVEMBER 21   Near Kojo, North Korea, the cruiser *Los Angeles* departs Task Force 77 to shell Communist forces attempting to cut off the ROK I Corps; the enemy forces are driven back.

1952

JANUARY 11   Projects Package and Derail commence, as coastal rail lines of North Korea become the object of a bombing and shelling campaign by warships of Task Force 95 and warplanes of Task Force 77.

JANUARY 29   Off the west coast of South Korea, Navy LSTs of Task Force 90 complete the evacuation of 20,000 civilians from offshore islands threatened by Communist attack.

JANUARY 30   In Western Europe, Vice Admiral Lynde D. McCormick gains appointment as the first Supreme Allied Commander, Atlantic, within the NATO alliance.

FEBRUARY 19   At Songjin, North Korea, the destroyer *Shelton*, the New Zealand frigate *Taupo*, and the minesweeper *Endicott* repel an attack by 45 North Korean sampans, crammed with troops, against the islands of Kil-chu and Myongchon.

APRIL 21   Near Kojo, North Korea, the cruiser *St. Paul* experiences a turret explosion that kills 30 men.

APRIL 26   In the North Atlantic, the destroyer *Hobson* collides with the carrier *Wasp* during naval exercises and is cut clean in half; 176 lives are lost.

APRIL 28   In Washington, D.C., the Navy Department approves a plan to install

British-style steam-launch catapults on all U.S. Navy aircraft carriers.

MAY 8   To improve gunner proficiency, the Navy establishes the Fleet Air Gunnery Unit for Pacific Fleet squadrons.

JUNE 14   At Groton, Connecticut, the keel of the *Nautilus*, the world's first nuclear-powered submarines, is laid. The Navy's atomic age comes to pass.

JUNE 23–25   Hydroelectric power plants at Suiho, Chosen, Fusen, and Kyosen, North Korea, are struck by 70 AD Skyraiders and F9F Panthers from the carriers *Boxer*, *Philippine Sea*, and *Princeton*. This is part of a two-day aerial offensive to neutralize North Korean electrical capacities.

JULY 1   In light of new technologies pouring into fleet usage, the Navy founds the Naval Guided Missile School at Dam Neck, Virginia, and the Naval Air Guided Missile School (Advanced) at Naval Air Center Station, Jacksonville, Florida.

JULY 11–12   The North Korean capital of Pyongyang is struck by 91 warplanes launched from the carriers *Bon Homme Richard* and *Princeton*, which bomb military targets in the vicinity.

Over North Korea, warplanes from Task Force 77 destroy the lead zinc mill at Sindok and the magnesite plant at Kilchu, two of the largest industrial facilities in that country.

JULY 14   At Newport News, Virginia, the keel is laid to the new supercarrier *Forrestal*.

AUGUST 6   Off the Korean coast, the carrier *Boxer* experiences a hangar fire that kills eight sailors; however, the vessel remains in the combat zone.

AUGUST 13   In South Korea, Hospital Corpsman John E. Kilmer treats several wounded marines while under enemy fire, until he is mortally wounded while shielding an injured soldier with his own body. He receives a posthumous Congressional Medal of Honor.

AUGUST 28   Over Hungham, North Korea, a F6F drone controlled by Guided Missile Unit 90 is used to strike a railroad bridge.

AUGUST 29   Pyongyang, North Korea, is struck by 1,000 UN aircraft, including many launched from the carriers *Boxer* and *Essex*. This is also the largest air raid of the war to date.

AUGUST 30   Near Hungham, North Korea, the ocean tug *Sarsi* strikes a mine and sinks, becoming the final U.S. Navy vessel lost in this war.

SEPTEMBER 1   Over North Korea, the largest carrier raid of the war transpires, as 144 warplanes launched from Task Force 77, the carriers *Boxer*, *Essex*, and *Princeton*, devastate the oil refinery at Aoji, eight miles from the Soviet border.

In the North Atlantic, OPERATION MAINBRACE unfolds as U.S. Navy forces join several European navies in NATO's first major naval exercise.

SEPTEMBER 3   At Inyokern, California, the first firing of a heat-seeking Sidewinder air-to-air missile is orchestrated by the Naval Ordnance Test Center.

SEPTEMBER 5   In South Korea, Navy Corpsman Third Class Edward C. Benford is attending several wounded marines when he is attacked by enemy soldiers. Benford picks up several grenades and charges the enemy troops, killing them and himself; he wins a posthumous Congressional Medal of Honor.

September 16 At Wonsan, North Korea, the destroyer *Barton* strikes a mine that kills five sailors.

October 8 Over North Korea, 12 F2H Banshee jets from the carrier *Kearsarge* escort Air Force B-29s, as they flatten the rail center at Kowon. This is the second and final time Navy jets accompany the heavy bombers.

October 9–July 1953 Vice Admiral J. J. Clark of the Seventh Fleet orders a battlefront bombing campaign against Communist supply facilities placed beyond UN artillery range. These are dubbed "Cherokee raids" in honor of the admiral's Indian ancestry.

October 28 The Douglas XA3D-1 Skywarrior jet-bomber prototype performs its maiden flight; it soon enters service as the largest aircraft ever committed to carrier operations.

November 1 Near Point Mugu, California, the missile ship *Norton Sound* fires an experimental Regulus I ballistic missile for the first time.

November 18 Around 100 miles southwest of Vladivostok, Soviet Union, three F9F Panthers from the carrier *Oriskany* engage seven MiG-15 fighters which are approaching the fleet; two MiGs are shot down.

Near Panama City, Florida, Navy development squadron VX-1 demonstrates the viability of using helicopters for mine sweeping operations with the so-called HRP-1 "Flying Banana."

December 4 The Grumman XS2F-1 Tracker prototype flies for the first time; this is the first aircraft specifically designed to perform antisubmarine warfare (ASW).

1953

January 18 In the Straits of Taiwan, antiaircraft fire shoots down a Navy P2V Neptune as it passes near a Communist-controlled island. Eleven crewmen survive the crash and are rescued by a Coast Guard PBM Mariner, which also crashes in heavy seas. The destroyer *Halsey Powell* ends up rescuing 10 survivors; 11 airmen are killed.

January 22 The carrier *Antietam* commences testing of its new angled flight deck with six types of aircraft under various conditions. Angled decks become standard equipment on all future carriers.

January 28 Near Cape Cod, Massachusetts, the former battleship *Mississippi* test-launches the first Terrier surface-to-air missile while at sea.

February 9–10 Warplanes launched from Task Force 77 carriers work over transportation lines and supply depots from Wonsan to Chongjin, North Korea.

February 13 At Point Mugu, California, the new Sparrow air-to-air missile makes its first full guidance flight test.

March 1–5 Carriers of Task Force 77 launch air strikes that badly damage the hydroelectric plant at Chosen, North Korea, then attack again.

March 6 The World War II-vintage submarine *Tunny* is recommissioned as the Navy's first submersible capable of launching Regulus I missiles while surfaced.

MARCH 13 Near Chongjin, North Korea, aircraft from Task Force 77 devastate a large part of the industrial sector there.

MARCH 19 Over Chongjin, North Korea, warplanes launched from Task Force 77 carriers bombard industrial targets.

MARCH 26 In South Korea, Navy Corpsman Francis C. Hammond bravely assists wounded marines under fire despite serious wounds. He is killed supervising the evacuation of wounded soldiers, winning a posthumous Congressional Medal of Honor.

MARCH 27 In South Korea, Navy Corpsman Third Class William R. Charette gives up his flak vest to a wounded marine, shields another from enemy fire with his own body, and suffers serious wounds in the course of assisting many wounded soldiers; he receives a Congressional Medal of Honor.

JUNE 11 The U.S. Navy evacuates 19,245 Korean civilians from islands on the western side of the peninsula and north of the 38th Parallel prior to the conclusion of truce talks.

JUNE 15 Aircraft from the carrier *Princeton* launch 184 sorties in a single day, which is a record for this war.

JULY 16 Four Navy F4U-5N radar-equipped nightfighters operating with the Fifth Air Force near Seoul, South Korea, shoot down the last of five North Korea Po-2 biplane night raiders, or "Bedcheck Charlies." In this manner Lieutenant Guy P. Bordelon becomes the only Navy ace of the Korean War and its only nightfighter ace ever.

JULY 27 At Panmunjon, North Korea, a cease-fire agreement between UN and Communist forces suspends hostilities in Korea.

AUGUST 12 The experimental missile ship *Mississippi* shoots down a F6F-5K drone with a Terrier surface-to-air missile. This is the first successful interception by a fully guided missile at sea.

SEPTEMBER 2 In Washington, D.C., the Navy Department declares that it will retrofit all *Midway*-class aircraft carriers with new steam catapults and angled flight decks.

OCTOBER 3 Over Muroc, California, a Douglas F4D Skyray piloted by Lieutenant Commander James F. Verdin establishes a new world speed record of 752.943 miles per hour.

OCTOBER 16 In Boston, Massachusetts, the carrier *Leyte* is wracked by an explosion and fire that kills 37 sailors.

1954

JANUARY 4 The antisubmarine warfare (ASW) carrier *Leyte* begins operations; this is a new concept involving carriers, destroyers, and other submarines to counter the Soviet underwater menace.

APRIL 1 Off the California coast, the carrier *Hancock* launches a S2F Tracker aircraft in the first successful test of the new C-11 steam catapult. This becomes standard equipment on all future carriers.

MAY 25 A ZPG-2 airship commanded by Commander Marion H. Eppes sets a record flight for this type of craft by remaining aloft for eight days and eight hours.

MAY 26   At Newport, Rhode Island, 103 sailors die and 201 are injured when the carrier *Bennington* is wracked by an explosion and fires.

MAY 27   In Washington, D.C., the Chief of Naval Operations supports a new program to retrofit aging *Essex*-class carriers with angled flight decks, enclosed hurricane bows, and other modern features.

JUNE 1   The carrier *Hancock* successfully tests its new steam catapult system by sending a S2F Tracker aloft; the vessel makes 254 other launches as part of the test program.

JUNE 22   The Douglas XA4D-1 Skyhawk prototype, a light jet attack craft, performs its maiden flight; it performs capably through the Vietnam War.

JULY 26   Off Hainan Island, South China Sea, two AD Skyraiders area attacked by a pair of Chinese LA-7 fighters; both of the intruders are shot down. They Navy planes are searching for survivors of an Air Cathay flight that had been shot down on July 24.

AUGUST 11   In Washington, D.C., President Dwight D. Eisenhower, reacting to comments made by Chinese Foreign Minister Chou En-lai that Taiwan must be liberated, declares that they will first have to "run over the Seventh Fleet."

AUGUST 16–MAY 18, 1955   In French Indochina (Vietnam), OPERATION PASSAGE TO FREEDOM commences as U.S. Navy vessels under Rear Admiral Lorenzo Sabin aid in the evacuation of 293,000 civilians and 17,846 military personnel escaping persecution from the Communist-controlled north.

SEPTEMBER 4   In international airspace over Siberia, Soviet MiGs shoot down a Navy P2V reconnaissance aircraft from VP-19; 9 of 10 crewmen are rescued by a Coast Guard cutter.

SEPTEMBER 13   In a show of solidarity with Taiwan, President Dwight D. Eisenhower orders the Seventh Fleet to provide logistical support to Nationalist Chinese units on the coastal island of Quemoy and Matsu.

SEPTEMBER 30   At Groton, Connecticut, the revolutionary submarine *Nautilus* is commissioned; this is the world's first atomic-powered submersible.

1955

JANUARY 17   Near Connecticut, Commander Dennis Wilkinson radios that the submarine *Nautilus* is "underway on nuclear power." This feat initiates a new era in submarine propulsion, as such craft no longer have to operate at the surface for extended periods, making them far less vulnerable to attack from aircraft and surface vessels.

FEBRUARY 1   The Navy establishes Task Force 43 under Rear Admiral George Dufek for the purpose of performing OPERATION DEEP FREEZE, the construction of several Antarctic bases for the International Geophysical Year (1957–1958).

FEBRUARY 6–13   Off the coast of China, Vice Admiral A. M. Pride's Seventh Fleet evacuates 29,000 Nationalist Chinese from the Tachen Islands. They are covered by warplanes from the carriers *Essex*, *Kearsarge*, *Midway*, *Wasp*, and *Yorktown*.

March 25 The Chance Vought XF8U-1 Crusader jet fighter prototype flies for the first time; this exceptional dogfighter performs well throughout the Vietnam War.

May 12 The Navy Department announces that all new naval aircraft will be equipped for inflight refueling, which is now a standard operational procedure.

June 1 At Iwakuni, Japan, the Navy commissions its first electronic countermeasures squadron, VQ-1, which is equipped with large and complex P4M Mercator aircraft.

June 22 Over the Bering Sea, Soviet MiGs shoot down a Navy P2V reconnaissance aircraft of VP-9 over international waters; it crash-lands on St. Lawrence Island without loss of life.

August 17 In Washington, D.C., famed destroyerman Admiral Arleigh Burke gains appointment as the 15th Chief of Naval Operations.

August 22–24 The carrier *Bennington* serves as a test bed for the new mirror landing system which replaces the prevailing system of paddle-waving landing officers. Testing is in the hands of Experimental Squadron (VX) 3.

September 13 In Washington, D.C., President Dwight D. Eisenhower orders the Department of Defense to develop a strategic ballistic missile with a range of 1,500 miles and the ability to be launched from either land or sea.

October 1 At Norfolk, Virginia, the new "supercarrier" *Forrestal*, weighing 59,630 tons, is commissioned. It is also the first carrier vessel especially designed to operate jet aircraft.

November 1 At Philadelphia, Pennsylvania, the guided missile cruiser *Boston* becomes the first Navy vessel of its kind, being capable of firing new Terrier surface-to-air missiles.

Burke, Arleigh A. (1901–1991)

Arleigh Albert Burke was born in Boulder, Colorado, on October 19, 1901, and he graduated from the U.S. Naval Academy in 1919. By 1937 Burke was executive officer onboard the destroyer *Craven* and commenced his long association with "Tin Cans." Two years later he commanded the *Mugford*, trained it to a razor's edge, and won the coveted Destroyer Gunnery Trophy for 1939. In March 1943 he took charge of the destroyer *Waller*, sank a Japanese destroyer in the Solomon Islands, then assumed control of Destroyer Squadron 23. At the Battles of Empress Augusta Bay and Cape St. George, his well-aimed torpedoes sank several more Japanese destroyers without loss, and Admiral William F. Halsey christened him "Thirty-One Knot Burke" on account of his high-speed tactics. After the war he served as director of research at the Bureau of Ordnance in Washington, D.C.

The postwar years were a period of fiscal entrenchment for the military, and Burke's vocal opposition to the Air Force B-36 bomber caused President Harry S. Truman to delete his name from the list of potential flag officers. In 1955 President Dwight D. Eisenhower nonetheless appointed him the youngest Chief of Naval Operations at age 53. Here Burke helped the Navy redefine itself by promoting nuclear-powered submarines, the Polaris ballistic missile, and the angle-deck *Forrestal*-class carriers. His success may be gauged by the fact that he served three terms, longer than another other incumbent. Burke retired in 1961 and died in Washington, D.C., on January 1, 1991, one of the Navy's most far-sighted and accomplished senior officers.

NOVEMBER 8 Development of the Jupiter medium-range ballistic missile is assigned to the new Joint Army-Navy Missile Committee.

NOVEMBER 17 In Washington, D.C., the Secretary of the Navy directs Rear Admiral William F. Raborn to take charge of the Special Projects Office, to develop a shipboard launching system for ballistic missiles.

NOVEMBER 28 In Washington, D.C., the Secretary of the Navy selects 1965 as the target date for completion of a solid-fuel ballistic missile capable of being fired by submarines.

1956

JANUARY 10 At New London, Connecticut, the Navy establishes its first nuclear power school.

JANUARY 25 The nuclear-powered submarine *Swordfish* is the first such vessel constructed entirely at a Navy shipyard.

MARCH 12 F7U Cutlasses of Attack Squadron 83 deploy to the Mediterranean onboard the carrier *Intrepid*; they are the first Navy squadron equipped with Sparrow air-to-air missiles.

JULY 20 The Navy commissions the *Thetis Bay*, the first amphibious assault vessel designed to carry and land 2,000 marines under combat conditions.

AUGUST 21 Over China Lake, California, an F8U Crusader flown by Commander Robert W. Windsor establishes a new world's speed record of 1,015.428 miles per hour.

AUGUST 22 Off the Chinese coast, a Navy P4M Mercator reconnaissance aircraft is shot down over international waters while conducting a routine patrol; the 16 crew members all perish.

SEPTEMBER 21 Off eastern Long Island, New York, an F11F-1 Tiger jet conducts firing tests at high altitude, dives to a lower altitude, and is struck by the projectiles previously fired—in effect, shooting itself down! The pilot survives the crash.

OCTOBER 11 Over the Atlantic, an R6D Skymaster transport of VR-6 crashes, killing 50 passengers and crew.

OCTOBER 29–NOVEMBER 3 As war breaks out in the Middle East, ships of the Sixth Fleet begin evacuating nearly 5,000 American citizens from Egypt, Israel, and Syria.

OCTOBER 31 At Antarctica, an R4D transport lands at the South Pole for the first time since Royal Navy Captain Robert F. Scott in 1912. The crew consists of Rear Admiral G. J. Dufek and seven officers.

DECEMBER 3 In Washington, D.C., the Navy Department receives permission to withdraw from the joint Jupiter missile project in order to concentrate on the solid-fuel Polaris missile capable of being fired from submarines.

The new destroyer *Gyatt* is commissioned, becoming the first vessel of its class to mount Terrier surface-to-air missiles. It is also fitted with the Denny-Brown stabilization system, consisting of two 45-foot retractable fins to reduce rolling in heavy seas.

DECEMBER 18 The government disbands the Joint Army-Navy Missile Committee.

DECEMBER 19 The Special Projects Office under Rear Admiral William F. Raborn is given priority funding to develop the new Polaris submarine-launched missile.

1957

FEBRUARY 8 In Washington, D.C., Chief of Naval Operations Admiral Arleigh Burke selects January 1965 as the deadline for developing a solid-fuel rocket with a 1,500-mile range, which can also be launched from submerged submarines.

FEBRUARY 13 In the Mediterranean, the guided-missile cruiser *Boston* test-launches a Terrier surface-to-air missile at sea for the first time.

MARCH 4–15 A ZPG-2 airship commanded by Commander Jack R. Hunt sets a 264-hour endurance record by flying roundtrip from the United States to Africa and back.

MARCH 17 At Cape Canaveral, Florida, the Navy launchers the Vanguard satellite, which only weighs 3.2 pounds.

MARCH 21 A Douglas A3D Skywarrior flown by Commander Dale Cox sets two new transcontinental speed records by flying roundtrip between Los Angeles and New York.

MARCH 30 The nuclear-powered submarine *Seawolf* is completed, being the first vessel of its kind driven by a liquid-metal-cooled atomic reactor. It has the capacity to circumnavigate the globe three times without surfacing.

JULY 8 At Pearl Harbor, Hawaii, the submarine *Gudgeon* sets out to be the first American submersible to circumnavigate the Earth.

AUGUST 12 The first test of an automatic "hands off" carrier landing system occurs as a F3D Skynight flown by Lieutenant Commander Don Walker touches down on the carrier *Antietam*.

AUGUST 27 At Portsmouth, New Hampshire, the nuclear-powered submarine *Swordfish* is completed; this is the first such vessel constructed entirely at a naval facility.

DECEMBER 9 In Washington, D.C., the Secretary of Defense moves up the deadline to develop the new Polaris submarine-launched missile to 1960. The design of the submarine destined to carry them has also been approved.

DECEMBER 23 The nuclear-powered submarine *Skate* is commissioned, becoming the first vessel of its class.

1958

JANUARY This month construction begins on the first three Polaris-class ballistic missile submarines. The first vessel of this class had originally been designed as an attack submarine, but then it was cut in two for the addition of a 120-foot midsection to accommodate the missiles.

January 11 Near Point Mugu, California, two years into the program, the Navy successfully conducts the first test-firing of a solid-fuel Polaris ballistic missile.

February 4 At Newport News, Virginia, the keel is laid for the nuclear-powered carrier *Enterprise*, destined to become the first such vessel of its kind in the world.

February 21 At Pearl Harbor, Hawaii, the submarine *Gudgeon* becomes the first American submersible to circumnavigate the Earth, covering 25,000 miles in eight months.

March 7 At Mare Island, California, the submarine *Grayback* becomes the first naval submersible capable of routinely firing ballistic missiles, in this instance a Regulus I. However, because the latter can only be launched while the vessel is surfaced, Polaris-armed submarines are much preferred.

March 15 In Washington, D.C., Congress authorizes a permanent memorial to be constructed over the remains of the sunken battleship *Arizona* at Pearl Harbor, Hawaii.

April 24 In Washington, D.C., the Navy Department unveils the first official Navy flag. The designed is approved by President Dwight D. Eisenhower.

May 27 The McDonnell Douglas XF4H-1 Phantom jet fighter prototype successfully flies. This is one of the most successful warplanes in aviation history, and is also adopted by the U.S. Air Force.

May 28 The cruiser *Galveston* becomes the first Navy vessel equipped to fire the new Talos antiaircraft missiles.

Near Pearl Harbor, the submarine *Stickleback* collides with the destroyer *Silverstein*, sinking without loss of life.

July 1 The Navy establishes Submarine Squadron 14, which is also the first Fleet Ballistic Missile Submarine Squadron.

July 15–October 25 At Lebanon, vessels of the Sixth Fleet under Admiral J. L. Holloway land marines ashore to help forestall a civil war there.

July 30 At New London, Connecticut, the nuclear-powered submarine *Skate* departs on a year-long voyage that will carry it under the Arctic ice for the first time.

August 3 At the North Pole, Commander William R. Anderson directs the nuclear submarine *Nautilus* under the polar ice cap for the first time.

August 8 In Washington, D.C., President Dwight D. Eisenhower awards the Presidential Unit Citation to the crew of the submarine *Nautilus*. This is the first peacetime presentation of the award.

August 11 The submarine *Skate* under Commander James F. Calvert is the first submersible to surface through the Polar ice cap, and repeats the feat on August 17 as part of an Arctic exploration voyage.

August 19 The Lockheed XP3V-1 prototype maritime patrol aircraft makes its maiden flight; it remains in service to present times as the P-3 Orion.

At China Lake, California, the Naval Ordnance Test Station successfully tests the new Tartar surface-to-surface antiaircraft missile system, which shoots down an F6F target drone.

August 23 In the Strait of Taiwan, the Seventh Fleet is ordered to help supply the Nationalist garrison on the offshore islands of Matsu and Quemoy. The Communist Chinese are shelling the island from the mainland and threatening to invade them.

AUGUST 25 Navy Commander Forrest S. Petersen successfully flies the Boeing X-15 high-speed research aircraft for the National Aeronautics and Space Administration (NASA).

SEPTEMBER 15 Lieutenant William P. Lawrence becomes the first naval aviator to routinely fly twice the speed of sound (1,200 miles per hour) in an F8U-3 Crusader.

SEPTEMBER 16 Off the coast of California, the submarine *Grayback* successfully test-launches the first Regulus I missile used in a mock attack against Edwards AFB.

OCTOBER 24 Near Nicara, Cuba, the transport *Kliensmith* evacuates 56 American citizens as they flee Communist revolutionary violence. They do so under the watchful eye of the carrier *Franklin D. Roosevelt*.

DECEMBER 12 In Washington, D.C., the Secretary of the Navy cancels further development of the Regulus II missile in favor of the new Polaris missile program.

1959

FEBRUARY 24 In Washington, D.C., the Navy Department declares that it is scrapping all its battleships save for the four fast *Iowa*-class vessels.

MARCH 11 The Sikorsky XHSS-2 Sea King antisubmarine helicopter successfully performs its maiden flight.

APRIL 6 The seven Mercury astronauts are introduced to the public, including Navy Lieutenant Commander Alan B. Shepard, Walter M. Schirra, and Lieutenant Malcolm Scott Carpenter.

APRIL 20 At Cape Canaveral, Florida, the Polaris ballistic missile makes an early and successful test flight.

APRIL 25 The carrier *Lexington* hosts Attack Squadron VA-212, which is the first jet squadron equipped with Bullpup guided air-to-ground missiles.

MAY 10 At Groton, Connecticut, the huge nuclear-powered submarine *Triton* is commissioned. This is the first submersible fitted with twin reactors and is 447 feet in length; it is intended to serve as a radar-equipped early-warning picket boat.

JUNE 9 The new ballistic-missile submarine *George Washington* is launched at Groton, Connecticut. This is the culmination of several radical new concepts including nuclear warheads, ballistic missiles, nuclear power, and a radical, streamlined shape.

JUNE 16 Off the North Korean coast, MiG fighters attack a Navy P4M *Mercator* reconnaissance craft of VQ-1, damaging it.

JUNE 19 At Naval Air Station, Lakehurst, New Jersey, the Navy commissions ZPG-3W, the largest non-rigid airship ever constructed.

JULY 14 At Quincy, Massachusetts, the 14,000-ton nuclear powered cruiser *Long Beach* is launched, becoming the very first vessel of its kind. It will possess a top speed of 30 knots and virtually unlimited cruising range.

August 27 Near Cape Canaveral, Florida, the ship *Observation Island* successfully test-fires a Polaris ballistic missile at sea.

September 21 In the North Pacific, the submarine *Barbero* makes the first deterrent cruise while equipped with Regulus I missiles.

October 6 At Nagoya, Japan, the carrier *Kearsarge* helps evacuate 6,000 people in the wake of a destructive typhoon. It also delivers 200,000 pounds of medicine and supplies to the city's inhabitants.

December 1 In Washington, D.C., the Bureau of Ordnance and the Bureau of Aeronautics are merged into a new entity, the Bureau of Naval Weapons.

December 6 An F4H-1 Phantom flown by Commander Larry E. Flint reaches a record altitude of 98,560 feet, breaking 12 previous altitude and time-to-climb marks.

December 31 The new ballistic-missile submarine *George Washington* is commissioned. In concert with Air Force B-52 bombers and Minuteman land-based missiles, these vessels form one leg of the strategic "triad" for American nuclear deterrence.

1960

January This month, the deep-sea diving bathyscaph *Trieste* under Lieutenant Don Walsh and Jacques Piccard reach a depth of 35,800 feet off the Marianas Islands.

January 7 Near Cape Canaveral, the Polaris missile completes its first fully guided test flight of 900 miles.

February 16 At Groton, Connecticut, the huge nuclear-powered submarine *Triton* departs on an 84-day voyage to circumnavigate the world while submerged.

February 25 Over Rio de Janeiro, Brazil, an R6D Liftmaster collides with a commercial airliner; 64 people are killed in all, including 38 on the Navy plane.

March 25 Near Oahu, Hawaii, the submarine *Halibut* successfully fires an operational Regulus I missile for the first time during naval maneuvers.

April 12 At Cape Canaveral, Florida, the Navy successfully launches Transit IB, its first navigational satellite.

April 19 The Grumman YA2F-1 prototype makes its maiden flight; it enters service as the A-6 Intruder all-weather attack aircraft, and serves capably up through the Gulf War of 1991.

May 6 In the San Nicholas Channel off the coast of Cuba, the cutter *Oriente* fires on the submarine *Sea Poacher*.

May 11 At New Groton, Connecticut, the nuclear-powered submarine *Triton* under Commander Edward L. Beach becomes the first submersible to circumnavigate the globe underwater. The voyage takes 84 days and covers 41,419 nautical miles; the Triton subsequently receives a Presidential Unit Citation.

July 19 Near Long Beach, California, a collision between destroyers *Ammen* and *Collett* results in 20 sailors dead and 20 injured; the *Ammen* is scrapped shortly afterwards.

July 20 Near Cape Canaveral, Florida, the ballistic submarine George *Washington* successfully launches a Polaris A-1 missile, while submerged, for the first time.

September 10 The new destroyer *Charles F. Adams* is commissioned. This is first of a 4,500-ton class utility vessel designed to carry Tartar missiles; 23 such vessels are acquired.

October 21 The Grumman W2F-1 prototype successfully flies for the first time; it enters the service as the E-2 Hawkeye and is still in service to present times.

November 1 In London, England, Prime Minister Harold Macmillan decides to allow U.S. Navy Polaris submarines to operate from Holy Loch, Scotland.

November 15 At Charleston, South Carolina, the *George Washington* commences the Navy's first Polaris submarine patrol of the Cold War. This vessel carries 16 such weapons, each with a range of 1,200 miles.

December 13 Over Edwards AFB, California, an A3J-1 Vigilante flown by Commander Leroy A. Heath establishes a new world altitude record of 91,450.8 feet.

December 19 At the Brooklyn Navy Yard, New York, a fire sweeps the carrier *Constellation* as it is under construction; 50 workers die, 150 are injured, and damage is estimated at $75 million.

1961

January 12 In Washington, D.C., President Dwight D. Eisenhower's defense budget for fiscal year 1962 has funding to support a Navy establishment of 817 ships.

April 17–20 During the failed Bay of Pigs invasion, Cuba, six warplanes from the carrier *Essex* are committed to protecting CIA flown B-26 bombers; the bombers arrive over the target before the jets do; two are shot down.

April 28 In the Gulf of Mexico, a Stratolab balloon is launched from the deck of the carrier *Antietam,* becoming the first manned balloon to rise to 6,000 feet and then return to the vessel that launched it.

April 29 At Camden, New Jersey, the carrier *Kitty Hawk*, the first vessel of its kind to be equipped to fire missiles, is commissioned.

May 4 In the Gulf of Mexico, Commander Malcolm D. Ross and Lieutenant Commander Victor A. Prather launch their balloon from the deck of the carrier *Antietam* and reach 113,740 feet. Prather, however, is killed by falling from the rescuing helicopter.

May 5 At Cape Canaveral, Navy Commander Alan B. Shepard is launched in a suborbital flight while in the space capsule Freedom 7, and subsequently recovered by helicopters from the carrier *Lake Champlain*. He is the first American in space, having reached an altitude of 116.5 miles.

June 29 At Cape Canaveral, Florida, the Navy Transit IVA communications satellite is placed in orbit 500 miles up. This is also the first spacecraft to carry a small nuclear generator aloft in the form of a radioisotope battery.

August 26 The new amphibious assault vessel *Iwo Jima*, especially designed to operate helicopters, is commissioned.

September 10 The guided-missile cruiser *Long Beach* is commissioned, being the first nuclear-powered vessel of that class. It is also the first warship armed entirely with missiles.

October 23 In the Atlantic, the submarine *Ethan Allen* test-fires a new Polaris A-2 missile for the first time; this new version has a range of 1,500 miles.

November 25 At Newport News, Virginia, the nuclear-powered carrier *Enterprise* becomes the first vessel of its kind in the world. The ship displaces 85,830 tons, is 1,123 feet in length, and is manned by a crew of 4,600 men; it remains the largest warship ever constructed.

December 11 In South Vietnam, the ferry-carrier *Core* delivers a shipment of 33 Army H-21 Shawnee helicopters and 400 pilots and ground crew.

1962

January 1 In light of President John F. Kennedy's preference for unconventional warfare in battling communist-inspired subversion, the Navy creates the first two Sea Air Land (SEAL) teams for operations in rivers and coastal areas.

May 6 In the Pacific Ocean, the missile submarine *Ethan Allen* fires the first live nuclear warhead on a Polaris submarine; the warhead detonates high above Christmas Island.

SEALs

The origins of naval commandos date back to World War II when the Navy employed specialized teams of Underwater Demolition Teams (UDTs) to clear debris from beaches prior to amphibious landings. However, it was not until after the Korean War and the invention of specialized scuba equipment for underwater breathing that they began taking on non-traditional skills like parachuting. In 1962 President John F. Kennedy, who was enamored of special operations, created the Navy Sea, Air, Land teams, generally known as SEALs. These are the naval equivalent of the Army's Green Berets, and are highly trained and especially equipped for non-conventional warfare. The SEALs first experienced combat in South Vietnam, where they conducted many successful forays against Viet Cong units in the Mekong Delta. In 1983 a SEAL team participated in Operation Urgent Fury, the liberation of Grenada, and rescued the British governor general. They also performed useful work in the 1991 Gulf war against Iraq by performing reconnaissance missions, and were among the first Coalition forces to enter the newly liberated Kuwait City.

Presently, the Navy maintains a force of 2,000 SEALs organized in six teams, one of which is a designated anti-terrorist unit. The standards for joining are severe, for all prospective candidates are subjected to one of the most grueling physical and mental training regimens ever devised. Consequently, SEAL teams are capable of operating in conditions from the Arctic to the tropics, and are in the front rank of forces waging the global war against terrorism.

MAY 24 At Cape Canaveral, Florida, Navy Commander Malcolm Scott Carpenter completes the second orbital flight of an American astronaut in his capsule Aurora 7.

JUNE 26 At Charleston, South Carolina, the missile submarine *Ethan Allen* departs on the first Polaris A-2 deterrent cruise of the Cold War.

AUGUST 7 At Cape Canaveral, the first test flight of a new A-3 Polaris missile unfolds; this version has a range of 2,500 miles.

AUGUST 17 At Seattle, Washington, the hydrofoil patrol craft *Long Point* becomes the first such craft in the U.S. Navy. This vessel achieves high speed by riding on three foils lowered from the hull, permitting it to "fly" through the water.

AUGUST 22 At the North Pole, the submarines *Skate* and *Seadragon* surface through the ice only 850 miles from Cape Cheyuskin in the Soviet Union.

AUGUST 31 At Naval Air Station, Lakehurst, New Jersey, the Navy's final lighter-than-air flight is made, and the program is finally disbanded.

SEPTEMBER 8 The *Raleigh*, first of an entire class of amphibious transport docks, is commissioned.

OCTOBER 3 At Cape Canaveral, Florida, Navy Commander Walter W. Schirra remains in low Earth orbit for 10 hours and 46 minutes in the capsule Sigma 7. He covers 160,000 miles in that period.

OCTOBER 6 The nuclear-powered guided missile frigate *Bainbridge* becomes the first vessel of its class in the world.

Banner headlines of Great Britain's daily newspapers announcing U.S. president John F. Kennedy's blockade of Cuba, October 23, 1962. (Library of Congress)

OCTOBER 15   At Jacksonville, Florida, RF-8A Crusaders of Light Photoreconnaissance Squadron (VPF) 62 begin flying regular missions over Cuba in concert with Air Force aircraft.

OCTOBER 22   In Washington, D.C., President John F. Kennedy declares a naval quarantine of Communist Cuba to force the Soviet Union to remove its nuclear missiles from the island. Accordingly, Task Force 136 arises under Vice Admiral Alfred G. Ward, which is built around the carrier *Essex*, heavy cruisers *Newport News* and *Canberra*, and several destroyer squadrons. Task force 135 is also created under Rear Admiral John T. Hayward, centered upon the carrier *Enterprise*, for the possible defense of Guantanamo, Cuba.

OCTOBER 24   Around Cuba, the American naval quarantine goes into effect as 25 Soviet vessels are headed for the island; all of them reverse course in a matter of hours.

OCTOBER 25   In the Atlantic, the Soviet tanker *Bucharest* is accosted by the destroyer *Gearing*, which search the vessel and allows it to continue when no weapons are found.

OCTOBER 26   The Soviet-chartered freighter SS *Marcula* is stopped at sea by the destroyers *Joseph P. Kennedy, Jr.*, and *John R. Pierce*; it is searched for weapons and allowed to continue.

OCTOBER 28   In Moscow, Soviet Union, Premier Nikita Khrushchev defuses the Cuban missile crisis by ordering all offensive Soviet missiles out of Cuba.

NOVEMBER 20   In Washington, D.C., President John F. Kennedy, having been assured by the Soviets that all missiles and bombers would be withdrawn in 30 days, declares the naval quarantine of Cuba at an end.

1963

APRIL 10   The nuclear submarine *Thresher* is lost during a test dive 240 miles east of Cape Cod, Massachusetts; the entire crew of 129 men dies. The wreckage is located on October 1, 1964, by the deep-diving vessel *Trieste II*.

APRIL 23   The *Lafayette* is commissioned, becoming the first of a new class of fleet ballistic-missile submarines.

OCTOBER 25   In Haiti, Navy ships conduct relief operations in the wake of Hurricane Flora by delivering 375 tons of relief supplies.

OCTOBER 26   The submarine *Andrew Jackson* successfully fires an A-3 Polaris missile while submerged for the first time. This new weapon possesses a range of 2,500 miles, twice that of the A-1 version.

DECEMBER 4   In Washington, D.C, the Navy Department unveils its new rocket-powered guided missile or SUBROC, which can be fired by submerged submarines. It can also be fitted with a nuclear warhead for destroying enemy submarines.

1964

January 13 Off the coast of Zanzibar, Africa, a revolution results in the destroyer *Manley* evacuating 55 American citizens to safety.

February 1 In Washington, D.C., the Navy Department announces that Vice Admiral Hyman Rickover of the Bureau of Ships for Nuclear Propulsion has reached the mandatory age for retirement, but that he will be allowed to serve as a retired officer at the request of the president. He is regarded as the "Father of the Nuclear Navy."

May 13 In the Mediterranean, Rear Admiral Bernard M. Strean commands the world's first nuclear-powered task group consisting of the carrier *Enterprise*, the cruiser *Long Beach*, and the frigate *Bainbridge*.

June 6 Over the Plaine des Jarres, Laos, the RF-8 reconnaissance jet flown by Lieutenant Charles F. Klusmann of the *Kitty Hawk* is shot down, and he is captured by Communist forces. He subsequently escapes, winning the Distinguished Flying Cross.

June 7 Over Laos, an F-8 Crusader belonging to the carrier *Kitty Hawk* is shot down while escorting a reconnaissance flight. However, Commander Doyle W. Lynn ejects and is rescued by helicopter.

July 31 Near Gibraltar, Spain, Operation Sea Orbit commences as the nuclear-powered carrier *Enterprise*, the cruiser *Long Beach*, and frigate *Bainbridge* depart on a circumnavigation of the globe. Their voyage concludes on October 1 when they anchor at Charleston, South Carolina, after a 30,565-nautical mile trek, in which they were neither refueled nor resupplied.

August 2 In the Gulf of Tonkin off North Vietnam, the destroyer *Maddox* under Captain Herbert L. Ogier is attacked by three Communist patrol boats while in international orders. Assisted by F-8 Crusaders from the carrier *Ticonderoga*, the *Maddox* sinks one patrol vessel and drives off the rest.

August 4 In the Gulf of Tonkin, the destroyers *Maddox* and *Turner Joy* under Commander Robert C. Barnhart are attacked in the dark by North Vietnamese torpedo boats. The engagement is handled entirely by radar and no visual contact is made, but the incident provides a convenient pretext for retaliation.

August 5 Over North Vietnam, Operation Pierce Arrow unfolds as warplanes from the carriers *Constellation* and *Ticonderoga* launch the first air raids of the Vietnam War, striking oil tanks and naval installations along the coast. Two aircraft from the former are shot down, resulting in the first Navy fatality and Lieutenant Everett Alvarez becoming the first Navy prisoner of war.

August 7 In Washington, D.C., Congress passes the Tonkin Gulf Resolution, which allows President Lyndon B. Johnson authority to expand the conflict in Southeast Asia at his discretion.

September 18 In the Gulf of Tonkin, the destroyers *Morton* and *Parsons* open fire on four fast-moving radar contacts believed to be North Vietnamese torpedo boats. No damage or casualties result.

September 28 At Charleston, South Carolina, the submarine *Daniel Webster* departs on the first Polaris A-3 patrol of the Cold War.

December 6 At Guantanamo, Cuba, the Navy installs three saltwater conversion plants after the Communist regime of Fidel Castro cuts off the water supply. The base is now independent of all outside sources for drinking water.

December 26 Near Guam, the missile submarine *Daniel Boone* begins the first Polaris A-3 patrol made in the Pacific.

1965

February 7 Over North Vietnam, Operation Flaming Dart commences as warplanes from the carriers *Hancock*, *Ranger*, and *Coral Sea* strike military installations near Dong Hoi. The attack comes in response of the bombing of an American army barracks at Pleiku; one aircraft is shot down.

February 11 Over North Vietnam, Operation Flaming Dart II unfolds as 99 warplanes from the carriers *Coral Sea*, *Hancock*, and *Ranger* bomb Communist military installations at Chan Hoa; a F-8 Crusader from the *Coral Sea* is shot down.

March 2–October 31 Over North Vietnam, Air Force and Navy warplanes join forces during Operation Rolling Thunder, a prolonged aerial bombardment campaign intended to dissuade the Communist government from infiltrating South Vietnam.

March 8 Near Da Nang, South Vietnam, the transport dock *Vancouver*, the flagship *Mount McKinley*, and the attack transport *Henrico* posit the 9th Marine Expeditionary Brigade ashore. This post subsequently serves as a major airbase.

March 11 Near South Vietnam, destroyers *Black* and *Higbee* commence Operation Market Time to halt the infiltration of supplies and weapons arriving by Viet Cong junks. By November more ships are assigned to the mission as Task Force 71, which boards and searches 6,000 vessels.

March 15 Over North Vietnam, warplanes from the carriers *Hancock* and *Ranger* attack a Communist ammunition dump at Phu Qui.

March 23 Above Earth, Navy Lieutenant Commander John Young and Air force Lieutenant Colonel Virgil Grissom complete three orbits in the new Gemini space capsule.

March 26 Warplanes from the carriers *Hancock* and *Coral Sea* attack four radar sites in North Vietnam; two aircraft are shot down, but their pilots are rescued.

April Commencing this month, naval aircraft fly over 55,000 sorties from Yankee Station (Gulf of Tonkin) against Communist targets in North Vietnam and elsewhere for the rest of the year. Targets include military installations, transportation networks, and power stations.

April 3 Over North Vietnam, warplanes from the carriers *Hancock* and *Coral Sea* attack the Dong Phoung highway bridge south of Hanoi. During the strike naval aviators catch their first glimpse of Communist MiG fighters.

April 15 Over South Vietnam, warplanes from the carriers *Coral Sea* and *Midway* attack Viet Cong positions for the first time. They are assisted by aircraft from the U.S. and South Vietnamese air forces. These same vessels also launch 10 reconnaissance aircraft over North Vietnam for the first time.

April 27 Off the coast of the Dominican Republic, the assault ship *Boxer* puts marines ashore during a period of civil strife.

April 30 In Washington, D.C., the government announces that Coast Guard units will be deployed for service in Vietnam.

May 10 In California, the LST *Tioga County* successfully test launches a Seaspar missile, a surface-to-air version of the Sparrow air-to-air missile.

May 12–18 In Washington, D.C., President Lyndon B. Johnson orders the first halt to the American bombing campaign of North Vietnam and calls for negotiations; the Communists fail to respond.

May 16 Southeast of Cam Ranh Bay, South Vietnam, a single Navy carrier stakes out the new Dixie Station to launch air strikes in support of U.S. and allied forces.

May 20 In North Vietnam, warships of the Seventh Fleet selectively bombard targets along the coast for the first time. These are the first fire-support missions for the U.S. Navy since the Korean War.

June 10 At Dong Xoai, South Vietnam, Construction Mechanic Third Class Marvin G. Shields helps fellow Seabees defend their position against a Viet Cong attack. Despite severe wounds he volunteers to help destroy an enemy machine gun nest and is successful, but dies of his injuries; Shields receive a posthumous Congressional Medal of Honor.

June 17 South of Hanoi, North Vietnam, two MiG-17 fighters are shot down by Sidewinder-wielding F-4 Phantoms from the carrier *Midway*.

June 20 When a pair of propeller-driven A-1 Skyraiders is attacked by Communist MiG-17s over North Vietnam, they turn on their attackers and shoot one of them down.

July 20–August 1 In South Vietnam, Coast Guard Division 1 arrives; this consists of 17 cutters tasked with monitoring coastal traffic as part of OPERATION MARKET TIME, to cut down the infiltration of arms and men from the north.

August 1 In South Vietnam, Rear Admiral Norvell G. Ward takes charge of OPERATION MARKET TIME, and he reorganizes his force as Task Force 155, the Coastal Surveillance Force.

August 11–12 A major escalation in the air war over North Vietnam occurs when a Soviet-supplied SAM (surface-to-air missile) downs an A-4 Skyhawk from the carrier *Midway*. This is the first Navy jet to fall to such a weapon.

August 13 Over North Vietnam, ground fire claims an A-1 Skyraider, two A-4 Skyhawks, and two F-8 Crusaders from carriers *Coral Sea* and *Midway* as they scout about looking for SAM sites; this is the worst day of the air war to date.

August 18 Near Chu Lai, South Vietnam, OPERATION STARLITE is supported by naval gunfire from the cruiser *Galveston* and two destroyers; the marines kill 964 enemy troops over the ensuing week.

AUGUST 28   Near La Jolla, California, three teams of 10 men (aquanauts) spend 15 days at sea nestled inside SeaLab II, which rests in water 210 feet deep. They are assisted by a specially trained dolphin named Tuffy, who acts as a courier.

SEPTEMBER 27   The Vought A-7 Corsair II light attack plane prototype flies for the first time; it renders distinguished service up through the 1991 Gulf War.

OCTOBER 15   In South Vietnam, the U.S. Naval Support Activity, Da Nang, is created to support naval operations in the vicinity.

OCTOBER 17   Over North Vietnam, an A-6 Intruder and four A-4 Skyhawks from the carrier *Independence* successfully knock out a SAM site at Kep without loss; this is the first successful attack on a missile base.

OCTOBER 26   In Vietnam, the destroyer *Turner Joy* suffers from an turret explosion that kills three sailors and injures three more.

OCTOBER 31   In South Vietnam, the Navy deploys the first of its "PCF Swift Boats," which are fast, heavily armed aluminum craft with a crew of five. They are intended for use in OPERATION MARKET TIME off the coast, but also support riverine operations in the Mekong region.

NOVEMBER 26   Off the coast of Vietnam, the U.S. Navy presence is bolstered by the nuclear powered carrier *Enterprise* and the nuclear-powered frigate *Bainbridge*.

DECEMBER 2   In South Vietnam, the carrier *Enterprise* becomes the first nuclear-powered ship in war once it launches 188 sorties against Viet Cong positions.

DECEMBER 4   Above the Earth, the Gemini VII space capsule flown by Navy Commander James A. Lovell and Air Force Colonel Frank Borman sets a record 14 days in orbit.

DECEMBER 7   In the South China Sea, the carrier *Kitty Hawk* experiences an onboard fire that kills 2 sailors and injures 28.

DECEMBER 15   The crew of Gemini VII is joined by Gemini VIII under Navy Captain Walter Schirra and Air Force Major Thomas P. Stafford. This is the first planned rendezvous of spacecraft in orbital flight.

DECEMBER 18   In the Mekong Delta of South Vietnam, Task Force 116, the U.S. Navy River Patrol Force, begins searching the area for Viet Cong between Saigon and the Rung Sat Special Area.

DECEMBER 22   Over North Vietnam, 100 warplanes from the carriers *Enterprise*, *Kitty Hawk*, and *Ticonderoga* devastate the thermal-power plant at Uong Bi; two planes are lost in this, the first attack against a purely industrial target.

DECEMBER 24   In Washington, D.C., President Lyndon B. Johnson orders a second halt in the air war over North Vietnam; it does not recommence until January 31, 1965.

1966

JANUARY 31   Over North Vietnam, a 37-day halt to OPERATION ROLLING THUNDER comes to an end after the United States fails to convince the North Vietnamese to enter into negotiations.

FEBRUARY 14 In South Vietnam, *PCF 4* becomes the first swift boat lost in action after it strikes a mine; four men are killed and two are wounded.

FEBRUARY 16 At Chu Lai, South Vietnam, the hospital ship *Repose* opens its medical facilities.

FEBRUARY 26 At Vung Tu, South Vietnam, Coast Guard Division 13 arrives with 9 additional cutters; a total of 26 such vessels are deployed in theater.

MARCH 29 At Naval Air Station, Pensacola, Florida, Ensign Gale Ann Gordon becomes the first woman to ever solo in a naval aircraft. This comes as part of her training in aviation experimental psychology.

MARCH 31 In South Vietnam, the Navy relieves Commander Marcus Aurelius Arnheiter from the destroyer *Vance*; he blames a cabal of disloyal subordinates, and several lawsuits and hearings result.

Rear Admiral Norvell G. Ward assumes command of the new U.S. Naval Forces, Vietnam, to control various coastal units.

APRIL 7 At Palomares, Spain, Navy divers retrieve an H-bomb lost after two Air Force bombers collided; the search took 80 days.

APRIL 10 In South Vietnam, OPERATION GAME WARDEN is bolstered by the arrival of two water-jet propelled river patrol boats (PBRs).

APRIL 17 In South Vietnam, the cruiser *Canberra* is the first U.S Naval vessel to employ the Syncom II communications satellite to relay a message 4,000 miles away to Hawaii.

MAY 1 In Washington, D.C., the Navy Department authorizes an administrative shake-up by reconfiguring the bureaus of Naval Weapons, Ships, Supplies and Accounts, and Yards and Docks into six new commands under the Office of Naval Material: Ordnance Systems, Air Systems, Ship Systems, Electronic Systems, Supply Systems, and Facilities Engineering. The Chief of Naval Operations' office also assumes control of the Office of Naval Materiel, the Bureau of Naval Personnel, and the Bureau of Medicine and Surgery.

MAY 9 On the Bassac River, South Vietnam, 10 Navy river patrol boats begin sweeping the Mekong Delta for Viet Cong units.

In South Vietnam, OPERATION MARKET TIME is bolstered by the arrival of the Navy's first three air-cushion patrol craft (PACVs); these are capable of 50 knots

A river patrol boat navigates inland waterways in Vietnam in an offensive against Viet Cong forces. Riverine craft were designed with shallow drafts, allowing them to operate in shallow rivers and canals. (National Archives)

and carry a heavy machine gun, but prove difficult to maintain in the field.

May 11 In South Vietnam, the vessels *Brister*, *Vireo*, and cutter *Point Grey* intercept and destroy a 150-foot freighter as part of OPERATION MARKET TIME; the vessel was carrying 50 tons of supplies and weapons to the Viet Cong.

May 12 Near Point Mugu, California, the Navy successfully tests the highly complex Phoenix air-to-air missile at the Pacific Missile Range; these are to be carried by the forthcoming F-14 Tomcat fighters.

May 22 On the Dinh Ba River, South Vietnam, swift boat *PCF 41* is holed by recoilless rifle fire in the Rung Sat Special Region and sunk.

May 23 Over the Gulf of Tonkin, the nuclear-powered cruiser *Long Beach* scores a long-range kill by downing a Communist MiG aircraft with a Talos missile.

June 3 Over Earth, Navy Lieutenant Commander Eugene A. Cernan and Air Force Lieutenant Colonel Thomas P. Stafford conduct Gemini IX on a three-day mission; Stafford becomes the second American to walk in space.

June 12 Over North Vietnam, an F-8 Crusader from the carrier *Hancock* obtains the first aerial kill for that type of aircraft by downing a MiG-17 with a Sidewinder missile.

June 16 Over North Vietnam, warplanes from the carrier *Hancock* attack the Thanh Hoa petroleum facility for the first time as part of a concerted effort to destroy enemy fuel reserves.

June 20 In the Mekong Delta, South Vietnam, Coast Guard cutters *Point League* and *Point Slocum* attack and run a 120-foot trawler that fired on them aground; this Communist Chinese vessel was carrying 250 tons of military supplies to the Viet Cong.

June 29 Over North Vietnam, 46 jets from the carrier *Constellation* bomb oil storage tanks outside Hanoi and Haiphong; this is the nearest attack made to either city and signals a new campaign to cripple Communist fuel supplies and distribution.

July 1 In the Gulf of Tonkin, three North Vietnamese torpedo boats attack the frigate *Coontz* and the destroyer *Rogers*; in turn they are all sunk by carrier aircraft. This is the first Communist naval aggression since August 1964.

On the Long Tau River, South Vietnam, the 12 vessels of Detachment Alpha, Mine Squadron 11, begin sweeping the waters around Saigon for hidden explosives.

July 13 Over North Vietnam, an F-4 Phantom from the carrier *Constellation* downs a Communist MiG-17; Air Force jets bag another 5, raising the total number of aerial kills to 15.

July 18–21 Over the Earth, Navy Commander John W. Young and Air Force Major Michael Collins ride Gemini X for 43 orbits and also dock with an Agena space vehicle.

August 3 Over Haiphong, North Vietnam, warplanes from the carrier *Constellation* hit oil refineries around the city; the Soviet Union charges that one of its freighters in the harbor was struck by American bullets.

August 6 In light of the growing significance of riverine and shallow-water operations in Southeast Asia, the navy commissions the new *Asheville* patrol gunboat, or PGM.

AUGUST 7   Over North Vietnam, Communist gunners shoot down a Navy A-1 Skyraider along with six Air Force jets, making this the costliest day of the air war so far.

AUGUST 23   In the Long Tau Channel east of Saigon, South Vietnam, the freighter SS *Baton Rouge*, working for the Military Sea Transport Service (MSTS), sinks after striking a mine; seven crewmen are killed.

AUGUST 29   Off the coast of North Vietnam, A-4 Skyhawks and A-6 Intruders from the carrier *Constellation* sink two Communist torpedo boats and damage a third after they fire on them. The Chinese government subsequently protests that the ships in question were merchantmen of theirs.

AUGUST 30   Over South Vietnam, Navy-crewed UH-1B Seawolfs of Helicopter Attack (Light) Squadron (HAL) 3 are called in to support OPERATION GAME WARDEN in the Mekong Delta; these replace the Army Huey helicopters used for the same purpose and become one of the most decorated Navy squadrons of the war.

SEPTEMBER 11   Over North Vietnam, Naval aviators perform a record 171 bombing missions without losing a single aircraft.

On the Co Chin River, South Vietnam, two river patrol boats with OPERATION GAME WARDEN are ambushed by Viet Cong units; one sailor is killed.

SEPTEMBER 15   Above Earth, the Navy's Commander Charles Conrad and Lieutenant Commander Richard F. Gordon complete 71 hours in orbit, then splash down and are rescued by the assault ship *Guam*.

SEPTEMBER 16   In Hong Kong harbor, the crew of the sinking merchant vessel *August Moon* is rescued by helicopters from the carrier *Oriskany*.

SEPTEMBER 22   On the Long Tau River, South Vietnam, the minesweeper *MSB 15* is attacked by Viet Cong recoilless rifle fire, which kills 1 man and wounds 11.

SEPTEMBER 29   Off the coast of Dominican Republic and Haiti, amphibious ships *Boxer*, *Rankin*, *Plymouth Rock*, *Ruchamkin*, and *Suffolk County* commence relief operations in the wake of Hurricane Inez.

OCTOBER 9   Over North Vietnam, an A-1 Skyraider from the carrier *Intrepid* shoots down a Communist MiG-21 near the Phy Ly Bridge, while a second MiG-21 is downed by an F-8 Crusader flown by Commander Richard Bellinger from the *Oriskany*.

OCTOBER 25   In North Vietnam, OPERATION SEA DRAGON commences, as vessels of the Seventh Fleet begin attacking enemy supply ships operating along the coastline, sinking 230 in the first month alone.

OCTOBER 26   On Yankee Station, the carrier *Oriskany* suffers from a hangar deck fire that kills 44 officers and men.

OCTOBER 31   Along the Mekong River, South Vietnam, 8 patrol boats of OPERATION GAME WARDEN, supported by Seawolf helicopters, destroy 51 Viet Cong junks in a three-hour battle; no Americans are hit. Boatswain's Mate First Class James E. Williams displays exemplary courage while operating a searchlight under fire, and wins a Congressional Medal of Honor.

On the Long Tau River, South Vietnam, the minesweeper *MSB-15*, the first vessel of its class, is lost after it strikes a mine; two crewmen are missing and four are wounded.

NOVEMBER 4 In the South China Sea, the carrier *Franklin D. Roosevelt* experiences an internal fire that kills seven sailors and injures four.

NOVEMBER 11–15 Above the Earth, Gemini XII, flown by Navy Captain James A. Lovell and Air Force Lieutenant Colonel Edwin E. Aldrin, completes the final mission of the Gemini series.

NOVEMBER 18 In North Vietnam, the destroyers *John R. Craig* and *Hammer* shell a Communist radar site two miles north of the Demilitarized Zone. This is the first such naval attack of the war.

NOVEMBER 23 In North Vietnam, destroyers *Mullany* and *Warrington* engage a convoy of 60 Communist supply barges as part of OPERATION SEA DRAGON, sinking 47.

DECEMBER 5 In North Vietnam, Communist shore batteries bracket the destroyer *Ingersoll* northeast of Dong Hoi, slightly damaging it.

DECEMBER 11 In the Mekong Delta, South Vietnam, two river-patrol boats with OPERATION GAME WARDEN engage a force of 40 Viet Cong sampans in a canal west of My Tho; 28 enemy vessels are sunk without loss.

DECEMBER 23 Near Dong Hoi, North Vietnam, a Communist shore battery lands a round on the destroyer *O'Brien*, killing two men and wounding four. This is the first time a Navy vessel receives a direct hit.

1967

JANUARY 13 Master Chief Gunner's Mate Delbert D. Black gains appointment as the Navy's first Senior Enlisted Advisor, although the position is subsequently changed to Master Chief Petty Officer of the Navy.

JANUARY 27 At Cape Canaveral, Florida, a fire in the cabin of the Apollo 1 spacecraft kills Navy Lieutenant Commander Roger B. Chaffee, as well as Air Force Lieutenant Colonel Virgil I. Grissom and Lieutenant Colonel Edward H. White.

FEBRUARY 4 On the Co Chien River, South Vietnam, river-patrol boat *PBR-113* is damaged by enemy fire and sinks, becoming the first vessel of its class scuttled and used for parts.

FEBRUARY 15 At Saigon, South Vietnam, the minesweeper *MSB-45* strike a mine and sinks, while *MSB-49* is struck by Viet Cong recoilless rifle fire; 1 sailor is killed and 16 are wounded.

FEBRUARY 16 In the Rung Sat Special Zone, South Vietnam, boats of River Assault Flotilla One support Army offensive operations for the first time.

FEBRUARY 26 In North Vietnam, A-6 Intruders from the carrier *Enterprise* begin sowing mines along the Communist coast for the first time. This tactic is aimed at coastal barges slipping supplies to enemy units further south.

Off the coast of North Vietnam, the cruiser *Canberra* and destroyers *Benner* and *Joseph Strauss* shell 16 targets near Thanh Hoa; this is the first time naval gunfire has been applied offensively and not in response to enemy shore fire.

FEBRUARY 28   In South Vietnam, the Mekong Delta Mobile Riverine Force, or Task Force 117, is created. It employs heavily armed and armored river patrol boats known as monitors.

MARCH 6   On the Mekong River, South Vietnam, Seaman David G. Ouellet of *PBR-124* rushes to place himself with between a Viet Cong Grenade and his captain, and dies in the blast; he wins a posthumous Congressional Medal of Honor.

MARCH 7   The Navy Department increases personnel total for the Women Accepted for Voluntary Emergency Services (WAVES) to 600 officers and 6,000 enlisted, a 20 percent increase.

MARCH 9–11   Near Vinh, North Vietnam, the heavy cruiser *Canberra* and destroyers *Ingersoll* and *Keppler* bombard and silence several enemy shore batteries, although the latter takes a direct hit on March 11, with no fatalities.

MARCH 11   Over Sam Son, North Vietnam, jets from the carrier *Oriskany* employ television-guided Walleye bombs for the first time against a military barracks.

MARCH 14   In South Vietnam, a North Vietnamese trawler is spotted by a P2V Neptune working with OPERATION MARKET TIME; it then beaches itself before being destroyed by the vessels *Brister*, *PCF 78*, and Coast Guard cutter *Point Ellis*.

APRIL 1   In Washington, D.C., the Coast Guard transfers from the Treasury Department to the new Department of Transportation after 177 years.

The Mobile Riverine Force base at Cat Lo, Vietnam. The Mobile Riverine Force was created in mid-1966 for search-and-destroy operations in the waterways of the Mekong Delta. (U.S. Coast Guard)

The *Will Rogers* is the last of 26 Polaris ballistic missile submarines commissioned b y the Navy.

APRIL 10   In South Vietnam, the hospital ship *Sanctuary* becomes only the second vessel of its class to operate there.

APRIL 20   Over North Vietnam, warplanes from the *Kitty Hawk* and *Ticonderoga* attack power plants on the outskirts of Haiphong harbor; this is the closest bombs have been dropped near that city.

APRIL 24   Over North Vietnam, warplanes from the *Bon Homme Richard* and *Kitty Hawk* strike at Communist airfields at Kep for the first time. Navy aviators down two MiG-17s as they attempted to take off.

APRIL 27   In South Vietnam, command of U.S. Naval Forces, South Vietnam, passes from Rear Admiral Norvell G. Ward to Rear Admiral Kenneth L. Veth.

MAY 1   Over Kep, North Vietnam, A-4 Skyhawks from the carriers *Bon Homme Richard* and *Kitty Hawk* shoot down two MiG-17s and destroy four more in a bombing raid in the air field.

MAY 15   In South Vietnam, the number of Coast Guard vessels rises, and three 311-foot cutters arrive; the *Barataria*, the *Bering Strait*, and the *Gresham*.

MAY 19   Over Hanoi, North Vietnam, F-8 Crusaders from the carrier *Bon Homme Richard* shoot down four MiG-17s, while covering a bombing raid on a thermal power plant.

MAY 27   At Camden, New Jersey, the *Truxtun* becomes the Navy's secondnuclear-powered guided-missile frigate.

JUNE 8   In the eastern Mediterranean, the signals intelligence ship *Liberty* is attacked by Israeli aircraft and torpedo boats north of the Sinai Peninsula; 34 sailors are killed and 171 are wounded. The Israeli government apologizes for the incident, as the vessel was mistaken for an Egyptian ship of similar size. Captain William L. McGonagle receives a Congressional Medal of Honor for his conduct during the attack.

JUNE 25   Near the Ca Mau Peninsula, South Vietnam, swift boat *PCF-97* is struck by recoilless rifle fire and sunk; one man is wounded.

JULY 15   Near Cape Batangan, South Vietnam, Navy and Coast Guard vessels performing OPERATION MARKET TIME patrols run a 120-foot trawler ashore; it was carrying tons of supplies and arms to the Viet Cong.

JULY 21   North of Haiphong, North Vietnam, F-8 Crusaders from the carrier *Bon Homme Richard* shoot down three MiG-17s during a bombing raid against oil storage facilities. Fighters from this vessel have downed nine Communist aircraft.

JULY 29   Near North Vietnam, the carrier *Forrestal* experiences a severe fire on the flight deck after a rocket explodes while being loaded; 134 sailors are killed and 21 aircraft are destroyed. This accident occurs only three days after arriving at Yankee Station.

AUGUST 1   In Washington, D.C., the Navy Department decides to reactivate the battleship *New Jersey* and employ its 16-inch cannon in North Vietnam.

AUGUST 10   South of Hanoi, South Vietnam, F-4 Phantoms from the carrier *Constellation* down two MiG-21s during an attack against a truck park.

August 30 Over Haiphong, North Vietnam, a campaign to isolate the port city begins as warplanes form the *Oriskany* begin attacking the four major bridges linking it to the mainland.

September 28 On the Mekong River, South Vietnam, a PBR is hit by a Viet Cong rocket and sinks, with two killed and four wounded.

October 25 Over North Vietnam, a carrier raid on the Phuc Yen airfield destroys 10 MiG fighters on the ground.

October 26 South of Hanoi, North Vietnam, a MiG-21 is shot down by an F-4 Phantom from the carrier *Constellation*.

October 30 Over North Vietnam, two F-4 Phantoms from the carrier *Constellation* engage four MiG-17s, downing one.

October 31 At Mare Island, California, the seaplane tender *Currituck* is decommissioned; this is the first time since 1911 such a vessel is not on the Navy inventory.

November 5 At Naval Air Station North Island, California, a SP-5B Marlin of VP-40 makes the last operational flying-boat mission in Navy history.

December 4 In Dinh Tuong Province, South Vietnam, vessels of the Mobile Riverine Force kill 235 Viet Cong in a series of protracted battles.

December 14 Over North Vietnam, a scrape between four F-8 Crusaders from the carrier *Oriskany* and four MiG-17s results in one Communist fighter shot down.

1968

January 1–5 Over North Vietnam, Communist gunners manage to claw down five Navy jets, rendering this one of the worst weeks of the air war.

January 15–18 In Washington, D.C., President Lyndon B. Johnson proclaims a bombing halt in the vicinity of Haiphong, North Vietnam.

January 22 In North Korea, the intelligence-collection ship *Pueblo* under Lieutenant Commander Lloyd M. Bucher is accosted and boarded in international waters by North Korean patrol vessels. The captured vessel is then taken into Wonsan harbor; one sailor is killed; three others, including Bucher, are wounded.

February 29–March 2 In South Vietnam, eight Coast Guard cutters and several small patrol ships intercept and destroy three Communist trawlers attempting to bring supplies and arms to the Viet Cong.

March 31 In Washington, D.C., President Lyndon B. Johnson declares that he will not seek reelection to the presidency. Furthermore, to encourage peace talks, he restricts bombing to south of North Vietnam's 20th parallel.

April 6 The World War II-vintage battleship *New Jersey* is recommissioned prior to being deployed in Southeast Asia.

April 10 The Navy drops the venerable Douglas A-1 Skyraider from its aerial inventory; these rugged craft have served with distinction since 1945.

May 21 The nuclear-powered attack submarine *Scorpion* under Lieutenant Francis A. Slattery suddenly vanishes 400 miles south of the Azores, triggering a massive salvage operation to locate its remains. These are found in 10,000 feet of water by the oceanographic research vessel *Mizar*. It has since been determined that it was ambushed and sunk by a Soviet submarine in retaliation for the accidental ramming and sinking of another Soviet submersible in the Pacific several months earlier.

May 25 The Grumman EA-6B Prowler, an electronic countermeasures aircraft, makes its maiden flight; it is still in operation.

June 10 On the Long Tau River, South Vietnam, the Navy turns over 14 river patrol boats to the South Vietnamese Navy, which is assuming responsibility for the region.

June 16 In South Vietnam, the cruiser *Boston* and the Australian destroyer *Hobart* are slightly damaged when mistakenly bombed by Air Force jets.

June 19 Over North Vietnam, a UH-2 Seasprite helicopter flown by Lieutenant Clyde E. Lassen flies through intense enemy ground fire to rescue the crew of a downed F-4 Phantom jet. After several attempts he finally returns to his ship with five minutes of fuel left, winning a Congressional Medal of Honor.

June 26 Over North Vietnam, two MiG-21s engage three F-8 Crusaders from the carrier *Bon Homme Richard*; one MiG is downed by a missile.

July 9 In South Vietnam, the Army-Navy Mobile Riverine Force begins its first operations along the Co Chien River.

July 12 At Patuxent Naval Air Station, Maryland, the Navy retires its last P5M Marlin seaplane. Seaplanes have served with distinction since World War I.

July 22 Over North Vietnam, Commander Samuel R. Chessman of Attack Squadron 195 (*Ticonderoga*) completes his 306th mission; he previously flew 77 combat missions during the Korea War.

July 29 In South Vietnam, the patrols of Operation Game Warden are extended up the Mekong and Bassac Rivers, right up to the Cambodian border. This is done in an attempt to halt Communist infiltration from across the border.

Over North Vietnam, four MiG-17s tangle with four F-8 Crusaders from the carrier *Bon Homme Richard*; one Communist craft is downed.

September 7 The carrier *John F. Kennedy*, a conventionally powered *Forrestal*-class vessel, is commissioned.

September 18 In South Vietnam, the Swift Boat PCF 21 attacks a convoy of Viet Cong sampans 35 miles south of Da Nang, sinking or damaging 44 vessels.

September 19 Over North Vietnam, a MiG-21 is shot down by an F-8 Crusader from the carrier *Intrepid*; this the Navy's 29th aerial victory and the last attributed to the F-8.

September 29 The recommissioned battleship *New Jersey* begins its tour of Vietnam by shelling Communist positions near Con Thein, north of the demilitarized zone.

In a significant move, the post of Commander, U.S. Naval Forces, Vietnam, passes from Rear Admiral Kenneth L. Veth to Vice Admiral Elmo R. Zumwalt.

OCTOBER 15   In South Vietnam, OPERATION SEALORDS begins as vessels of OPERATION GAME WARDEN and the Army-Navy Mobile Riverine Force are combined in a joint operation against Viet Cong forces in the Mekong Delta.

OCTOBER 29   In South Vietnam, the LST *Washoe County* and Coast Guard cutter *Wachusetts* attack Viet Cong positions on the Cua Lon-Bo De River, destroying 242 enemy junks and 167 structures; five sailors are wounded.

OCTOBER 31   In Washington, D.C., President Lyndon B. Johnson orders all air attacks against North Vietnam halted. This proves disconcerting to American aviators, as, following each prior bombing halt, Communist air defenses were repaired and noticeably improved.

NOVEMBER 1–30   In a single month of action, the battleship *New Jersey* accounts for 182 enemy bunkers, 800 structures, 15 cave complexes, and 9 sampans. The long reach of its 16-inch guns is devastating.

DECEMBER 6   In South Vietnam, OPERATION GIANT SLINGSHOT commences, as Navy river-patrol boats begin regular forays up the Vam Co Dong and Van Co Tay rivers, in an attempt to close off the Viet Cong smuggling routes in the so-called "Parrot's Beak" along the Cambodian border.

DECEMBER 21   The Apollo VIII spacecraft, which includes Navy commander

Artillery is blasted toward targets in Vietnam by the main battery of the battleship USS New Jersey in the South China Sea. The U.S. Navy played a significant role in the Vietnam War, performing a diverse array of functions, including direct combat, logistical support, refugee evacuation, intelligence, and communications. (U.S. Naval Institute)

James A. Lovell, reaches the moon, circles it, then safely returns to Earth.

DECEMBER 23   In North Korea, the 82 crewmen of the intelligence ship *Pueblo* are released across the DMZ into South Korea.

In South Vietnam, four Navy Swift Boats, supported by Army helicopter gunships, attack Viet Cong positions in An Xuyen Province; they destroy 167 sampans, 125 structures, and 8 bunkers.

1969

JANUARY 3   At Naval Air Station, North Island, California, the Navy establishes Light Attack Squadron (VAL) 4, equipped with OV10 Bronco aircraft. This mission is to provide close support missions to river-patrol boats in Vietnam.

JANUARY 13   In South Vietnam, the battleship *New Jersey* and two destroyers support OPERATION BOLD MARINER as marines from the Seventh Fleet land on the Batangan Peninsula.

JANUARY 14   South of Hawaii, a fire sweeps the flight deck of the carrier *Enterprise*, which is brought under control in 45 minutes; 28 sailors die and 65 are injured.

FEBRUARY 1   In the Mekong Delta, South Vietnam, the U.S. Navy hands over 25 river gunboats to the South Vietnamese Navy.

MARCH 5   The carrier *Ticonderoga* becomes the first carrier in the fleet to begin its fifth combat tour of Vietnam.

MARCH 14   In Nha Trang Bay, South Vietnam, Lieutenant Joseph R. Kerrey directs his SEAL team during an island assault despite severe wounds, then oversees their successful extraction under fire; he wins a Congressional Medal of Honor.

MARCH 19   In Quang Nam Province, South Vietnam, Hospital Corpsman David R. Ray helps a wounded marine in combat, fighting off several Viet Cong before being fatally wounded; he wins a posthumous Congressional Medal of Honor.

MARCH 25   OV-10A Broncos of Light Attack Squadron VAL 4 are assigned to support the River Patrol Force from their bases at Vung Tau and Binh Thuy, South Vietnam.

MARCH 27   In waters off South Vietnam, the battleship *New Jersey* destroys 72 enemy bunkers near Phan Thiet, II Corps region.

MARCH 31   The battleship *New Jersey* concludes six months of active duty, and leaves the gun line.

APRIL 14   Near North Korea, a Navy Lockheed EC-121 of the Fleet Reconnaissance Squadron is shot down by Communist MiGs over international waters; all 31 crew members perish.

APRIL 18   The carrier *Bon Homme Richard* returns to Yankee Station on its fifth combat tour.

APRIL 20   In the Sea of Japan, Rear Admiral Malcolm W. Cagle's Task Force 71, consisting of 23 warships, makes a show of force in response to the downing of the Navy EC-121 aircraft. The battleship *New Jersey* is also ordered back to Japan.

May 3 At Groton, Connecticut, the huge nuclear-powered submarine *Triton*, the first vessel to entirely circumnavigate the globe while submerged, is decommissioned.

May 15 In San Francisco, California, the nuclear submarine *Guitarro* accidentally sinks at dockside while it is under construction. A Special House Armed Services Committee report notes "culpable negligence" on the part of shipyard workers.

May 16 The Coast Guard transfers the cutters *Point Garnet* and *Point League* over to the South Vietnamese Navy. Since June 1968 a total of 101 vessels of various sorts have been transferred.

May 18–26 At Cape Kennedy, Florida, Apollo X lifts off with Navy Captain John W. Young and Commander Eugene A. Cernan and Air Force Colonel Thomas P. Stafford. They pass within nine miles of the lunar surface before returning back to Earth.

June 1 Responsibility for the Fourth Coastal Zone, which stretches from the South China Sea to the Gulf of Thailand, is assumed by the South Vietnamese Navy.

June 2 In the South China Sea, the destroyer *Frank E. Evans* is struck by the Australian carrier *Melbourne* and cut in half, and sinks, with a loss of 74 crewmen. The two ships had been participating in a SEATO exercise.

June 9 A Joint Board of Investigation concludes that captain and deck officer of the destroyer *Frank E. Evans* are responsible for the loss of their ship; the two are reprimanded. No blame is attached to the captain of the Australian vessel.

June 15 On the bank of the Ong Muong Canal, South Vietnam, Lieutenant Thomas G. Kelley directs eight river assault craft, despite severe head wounds, and rescue a craft experiencing mechanical difficulties; he receives a Congressional Medal of Honor.

July 1 At this date the U.S. Navy commands 886 vessels, with an average age of 17 years.

July 10 In the Gulf of Thailand, OV-10A Broncos of VAL 4, attached to the River Patrol Force, destroy six Viet Cong boats off Kien Giang Province, South Vietnam.

July 20 Former Navy pilot Neil A. Armstrong departs the Apollo 11 landing craft, becoming the first man to walk on the moon.

August 5 North Vietnam releases the first three American prisoners of war, Lieutenant Robert F. Frishman, Seaman Douglas B. Hegdahl, and Captain Wesley L. Rumble. During a press conference on October 3, they report that American captives are subject to beating and other torture.

September 4 In North Vietnam, Captain James B. Stockdale, having suffered constantly from bouts of torture and abuse, deliberately attempts committing suicide to defy his captors; he is revived by the enemy, and subsequently wins a Congressional Medal of Honor.

October 10 In South Vietnam, the U.S. Navy turns over 80 river-patrol boats to the South Vietnamese Navy, for a total of 229 vessels transferred to date.

October 26 Off the coast of Vietnam, the carrier *Coral Sea* begins its fifth combat tour of duty.

OCTOBER 27 The *NR-1* becomes the Navy's first nuclear-powered deep-sea submarine, capable of underwater research and recovery missions.

NOVEMBER 14–24 At Cape Kennedy, Florida, Apollo XII lifts off with an all-Navy crew of Commander Charles Conrad, Commander Richard Gordon, and Lieutenant Commander Alan Bean.

NOVEMBER 24 The crew of Apollo XII is safely rescued at sea by the carrier *Hornet*.

NOVEMBER 29 In the Mekong Delta, South Vietnam, the U.S. Navy turns over the My Tho Naval Base to the South Vietnamese navy.

DECEMBER 17 At the Naval Inactive Ship Maintenance Facility, Bremerton, Washington, the battleship *New Jersey* is decommissioned as a result of defense cuts. It will return to active service 13 years later.

DECEMBER 30 On the Saigon River, South Vietnam, a Navy river patrol boat surprises Viet Cong forces crossing a river; it attacks in concert with a helicopter gunship, killing 27 of the enemy for no loss.

1970

JANUARY 1 On the Saigon River, South Vietnam, Navy and South Vietnamese vessels rush to the scene of a stricken river-patrol boat battling with Viet Cong attempting to capture it; 12 enemy soldiers are slain, and the vessel is recovered.

JANUARY 9 In Tay Ninh Province, South Vietnam, a Sealords patrol, assisted by Seawolf helicopters and OV1-Broncos, gives battle with a large force of Viet Cong; 32 Communists are killed.

JANUARY 28 At Vung Tau, South Vietnam, the destroyer *Mansfield* provides close supporting fire to the 1st Australian Task Force.

FEBRUARY 14 The Coast Guard transfers another three 82-foot cutter vessels to the South Vietnamese Navy; six more are also given by year's end.

FEBRUARY 28 At Da Nang, South Vietnam, the Navy transfers 11 Swift Boats to the South Vietnamese Navy, which now assumes responsibility for patrolling coastal provinces along the five northernmost provinces.

MARCH 14 After four years of dedicated service, the hospital ship *Repose* returns to the United States.

MARCH 16 At Da Nang, South Vietnam, the Navy transfers four support ships and two more cutters to the South Vietnamese Navy. The Coast Guard now maintains only the 13th Division off the Mekong Delta.

MARCH 28 Over North Vietnam, a MiG-21 is shot down by an F-4 Phantom from the carrier *Constellation*; this is the Navy's first aerial kill in 16 months.

In the IV Corps area, South Vietnam, the destroyer *Orleck* shells and destroys 44 enemy structures while supporting the South Vietnamese 21st Infantry Division.

APRIL 11 In space, the Apollo XIII spacecraft under Navy Captain James A. Lovell experiences an on-board explosion en route to the moon, but is gingerly brought back to Earth, and the crew is safely recovered.

MAY 5   Patrolling the Vam Go Dong and Vam go Tay Rivers, South Vietnam, is handed over to the South Vietnamese Navy as OPERATION GIANT SLINGSHOT concludes. Since December 1968, U.S. Navy forces have waged 1,200 firefights and accounted for 2,400 Viet Cong.

MAY 6   On the Kham Span River, a force of 40 U.S. Navy patrol boats enters Cambodia, and is fired upon less than two miles from the border.

MAY 8   On the Mekong River, over 100 Navy and South Vietnamese patrol boats sail across the Cambodian border; they remain within the 21-mile limit established by President Richard M. Nixon.

MAY 12   U.S. Navy and South Vietnamese patrol craft ring the Gulf of Thailand to blockade the Cambodian coastline and cut Communist infiltration there.

JUNE 23   The Navy transfers an additional 273 river patrol raft to the South Vietnamese Navy, bring the total number of vessels turned over to 525.

JULY 1   In Washington, D.C., 49-year-old Admiral Elmo R. Zumwalt becomes the youngest officer to serve as Chief of Naval Operations. His tenure here will be marked by controversy.

JULY 22   At Newport, Rhode Island, 60 South Vietnamese officers graduate the U.S. Navy's Officer Candidate School at the Naval War College.

AUGUST 1   In Washington, D.C., the Navy Department orders the Military Sea Transport Service renamed the Military Sealift Command; it remains under Navy jurisdiction.

AUGUST 3   Near Cape Kennedy, Florida, the submarine *James Madison* successfully test-launches the first Poseidon C-3 multi-warhead ballistic missile, while submerged.

Zumwalt, Elmo R. (1920–2000)

Elmo Russell Zumwalt was born in San Francisco, California, on November 29, 1920, and he graduated from the U.S. Naval Academy in 1943. He saw service in World War II and subsequently commanded a destroyer during the Korean War. Zumwalt made history in July 1965 by becoming the Navy's youngest rear admiral at the age of 44. Three years later he advanced to commander of all U.S. naval forces in Southeast Asia as a vice admiral. Zumwalt determined that the Navy should have a higher profile in that conflict, which he achieved through creation of the so-called "Brown-Water Navy." More controversial was his use of the Defoliant Agent Orange to strip away the thick jungle coverage used by the enemy. By 1969 Zumwalt's efforts had greatly impeded Communist infiltration, but the process of "Vietnamization" had begun, and Zumwalt's responsibilities were subsequently assumed by the South Vietnamese Navy.

In July 1970 Zumwalt again made history when President Richard M. Nixon appointed him Chief of Naval Operations; at 49, he remains the youngest officer to hold that post. He now began the most controversial phase of his career by issuing a series of 120 "Z-grams" whereby beards were allowed, clothing standards relaxed, and numerous traditional duties dispensed with. Zumwalt faced an even greater challenge posed by the invigorated Soviet Navy, so he adopted the "High-Low" strategy of mothballing obsolete vessels and purchasing numerous, smaller vessels. He retired from the Navy in July 1974 and died in Durham, North Carolina, on January 2, 2000, possibly the most controversial reformer in U.S. Navy history.

SEPTEMBER 14   In Washington, D.C., the Pentagon reports that the South Vietnamese Navy consists of 35,000 men and 1,500 surface vessels, with 600 of these being river-patrol boats transferred there.

SEPTEMBER 17   In a cost-cutting measure, the Navy declares plans to deactivate 58 older vessels, including the carrier *Shangri La*; since January 1969 no less than 286 ships have been mothballed.

OCTOBER 29   In Washington, D.C., Secretary of the Navy John R. Chaffee projects that the U.S. Navy will consist of less than 700 vessels as of July 1971; he also warns that dipping below that level is potentially dangerous.

NOVEMBER 21   In North Vietnam, warplanes from the carriers *Hancock*, *Oriskany*, and *Ranger* support Marine and Air Force jets in attacking Communist antiaircraft sites below the 19th Parallel.

DECEMBER 15   In Washington, D.C., the State Department reveals that the Navy is constructing a $19-million communications facility on the British Indian Ocean island of Diego Garcia.

DECEMBER 30   The Navy ends its participation in inland waterway patrolling, after turning over the remaining 125 small vessels to the South Vietnamese Navy.

1971

FEBRUARY 11   In Washington, D.C., reform-minded Admiral Elmo R. Zumwalt abolishes the traditional practice of enlisting Filipino mess stewards.

The United States and Soviet Union conclude a treaty prohibiting the placement of nuclear weapons on the ocean bottom.

JANUARY 22–FEBRUARY 8   Commander Donald H. Lillienthal flies a P-3 Orion to eight world distance, speed, and time-to-climb records, while covering 5,963 nautical miles from Naval Air Station, Atsugi, Japan, to Naval Air Station, Patuxent River, Maryland.

JANUARY 31   In space, Navy Captain Alan B. Shepard, the first American in space, becomes the seventh man to walk on the moon, as part of Apollo XIV.

MARCH 5   In Washington, D.C., the Navy Department establishes the Deputy Chiefs of Naval Operations for Air, Surface, and Submarine Warfare, in concert with a scheme promulgated by Chief of Naval Operations Admiral Elmo R. Zumwalt.

MARCH 16   The prototype SH-2D Seasprite multipurpose system helicopter completes its first flight. This version carries advanced sensors for detecting enemy vessels at night, on the surface or underwater.

APRIL 1   At Charleston, South Carolina, the missile submarine *James Madison* departs on the first Poseidon C-3 patrol of the Cold War.

At Norfolk, Virginia, the Helicopter Mine Countermeasures Squadron (HM) 12 becomes the first organization of its kind in the Navy.

APRIL 12   Near South Vietnam, a 160-foot North Vietnamese trawler is cornered and sunk by a Navy gunboat, two Coast Guard cutters, a South Vietnamese patrol craft, and two Navy patrol planes.

APRIL 28   In Washington, D.C., Captain Samuel L. Gravely becomes the first African American to reach the rank of rear admiral; he is one of a new group of 49 fleet officers chosen.

MAY 1   The hospital ship *Sanctuary* departs Southeast Asia after four years of conspicuous medical service.

AUGUST 19   Off the coast of North Vietnam, vessels of the Seventh Fleet bombard Communist positions along the Demilitarized Zone.

AUGUST 26   Captain Alan B. Shepard, America's first man in space, is promoted to rear admiral.

OCTOBER 1   At San Diego, California, the carrier *Constellation* departs on its sixth combat tour of Vietnam.

DECEMBER 11   As war rages between Indian and Pakistan, a task force based on the carrier *Enterprise* sails to the Bay of Bengal to evacuate American citizens, if necessary.

DECEMBER 31   At the Boston Naval Shipyard, Massachusetts, the service shuts down its only rope-making facility. Hereafter private firms will provide that commodity.

1972

JANUARY 21   The Lockheed S-3 Viking antisubmarine aircraft prototype makes its maiden flight; it is still in service to present times.

JANUARY 19   Over North Vietnam, a MiG-21 is downed by an F-4 Phantom from the carrier *Constellation*. The crew, consisting of Lieutenant Randall F. Cunningham and Lieutenant William P. Driscoll, end up as the Navy only aces of this war.

MARCH 28   Over North Vietnam, a MiG-17 is shot down by two F-4 Phantoms from the carrier *Coral Sea*.

APRIL 1   Light Attack Squadron VAL-4, the Navy's final in-country unit, is ordered out of the Mekong Delta region of South Vietnam.

APRIL 10–13   In South Vietnam, SEAL Lieutenant Thomas R. Norris dons the disguise of a South Vietnamese fisherman and rescues two downed pilots deep within enemy territory; he receives a Congressional Medal of Honor.

APRIL 27   Captain Alene B. Duerk, a Navy nurse, becomes the first woman promoted to rear admiral.

MAY   This month Navy plots shoot down a total of 16 MiGs, making this their best month of the war. The cruiser *Chicago* also bags an unidentified aircraft over North Vietnam with a long-range Talos missile shot.

MAY 8   In response to renewed Communist aggression, Navy A-6 Intruder aircraft begin sowing mines in North Vietnamese harbors. This act completely cuts all seaborne supplies to Communist forces operating in the south, although 31 neutral vessel are trapped in the harbor.

A helicopter carrying Rear Admiral Rembrandt C. Robinson, who commands Cruiser-Destroyer Division 11, crashes, killing him. He is the first flag officer to die in this war.

Over North Vietnam, a second MiG-17 is downed by an F-4 Phantom flown by Lieutenants Randall F. Cunningham and William P. Driscoll.

MAY 10   Over North Vietnam, Navy jets claim seven MiGs; Lieutenants Randall F. Cunningham and William P. Driscoll bag three, making them the first American aces of the war. They are struck by a missile on their way back to the carrier and forced to bail out over the ocean.

MAY 25   In Moscow, Soviet Union, Secretary of the Navy John W. Warner and Soviet Admiral of the Fleet Sergei G. Gorshkov signs the Incidents at Sea Agreement to reduce the hostile encounters and accidents on the high seas.

JUNE 30   In Washington, D.C., the Senate approves Admiral Thomas Moorer to serve a second two-year term as chairman of the Joint Chiefs of Staff.

AUGUST 27   Near Haiphong, North Vietnam, a four-ship formation from the Seventh Fleet begins a nighttime bombardment of this strategic port; two torpedo boats which sally to confront them are sunk.

SEPTEMBER 22   Over North Vietnam, Commander Dennis R. Weichman completes his 501st combat mission, setting a new Navy record.

OCTOBER 11   In South Vietnam, the cruiser *Newport News* experiences a turret explosion that kills 19 sailors and injures 10.

OCTOBER 12   In North Vietnam, racial tensions explode into a race riot on the carrier *Kitty Hawk*, whereby 60 sailors are injured.

OCTOBER 16   At Subic Bay, the Philippines, racial unrest surfaces on the fleet oiler *Hassayampa* when 12 black sailors, who accuse their white counterparts of stealing their money, refuse to go to sea.

OCTOBER 17   The new Harpoon anti-ship missile is flight-tested for the first time. This highly accurate weapon boasts a range of 60 miles and can be mounted on ships, aircraft, or submarines.

OCTOBER 23   In Washington, D.C., President Richard M. Nixon, to facilitate peace talks, halts bombing raids over North Vietnam above the 23rd Parallel.

OCTOBER 31   In North Vietnam, SEAL adviser Engineman Second Class Michael E. Thornton rescues his wounded squad leader while under fire, kills two enemy soldiers, then safely evacuates the wounded man out to sea; he receives a Congressional Medal of Honor.

DECEMBER 6   The final Apollo moon mission is carried out by Navy Captain Eugene A. Cerman, Commander Ronald E. Evans, and civilian Dr. Harrison H. Schmidt.

1973

JANUARY 12   Over the Gulf of Tonkin, an F-4 Phantom from the carrier *Midway* shoots down a Communist MiG-17, being the last American aerial victory of this conflict. Naval aircraft have claimed 59 MiGs and two AN-2 biplanes.

January 27 Over North Vietnam, an F-4 Phantom from the carrier *Enterprise* is shot down, becoming the final American aerial loss in the war; the radar operator is rescued, but Commander Harley H. Hall is declared missing in action.

January 28 Warplanes from the carriers *Ranger* and *Enterprise* continue flying strike missions against Communist positions over Laos, despite the cease-fire with Vietnam.

February 24–July 18 In North Vietnam, OPERATION ENDSWEEP begins as Helicopter Mine Countermeasure Squadron 12 begins clearing Communist waterways of all mines laid there since May 1972. This action takes place in consequence of the Paris Peace Accords.

May 25–June 22 Over the Earth, Skylab I, America's first orbiting space station, receives an all-Navy crew consisting of Captain Charles P. Conrad, Commander Joseph P. Kerwin, and Commander Paul J. Weitz; they remain on the station for 28 days.

July 28–September 5 Above the Earth, Skylab III sets a new record in space when Navy Captain Alan L. Bean beats the old record of 49 days, 3 hours, 37 minutes.

July 31 At Naval Air Station, Imperial Beach, California, the Light Helicopter Antisubmarine Squadron (HSL) 33 is activated as the first unit of its kind in the Navy.

October 5 At Yokosuka, Japan, the carrier *Midway* arrives at its new homeport, becoming the first forward-deployed vessel operating at a foreign base.

November 19 In Washington, D.C., Vice Admiral Hyman G. Rickover, "Father of the Nuclear Navy," receives his fourth star of full admiral.

USS Washtenaw County (MSS-2, formerly LST-1166) cruises in Haiphong Harbor, North Vietnam, in a final demonstration that the channel is safe for shipping at the completion of minesweeping operations, June 20, 1973. (U.S. Naval Historical Center)

> ### Rickover, Hyman G. (1900–1986)
>
> Hyman George Rickover was born in Makow, Poland, on January 27, 1900, a son of Russian Jews. He immigrated to the United States, and in 1922 he graduated from the U.S. Naval Academy. The turning point in his career occurred in 1946 when he was one of a handful of officers to study at the Manhattan Engineering District at Oak Ridge, Tennessee. Rickover immersed himself in the new science of atomic energy and began crusading for its application to sea power. In 1947 Rickover maneuvered himself into serving as both chief of the nuclear power division at the Bureau of Ships and head of the naval reactor branch of the Atomic Energy Commission. He also had a hand in designing and building all essential components, and his efforts culminated in March 1953 when the *Nautilus*, the world's first atomic-powered submarine, was launched.
>
> Rickover's outspoken nature made him unpopular, and he was passed over for promotion twice in 1951 and 1952. However, Congress pressured the Navy to make him an admiral in July 1953, whereupon Rickover pushed harder for a fleet of nuclear-powered surface vessels. In the early 1960s the carrier *Enterprise*, the guided missile cruiser *Long Beach*, and the frigate *Bainbridge* all demonstrated the viability of nuclear propulsion. Rickover was considered so indispensable that he remained on active duty past retirement age, and in 1973 he advanced to full admiral. Rickover retired in January 1982 after six decades of conscientious service to the nation. He died in Washington, D.C., on July 8, 1986, the "Father of the Nuclear Navy."

DECEMBER 20 The distinction of being the first female Naval Flight Surgeons falls to Lieutenants Jane O. McWilliams and Victoria M. Voge.

1974

FEBRUARY 22 Lieutenant Barbara Ann Allen successfully completes the Navy's flight-training program, becoming the first woman to earn a naval aviator's gold wings.

APRIL 24–JUNE 3 In Egypt, helicopters of MH-12, Task Force 65, begin sweeping the Suez Canal clear of mines laid during the most recent Arab-Israeli War in 1972.

JULY 1 In Massachusetts, the Boston Naval Shipyard closes after 174 years of continuous operation. This was the Navy's oldest facility and one of the most historic.

JULY 2 In Washington, D.C., Admiral Thomas H. Moorer steps down as chairman of the Joint Chiefs of Staff and is replaced by Air Force General George S. Brown.

JULY 22 In the eastern Mediterranean, Navy and Marine Corps helicopters evacuate 400 American and British civilians from Cyprus two days after a Turkish invasion of the island.

JULY 25 The General Dynamics Corporation contracts with the Navy to design and construct the nuclear powered *Trident* ballistic-missile submarine.

NOVEMBER 24 In the Persian Gulf, the carrier *Constellation* becomes the first American vessel of its type to visit since 1948.

1975

January 27 At Corfu, Greece, anti-American activity forces the destroyer *Richard E. Byrd* to leave the port.

March 3 In Washington, D.C., the Navy Department declares that its fleet strength will drop to 490 vessels as of June 30, 1976.

April 29–30 In South Vietnam, OPERATION FREQUENT WIND unfolds as Navy and Marine Corps helicopters evacuate 9,000 people fleeing Communist tyranny in Saigon. Other individuals are assisted by vessels of the Military Sealift Command. The effort is covered by aircraft from the carriers *Coral Sea*, *Enterprise*, *Hancock*, and *Midway*; this is also the combat debut of the new F-14 Tomcat variable-geometry (swing-wing) jet.

May 2 The Northrop YF-17 prototype, which lost out in an Air Force competition, is chosen by the Navy to serve as the basis for its new strike-fighter, the F/A-18 Hornet.

May 3 The Navy commissions the new 81,600-ton *Nimitz*, its second nuclear-powered carrier. This huge vessel carries 100 aircraft and helicopters at speeds in excess of 30 knots.

May 12–15 Off the coast of Cambodia, Communist Khmer Rouge forces seize the American transport *Mayaguez*, and a rescue effort is mounted with aircraft from the carrier *Coral Sea* and the destroyer *Harold E. Holt*. Both the ship and its crew are released by the Communists after a stiff fight on Koh Tang Island; 1 Navy corpsman is among the 18 servicemen killed in this operation.

June 5 In Egypt, the cruiser *Little Rock* is the only foreign vessel allowed to transit the newly opened Suez Canal.

September 20 At Pascagoula, Mississippi, the new destroyer *Spruance* is commissioned, being the first gas-turbine powered vessels of its class; 30 will be built.

November 22 In the Mediterranean, the cruiser *Belknap* collides with the aircraft *John F. Kennedy*; 7 sailors are killed and 24 injured. A court of inquiry finds the cruiser captain negligent.

1976

February 12 Captain Fran McKee is selected for promotion to rear admiral; she is the first female line officer selected.

March 28 Near California, an A-6 Intruder launches the first Tomahawk guided cruise missile. This represents a new generation of computer-guided "smart" weapons.

May 29 The new assault ship *Tarawa* is commissioned, unique in its ability to house and operate AV-8 Harriet vertical take-off jets.

June 20 Offshore at Beirut, Lebanon, vessel of the Sixth Fleet arrives to evacuate American citizens during the latest round of factional strife.

JUNE 30   A long-standing naval aviation tradition ends when officers and chief petty officers lose their distinctive brown shoes in favor of regulation black.

JULY 6   At Annapolis, Maryland, 81 women are accepted into the Naval Academy's class of 1980.

JULY 27   In Lebanon, carriers *American* and *Nimitz* cover the amphibious dock ship *Coronado* as it helps evacuate 160 Americans and 148 foreign nationals from the latest outburst of civil strife.

AUGUST 28   In the Ionian Sea, the frigate *Voge* collides with a Soviet Echo II submarine after the latter surfaces in its path; one sailor is injured.

SEPTEMBER 14   North of Scotland, the carrier *John F. Kennedy* collides with the destroyer *Bordelon*; six sailors are injured, and the destroyer has to be scrapped.

SEPTEMBER 30   The *Essex*-class carrier *Oriskany*, a distinguished veteran of Korea and Vietnam, is decommissioned.

OCTOBER 7   The Navy Department reduces the number of naval districts from 12 to 4 with headquarters at Seattle, Washington; Great Lakes, Illinois; Philadelphia, Pennsylvania; and Washington, D.C.

NOVEMBER 13   At Newport News, Virginia, the new nuclear-powered attack submarine *Los Angeles* is commissioned. At a length of 340 feet, this is the largest submersible built to date, has speeds in excess of 30 knots, and can fire Tomahawk, Harpoon, and Subroc missiles.

1977

JANUARY 10   In Washington, D.C., Admiral Arleigh Burke receives the Medal of Freedom, the highest civilian decoration.

JANUARY 18   Near Cape Kennedy, Florida, the Navy successfully launches its new Trident C-4 ballistic missile for the first time.

MAY 9   In Washington, D.C., the Navy announces that its fleet strength for the following year will reach an all-time low of 462 active vessels.

JUNE 28   Near Portsmouth, England, the cruiser *California* and the submarine *Billfish* are 2 of 150 vessels participating in Queen Elizabeth's Silver Jubilee Naval Review.

OCTOBER 18   The nuclear-powered carrier *Dwight D. Eisenhower* is commissioned, being the second vessel of the *Nimitz*-class.

DECEMBER 17   The guided-missile frigate *Oliver H. Perry* is commissioned, the first of 50 vessels assigned to this class. This is also the most numerous type of warship built by the Navy since World War II and is designed as a convoy escort.

1978

FEBRUARY 1   Off the coast of California, the submarine *Barb* successfully launches the first Tomahawk missile while submerged. This revolutionary weapon is computer-guided and has a terrain-following internal navigation system.

February 9 The new Fleet Satellite Communications System is successfully launches, which ushers in a new era in naval communications.

March 11 The missile submarine *Abraham Lincoln* becomes the first American submarine to complete 50 nuclear deterrent patrols. During a 17-year period it covered 420,000 miles and remained underwater for the equivalent of 8.5 years.

October 20 In Chesapeake Bay, the Coast Guard training cutter *Cuyahoga* collides with the Argentine freighter *Santa Cruz II* and sinks, with a loss of 11 lives. The captain of the former is found guilty of dereliction of duty and is reprimanded.

November 1 Another gender barrier falls as nine female ensigns are assigned to five non-combat vessels in the North Atlantic Fleet. This is also the first time that females have served on vessels other than hospital ships or troop transports.

November 18 The prototype McDonnell Douglas F/A-18 Hornet flies for the first time; this is a new generation of jet attack aircraft, and will replace the elderly A-6 Intruder and A-7 Corsair II in carrier attack groups.

December 27 The carrier *Constellation* deploys to waters west of Singapore in light of continuing revolutionary unrest in Iran.

1979

February 6 At Bandar Abbas and Char Bahar, Iran, the command ship *La Salle*, destroyers *Blandy*, *Decatur*, *Hoel*, and *Kincaid*, and the frigate *Talbot* evacuate 200 Americans and 240 foreign nationals.

April 1 Lieutenant Beverly Kelly is the first woman to captain a U.S. warship after she assumes control of the Coast Guard Cutter *Cape Newagen*.

April 10 Near Cape Kennedy, Florida, the submarine *Francis Scott Key* performs the first submerged launching of a C-4 Trident ballistic missile.

June 20 On the carrier Independence, Lieutenant Donna A. Sprull successfully lands her C-1 Trader into the traps, becoming the first woman carrier-qualified for fixed-wing aircraft.

July 19 In Washington, D.C., President Jimmy Carter instructs the Seventh Fleet to begin rescuing thousands of Vietnamese "boat people" fleeing Communist oppression; 1,800 are taken aboard this year, but many more perish at sea.

September 30 On this day the United States releases all control of the Panama Canal Zone to the government of Panama; it continues to be a vital waterway for trade and U.S. warships.

December 3 Near San Juan, Puerto Rico, terrorists fire upon a bus carrying naval personnel; 2 sailors die and 10 are wounded.

December 12 The prototype Sikorsky SH-60 Seahawk, a navalized verison of the Army's UH-60 Blackhawk, flies for the first time.

1980

January 10 Ensign Roberta McIntyre becomes the first female naval officer to qualify in surface warfare by serving aboard the submarine tender *Dixon*.

January 14 The carriers *Nimitz* and *Kitty Hawk* battlegroups are ordered to join the *Midway* in the Persian Gulf in light of continuing tensions with Iran.

January 28 In Tampa Bay, Florida, the Coast Guard buoy tender *Blackthorn* accidently strikes the oil tanker *Capricorn* near the Skyway Bridge; 23 sailors die.

March 1 The repair ship *Vulcan* becomes the first vessel to complete six months at sea, with 57 women as part of its regular crew.

April 24 In Iran, OPERATION BLUE LIGHT commences as the carrier *Nimitz* launches eight RH-53D helicopters crammed with joint service commandoes in an attempt to rescue the American hostages in Tehran. The mission is canceled when three helicopters experience mechanical difficulties, and all are abandoned after one collides with an Air Force C-130 transport on the ground.

May 28 The first women officers graduate from the service academies, with 61 from West Point, 55 from Annapolis, and 97 from the Air Force Academy.

July 8 Off the coast of Cuba, 11 Navy vessels assist 115,000 refugees fleeing from the Communist dictatorship of Fidel Castro; this becomes known as the Mariel Boat Lift.

September 30 The carrier *Saratoga* is the first vessel to undergo the Service Life Extension Program designed to increase the longevity of ships still in active service.

October 1 In Washington, D.C., the Office of Antisubmarine Warfare and Ocean Surveillance is redesignated the Office of Naval Warfare.

October 11 The guided-missile cruiser *Leahy* is ordered to the Persian Gulf, where it will assist Air Force E-3 Airborne Warning and control Systems (AWACS) aircraft in theater.

October 18 The guided-missile cruiser *Arkansas* becomes the last nuclear-powered vessel acquired by the U.S. Navy; eight are now in service.

November 13 In Washington, D.C., the Navy Department announces the retirement of 81-year-old Admiral Hyman Rickover as of January 31, 1982; he has been the guiding force behind the American nuclear navy for over three decades.

December 22 At Norfolk, Virginia, the *Dwight D. Eisenhower* and cruisers *South Carolina* and *Virginia* return home after 251 days at sea; this is the longest deployment of vessels since World War II, and it is mostly spent in the Indian Ocean/Persian Gulf region, one of the world's hottest hot spots.

1981

February 5 In Washington, D.C., John F. Lehman, Jr., gains appointment as the 65th Secretary of the Navy. His quest to obtain a 600-ship Navy, built around 15 carrier battlegroups, is a centerpiece of the Reagan administration's defense build-up.

MARCH 4   In Washington, D.C., Secretary of Defense Caspar Weinberger reactivates the battleships *Iowa* and *New Jersey* and the carrier *Oriskany* from mothballs. Naval appropriations will rise 11 percent and 15 percent over current level over the next two years.

APRIL 9   South of Sasebo, Japan, the missile submarine *George Washington* collides with the Japanese merchantman *Nissho Maru* while surfacing, killing two crew from the latter; the submarine captain is relieved of duty.

APRIL 12–14   At Cape Kennedy, Florida, the space shuttle Columbia blasts off with an all-Navy crew consisting of Captains John W. Young and Robert L. Crippen.

APRIL 27   In New York City, the 37-year-old carrier *Intrepid* is retired as a floating sea-air-space museum for the public.

MAY 28   In Florida, a Marine EA-6B Prowler crashes while landing on the deck of the carrier *Nimitz*, killing 14 sailors and injuring 48.

JUNE 17   At Charleston, South Carolina, the missile submarine *James K. Polk* concludes the 2,000th Cold War deterrent patrol made by Navy vessels, and returns to port.

JULY 27   The destroyer *Kidd*, originally intended for service with the Iranian navy, is commissioned; it differs from other *Spruance*-class vessels in being armed with missiles.

AUGUST 19   Over the Gulf of Sidra, Mediterranean Sea, VF-41 F-14 *Tomcats* from the carrier *Nimitz* down two Libyan Su-22 jets after they fire on the Americans in international airspace. Libyan dictator Moammar Qaddafi had proclaimed a "line of death" to any American vessel that crosses it.

OCTOBER 1   The missile submarine *Robert E. Lee* completes the final Cold War deterrent cruise carrying Polaris A-3 missiles.

NOVEMBER 11   At Groton, Connecticut, the new 18,700-ton missile submarine *Ohio* is commissioned. This craft is the largest class of submarine ever launched and is specifically designed to carry 24 new Trident missiles; eighteen vessels are planned for this class.

1982

JANUARY 7   On Moolokai, Hawaii, a Coast Guard HH-52A helicopter crashes while responding to a distress signal, and Lieutenant Colleen A. Cain is the first woman pilot killed in the line of duty.

JANUARY 17   At Cape Kennedy, Florida, the missile submarine *Ohio* fires a Trident missile while submerged, for the first time.

FEBRUARY 13   On the carrier *Nimitz*, F-14 Tomcats of VF-84 complete the first missions utilizing the new Tactical Air Reconnaissance Photographic System (TARPS); this provides low- to medium-altitude photographic capabilities for fleet intelligence.

MARCH 1   The *Robert E. Lee*, the Navy's last Polaris submarine, is redesignated an attack submarine; this class of vessel served with distinction for 21 years.

MARCH 13   The supercarrier *Carl Vinson* is commissioned, giving the U.S. Navy a total of 14 carriers in service.

March 16 In Washington, D.C., Vice President George H. W. Bush announces that Navy Grumman E-2 Hawkeye airborne early warning aircraft, along with several Coast Guard vessels, will be deployed in the war against drug smugglers.

May 16 In San Juan, Puerto Rico, terrorists kill one sailor from the amphibious vessel *Pensacola* and wound three more.

June 20 In the South China Sea, an unidentified vessel fires a machine gun at the guided missile cruiser *Sterett* and destroyers *Lynde McCormick* and *Turner Joy*; warning shots are fired back at the intruder, who sails off.

June 24–25 At Juniyah, Lebanon, the amphibious ships *Nashville* and *Heritage* evacuate 600 Americans and foreign nationals during Israel's invasion of that nation.

August 25 At Beirut, Lebanon, the Sixth Fleet lands part of the 32nd Marine Amphibious Unit as part of an international peacekeeping force and to help supervise the evacuation of 12,000 Palestinian refugees onto merchant vessels during a major relocation. The operation lasts nearly a month.

September 15 At Pascagoula, Mississippi, the World War II-vintage battleship *Iowa* arrives for modernization and a refit, and is scheduled to be activated with the fleet by June 1984.

September 29 At Beirut, Lebanon, the Sixth Fleet debarks 1,200 men of the 32nd Marine Amphibious Unit as part of an international peacekeeping force.

October 1 At Bangor, Washington, the missile submarine *Ohio* begins the first Cold War deterrence cruise to include Trident missiles.

November 23 The guided-missile cruiser *Mississippi* becomes the first U.S. Navy vessel to seize a drug-smuggling vessel at sea; it is boarded by a Coast Guard party.

December 28 At Long Beach, California, the battleship *New Jersey* is recommissioned into active service at the behest of President Ronald W. Reagan; the vessel is outfitted with 16 Harpoon anti-ship missiles and 32 Tomahawk cruise missiles. This is the third time it is called back to the colors.

1983

January 22 The guided-missile cruiser *Ticonderoga* is commissioned; it is the first vessel equipped with the Aegis weapon system and first of a class that ultimately includes 27 vessels.

June 10 At the Naval Air Station, Patuxent River, Maryland, Lieutenant Colleen Nevius is the first female naval aviator to pass through the U.S. Naval Test Pilot School.

July 26–September 12 The carriers *Ranger* and *Coral Sea* and the battleship *New Jersey* deploy off the west coast of Central and South America in a show of force against Communist insurgencies.

September 1 Off the Kamchatka Peninsula, Soviet Union, U.S. Navy vessels search for wreckage of Korean Air Line Flight 007, which was shot down after straying into Soviet airspace.

September 8 In Beirut, Lebanon, the frigate *Bowen* trains its 5-inch guns on Druze militiamen who had been firing on the marines with small arms and mortars.

September 19 In Lebanon, the guided missile cruiser *Virginia* and the destroyer *John Rodgers* fire 338 5-inch rounds near Sug el Gharb village to support the Lebanese army. This act is considered a shift in American policy, which heretofore only fired to defend U.S. positions ashore.

September 25 The revamped battleship *New Jersey* arrives off the coast of Lebanon, a symbol of American determination to support that war-torn nation.

October 1 The Naval Space Command is organized by consolidating several space services into one centrally administered unit. It is administered by Captain Richard Truly, a former astronaut.

October 25–30 In Grenada, Operation Urgent Fury unfolds under Vice Admiral Joseph Metcalf III, when Navy SEALs infiltrate the capital of St. George's and capture Government House; Governor General Sir Paul Scoon is released from captivity. Operations ashore are also abetted by a 12-vessel task force including the carrier *Independence* and the amphibious assault ship *Guam*.

November 1 In Washington, D.C., retired Admiral Hyman G. Rickover receives a second congressional gold medal for his distinguished service to the nation. This a distinction shared only with Zachary Taylor.

In the Arabian Sea, the carrier *Ranger* experiences a fire in its engine room; 6 sailors die and 35 are injured.

November 8 In Washington, D.C., 76-year-old Captain Grace M. Hopper is promoted to commodore. Previously, she was partly responsible for inventing computer-programming languages.

November 17 In the Arabian Sea, the destroyer *Fife* collides with the Soviet missile frigate *Razyashchiy*; minor damage results and there are no casualties.

November 28 In Washington, D.C., the Navy Department declares that the battleship *New Jersey* will be retained off Lebanon in light of the situation there, although the crew may be rotated in the process.

December 4 Near Beirut, Lebanon, 28 Navy warplanes from the *Independence* and *John F. Kennedy* bomb Syrian anti-aircraft and missile batteries. An A-6 Intruder flown by Lieutenant Mark A. Lange is shot down; Lange is killed and his navigator, Robert O. Goodman, is captured. An A-7 Corsair II flown by Commander Edward K. Andrews is also downed; he is wounded but rescued. This action comes in response to Syrian anti-aircraft batteries firing on a U.S. reconnaissance aircraft over the Bekaa Valley.

December 14 In Beirut, Lebanon, the battleship *New Jersey* unleashes its 16-inch guns against militant Druze positions; they are also the first such projectiles fired anywhere since 1969.

1984

January 3 Naval aviator Robert O. Goodman is released by the Syrian government at the behest of the Reverend Jesse Jackson, who negotiates with President Haffez Assad.

February 7 High above Earth, Navy Captain Bruce McCandless makes the first untethered spacewalk from the space shuttle Challenger, using the manned maneuvering unit (MMU).

February 8 In light of continuing tensions in Lebanon, the battleship *New Jersey* lobs 288 16-inch shells upon Syrian and Druze positions in the Bekaa Valley, wiping out eight artillery batteries and killing the Syrian general in charge of Lebanon.

February 9 In Beirut, Lebanon, destroyers *Caron* and *Moosbrugger* unleash 400 5-inch rounds against hostile Syrian positions; this is the heaviest American bombardment of the Lebanese civil war.

February 10–11 In Beirut, Lebanon, Navy and Marine helicopters evacuate American citizens and foreign nationals from Beirut, as the civil war continues spiraling out of control.

February 14 In Beirut, Lebanon, the guided-missile destroyer *Claude V. Ricketts* shells Syrian-held positions east of the city.

February 26 In Beirut, Lebanon, the Sixth Fleet completes the evacuation of the 22nd Marine Amphibious Brigade.

March 21 In the Sea of Japan, the carrier *Kitty Hawk* collides with a Soviet Victor I-class nuclear attack submarine surfacing in its path; the latter is heavily damaged and is towed back to the Soviet naval base at Vladivostok.

April 2 In the South China Sea, the frigate *Harold E. Holt* is struck by three signal flares fired at it by the Soviet aircraft carrier *Minsk*; no damage results.

April 28 The World War II battleship *Iowa* is recommissioned into active service as part of the overall naval buildup.

May 2 In New Orleans, Louisiana, the Bell Aerospace Textron landing-craft air-cushion (LCAC) debuts; this new hovercraft is designed to give amphibious operations better speed and flexibility.

May 5 The battleship *New Jersey*, having sailed 76,000 nautical miles in 322 days, completes its first post-reactivation deployment.

June 25–26 In the Gulf of Sidra off Libya, F-14 Tomcats from the carrier *Saratoga* demonstrate America's confirmation of its status in international waters.

August 7–October 2 In the Red Sea, OPERATION INTENSE LOOK unfolds, as Navy vessels begin minesweeping efforts at the request of Egypt and Saudi Arabia. Previously, several commercial vessels mysteriously exploded and sank in the region.

August 17 In the Gulf of Suez, Egypt, Helicopter Mine Countermeasure Squadron 14 (HM-14) from the amphibious transport dock *Shreveport* begins clearing mines from that strategic waterway. The operation will last 22 days.

September 20 In East Beirut, Lebanon, a terrorist bomb explodes in the U.S. Embassy Annex, killing 23 people; among the dead is Petty Officer Michael R. Wagner. Two sailors are also injured.

November 30 The *Nimitz* battlegroup deploys near Cuba, after the government refuses to allow a Coast Guard vessel to rescue a disabled American ship drifting into its waters. Upon further reflection, the Cubans allow the vessel to be towed.

December 2–4 At Vladivostok, Soviet Union, the *Carl Vinson* and *Midway* carrier battlegroups sail to within 50 miles of the coastline as part of Fleet Exercise 85–1; the Russians respond by dispatching 100 aircraft and vessels in their direction.

1985

February 2 Diplomacy: The government of New Zealand denies permission for the destroyer *Buchanan* to dock, citing its undesirability as a nuclear-armed vessel. This act leads to a rift in U.S.-New Zealand military relations.

May 20 Navy Chief Warrant Officer John A. Walker, Jr., is arrested by the FBI and charged with providing top secret information to Soviet operatives since 1967. Two of his sons in the Navy are also apprehended; the damage inflicted by the Walker family to national security by providing keys for encrypted naval radio transmissions is considered incalculable.

June 14 Islamic terrorists hijack TWA Flight 847 over Athens, Greece, and make it land at Beirut, Lebanon. There they murder Navy diver Steelworker 2nd Class Robert D. Stetham, dumping his body on the tarmac.

August 28 In Washington, D.C., the Navy Department reveals its new Surface Warfare insignia, which is a ship's bow set against a pair of crossed swords.

August 29 In the North Atlantic, NATO exercise Ocean Safari '85 commences, which involves ships from 10 nations including the United States. This is the largest NATO exercise held to date, and involves no less than 157 vessels and 70,000 personnel.

October 10 South of Crete in the Mediterranean, an Egyptian Boeing 737 airliner carrying terrorists responsible for the hijacking of the Italian cruise ship *Achille Lauro* is intercepted by seven Navy F-14 *Tomcat* fighters from the carrier *Saratoga*, and forced to fly to Italy.

November 8 In Washington, D.C., the Navy Department replaces the rank of commodore with that of rear admiral.

November 21 Jonathan Jay Pollard, a former naval intelligence analyst, is arrested and charged with spying for Israel; he is currently serving a life sentence in a military prison.

1986

January 24–21 Off the coast of Libya, the carriers *Coral Sea* and *Saratoga* commence OPERATION ATTAIN FREEDOM I in the Gulf of Sidra, again demonstrating American resolve to defy that government's claim over the region.

January 28 Over Cape Kennedy, Florida, the space shuttle Challenger explodes after takeoff, killing the crew of seven including Commander Michael Smith.

January 29 In waters off the Florida coast, the nuclear-powered submersible *NR-1* is instrumental in retrieving pieces of the exploded space shuttle *Challenger* from the ocean floor.

February 10–15 Once again, carriers *Coral Sea* and *Saratoga* ply the waters of the Gulf of Sidra in defiance of the Libyan government's claim to these waters.

March 22 Near Midway Atoll, the missile submarine *Georgia* collides with the ocean-going tug *Secota*; the latter sinks, and two deaths result.

March 24–25 In the Gulf of Sidra, North Africa, Libyan anti-aircraft batteries fire missiles at Navy aircraft from the *Coral Sea* and *Saratoga*. The next day OPERATION PRAIRIE FIRE unfolds as six A-6 Intruder aircraft from the *America* sink two Libyan patrol boats and a guided missile corvette with Harpoon anti-ship missiles. Several missile batteries on shore are also knocked out by HARM missiles launched from A-7 Corsair IIs.

March 27 Having demonstrated their point, U.S. Naval forces withdraw from the Gulf of Sidra without interference from Libya.

March 29 This season's first flight demonstration performance by the Navy Blue Angels is accompanied by Lieutenant Commander Donnie L. Cochran, the first African American to fly with them.

April 15 Over Libya, OPERATION EL DORADO CANYON unfolds as Air Force F-111F bombers join aircraft from the *America* and *Coral Sea* on a retaliatory strike against Tripoli. Heavy damage is inflicted on the Jumahiriya Military Barracks and Benina Military Airfield. The raid comes in retaliation for Libyan-supported acts of terror in Germany.

May 6 In the Arctic Circle, nuclear-powered submarines *Archerfish*, *Hawkbill*, and *Ray* all simultaneously surface at the North Pole as part of Exercise Icex-I-86. This is the first time three submarines have gathers at the pole for one mass surfacing.

May 10 The historic battleship *Missouri*, upon which the ceremonies ending World War II took place, is the third such vessel recommissioned along with the *Iowa* and *New Jersey*.

May 13 At Long Beach, California, the reconditioned battle ship *New Jersey* sails for the Pacific as a battlegroup and accompanied by the cruiser *Long Beach*, the destroyer *Merrill*, and the frigate *Thatch*. They return to port on October 20.

September 20 In Washington, D.C., Secretary of the Navy John F. Lehman orders brown shoes reissued to uniforms of naval officers and chief petty officers assigned to aviation units.

October 25 The new nuclear-powered carrier *Theodore Roosevelt* is commissioned, bringing the total number of carriers in service up to 15. Two other vessels, the *George Washington* and the *Abraham Lincoln*, are under construction.

November 5 In China, the cruiser *Reeves*, the destroyer *Oldendorf*, and the frigate *Rentz* are first U.S. Navy warships to call in 37 years.

December 31 In San Juan, Puerto Rico, H-3 Sea King helicopters of Composite Squadron (VC) 8 rescue 75 people from the rooftop of a burning hotel.

1987

March 7 In the Persian Gulf, the so-called tanker war begins, as Iran and Iraq begin attacking oil tankers carrying each other's oil. President Ronald W. Reagan is determined that the flow of petroleum to the West continue, and announces that 11 Kuwaiti tankers will be reflagged with American colors to protect them from attack.

April 15 To bring special forces of all four branches, including Navy SEALS, under a unified command, the Navy initiates the Special Operations Command (SOCOM).

April 21 In foggy weather off the Virginia coast, the frigate *Richard L. Page* collides with the fishing boat *Chickadee*, and it sinks.

May 14 In the Persian Gulf, the destroyer *Coontz* prepares to engage an Iraqi Mirage F-1 fighter approaching within 10 miles, when it suddenly turns around.

May 17 In the Persian Gulf, the frigate *Stark* under Captain Glenn R. Brindel is struck by two French-made Exocet missiles fired by an Iraqi F-1 Mirage; 37 sailors are killed, and the vessel is badly damaged. Brindel and his tactical action officer, Lieutenant Basil Moncreif, are allowed to resign rather than face a court-martial.

July 1 The United States commences Operation Earnest Will whereby the cruiser *Fox*, the frigate *Crommelin*, and the destroyer *Kidd* provide escort protection to reflagged Kuwaiti oil tankers as they transit the Persian Gulf.

July 27 In the Persian Gulf, helicopter mine-countermeasure squadron HM-14 arrives after an Iranian mine damages the reflagged tanker *Bridgeton* on July 24.

August 4 At Pascagoula, Mississippi, the amphibious assault ship *Wasp* is launched; this new class of vessel will gradually replace the *Iwo Jima*-style helicopter carriers.

August 24 In the Persian Gulf, the destroyer *Kidd* is approached by two Iranian dhows, until warning shots force them back. The frigate *Jarrett* also interposes his vessel between the convoy he is escorting and an approaching Iranian warship.

August 26 In Washington, D.C., Secretary of the Navy James Webb announces that the newest Aegis-class cruiser will be named the *Hue Cry* after the 1968 victory over the Viet Cong. This is the first vessel to carry a battle name from the Vietnam War.

September 10 VC-6, Detachment One, one of the first squadrons of Pioneer remotely controlled vehicles, deploys on the battleship *Iowa*.

September 21 In the Persian Gulf, an Army Special Forces MH-6 helicopter from the frigate *Jarrett* damages the Iranian landing craft *Iran Ajr* after it is caught deploying mines. The vessel is then stormed by SEALs and taken under tow; 3 Iranians are killed, and the remaining crew of 26 is released shortly afterwards.

October 8 In the Persian Gulf, an Army Special Forces MH-6 helicopter launched from the frigate *Ford* attacks four Iranian speedboats (boghammers) who had been firing at U.S. helicopters; one is sunk and two are captured.

October 13 In Washington, D.C., 7,000 active duty sailors, retirees, and family members attend ceremonies dedicating the new "Lone Sailor" statue as a tribute to all naval personnel, past and present.

October 19 In the Persian Gulf, guided-missile destroyers *Hoel* and *Kidd*, along with the destroyers *John Young* and *Leftwich,* destroy two older Iranian oil platforms 80 miles east of Qatar to retaliate for missile attacks against neutral shipping.

DECEMBER 12   In the Persian Gulf, a helicopter from the destroyer *Chandler* evacuates 11 crewmen from the Cypriot tanker *Pivot,* after Iranian speedboats attack it.

DECEMBER 25   In the Persian Gulf, helicopters from the frigates *Elrod* and HMS *Scylla* rescue 20 crewmen from the South Korean tanker *Hyundai,* after an Iranian frigate attacks it.

DECEMBER 27   In Barcelona, Spain, a terrorist bomb rips through the United Service Organization club, killing one sailor and injuring five.

1988

FEBRUARY 12   Near Sebastopol in the Black Sea, the guided-missile cruiser *Yorktown* and the destroyer *Caron* are bumped by two Soviet patrol frigates protesting their proximity to this major Soviet naval base.

FEBRUARY 22   In Washington, D.C., Secretary of the Navy James H. Webb resigns over Secretary of Defense Frank Carlucci's failure to support the so-called 600-ship Navy. In reality, Carlucci had authorized the retirement of 16 elderly frigates.

APRIL 14   In the Persian Gulf, the frigate *Samuel B. Roberts* strikes a mine that injures 10 sailors and inflicts a 21-foot-long hole in its hull. Iran is suspected to have planted the mine.

In Naples, Italy, a terrorist bomb explodes in a United Services Organization club; one sailor is killed and four are wounded. Libyan agents are suspected.

APRIL 18   In the Persian Gulf, OPERATION PRAYING MANTIS unfolds, as U.S. Navy warships and jet bombers retaliate for a mine strike on the frigate *Samuel B. Roberts.* The destroyer *Merrill* shells and destroys the Sassan oil platform, while a second structure, the Sirri platform, is also eliminated by the guided-missile cruiser *Wainwright* and frigates *Simpson* and *Bagley.* A-6 Intruders from the carrier *Enterprise* fire Harpoon missiles that sink the fast patrol boat *Joshan* and the frigate *Sahand.* A-6 and A-7 aircraft also pummel the Iranian frigate *Sabalan,* which is allowed to return to port in severely damaged condition.

APRIL 24   Near Cape Kennedy, Florida, the diesel-electric submarine *Bonefish* is decommissioned, following a battery explosion that kills three sailors.

APRIL 29   In Washington, D.C., Secretary of Defense Frank Carlucci announces that the United States will protect neutral shipping in the Persian Gulf by force of arms, if necessary.

JUNE 28   In Athens, Greece, a terrorist bomb kills Naval attache Captain William E. Nordeen, as he drives to work.

JULY 2   In the Persian Gulf, the frigate *Elmer B. Montgomery* fires warning shots at an Iranian speedboat harassing a Danish supertanker.

JULY 3   In the Persian Gulf, the guided-missile cruiser *Vincennes* picks up a radar contact indicating that a large aircraft is approaching. This turns out to be an

Iranian A-300 Airbus, yet it is mistaken at long range for an Iranian F-14 fighter. Fearing a suicide attack, the *Vincennes* shoots it down after the craft ignores repeated warnings, killing all 290 passengers. A Navy investigation subsequently exonerates Captain Will C. Rodgers for his actions.

SEPTEMBER 26 In Washington, D.C., President Ronald Reagan, reacting to an end of the Iran-Iraq War, declares that Navy convoy-style operations in the Persian Gulf will be replaced by a zone-defense system.

OCTOBER 22 The battleship *Wisconsin* is recommissioned; this is the first time that all four *Iowa*-class battleships are in service since World War II.

DECEMBER In the Persian Gulf, tensions have declined, and the role of the Navy reverts back to monitoring U.S.-flagged vessels and OPERATION EARNEST WILL concludes. Since July 1987, Navy vessels had escorted 270 merchant ships plying these dangerous waters in 136 convoys; the tanker *Bridgeton* was damaged.

1989

JANUARY 4 Over the Gulf of Sidra, F-14 Tomcats from the *John F. Kennedy* shoot down two Libyan MiG-23 jets which had approached the American jets in a hostile manner.

MARCH 21 Near Cape Kennedy, Florida, the missile submarine *Tennessee* launches the Trident II D-5 missile underwater for the first time; the test fails, and the missile has to be destroyed in mid-flight.

APRIL 19 Near Puerto Rico, the battleship *Iowa* suffers a turret explosion that kills 47 sailors; only quick flooding of the powder magazine below the turret prevents an even larger, more catastrophic explosion.

MAY 30 Near Okinawa, a CH-46 Skyknight helicopter crashes moments after being launched from the amphibious transport *Denver*; 13 marines and a Navy corpsman are killed.

JUNE 14 Near California, the submarine *Houston* snares a tow bale dangling from the tugboat *Barcelona* and drags it underwater; one civilian dies.

JULY 21–AUGUST 8 At Norfolk, Virginia, the Soviet missile cruiser *Marshal Ustinov*, the missile destroyer *Otlichny*, and oiler *Genrikh Gasanov* pay a friendly port visit.

AUGUST 4–8 The guided-missile cruiser *Thomas Gates* and guided-missile frigate *Kauffman* concurrently drop anchors at Sevastopol, Crimea, in the Soviet Union.

SEPTEMBER 7 An investigation concludes that the turret accident on the battleship *Iowa* resulted from a suicidal act of sabotage by Gunner's Mate Second Class Clayton Hartwigg. Hartwigg's family strongly contests the finding.

SEPTEMBER 16 At Bath, Maine, the guided-missile destroyer *Arleigh Burke*, the first of a class of 25 vessels, is launched. This represents a new generation of highly automated, computer-linked warships.

October 11 An officer and a seaman die on the amphibious assault ship *Iwo Jima*, when struck by rounds accidentally fired from a Phalanx gun on the cargo ship *El Paso*.

October 29 Near Pensacola, the pilot and four deck crewmen die following the crash of a T-2 Buckeye trainer on the flight deck of the training carrier *Lexington*.

October 30 In the Indian Ocean, an F/A-18 Hornet accidently drops a 500-pound bomb on the guided missile cruiser *Reeves*; five sailors are injured.

November 11 The nuclear-powered carrier *Abraham Lincoln* is commissioned; this is the fifth of the ultra-modern *Nimitz*-class carriers constructed.

November 14 In Washington, D.C., Chief of Naval Operations Admiral Carlisle Trost orders the entire fleet to stand down for a review of basic safety procedures. He subsequently testifies before Congress that 67 major mishaps have cost $1 million to repair.

December 2 Near Malta, the guided-missile cruiser *Belknap* arrives as a meeting place for talks between Presidents George H. W. Bush and Mikhail S. Gorbachev.

December 7 In the Persian Gulf, the *New Jersey* becomes the first battleship to visit these waters on a five-day goodwill cruise to Bahrain and the United Arab Emirates.

December 16 In Panama City, Panama, a Navy officer and his wife are taken into custody and physically abused by Panamanian guards. This incident proves a catalyst for President George H. W. Bush to take direct action against the dictatorship of General Manuel Noriega.

December 20–24 In Panama, several SEAL teams participate in OPERATION JUST CAUSE, disabling a boat and a car used by dictator Manuel Noriega, thereby preventing his escape. They also engage in a heavy firefight with Panamanian security forces at Paitilla Airport; four Navy personnel are killed and nine wounded.

1990

January 25 In Washington, D.C., Secretary of Defense Dick Cheney announces the retirement of 54 warships, including 2 battleships and 5 nuclear attack submarines, as a cost-cutting expedient.

March 29–April 23 The missile submarine *Tennessee* makes the first deterrent patrol while armed with new Trident D-5 missiles.

April 30 At Norfolk, Virginia, the aircraft carrier *Coral Sea* is decommissioned after 42 years of service; the number of carrier battlegroups in service is reduced to 14.

May 8 Near Norfolk, Virginia, a boiler-room fire on the guided-missile destroyer *Conyngham* kills one sailor and injures 18; the ship is decommissioned shortly afterwards.

June 20 Off the coast of Japan, a storeroom fire on the carrier *Midway* kills two sailors and injures 16.

JUNE 27–29 At Gdansk, Poland, the guided-missile carrier *Yarnell* and the guided-missile frigate *Kaufman* conduct a goodwill tour; they are the first American warships to visit in 45 years.

JULY 12 Commander Rosemary B. Mariner takes control of Tactical Electronics Warfare Squadron 34 (VAQ-34), becoming the first woman to head an operational aircraft squadron.

AUGUST 2 In a military miscalculation of mammoth proportions, Iraqi dictator Saddam Hussein orders his army to invade the neighboring, oil-rich country of Kuwait. President George H. W. Bush condemns the move as "naked aggression," and orders the U.S. military to take measures to drive him out.

AUGUST 3 In response to the Iraqi invasion of Kuwait, the carrier *Independence* battlegroup is ordered from the Indian Ocean to the Persian Gulf region, while the carrier *Eisenhower* battlegroup relocates from the Mediterranean to the Red Sea.

AUGUST 5 In Liberia, OPERATION SHARP EDGE commences as the amphibious assault ship *Saipan* evacuates 2,609 American and foreign nationals from the capital of Monrovia.

AUGUST 7 In the Red Sea, the carrier *Dwight D. Eisenhower* joins the carrier *Independence* in the Gulf of Oman. Their combined air wings are the only aircraft available for use in the Persian Gulf.

AUGUST 11 In the Persian Gulf, U.S. Navy vessels enforce a United Nations embargo of Iraq by enacting a naval quarantine. The hospital ship *Comfort* also sails from Norfolk to the Persian Gulf, becoming the first vessel of its type fully activated since Vietnam.

AUGUST 18 In the Persian Gulf, the guided-missile frigate *Reid* and frigate *Bradley* independently fire warning shots at two Iraqi tankers attempting to leave. The guided-missile cruiser *England* and the guided-missile destroyer *Scott* also divert several freighters from docking there.

AUGUST 28 In the Gulf of Aqaba, U.S. Navy warship halt the Greek container vessel *Zorba Express* and the Indian merchant ship *Kalidas*, search for contraband items, then allow them to proceed.

AUGUST 31 In the Persian Gulf, the guided-missile cruiser *Biddle* searches the Iraqi freighter *Al Karamah*; it is subsequently allowed to proceed to Jordan. To date, Navy vessels have stopped 350 ships and boarded 11.

SEPTEMBER 5 In San Diego, California, the fleet tender *Acadia* departs with a crew of 1,260, including 360 women. This becomes the first test of a combined-sex crew in wartime.

SEPTEMBER 12 The battleship of *Wisconsin* test-fires its 16-inch guns for the first time since the turret explosion aboard its sister ship *Iowa* on April 19, 1989.

SEPTEMBER 16 In the Persian Gulf, the Bahamian-rigged tanker *Daimon* becomes the 1,000th vessel to be searched after it is intercepted by the destroyer *O'Brien*.

SEPTEMBER 27 In the Gulf of Aqaba, Jordan, the Iraqi tanker *Tadmur* is intercepted and searched by the frigate *Elmer B. Montgomery* after firing shots across its bow.

OCTOBER 1–4 In the Persian Gulf, the carrier *Independence* becomes the first vessel of its kind to operate in such cramped waters since 1974.

OCTOBER 8 In the Gulf of Oman, the frigate *Reasoner*, British frigates *Battleaxe* and *London*, and Australian frigate *Adelaide* accost the Iraqi tanker *Al-Wasitti* by firing across its bow. The vessel is searched, found empty, then allowed to proceed.

OCTOBER 20 To date, U.S. and Coalition warships enforcing the naval quarantine against Iraq have stopped 2,500 vessels at sea and boarded no less than 240.

OCTOBER 26 At Norfolk, Virginia, the battleship *Iowa* is decommissioned and returned to mothballs; this leaves three battleships on active duty.

OCTOBER 30 In the Persian Gulf, a steam leak on the amphibious assault ship *Iwo Jima* kills 10 sailors.

NOVEMBER 8 In Washington, D.C., Vice Admiral Peter M. Hekman testifies before Congress that he is willing to decommission the battleships *Missouri* and *Wisconsin*, unless the two have unique utilities applicable to the present Middle Eastern crisis.

DECEMBER 10 In Washington, D.C., Pentagon Inspector General Susan Crawford tells the House Armed Service Committee that a criminal investigation is underway relative to overpayments in the A-12 Avenger stealth-attack aircraft jointly developed by McDonnell Douglas and General Dynamics.

DECEMBER 21 Near Haifa, Israel, tragedy strikes as the chartered ferry *Tuvia* capsizes while returning to the carrier *Saratoga*; 21 sailors are drowned.

DECEMBER 26 In the Arabian Sea, the destroyers *Fife* and *Oldendorf*, the guided-missile frigate *Trenton*, and the amphibious transport dock *Shreveport* intercept and board the so-called "peace ship" *Ibn Khaldoon*. It is found carrying contraband cargo, and is redirected into a port in Oman.

DECEMBER 27 At Naples, Italy, Lieutenant Commander Darlene Iskra becomes the first female to head up a U.S. Navy vessel when she takes charge of the salvage ship *Opportune*.

1991

JANUARY 4 In the Red Sea, the Soviet freighter *Dmitri Firmanov* is halted by a Spanish warship and boarded by U.S. naval personnel present, who uncover military equipment; the vessel is thereupon detained.

JANUARY 5 Off the Horn of Africa, the assault ship *Guam* and the transport dock *Trenton* assist in the evacuation of 500 American diplomats and foreign nationals from war-torn Somalia.

JANUARY 7 In Washington, D.C., Secretary of Defense Richard Cheney cancels the behind-schedule, over-budget A-12 Avenger stealth aircraft, after $52 billion has been spent. To date, this is the largest defense project ever cancelled.

JANUARY 16 Six carriers begin launching strikes against targets in Kuwait and Iraq as part of OPERATION DESERT STORM. The F/A-18 Hornet flown by Lieutenant Commander Michael S. Speicher of

VFA-81 (*Saratoga*) is shot down, and the pilot is declared killed in action; his remains are discovered in July 2009.

In the Persian Gulf region, Navy vessels fire 122 precision-guided Tomahawk cruise missiles; the honor of the first shot goes to the cruiser *San Jacinto* in the Red Sea. Tomahawk missiles are also launched from the battleships *Wisconsin* and *Missouri*.

JANUARY 18   Over Iraq, a pair of MiG-29s falls to a pair of F/A-18s piloted by Commander Mark I. Fox and Lieutenant Nick Mongillo from VFA-81 of the *Saratoga*.

In the Persian Gulf, the frigate *Nicholas*, assisted by Helicopter Antisubmarine Squadron (Light) (HSL-44) and a Kuwaiti patrol boat, neutralizes Iraqi oil platforms launching shoulder-launched missiles at coalition aircraft; 5 Iraqis die, 8 are wounded, and 23 become captives. The destroyer *Moosbrugger* also dispatches a SEAL team on board the Sudanese vessel *El Obeid*; this becomes the first vessel apprehended since hostilities commenced.

JANUARY 19   Over Iraq, the new Standoff Land Attack Missiles(SLAM) are fired by A-6 Intruders and A-7 Corsair IIs from the *John F. Kennedy* and *Saratoga* for the first time.

In the Red Sea, the submarine *Louisville* fires the first-ever submerged Tomahawk cruise missile at targets in Iraq.

JANUARY 22   Over the Persian Gulf, A-6 Intruder aircraft sinks an Iraqi T-43 class vessel capable of laying mines.

JANUARY 23   In the Persian Gulf, A-6 Intruders disable an Iraqi *Al Qaddisiyah*-class tanker collecting military intelligence, while an enemy hovercraft and patrol ship moored alongside are sunk.

A diver from Detachment B, Explosive Ordnance Disposal (EOD) Mobile Unit 6 attaches an explosive charge to the side of an Iraqi mine in the Persian Gulf on January 1, 1991. While operating with the U.S. Mine Countermeasures Group, the divers of Detachment B recovered or destroyed forty Iraqi mines in the Persian Gulf and Kuwait's harbors. (United States Navy)

JANUARY 24 In the Persian Gulf, A-6 Intruder aircraft sink an Iraqi minelayer and minesweeper; 22 survivors are airlifted to safety by an SH-60 Seahawk from the guided missile frigate *Curts*. A SEAL team also lands on a small island and captures 51 Iraqis shooting at coalition aircraft. These are evacuated by helicopters from the destroyer *Leftwich* and the guided-missile frigate *Nicholas*; this is also the first Kuwaiti territory liberated from Iraq.

JANUARY 29 Over the Persian Gulf, Navy warplanes sink three Iraqi patrol boats near Bubiyan Island, while a further three are destroyed in gulf waters.

FEBRUARY 4 In Washington, D.C., the new defense budget includes $2.8 billion for a new *Seawolf* nuclear attack submarine, the first in its class, but the battleships *Missouri* and *Wisconsin* are to be mothballed.

FEBRUARY 4–9 In the Persian Gulf, the battleship *Missouri* fires its 16-inch guns for the first time since World War II, destroying Iraqi command and control bunkers. Three days later the battleship *Wisconsin* takes its place and fires its big guns for the first time since the Korean War.

FEBRUARY 6 Over Iraq, an F-14 Tomcat from the *Ranger* shoots down an Iraqi Mi-8 helicopter.

FEBRUARY 8 At Long Beach, California, the venerable battleship *New Jersey* is decommissioned and sent to mothballs.

FEBRUARY 18 In the Persian Gulf, Iraqi mines damage the amphibious assault ship *Tripoli* and the guided-missile cruiser *Princeton*; seven crewmen are injured. American and British minesweepers begin clearing out the area.

FEBRUARY 25 In the Persian Gulf, the battleships *Missouri* and *Wisconsin* join 29 other allied vessels in shelling Iraqi positions along the Kuwaiti coast and on Faylakah Island. The British destroyer *Gloucester* also fires two Sea Dart missiles, which destroy an Iraqi Silkworm missile apparently headed for the *Missouri*.

MARCH 4 In Iraq, among the 10 Coalition prisoners released are Navy lieutenants Lawrence R. Slade, Robert Wetzel, and Jeffrey N. Zaun.

MARCH 18 At Norfolk, Virginia, the combat stores ship *Sylvania* becomes the first vessel from OPERATION DESERT STORM to reach home port. Previously, it delivered 20,500 tons of supplies and 31,000 piles of mail over a seven-month period.

APRIL 11 During OPERATION DESERT SHIELD/STORM, U.S. Navy vessels have destroyed 533 mines, intercepted 8,770 merchant ships, and boarded 590.

JUNE 16–25 Near Luzon, the Philippines, vessels of the Seventh Fleet help evacuate 19,000 people following the violent eruption of Mount Pinatubo.

JULY 4 At Norfolk, Virginia, the *Arleigh Burke* is commissioned as the first Aegis guided-missile destroyer; the honor is conferred while Admiral Burke is still alive. In time this class of Navy vessels will become the most numerous in operation.

SEPTEMBER 8 In Las Vegas, Nevada, during the 35th annual Tailhook Convention, bawdy behavior brings charges of groping and other forms of sexual harassment from 83 women (including several active-duty officers) and 7 men. A total of 69 officers receive reprimands for their conduct, and the Navy institutes gender sensitivity training for the first time in its history.

SEPTEMBER 11   At Yokosuka, Japan, the *Independence* replaces the *Midway* as the Navy's only forward-deployed carrier.

SEPTEMBER 16   In Manila, Philippines, the Philippine senate rejects renewing the Subic Bay Naval facility lease on a vote of 12 to 11, despite the urging of President Corazon Aquinio.

SEPTEMBER 27   In Washington, D.C., President George H.W. Bush declares that the United States will unilaterally reduce its nuclear weapons stockpile, including those carried at sea.

SEPTEMBER 30   The venerable battleship *Wisconsin* is decommissioned and consigned to mothballs.

OCTOBER 17   The Navy formally exonerates sailor Clayton Hartwigg for the accidental explosion on board the battleship *Iowa*; they also apologize to his family for earlier accusations.

NOVEMBER 15   A U.S. federal appeals court orders all charges against Rear Admiral John M. Poindexter dropped over for his role in the Iran-Contra scandal; he was a member of the president's National Security Advisory at the time.

NOVEMBER 24   The Navy relinquishes Subic Bay and all its naval facilities once the Philippine government refuses to renew its lease; thus ends an American naval presence going back to 1898.

DECEMBER 8   At the Naval Air Station, Pensacola, Florida, the training carrier *Lexington*, last of the World War II *Essex*-class carriers, is decommissioned. It ends up a floating museum in Corpus Christi, Texas.

1992

FEBRUARY 12   Near Wake Atoll in the mid-Pacific, the salvage vessel *Salvor* brings up parts of a helicopter from 17,250 feet; this is the deepest-known oceanic recovery.

MARCH 31   The venerable battleship *Missouri*, on whose decks the World War II surrender documents were signed, is decommissioned.

JUNE 22   In Washington, D.C., Secretary of the Navy H. Lawrence Garrett III resigns due to criticism arising from his handling of the "Tailhook" scandal.

JULY 4   The nuclear-powered supercarrier *George Washington* is commissioned, being the sixth member of the *Nimitz* class.

JULY 22   In Washington, D.C., the Assistant Chiefs of Naval Operations for Surface, Submarine, Air, and Naval Warfare are all consolidated under the Deputy Chief of Naval Operations for Resources, Warfare, Requirements, and Assessment.

JULY 24   In the Adriatic Sea, the carrier *Saratoga* becomes the first such vessel to conduct operations relative to ethnic unrest in the former Yugoslavian province of Bosnia-Herzegovina.

JULY 27   Over Iraq, warplanes launched from the carrier *Independence* are among the first to enforce no-fly provisions of OPERATION SOUTHERN WATCH.

SEPTEMBER 24 A government inquiry into the so-called "Tailhook Scandal" reveals that several high-ranking officers tried to obstruct the matter to avoid adverse publicity; two admirals are retired and one is reassigned.

SEPTEMBER 28 In Washington, D.C., a far-sighted policy statement entitled " . . . From the Sea" emerges to address post-Cold War requirements and concerns for the Navy and Marine Corps. It argues that the services must be retooled for a variety of global missions, and in the face of shrinking defense appropriations.

OCTOBER 1 In the Mediterranean, the bridge of the Turkish destroyer *Muavenet* is struck by a Sea Sparrow missile accidentally launched from the aircraft carrier *Saratoga*; five sailors die, including the ship's captain.

DECEMBER 9–10 In Mogadishu, Somalia, OPERATION RESTORE HOPE commences as SEAL and marine reconnaissance teams go ashore to facilitate the transfer of humanitarian aid. The effort is assisted offshore by the carrier *Ranger* and the supply vessel *Tripoli*, which also monitor air traffic in the capital.

1993

JANUARY 13 The carrier *Kitty Hawk* launches 35 warplanes which strike at 32 Iraqi missile and radar sites, after they deliberately locked onto Coalition aircraft. This action comes is spite of repeated warnings to desist.

JANUARY 15–NOVEMBER 26, 1994 Near Haiti, OPERATION ABLE MANNER unfolds as 17 Coast Guard vessels and 5 Navy ships intercept 40,000 migrants attempting to illegally enter the United States; most are returned to Haiti.

JANUARY 17 In the Persian Gulf, the destroyers *Caron*, *Hewitt*, and *Stump* launch cruise missiles against the Zaafaraniyah nuclear fabrication plant in Baghdad, Iraq; the facility is demolished.

MARCH 12 In Norfolk, Virginia, the Naval Doctrine Command is founded.

APRIL 12 In the Adriatic Sea, warplanes from several carriers offshore, along with those based at Aviano, Italy, are engaged in OPERATION DENY FLIGHT over Bosnia, to suppress Serbian and Yugoslavian air support to their ground forces. The operation remains in place until December 20, 1995.

APRIL 28 In Washington, D.C., Defense Secretary Les Aspin eliminates the ban on women flying combat missions.

JUNE 15 In the Adriatic Sea, Navy vessels embark on OPERATION SHARP GUARD to enforce economic sanctions against Croatia, Serbia, and the Republic of Yugoslavia. The operation lasts until June 19, 1996; during this time 73,000 vessels are challenged and 7,200 searched.

JUNE 26 In the Persian Gulf, the cruiser *Chancellorsville* and the destroyer *Peterson* unleash 23 Tomahawk cruise missiles at Iraqi Intelligence Service headquarters. This action comes in response to a revelation that the Iraqis were plotting to kill President George H. W. Bush when he visited Kuwait in the previous April.

JULY 29 Over southern Iraq, EA-6B Prowlers unleash HARM missiles at anti-aircraft sites that had established radar locks on them.

SEPTEMBER 1 The Navy Department releases its "Bottom Up Review" that declares the fleet should consist of 346 ships, including 11 carrier battlegroups and 1 training/reserve carrier battlegroup. Thus armed, it could wage two major regional conflicts and one low-intensity conflict simultaneously.

SEPTEMBER 11 At the Philadelphia Naval Yard, Pennsylvania, the first supercarrier *Forrestal*, which entered service in 1955, is decommissioned.

OCTOBER 1 The Joint Primary Aircraft Training Program begins with Air Force pilots arriving at Naval Air Station Whiting Field, Florida, and Navy, Marine Corps, and Coast Guard aviators deploying at Randolph Air Force Base, Texas.

OCTOBER 15 In Washington, D.C., Pentagon officials censor 3 admirals and 30 senior naval officers for failing to properly supervise the annual Tailhook Convention in Las Vegas, Nevada.

OCTOBER 18 In Haiti, Navy and Coast Guard vessels enforce United Nations sanctions against the military regime by enacting OPERATION SUPPORT DEMOCRACY and enforcing an economic quarantine. These sanctions remain in place until President Aristide is allowed to return.

NOVEMBER 30 In Washington, D.C., President William J. Clinton signs legislation permitting women to serve on Navy combat vessels.

1994

FEBRUARY 27 Lieutenant Shannon Workman becomes the first female pilot to carrier-qualify by landing her EA-6B Prowler on the carrier *Dwight D. Eisenhower*.

MARCH 7 The carrier *Dwight D. Eisenhower* is the first Navy warship with a permanent female complement of 67 women officers and sailors.

APRIL 11 In Bosnia, a pair of A/F-18 Hornets strafe Serbian targets near the Gorazde safe zone in support of UN peacekeeping forces.

APRIL 23 In Washington, D.C., Admiral Jeremy M. Boorda becomes the 25th Chief of Naval Operations; he is the first to do so by rising through the enlisted ranks.

JULY 31 Off the coast of California, Lieutenants Kara Hultgreen and Carey Dunai are the first women qualified in F-14 Tomcats by landing on the carrier *Constellation*.

AUGUST 19–24 In waters off Cuba, OPERATION ABLE VIGIL unfolds as Coast Guard vessels intercept 30,224 refugees attempting to escape Communism. This is the biggest Coast Guard operation since the Vietnam War, and involves 38 cutters and 9 naval vessels.

> **Boorda, Jeremy M. (1938–1996)**
>
> Jeremy Michael Boorda was born in South Bend, Indiana, on November 28, 1938, and he joined the Navy in 1954 after dropping out of high school. He passed officer candidate's school in 1962, rose rapidly through the ranks, and in 1981 he commanded Destroyer Squadron 22. Boorda next rose to rear admiral and commander of Destroyer-Cruiser Force 8 in 1984; then, in 1991, he advanced to four-star admiral and commander, Allied Forces, South Europe, and commander, U.S. Naval Force Europe. In this capacity he orchestrated NATO's first-ever offensive action by ordering air strikes against Serbian forces in Bosnia, to halt "ethnic cleansing" operations there. The performance of naval air units involved was judged to be excellent, and he was much praised for the effort.
>
> Boorda's career crested on April 23, 1994, when President Bill Clinton appointed him the 25th Chief of Naval Operations, becoming the first CNO to have risen from the ranks. Boorda inherited a force boasting great technical competence, but buffeted by internal morale problems. So he worked the halls of Congress to preserve long-range strategic spending, while securing pay and benefit raises to maintain skilled personnel. He also preserved funding for newer and better ships and aircraft, along with highly sophisticated technical systems to enhance combat effectiveness. Unfortunately, Boorda's otherwise successful tenure as CNO was interrupted over the issue of combat medals that he apparently did not earn in Vietnam. Boorda, in fact, was never in combat, and when it became apparent that *Newsweek* magazine was about to break the story nationally, he committed suicide on May 16, 1996. Boorda was interred with full honors at Arlington National Cemetery.

SEPTEMBER 19 Off the coast of Haiti, 24 Navy vessels participate in OPERATION SUPPORT DEMOCRACY. These include carriers *Dwight D. Eisenhower* and *America*, which remove their usual air groups to accommodate Army helicopters. Crisis is averted when General Manuel Cedras agrees to depart peacefully.

OCTOBER 8–DECEMBER 22 In the Persian Gulf, recent Iraqi maneuvers near the Kuwaiti border require the guided-missile cruiser *Leyte Gulf* to be deployed there as part of OPERATION VIGILANT WARRIOR. The carrier *George Washington* battlegroup is also ordered to deploy in the Red Sea, if needed.

OCTOBER 25 On the carrier *Abraham Lincoln*, Lieutenant Kara S. Hultgreen, the first woman qualified in an F-14 Tomcat, dies in a landing accident, when her aircraft suddenly loses power.

NOVEMBER 15 Another racial barrier falls as Commander Donnie L. Cochran becomes the first African American to head up the Blue Angels Flight Demonstration Team.

1995

JANUARY 12 As a cost-cutting expedient, the four mothballed *Iowa*-class battleships are finally removed from the Naval Vessel register.

FEBRUARY 27–MARCH 3   Near Mogadishu, Somalia, the amphibious assault ship *Essex* removes the last remaining United Nations troops from that war-torn land.

MARCH 3   At Cape Kennedy, Florida, Lieutenant Commander Wendy Lawrence is the first female naval aviator in space when she launches aboard the space shuttle *Endeavor* as a mission specialist.

MAY   This month Admiral Paul J. Reason, the first African American to reach four-star rank, assumes command of the Atlantic Fleet.

JUNE 8   In the Adriatic Sea, the amphibious assault ship *Kearsarge* launches a marine reconnaissance unit that successfully locates and rescues Air Force F-16 pilot Captain Scott Grady, who had been shot down over Banja Luka on June 2.

JUNE 27–JULY 7   Over Earth, the space shuttle Atlantis under Captain Robert Gibson docks with the Russian space station Mir.

JULY 1   To better exercise operational control of U.S. naval forces in the Persian Gulf and Indian Ocean region, the Fifth Fleet is established under the aegis of the U.S. Central Command (CENTCOM).

AUGUST 4   Over Croatia, EA-6B Prowlers from the *Theodore Roosevelt* and two Marine Corps F/A-18 Hornets from Aviano, Italy, fire HARM missiles at Serbian missile sites near Knin and Ubdina.

AUGUST 17   Iraqi troop movements along the Kuwaiti border result in the *Abraham Lincoln* and *Independence* carrier battlegroups being placed on alert, along with the *New Orleans* amphibious ready group. In the eastern Mediterranean, the carrier *Theodore Roosevelt* also steams within bombardment range.

AUGUST 30–SEPTEMBER 21   Over Serbia, warplanes launched from the carriers *Theodore Roosevelt* and *America* pound Serb missile and radar installations, command posts, and ammunition dumps in response to a mortar attack on Sarajevo, capital of Bosnia. The Aegis cruiser *Normandy* also weighs in by launching Tomahawk cruise missiles at air defense targets in Banja Luka.

NOVEMBER 29   Over St. Louis, Missouri, the Navy's ultra-modern McDonnell-Douglas F/A-18E Super Hornet is test-flown for the first time.

DECEMBER 9   The supercarrier *John C. Stennis* is commissioned, being the eighth *Nimitz*-class vessel to join the fleet.

1996

JANUARY 22   In Washington, D.C., a defense appropriations act signed this day allows the Navy to put the two best-preserved battleships back on the list. A conundrum develops, as *Iowa*-class battleships are prohibitively expensive to maintain in mothballs. Naval authorities request clarification on the issue before placing the *Iowa* and *Wisconsin* in Category B Mobilization Assets.

February 24 Off the coast of Cuba, the guided-missile cruiser *Mississippi* and the amphibious assault ship *Nassau* assist Coast Guard vessels to search for survivors of two Cessna aircraft downed by Cuban Air Force MiGs.

March 5–24 In the western Pacific, the Navy rushes the *Nimitz* and *Independence* carrier battlegroups into the Taiwan Strait as a sign of solidarity with the Nationalist regime. The People's Republic of China has apparently closed part of that waterway to conduct live-fire naval exercises on the eve of Taiwan's national election.

March 23 In the China Sea, the *Nimitz* and *Independence* carrier battlegroups cruise the vicinity of Taiwan as the People's Republic of China conducts live-fire exercises nearby.

April 9–25 At Monrovia, Liberia, Navy SEALS and other special forces arrive from the assault ship *Guam* to facilitate implementation of a major evacuation effort, dubbed Operation Assured Response.

April 15 At Randolph Air Force Base, Texas, Navy and Air Force navigator trainees will study in a single class for the first time.

April 20 Near Monrovia, Liberia, the amphibious assault ship *Guam*, the amphibious transport dock *Trenton*, the dock-landing ship *Portland*, and guided-missile destroyer *Conolly* evacuate 1,250 Americans and foreign nationals as part of Operation Assured Response.

May 9 Several geography experts determine that Admiral Robert E. Byrd falsified his diary in claiming to be the first person to fly over the North Pole on May 9, 1926.

May 13 In Washington, D.C., Vice Admiral Paul Reason is nominated to become the Navy's first four-star admiral of African American descent.

May 16 In Washington, D.C., Chief of Naval Operations Admiral Jeremy M. Boorda commits suicide after accusations surface that he was wearing Vietnam combat decorations that he never earned.

June 4 In the Pacific, the Japanese destroyer *Yuugiri* accidentally shoots down an A-6 Intruder from the carrier *Independence* as it was engaged in target-towing activities; both crewmen eject and are rescued.

June 21 At Randolph Air Force Base, Texas, Commander David J. Cheslak becomes the first naval officer to lead an Air Force squadron when he assumes control of the 562nd Flying Training Squadron; this unit is responsible for training navigators for both services.

In Washington, D.C., Congress scales back procurement plans for the the new and highly capable *Seawolf* submarines, costing $2.1 billion apiece, from 28 units to only 3.

July 1 On the carrier *Constellation*, an Air Force crew flies a EA-6B Prowler off a deck for the first time; this aircraft is intended to replace the EF-111, as it is being phased out operationally.

July 5 The nuclear attack submarine *Seawolf* successfully completes its sea trials, but only three will be acquired due to their great expense.

July 10 In Washington, D.C., Rear Admiral Patricia Tracey is promoted to Vice Admiral; she is the first three-star female officer of any service.

JULY 11 At Naval Air Station, Fallon, Nevada, the new Naval Strike and Air Warfare Center arises as the Naval Strike Warfare Center, Navy Fighter Weapons School, and Carrier Airborne Early Warning Weapons School are consolidated.

JULY 17 Off the coast of New York, salvage ships *Grasp* and *Grapple*, along with the landing-dock ship *Oak Hill*, comb the waters for wreckage from TWA Flight 800 after it crashes.

JULY 27 At Groton, Connecticut, the submarine *Louisiana* is commissioned, being the 18th and final *Ohio*-class ballistic-missile submarines.

AUGUST 8 Lieutenant Manje Malak Abd Al Mut'a Ali Noe becomes the Navy's first Muslim chaplain.

SEPTEMBER 3–4 Reacting to Iraqi occupation of Kurdish territory, OPERATION DESERT STRIKE unfolds as the guided-missile cruiser *Shiloh*, the guided-missile destroyers *Laboon* and *Russell*, the destroyer *Hewitt*, and submarine *Jefferson City* fire Tomahawk missiles against air defense targets.

SEPTEMBER 13 The submarine *Cheyenne* is commissioned, being the last of the *Los Angeles*-class attack submarines; a total of 56 have been constructed over the past 22 years.

1997

JANUARY 18 The A/F-18F Super Hornet performs its carrier sea trials on board the *John C. Stennis*; this model is 25 percent larger than existing Hornets and enjoys greater range, payload, and combat survivability.

MARCH 13–17 In the Adriatic Sea, OPERATION SILVER WAKE commences as 877 people are evacuated from Tirana, Albania, to the amphibious transport dock *Nashville* offshore.

MARCH 18 Over California, a Navy F/A-18 Hornet fires the Standoff Land Attack Missile-Expanded Response for the first time; this weapon has the unique capacity of loitering over a target for considerable time.

MARCH 21 At Naval Air Station, Pensacola, Florida, Lieutenant Colonel Marcelyn A. Atwood is the first Air Force officer to lead a Navy squadron.

MAY 19 In Washington, D.C., the Quadrennial Defense Review allows the Navy to retain 12 carrier battlegroups and 12 amphibious ready groups, but reduces the surface fleet from 128 to 116 vessels, and cuts the number of attack submarines from 73 to 50. However, a 10th *Nimitz*-class supercarrier will be built to replace the aging *Kitty Hawk*. The number of F/A-18E/F purchases is also cut back by a third, to between 548 and 785 aircraft, but acquisition of the Navy's planned Joint Strike Fighter (JCF) is kept alive. Furthermore, naval personnel will be reduced by 18,000, while the Reserves are allowed to decline by 4,100.

MAY 30–JUNE 4 Off the coast of Sierra Leone, OPERATION NOBLE OBELISK unfolds as the *Kearsarge* amphibious ready group evacuates 2,500 American citizens and foreign nationals.

JULY 21 At Boston, Massachusetts, the frigate *Constitution*, still the world's oldest commissioned warship, sets out on a one-hour voyage to cap a three-year, $12-million restoration. This is the first time the venerable vessel has sailed in 116 years.

AUGUST 6 On Guam, Navy Seabees cut through dense jungle to reach the crash site of Korea Air Lines Flight 801, while CH-46 Skyknight helicopters rescue 30 survivors.

SEPTEMBER 1 The carrier *Nimitz* accepts the first shipment of the advanced Joint Standoff Weapon (JSOW).

1998

FEBRUARY 12 Consistent with the Department of Defense authorization bill of January 22, 1996, the retired battleships *Wisconsin* and *New Jersey* are returned to the Naval Vessel Register, while the *Iowa* is kept as a spare-parts source.

MAY 4 At Pearl Harbor, Hawaii, the venerable battleship *Missouri* transfers to the USS *Missouri* Memorial Association as part of historic battleship row.

JUNE An important threshold passes as the landing-dock ships *Mount Vernon*, *Carter Hall*, and *Gunston Hall*, the tank-landing ship *La Moure County*, and the guided-missile frigate *Jarrett* receive female commanding officers.

JUNE 12 In Washington, D.C., the Navy contracts with the Bath Iron Works and Ingalls Shipbuilding, Maine, to construct the new DD 21 *Zumwalt*-class destroyer. This futuristic vessel will replace the *Perry* and *Spruance* class destroyers in service, and is capable of fighting at sea or assisting landing forces. Among its many features is a 155-mm Advanced Gun System capable of hitting targets 100 miles away.

JULY 18 In Yokosuka, Japan, *Kitty Hawk* replaces *Independence* as the Navy's forward-deployed aircraft carrier.

JULY 25 The new supercarrier *Harry S. Truman* is commissioned.

AUGUST 20 Naval vessels launch 75 cruise missiles at suspected chemical-weapons facilities at Khartoum, Sudan, and terrorist training camps in Afghanistan. This action comes in response to terrorist bombings of American embassies in Kenya and Tanzania, attributed to Saudi terrorist Osama bin Laden.

SEPTEMBER 4 The *South Carolina* is deactivated, being the Navy's last operating nuclear-powered surface ship.

SEPTEMBER 9 Off the coast of Nova Scotia, Canada, salvage ship *Grapple* helps recover wreckage from the crashed Swissair Flight 111.

DECEMBER 16–19 Over Iraq, OPERATION DESERT FOX commences as aircraft from the *Enterprise*, assisted by 325 Tomahawk cruise missiles, strike at Iraqi nuclear, biological, and chemical-weapon facilities; this is also the first time that female aviators fly combat missions. The action comes in response to Iraqi obstruction and deceit connected with the UN arms inspection mission.

1999

January 4 The battleship *Iowa* replaces the *New Jersey* on the Naval Vessel Register after it is discovered that the latter's guns had been damaged by its last mothballing in 1995. It is deposited at Camden, New Jersey as a war memorial.

January 24 Over Mosul, Iraq, a Navy EA-6B Prowler fires an AGM-154A standoff weapon at a hostile radar site for the first time. Saddam Hussein nonetheless challenges United Nations enforcement of Operation Northern Watch to assist the Kurds.

January 25 Over Iraq, Operation Southern Watch commences as United States and British warplanes pound Iraqi anti-aircraft missile sites near Basra. Navy F/A-18 Hornets of VFA-22 and VFA-94 continue firing advanced AGM-154A Joint Standoff Weapons.

February 4 Off the Virginia coast, the destroyer *Arthur W. Radford* collides with a Saudi Arabian cargo vessel. It suffers $24 million in damage, and 10 months lapse before it is back in service.

February 17 In Antarctica, the Antarctic Development Squadron 6 (VXE-6), which had logged more than 200,000 hours since 1955, departs for the last time. The Navy is concluding its presence in the region.

February 24 At Naval Air Station, Point Mugu, California, three LC-130R Hercules transports of Antarctic Development Squadron 6 (VXE-6) return after assisting the National Science Foundation's Operation Deep Freeze for four decades.

March 24–June 10 In the Adriatic Sea, Operation Allied Force unfolds as the cruiser *Philippine Sea*, destroyers *Gonzalez*, *Nicholson*, and *Thorn*, and submarines *Miami* and *Norfolk* launch Tomahawk cruise missiles at targets throughout Yugoslavia.

April 3 In the Adriatic Sea, the carrier *Theodore Roosevelt* arrives and its air wings go on to fly 4,270 sorties against Serbian forces.

April 11 In the Adriatic, Operation Shining Hope unfolds, as MH-53 Sea Dragon and CH-46 Skyknight helicopters from the assault vessel *Inchon* transport 6,000 pounds of relief supplies to refugees huddling in Kukes, Albania.

April 19 On Vieques Island, Puerto Rico, an F/A-18 Hornet releases a bomb that goes astray and kills a civilian security guard; ensuing protests lead to a halt in operations, which have been ongoing since 1946.

May 3 At the North Pole, the nuclear-powered submarine *Hawkbill* surfaces through the ice as part of the final Navy-National Science Foundation Science expedition.

May 17–November 17 Over southern Iraq, Navy F/A-18 Hornets assist Air Force A-10 Thunderbolt IIs attack Iraqi missile and antiaircraft artillery sites after being fired upon.

June 16 In the southern no-fly zone of Iraq, Navy F/A-18 Hornets and British GR-1 Tornadoes respond to Iraqi antiaircraft fire by launching missiles against two radar sites.

JULY 18 In southern Iraq, F-14D Tomcats, F/A-18 Hornets, and F-16C Falcons retaliate against antiaircraft fire directed at them by knocking out offending missile and radar sites.

AUGUST 10 An Iraqi missile launch in the southern no-fly zone prompts a sharp response from Navy F-14D Tomcats, F/A-18 Hornets, and Air Force F-16 Fighting Falcons, which attack and knock out the offending launch sites and radar installations.

AUGUST 23–SEPTEMBER 12 In Turkey, the *Kearsarge* amphibious ready group reacts to a 7.4-magnitude earthquake that killed an estimated 24,000 people, by ferrying emergency aid by helicopter.

SEPTEMBER 2 The keel of the *Virginia* is laid; this is the Navy's newest class of nuclear attack submarines and capable of launching Tomahawk cruise missiles. They will replace older *Los Angeles*-class attack submarines, and 30 will be acquired over the next two decades.

OCTOBER 7–26 Near East Timor, the *Belleau Wood* amphibious ready group stations itself in support of Australian peacekeepers during a period of civil unrest.

OCTOBER 26–NOVEMBER 26 Near East Timor, the *Peleliu* amphibious ready group replaces the *Belleau Wood* as peacekeeping efforts on the island continue.

OCTOBER 28 Cryptologic Technician First Class Daniel King is arrested for passing classified materials to the Soviet embassy in Washington, D.C., during the Cold War.

OCTOBER 31 Near Nantucket, Massachusetts, the amphibious transport dock *Austin* and salvage ship *Grapple* comb the waters for wreckage from Egyptian Air Flight 900, which had crashed.

NOVEMBER 17 Over southern Iraq, an F/A-18 Hornet patrolling the no-fly zone fires a HARM missiles at an Iraqi radar site which had locked onto it.

DECEMBER 3 On Puerto Rico, the government asks the Navy to suspend live-fire exercises on the island of Vieques immediately; it also rejects the Navy's suggestion to end such maneuvers within five years.

2000

JANUARY 31 In Puerto Rico, civilian authorities will allow the Navy to continue exercises on Vieques Island for the next three years, although using non-explosive ammunition.

Near Point Mugu, California, the destroyer *Fife*, guided-missile frigate *Jarrett*, and amphibious transport dock *Cleveland* comb the waters for wreckage from Alaska Airlines Flight 261.

MAY 6 At Vieques, Puerto Rico, the destroyer *Stump* is the first vessel to conduct fire exercises since April 1999.

JULY 5 In Washington, D.C., the Assistant Chief of Naval Operations for Missile Defense is created; it is responsible for developing defenses against ballistic and cruise-type weapons.

JULY 13 West of Oahu, Hawaii, the amphibious transport dock *Denver* collides with the Military Sealift Command oiler *Yukon*; both vessels sustain $7 million in damage.

AUGUST 8 At Charleston harbor, South Carolina, the Confederate submarine *H. L. Hunley*, which sank in 1864, is raised from the bottom and taken ashore for restoration.

AUGUST 27 Off the coast of Virginia, the destroyer *Nicholson* and the combat support ship *Detroit* collide during a replenishment exercise. Consequently, the Chief of Naval Operations institutes a safety standdown for all vessels.

OCTOBER 12 At Aden, Yemen, an inflatable speedboat laden with a half-ton of high explosives strikes the guided-missile destroyer *Cole*, killing 17 sailors, wounding 39, and ripping a 40-foot hole in the *Cole's* port side. The vessel returns to the United States atop of the Norwegian commercial heavy-lift ship *Blue Marlin*, and resumes active duty on April 19, 2002. American intelligence points to fugitive Saudi Osama bin Laden as the mastermind behind the attack.

OCTOBER 30 In Washington, D.C., President Bill Clinton signs a "Sense of Congress" resolution to rehabilitate the reputations of Admiral Husband E. Kimmel and Lieutenant General Walter C. Short. Previously held as scapegoats for the Japanese attack on Pearl Harbor, their personnel files are amended and they are allowed to retire posthumously at their highest rank.

Damage sustained on the port side of the Arleigh Burke-class guided missile destroyer USS Cole *after a bomb exploded during a refueling operation in the port of Aden, Yemen, in 2000. The Pentagon has said it is charging a Saudi Arabian citizen with "organizing and directing" the bombing of the* Cole. *(AP/Wide World Photos)*

2001

January 13 In Puerto Rico, Governor Sila Maria Calderon reneges on allowing live bombing practice at the Vieques firing range; negotiations by President Bill Clinton fail to resolve this issue.

February 9 Near Pearl Harbor, Hawaii, the nuclear submarine *Greeneville* strikes the Japanese trawler *Ehime Maru* while surfacing, killing nine crewmen. The Navy issues an apology, recovers the bodies of the deceased, and pays out $11 million as compensation.

February 16 Over Iraq, 24 aircraft from the *Harry S. Truman* strike radar sites and air-defense command centers over a series of violations in the northern and southern no-fly zones.

March 4 The new aircraft carrier *Ronald Reagan*, the first such vessel christened after a living former chief executive, is commissioned by former First Lady Nancy Reagan.

March 12 Over Kuwait, during a nighttime, live-fire exercise, an F/A-18 Hornet from the *Harry S. Truman* accidentally drops a 500-pound bomb on an observation bunker; five Americans die along with a New Zealand Army officer.

April 1 Near Hainan Island, China, an EP-3E *Aries II* reconnaissance craft collides with a J-8 Chinese jet fighter; Lieutenant Shane Osborne manages to safely land at Lingyuan military airfield, where the crew is detained for 11 days. The aircraft is also ransacked by the Chinese, who gain an intelligence windfall.

April 4 The Navy announces that it has eliminated all remaining stocks of napalm weapons.

April 12 The Navy declares that it will resume live-fire training exercises on Vieques, Puerto Rico, for the first time since December 2000; protests are ignored.

April 23 At Pearl Harbor, Hawaii, a court-martial finds Commander Scott Waddle of the submarine *Greeneville* guilty of neglect for colliding with a Japanese fishing trawler. Waddle is reprimanded, suffers a 50 percent reduction in pay, and is forced to retire on October 1.

April 24 In Puerto Rico, Governor Sila Maria Calderon sues to stop the Navy from conducting live-fire exercises on Vieques, because it violates restrictions on decibel levels passed by the legislature.

In Washington, D.C., President George W. Bush declares his intention to sell P-3 Orion maritime patrol aircraft to Taiwan as a sign of his support for the regime.

April 25 In Washington, D.C., Judge Gladys Kessler of the U.S. district court rejects a temporary restraining order to halt Navy bombing practice at Vieques, Puerto Rico.

April 27–May 1 At Vieques, Puerto Rico, anti-Navy demonstrators protest a scheduled live-fire exercise held by the carrier *Enterprise* and the *Kearsarge* amphibious ready group; 183 people are arrested.

June 12 In Washington, D.C., a naval panel reports that the proposed *Zumwalt*-class DD 21 destroyer is not a substantial improvement of existing systems, which casts the future of this class in jeopardy.

June 15 In Washington, D.C., Secretary of the Navy Gordon R. England declares that the Navy will terminate training exercises on Vieques Island, Puerto Rico, as of May 1, 2003.

July 5 At Hainan island, China, the Navy EP-3 forced to land on April 1 is disassembled and loaded on board a Russian AN-124 transport. It is flown to Dobbins Air Reserve Base, Marietta, Georgia, and has since resumed active service.

July 12 The Navy, responding to a Congressional resolution in the 2001 defense authorization act, amends the personnel record of Captain Charles B. McVay III and clears him for the loss of the heavy cruiser *Indianapolis* in 1945.

July 16 Near Hatteras Island, North Carolina, the 30-ton steam engine from the Union ironclad *Monitor*, which sank there in a storm on December 31, 1862, is recovered by the joint Navy-National Oceanic and Atmospheric Administration Team; the artifact is displayed at the Mariners' Museum, Newport News, Virginia.

August 10 Southeast of Baghdad, Iraq, 50 F-14 and F/A-18 aircraft from the *Enterprise* join British jets in punitive strikes against antiaircraft emplacements. This is the 25th airstrike for violations of OPERATIONS NORTHERN and SOUTHERN WATCH.

September 11 After the destruction of the World Trade Center and terrorists attacks in Washington, D.C., naval vessels sortie to patrol coastal waters. The attack on the Pentagon kills 33 sailors and 6 civilians, and wounds 4 sailors and 2 civilians.

September 14 In New York City, the hospital ship *Comfort* docks to proffer assistance to survivors of the World Trade Center attack.

September 30 In Washington, D.C., the 2001 Quadrennial Defense Review (QDR) advises that the Navy increase carrier battlegroups in the Pacific and home-port more surface vessels and submarines there. Presently, the Navy fields 12 carrier battlegroups, 12 amphibious ready groups, 108 surface combatants, and 55 attack submarines.

October 7 Over Afghanistan, United States and British warplanes commence OPERATION ENDURING FREEDOM to drive the Taliban and Al-Qaeda out of power. The attacks include aircraft from carriers *Enterprise* and *Carl Vinson*, while 50 Tomahawk cruise missiles are also launched from a variety of vessels.

October 12 In the Arabian Sea, the carrier *Kitty Hawk* serves as a floating base for Special Forces operations in Afghanistan; most of its air assets are transferred ashore to make room.

October 26 Lockheed Martin receives a contract to construct the advanced F-35 Joint Strike fighter, which will see service in the Air Force, Navy, and Marine Corps.

November 1 In Washington, D.C., the Navy Department announces that it is scrapping the new DD-21 *Zumwalt*-class destroyer and is opting to acquire the very advanced and highly capable DD(X). This revolutionary design carries a gun system capable of striking targets at ranges of 100 miles, while presenting a radar cross-section that is a fraction of most vessels.

November 18 Petty Officer Vincent Parker and Petty Officer Third Class

Benjamin Johnson drown while searching a dangerously overloaded Iraqi tanker that suddenly sinks in heavy seas.

NOVEMBER 26 Over Afghanistan, F-14Ds from the *Carl Vinson* wipe out a 15-vehicle Taliban convoy; they were directed to the target by Marine AH-1W Super Cobra helicopters operating from Camp Rhino.

DECEMBER 12 In Washington, D.C., the Navy Department postpones action on bombing activities at Vieques, Puerto Rico, once the House and Senate Armed Service Committees pass a resolution requiring that it be maintained until a suitable replacement is found.

An Air Force B-1B bomber, returning from a bomb run over Afghanistan, crashes in the Indian Ocean. The crew is safely rescued within two hours by the destroyer *Russell*.

DECEMBER 15 In the Gulf of Arabia, the carrier *Enterprise* is relieved by the *John C. Stennis*; to date its air groups had flown 4,200 sorties against Taliban targets in Afghanistan.

DECEMBER 27 In Washington, D.C., the Department of Defense announces that Taliban and Al-Qaeda captives seized in Afghanistan will be interred in special facilities at the Guantanamo Bay naval base, Cuba.

DECEMBER 31 Over Afghanistan, Navy aircraft account for 72 percent of all tactical airstrikes and over half of all precision-guided weapon launches against Taliban and Al-Qaeda targets.

2002

JANUARY 21 Over southern Iraq, Navy, Air Force, and Coalition aircraft strike at Iraqi antiaircraft artillery emplacements at Tallil, and it opens fire on them.

MARCH 4 In eastern Afghanistan, Aviation Boatswain's Mate First Class Neil C. Roberts, a Navy SEAL, is killed in action during OPERATION ANACONDA.

MARCH 27 Near Kandahar, Afghanistan, Chief Hospital Corpsman Matthew J. Bourgeois, a Navy SEAL, dies during a small unit training exercise.

APRIL 1 At Vieques, Puerto Rico, protests resume once the *George Washington* carrier battlegroup resumes live-fire training exercises offshore.

MAY 19 At the Naval Air Systems Command Western Test Range, California, tests begin on the Navy's Fire Scout unmanned takeoff and landing tactical aerial vehicle.

MAY 21 Offshore at San Diego, California, the frigate *Thatch* assists the research submarine *Dolphin* after it experiences a fire and flooding.

JUNE 6 Off the North Carolina coast, the dock-landing ship *Tortuga* runs aground during the night; fortunately, it is refloated the following day.

JUNE 12 At the Naval War College in Newport, Rhode Island, Chief of Naval Operations Admiral Vern Clark unveils "Sea Power 21," his vision for the U.S. Navy during the new century. This proffers three basic concepts: Sea Strike, projecting power anywhere in the world; Sea Shield, defending the nation and its assets at sea; and Sea Basing, to maintain sovereignty abroad. These programs are designed to more fully integrate sea, land, air, space, and cyberspace forces more closely than ever before attempted.

JUNE 13   The United States having withdrawn from the 1972 Anti-Ballistic Missile Treaty, the guided-missile cruiser *Lake Erie* successfully test-fires an SM-3 Standard missile. This weapon is designed to intercept incoming ballistic missiles midway through their trajectory and 100 miles above the earth.

JUNE 17   Near Oman, 16 merchant sailors that had been adrift for 11 days are rescued by the cruiser *Vicksburg*.

JULY 24   The new F/A-18E Super Hornet deploys with Attack Squadron VFA-115 on the carrier *Abraham Lincoln*.

JULY 26   In Somerset, Pennsylvania, eight medical and diving experts from various Navy commands arrive with a portable recompression chamber, after a mineshaft collapses 240 feet below the surface.

SEPTEMBER 3   At Yokosuka, Japan, the Commander, Seventh Fleet, relieves the captain of the forward-based carrier *Kitty Hawk*.

SEPTEMBER 4   At Vieques Island, Puerto Rico, protestors pelt naval security personnel with rocks as the *Harry S. Truman* carrier battlegroup conducts live-fire exercises.

SEPTEMBER 8   In Washington, D.C., the Secretary of the Navy announces that the Navy's newest amphibious transport dock will be christened the *New York* in honor of the 9/11 victims.

SEPTEMBER 11   In Washington, D.C., the Secretary of the Navy orders all vessels to fly the First Navy Jack of 1775, consisting of thirteen red and white stripes with the motto "Don't Tread on Me," until the war against terrorism ends. This is also the first anniversary of the 9/11 terrorist attack.

NOVEMBER 5   Over southern Iraq, the Navy's new F/A-18 Super Hornet makes its combat debut by firing weapons against Iraqi radar and missile sites.

NOVEMBER 13   In the mid-Atlantic, the nuclear attack submarine *Oklahoma City* accidentally collides with a Norwegian commercial vessel; the captain is subsequently relieved of command and reassigned.

DECEMBER 6   In the North Arabian Gulf, the destroyer *Paul Hamilton* accidentally collides with a merchant vessel and receives damage.

DECEMBER 8   On Guam, Naval Mobile Construction Battalion 74 spends the next several days restoring water supplies to the inhabitants after Typhoon Pongsona lashes the island with 180-miles-per-hour winds.

DECEMBER 9   In Washington, D.C., the Secretary of the Navy announces that the tenth *Nimitz*-class carrier will be named in honor of former President George H. W. Bush.

DECEMBER 12   In their first year of deployment, F/A-18 Hornets log 5 million hours of flight time in Navy and Marine Corps squadrons.

2003

JANUARY This month the missile submarine *Florida* test-launches two Tomahawk missiles while submerged for the first time. Success here lends greater emphasis on converting four nuclear-powered *Ohio*-class missile submarines into guided-missile submarines.

JANUARY 10 At San Diego, California, the carrier *Nimitz* battlegroup commences a highly compressed, three-week training cruise before deploying to the Persian Gulf.

JANUARY 21 Off the coast of Australia, the carrier *Abraham Lincoln* and its battlegroup are ordered to the Persian Gulf, just as it was returning home from a six-month Middle Eastern deployment. In the Caribbean, the carrier *Theodore Roosevelt* and its battlegroup are also ordered to steam with all speed to that troubled region.

JANUARY 23 In Fremantle, Australia, the Navy's new Sea Swap Initiative allows three ship crews to rotate through a vessel at sea, allowing it more time on station. The destroyer *Fletcher* is the first participant, and is re-crewed by personnel from the recently decommissioned *Kinkaid*.

JANUARY 24 In Washington, D.C., Gordon England relinquishes the post of Secretary of the Navy to serve as Deputy Secretary of the Department of Homeland Security. He is temporarily replaced by Acting Secretary of the Navy Susan M. Livingston.

FEBRUARY 1 Over Texas, the space shuttle Columbia disintegrates, killing the entire crew of seven including Navy Captain David M. Brown, Marine Corps Captain Laurel Clark, and Commander William C. McCool.

FEBRUARY 13 At Naval Station, Mayport, Florida, President George W. Bush arrives for lunch aboard the guided-missile cruiser *Philippine Sea*.

MARCH 10 In the Mediterranean, OPERATION ACTIVE ENDEAVOR commences, as the destroyer *Halyburton* escorts civilian shipping through the Strait of Gibraltar.

MARCH 14 At Amphibious Naval Base, Little Creek, Virginia, the Center for Naval Leadership arises.

MARCH 19 Over Iraq, OPERATION IRAQI FREEDOM commences 42 Tomahawk cruise missiles are fired by the destroyers *Donald Cook* and *Milius*, the cruisers *Cowpens* and *Bunker Hill*, and submarines *Cheyenne* and *Montpelier* at various targets. Several buildings thought to house Saddam Hussein, his two sons, and several ranking government officials are targeted and destroyed.

MARCH 20 In the Persian Gulf, the destroyer *John S. McCain* and submarines *Columbia* and *Providence*, assisted by two British submersibles, fire an additional 50 Tomahawk missiles at targets in Baghdad, Iraq. Teams of Navy SEALS and Royal Marines also raid the Kaabot and Mabot oil terminals.

MARCH 21 Over Baghdad, Iraq, aircraft from the *Abraham Lincoln, Constellation, Harry S. Truman, Kitty Hawk*, and *Theodore Roosevelt* participate in the "shock and awe" campaign against the Iraqi capital. Other vessel fire a further 320 Tomahawk cruise missiles against military targets.

The first Tomahawk missile to be fired on Iraq is launched from the USS Bunker Hill at 5:25 A.M. on March 20, 2003. (Department of Defense)

In the Arabian Gulf, a Navy P-3 Orion of VP-46 tracks an Iraqi fast attack patrol boat, which is then sunk by an Air Force AC-130 Spectre gunship.

MARCH 22   Over the Arabian Gulf, exchange officer Navy Lieutenant Thomas M. Adams is killed as two Royal Navy Sea King helicopters collide and crash.

MARCH 23   In the eastern Mediterranean, the *Cape St. George*, *Anzio*, and the destroyer *Winston S. Churchill* begin launching Tomahawk missiles against targets in distant Iraq.

MARCH 24   In the Khor Abd Allah waterway, Iraq, four Iraqi vessels carrying nearly 100 mines are boarded by coalition naval forces.

MARCH 25   Over Basra, Iraq, a Lockheed S-3 Viking from Sea Control Squadron 38 (VS-38) directs a raid by F/A-18 Hornets from VFA-151. This is the first time the 30-year-old Viking design has seen combat operations.

In Iraq, Hospital Corpsman Third Class Michael Vann Johnson, Jr., dies in action.

MARCH 28   In the Persian Gulf, Mine Countermeasures Squadron HM-14 and Commander Task Unit 55.4.3 clear mines and other obstacles out of the port of Umm Qasr, and the British auxiliary vessel *Sir Galahad* lands with tons of food and humanitarian aid.

MARCH 31   Over northern Iraq, aircraft from the *Theodore Roosevelt* bombard artillery emplacements, barracks, and surface-to-air missile installations in support of the Kurds.

Over St. Inigoes, Maryland, the NP-3C Orion dubbed "Hairy Buffalo" demonstrates the Aerolight unmanned aerial vehicle (UAV) in mid-air; this is the first time a UAV has been controlled by another aircraft.

APRIL 1–2   A combined Special Forces task force, including Navy SEALS, rescues Army private Jessica Lynch from a hospital in Al Nasiriya, Iraq.

APRIL 2   Over Kuwait, a Patriot missile battery mistakenly locks onto a Navy F/A-18 Hornet jet fighter of VFA-195 (*Kitty Hawk*), downing the craft and killing Lieutenant Nathan White.

APRIL 5   Off the coast of California, the guided-missile destroyer *Stethem* launches the first Tactical Tomahawk, the latest version of this weapon system.

APRIL 11   At Naval Amphibious Base, Little Creek, Virginia, the amphibious dock-landing ship *Portland* becomes the first vessel returning from OPERATION IRAQI FREEDOM.

April 16 At Baghdad, Iraq, a P-3 Orion from VP-46 is the first Coalition aircraft to touch down at Baghdad International Airport. It is conveying Vice Admiral Timothy Keating, Commander, U.S. Naval Forces, Central Command.

April 22 In Hawaii, the frigate *Crommelin* concludes a six-month cruise, during which time it seized six tons of narcotics worth $183 million; it also rescued 157 Ecuadorians from a sinking vessel and transported them home.

April 30 On Puerto Rico, the Navy transfers its property on Vieques Island to the Department of the Interior; the area will be developed into a wildlife refuge.

May 1 Off the coast of California, President George W. Bush lands aboard the carrier *Abraham Lincoln* and announces an end to offensive military operations in Iraq. "Mission accomplished!" he declares to loud applause.

May 6 At Bremerton, Washington, the *Abraham Lincoln* returns to port after 10 months at sea; this is a record deployment for a nuclear-powered carrier. The vessel partook of Operations Southern Watch, Enduring Freedom, and Iraqi Freedom, before hosting the commander in chief.

May 8 Off the California coast, the destroyer *Stetham* fires the first live warhead demonstration of the new Tactical Tomahawk missile system.

October 31 In Washington, D.C., President George W. Bush reappoints Admiral Veron Clark to serve another two-year stint as Chief of Naval Operations, making him the longest-serving incumbent since Admiral Arleigh Burke in the late 1950s and early 1960s.

July 17 In Washington, D.C., the Navy Department announces a new contract with the General Dynamics, Lockheed Martin Naval Electronics, and Raytheon Integrated Defense Systems to commence preliminary designs for the new Flight O Littoral Combat Ship (LCS). This new class of warship is designed for mine countermeasures, antisubmarine warfare, and antisurface warfare.

2004

December 15 In Washington, D.C., the Navy announces a $188.2 million contract with Lockheed Martin to detail design and construction of the first Flight O Littoral Combat Ship (LCS).

December 26 After a huge tsunami ravages the coast of Indonesia, the carrier *Abraham Lincoln* battlegroup arrives in the region as part of Operation Unified Assistance.

2005

January 1 Offshore at Aceh province, Indonesia, the carrier *Abraham Lincoln* and its escort vessel arrive to support humanitarian efforts after the region was devastated by tidal waves.

Navy personnel form a chain and unload relief supplies for tsunami victims in Banda Aceh on the island of Sumatra, Indonesia. (United States Navy)

JANUARY 8   The nuclear submarine *San Francisco*, running a submerged, high-speed test 350 miles south of Apra, Guam, strike an uncharted, underwater mountain. The vessel sustains heavy damage estimated at $90 million; 1 sailor is killed and 23 are injured.

FEBRUARY 3   The hospital ship *Mercy* arrives off the island of Sumatra, recently devastated by a huge tidal wave. Over the next two months the vessel's medical facilities treat 9,200 patients and perform 285 surgical procedures, while also pulling 1,300 bad teeth and issuing 4,000 eye exams and new glasses.

MAY 9   At Pearl Harbor, Hawaii, the Commander Pacific Fleet releases a final report that finds Commander Kevin Mooney of the nuclear submarine *San Francisco* and his entire navigation team responsible for the near-fatal accident off Guam; Mooney is reassigned and allowed to retire.

AUGUST 7   Acting upon a plea from the Russian government, a combined American/British "Scorpio" underwater remotely controlled vehicle (ROV) helps rescue the crew of the mini-submarine *Friz* (Prize) in waters off the Kamchatka Peninsula. The minisub was on maneuvers with the Russian fleet at a depth of 600 feet when its propellers became entangled in a fishing net.

AUGUST 17   At Apra, Guam, the damaged nuclear submarine *San Francisco* sets sail for the Puget Sound Shipyard, Washington state, for extensive repairs to its bow and sonar dome.

OCTOBER 8   After a remote part of Pakistan is devastated by a powerful earthquake, Expeditionary Strike Group One under Rear Admiral Michael LeFever sets up headquarters in Islamabad to coordinate the delivery of food, water, and relief supplies.

2006

MAY 17   Off the coast of Pensacola, Florida, the aged carrier *Oriskany* is deliberately sunk 24 miles at sea, to form the world's largest man-made reef.

MAY 20–27   The hospital ship *Mercy* arrives in the Philippines to assist thousands of victims of a large tsunami. On the 27th it also deploys a medical team to Java, after a large earthquake strikes Yogyakarta Province.

JUNE This month the Aegis missile cruiser *Shiloh* fires a SM-3 Standard missile which successfully intercepts a separating ballistic missile target. This is the seventh hit out of eight tries in the most recent round of testing.

NOVEMBER 28 In Marietta, Georgia, the Lockheed Martin Corporation delivers its 100th Aegis Weapons system for installment in the new destroyer DDG-108, the *Wayne E. Meyer*. Rear Admiral Meyer is considered the "Father of the Aegis" system.

2007

JANUARY 23 In Washington, D.C., the Deputy Secretary of Defense grants the Navy a two-year exemption to continue experimenting with mid-frequency active sonar, despite its alleged dangerous effects on marine mammals.

APRIL 2 The Military Sealift Commands pre-positions ship *Fred W. Stockham* at the Solomon Islands to distribute emergency aid following a destructive tsunami.

APRIL 12 At Gizo, Solomon Islands, Navy helicopters rescue the crew and passengers of a Taiwanese-flagged freighter that has run aground on a reef; the vessel was carrying Red Cross aid workers from New Zealand at the time.

AUGUST 1 In Minneapolis, Minnesota, a bridge on I-35 spanning the Mississippi River collapses, killing 13 people and injuring over 100. The Navy dispatches 18 divers from the Mobile Diving and Salvage Unit (MDSU) to assist; they eventually locate eight victims and removed 50 tons of debris.

SEPTEMBER 2 Off the coast of Nicaragua and Honduras, the amphibious assault vessel *Wasp* and the frigate *Samuel B. Roberts* arrive to distribute relief supplies in the wake of Hurricane Felix, a category-five storm.

OCTOBER In Washington, D.C., President George W. Bush honors SEAL Lieutenant Michael P. Murphy, who was killed in Afghanistan in June 2005, after he wins the Congressional Medal of Honor. This is the first such award for naval personnel in 35 years.

NOVEMBER 15 Task Force 76 under Rear Admiral Carol M. Pottenger arrives off Bangladesh in the wake of Tropical Cyclone Sidr, which packs winds of 156 miles per hour and leaves thousands of people homeless.

DECEMBER By year's end, the Navy reports having seized five smuggling vessels, sunk 13 more, arrested 68 suspected drug runners, and confiscated 189,900 pounds of cocaine attempting to enter the country by sea.

2008

FEBRUARY 20 OPERATION BURNT FROST unfolds as the guided-missile cruiser *Lake Erie* successfully fires an SM-3 Standard missile, which successfully intercepts a decaying satellite at an altitude of 153 miles above the Earth and a closing speed of 22,000 miles per hour. The satellite is carrying a supply of highly toxic hydrazine propellant, so President George W. Bush seeks to destroy it before it strikes a populated area.

FEBRUARY 28   At New London, Connecticut, the nuclear submarine *Annapolis* under Commander Dennis McKelvy concludes a six-month tour of Europe and Africa which included port calls at Rota, Spain, Toulon and Brest, France, Praia, Cape Verde, and Ghana.

JUNE 5   West of Hawaii, the guided-missile cruiser *Lake Erie* successfully test-fires two SM-3 Standard missiles as part of an anti-ballistic missile program. This is the 14th successful intercept of the Aegis Ballistic Missile Defense system.

JULY 31   In Washington, D.C., Navy officials testify before a House Committee that production of the ultra-modern and highly expensive *Zumwalt* DDG-1000 class destroyers should be capped at three vessels, because they cannot deploy SM-3 or SM-6 Standard missiles for ballistic missile defense. They insist that the nation would be better served by purchasing somewhat older but far more capable *Alreigh Burke* destroyers with updated electronic suites.

AUGUST 17   In the Black Sea, the guided missile destroyer *McFaul* and the Coast Guard Cutter *Dallas* arrive at Batumi, Georgia, to provide humanitarian relief to 118,000 displaced survivors of a Russian invasion of South Ossetia.

SEPTEMBER 5–26   On Haiti, the amphibious landing ship *Kearsarge* arrives to provide 3.3 million pounds of food and emergency aid to victims of several severe tropical storms.

NOVEMBER 12   In Washington, D.C., the U.S. Supreme Court rules 6–3 in favor of the U.S. Navy to resume oceanic testing of advanced mid-frequency active (MFA) sonar systems. Previously, groups like the Natural Resources Defense Council feared that such testing may hurt marine mammals and sued to stop the tests.

DECEMBER 27   The Navy enters into a comprehensive settlement with the Natural Resources Defense Council, the International Fund for Animal Welfare, the Cetacean Society International, and other environmental groups which would allow the continued testing mid-frequency active (MFA) sonar, which is conducting a long-range environmental analysis as it relates to sonar.

2009

JANUARY   The Navy and the National Marine Fisheries draw up a marine-mammal-stranding-response plan to assist whales that are beached near the Hawaiian Range Complex, the Southern California Complex, and the Atlantic Fleet Sonar Training area.

JANUARY 8   In light of rising piracy in the Red Sea and off the Horn of Africa, Task

Forces 150 and 151 are created under Rear Admiral Terence McKnight to counter the threat.

APRIL 6 In Washington, D.C., Secretary of Defense Robert M. Gates strongly urges Congress to supply $700 million to field additional SM-3 Standard missiles as the first line of defense against hostile ballistic missile launches.

Bibliography

Alden, John D. *United States and Allied Submarine Successes in the Pacific and Far East during World War II*. Jefferson, N.C.: Mcfarland, 2009.

Alden, John D., and Ed Holm. *The American Steel Navy: A Photographic History of the U.S. Navy from the Introduction of the Steel Hull in 1883 to the Cruise of the Great White Fleet, 1907–1909*. Annapolis, Md.: Naval Institute Press, 2008.

Allen, Robert L. *The Port Chicago Mutiny: The Story of the Largest Mass Mutiny Trial in U.S. Naval History*. Berkeley, Calif.: Heyday Books, 2006.

Allen, Thomas B., and Norman Polmar. *Rickover: Father of the Nuclear Navy*. Washington, D.C.: Potomac Books, 2007.

Allison, Robert J. *Stephen Decatur: American Naval Hero, 1779–1820*. Amherst: University of Massachusetts Press, 2005.

Althoff, William F. *Forgotten Weapon: U.S. Navy Airships and the U-boat War*. Annapolis, Md.: Naval Institute Press, 2009.

Bachner, Evan. *Making WAVES: Navy Women of World War II*. New York: Abrams, 2008.

Bahmanyar, Mir. *SEALs: The U.S. Navy's Elite Fighting Force*. New York: Osprey, 2008.

Baldwin, John, and Ron Powers. *Last Flag Down: The Epic Journey of the Last Confederate Warship*. New York: Crown Publishers, 2007.

Barlow, Jeffrey G. *From Hot War to Cold War: the U.S. Navy and National Security Affairs, 1945–1955*. Stanford, Calif.: Stanford University Press, 2009.

Bartholomew, Charles A. *Mud, Muscle and Miracles: Marine Salvage in the United States Navy*. Washington, D.C.: Naval History & Heritage Command, 2009.

Beaver, Floyd. *Sailor from Oklahoma: One Man's Two-Ocean War*. Annapolis, Md.: Naval Institute Press, 2009.

Berube, Claude G. *A Call to the Sea: Captain Charles Stewart of the USS Constitution*. Washington, D.C.: Potomac Books, 2005.

Billy, George J., and Christine M. Billy. *Merchant Mariners at War: An Oral History of World War II*. Gainesville: University Press of Florida, 2008.

Black, Jeremy. *The War of 1812 in the Age of Napoleon*. Norman: University of Oklahoma Press, 2009.

Block, Leo. *Aboard the Farragut Class Destroyers in World War II: A History with First-Person Accounts of Enlisted Men*. Jefferson, N.C.: McFarland, 2009.

Bonner, Kit. *Cold War at Sea: An Illustrated History*. Osceola, Wis.: MBI, 2000.

Bradley, James. *The Imperial Cruise: A Secret History of Empire and War*. New York: Little, Brown, 2009.

Braisted, William R. *Diplomats in Blue: U.S. Naval Officers in China, 1922–1933*. Gainesville: University Press of Florida, 2009.

———. *The United States Navy in the Pacific, 1897–1909*. Annapolis, Md.: Naval Institute Press, 2008.

Broadwater, Robert P. *Civil War Medal of Honor Recipients: A Complete Illustrated Record*. Jefferson, N.C.: McFarland, 2007.

Brockman, R. John. *Commodore Robert F. Stockton, 1795–1866: Protean Man for a Protean Nation*. Amherst, N.Y.: Cambria Press, 2009.

Brodine, Charles E., Michael J. Crawford, and Christine F. Hughes. *Against All Odds: U.S. Sailors in the War of 1812*. Washington, D.C.: Naval Historical Center, 2004.

———. *Interpreting Old Ironsides: An Illustrated Guide to the USS Constitution*. Washington, D.C.: Naval Historical Center, 2007.

Buell, Thomas B. *Naval Leadership in Korea: The First Six Months.* Washington, D.C.: Naval Historical Center, 2002.

Burgess, Richard R. *U.S. Navy A-1 Skyraider Units of the Vietnam War.* New York: Osprey, 2009.

Burkhardt, George S., ed. *Double Duty in the Civil War: the Letters of Sailor and Soldier Edward W. Bacon.* Carbondale: Southern Illinois University Press, 2009.

Callo, Joseph F. *John Paul Jones: America's First Sea Warrior.* Annapolis, Md.: Naval Institute Press, 2006.

Camp. Richard D. *Iwo Jima Recon: The U.S. Navy at War, February 17, 1945.* St. Paul, Minn.: Zenith Press, 2007.

Campbell, R. Thomas, ed. *Confederate Naval Cadet: The Diary and Letters of Midshipman Hubbard T. Minor, with a History of the Confederate Naval Academy.* Jefferson, N.C.: McFarland, 2007.

———. *Voice of the Confederate Navy: Articles, Letters, Reports, and Reminiscences.* Jefferson, N.C.: McFarland, 2008.

Carlisle, Rodney P. *Sovereignty at Sea: U.S. Merchant Ships and American Entry into World War I.* Gainesville: University Press of Florida, 2009.

Carter, Alden R., ed. *The Sea Eagle: The Civil War Memoir of LCDR William B. Cushing.* Lanham, Md.: Rowman & Littlefield, 2009.

Carter, William A. *Why me, Lord?: The Experiences of a U.S. Navy Armed Guard Officer in World War II's Convoy PQ 17 on the Murmansk Run.* Millsboto, Del.: W. A. Carters, 2007.

Chaffin, Tom. *Sea of Gray: The Around-the-World Odyssey of the Confederate Raider Shenandoah.* New York: Hill & Wang, 2007.

———. *The H. L. Hunley: The Secret Hope of the Confederacy.* New York: Hill & Wang, 2008.

Cherpak, Evelyn C., ed. *Three Splendid Little Wars: The Diaries of Joseph Knefler Taussig, 1898–1901.* Newport, R.I.: Naval War College Press, 2009.

Christley, Jim. *US Submarines, 1941–45.* Oxford: Osprey, 2006.

Cope, Jeffrey. *U.S.S. Holt (DE-706) Destroyer Escort.* Bloomington, Ind.: AuthorHouse, 2008.

Cope, Tony. *On the Swing Shift: Building Liberty Ships in Savannah.* Annapolis, Md.: Naval Institute Press, 2009.

Cotham, Henry O., ed. *The Southern Journey of a Civil War Marine: the Illustrated Notebook of Henry O. Gusley.* Austin: University of Texas Press, 2006.

Couch, Dick. *Sheriff of Ramadi: Navy SEALS and the Winning of Al-Anbar.* Annapolis, Md.: Naval Institute Press, 2008.

Craven, John P. *The Silent War: The Cold War Battle Beneath the Sea.* New York: Simon & Schuster, 2001.

Crawford, Michael J., and Donald C. Winter. *The World Cruise of the Great White Fleet: Honoring 100 Years of Global Partnerships and Security.* Washington, D.C.: Naval Historical Center, 2008.

Crew, Thomas E. *Combat Loaded: Across the Pacific on the USS Tate.* College Station: Texas A&M University Press, 2007.

Cross, Coy F. *Lincoln's Man in Liverpool: Consul Dudley and the Legal Battle to Stop Confederate Warships.* Dekalb: Northern Illinois University Press, 2007.

Daniels, Josephus. *Our Navy at War.* Cranbury, N.J.: Scholars Bookshelf, 2006.

Daughan, George C. *If by Sea: The Forging of the American Navy: From the American Revolution to the War of 1812.* New York: Basic Books, 2008.

Davis, William E. *Sinking the Rising Sun: Dog Fighting & Dive Bombing in World War II: A Navy Fighter Pilot's Story.* St. Paul, Minn.: Zenith Press, 2007.

Deal, Harry W. *Venus Rising.* Los Angeles, Calif.: Orsini Press, 2007.

De Kay, James T. *A Rage for Glory: The Life of Commodore Stephen Decatur, USN.* New York: Free Press, 2004.

Dickon, Chris. *The Enduring Journey of the USS Chesapeake: Navigating the Common History of Three Nations.* Charleston, S.C.: History Press, 2008.

Dingman, Roger. *Deciphering the Rising Sun: Navy and Marine Corps Codebreakers, Translators, and Interpreters in the Pacific War.* Annapolis, Md.: Naval Institute Press, 2009.

Dockery, Kevin. *Navy Seals: A Complete History: From World War II to the Present.* New York: Berkley Books, 2004.

Dorny, Louis B. *US Navy PBY Catalina Units of the Pacific War.* New York: Osprey, 2009.

Driscoll, John K. *The Civil War on Pensacola Bay, 1861–1862.* Jefferson, N.C.: Macfarland, 2007.

Drury, Bob, and Thomas Calvin. *Halsey's Typhoon: The True Story of a Fighting Admiral, an Epic

Bibliography

Storm, and an Untold Rescue. New York: Atlantic Monthly Press, 2007.

Dudley, William S., and Michael J. Crawford, eds. *The Early Republic and the Sea: Essays on the Naval and Maritime History of the Early United States.* Washington, D.C.: Brassey's, 2001.

Dunn, Robert F. *The Reminiscences of Vice Admiral Robert F. Dunn, U.S. Navy (Retired).* Annapolis, Md.: Naval Institute Press, 2008.

Edgemon, Carol. *Radioman: An Eyewitness Account of Pearl Harbor and World War II in the Pacific.* New York: Thomas Dunne Books, 2008.

Edwards, Paul M. *Small United States and United Nations Warships in the Korean War.* Jefferson, N.C.: McFarland, 2008.

Elphick, Peter. *Liberty: The Ships that Won the War.* Annapolis, Md.: Naval Institute Press, 2006.

Elward, Brad A. *US Navy F-4 Phantom II MiG Killers: 1965–1970.* New York: Osprey Aviation, 2001.

Evans, Thomas. *John Paul Jones: Sailor, Hero, Father of the American Navy.* New York: Simon & Schuster, 2007.

Faram, Mark D. *Faces of War: The Untold Story of Edward Steichen's WWII Photographers.* New York: Berkley Caliber, 2009.

Fawcett, Bill. *Hunters & Shooters: An Oral History of the U.S. Navy Seals in Vietnam.* New York: Harper, 2008.

Felker, Craig C. *Testing American Sea Power: U.S. Navy Strategic Exercises, 1932–1940.* College Station: Texas A&M University Press, 2007.

Field, Ron. *Confederate Ironclad vs. Union Ironclad: Hampton Roads, 1862.* New York: Osprey, 2008.

Forbes, Bernard B. *The Reminiscences of Vice Admiral Bernard B. Forbes, Jr., U.S. Navy.* Annapolis, Md.: Naval Institute Press, 2008.

Fowler, Mary Lee Coe. *Full Fathom Five: A Daughter's Search.* Tuscaloosa: University of Alabama Press, 2008.

Fox, Stephen R. *Wolf of the Deep: Raphael Semmes and the Notorious Confederate Raider CSS Alabama.* New York: Vintage Civil War Library, 2007.

Frazier, Donald S. *Fire in the Cane Field: the Federal Invasion of Louisiana and Texas, January 1861–January 1863.* Buffalo Gap, Tex.: State House Press, 2009.

Freeman, Gregory A. *Troubled Water: Race, Mutiny, and Bravery on the USS Kitty Hawk.* New York: Palgrave Macmillan, 2009.

Fremont-Barnes, Gregory. *The Wars of the Barbary Pirates: To the Shores of Tripoli: The Rise of the U.S. Navy and Marines.* Oxford: Osprey, 2006.

Friedman, Barry, and Robert Robinson. *The Short Life of a Valiant Ship: USS Meredith (DD434).* New York: iUniverse, 2007.

Friedman, Hal M. *Arguing Over the American Lake: Bureaucracy and Rivalry in the U.S. Pacific, 1945–1947.* College Station: Texas A&M University Press, 2009.

Friedman, Norman. *Network-Centric Warfare: How Navies Learned to Fight Smarter Through Three World Wars.* Annapolis, Md.: Naval Institute Press, 2009.

Fuller, Howard J. *Clad in Iron: The American Civil War and the Challenge of British Naval Power.* Westport, Conn.: Praeger Security International, 2008.

Gaines, W. Craig. *Encyclopedia of Civil War Shipwrecks.* Baton Rouge: Louisiana State University Press, 2008.

Galantin, I. J. *Take Her Deep! A Submarine Against Japan in World War II.* Annapolis, Md.: Naval Institute Press, 2007.

Gallery, Daniel V. *Playships of the World: The Naval Diaries of Admiral Dan Gallery, 1920–1924.* Columbia: University of South Carolina Press, 2008.

Gannon, Michael. *Operation Drumbeat: The Dramatic True Story of Germany's First U-boat Attacks Along the American Coast in World War II.* Annapolis, Md.: Naval Institute Press, 2009.

Gilje, Paul A. *Liberty on the Waterfront: American Maritime Culture in the Age of Revolution.* Philadelphia: University of Pennsylvania Press, 2007.

Goldman, Ken. *Attack Transport: USS Charles Carroll in World War II.* Gainesville: University Press of Florida, 2008.

Graff, Cory. *F6F Hellcat at War.* Minneapolis, Minn.: MBI, 2009.

Gross, Jerome S. *Silently We Served: U.S. Submarines WWII.* Bellmore, N.Y.: Sheron Enterprises, 2007.

Guttridge, Leonard F. *Our Country, Right or Wrong: The Life of Stephen Decatur, the U.S. Navy's Most Illustrious Commander.* New York: Forge, 2006.

Hagan, Kenneth J., and Michael T. McMaster, eds. *In Peace and War: Interpretations of American Naval History.* Westport, Conn.: Praeger Security International, 2008.

Halberstadt, Hans. *U.S. Navy Seals.* 2nd ed. Grand Rapids, Mich.: Zenith, 2006.

Harris, Gail. A *Woman's War: The Professional and Personal Journey of the Navy's First African American Female Intelligence Officer*. Lanham, Md.: Scarecrow Press, 2010.

Hawley, Samuel J., ed. *America's Man in Korea: The Private Letters of George C. Foulk, 1884–1887*. Lanham, Md.: Lexington Books, 2008.

Hearn, Chester G. *Navy: An Illustrated History; the U.S. Navy from 1775 to the 21st Century*. St. Paul, Minn.: Zenith Press, 2007.

Henderson, Bruce B. *Down to the Sea: An Epic Story of Naval Disaster and Heroism in World War II*. New York: Collins, 2008.

Hendrix, Henry J. *Theodore Roosevelt's Naval Diplomacy: The U.S. Navy and the Birth of the American Century*. Annapolis, Md.: Naval Institute Press, 2009.

Herman, Jan K. *Navy Medicine in Vietnam: Oral Histories from Dien Bien Phu to the Fall of Saigon*. Jefferson, N.C.: McFarland, 2009.

Hogenboom, Ari A. *Gustavus Vasa Fox of the Union Navy: A Biography*. Baltimore, Md.: Johns Hopkins University Press, 2008.

Holloway, James L. *Aircraft Carriers at War: A Personal Retrospective of Korea, Vietnam, and the Soviet Confrontation*. Annapolis, Md.: Naval Institute Press, 2007.

Hollwit, Joel I. *"Execute Against Japan": The U.S. Decision to Conduct Unrestricted Submarine Warfare*. College: Texas A&M University Press, 2009.

Holmes, Tony. *F-14 Tomcat Units of Operation Enduring Freedom*. New York: Osprey, 2008.

Holzer, Harold, and Tim Mulligan, eds. *The Battle of Hampton Roads: New Perspectives on the USS Monitor and CSS Virginia*. New York: Fordham University Press, 2006.

Hone, Thomas C., and Trent Hone. *Battle Line: The United States Navy, 1919–1939*. Annapolis, Md.: Naval Institute Press, 2006.

Hough, Louis A. *A Fleet to be Forgotten: The Wooden Freighters of World War One*. San Francisco, Calif.: San Francisco Maritime History Press, 2009.

Huchthausen, Peter A., and Alexandre Sheldon-Duplaix. *Hide and Seek: The Untold Story of Cold War Espionage at Sea*. Hoboken, N.J.: J. Wiley & Sons, 2008.

Jernigan, Emory J. *Tin Can Man*. Annapolis, Md.: Naval Institute Press, 2008.

Johnson, Stephen R. *Silent Steel: The Mysterious Death of the Nuclear Attack Submarine USS Scorpion*. Hoboken, N.J.: John Wiley, 2006.

Johnston, James C. *The Yankee Fleet: Maritime New England in the Sage of Sail*. Charleston, S.C.: History Press, 2007.

Joiner, Gary D. *Mr. Lincoln's Brown Water Navy: The Mississippi Squadron*. Lanham, Md.: Rowman & Littlefield, 2007.

Jones, Joseph F. *John Paul Jones: America's First Sea Warrior*. Annapolis, Md.: Naval Institute Press, 2006.

Jones, Wilbur D. *"Football! Navy! War!": How Military "Lend-Lease" Players Saved the College Games and Helped Win World War II*. Jefferson, N.C.: McFarland, 2009.

Kaplan, Robert D. *Hog Pilots, Blue Water Grunts: The American Military in the Air, at Sea, and on the Ground*. New York: Vintage Books, 2008.

Karsten, Peter. *The Naval Aristocracy: The Golden Age of Annapolis and the Emergence of Modern American Navalism*. Annapolis, Md.: Naval Institute Press, 2008.

Kehn, Donald M. *A Blue Sea of Blood: Deciphering the Mysterious Fate of the USS Edsall*. Minneapolis, Minn.: MBI, 2008.

Keith, Don. *Final Patrol: True Stories of World War II Submarines*. New York: NAL Caliber, 2006.

Keith, Thomas H. *SEAL Warrior: Death in the Dark: Vietnam, 1968–1972*. New York: Thomas Dunne Books/St. Martin Press, 2009.

Kelso II, Frank B. *The Reminiscences of Admiral Frank B. Kelso II, U.S. Navy (Retired)*. Annapolis, Md.: Naval Institute Press, 2009.

Kennedy, Maxwell T. *Danger's Hour: The Story of the USS Bunker Hill and the Kamikaze Pilot Who Crippled Her*. New York: Simon & Schuster, 2008.

Kernan, Alvin B. *The Unknown Battle of Midway: The Destruction of the American Torpedo Squadrons*. New Haven, Conn.: Yale University Press, 2007.

———. *Crossing the Line: A Bluejacket's Odyssey in World War II*. New Haven, Conn.: Yale University Press, 2007.

Kershaw, Alex. *Escape the Deep: The Epic Story of a Legendary Submarine and Her Courageous Crew*. Philadelphia: Da Capo, 2009.

Kimble, David L. *Chronology of U.S. Navy Submarine Operations in the Pacific, 1939–1942*. Bennington, Vt.: Merriam Press, 2008.

Knoblock, Glenn A. *Black Submariners in the United States Navy, 1940–1975*. Jefferson, N.C.: McFarland, 2005.

———. *African American World War II Casualties and Decorations in the Navy, Coast Guard, and Merchant Marine: A Comprehensive Record. Jefferson, N.C.: McFarland, 2009.

Knott, Richard C. *Attack from the Sky: Naval Air Operations in the Korean War.* Washington, D.C.: Naval Historical Center, Department of the Navy, 2004.

Kuehn, John T. *Agents of Innovation: The General Board and Design of the Fleet that Defeated the Japanese.* Annapolis, Md.: Naval Institute Press, 2008.

Lambeth, Benjamin S. *American Carrier Air Power at the Dawn of a New Century.* Santa Monica, Calif.: RAND, National Defense Research Institute, 2005.

Lambert, Frank. *The Barbary Wars: American Independence in the Atlantic World.* New York: Hill & Wang, 2007.

Lardas, Mark. *American Light and Medium Frigates, 1794–1836.* New York: Osprey, 2008.

———. *Ships of the American Revolution.* New York: Osprey, 2009.

———. *Constitution vs Guerriere: Frigates During the War of 1812.* New York: Osprey, 2009.

LaVo, Carl. *The Galloping Ghost: The Extraordinary Life of Submarine Legend Eugene Fluckey.* Annapolis, Md.: Naval Institute Press, 2007.

Lawrence, Frederick V. *A Journal of Occurrences along the Rebel Coast: A Chronology of Revolutionary War Naval Events in the Waters South and West of Cape Cod.* Westminster, Md.: Heritage Books, 2008.

Leek, Jim. *Manila and Santiago: The New Steel Navy in the Spanish-American War.* Annapolis, Md.: Naval Institute Press, 2009.

Leiner, Frederick C. *Millions for Defense: The Subscription Warships of 1798.* Annapolis, Md.: Naval Institute Press, 2006.

Leiner, Frederick C. *The End of Barbary Terror: America's 1815 War Against the Pirates of North Africa.* New York: Oxford University Press, 2006.

Levy, David M. *Fast Boats and Fast Times: Memories of a PT Boat Skipper in the South Pacific.* Bloomington, Ind.: AuthorHouse, 2008.

Lundstrom, John B. *Black Shoe Carrier Admiral: Frank Jack Fletcher at Coral Sea, Midway, and Guadalcanal.* Annapolis, Md.: Naval Institute Press, 2006.

Luttrell, Marcus. *Lone Survivor: The Eyewitness Account of Operation Redwing and the Lost Heroes of SEAL Team 10.* New York: Little, Brown, 2007.

McCarthy, Donald J. *MiG Killers: A Chronology of U.S. Air Victories in Vietnam, 1965–1973.* North Branch, Minn.: Specialty Press, 2009.

McConaghy, Lorraine. *Warship under Sail: The USS Decatur in the Pacific West.* Seattle, Wash.: Center for the Study of the Pacific Northwest, 2009.

McCullough, Jonathan J. *A Tale of Two Subs: An Untold Story of World War II, Two Sister Ships, and Extraordinary Heroism.* New York: Grand Central Pub., 2008.

McDonald, Craig R. *The USS Puffer in World War II: A History of the Submarine and Its Wartime Crew.* Jefferson, N.C.: McFarland, 2008.

McHale, Gannon. *Stealth Boat: Fighting the Cold War in a Fast Attack Submarine.* Annapolis, Md.: Naval Institute Press, 2008.

Macomber, Robert N. *A Different Kind of Honor: Lt. Cmdr. Peter Wake, U.S.N., in the War of the Pacific, 1873.* Sarasota, Fla.: Pineapple Press, 2007.

McPartlin, Greg. *Combat Corpsman.* New York: Penguin, 2005.

Madgwick, Gary, Mark Attrill, and Mark Rolfe. *F/A-18A/B/C/D in Worldwide Service.* Wantage, UK: Aviation Workshop Publications, 2008.

Magra, Christopher P. *The Fisherman's Cause: Atlantic Commerce and Maritime Dimensions of the American Revolution.* New York: Cambridge University Press, 2009.

Malcomson, Robert. *Capital in Flames: The American Attack on York, 1813.* Montreal: Robin Brass, 2008.

Mardola, Edward J. *The U.S. Navy in Korea.* Annapolis, Md.: Naval Institute Press, 2007.

———. *The Approaching Storm: Conflict in Asia, 1945–1965.* Washington, D.C.: Naval History & Heritage Command, 2009.

Mardola, Edward J., and Robert J. Schneller, eds. *Shield and Sword: The United States Navy in the Persian Gulf War.* Annapolis, Md.: Naval Historical Center, 2001.

Melton, Buckner F. *Sea Cobra: Admiral Halsey's Task Force and the Great Pacific Typhoon.* Guilford, Conn.: Lyons Press, 2007.

Miller, Edward S. *War Plan Orange: The U.S. Strategy to Defeat Japan, 1897–1945.* Annapolis, Md.: Naval Institute Press, 2007.

Millet, Wesley, and Gerald White. *The Rebel and the Rose: James A. Semple, Julia Gardiner Tyler, and the Lost Confederate Gold.* Nashville, Tenn.: Cumberland House, 2007.

Mills, Eric. *The Spectral Tide: True Ghost Stories of the U.S. Navy*. Annapolis, Md.: Naval Institute Press, 2009.

Moore, Stephen L. *Presumed Lost: The Incredible Ordeal of America's Submarine POWs during the Pacific War*. Annapolis, Md.: Naval Institute Press, 2009.

Moses, Sam. *At All Costs: How a Crippled Ship and Two American Merchant Mariners Turned the Tide of World War II*. New York: Random House Trade Paperbacks, 2007.

Mrazek, Robert J. *A Dawn Like Thunder: The True Story of Torpedo Squadron Eight*. New York: Little, Brown, 2008.

Muir, Malcolm. *Sea Power on Call: Fleet Operations, June 1951–July 1953*. Washington, D.C.: Naval Historical Center, Department of the Navy, 2005.

Nalty, Bernard C. *Long Passage to Korea: Black Sailors and the Integration of the U.S. Navy*. Washington, D.C.: Naval Historical Center, 2003.

Nash, Peter V. *The Development of Mobile Logistics Support in Anglo-American Naval Policy, 1900–1953*. Gainesville: University Press of Florida, 2009.

Nelson, James L. *George Washington's Secret Navy*. Chicago: McGraw-Hill, 2008.

Newpower, Anthony. *Iron Men and Tin Fish: The Race to Build a Better Torpedo During World War II*. Westport, Conn.: Praeger Security International, 2006.

Nichols, Gina. *The Seabees at Gulfport*. Charleston, S.C.: Arcadia Pub., 2007.

———. *The Seabees at Port Hueneme*. Charleston, S.C.: Arcadia Pub., 2006.

Norton, Louis A. *Captains Contentious: The Dysfunctional Sons of the Brine*. Columbia: University of South Carolina Press, 2009.

Offley, Edward. *Scorpion Down: Sunk by the Soviets, Buried by the Pentagon: The Untold Story of the USS Scorpion*. New York: Basic Books, 2007.

O'Hara, Vincent P. *The U.S. Navy Against the Axis: Surface Combat, 1941–1945*. Annapolis, Md.: Naval Institute Press, 2007.

———. *Struggle for the Middle Sea: The Great Navies at War in the Mediterranean Theater, 1940–1945*. Annapolis, Md.: Naval Institute Press, 2009.

Olsen, A. N. *The King Bee: A Biography of Admiral Ben Moreell, Founder of the U.S. Navy Seabees*. Victoria, BC: Trafford Publishing, 2007.

O'Rourke, Ronald. *The Impact of Chinese Naval Modernization on the Future of the United States Navy*. New York: Nova Science Publishers, 2006.

Ostlund, Mike. *Find 'em, Chase 'em, Sink 'em: The Mysterious Loss of the WWII Submarine USS Gudgeon*. Guilford, Conn.: Lyons Press, 2006.

Ostrom, Thomas P. *The United States Coast Guard in World War II: A History of Domestic and Overseas Actions*. Jefferson, N.C.: McFarland, 2009.

Park, Carl D. *Ironclad Down: The USS Merrimack-CSS Virginia from Construction to Destruction*. Annapolis, Md.: Naval Institute Press, 2007.

Patton, Robert H. *Patriot Pirates: The Privateer War for Freedom and Fortune in the American Revolution*. New York: Vintage Books, 2009.

Polmar, Norman. *Historic Naval Aircraft*. Dulles, Va.: Potomac Books, 2006.

Polmar, Norman, and Christopher P. Cavas. *Navy's Most wanted: The Top 10 Book of Admirable Admirals, Sleek Submarines, and Other Naval Oddities*. Washington, D.C.: Potomac Books, 2009.

Puryear, Edgar F. *American Admiralship: The Moral Imperatives of Naval Command*. Annapolis, Md.: Naval Institute Press, 2006.

Rains, Calvin E. *The Story of One Navy Fighter Pilot*. Bloomington, Ind.: AuthorHouse, 2006.

Rawson, Andrew. *The Vietnam War Handbook: U.S. Armed Forces in Vietnam*. Stroud, UK: History Press, 2008.

Ray, William, and Hester Blum. *Horrors of Slavery, or, the American Tar in Tripoli*. New Brunswick, N.J.: Rutgers University Press, 2008.

Reardon, Carol. *Launch the Intruders: A Naval Attack Squadron in the Vietnam War, 1972*. Kansas: University of Kansas Press, 2005.

Reminick, Gerald. *Action in the South Atlantic: The Sinking of the German Raider Stier by the Liberty Ship Stephen Hopkins*. Palo Alto, Calif.: Glencannon Press, 2006.

Reynolds, Clark G. *On the Warpath in the Pacific: Admiral Jocko Clark and the Fast Carriers*. Annapolis, Md.: Naval Institute Press, 2005.

Riker, H. Jay. *The Silent Service. Seawolf Class*. New York: Avon Books, 2002.

Roberts, Mark K. *Sub: An Oral History of U.S. Submarines*. New York: Berkley Caliber, 2008.

Roberts, William H. *Civil War Ironclads: The U.S. Navy and Industrial Mobilization*. Baltimore, Md.: John Hopkins University Press, 2007.

Bibliography

Rottman, Gordon L. *US Patrol Torpedo Boats: World War II.* New York: Osprey, 2008.

Sasgen, Peter T. *Stalking the Red Bear: The True Story of a U.S. Cold War Submarine's Covert Operations Against the Soviet Union.* New York: St. Martin's Press, 2008.

Schneller, Robert S. *Blue & Gold and Black: Racial Integration of the U.S. Naval Academy.* College Station: Texas A&M University Press, 2008.

———. *Anchor of Resolve: A History of U.S. Naval Forces Central Command/Fifth Fleet.* Washington, D.C.: Naval Historical Center, 2007.

Schroeder, John H. *Commodore John Rodgers: Paragon of the Early American Navy.* Gainesville: University Press of Florida, 2006.

Schultz, Robert. *We Were Pirates: A Torpedoman's Pacific War.* Annapolis, Md.: Naval Institute Press, 2009.

Schwab, Stephen I. *Guantanamo, USA: The Untold History of America's Cuba Outpost.* Lawrence: University Press of Kansas, 2009.

Scott, James. *The Attack on the Liberty: The Untold Story of Israel's Deadly 1967 Assault on a U.S. Spy Ship.* New York: Simon & Schuster, 2009.

Sendzikas, Aldona. *Lucky 73: USS Pampanito's Unlikely Rescue of Allied POWs in WWII.* Gainesville: University Press of Florida, 2010.

Sewell, Kenneth R. *All Hands Down: The True Story of the Soviet Attack on the USS Scorpion.* New York: Simon & Schuster, 2008.

Sherwood, John D. *Black Sailor, White Navy: Racial Unrest in the Fleet During the Vietnam War Era.* New York: New York University Press, 2007.

———. *Nixon's Trident: Naval Power in Southeast Asia, 1968–1972.* Washington, D.C.: Naval Historical Center, Department of the Navy, 2008.

Shomette, Donald. *Flotilla: The Patuxent Naval Campaign in the War of 1812.* Baltimore: Johns Hopkins University Press, 2009.

Silverstone, Paul H. *The Navy of World War II, 1922–1946.* London: Routledge, 2007.

———. *The Navy of the Nuclear Age, 1947–2007.* New York: Routledge, 2009.

Simmons, Rick. *Defending South Carolina's Coast: The Civil War from Georgetown to Little River.* Charleston, S.C.: History Press, 2009.

Simpson, Michael. *Anglo-American Naval Relations, 1919–1939.* Burlington, Vt.: Ashgate, 2009.

Smith, Douglas V. *Carrier Battles: Command Decision in Harm's Way.* Annapolis, Md.: Naval Institute Press, 2006.

Smith, Myron J. *Le Roy Fitch: The Civil War Career of a Union River Gunboat Commander.* Jefferson, N.C.: McFarland, 2007.

———. *The Timberclads in the Civil War: The Lexington, Conestoga, and Tyler on the Western Waters.* Jefferson, N.C.: McFarland, 2008.

Steely, Skipper. *Pearl Harbor Countdown: Admiral James O. Richardson.* Gretna, La.: Pelican Pub. Co., 2008.

Stein, Stephen K. *From Torpedoes to Aviation: Washington Irving Chambers and Technological Innovation in the New Navy, 1876–1913.* Tuscaloosa: University of Alabama Press, 2007.

Still, William N. *Crisis at Sea: The United States Navy in European Waters in World War I.* Gainesville: University Press of Florida, 2006.

Stille, Mark. *USN Carriers vs IJN Carriers: The Pacific, 1942.* New York: Osprey, 2007.

———. *USN Cruiser vs IJN Cruiser.* New York: Osprey, 2009.

Stillwell, Paul. *Submarine Stories: Recollections from the Diesel Boats.* Annapolis, Md.: Naval Institute Press, 2007.

Stoffey, Robert E. *Fighting to Leave: The Final Years of America's War in Vietnam, 1972–1973.* Minneapolis, Minn.: MBI, 2008.

Sumrall, Robert F. *Sumner-Gearing Class Destroyers: Their Designs, Weapons, and Equipment.* Annapolis, Md.: Naval Institute Press, 2008.

Symmes, Weymouth D. *This is Latch: The Rear Admiral Roy F. Hoffman Story.* Missoula, Mont.: Pictorial Histories Pub. Co., 2007.

Symonds, Craig L. *Lincoln and His Admirals.* New York: Oxford University Press, 2008.

———. *The Civil War at Sea.* Santa Barbara, Calif.: Praeger, 2009.

Taaffe, Stephen R. *Commanding Lincoln's Navy: Union Naval Leadership During the Civil War.* Annapolis, Md.: Naval Institute Press, 2009.

Thomas, Evan. *Sea of Thunder: Four Commanders and the Last Great Campaign, 1941–1945.* New York: Simon & Schuster, 2007.

Thomason, Tommy H. *Strike from the Sea: Development of U.S. Navy Attack Aircraft.* North Branch, Minn.: Specialty Press, 2009.

———. *U.S. Naval Air Superiority: Development of Shipborne Jet Fighters, 1943–1962.* North Branch, Minn.: Specialty Press, 2008.

Thompson, Warren. *F4U Corsair Units of the Korean War.* New York: Osprey, 2009.

Toll, Ian W. *Six Frigates: The Epic History of the Founding of the U.S. Navy.* New York: W. W. Norton, 2007.

Tomblin, Barbara. *Bluejackets and Contrabands: African Americans and the Union Navy.* Lexington: University Press of Kentucky, 2009.

Trimble, William F. *Admiral William A. Moffett: Architect of Naval Aviation.* Annapolis, Md.: Naval Institute Press, 2007.

———. *Attack from the Sea: A History of the U.S. Navy's Seaplane Striking Force.* Annapolis, Md.: Naval Institute Press, 2005.

Tuohy, William. *The Bravest Man: The Story of Richard O'Kane and the Amazing Submarine Adventures of the USS Tang.* New York: Ballantine Books, 2006.

———. *America's Fighting Admirals: Winning the War at Sea in World War II.* St. Paul, Minn.: MBI, 2007.

Underwood, Rodman L. *Waters of Discord: The Union Blockade of Texas During the Civil War.* Jefferson, N.C.: McFarland, 2008.

Venzon, Anne C. *America's War with Spain: A Selected Bibliography.* Lanham, Md.: Scarecrow Press, 2003.

Victor, George. *The Pearl Harbor Myth: Rethinking the Unthinkable.* Washington, D.C.: Potomac Books, 2007.

Volo, James M. *Blue Water Patriots: The American Revolution Afloat.* Westport, Conn.: Praeger Publishers, 2007.

Wahl, Andrew J. *Sea Raptors: Logs of the Private Armed Vessels Comet and Chasseur, Commanded by Tom Boyle, 1812–1815.* Westminster, Md.: Heritage Books, 2008.

Walker, Frank. *John Paul Jones: A Maverick Hero.* Stroud, Gloucestershire, UK: Spellmount, 2007.

Warner, Jeff. *U.S. Naval Amphibious Forces.* Atglen, Penn.: Schiffer Military History, 2007.

———. *Weapons, Equipment, Insignia: Submarine Service, PT Boats, Coast Guard, Other Sea Service.* Atglen, Penn.: Schiffer Military History, 2008.

Westwell, Ian. *U.S. Forces in the Pacific.* Edison, N.J.: Chartwell Books, 2007.

Wheelan, Joseph. *Jefferson's War: America's First War on Terror, 1801–1805.* New York: Carroll & Graf Publishers, 2003.

Whitlock, Flint. *The Depths of Courage: American Submariners at War with Japan, 1941–1945.* New York: Berkeley Caliber, 2007.

Wiche, Glen N., ed. *Dispatches from Bermuda: The Civil War Letters of Charles Maxwell Allen.* Kent, Ohio: Kent State University Press, 2008.

Wildenberg, Thomas. *All the Factors of Victory: Admiral Joseph Mason Reeves and the Origins of Carrier Airpower.* Washington, D.C.: Potomac Books, 2005.

Wiley, Ken. *Lucky Thirteen: D-Days in the Pacific with the U.S. Coast Guard in World War II.* Philadelphia: Casemate, 2007.

Wilkes, James W. *Down Under: My Life as a WWII Submariner.* Philadelphia: Xlibris, 2007.

Williams, Greg H. *The French Assault on American Shipping, 1793–1813: A History and Comprehensive Record of Merchant Marine Losses.* Jefferson, N.C.: McFarland, 2009.

Winkler, David F. *Cold War at Sea: High-Seas Confrontation between the United States and the Soviet Union.* Annapolis, Md.: Naval Institute Press, 2000.

Wise, Harold E. *Inside the Danger Zone: The U.S. Military in the Persian Gulf, 1987–1988.* Annapolis, Md.: Naval Institute Press, 2007.

Wise, James E., and Scott Baron. *The Navy Cross: Extraordinary Heroism in Iraq, Afghanistan, and Other Conflicts.* Annapolis, Md.: Naval Institute Press, 2007.

———. *The Silver Star: Navy and Marine Corps Gallantry in Iraq, Afghanistan, and Other Conflicts.* Annapolis, Md.: Naval Institute Press, 2008.

Wordell, M. T., E. N. Seiler, and Keith Ayling. *"Wildcats" Over Casablanca: U.S. Navy Fighters in Operation Torch.* Washington, D.C.: Potomac Books, 2007.

Wragg, David M. *Fighting Admirals of the Second World War.* Annapolis, Md.: Naval Institute Press, 2009.

Zacks, Richard. *The Pirate Coast: Thomas Jefferson, the First Marines, and the Secret Mission of 1805.* New York: Hyperion, 2005.

Zatarain, Lee A. *Tanker War: America's First Conflict with Iran, 1987–88.* Philadelphia: Casemate, 2008.

Zichek, Hared A. *Secret Aerospace Projects of the U.S. Navy, Vol. 1: The Incredible Attack Aircraft of the USS United States, 1948–1949.* Atglen, Pa.: Schiffer Publishing, 2009.

Zimmerman, W. Frederick. *CVN-68 Nimitz: U.S. Navy Aircraft Carrier.* Ann Arbor, Mich.: Nimble Books, 2008.

Index

Note: Page numbers followed by *f* refer to citations found in photo captions.

Adams, John, vii, 2, 11, 21, 22, 23, 25, 28, 30
Admiralty courts, creation of, 2
Aegis Ballistic Missile Defense system, 342, 343
Aerial bombing tests, 176
Aerial reconnaissance, 81, 83, 156, 158
Aerial refueling, 273
Aerial spotting, 149, 150, 178
Aerial torpedoes, 162, 167
Aeronautical engineering, 151
Aerospace activities, 277
    Apollo missions, 290, 295–296, 297, 298–299, 302
    Challenger, explosion of, 313
    Columbia, disintegration of, 338
    communications satellites, 279, 287
    first American in space, 279
    first female aviator in space, 327
    Gemini missions, 287–290
    Mercury astronauts, Navy representation, 277
    Naval Space Command, 311
    navigational satellites, 278
    second orbital flight, 281
    Skylab, 303
    space shuttle program, 309, 311, 313, 338
    space walks, 288, 311
    Vanguard satellite, launching of, 275
Afghanistan, U. S. involvement in, 209, 330, 335–336
African Americans
    E. A. Bryant, explosion of, 240
    enlistment of into the naval service, Civil War, 82
    first admitted to the U.S. Naval Academy, 118
    first ensign commission in the regular naval service, 261
    first four-star admiral, 328
    first in Navy Nurse Corps, 251
    first naval officer, 213
    first Navy pilot, 266
    first rear admiral, 301
    first to fly with the Blue Angels Flight Demonstration Team, 314
    first to graduate from the U.S. Naval Academy, 262
    first to head up Blue Angels Flight Demonstration Team, 326
    first to reach four-star rank, 327
    mutiny aboard *S. J. Waring,* Civil War, 80
    racial tensions aboard *Kitty Hawk,* 302
    recruitment of, prohibition against, 23
    recruitment of, for World War II service, 213
    theft of Confederate tug *Planter,* Civil War, 91
African Squadron, 49, 75
Aguinaldo, Emilio, 135, 138
Ainsworth, Walden L., 220, 225, 238
Air Force, monopoly on strategic bombing, 261
Airtime Warning and Control Systems (AWACS), 308
Alabama
    in the Civil War, 79, 89
    Mobile, battle for, 89, 96–97, 104–105, 108–109, 114
    piracy off the coast of, 35
    in the Revolutionary War, 15
Alabama (commerce raider), 93, 94, 95, 96, 107–108, 113
Albania, Operation Silver Wake, 329
Aleutian Islands, in World War II, 213, 224, 225, 236
Algiers, U.S. declaration of war against (1815), 46
Allen, William Henry, 39, 40
Amazon River, exploration of, 71
America (British racing yacht), 88
America (dirigible), 144
America (Revolutionary War ship), 17
Amistad, slave mutiny aboard, 59
Amphibious hydroaeroplanes. *See* Flying boats
Amphibious operations
    aircraft suited for, 184, 186
    assault vessels, 274, 279, 315, 322, 328
    in the Civil War, 81, 83, 107
    invasion of Italy, World War II, 225
    in the Korean War, 264, 265

Amphibious operations (*continued*)
  by Native Americans, 59
  Revolutionary War, 1, 13
  SEALs, 280
  transport docks, 281
  in the War of 1812, 39–40
  in World War II, 197, 214, 215, 220, 224–225, 227, 230, 232, 233
Andrew Doria, 4, 5, 7, 8, 10
Angled decks, aircraft carriers, 270, 271–272
Antarctica, 274
  conclusion of naval operations in, 331
  Operation Deep Freeze, 272, 331
  Operation Highjump, 261
  U.S. Exploring Expedition survey of, 57–61
Antiaircraft fire control system, 184
Antiaircraft weapons, 198
Arcadia Conference, 205, 206
Arctic, exploration of
  DeLong's expedition, 120–121
  Greely's expedition, 122
  Grinnell Expedition, 70–71
  Macmillan Arctic Expedition, 183
  Operation Frostbite, 260
  Polaris expedition to, 118
  Second Grinnell Expedition, 72, 74
Argentina, civil unrest, protection of American lives and interests, 71
Arizona (battleship), loss of at Pearl Harbor, 11, 160, 203, 276
Arkansas, Civil War, 91, 94, 96
Arkansas (ironclad), 93
Arlington National Cemetery, 177, 326
Armed Ship Bill (1917), 161
Arms and supplies
  Aegis Ballistic Missile Defense system, 342, 343
  air-launched torpedo, 148
  air-to-air missile, 269, 270, 274
  air-to-ground missile, 195
  antiaircraft weapons, 198
  ballistic missiles, 273–274, 282
  computer-guided "smart" weapons, 305
  Explosive Ordnance Disposal (EOD) Mobile Unit, 321*f*
  machine guns, use of aboard aircraft, 164
  nuclear weapons, 257–258, 262, 264, 255, 300, 323
  "Old Sow," 36
  "Peacemaker," 62
  Polaris missile, 274–276, 277, 278–280, 281, 282
  Poseidon multiwarhead ballistic missile, 299–300
  recoil-less gun, 149
  rocket-powered guided missile (SUBROC), 282
  solid-fuel rocket, 275
  SM-3 standard missiles, 344
  Standoff Land Attack Missiles (SLAM), 321
  surface-to-air missile, 268, 271, 273, 285
  surface-to-surface antiaircraft missile system, 276
  Tomahawk guided cruise missile, 305, 306–307, 339
  Trident missile, 317
Army Air Corps, 188
Army Medal of Honor, 84
Arnold, Benedict, 1, 6, 7
Arthur, Chester A., 122
Asiatic Squadron, 128
Asiatic Station, submarines ordered to, 196–197
Assistant Secretary of the Navy, 80, 125
Assistant Secretary of the Navy for Aeronautics, 184
Astronomical observations, as navigational tool, 70
Atlantic Charter, 201
Atlantic Fleet, World War II, 199, 202, 205
Atlantic Ocean
  mission to test winds and currents in, 71
  transatlantic cable, laying of, 75
Atlantic Squadron, 114
Autopilot, 175
Aviation Cadet Act (1935), 192

Bahamas
  in the Civil War, 88, 90, 93, 112
  in the Revolutionary War, 4
Bailey, Joseph, 106, 107
Bainbridge, William, 24, 27, 30, 31, 33, 37, 42, 47
Bainbridge (torpedo-boat destroyer), 139*f*, 179
Balloons, 81, 83, 158, 164, 171, 279
Baltimore (minelayer), 124, 155
Baltimore (sloop), 23–24
Bancroft, George, 62, 63, 64
Banks, Nathaniel P., 105, 106
Barbados, in the Revolutionary War, 11
Barbary Wars, vii
  blockade, port of Tripoli, 28, 30, 31
  captives taken by U.S., 28
  de facto state of war with, 29–33
  declaration of war by Pasha of Tripoli (1801), 28
  end of, 48
  Jefferson's response to, 28
  Mediterranean squadron organized to repel, 46–47
  national insult weathered by Captain Bainbridge, 27
  peace treaty, ratification of, 31, 33
  peace treaty with Tripoli (1805), 33
  Philadelphia, deliberate burning of, 46
  ransom demanded by, 18, 20
  restitution paid by, 47
  seizure of American vessels by, 18, 20
  treaties with Pasha of Tripoli, 21, 47–48
  treaty to placate Dey of Algiers (1795), 20
  U.S. response to, 19
Barbey, Daniel E., 225, 228, 229, 232, 233, 236, 242
Barney, Joshua, 11, 17, 20, 42, 43
Barron, James, 34, 46, 49

Index

Barron, Samuel, 26, 32, 33
Barry, John, vii, 3, 5, 11, 12, 15, 16, 17, 20, 21, 140
"Battle of the Kegs," 11
Beach, Edward L., 154, 160, 278
Beall, John Y., 103, 109
Bean, Alan, 298, 303
Beauregard, Pierre G. T., 102, 103, 104
Belknap, George C., 116, 119
Bellinger, Patrick N. L., 151, 152, 153, 155, 156
Benson, William S., 147, 155
Berkey, Russell S., 254, 256
Berlin Airlift, 262
Bermuda, naval operations near, 6, 24
"Bermuda Triangle," 259
Biddle, James, 48, 51, 63, 64–65, 68, 69
Biddle, Nicholas, 3, 6, 11
Biddle, Thomas, 5, 46
Bin Laden, Osama, 330, 333
"Black Cat Squadron," 219
Blackouts, pilot, 191
Blakeley, Johnston, 42, 43, 44
Blandy, William H. P., 243, 250
Blimps, use of in World War II, 215–216, 226
Blind landings, 190, 193
Blockade(s)
　of Americans, Revolutionary War, 1
　by British, War of 1812, 37, 39, 40, 41, 42
　California coast, during Mexican-American war, 64
　in Civil War, official end of, 114
　of Cuba, Spanish-American War, 128, 132
　economic effects of, 42, 78, 115
　of Mexican ports in preparation for and during Mexican-American War, 63, 64, 65
　naval quarantine, Cuban Missile Crisis, 281f, 282
　North Korean coastline, 264–265, 266
　port of Tripoli, 28, 30, 31
　of southern Florida, Seminole Wars, 56, 59
　Union against Confederate coastline, 77–78, 80, 82, 93, 95, 104, 110, 115
Blockade Strategy Board, 80
Blue Angels Flight Demonstration Team, 260, 267, 314, 326
"Blue-Water Navy," 33
Blunt, S. F., 63, 75
Board of Navy Commissioners, 48, 61
Bombers
　equipped with brakes, 187
　mock dive-bombing attacks, 184, 185
　premature detonation of bombs, 160
　prototype dive bombers, 186, 188, 191, 195
　trapeze-type delivery mechanism, 188
Bombsight, 158, 186
Bonhomme Richard, 12, 14f
Boorda, Jeremy M., 325, 326, 328
Bosnia-Herzegovina, ethnic unrest in, 324, 326
Boston Naval Shipyard, 301, 304

Braine, John C., 104, 109
Brazilian Squadron, 75, 115
Brennan (first destroyer escort), 220
Bristol, Mark L., 151, 153, 154, 157, 158
Brown, Francis E., 215, 229
Brown, Isaac N., 92, 100
"Brown-Water Navy," 299
Buchanan, Franklin, 63, 78, 86, 87, 88, 93
Bureau(s)
　Aeronautics, 176–177, 180, 181, 183, 187, 197, 208, 278
　Construction and Repair, 144, 162, 169
　Engineering, 176
　Naval Weapons, 278
　Navigation, 145, 146, 179, 212
　Ordnance, 176, 197, 278
　Ordnance and Hydrography, 67
　Personnel, 212
　Ships, 198
　Ships for Nuclear Propulsion, 283
　Steam Engineering, 170, 175, 181
Burke, Arleigh A., 230, 231, 267, 273, 275, 306
Burnside, Ambrose E., 85, 86, 88
Bush, George H. W., 242, 310, 318, 319, 323, 325
Bush, George W., 334, 337, 340, 342, 343
Bushnell, David, 6, 10
Butler, Benjamin F., 81, 110, 111
Byrd, Richard E., 172, 183, 184–185, 186, 187, 261, 328

California, in Mexican-American War, 64
Cambodia
　Khmer Rouge, 305
　U.S. incursion into, 294, 299
Campaign medals. 131
Campbell, David, 239, 244
Canada
　boundary dispute, settlement of, 61
　Confederate sympathizers in, 104
　naval operations, 1, 8, 9, 10, 12, 13
　naval operations, Revolutionary War, 1, 8, 9, 10, 12, 13
　War of 1812, 36, 37, 39, 40
Canadian Royal Flying Corps, 165, 168
Canary Islands, in World War II, 224, 226, 232, 236
Cape of Good Hope, first American warship to round, 26
Caperton, William B., 155, 156, 157, 158
Caribbean region
　naval operations, War of 1812, 38, 41
　piracy in by France against U.S. vessels, 21, 22, 23–24
　See also individual islands by name
Caroline Islands, in World War II, 231, 234, 236, 238, 241, 246, 251
Carpenter, Malcolm Scott, 277, 281
Carter, Jimmy, 307

Catapult(s)
  compressed air, 177, 178
  flush-deck hydraulic, 191, 196
  flywheel, 172
  gunpowder, 182
  steam-launch, 269, 271
Central Command (CENTCOM), 327
Cernan, Eugene A., 288, 297, 302
Cervera, Pascual, 128, 130, 131, 133
Chain of command, violations of, 163
Chambers, Washington I., 144, 146, 147, 148, 150, 151
Chauncey, Isaac, 32, 36, 37, 38, 39, 40, 41, 48
Chemical weapons
  napalm, elimination of remaining U.S. stocks, 334
  suspected, Sudan, 330
Cheney, Dick, 318
Chesapeake (frigate), 24, 26, 29
  American revenge for attack on, 35
  British attack on, 34, 35
  reputation as "unlucky vessel," 26
Chesapeake-Leopold Affair, 34
Chevalier, Godfrey DeC., 150, 159, 179
China
  civil unrest, protection of American interests during, 73, 74–75, 181
  Dagu Forts, British/American attack on, 75
  opening of trade relations with (1845), 63
  protection of U.S. Consulate from Japanese, 195
  U.S. reconnaissance craft, detaining of, 334
Churchill, Winston, 198, 201, 205, 206, 212, 220, 223, 227, 231, 242, 249, 257
Civil unrest, protection of American lives and interests during
  Argentina, 71
  China, 73, 74–75, 181
  Cuba, 119, 141, 148, 161, 162
  Cyprus, 304
  Dominican Republic, 140, 158, 285
  Egypt, 121
  Fiji Islands, 74
  Greco-Turkish War, 176
  Greece, 260
  Haiti, 154, 155, 156
  Hawaii, 119, 125
  Iran, 307
  Japan, 116
  Korea, 123, 140, 264
  Lebanon, 139, 305–306, 310
  Liberia, 319, 328
  Nicaragua, 125–126, 127, 135, 144, 185
  Panama, 119, 123, 138–139
  Samoa, 136
  Spanish Civil War, 193
  Uruguay, 74, 116
  Vietnam, Operation Passage to Freedom, 272
  Zanzibar, 283

Civil War, vii, 76–115
  amphibious operations, 81, 83, 107
  anti-torpedo squadron, 107
  Blockade Strategy Board, 80
  blockades, official end of, 114
  coastal defense, 78
  cotton, capture of, 97
  end of, 114
  final report, Gideon Welles, 115
  final shots of, 114–115
  first hostile shots, 76
  first offensive action by U.S. Navy, 79
  first Union vessel captured, 82
  Fort Sumter, naval activities related to, 76–77, 102, 104
  fort-reducing tactics, Union, 81
  Great Britain, rocky relations with, 104
  improvisations, 99
  ironclad ships, use of, 79, 80, 81, 82, 85, 86, 87*f*, 89–90, 93
  international law, violations of, 83, 98
  naval shipyards in, 76
  Navy's first officer fatality, 80
  observation balloons, use of, 81, 83
  Russian warships, official visit to New York, 103–104
  shallow-water gunboats, use of by Union on western waters, 79
  steam rams, construction and use of, 88, 97, 104
  steam-powered ships in, 77
  "Stone Fleet," 84
  Union blockades against Confederate coastline, 77–78, 80, 82, 93, 95, 104, 110, 115
  See also individual states
Civilian Engineer Corps, 209
Clinton, Bill, 325, 333, 334
Coastal fortifications
  acquisition of gunboats for defense, 34
  funding for, 33
  ports, U.S. Coast Guard protection of, 208
Cochran, Donnie L., 314, 326
Cockburn, Sir George, 38, 43
Cockpit, enclosed, 189, 192
Cold War, viii, 259
  first military crisis, Korea, 264
  Incidents at Sea Agreement, 302
  Polaris A-2 deterrent cruise, 281
  rising tensions with the Soviet Union and its allies, 262, 264
Cold-weather equipment, 192
Cole, terrorist bombing of, 333
Collins, Napoleon, 109, 116
Collisions
  between aircraft, 181, 194
  Ammen and *Collett*, 278
  Blackthorn and oil tanker, Tampa, Florida, 308
  Hobson and *Wasp*, North Atlantic, 268

Index

hospital ship and freighter, San Francisco, 265
Oneida and British vessel *City of Bombay*, 117
S-1 submarine with *City of Rome*, 183
Woolsey and *Steel Inventor*, 176
Colt, Samuel, 60, 61
Commander, Carrier Air Group, 195
Commerce, U.S.
  protection of, 20, 29, 32–33, 35, 47, 49, 53
  Treaty of Wanghia, promoting trade with China, 63
Commercial aircraft disasters, search and recovery operations
  Air Cathay, 272
  Alaska Airlines Flight 261, 332
  Egyptian Air Flight 900, 332
  Korean Air Lines Flight 007, 310
  Korean Air Lines Flight 801, 330
  Swissair Flight 111, 330
  TWA Flight 800, 329
Computer-guided "smart" weapons, 305
Conestoga (gunboat), 84, 85, 86, 195
Confederate States of America (CSA)
  acquisition of naval vessels from Britain, 79
  blockade running, 78, 79, 81, 82, 86, 88, 94, 107, 110
  Committee of Naval Affairs, 79
  Confederate River Defense Fleet, 90–91
  "Cottonclads," 86, 95, 96, 97
  defection of U.S. Navy officers and public officials to, 76–77
  Department of the Navy, 76
  first rear admiral, 93
  first Union vessel captured by, 82
  foreign-made warships acquired by, 93
  ironclad ships, use of, 79, 80, 82, 89–90, 93
  Keokuk, sinking of, 99, 103
  mines, use of, 80, 85, 92, 95, 102, 105, 106, 111, 112
  naval academy, establishment of, 90
  naval forces, weakness of, 106
  Naval Submarine Battery Service, 94
  privateering activities, 77, 79
  Secretary of the Navy, 77
  ship seizures by, 77
  submersibles ("infernal machine"), construction of, 79–80
  Torpedo Bureau, 94
  See also Civil War
Congress (frigate), 23, 25, 35, 51, 87
Congressional Medal of Honor, 104, 107, 118, 155, 179, 180, 186
  awarded in Korean War, 266, 271
  awarded posthumously, 166, 176, 182, 194, 212, 221, 225, 228, 231, 242, 245, 248, 249, 250, 251, 255, 256, 267, 269, 271, 285, 291, 296
  awarded in Vietnam War, 285, 289, 291, 292, 294, 296, 297, 302
  awarded in war on terror, 342
  awarded in World War I, 166, 168, 169, 170, 172, 173
  awarded in World War II, 207, 208, 210, 234, 237, 238, 241, 242, 244, 250, 251, 253, 254, 256, 258
  Bennington boiler explosion, 140
  Decatur, explosion aboard, 157
  for exploration activities, 184–185
  Kearsarge, turret fire aboard, 141
  Memphis, sinking of, 160
  Mexican incident (1914), 153, 157
  New York, shipmate rescue, 158
  Pearl Harbor, Japanese attack on, 203
  Philippine Insurrection, 136, 138
  Pittsburg, explosion aboard, 165
  powder incident aboard battleship *Missouri*, 140
  for response to natural disasters, 180
  Spanish-American War, 129, 130, 131, 133, 135
  two-time recipients, 311
Connecticut, War of 1812, 36, 39
Conner, David, 62–63, 64, 65, 66, 67, 68, 72
Conrad, Charles, 289, 298, 303
Constellation (frigate), 20, 21, 23, 24, 26, 29, 40, 50
Constitution (frigate), 20, 21, 23, 25, 29, 31, 32, 36, 37, 56, 78, 79, 330
Continental Congress
  Agent of Marine, creation of, 16, 18
  appointment of surgeons and surgeon's mates to naval vessels, 4
  Board of the Admiralty, creation of, 14–15
  Continental Naval Board, creation of, 7
  Declaration of Independence, promulgation of, 6
  funding and construction of Continental Navy, 1–2, 3, 8
  General Letter of Marque and Reprisal, 4
  instructions to Continental Navy, 3–4
  Marine Committee, 2, 3, 4, 7, 8
  Naval Committee, 3
  Navy Board of the Eastern Department, creation of, 8
  officers and rank, regulations for, 7
  privateering, authorization of, 4
  Secretary of Marine, creation of, 16
  ship purchases, 4, 6, 12
Continental Navy, vii
  borrowed vessels, 17
  Congressional funding and construction of, 1–2, 3, 8
  Continental Congress instructions to, 3–4
  delivery of diplomatic envoys by, 8, 11, 12, 15
  disbanding of, 18
  discipline, 2, 7
  first American warship, 1
  first commander in chief, 2, 3
  first frigate launched, 5
  first officers, appointment of, 3
  first planned offensive, 4

Continental Navy (*continued*)
   first prize taken at sea by an American warship, 4
   first sortie in strength, 4
   founding and construction of, 1, 2, 5
   merchant vessels, purchase and arming of, 2
   officers, pay scales, 7
   only officer officially honored, 18
   only officer with professional training, 11
   pay rations, regulations for, 2
   prize money, division of, 2, 7
   purchases of ships for, 4, 6, 12
   recruitment process, improvements in, 7
   regulations governing, 2, 6
   uniforms, 6
   war ships, sell-off of, 18
Corregidor Island, Philippines
   in the Spanish-American War, 129
   in World War II, 210, 212
"Cottonclads," 86, 95, 96
Court-martials
   Alexander Mackenzie for mutiny aboard *Somers*, 61
   Charles G. Hunter, for interfering with Home Squadron plans, 68
   Chester Nimitz, for neglect of duty, 142
   David Porter, for overly aggressive actions, 52
   for dereliction of duty, Pearl Harbor attack, 206, 333
   E. A. Bryant explosion, 240
   Indianapolis, sinking of, 257
   Oliver Hazard Perry, for ship run aground, 34
   Thomas T. Crave, for not engaging the enemy, 113
Craven, T. A. M., 69, 70, 76
Crowinshield, Benjamin, 45, 46
Cruiser Act (1929), 187
Crutchley, Victor A. C., 232, 237
Cuba
   American sugar mills, protection of, 141, 148
   Bay of Pigs invasion, 279
   blockade, Cuban Missile Crisis, 281f, 282
   civil unrest, protection of American interests, 119, 141, 148, 161, 162
   Communist revolution, 277
   Confederate raiding activities near, 80
   delivery of captured Spanish soldiers to (1821), 50
   Guantanamo, use of for naval base, 139, 282, 336
   Mariel Boat Lift, 308
   naval operations near during Quasi-War with France, 24, 25
   Operation Able Vigil, 325
   piracy off of, 50–51, 52
   protection of American lives and property, 161
   saltwater conversion plants, 284
Cubi Point, Naval Air Station (NAS) at, 209
Cunningham, Randall F., 301, 302
Curacao, during the Quasi-War with France, 27
Curtiss, Glenn H., 145, 146, 147, 159
Curtiss Marine Trophy race, 173

Cushing, William B., 95, 105, 110
Cushing (first torpedo boat), 124
Cyprus, civil unrest, protection of American interests, 304

Dahlgren, John A. B., 67, 73, 76, 78, 101, 102, 103, 105, 113, 122
Dale, Richard, 8, 16, 20, 22, 28, 29
"Damn the torpedoes, full speed ahead!" battle cry, 89, 109
Daniels, Josephus, 151–152, 155, 156, 157
Davis, Charles H., 90, 91, 92, 94, 115, 116, 134
Davis, Jefferson, 77, 110
Decatur, Jr., Stephen, 30, 31, 32, 34, 37, 39, 45, 46, 47–48, 49
Decatur, Sr., Stephen, 22, 24, 25, 26
Declaration of Independence, promulgation of, 6
Delaware
   Chesapeake Bay blockade, War of 1812, 37, 38, 39
   naval operations, Revolutionary War, 5, 9
DeLong, George W., 120–121
Demologos. See *Fulton the First*
Denfield, Louis E., 262, 263
Denny-Brown stabilization system, 274–275
Department of Defense (DoD), creation of, 261
Depot of Charts and Instruments, 55, 61
Dewey, George, 127, 128, 129, 130, 132, 134, 135, 137, 139, 146, 151
Dewey Medal, 131
Deyo, Morton L., 239, 252
Diego Garcia, Navy communications facility on, 300
Dirigibles, 144, 155, 159, 163, 168, 181, 185, 187, 189, 190, 192
Disease, Navy deaths and incapacitation from, 25, 69
Distinguished Flying Cross, 193, 266, 283
Distinguished Service Cross, 187, 220
Diving bells, 62, 195
Dominican Republic
   civil unrest, protection of American interests, 140, 158, 285
   military coup in, 148
   national customs service, U.S. naval control of, 140
"Don't give up the ship!" battle cry, origin of, 39
Doolittle, James "Jimmy," 211, 218, 234
Doorman, Karel W. E. M., 207, 208
Doyle, James H., 264, 265, 266
Draft, 44, 84
Driscoll, William P., 301, 302
Drone, radio-controlled, 195, 210–211, 269
Drummond, George, 42, 43
Dry dock(s), 29, 53, 56, 67, 78
Du Pont, Samuel F., 65, 66, 82, 83, 87, 94, 97, 99, 101
Dufek, D. J., 272, 274

East Gulf Blockading Squadron, 85, 95, 114
East India Squadron, 61, 75, 115
East Pacific Squadron, 61

Index

Egypt, civil unrest, protection of American interests, 121
Eisenhower, Dwight D., 272, 273, 276, 279
Ejection seat, first emergency use of, 262
Electric lighting, first navy vessel fitted with, 121
Elliott, Jesse D., 37, 38, 43
Ellyson, Theodore G. (Naval Aviator No. 1), 145, 146, 147, 148, 149, 186
Embargo Act of 1807, 34
Engineering
   chief engineer, institution of on every steam vessel, 61
   General Order delineating duties of engineering officers, 62
   importance of to Navy, 57, 61
Enola Gay, 257
Enterprise (aircraft carrier), 194, 196, 202, 204, 206–207, 208, 209, 216, 219, 282, 301, 303, 336
Enterprise (brig), 40, 41, 50, 51, 62
Enterprise (nuclear-powered), 276, 280, 283
Enterprise (re-christened British Revolutionary War sloop), 1
Enterprise (schooner), 29, 31
Ericsson, John, 62, 81, 82, 85, 124
Essex (aircraft carrier), 194, 220, 229, 339
Essex (frigate), 35–36, 38, 39, 41, 89
Essex (ironclad), 92
Essex (screw steamer), 123
European Squadron, 89

Farragut, David G., 39, 41–42, 52, 73, 84, 85, 86, 89–90, 92, 93, 98, 100, 102, 104, 105, 109, 111, 116, 118, 129
Favored-nation status, 53
Fechteler, William M., 234, 237, 238, 239, 241, 249, 250
Federation Aeronautique Internationale, 150
Fiji Islands, 59
   civil unrest, protection of American interests, 74
Fillmore, Millard, 72, 73
First International Conference on Limits of Naval Armaments, 177
Fitch, Le Roy, 97, 101, 102, 111
Five Powers Treaty (1922), 178, 191
Flag, U.S.
   first Navy Jack of 1775 ("Don't Tread on Me"), 337
   first official salute by sovereign nation, 11
   Grand Union, first use of aboard a naval vessel, 2–3, 7
   Mexican refusal to salute, 152
   Stars and Stripes, first navy use of, 9
   U.S. Navy, first official, 276
Fleet Air Gunnery Unit, 269
Fleet Air Tactical Unit, 196
Fleet exercises, 179, 187, 193, 194, 197, 312
Fleet Satellite Communications System, 307
Fletcher, Frank F., 152–153, 157, 204, 211, 212, 213, 214, 215, 216

Flight Surgeon, 182, 185, 304
Flogging, 55, 71
Florida
   in the Civil War, 76, 77, 79, 81, 83, 85, 88, 91, 96
   defense of Fort Brooke, Seminole Wars, 56
   Indian Key, Seminole amphibious assault on, 59
   salt works, destruction of, 96, 104
   Seminole Indians, removal of, 56–57, 59
   suppression of piracy off coast of, 48
   in the War of 1812, 42
Florida Expedition, 59
Florida Keys
   claimed by the U.S., 51
   securing of Forts Taylor and Jefferson against secessionists, 76
"Flying Banana," 270
"Flying Barrel," 192
Flying boats, 145, 149, 151, 166, 174, 186, 191, 193, 194, 195, 261
"Flying Flapjack," 197
"Flying Squadron," 127, 130
Flying torpedo, 173
Foote, Andrew H., 75, 81, 84, 85, 86, 88, 89, 90, 101
Ford Trimotor, 187
Formosa (Taiwan)
   proposed invasion of, World War II, 243
   raids, in retaliation for massacre of merchant crew, 116
Forrestal, James V., 236, 261, 262
Fox, Gusavtus V., 77, 80, 88, 94, 115
Foxardo Affair, 53
France
   American naval operations in French waters during Revolutionary War, 8, 9–10, 16
   Quasi-War with, 3, 22, 23, 24–25
   rising maritime tensions with following Revolutionary War, 21, 22
Franklin, Benjamin, 8, 10, 12
Franklin D. Roosevelt (aircraft carrier), 259, 260
Fulton, Robert, 44
Fulton the First (first steam-powered warship), 44, 54
Fulton II, 54, 72

Galena (ironclad), 81
George Washington (sloop), 27
Georgia, Civil War, 85, 101, 111
   Cumberland Island, capture of, 87
   Fort Clinch, retaking of, 87
   Savannah, blockade of, 84
   Tybee Island, Union seizure of, 84
Gibraltar, naval operations on or near, 29
   Operation Sea Orbit, 283
Giffen, Robert C., 210, 220
Gilbert Islands, in World War II, 207, 216, 229, 231, 232
Gleaves, Albert, 160, 164
Goldsborough, Louis M., 59, 82, 84–85, 86, 93

Good Conduct Medal, 117
Gordon, Richard F., 289, 298
Gosport Navy Yard, 78
Grant, Ulysses S., 81, 83, 84, 98, 99, 100, 109, 112
Great Lakes, War of 1812
    Battle of Lake Erie, 40–41, 43, 72
    Lake Ontario, battles on, 36, 37, 39, 40, 41, 43
    ship-building program for, 36
"Great White Fleet," 141, 143
Greco-Turkish War, 176, 178
Greece, civil unrest, protection of American interests, 260
Greenbury Point (first naval aviation base), 146, 147
Gregory, Francis H., 35, 42, 51, 52
Grenada invasion, Operation Urgent Fury, 311
Griffith, Virgil C., 178–179
Grinnell, Henry, 70–71, 72
Grinnell Expedition, 70–71
Grinnell Land (Ellesmere Island), 122
Grissom, Virgil, 284, 290
Guadalcanal, in World War II, 215, 216–219, 224, 249
Guadalupe, in the Quasi-War with France, 24, 26, 27
Guam, 137, 337, 441
    first American warship to visit, 56
    Navy responsibility for administering, 135
    in the Spanish-American War, 132
    surrender of to Japanese, 204
    in World War II, 238, 239, 240–241
Guerilla warfare, 94, 135, 224
Gulf Blockading Squadron, 82, 85. *See also* East Gulf Blockading Squadron; West Gulf Blockading Squadron
Gulf Coast Squadron, 72, 114. *See also* Home Squadron
Gunboat flotillas, Civil War, 79, 81, 85, 88, 92, 96f
Gyrocompass navigation, 148
Gyroscope, first successful flight of airplane guided by, 160
Gyroscopic bombsight, 158
Gyroscopic stabilizers, 150

Hacker, Hoysted, 7, 13
Haiti
    civil unrest, protection of American interests, 154, 155, 156
    naval operations in or near during the Quasi-War with France, 26, 27
    Operation Support Democracy, 325, 326
    in Revolutionary War, 16
    tropical storms, recovery efforts, 343
    wrongfully detained steamer, efforts to free, 124
Halsey, William F., 202, 206, 208, 211, 218, 222, 225, 233, 245, 247, 248, 249, 255, 259, 273
Hamilton, Paul, 34, 36, 37
Hampton Naval Air Station, Experimental and Test Department, 168, 188
Harding, Seth, 5, 13, 16

Harrison, William Henry, 41
Hart, Thomas C., 199, 206, 207
Hartwigg, Clayton, 317, 323
Hawaiian Islands
    charting of (North Pacific Surveying and Exploring Expedition), 72
    civil unrest, protection of American interests, 119, 125
    first U.S. arrival at, 53
Helicopters, 317
    for anti-submarine warfare (ASW), 268, 270, 271, 277
    collision of, 339
    early hybrid, testing of, 189
    Helicopter Antisubmarine Squadron (Light) (HSL-44), 321
    Helicopter Attack (Light) Squadron (HAL), 289
    Helicopter Mine Countermeasure Squadron (HM), 300
    Helicopter Utility Squadron (HU-1), activation of, 261
    Light Helicopter Antisubmarine Squadron (HSL), 303
    for minesweeping operations, 270
    Sikorsky SH-60 Seahawk, 307
    use of at sea, 223
Helium, use of in place of hydrogen gas, 177
Helldiver, 195
Henley, John D., 38, 44, 45, 48, 49, 50
Hewitt, H. Kent, 218, 225, 228, 241
High-speed flutter analysis, 200
Hill, Harry W., 234, 241
Hillar, Benjamin, 26, 27
Hinman, Elisha, 9, 11
Hispaniola, 24, 25. *See also* Dominican Republic; Haiti
Hollins, George N., 73, 80, 82
Hollis, George N., 88, 89
Holloway, James L., 260, 276
Home Squadron, 60, 62–63, 65, 66, 67, 68, 69
Hopkins, Esek, 2, 3, 4, 5, 7, 8
Hopkins, John B., 3, 12–13
Hudson, William L., 54, 60, 75
Huerta, Victoriano, 152–153
Hull, Isaac, 26–27, 31, 33, 36
Humphreys, Joshua, 20, 21
Huse, Henry P., 134, 138
Hydraulic-type arresting gear, 187, 190
Hydrofoil patrol craft, 281
Hydrographic Office, establishment of, 115–116

Idaho (battleship), 142
Illegal seizure, U.S. response to, 55
Impressment, 24–25, 33, 35
Indian Wars, Navy participation in, 56–57, 74
Indiana (battleship), 126
Indianapolis (heavy cruiser), 187

Index

Indonesia
    Operation Unified Assistance, 340
    tsunami, humanitarian response to, 340–341
The Influence of Sea Power upon the French Revolution and Empire, 122
The Influence of Sea Power upon History, 1660–1783, 122, 124
Ingraham, Duncan J., 64, 72, 97
Ingram, Osmond K., 166, 174
Intelligence gathering
    Civil War, 85
    in Europe, World War II, 197
    Korean War, 268
    Mexican-American War, 69
    ships used for, 321
Intrepid (aircraft carrier), 234, 253, 274, 309
Intrepid (ketch), 31, 32
Intrepid (screw steamer), 119
Iowa (steel battleship), 125, 126
Iowa (World War II battleship), 221, 224, 231, 232, 238, 314
Iran
    American hostages, rescue of, 308
    civil unrest, protection of American interests, 307
    Operation Blue Light, 308
    war with Iraq, 317
Iran-Contra Scandal, 323
Iraq
    invasion of Kuwait (1990), 319
    naval quarantine of, 319–320
    Operation Desert Strike, 329
    Operation Northern Watch, 331, 335
    Operation Southern Watch, 323–324, 331, 335, 340
    Persian Gulf War, 280
    plot to kill President George H. W. Bush, 325
    troop movements along Kuwait border, 327
    war with Iran, 317
    weapons of mass destruction, monitoring of (Operation Desert Fox), 336
Iraq War, 338–340
    "Mission accomplished!," 340
    Operation Iraqi Freedom, viii, 338, 339, 340
    Seabees in, 209
    "shock and awe" campaign, 338
Ironclad Board, 80, 81
Ironclad ships
    Arkansas, 93
    call for additional funding, after Civil War, 123
    first to cross Atlantic, 115
    Galena, 81, 92
    impact of on naval warfare, 81, 87f
    Ironclad Board, recommendations for construction of, 81
    Keokuk, 99, 103
    lengthy voyages, return from, 116
    Lincoln's approval for acquisition of, 82

Monitor, vii, 81, 82, 84, 85, 86, 87f, 90, 91, 95, 124
Virginia, 79, 82, 86, 87f, 91, 93
Iwo Jima, in World War II, 236, 238, 242, 243, 248, 250–251

Jackson, Andrew
    Battle of New Orleans, 45
    capture of East Florida, 50
    response to Sumatran piracy, 55
    in War of 1812, 44, 45
James River Squadron, 113, 114
Japan
    American response to *Pembroke* incident, 101, 102
    civil unrest, protection of American interests, 116
    first visit of American warships to, 65
    "floating chrysanthemums," 253
    Orange Plan, 141
    Panay, sinking of, 194
    Perry's mission to open, 71, 72–73
    protection of American lives and property (1868), 116
    Shanghai, China, bombing of *Tutila*, 199, 200–201
    surprise attack on Pearl Harbor, 202, 203–204f
    surrender of, 258, 259f
    Treaty of Kanagwa, 73
    Treaty of Naha, 73, 74
    U.S. attacks on, World War II, 211, 218, 234, 251, 255, 257–258
Jefferson, Thomas, 20, 28, 29, 32, 33, 34
Jet aircraft
    bomber, prototype, 270, 273
    first landing of on a naval vessel, 259, 260
    Phantom fighter, 276
Jet propulsion, committee tasked to review, 199
Johanna Island, bombardment of, 71
John Adams (frigate), 25, 27, 29, 30, 32, 42, 43, 48, 51, 74
Johnson, Andrew, 114
Johnson, Lyndon, 283, 293, 295
Joint Army-Navy Airship Board, 162
Joint Army-Navy Missile Committee, 274, 275
Joint Army/Navy Technical Board, 168
Joint Chiefs of Staff, 207, 243, 261, 302, 304
Joint operations
    Alliance (America and France), 12
    Army-Navy, 28, 57, 99, 100, 161, 162
Joint Primary Aircraft Training Program, 325
Joint Strike Fighter (JCF), 329
Joint Technical Board on Airplanes, 163, 164, 166
Jones, Catesby ap Roger, 87, 91
Jones, John Paul, vii, 13–14
    Alfred, command of, 7, 8
    death and burial of in France, 19
    naval victories, 7, 8, 10, 11–12
    official recognition of, 16, 18–19
    promotion of, 6
    Providence, command of, 5

Jones, John Paul (continued)
　Ranger, command of, 10, 11–12
　reburial of at U.S. Naval Academy, 140
　U.S. flag, first hoisting of, 2–3, 9
Jones, Thomas ap Catesby, 44, 53, 61, 70
Jones, William, 38–39, 44

Kane, Dr. Elisha Kent, 72, 74
Kearny, Lawrence, 41, 45, 50, 52, 54, 61
Kearsarge (battleship), 126, 136, 141
Kearsarge (screw sloop), 105, 108*f*, 125
"Kedging," 36
Kennedy, John F.
　PT-109 incident, World War II, 226
　special operations, interest in, 280
Kentucky, Civil War, 81, 86–87, 92, 105
Keokuk (ironclad), 99, 103
Kimberly, L. A., 118, 124
Kimmel, Husband E., 199, 205, 206, 333
King, Ernest J., 196, 199, 201, 205, 210, 211, 222, 223, 242, 243, 247
Kinkaid, Thomas C., 217, 227, 244, 248
Knox, Frank, 211, 235
Korea
　attempts to establish diplomatic relations with, 116, 121
　civil unrest, protection of American interests, 123, 140, 264
　retaliation for firing on American squadron, 118
　U.S. legation, protection of (1904), 140
Korean War, viii, 264–271
　amphibious operations, 264, 265
　"Bedcheck Charlies," 271
　cease-fire agreement, 271
　"Cherokee raids," 270
　Chinese offensive, U.S. response to, 266
　civilians, evacuation of, 268, 271
　deployment of U.S. troops, logistics of, 265*f*
　final U.S. Navy vessel lost, 269
　first naval airstrikes, 264
　first naval aviator killed in, 264
　first Navy vessel lost in, 366
　first Soviet-built MiG jet fighter shot down, 266
　jet fighters, use of, 261, 264, 267
　military crisis triggering, 264
　minesweeping, 266
　Naval Air Reserve, participation in, 266
　naval blockade of North Korea, 264–265, 266
　only purely naval engagement of, 264
　Operation Mainbrace, 269
　Operation Strangle, 267
　Seabees in, 209
　U.S. troop authorization for, 264
Kuwait
　Iraqi invasion of, 319
　oil tankers, protection of (Operation Earnest Will), 315, 317

Operation Desert Shield, 321
Operation Desert Storm, 320–321

Landing-craft air-cushion (LCAC), 312
Landing Craft Infantry (LCI), 225
Landing Craft Mechanized (LCM), 212
Landing Craft Tank (LCT), 225
Landing Craft Vehicle Personnel (LCVP), 200
Landing gear
　retractable, 188, 189, 192
　shock-absorbing, 183
Landing Ship Dock (LSD), 227
Landing Ship Tank (LST), 225, 265*f*
Landing system
　automatic "hands off," 275
　mirror, 273
Langley (aircraft carrier), 178–179, 182, 189
　carrier squadron on, 182
　crash barriers, 184
　damage to, 208
Laos, flyer shot down over, 283
Lawrence, James, 33, 38, 39
League of Nations, 174
Leahy, William D., 214, 247
Lebanon, civil unrest, protection of American interests, 139, 305–306, 310–312
Lee, Stephen D., 91, 93, 109
Lee, Willis A., 219, 238
Lehman, Jr., John F., 308–309, 314
Letters of Marque and Reprisal, 2, 4, 23, 77, 78, 82
Lexington (aircraft carrier), 186, 187, 196, 203, 207, 212, 277, 323
Lexington (Revolutionary War ship), 4, 5, 8, 10
Liberia
　civil unrest, protection of American interests, 319, 328
　Navy assistance to, 49, 50
　Operation Assured Response, 328
　Operation Sharp Edge, 319
Libya
Operation Attain Freedom I, 313
Operation El Dorado Canyon, 314
Operation Prairie Fire, 314
Lighter-than-air aircraft
　dangers of, 177, 180, 192
　final flight, 281
　purchase of for World War II service, 213
Lincoln, Abraham, 98
　approval for Union acquisition of ironclad ships, 82
　assassination of, 114
　call for enlistment of sailors, 78
　commendation for naval personnel, 95
　defense of Fort Sumter, 77
　election of, 76
　naval rank, changes in, 92, 111
　rocket explosion at Washington Navy Yard, 95

Index

temporary expansion of U.S. Navy, 80
transport of to talks with General George B. McClellan, 92
and Union blockade against Confederate coastline, 77–78
visit to John L. Worden's bedside, 87
"Lone Sailor" statue, 315
Long Beach (nuclear-powered cruiser), 277, 228
Long Range Navigation Equipment (LORAN), 213
Louisiana, Civil War, 94–95, 97, 98, 100
    Baton Rouge, expedition against, 93
    fall of New Orleans, 89–90, 91
    forts, fall of to Union naval forces, 90
    New Orleans campaign, preparation for, 83, 84, 86, 89
    Red River, gunboat activities on, 105–107
    Shreveport Expedition, 105, 106
Louisiana, War of 1812, 44, 45
Lovell, James A., 286, 290, 296, 298–299
Luce, Stephen B., 112, 122
Lusitania, sinking of, 155
Lynch, William F., 70, 82, 86, 107

MacArthur, Douglas, 188
    Commander, Southwest Pacific Area, 210, 211
    Pacific military strategy, formulation of, 241, 242
    in the Philippines, 205
    return to the Philippines, 218, 243
MacDonough, Thomas, 36, 38–39, 43–44
Macedonian (frigate), 37, 39, 49, 50, 51
Mackenzie, Alexander S., 61, 116
MacKenzie, George K., 220–221
Mackenzie, John, 167–168
Macmillan Arctic Expedition, 183
Maddox, Charles H., 148, 149
Maffitt, John N., 93, 97, 103
Magnetic Anomaly Detection (MAD) equipment, 234
Mahan, Alfred Thayer, vii, 59, 122, 124, 154
Maine
    in the Civil War, 101
    in the Revolutionary War, 1, 13
    in the War of 1812, 43
Maine (armored cruiser lost in Havana Harbor), 123, 126–127, 128, 148
Maine (replacement battleship), 139
Mallory, Stephen R., 76–77, 79, 86, 88, 89, 106, 110
Malta, in World War II, 212
Manley, John, 2, 5, 9
Mare Island Navy Yard, 73, 75
Marianas Islands, in World War II, 227, 234, 235, 236, 238, 240–241
Marine Corps, 25, 259
Maritime disasters
    explosion of the *Sultana*, 114
    Lusitania, sinking of, 155
    rescue of passengers from German liner *Columbus*, 197

Titanic, sinking of, 114, 148
Vinh-Long, explosions aboard, 179
Marquesas Islands, U.S. claim to (1813), 41
Marquis de Lafayette, 12, 53
Marshall Islands
    Operation Crossroads, 260
    in World War II, 231, 232, 233–234, 238, 239, 240–241
Martinique
    in the Civil War, 94
    and Quasi-War with France, 23
    in the Revolutionary War in, 6, 15
    in World War II, 213
Maryland, Civil War, 108
Maryland, War of 1812
    Battle of Bladensburg, 43
    Chesapeake Bay Flotilla, destruction of, 43
    Fort Warburton, evacuation of, 43
    naval attacks on, 42, 43
Massachusetts
    naval militia, establishment of, 123
    naval operations, Revolutionary War, 1, 4, 5, 13
    in the War of 1812, 35
Maury, Matthew Fontaine, 61, 71, 94
Maury, William L., 99, 104
Maxfield, Louis H., 168, 177
Mayo, Henry T., 152, 222
McCain, John S., 211, 213, 246, 248, 255–258
McCalla, Bowman H., 131, 132, 137
McCann Rescue Chamber (diving bell), 195
McCauley, Charles S., 77, 78
McDonnell, Edward O., 165–166, 174
McGinnis, Knefler, 191, 193
McKean, William W., 79, 82
McKeever, Isaac, 44, 53, 71
McKinley, William T., 128, 132
McLaughlin, John T., 59, 60
McVay III, Charles B., 257, 335
Medal of Freedom, 306
Mediterranean Command (Sixth Fleet), 260, 263, 305
Mediterranean Sea
    Operation Active Endeavor, 338
    strategic importance of, to Western security, 260
Mediterranean Squadron, 30, 32, 33, 81, 114
Merrimack (frigate), 79, 82, 87f. See also *Virginia* (ironclad ship)
Mexican-American War, vii, 63–70
    amphibious operations, 64
    Battle of Veracruz, 68f
    California, naval operations in, 64–65, 67
    final shots fired by U.S. Navy personnel, 70
    formal declaration of, 64
    Home Squadron, role of, 63–64, 65, 66, 67, 68, 69
    interception of vessels bound for, 64
    Mazatlan, capture of, 68
    Monterrey, mistaken U.S. seizure of, 61

Mexican-American War (*continued*)
  naval support for, 63–64
  San Juan de Ulúa, U.S. bombardment of, 66*f*, 67
  Tampico, U.S. seizure of, 66–67
  Treaty of Guadalupe Hidalgo (1849), 70
  U.S. blockades during, 63, 64, 65
Mexico, American sailors, arrest of (1914), 152
Michigan (battleship), 144
Michigan (first prefabricated warship), 62
Michigan Territory, War of 1812, 41, 42–43
Middle East
  Arab-Israeli War, 304
  evacuation of American citizens (1956), 274
  Lebanon, civil war in, 310–312
  Liberty (intelligence ship), Israeli attack on, 292
  Operation Intense Look, 312
  "peace ship" *Ibn Khaldoon*, smuggling by, 320
  survey mapping of, 70
Mid-frequency active (MFA) sonar, 342, 343
Midway Island
  annexation of as American territory, 115
  Battle of, World War II, 213
  in World War II, 203, 213, 218, 224, 233
Military Naval Affairs Committee, 262
Military Sea Transport Service (MSTS), 264, 265*f*, 289, 299
Military Sealift Command, 299, 305, 333
Mines, 171
  anti-torpedo squadron, Civil War, 107
  Baltimore, first American minelayer, 124, 155
  Confederate, 80, 85, 92, 95, 102, 105, 106, 111, 112
  floating, use of in Revolutionary War, 10–11
  minesweeping, Korean War, 266
  underwater, Samuel Colt's experiments with, 60, 61
Missionaries, naval protection for, 62, 147
Mississippi, Civil War
  Biloxi, capture of, 84
  Pass Christian, naval battle at, 88
  Vicksburg, battle for, 91, 92–93, 95, 97–101
  Yazoo River, gunboat activities on, 98, 100, 101, 106
Mississippi (battleship), 141
Mississippi (ironclad ship), 90
Mississippi River, 82
  blockade of in the Civil War, 79
  Confederate River Defense Fleet, 90–91
  guarding confluence of with Ohio at Cairo, Illinois, 81
  gunboat activity on, Civil War, 84, 88, 90, 91, 93
  obstacles, placed by Confederates, 98
  pirate vessels off the mouth of, 34
  trading rights on, enforcement of, 29
  Union efforts to control, 88–89, 91
  in War of 1812, 45
Mississippi River Squadron, 89, 101
Mississippi Squadron, 94

Missouri, Civil War
  gunboat victories in, 81, 83
  New Madrid, Confederation evacuation of, 88
Missouri (battleship), 139, 140, 156
Missouri (first side-paddle warship), 60
Missouri (World War II battleship), 218, 238, 248, 253, 258, 259*f*, 260, 314, 323, 330
Missroon, John S., 68–69
Mitchell, John K., 109, 112
Mitscher, Marc A., 202, 222, 223, 233, 234, 236, 239, 241–244, 250–253, 255
Mobile Diving and Salvage Unit (MDSU), 342
Moffett, William A., 176, 177, 183, 187, 189, 190
"Momsen Lung," 187
Monitor (ironclad), vii, 81, 82, 84, 85, 86, 87*f*, 90, 91, 95, 124, 335
Monroe, James, 48
Montgomery, Alfred E., 229, 231–232, 237, 241
Montgomery, James E., 90, 91
Montgomery, John B., 64, 69
Montojo, Patricio, 127, 128, 129
Moorer, Thomas H., 207, 302, 304
Morgan, John H., 101, 102
Moros (Muslim insurgents), 138, 141, 147
Morris, Charles M., 105, 109
Morris, Richard V., 25, 29, 30
Morton, Dudley W. "Mush," 220, 222, 230
"Mosquito Squadron," 59, 60, 61, 89
Mugford, James, 1, 5
Murray, Alexander, 16, 25, 29
Mustin, Henry C., 157, 160
Mutiny
  by African Americans aboard *S. J. Waring*, 80
  only instance of aboard a U.S. Naval warship, 61
  of slaves, aboard the *Amistad*, 59

National Aeronautics and Space Administration (NASA), 277
National Industrial Recovery Act, 190, 191
National Naval Medical Center, dedication of, 216
National Naval Volunteers (NNV), 171
National Security Act of 1947, 261
Natural disasters, Navy response to
  Congressional Medal of Honor awarded for, 180
  earthquakes, 141, 179, 180, 189
  hurricanes/typhoons, 184, 278, 282, 337, 342
  mine collapse, 337
  ships lost to, 117, 137
  tsunami, Southeast Asia, 340–341
  volcano eruptions, 322
  wrecks due to storms, 119
Nautical Almanac Office, Harvard University, 70
Naval Act
  of 1794, 20
  of 1915, 154
  of 1916, 174
Naval Advisory Board, establishment of, 120

Index

Naval aeronautics, birth of, 81
Naval Air Detail, Macmillan Arctic Expedition, 183
Naval Air Guided Missile School (Advanced), 269
Naval Air Missile Test Center, 260
Naval Air Reserve, first unit called into combat, 266
Naval Air Test Center, founding of, 256
Naval Air Transportation Service, creation of, 204
Naval Aircraft Factory, 165, 166, 169, 171, 175, 176, 179, 185, 188, 191, 192, 193, 196, 200
Naval Aircraft Radio Laboratory, 178
Naval Appropriations Act
   of 1844, 62
   of 1847, 67
   of 1914, 150
   of 1917, 159, 162
   of 1919, 174
Naval arms race, 122
Naval Asylum board, 63
Naval attaché, first, 121
Naval aviation
   aerial attacks, 169
   Aeronautical Engine Laboratory, 179
   aircraft camouflage scheme, 199
   aircraft color regulations, 160, 162, 169, 181, 195
   aircraft construction, high-strength components for, 176
   aircraft identification, letter symbols, 176
   aircraft identification, numbering system for, 158, 205
   aircraft launched from warships, 149
   aircraft production program, 182
   birth of, 146
   cameras, use of aboard aircraft, 161
   carrier aviation, offensive potential of, 187, 188
   Director of, 176
   direct-voice communication, availability of, 170
   emergency landing sites, 181
   endurance records, 149
   experimental aircraft, 180
   first aerial casualty, 153
   first aircraft launch from a warship, 145
   first all-jet fighter squadron, 261
   first all-metal airplane, 178, 182, 188
   first American-made warplane assembled in Europe, 171
   first appropriations for, 145
   first aviation base, 146, 147
   first awareness of aviation within the U.S. Navy, 144
   first capital ship outfitted for aircraft operations, 159
   first communications equipment installed in single-seat aircraft, 185
   first fatality, 151
   first military trial of Wright brothers' aircraft, 142
   first monoplane design evaluated by, 188
   first naval air station, 152
   first night flight, 146
   first night-patrol mission, 171
   first nighttime landing, 183
   first seaplane, 147
   first shipboard launch from a vessel underway, 157
   first transatlantic crossing by large aircraft, 174
   flight controls, 159
   flight pay, increase in, 150
   formal flight testing program, 160
   "heavier than air flying machines," request for, 143
   long-range patrolling aircraft, 181
   malfunctioning aircraft, 167
   meteorological equipment, installation of on aircraft, 154
   national insignia regulations for aircraft, 168
   night flying, 146, 171, 186
   Night Wing, genesis of, 171
   non-stop flights, 180, 260
   Office of the Director of Naval Aviation, 169
   official aircraft designations, 152
   onboard hangar, 190
   pilots. *See* Navy pilot(s)
   radial engines, 178
   radio, experiments with aboard aircraft, 158, 160, 161, 164, 166, 174, 181, 190, 191
   radio-controlled aircraft, 176, 181, 195, 196
   reconnaissance missions, 156
   records related to, 180
   rotary engine, evaluation of, 149
   safety measures, 160, 180, 182
   scouting missions, 146*f*, 148
   spotter aircraft, 178
   standard equipment, naval aircraft, 150, 156, 159
   violent maneuvers and inverted flight profiles, 187
Naval Aviator, 155
Navy Band, official recognition of, 182
Navy Bureau of Equipment, 143
Naval Conference (1908), 143
Naval Conference (1936), 198
Naval Construction Battalion (Seabees), 206, 207, 209, 227, 237, 285, 330
Naval Construction Corps, abolishment of, 198
Naval Expansion Act
   of 1938, 194
   of 1940, 198
Naval Flying Reserve Corps, 159
Naval Guided Missile School, 269
Naval intelligence
   Office of Naval Intelligence (ONI), 121
   See also Intelligence gathering
Naval Medical School, Aviation Section, 185
Naval medicine
   first certified dentist to serve on a naval vessel, 150
   hospital ships, 89, 175, 287, 301, 319, 335, 341
   medical school, first unofficial, 52
   National Naval Medical Center, dedication of, 216
   naval hospitals, construction of, 34, 48, 53
   Navy Nurse Corps, 89, 142*f*, 251
   origins of, 4

Naval militia, 123, 152
   aeronautics corps within, 154
   aircraft identification, system for, 160
   qualifications for officers and enlisted men in, 158
Naval ordnance, 48
   Bureau of Ordnance and Hydrography, 67
   design of, 67
   Test Center, 269, 276
Naval Overseas Transport Service (NOTS), 168, 170, 171, 173
Naval Personnel Act of 1899, 135–136
Naval Preparedness Act of 1916, 159–160
Naval Reorganization, Commission on, 143
Naval Research Laboratory, 190, 191
   Underwater Sound Reference Division (USRD), 250
Naval Reserve
   creation of, 123
   First Yale Unit, 162
   mobilization of, World War II, 200
   Second Yale Unit, 166
Naval Reserve Flying Corps, 165
Naval Reserve Officers' Training Corps (NROTC), 182–183, 260
Naval School, 63, 71. *See also* U.S. Naval Academy
Naval Strike and Air Warfare Center, 329
Naval Supply Act of 1940, 198
Naval Test Pilot Center, 222, 310
Naval Vessel Register, 330, 331
Naval warfare, rules of, 143
Navy, Department of, creation of, 22
Navy Cross, 174, 217, 218, 220, 224
Navy Day, 179
Navy Distinguished Service Medal, 174
Navy Flight Demonstration Team (Blue Angels), 260
Navy Library, 122
Navy Medal of Honor, 84, 86
Navy pilot(s)
   from enlisted ranks, minimum percentage of, 185
   entrants into program increase in, 198
   first certificates, 154
   first female to carrier-qualify, 325
   first female to carrier-qualify for fixed-wing aircraft, 307
   first female to earn naval aviator's gold wings, 304
   first female to pass through the U.S. Naval Test Pilot School, 310
   first female to solo, 287
   ground instruction at Massachusetts Institute of Technology (MIT), 165
   length of time for training, World War II, 196, 208
   qualification standards, 150, 192
   training of, 145, 168, 193, 198, 208
Nebraska, 140
Neutrality, violations of, 125
Nevada (battleship), 158
Nevis, in the Quasi-War with France, 24

New England, War of 1812, 41, 42
New Guinea, in World War II, 212, 220, 223, 228, 229, 232, 233, 236, 237–238, 241
New Hampshire, first shipyard constructed in, 27
New Ironsides (ironclad), 81, 104
New Jersey
   naval operations, Revolutionary War, 6
   War of 1812, 36
New Mexico (battleship), 162, 170
New York (first modern warship), 125
New York, Revolutionary War, 10
New York, War of 1812, 35–36, 41
   Battle of Lake Champlain, 43
   Battle of Sackets Harbor, 36
   British capture of arms at Oswego, 42
   first steam-powered warship launched, 44
Nicaragua
   civil unrest, protection of American interests, 125–126, 127, 135, 144, 185
   detainment of American ambassador (1854), 73
   post-earthquake assistance, 189
   safeguarding of American interests in, 125–126, 135, 144, 149, 185
Nicholson, James, 11, 15, 16
Nicholson, Samuel, 20, 21, 23, 24, 25
Night Fighter Development Unit, 211
Nimitz, Chester W., 142, 148, 205, 210, 211, 217, 223, 241, 242, 243, 247, 259
Nimitz (nuclear-powered carrier), 305
Nixon, Richard M., 299, 302
Norfolk Navy Yard, 90
Noriega, Manuel, 318
Normandie, 200, 207
North Atlantic Blockading Squadron, 82, 93, 109, 114
North Atlantic Squadron, 126, 128
North Atlantic Treaty Organization (NATO), 262, 268, 269
   Ocean Safari exercise, 313
North Carolina (battleship), 159, 200, 216–217
North Carolina, Civil War, 80, 82, 98, 112–113
   attack on Roanoke Island, 84–85, 86
   blockade off the coast of, 80, 82
   Fort Macon, fall of, 90
   forts Clark and Hatteras, Union attacks on, 81
   naval bombardment of Confederate positions near Plymouth, 94, 106, 107, 110
   Wilmington, defense of, 110, 111, 112, 113
North Carolina, War of 1812, 41
North Island, San Diego training facility, 165
North Pacific Surveying and Exploring Expedition (1855), 72
North Pole, exploration of, 120, 141, 142, 143, 184–185, 276
Northern Blockading Squadron, 91
Northern Bombing Group, 173
Norton Sound (first guided-missile test ship), 262

Index

Nuclear weapons
   on aircraft carriers, procedures for, 262
   bomber expressly designed to carry, 264
   first aircraft designed specifically to deliver, 266
   treaty prohibiting placement of on ocean floor, 300
   U.S. stockpile of, 323
   use of on Japan, World War II, 257–258

Oceanography, origins of, 61
Office of General Counsel, creation of, 241
Office of Naval Intelligence (ONI), founding of, 121
Office of Naval Records, 122
Office of Naval Research, 260
Office of Naval Warfare, 308
Office of Purveyor of Supplies, creation of, 20. *See also* Supply Corps
Ohio (battleship), 139, 156
Okinawa
   first American vessel to drop anchor at, 70
   in World War II, 233, 243, 249, 250, 251, 252–256, 258
Oklahoma (battleship), 158
"Old Ironsides," 36, 55. *See also* Constitution (frigate)
Oldendorf, Jesse B., 236, 238, 245
onboard post offices, first naval vessels with, 142
101st Airborne Division, 238
Orange Plan, 141
O'Reagan, William, 239–240
Oregon Territory, exploration of, 48–49, 65
Ormsbee, Francis E., 166, 172–173

Pacific Fleet, World War II, 199, 202, 205, 211
Pacific Squadron, 49, 50, 65, 67, 68, 69
Panama
   civil unrest, protection of American interests, 119, 123, 138–139
   new naval base in, 196
   Operation Just Cause, 318
Panama Canal
   air attacks against, potential for, 179
   explorations of the Isthmus of Panama in advance of building, 73, 117, 119
   first capital ships to pass through, 155
   first navy vessel to pass through, 154
   need for, 127, 131
   official opening of, 153
   U.S. military presence at in World War I, 156*f*
   U.S. release of control for, 307
Parachutes, 181
Pay Corps, 118, 174
Peace Establishment Act of 1801, 28, 29
Peacekeeping mission, Bosnia-Herzegovina, 323, 326
Peacock (sloop), 47*f*
Pearl Harbor
   concentration of U.S. ships at (1940), 197
   first American warship to enter, 147
   Japanese attack on, 202, 203–204*f*
   mock surprise attack by *Saratoga*, 194
   permanent memorial, 276
   salvage operations at, 250
   U.S. naval facilities at, 143, 179
Peary, Robert E., 141, 142, 143
Pennsylvania
   in the Revolutionary War, 10
   in the War of 1812, 38, 39, 40
Pensacola Naval Air Station, 152, 154, 159, 167
Pensacola Navy Yard
   in the Civil War, 76
   Confederate bombardment of, 83
   dry dock facilities at, 67
   Navy Flying School at, 153, 155, 157, 158
Perry, Matthew C., 51, 62, 66, 67, 68, 69, 71, 72–73
Perry, Oliver Hazard, 34, 38, 39, 40–41, 49, 72
Persian Gulf, curbing tensions in, 316–317
   New Jersey, goodwill tour, 318
   Operation Earnest Will, 315, 317
   Operation Praying Mantis, 316
   Operation Vigilant Warrior, 326
   tanker war, 314–316
Persian Gulf War, viii
   Kuwait, Iraqi invasion of, 319
   Operation Desert Shield, 321
   Operation Desert Storm, 320–321
   SEALs in, 280
Philadelphia Navy Yard, 52
   Naval Aircraft Factory, 165, 166, 169, 171, 175, 176, 179, 185, 188, 191, 192, 193, 196, 200
Philippines
   Baatan, U.S. defense of, 206
   Battle of Manila Bay, Spanish-American War, 129, 131
   Corregidor Island, 129, 210, 212
   evacuation of American forces from, 208
   Insurrection, 135–138
   Manila, fall of to Japanese, World War II, 205
   Moros (Muslim insurgents), 138, 141, 147
   Navy nurses, evacuation of, 212
   in the Spanish-American War, 128–129, 134
   Subic Bay naval facility, 323
   U.S. aircraft based in, 196
   U.S. invasion of, World War II, 242, 243–248, 250–251
Piracy
   attack on schooner *Experiment*, 26
   along Barbary Coast, 18, 19, 20, 21
   in the Caribbean, U.S. efforts to control, 50–53
   Confederates tried for, 82
   Congressionally sanctioned Navy actions against, 49
   efforts to suppress in Gulf of Mexico, 35
   and first armed intervention in Asia by the U.S., 55
   by France against U.S. vessels, 21, 22, 23–24

Piracy (*continued*)
  Jean Lafitte, 44
  junks near Hong Kong, destruction of, 74
  in the Mediterranean, efforts to repel, 45–47, 54
  Mississippi River, off mouth of, 34
  search for in Mexico, 117
  Somalia, off coast of, 343–344
  Sumatran, U.S. response to, 55
  suppression of off Amelia Island, Florida, 48
  in waters off Greece, 54
Polk, James K., 63, 65
"Pook's turtles," 81
Porter, David, 30, 35–36, 37, 38, 39, 41, 51, 52, 53, 89
Porter, David D., 77, 79, 84, 85, 89, 93, 94, 95, 96, 97, 98, 99–100, 101, 102, 105–107, 109, 110, 111, 112, 113, 115, 116, 117
Potsdam Conference, World War II, 256–257
Pownall, Charles A., 227, 229, 232
Preble, Edward, 25, 26, 27, 29–32, 33
"Preble's Boys," 31
President (frigate), 23, 35, 40, 45, 46
Presidential Unit Citation, 276, 278
Princeton (aircraft carrier), 244
Princeton (screw sloop), 61
Princeton (steam frigate), 62
Prisoners of war
  Americans, in Korea, 267
  Americans, in Tripoli, 31, 33
  Confederate privateersmen as, 85
  exchange, at Guadalupe, 24
  German, seized near Greenland, 201–202
  in Japan, liberation of, 258
  Navy nurses in Manila, World War II, 205
  release of, 18
  Revolutionary War, 5, 8, 18
Privateers and privateering
  authorization of by Continental Congress, 4
  Confederates, treatment of as prisoners, 85
  encounters with British ships, 16, 17
  Letters of Marque and Reprisal, 2, 4, 23, 77, 78
  prize money, 2, 7, 22
Propellers, variable-pitch, 189, 190
Pueblo (intelligence ship), North Korean seizure of, 293, 296
Puerto Rico
  hotel rescue, 314
  new naval base in, 196
  in the Revolutionary War, 8
  in the Spanish-American War, 132, 134
  Vieques Island, bomb testing at, 331, 332, 334–336, 337, 340

Qaddafi, Moammar, 309
Quadrant Conference, 227
Quasi-War with France, vii, 3, 22, 23, 24, 28, 30
Queenstown (Ireland) Naval Air Station, 168
Quonset Point, Naval Air Station (NAS) at, 211

Radar
  acronym for "radio detection and ranging," 199
  aircraft identification, 199
  aircraft interception, 199
  developments in, 188, 190, 191, 193, 195, 198–199
  firing system directed by, 210
  first observations using, 178
  Project Roger, 200
  surface vessel detection, 199
Radford, Arthur W., 255, 256
Radio-wave detection device. *See* Radar
Ranger (aircraft carrier), 190, 191, 192, 212, 214, 218
Rathbun, John P., 11, 13
Read, Charles W., 100, 101, 114
Reagan, Ronald W., 314–315, 317
Reason, Paul J., 327, 328
Reeves, Joseph M., 184, 187
Refueling
  inflight, 273
  at sea, 94, 199
Refugees, evacuation of, 176, 178
Reifsnider, Lawrence F., 235, 254
"Remember the Maine!" battle cry, 127
Remotely controlled vehicle (ROV), 341
Renshaw, William B., 94, 96
Reuben James (destroyer), 202
Revenue Cutter Service, 120, 154
Revenue Marine Service, creation of, 19
"Revolt of the Admirals," 263
Revolutionary War
  American arms, capture of by British during Revolutionary War, 5
  American naval operations in European waters, 8, 9–10, 15, 16
  Bahamas, Revolutionary War, naval operations in, 4, 11
  British ships, capture of, 1, 2, 3, 6, 8
  end of, Congressional declaration, 18
  final naval engagement, 17
  first American naval victory at sea, 3
  largest American naval defeat, 13
  Philadelphia, fall of to British, 10
  privateering in, 2, 4
  Treaty of Paris, 17, 18
  victory at Saratoga, 10
  See also individual states
Rhode Island
  naval operations, Revolutionary War, 1, 5, 8
  War of 1812, 40, 41
Richardson, Holden C., 147, 151, 153, 173, 177
Rickenbacker, Eddie, 219
Rickover, Hyman G., 283, 303, 304, 308, 310
Riverine warfare
  "Mosquito Squadron," 59, 60, 61
  Navy's first experience with, 57, 60

Index

"Pook's turtles," 81
   in the Vietnam War, 287*f*, 288–289, 290, 291*f*, 293, 294, 296
Robin Moore (merchantman), 200
Rocket propulsion system, 190
Rodgers, John, 29, 30, 33, 35, 36, 40
Rodgers, John (Naval Aviator No. 2), 143, 149, 183
Rodgers, Jr., John, 72, 79, 81, 83, 91, 101, 118, 120
Rodman, Hugh, 167, 173
Roosevelt, Franklin, 179
   Chief of Staff, 214
   death of, 253
   declaration of war against Japan, 203
   expansion of U.S. Navy during World War II, 197–198
   instructions to Asiatic Fleet, 202–203
   meetings with Winston Churchill, 201, 205, 206, 220, 223, 227, 231, 242, 249
   military strategy conference at Pearl Harbor (1944), 241
   response to start of war in Europe, 196
   search for Amelia Earhart, 194
   War Shipping Administration, creation of, 207
   WAVES, creation of, 214
   Yalta Conference, 249
Roosevelt, Theodore, 138
   Guantanamo Bay, utilization of for Navy base, 139, 282, 336
   Inspection tour, Panama Canal, 141
   Monroe Doctrine, efforts to enforce, 139
   naval expansion program, 140
   naval reorganization, 143, 163
   request for additional navy funding, 142
   as Secretary of the Navy, 127, 129, 130
   USS designation for Navy ships, 141
Rowan, Stephen C., 57, 65, 69, 79, 86, 88
Royal, Forrest B., 251, 254, 256
Royal Flying Corps, 169
Rules for the Regulation of the Navy of the United Colonies of North America, 2
Russian Civil War, evacuation of refugees, 176
Ryukyu Islands, Treaty of Naha, 73, 74

Safety belts, 151
St. Barts, during the Quasi-War with France, 27
St. Kitts, as Navy's Caribbean base of operations, 24
Saltonstall, Dudley, 3, 8, 13
Samoa
   administration by U.S. Navy, 136
   civil unrest, protection of American interests, 136
   German activity in, 124
   landing at in retaliation for murder of American merchant seaman, 60
   as Pacific coaling station for U.S. Navy, 120
   protection of American interests in, 123–124, 136
Sampson, William T., 127–128, 130, 131, 132, 133, 138
San Cristobal Island, World War II, 217, 218, 227, 233

Sandwich Islands, U.S. arrival at, 53. *See also* Hawaii Islands
Santo Domingo, in the Quasi-War with France, 26
Satellite, destruction of (Operation Burnt Frost), 342–343
Saufley, Richard C., 153, 157, 158, 159
Schirra, Walter M., 277, 281, 286
Schley, Winfield S., 122, 125, 127, 130, 131, 133, 138
Scott, Norman, 217, 219
Scott, Percy, 138, 163
Scott, Winfield, 40, 57, 67, 72, 76
Sea sled, 174
"Sea trials," 93
Seabees, 206, 207, 209, 227, 237, 285, 330
SeaLab II, 286
SEALs (Sea Air Land teams), 280, 311, 315, 322, 336
Seaplanes, 160
   altitude records, 151, 155, 188
   biplane observation, 191
   capable of transatlantic flight, 166
   "Dunkirk Fighter," 167
   experiments with, Naval Operating Base, 166
   first ender designed specifically for the Navy, 197
   first flight assisted by radio compass, 175
   Navy's first, 147
   "Seagull" scout-observation aircraft, 192*f*
   speed records for, 180
   world endurance record, 183
Searchlights, 182
Second Grinnell Expedition, 72, 74
Secretary of the Navy
   annual report to Congress, 24
   creation of, 22
Secretary of War, creation of, 19
Security
   coastal defense, 161, 188
   National Security Act of 1945, 261
   U.S. ports, Coast Guard protection of, 208
   Western, significance of Mediterranean Sea to, 260
Selfridge, Thomas O., 69, 95, 105, 117
Seminole Wars
   defense of Fort Brooke, 56
   removal of Seminole Indians from Florida, 56–57, 59
Semmes, Raphael, 67, 76, 80, 88, 93, 94, 96, 99, 107–108, 113, 114
Senior Enlisted Advisor, 290
Service aircraft, 195
Service Life Extension Program, 308
Service medals, 42. *See also* Congressional Medal of Honor
Seventh Fleet, 263
Shafter, William T., 132, 133
Shepard, Alan B., 277, 279, 300, 301
Sherman, Forrest P., 217, 243, 255, 263
Sherman, Frederick C., 230, 231
Sherman, William Tecumseh, 95, 98, 111, 112, 113

Ship-model testing tank, 126
Ships run aground
   Alligator, wrecked on Corysfort Reef, 51, 52
   Atlanta, Civil War, 101
   Cabot, Revolutionary War, 8
   Columbine, St. John's River, Florida, 107
   Concord, in the Mozambique Channel, 62
   Decatur, Philippines, 142
   Delaware, Revolutionary War, 10
   Hannah, Revolutionary War, 1–2
   Independence, Revolutionary War, 12
   Milwaukee, California, 161
   Raleigh, Revolutionary War, 12
   Revenge, 34
   Tacoma, wrecked on Blanquilla Reef, 181
   Virginia, Revolutionary War, 11
Shipyards
   Boston Naval Shipyard, 301, 304
   Gosport Navy Yard, 78
   Mare Island Navy Yard, 73, 75
   Norfolk Navy Yard, 90
   Pensacola, 67, 76,
   Pensacola Navy Yard, 67, 76, 83, 153, 155, 157, 158
   Philadelphia Navy Yard, 52, 165, 166, 169, 171, 175, 176, 179, 185, 188, 191, 192, 193, 196, 200
   Washington Navy Yard, 26, 43, 76, 95, 126, 150, 155
Short, Walter C., 206, 333
Shreveport Expedition, 105, 106
Shubrick, John T., 47, 67, 68, 69, 70, 75
Shufeldt, Robert W., 120, 121
Sicard, Montgomery, 118, 126, 128
Sierra Leone, Operation Noble Obelisk, 329–330
Sigsbee, Charles D., 126, 127, 132, 140
Sims, William S., 138, 162, 163, 173
Sinclair, Arthur, 41, 42, 43
Singapore, ABDA (American, British, Dutch, Australian) command, 205, 209
Sino-Amrican Cooperative Organization, 223
Sixth Fleet, 260, 263, 305
Skipjack (first diesel-powered submarine), 148
Slaves
   African Squadron, genesis of, 49
   Amistad, mutiny aboard, 59
   anti-slavery patrols, 50, 61
   apprehension of slavers in South Atlantic, 76
   Navy seizure of, 49, 50
   role of navy in suppressing trade off West Africa, 49
   smuggling, efforts to suppress, 34–35
   U.S. seizure of slave vessels in Africa, 63, 75, 76
   See also African Americans
"Sled profile float," 145
Slidell, John, 82, 83, 84
Sloat, John D., 53, 64, 65

Smuggling
   efforts to suppress, 19, 34–35, 51, 184
   slaves, 35
   See also Piracy
Soley, James R., 122, 125
Solomon Islands, World War II, 214, 215, 216, 217, 220, 222, 227, 229, 243
Somalia, U.S. troop deployment to, 320–321, 327
   Operation Restore Hope, 324
Soucek, Apollo, 187, 188
South Atlantic Blockading Squadron, 83, 97, 101, 114
South Carolina, Civil War, 113
   Beaufort, seizure of by Union gunboats, 83
   blockade running by Confederates, 78, 79, 81, 82, 86, 88, 107, 110
   Charleston, battle for, 91, 94, 98, 99, 102, 103–105, 113
   Charleston, Union blockade of, 82, 94, 97
   Fort Sumter, naval activities related to, 76–77, 102, 104
   Otter Island, capture of, 84
   Port Royal, Union victory at, 83
South Carolina, Revolutionary War
   Charleston, defense of, 15, 16
South Pole, exploration of, 185, 186, 187
   Operation Deepfreeze, 185
   Operation Highjump, 185
Spanish-American War, 126–135
   Battle of Manila Bay, 129
   Battle of Santiago, 133*f*, 134
   explosion of *Maine* in Havana Harbor, 127
   first blood, 128
   first official report on loss of *Maine*, 128
   Maine, arrival of in Havana, 126–127
   naval actions in anticipation of, 126, 127
   naval operations in Cuba, 132–135
   only officer fatality in, 129
   "Remember the Maine!" battle cry, 127
   treaty ending, 135
   U.S. declaration of war on Spain, 128
Spanish Civil War, 193
Special Operations Command (SOCOM), 315
Speed records, 274, 275
Sperry, Elmer B., 160, 161
Spies and spying
   Civil War, 109
   Pollard, Jonathan Jay, 313
   submarine surveillance operations, 262
   Walker, Jr., John A., 313
"Splinter Fleet," 170
Spruance, Raymond, 213, 222, 233, 234, 238, 249, 252, 255
Squadron of Evolution, 124
Stafford, Thomas P., 286, 288, 297
Stalin, Joseph, 231, 249, 256
Standoff Land Attack Missile-Expanded Response, 329

Index

Stanton, Edwin M., 88, 112
Stark, Harold R., 196, 198, 202, 210, 212
Steam-powered ships
    chief engineer, position of, 61
    conversion of sailing ships to steam, 76
    experiments with, 56
    first, in War of 1812, 44
    first side-paddle steamship to cross the Atlantic, 61
    first side-paddle warship, 60
    first to undertake global voyage, 120
    second, 45, 51
    sidewheel steamer, first seaworthy, 57
"Steel Navy," 121
Stockton, Robert F., 50, 62, 65, 67
Stoddert, Benjamin, 22, 23, 24, 25, 28
"Stone Fleet," 84
Struble, Arthur D., 244, 247, 249, 250, 251, 252, 264, 266
Submarine(s)
    American, first major warship destroyed by, 215
    anti-submarine activity, World War II, 210
    appendectomy performed on while submerged, 216
    blimp as anti-submarine weapon, 195
    circumnavigation of the Earth, 275, 276, 278
    in Civil War, to break Union blockade, 102
    construction of first, 126
    escape from, 187
    experimental, *Hunley*, 102, 105
    first American casualties aboard, 155
    first diesel-powered, 148
    first experimental, 6
    first practical for naval warfare, 120
    first transatlantic voyage, 167
    George Taylor's plans for developing, 62
    Holland, Navy's first commissioned, 127, 137
    lost at sea, 282
    Narwal, 188
    Nautilus, 175, 216
    Naval Submarine Battery Service, Confederate States of America, 94
    at the North Pole, 281
    nuclear-deterrent patrols, 307, 309
    nuclear-powered, 267, 268, 272, 274, 275, 276, 277, 278, 304
    propulsion, 272
    radio transmission aboard, 175
    refueling, 199
    retro-rocket antisubmarine weapon, 213
    Scorpion, disappearance of, 294
    Squadron 14, 276
    station at New London, 157
    submerged, aerial spotting of, 149, 150
    sub-stowed aircraft, 180
    suicide (kaitens), 257
    World War II, 204, 206, 210, 231, 239, 257

Submersibles, 79–80, 188
Suez Canal, first American warship through, 118
Sunken ships
    Chauncey, accidental ramming of, 167
    deliberate, 42
    following a collision, 117, 119, 176
    Kearsarge (screw sloop), 125
Supercarriers, 262–263, 273, 309, 327
Supply Corps, 20, 118, 174
Surgeon General, first appointed, 117
Surveying expedition. *See* U.S. Exploring Expedition, survey of the Antarctic shelf
System of Orders and Instructions, 72

Tactical Reconnaissance Photographic System (TARPS), 309
Taft, William H., 150, 163
Talbot, Silas, 12, 13, 14, 20, 25
Tattnall, Josiah, 67, 68, 75, 83, 84, 88, 91
Taylor, David W., 158, 159, 166
Taylor, Zachary, 63–64, 311
Teaser (first Confederate minelayer), 92
Telegraphic cables, cutting of, 130
Television technology, 200
Teller Amendment, War Resolution, 128
Tennessee, Civil War
    Battle of Fort Donelson, 97
    Battle of Shiloh, navy involvement in, 88
    Fort Henry, attack on, 85
    gunboat activities along the Cumberland River, 84, 85–86
    Union attack on Fort Henry, 84, 85
Tennessee River, naval operations on, 110
Terrorism
    hijacking of TWA 847, 313
    interception of Egyptian airliner, 313
    in Puerto Rico, 307, 310
    U.S. Embassy Annex, Lebanon, 312
    USO bombings, in Europe, 316
    World Trade Center, destruction of, 335
    See also War on Terror
Texas
    annexation of, 62
    in Civil War, 93, 94, 95–96, 97, 103
    Galveston, importance of in Civil War, 96f
    invasion of, to cut off Confederate supplies, 105
Texas (armored battleship), 126, 144, 152
Thailand, commercial treaty between U.S. and, 56
Theobald, Robert A., 211, 213
Tilghman, William, 80, 85
Tingey, Thomas, 24–25, 43
Torpedoes. *See* Mines
Towers, John H. (Naval Aviator No. 3), 146, 147, 148, 149, 150, 151, 152, 153, 164, 174, 261
Transatlantic cable, 75
Treasury Department, U.S., 19, 120, 154, 260

Treaties
- between America and France during the Revolutionary War, 11
- Anti-Ballistic Missile, 337
- commercial, 55–56
- Convention of 1800 ending Quasi-War with France, 28
- ending Spanish-American War, 135
- final, to end Barbary Wars, 48
- Five Powers (1922), 178, 191
- Ghent (1813), 44
- Guadalupe Hidalgo (1849), 70
- Kanagwa (1854), 73
- Naha (1854), 73, 74
- Paris (1783), 17, 18
- with Pasha of Tripoli, 21, 47–48
- peace, with Tripoli (1805), 33
- to placate Dey of Algiers (1795), 20
- with Tunis (1797), 21
- Versailles (1919), 174
- Wanghia (1845), 63
- Washington Naval, 177, 185, 188
- Webster-Ashburton (1842), 61

Trident (nuclear-powered submarine), 304, 306, 307, 309
Truman, Harry S, 214, 253, 256–257, 259, 260, 263, 273
Truxtun, Thomas, 20, 21, 23, 24, 25, 26, 28, 29
Turner, Richmond K., 213–214, 215, 224–225, 252
Twenty Thousand Leagues under the Sea, 120

U.S. Aeronautical Reserve, 144
U.S. Antarctic Service, 185
U.S. Coast Guard
- Aviation Division, 159
- first officers to receive flight training, 158
- formation of, 120
- ice patrols, 148
- Lighthouse Bureau, 196
- official creation of, 154
- origin of, 19
- Revenue Marine Service as precursor to, 19
- search and recovery operations, 328
- strength of, World War II, 208, 248, 258
- transfer of to Navy jurisdiction during war, 154, 162
- transfer back to Treasury Department, 260
- transfer of to new Department of Transportation, 291
- U.S. ports, protection of, 208
- in Vietnam War, 285, 292, 297, 298
- Volstead Act, enforcement of, 175
- in World War II, 203

U.S. Exploring Expedition, survey of the Antarctic shelf, 57–61
U.S. Fleet into Battle, Scouting, Submarine, and Base Forces, 189

U.S. Military Academy (West Point), 124
U.S. Naval Academy, vii
- acceptance of women at, 305
- aviation classes at, 183
- burial of John Paul Jones at, 140
- Class of 1941, 199
- curriculum, changes to, 63, 71, 136, 183
- early graduations, World War II, 205, 224, 256
- examination of, 114
- female graduates, 408
- first African American admitted to, 118
- first African American graduate, 118, 262
- first interservice football game with U.S. Military Academy (West Point), 124
- first Japanese national admitted to, 117
- first superintendent, appointment of, 63
- flight instruction requirements for graduates of, 183–184
- initial plans for, 44
- Japanese midshipmen, congressional approval to attend, 117
- naming of, 71
- Naval Postgraduate School, 150
- opening ceremonies for, 63
- proposed site of, 63
- *Reina Mercedes* (receiving ship), 134
- relocation of to Newport, Rhode Island, during Civil War, 78, 79
- superintendent, 117
- transfer back to Annapolis at close of Civil War, 115

U.S. Naval Forces Operating in European Waters, 172
U.S. Naval Hospital, first, construction of, 53
U.S. Naval Reserve, 154
U.S. Naval War College, 112
- establishment of, 122
- first formal classes, 123
- Joint Chiefs of Staff gathering at, 262

U.S. Navy
- academic standards for enlisted men, 151
- administrative reform, 143, 287
- Admiral of the Navy, 135
- admiral rank, calls for adoption of, 48
- alcoholic rations, elimination of, 92, 153
- appropriations bill (1816), 48
- Army cooperation with, 28
- birthday of, 2
- "Bottom Up Review," 325
- British gunnery system, adoption of, 138
- calls for, 21
- capabilities, weakening of in the Pacific, 188, 193
- chief engineer position, institution of, 61
- Chief of Naval Operations (CFO), 154, 155, 157, 167, 168, 199, 210, 259, 262–263, 318, 325
- combat capabilities, acquisition of, 21
- combined-sex crews on warships, 319
- construction, Spanish-American War, 129
- conversion of sailing ships to steam power, 76

Index

corporal punishment, regulations governing, 72
Defense Appropriations Act (1996), 327
delivery of diplomatic envoys by, 8, 11, 12, 15, 39, 42
Department of Navy, creation of, 22
Depot of Charts and Instruments, 55, 61
dry docks, call for construction of, 48
"engineering duty only" classification, 198
establishment of, 21, 22, 30
expansion of, 22, 24, 25, 33, 80, 123, 124, 140, 157, 194–195, 197–198
exploration activities of, 48–49, 53, 57, 70–71, 72, 74, 119, 120, 141, 142. *See also* U.S. Exploring Expedition
"Father of," 3, 14*f*
first aircraft carrier, 178–179, 182
first all-iron vessel, 62
first American squadron in European waters, 9
first American to command a battleship, 126
first American warship to pass through the Suez Canal, 117
first American warship to reach the Pacific Ocean, 38
first armed intervention in Asia by U.S., 55
first armored battleship, 126
first blood drawn by, 22
first commissioned submarine, 127
first convoy, 27
first enemy warship taken in a formal ship-to-ship encounter, 5
first experimental torpedo ram, 119
first guided-missile program, 162, 197
first gunnery school, 72
first hospital ship, 89
first Jewish officer to gain rank of captain, 62
first mass torpedo launch, 178
first Muslim chaplain, 329
first naval attaché, 121
first officer to receive medal, 33
first officers, appointment of, 20
first official seal, 15
first official warship, 21
first prefabricated warship, 62
first rear admiral, 89, 92
first recorded underwater accident, 144
first rigid airship, 180, 181, 190
first ship constructed from keel up, 140
first surface action, World War II, 206
first Surgeon General appointed, 117
first torpedo boat, 124
first torpedo-boat destroyer, 139*f*
first torpedo station, 117
first vessel constructed entirely as a hospital ship, 175
first vessel driven by a propeller, 61–62
first warship to circumnavigate the globe, 54
fleet strength, declines in, 305, 306
General Board of senior admirals, founding of, 136–137
George Washington's endorsement for creation of, 21
"Great White Fleet," 141, 143
Hepburn report, 195
lack of, following Revolutionary War, 18
mandatory retirement age, 135
manpower ceilings, limits on, 62
manpower levels, increases in, 65, 206
mapping activities, 70, 115, 261
Medal of Honor, 84, 86
modern battleships, introduction of, 123
Naval Personnel Act of 1899, 135–136
naval yard and depot, construction of at Pensacola, Florida, 53
officer corps, reduction in, 27, 29
officer training, plans to transform, 62
only officer to attain rank of both general and admiral, 121
ordnance and equipment, standardization of, 44
overseas airbases, call for more, 195
pay, increases in, 154
pensions, 25
plans to reduce sailors' affection for (rum), 55, 92
Quadrennial Defense Review (QDR), 329, 335
rank, changes in, 92, 116, 135–-136
recruitment efforts, 54
regulations, first set of, 21
reorganization of, 44, 48, 61, 92, 143, 175
resignation of officers to join Confederacy, 76
scientific activities, 183, 260
Sea Swap Initiative, 338
"Sea Power 21," 336–337
secret plan to secure battleships and auxiliaries (1903), 139
ships, letter identification system for, 176
single largest loss of personnel, 11
size of, 146
strategy, shift in, 33
strength of, in Civil War, 84, 95, 104, 111, 115
strength of, in World War II, 198, 199
supercarrier, cancellation of, 262–263
Surface Warfare insignia, ships, 313
surgeons, General Order granting naval rank to, 63
"System of Orders and Instructions," 72
Tailhook scandal, 322–323, 325
temporary expansion of, Civil War, 80
uniforms, 60, 147, 159, 162, 188, 223, 314
USS ship designation, 141
vessels lost to submerged Confederate ordnance, 95
V-12 training program, 225
warships, construction of to support America's global responsibilities, 138
warships, official naming policy, 49
WAVES, 214, 215*f*, 248
women in (*see* Women, U.S. Navy)
Unanimity (schooner), 23

Undersecretary of the Navy, creation of, 198
Underwater Demolition Team (UDT), 230, 250, 265, 280
Underwater ordnance, 102. *See also* Mines
Uniform(s)
   aviation personnel, 147
   British, capture of in Revolutionary War, 7
   carrier deck gear for adverse weather conditions, 189
   change of color, naval aviation, 306
   clothing allowances for flight personnel, 159
   Continental Navy, 6
   first dress regulations for enlisted personnel, 60
   khaki-colored, 223
   protective flight clothing, testing of, 189
   shoes, 314
U.S. Navy Nurse Corps, 89, 142*f*
U.S. Navy Reserve Force, 159
United States (frigate), 20, 21, 24, 24, 35, 39, 46
United States (supercarrier), 263*f*
United States Life-Saving Service, 120, 121, 154
United States Naval Institute, 119
United States Naval Policy, 178
United States Shipping Board, 160
Unknown Soldier, 177
Unmanned aerial vehicle (UAV), 339
Uruguay, civil unrest, protection of American interests, 74, 116

Van Buren, Martin, 56
Venezuela, German warships at (1903), 139
Vessels lost at sea
   Albany (off Panama), 74
   Conestoga (en route to Samoa), 176
   Donado (Atlantic in World War II), 230
   Ferret (off Cuba), 53
   Grampus (en route from Charleston, South Carolina), 61
   Levant (between Hawaii and Colombia), 76
   Lynx (Carysfort Reef), 50
   Monitor (off Cape Hatteras, North Carolina), 95
   Narcissus (off Florida coast), 115
   Porpoise (Formosa Straits), 73
   Urdameta, Philippine Insurrection, 136
   Wildcat (off Cuba), 52
Veth, Kenneth L., 292, 295
Vietnam War, viii
   Agent Orange defoliant, 299
   air attacks over North Vietnam, 288
   air raids, 283
   American prisoners of war, release of, 297
   Army-Navy Mobile Riverine Force, 294, 295
   attacks against purely industrial targets, 286, 292
   "boat people," flight of, 307
   Cambodian incursion, 294, 299
   Coast Guard, participation of, 285, 292, 297, 298
   evacuation of civilians fleeing Communist tyranny, 305
   expansion of, 283, 285
   fire-support missions, 285
   first air raids of, 284
   first offensive naval gunfire, 290–291
   flying boats, use of, 261
   last American aerial victory, 302
   Mekong Delta Mobile Riverine Force, 291
   minesweeping operations, 303*f*
   Operation Bold Mariner, 296
   Operation Endsweep, 303
   Operation Flaming Dart, 284
   Operation Flaming Dart II, 284
   Operation Frequent Wind, 305
   Operation Game Warden, 287, 289–290, 294, 295
   Operation Giant Slingshot, 295, 299
   Operation Market Time, 284, 285, 287, 288, 291, 292
   Operation Passage to Freedom, 272
   Operation Pierce Arrow, 283
   Operation Rolling Thunder, 284, 286
   Operation Sea Dragon, 289, 290
   Operation Sea Lords, 295
   Operation Starlite, 285
   Operation Urgent Fury, 280
   Paris Peace Accords, 303
   "Parrot's Beak," 295
   riverine operations, 287*f*, 288–289, 290, 291*f*, 293, 294, 296
   Seabees in, 209, 285
   SEALs in, 301, 302
   swift boats, 287, 296, 298
   temporary halts to, 285, 286, 293, 302
   Tonkin Gulf Resolution, 283
   U.S. Navy, significant role of, 295*f*
   "Vietnamization," 299
Vincennes, 58*f*
Vinson-Trammel Act (1934), 191
Virginia (ironclad), 79, 82, 86, 87*f*, 91, 93
Virginia, Civil War, 79–80, 81, 82–83
   Alexandria, surrender of to Union forces, 79
   first offensive action by U.S. Navy, 79
   gunboat activities in, 90
   Norfolk Navy Yard, Union reoccupation of, 90
   riverine naval activities, 91
Virginia, War of 1812, 39–40
VT proximity fuze ammunition, 198, 220

Waddell, James I., 110, 114, 115
Wake Island
   claimed for U.S., 135
   construction of air station on (1941), 199
   salvage operations, 323
   surrender of to Japan, 205
   U.S. discovery of, 60
   in World War II, 202, 204, 208, 229, 233, 237, 254

Index

War, Department of
  joint operations with Department of the Navy, 162, 163
  merger of with Department of the Navy, 259
  naval operations, oversight of, 22
War of 1812
  American motives for, 35
  amphibious assault, use of, 39–40
  Azores, American repulsion of British, 37, 44, 45
  Battle of Bladensburg, 43
  Battle of Lake Champlain, 43–44
  Battle of Lake Erie, 40–41, 43, 72
  Battle of New Orleans, preparations for, 44–45
  blockades, use of, 37, 39, 40, 41, 42
  Canada, campaigns in, 36, 37, 39, 40
  capture of HMS Macedonian, 37
  Congressional declaration of war, 35
  Detroit, recapture of, 41
  "Don't give up the ship!," battle cry, 39
  effects of on American economy, 42
  English Channel, U.S. foray into, 39–40, 42
  final naval action, 47
  first American warship lost in, 36
  first British naval vessel taken in, 36
  and impressment of American seamen by British, 35, 45
  and Indians, British arming of, 35
  Lake Ontario, battles on, 36, 37, 39, 40, 41, 43
  Mackinac, recapture of, 42–43
  Marquesas Islands, U.S. claim to, 41
  naval construction during, 36, 37, 38
  naval strategy, changes in, 36
  New England, exemption from British blockade, 41
  primary causes of, 35
  recruitment of naval forces, 38–39
  single-ship duels, British avoidance of, 37
  South America, U.S. naval operations in, 37, 38, 41–42
  steam-powered ships, use of, 44
  Treaty of Ghent, 45–46
  U.S. Navy strength at onset of, 35
  Washington, D.C., defense of, 43
  See also individual states
War on terror
  Afghanistan, U.S. involvement in, 209, 330, 335–336
  Operation Anaconda, 336
  Operation Enduring Freedom, viii, 335, 340
  prison at Guantanamo Bay, 336
  SEALs in, 280, 336, 342
  September 11 attacks, 335
"War Order No. 1," 202
Ward, Norvell G., 285, 287, 292
Warrington, Lewis, 42, 47, 52
Warships
  first American to visit China, 49
  first prefabricated, 62
  first to circumnavigate the globe, 54
  official naming policy, 49
  steam-powered, 44, 45
Washington, George, 1, 2, 3
  endorsement for creation of standing navy, 21
  first military commission issued by, 19
  first naval officers, appointment of, 20
  "George Washington's Navy," 1, 10
  recommendations for countering Algerian piracy, 20–21
Washington Naval Treaty, 177, 185, 188
Washington Navy Yard
  Aeronautical Engine Laboratory, 155
  dry dock, construction of, 26
  efforts to avoid British capture of, 43
  establishment of, 26
  protection of from secessionist capture, 76
  rocket explosion at, 95
  ship-model testing tank, 126
  wind tunnel, construction of, 150
Water Witch (side-wheel steamer)
  at Biloxi, Mississippi, 84
  capture of, 107
  inexplicable firing on by Paraguayan forces (1855), 74, 75
  return to New York (1859), 74
Watson, William H., 51, 52
WAVES (Women Accepted for Volunteer Emergency Service), 214, 215*f*, 248, 291
Webb, James, 315, 316
Webster-Ashburton Treaty (1842), 61
Welles, Gideon, 77, 78, 81, 82, 84, 86, 95, 101, 104, 106, 107, 109, 111, 112, 113, 114, 115
Wellings, Joseph H., 200, 225
West Gulf Blockading Squadron, 84, 85, 86, 89–90, 92, 114
West India Squadron, 51, 52, 56, 93–94, 115
West Indies
  in the Revolutionary War, 7, 9, 16
  in the War of 1812, 37
West Virginia (battleship), 203*f*
Western Gunboat Fleet, 94
Western Gunboat Flotilla, 92
Whipple, Abraham, 1, 3, 4, 11, 13, 15
Whiting, Kenneth, 164, 171, 178, 179
Wickes, Lambert, 6, 8, 9–10
Wilkes, Charles, 57–61
Wilkes, John, 83, 93–94
Wilkes Expedition, 57–61
Wilkes Land, 59
Wilkinson, Theodore S., 227, 230, 234, 242
Wilson, Woodrow, 152, 155, 156, 157, 161–162, 173
Wind power, 117
Wings, hydraulically folding, 193
Winslow, John A., 105, 108

Wireless transmission
    adoption of along the Atlantic Seaboard, 168
    experiments with, 145, 148
Wisconsin (battleship), 156
Wisconsin (World War II battleship), 235, 322
Women, U.S. Navy
    assignment of to non-combat vessels, 307
    first female Flight Surgeons, 304
    first female killed in the line of duty, 309
    first female officer to qualify for surface warfare, 308
    first female rear admiral, 301
    first female to head an operational aircraft squadron, 319
    first female to head a U.S. Navy vessel, 320
    first female to solo in a naval aircraft, 287
    legislation permitting women to serve on Navy combat vessels, 325
    pilots, firsts among, 287, 304, 307, 310, 325
    recruitment of, 142, 162, 214
    sexual harassment, 322–323
    at the U.S. Naval Academy, 305, 408
    WAVES, 214, 215f, 248
    Women's Armed Services Integration Act, 214, 261–262
Wood, John Taylor, 94, 103, 105, 109
Woodbury, Levi, 55, 56
Worden, John L., 77, 85, 86, 87, 95, 97, 98, 117
World War I, viii
    Anglo-American occupation force, 170
    defense expenditures, 156
    deployment of navy battleships to Europe, 167
    first aerial attack, 169
    first American convoy bound for England, armed escort, 164
    first American merchant vessel sunk in, 154
    first American sailor killed in action, 166
    first American troopship lost to hostile fire, 168
    first and only enemy vessel destroyed by American warships, 167
    Lusitania, sinking of, 155
    merchant vessels, arming of, 161–162
    Naval Consulting Board, 155
    naval preparations for entry into, 159–160
    only enemy action on American soil, 171
    recruitment of women, 162
    "sea frontiers," coastline designations, 201
    specialized unit for operations against German U-boats, 170
    submarine warfare, U.S. demand to end, 173
    Treaty of Versailles, signing of, 174
    U-boats, attacks on neutral vessels, 155, 162, 164–165f
    U-boats, in American coastal waters, 170
    U.S. declaration of war, 162
    U.S. naval air stations in Europe, construction of, 164, 167, 168
    U.S. Patrol Squadron, 164
World War II, viii, 197–259f
    ABC-1 Staff Agreement, 199, 201
    African Americans, recruitment of, 213
    Aleutian Islands, 213, 224, 225, 236
    Atlantic Charter, signing of, 201
    atomic bombs, dropping of on Japan, 257–258
    Attu, invasion of, 223
    Australia in, 207, 208, 220–221, 227, 228
    Battle of Badoeng Strait, 207
    Battle of Cape Esperance, 217
    Battle of Empress Augusta Bay, 230, 273
    Battle of Kolombaranga, 225, 226
    Battle of Kula Gulf, 225
    Battle of Leyte Gulf, 244
    Battle of Makassar Straits, Borneo, 206
    Battle of Savo Island, 215
    Battle of Suriago, 245
    Battle of Tassafaronga, 219
    Battle of the Eastern Solomons, 216
    Battle of the Java Sea, 208
    Battle of the Philippine Sea, 239
    Battle of the Santa Cruz Islands, 217–218
    Battle of Vella Lavella, 229
    "Black Cat Squadron," 219
    Brazil, naval operations off of, 220, 225, 229
    British Home Fleet, U.S. reinforcement of, 210, 229
    Canary Islands, 224, 232, 236
    Caroline Islands, 231, 234, 236, 238, 241, 246, 251
    Coral Sea, naval battle in, 211, 212, 218, 221
    escort carriers, 224
    "Exercise Tiger," 236
    final American warship damaged, 259
    final German vessel destroyed by American forces, 255
    final surface engagement, 258
    first aggression by a U.S. warship toward the Axis, 200
    first American naval victory, Mediterranean Sea, 219
    first American ship lost in, 200
    first American torpedo attack, 204
    first American warship lost in, 202
    first recorded U.S. submarine victory in, 204
    "floating chrysanthemums," 253
    German propaganda, U.S. efforts to refute, 198
    "Germany first" strategy, 205, 206, 222, 223
    Gilbert Islands, 207, 216, 229, 231, 232
    "Great Marianas Turkey Shoot," 239
    Guadalcanal, 215, 216–219, 224, 249
    Guam, 238, 239, 240–241
    homing missiles, use of, 254
    "Hydeman's Hellcats," 256
    invasion of Poland, 196
    Italy, U.S. invasion of, 223, 228, 229, 233
    Iwo Jima, 236, 238, 242, 243, 248, 250–251
    Japan, U.S. attacks on, 211, 218, 234, 251, 255, 257–258

Index

Japanese codes, cracking of, 213
kamikaze attacks, 244–247, 248, 250, 251, 252–253, 254, 255–256
Kurile Island, 234
  last air strike of, 258
"leap-frogging" campaign, 239
Lend-Lease Program, 198
"Liberty Ships," 199, 201
as a "Limited National Emergency" for the U.S., 196
Marianas Islands, 227, 234, 235, 236, 238, 239, 240–241
Marshall Islands, 231, 232, 233–234, 238, 239, 240–241
merchant vessels, arming of, 202, 210
Midway Island, 203, 213, 218, 224, 233
naval campaign, cost of, 256
naval procurement, increased levels of, 198
Naval Reserve, mobilization of, 200
Navy construction program, 199
Navy manpower, increases in, 196
Netherlands East Indies, 209
neutral shipping, protection of, 201
Neutrality Act, amendments to, 202
Neutrality Patrol, 196, 197
New Guinea, 212, 220, 223, 228, 229, 232, 233, 236, 237–238, 241
Normandy, invasion of, 236, 237–238
North Africa, 219, 236–237
Okinawa, 233, 243, 250, 251, 252–256, 258
101st Airborne Division, activation of, 238
Operation Avalanche, 228
Operation Barney, 256
Operation Dragoon, 241
Operation Forager, 238
Operation Galvanic, 231
Operation Husky, 225
Operation Iceberg, 252
Operation Ke, 221
Operation Magic Carpet, 258
Operation Overlord, 237–238
Operation SHO-1, 244
Operation Stalemate II, 242
Operation Stevedore, 241
Operation Ten-Go, 253
Operation Toenail, 223–224
Operation Torch, 218
Operation Watchtower, 215
Pearl Harbor, Japanese attack on, 202, 203–204f, 250

Philippines, U.S. invasion of, 242, 243–248, 250–251
Potsdam Conference, 256–257
Quadrant Conference, 227
San Cristobal Island, 217, 218, 227, 233
Seabees in, 206, 207, 209, 227, 237
Second Quebec Conference, 242
Singapore, 205
Solomon Islands, 214, 215, 216, 217, 220, 222, 227, 229, 243
surrender of Japan, 258, 259f
Tehran Conference, 231
"Tokyo Express," 219, 221, 225
Trident Conference, 223
"Two Ocean Navy," need for, 198
U-boat attacks, 201, 202, 206, 209, 216, 221, 224
as an "Unlimited National Emergency" for the U.S., 200
Wake, capitulation of, 203
Wake Island, 202, 204, 205, 208, 229, 233, 237, 254
WAVES, creation of, 214, 215f, 291
women in, 212, 214
Yalta Conference, 249
Women Accepted for Volunteer Emergency Service. *See* WAVES (Women Accepted for Volunteer Emergency Service)
Women's Armed Services Integration Act, 214, 261–262
Workman, Shannon, 325

Yalta Conference, World War II, 249
Yangtze Patrol (YangPat), 175
Yazoo River Expedition, Civil War, 98
"Yellow Peril," 192
Yemen, bombing of the *USS Cole*, 333
Yeo, Sir James L., 37, 40, 41, 42
Yorktown (aircraft carrier), 194, 207, 209, 212
Young, John, 12, 15, 16
Young, John W. (astronaut), 284, 288, 297, 309
Yugoslavia, former, U.S. involvement in
  Bosnia-Herzegovina, ethnic unrest in, 323, 326
  Operation Allied Force, 331
  Operation Deny Flight, 324
  Operation Sharp Guard, 324
  Operation Shining Hope, 331

Z-grams, 299
Zanzibar, civil unrest, protection of American interests, 283
Zumwalt, Elmo R., 295, 299, 296, 300

About the Author

JOHN C. FREDRIKSEN is an independent historian and the author of 20 reference books on various subjects. He received his doctorate in military history from Providence College.